Today's Mathematics

TWELFTH EDITION

Concepts, Methods, and Classroom Activities

JAMES W. HEDDENS

Professor Emeritus, Kent State University

WILLIAM R. SPEER

Professor, University of Nevada, Las Vegas

DANIEL J. BRAHIER

Professor, Bowling Green State University

WILEY

JOHN WILEY & SONS, INC.

VP & EXECUTIVE PUBLISHER	Jay O'Callaghan
EXECUTIVE EDITOR	Christopher Johnson
ACQUISITIONS EDITOR	Robert Johnston
SENIOR PRODUCTION EDITOR	Nicole Repasky
MARKETING MANAGER	Danielle Torio
DESIGNER	Jim O'Shea
PRODUCTION MANAGEMENT SERVICES	Katie Boilard/Pine Tree Composition, Inc.
SENIOR MEDIA EDITOR	Lynn Pearlman
EDITORIAL ASSISTANT	Carrie Tupa
COVER PHOTO	© Johner Images/MediaBakery

This book was set in Times New Roman by Laserwords Private Limited, Chennai, India and printed and bound by Bind-Rite. The cover was printed by Bind-Rite.

This book is printed on acid-free paper. ∞

ISBN-13: 978-0470-28690-6

Printed in the United States of America

10 9 8 7 6 5 4 3 2 1

Preface

The adoption and implementation of mathematics standards by states, local districts and individual schools provide students with an unparalleled opportunity to learn valuable mathematical skills and abilities as well as develop an understanding of important mathematical processes. At the same time, teachers find themselves faced with new problems such as: how to reorganize instruction to meet higher standards; how to best prepare themselves for dealing with the mathematics content demanded by local, state, and national standards; how to present mathematics lessons in the most effective manner, and how to best assess and evaluate mathematics teaching and learning.

The value of a mathematics program at any level will often be determined by the teacher's ability to thoroughly understand what mathematical ideas are to be taught and how to present the material in the most effective way. The adoption of programs based on analysis of the meaning of concepts and the *guided* and *facilitated* exploration of mathematics through hands-on and minds-on activities places new demands on teachers. This text represents a major effort to assist the teacher in meeting these demands.

The unique format of *Today's Mathematics* makes it adaptable to a wide range of course syllabi and a variety of student groups. *Today's Mathematics* has been used successfully in undergraduate and graduate courses in education and mathematics. Specifically, this text is designed for use

- in mathematics methods classes,
- in "mathematics content for teachers" classes,
- as a tool for in-service professional development work with teachers, and,
- as a valuable personal reference resource for *anyone* concerned with the mathematics education of elementary and/or middle school students and the development of sound and effective mathematics teaching.

While *Today's Mathematics* is designed to aid the teacher in understanding the mathematical concepts and relationships commonly found in elementary and middle school programs, this text also assists the teacher in presenting these concepts to students of all grades and abilities, emphasizing how a given concept is introduced at a particular level and how it is expanded and reinforced at successive levels.

Let's look at the organization of this text to see how these goals are accomplished. The chapters of the book are arranged in a manner that allows flexibility in their coverage. The logic and presentation of text material allows the instructor to choose to begin study with any of the Chapters including 1, 4, 5, 6, 10, 14 or Chapter 16. The NCTM *Principles and Standards for School Mathematics* (2000) are summarized in early chapters and then reflected throughout the remainder of this text. The first three chapters establish the tone of the book and provide an *overview* of contemporary philosophies and psychologies of learning, teaching, and assessing mathematics. The fourth chapter discusses tools such as calculators, computers, and other technologies to enhance learning, teaching, and assessing mathematics. The fifth chapter extends this thinking by identifying and examining the roles of problem solving, decision making, and communication in mathematics learning. The sixth chapter describes the nature and scope of a beginning mathematics program for the primary grades and the development of number sense and numeration. The remaining chapters, 7-17, deal with the content strands of computation with whole numbers, number theory and systems, algebraic reasoning, fraction and decimal concepts and operations, data handling and analysis, measurement, and the fundamental concepts of geometry.

Changes for the twelfth edition of *Today's Mathematics* include revision and reorganization of material into chapters that reflect the vision of mathematics learning, teaching, and assessment as described in the **National Council of Teachers of Mathematics *Principles and Standards for School Mathematics*** (2000) as well as earlier NCTM documents entitled *Curriculum and Evaluation Standards for School Mathematics* (1989), *Teaching Standards for School Mathematics* (1991), and *Assessment Standards for School Mathematics* (1995). In addition, this edition of *Today's Mathematics* reflects the content and vision present in the NCTM *Curriculum Focal Points* (2006) and the **most recent NCTM Teaching Standards entitled, *Mathematics Teaching Today: Improving Practice, Improving Student Learning*** (2007).

A notable continuation from the previous edition of *Today's Mathematics* is the extremely valuable inclusion of **virtual manipulatives** on the CD that accompanies the text along with hands-on activities supporting these virtual manipulatives found throughout the text. These virtual manipulatives represent a richly effective library of uniquely interactive, CD-based virtual manipulatives or concept tutorials for mathematics instruction. Virtual manipulatives are among the newest technologies being used by teachers of mathematics. Teachers who have interactive white boards in their classrooms often rely on virtual manipulatives to use as visual models for instruction. The virtual manipulative materials are of importance for the mathematical preparation of both pre-service and in-service elementary/middle schoolteachers. They represent an effort to enhance the effectiveness of physical manipulatives and other classroom tools by addressing or overcoming limitations of access, cost, and adaptability. All of the resources found on this CD, not only the virtual manipulatives, can be used independently of the text and have considerable value for planning and teaching mathematics far beyond the course in which this text is

used. Consequently, the virtual manipulatives on the CD that accompanies this edition of *Today's Mathematics* represent a most important contribution to professional development.

Another dramatic and substantive element in the format that resurfaces in this edition is the incorporation into a single, manageable volume of a previously separate but fully integrated companion text of teacher resources. As with the previous edition, one book represents the *Today's Mathematics* package of **"Concepts and Classroom Methods,"** that delineates the underlying theory and principles of sound mathematics instruction and **"Activities and Instructional Ideas"** including a host of activities reflecting benchmarks of the NCTM grade bands of PreK–2, 3–5, and 6–8 for students have been revised.

The book is also strengthened by the inclusion of:

- a discussion of changes in content and emphasis in PreK–8 mathematics;
- a listing of the NCTM standards for grades PreK–2, 3–5, and 6–8 and a supporting set of references;
- an example of a complete NCTM standard.

The chapter on **Technology in Mathematics** introduces the teacher to a discussion of the role of calculators in the classroom, supported by the complete text of the NCTM position paper on calculator use, and a set of **activities for grades PreK–8**; and a discussion of the role of computer technology in elementary/middle grades, including software, applications, multimedia, and the Internet), supported by the **complete text of the NCTM position paper on technology** in the classroom, and a set of activities for grades PreK–8.

Today's Mathematics also includes useful **Research Snapshots** designed to generate classroom and small-group discussion that, perhaps, will lead to action research projects on the part of your students. On the CD that accompanies the text, students will find that each chapter has **both primary and intermediate sample lesson plans** for each of the content chapters to aid in putting research theory into classroom practice.

In addition to the new features of the twelfth edition of *Today's Mathematics*, popular features of previous editions have been retained. These include:

- **motivational openings for each chapter** (with the themes of problem solving, decision making, and the role of communication in mathematics) that focus on connections to the real world as well as to other areas of mathematics;
- a special section of the CD that accompanies this text is designed to assist student teachers in becoming familiar with some of the practical

concerns every teacher faces when making instructional decisions. These aids include:

- **a comprehensive content scope and sequence for grades PreK–8** that reflects the vision of the NCTM standards,
- **a comprehensive checklist of mathematical concept clusters**, a variety of **thematic mathematics activity idea-packs**, and
- **a vignette from the NCTM assessment standards** that is designed to emphasize the importance and integration of content, teaching, and assessment.

Other features that have contributed to the widespread popularity of previous editions of *Today's Mathematics* have been maintained in this twelfth edition. Chapters are consistently structured in the following manner:

- **Chapter objectives** and **teaching competencies** are identified for each chapter to serve as advance organizers and to set the stage for what should be the major outcomes as a result of completing the chapter. A list of virtual manipulatives that are used in the chapter are included here.

- The body of each chapter presents a comprehensive focus on **appropriate content *and* methods** for the topics presented.

- The CD that accompanies the text includes a comprehensive **glossary of terminology, symbols, and procedures** that are discussed in each chapter—allowing the user to quickly and easily review these important definitions.

- A complete set of **content-oriented practice exercises** appears in Chapters 5–17. The student using the text can **self-check comprehension of the content** examined through use of the **accompanying CD with answers** to all of these practice exercises.

- Each chapter includes a set of revised **open-ended self-assessment questions** corresponding to each of the teaching competencies identified for the chapter. These are designed to encourage individual and cooperative reflection and to engage students in spirited discourse and debate centered on various issues raised in the chapter.

- Each chapter of the book includes a representative sample of appropriate classroom and individual instructional activities for students across the grades. A **much larger, comprehensive collection of classroom activities** for use with students in the PreK-8 grade ranges is provided for Chapters 5–17 on the CD that accompanies the text. These activities, which help the student translate theories and concepts discussed in the chapter, include many experiences with manipulatives and hands-on learning and suggest ways to anchor skills. There are also exercises in each chapter that focus on activities that use calculators, computers and virtual manipulatives in instruction.

- The CD that accompanies the text includes **a bibliography and collection of relevant references** that support the ideas found in each chapter. These bibliographies are drawn from readily available recent resources so that students can easily and readily locate additional readings to support and expand their understanding and efforts in planning for instruction.

We are certain that students, teachers and professors will find that the twelfth edition of *Today's Mathematics* continues to contribute to the long-standing tradition of relevance and insight established by previous editions of this text over the past forty-five years. The combined coverage of content and methods creates a long-lasting resource that helps pre-service and in-service teachers see the relationship between what they teach and how they teach. This interdependent structure helps illustrate the development of elementary and middle school mathematics curriculum from the primary grades through preparation for high school.

Supplements— Manual and Test Bank

Continuing a service begun with four previous editions of *Today's Mathematics*, we have revised the ***Instructor's Manual*** for the twelfth edition. Each of the chapters the *Today's Mathematics Instructor's Manual* includes:

- an overview of the content
- a list of teaching competencies
- a collection of group or individual activities
- a set of appropriate blackline masters for use in Powerpoint or overhead presentations
- a number of multiple-choice discussion questions with detailed analyses of correct and incorrect answers.

We are also pleased to provide a revised **computerized bank of test items** for each chapter of the twelfth edition of *Today's Mathematics*. The item bank and manual are available to adopters on the Wiley website at http://www.wiley.com/WileyCDA/WileyTitle/productCd-0470286903.html. The test bank allows the teacher to use simple word processing features to create a test for each chapter by selecting from the existing 60-plus multiple-choice, 10 true-false, 3 matching, 5 open-ended short answer essay questions, 3 short-term performance assessment tasks, and 3 long-term performance assessment tasks. Questions can be selected and sorted by the user, so tests can be created for individual chapters, groups of chapters, or the entire book. The teacher can also add questions to any chapter test by appending or replacing existing questions. The teacher can, in addition, build a test bank of his or her own by transferring work from an existing word processing file. The teacher has the option of labeling criteria on each item using any desired scheme such as level of difficulty or objective being tested. Created tests can be stored for future use and can be previewed, edited, scrambled, and printed in different fonts. Of course, an answer key can be printed for any created test.

Acknowledgments

A special acknowledgment must be given to Marge Speer for her continued assistance, support, and patience in life as well as in the preparation of this manuscript.

The authors would also like to express a sincere and hefty gratitude to Dr. Jeff Shih for his dedication to the improvement of this text most notably through the integration and implementation of the various virtual manipulatives referred to throughout the text and for organizing and updating the Research Snapshots in each chapter. His partnership and fellowship make an effort such as the revision of this text infinitely more enjoyable and rewarding. The authors also wish to sincerely acknowledge the important contributions of Eugene Paik, currently a doctoral student at the University of Nevada Las Vegas, for his insights in Chapter Four on the changing role of technology in teaching mathematics to children.

A special thank you is also reserved for Dr. Larry Cannon, Dr. Robert Heal, Dr. James Dorward, and Dr. Joel Duffin, the team at the Utah State University National Library of Virtual Manipulatives, for their efforts to enrich the previous edition of *Today's Mathematics* with the many virtual manipulatives and their continued support through the twelfth edition evident on the CD that accompanies this book. These invaluable applets will prove useful to any teacher for years to come.

It is also important to reaffirm our appreciation for the contributions made to the previous editions of *Today's Mathematics* that have been carried through to the twelfth edition. Special thanks to Dr. Juli K. Dixon, and Dr. Christy Falba for contributing chapters focusing on algebra and technology tools for enhancing instruction; to Dr. Marilyn Sue Ford for translating the vision of this text into exemplary primary and intermediate lesson plans for each content chapter; and Dr. Virginia Usnick for her valued input on the geometry chapters and the activities for students.

Special thanks for unbounded patience, understanding and assistance go to Robert Johnston and Carrie Tupa of John Wiley and Sons Publishing.

William R. Speer
Daniel J. Brahier
James W. Heddens

An Important Message for Students Using this Text

Helping You Make the Most of the Resources in *Today's Mathematics*

The Activities and Instructional Ideas sections in the book and on the CD of the twelfth edition of *Today's Mathematics* are designed to aid you in your quest to understand more mathematics and to develop successful approaches to teaching mathematics. By presenting the material from this section in an activity format, this offers you the opportunity to closely examine the translation of theory into practice. Ideas that, for whatever reason, were not as clear as you might have hoped upon the first reading of each chapter are often unveiled when seen in the activity format. Also, the material in the activities portion can serve as a springboard for you to explore alternative ways of presenting, discussing, and assessing the material as you work with children.

Today's Mathematics provides a wealth of support material that teachers need to successfully deliver the current vision of mathematics teaching and learning. Teachers quickly discover that even the best and/or most popular grade-level mathematics textbooks do not (in fact, *cannot*) present the mathematics to be learned in the countless ways that are often required by the learners in a classroom. Supplementary material is absolutely necessary, not only for individual teaching styles, but also to deal effectively with individual learning styles and individual levels of process and skill development.

This book begins with three chapters dealing with the learning of mathematics, the teaching of mathematics, and the assessment process in Mathematics. In these chapters you will find invaluable reference material to help you implement the NCTM standards.

- The first chapter, *Learning Mathematics*, includes a summary of the content recommended in the NCTM *Principles and Standards for School Mathematics* (2000). All of the Curriculum Standards for grades PreK–2, 3–5, and 6–8 are found here, along with a current bibliography on the CD. This bibliography should prove to be an excellent resource of supplementary ideas as you plan lessons for your students now and in the future. If you need to design a unit or set of lessons on a particular topic, these bibliographies will provide you with excellent starting points. Finally, to ensure that you comprehend the nature of the standards, an example of a complete standard has been reprinted in full on the CD.

- The second chapter, *Teaching Mathematics*, includes a list of the Teaching Standards drawn from the NCTM Professional Standards for Teaching and Learning Mathematics, *Mathematics Teaching Today* (2007), with a comprehensive bibliography included on the CD to help you find supporting and clarifying articles and resources. In addition to these features, Chapter 2 includes a discussion of lesson planning processes and purposes, a thorough description of lesson plan components, a scheme for self-evaluating the effectiveness of your planning and teaching, a sample template for creating lesson plans, and a list of all 28 sample lesson plans for Chapters 4–17 found on the CD that accompanies the text.

The CD also provides the names, addresses, toll-free telephone numbers, and Web addresses of the suppliers of mathematics resource materials. It would be to your advantage to add your name to the mailing lists of these companies to keep abreast of new developments, to become familiar with existing teaching and review materials, and to get ideas of materials that you can adapt and "manufacture" for your classroom use.

- The third chapter, *Assessing Mathematics*, draws from NCTM's *Assessment Standards for School Mathematics* (1995) and fully lists the six assessment standards that can be used to judge the quality of an assessment system and presents a supporting bibliography on the CD. A complete example of an assessment standard is included and supported with a classroom discussion that describes how assessment might occur in practice.

- Chapter 4 provides an overview of technology tools for enhancing instruction and learning. This chapter includes a discussion of technology in the elementary and middle grades by examining the role and applications of calculator and computer use in K–8 mathematics. It also incorporates an overview of software types, applications, hypermedia, and telecommunications—including email and the Internet Additional activities can be found throughout the text, but this chapter provides the framework for incorporating technology in instruction and assessment.

  Chapter 4 also provides a rich resource for teachers looking for computer software that supports various mathematics concepts. The CD includes several software publishers that are identified by names, addresses, toll-free telephone numbers, and Web addresses and a listing of popular software and a coding of concepts that the software helps attain.

For each of the remaining content-oriented chapters (Chapters 4–17) the CD that accompanies the text incorporates two sample lesson plans that illustrate the application of the content of the chapter, one at the primary level and another at the intermediate level. These lessons can form a guide and a foundation on which to build your planning skills and abilities.

You will also find samples and more extensive instructional and assessment ideas, reflecting the grade-range lines of NCTM's *Principles and Standards for School Mathematics*, that may be used either during initial instruction or as follow-up activities. These activities, in each chapter and on the CD, are easily transformed into seatwork, homework, motivations for new or extended lessons, learning center resources, or project-based activities. Many of these activities can be modified for either individual or cooperative group format and incorporate manipulatives, calculators, and computers where appropriate. The manipulatives used throughout this text are either commercial materials that are commonly found in mathematics curricula or are of a "homemade" nature using materials readily available in the school or brought in from home. In addition, the virtual manipulatives referred to in this text are readily available on the CD that accompanies this book or on the Internet.

The CD that accompanies this text may prove to be a most valuable resource for student teacher or a beginning teacher. The CD offers an opportunity to "look back as you move forward" in pursuing your goal to become a teacher.

- The CD includes an overview of eight content strands commonly found in elementary and middle school mathematics curricula. This is followed by a comprehensive discussion and a listing of critical objectives designed to make you feel more comfortable about how these strands unfold and interplay in grades PreK–8.

- Another feature of the CD is the inclusion of a checklist of mathematical concepts organized by concept clusters. This checklist allows you the opportunity to identify a particular concept and explore that concept through its step-by-step development from its earliest foundations. Even though several concepts are intertwined in instruction, each often needs to be examined in isolation by the teacher to identify important prerequisite knowledge, skills, and experiences. The format of this checklist allows for this sort of in-depth analysis.

- Several thematic mathematics activities are included on the CD. These are excellent resources for those teachers wishing to integrate mathematics with other disciplines. Even a cursory examination of the ideas presented in this section should give you the confidence to explore mathematics from a thematic base. What mathematics can we find at the zoo? At the grocery store? In health? In transportation? In geography? This is the place not only to find out but also to extend these ideas to other themes.

- Finally, The CD includes a vignette from the NCTM that is designed to show how the standards of curriculum, teaching, and assessment come together in practice. Reading and reflecting on this vignette can help you envision the environment your own classroom should, and hopefully will, embody.

The wealth of resources found in the entire *Today's Mathematics* "package" provides even more information to not only help you successfully complete this course, but also to aid you as you begin extended experiences in teaching children.

The completion of this text and this course is not a finish line; it is a starting line. The process of becoming a teacher is life-long, and, consequently, professional development is a part of your "job" that cannot be ignored. As you set out on this journey, it is to your advantage to familiarize yourself with any and all resources that may help you become a master teacher. We sincerely believe that *Today's Mathematics* can be such a resource for you – today AND tomorrow.

William R. Speer
Daniel J. Brahier
James W. Heddens

Contents

chapter 14

Data Analysis: Graphs, Statistics, and Probability   317

chapter 15

Measurement   339

chapter 16

Geometry: Basic Concepts and Structures   361

chapter 17

Geometry: Polygons and Polyhedra   385

Index   417

1

Learning Mathematics

TEACHING COMPETENCIES

Upon completing this chapter, you will be able to:

- Describe the vision of mathematics education put forth in the NCTM *Principles and Standards for School Mathematics*.

- Describe characteristics of an effective contemporary elementary/middle-school mathematics program.

- Contrast characteristics of a contemporary mathematics program with those of a more traditional program, relating the benefits and shortcomings of each.

- Describe a basic personal philosophy of teaching mathematics that promotes effective learning.

- Relate prominent learning theories to classroom mathematics teaching and learning.

- Describe, in general terms, mathematics content as appropriate for any given age/grade level or range, preK–8.

- Describe several roles a teacher may play in successfully implementing the NCTM *Principles and Standards for School Mathematics*.

Katie sat at the table in her college residence hall, doing a simple addition problem to balance her checkbook. She wrote the problem on a piece of paper, as shown here:

$$\begin{array}{r} \overset{2}{35} \\ \times\ 47 \\ \hline 91 \end{array}$$

As she entered the sum into her checkbook, she thought for a moment. In her head, a debate began, "If you add two numbers that are about 35 and 45, you can't get an answer greater than 90, can you? The problem has to be with the '2' that I carried. I must have made some careless mistake. Maybe I wrote down the wrong number or carried the wrong number." She reworked the problem by "carrying" the 1 and got an answer of 82. Since this was her checkbook we're talking about, to be sure, she finally took out her calculator, using it to verify that 82 was, in fact, the correct answer. She made the change in her checkbook and went on with her day.

Perhaps you know someone like Katie. Maybe you *are* a Katie—a person who memorized procedures for everything from addition and subtraction of whole numbers to dividing fractions and finding the circumference of a circle but never understood *why* the procedures worked and often not remembering what, to many people, are considered "easy" mathematical calculations. You may or may not consider yourself a "math person." Some people are convinced that either they are born with the math gene or they're not. Sadly, this misconception about mathematical ability being genetic and inherited is commonly discussed but is simply not true. There is no scientific evidence to support that some people are innately "good at math," while others are destined to struggle. In fact, most people who are excited about the field of mathematics and have excelled in it over the years can point back to a parent or teacher whose influence had lifelong implications. Many people will tell you, "I have liked math ever since the fifth grade when we did a big probability experiment and presented our results at a school curriculum fair." Conversely, others will say, "I have never liked math. It was my third-grade teacher who started me down the wrong road with all of those timed tests and publicly displayed scores that showed me that I was far behind the rest of the students."

Indeed, the teacher of mathematics *does* make a difference. Not only will an effective teacher help us make sense of mathematical ideas but he or she also has the potential to instill in us an appreciation for the content area that will affect us the rest of our lives. In this sense, *everyone* has the potential to be a "math person." You simply have to be exposed to the right kind of teachers who are emphasizing the types of mathematics problems that are relevant and interesting. Everyday in the classroom, we are not just teaching "mathematics"; we are teaching the *child* about mathematics. Consequently, the focus of our efforts should be on addressing student needs—placing their concerns, fears, and needs at the center of our work. Let's turn our attention to those student needs and the general ideas involved in the learning of mathematics.

Societal Needs

Society is in constant change. Elementary school mathematics programs must keep pace and, in some sense, contribute to that change. For too many years, mathematics programs have been static—unwavering in the face of new demands and challenges. But our contemporary world demands a kind of mathematical knowledge that is different from that required in the past. The Society for Industrial and Applied Mathematics described the mathematical content that mathematicians say they are using in their work. This list included modeling and simulation, probability and statistics, optimization, and discrete mathematics. This is a very different list than one generated 10 years ago (or even 10 years from now). The lead engineer of a major manufacturing company recently stated that he has to entirely relearn his job every five years, as technology and societal needs are changing that rapidly! Clearly, the need has never been greater for students to learn in a way that ensures that success in the present translates to success in the future. The Report of the Senior Assessment Panel for the International Assessment of the U.S. Mathematical Sciences (1998) argued that the economic health and the security of the nation have come to depend heavily on mathematics. Today, and even more so in the future, the need is for individuals who can formulate, define, and analyze significant problems as well as discover creative ways to solve them through disciplined imagination.

Previous generations needed to be able to calculate efficiently and accurately. There is still a need for such skill, but now it is more common to employ technology for lengthy and cumbersome calculations. Calculators are inexpensive, compact, and easily obtainable. In fact, many people carry calculators with them for immediate use when appropriate situations arise. Calculators and computers are, for the most part, readily available to assist people with involved computational demands in our technological society. Consequently, we need to reexamine and redefine the roles of calculators and computers in the classroom as well as the role of arithmetic in the study of mathematics.

An effective elementary/middle school mathematics program must consider a wider range of objectives than just computational skill. Certainly, skills necessary for daily life must be taught, but this should be combined with the development of understandings that free students from *mindless* rote memorization. In Katie's case, described at the beginning of this chapter, we would hope that she could simply look at the addition problem and think, "30 + 40 is 70, and 5 + 7 is 12, so 70 + 12 means the sum is 82," with neither paper and pencil nor a calculator in hand. A contemporary mathematics program should attempt to provide a satisfactory foundation for further study and exposure to a cultural and historical perspective of the role of mathematics in our society. To do so requires a firm understanding of mathematics—not simply skill in mathematics. A healthy combination of skill and understanding offers mathematical power to the learner.

Calls for Change

The content of school mathematics programs is, and should be, constantly evaluated and revised. During the past 50 years, substantial changes have occurred in both teaching strategies and the curricula of school mathematics programs. Learning theories—particularly the work of Jean Piaget, Jerome Bruner, Lev Vygotsky, and the van Hieles—have greatly informed us about how students learn and have influenced how mathematics is taught. Such phenomena as the experimental curricular projects of the 1950s and 1960s, "new math," the "back-to-basics" approach, integrated curricula, cooperative learning approaches, differentiated instruction, and focused attention on problem solving have greatly changed the content and focus of mathematics programs.

A number of reports offering direction for the future have been issued since the 1980s. The earliest of these signaled a need for careful examination of past assumptions regarding mathematics education. These early reports included *A Nation at Risk* (1983), *The Underachieving Curriculum: Assessing U.S. School Mathematics from an International Perspective* (1987), *Everybody Counts: A Report to the Nation on the Future of Mathematics Education* (1989), and *America 2000: An Education Strategy* (1991). The discussion and analysis of these and other reports led to plans of action such as *Standards for All: A Vision for Education in the 21st Century* (1993), *First in the World* (1993), *Foundation for the Future* (1994), *A Perspective on Reform in Mathematics and Science Education—Project 2061* (1996), *What Matters Most: Teaching for America's Future* (1996), *The National*

Education Goals Report (1997), *The Condition of Education* (1998), *Before It's Too Late: A Report to the Nation* (2000), and *Helping Children Learn Mathematics* (2002).

It was also during this period that the National Council of Teachers of Mathematics (NCTM) launched three separate landmark publications on mathematics curriculum, teaching, and assessment. These were the *Curriculum and Evaluation Standards for School Mathematics* (1989), the *Professional Standards for Teaching Mathematics* (1991), and the *Assessment Standards for School Mathematics* (1995). In response to the publication of NCTM's *Curriculum and Evaluation Standards for School Mathematics*, the Mathematical Association of America produced *A Call for Change: Recommendations for the Mathematical Preparation of Teachers of Mathematics* (1991). Each of these documents has had widespread influence on mathematics education, and each has been revisited to reflect both the changing needs of society and what we continue to discover regarding how students learn and how we might best contribute to and assess this learning.

In turn, each state has developed and implemented a mathematics curriculum framework that is consistent with the national standards. A report of the major findings of analysis of state standards and assessments (Achieve, 1999) noted that states, as a whole, (1) do not have expectations that are rigorous by international standards, (2) do not have a tightness of alignment between state standards and state assessment tools used to measure attainment of the standards, and (3) do not effectively address the "mile wide and inch deep" phenomenon—covering too many topics in too shallow a fashion as opposed to providing the greatest depth of understanding possible by delving into fewer topics. The Department of Education for each state has a Web site that describes that state's interpretation of mathematics standards—**see the list of state URLs on the CD that accompanies this text.**

The reports and position papers mentioned earlier, as well as others, have served to raise questions about the content of our mathematics programs, the mathematical performance of our students, and the performance of our mathematics teaching. Some people may brush these reports off as the cyclical moaning of longtime critics of education. However, the reports are deserving of a closer look and greater attention from those seeking to improve education.

National and International Achievement

Results of the 2007 National Assessment of Educational Progress (NAEP) indicates that the national performance in mathematical proficiency for fourth- and eighth-grade students was higher than for any previous year (National Center for Education Statistics, 2007). In addition, the average score on the mathematics SAT has increased steadily since 1967, reaching its highest point in 2005 (Arenson, 2005). (The test structure of the SAT was significantly changed in 2005, so recent scores are more difficult to compare to those of previous years.) Nevertheless, there are some troubling findings that cloud these improvements. For example, black, Hispanic, and American Indian students' scores are consistently lower than those of white students. Students from relatively wealthy households continue to outperform students from low-income families. Clearly, much work remains to get all students where we want them to be.

Perhaps one of the most significant indicators of the need for reform in mathematics education has come from the analysis of findings from the Third International Mathematics and Science Study (TIMSS) and the subsequent Trends in Mathematics and Science Study—an extended ongoing study using the same acronym. The 1995 TIMSS study was the most extensive in-depth study of international comparisons of mathematics and science education ever undertaken. Its purpose was to not only examine student achievement in 45 nations at three grade levels—4, 8, and 12—but also to analyze curricula and teaching practices of these countries. A TIMSS-Repeat study showed no significant gains over the 1995 results (1999).

Let's consider a problem that was featured on the 2003 fourth-grade TIMSS exam, shown below (National Center for Education Statistics, 2007). In the problem, students are expected to be able to determine that the gap between the high and low temperatures on Monday is greater than that for any other day of the week, making choice A the correct answer. Internationally, 42 percent of the fourth graders got the item correct, with 73 percent of Japanese students answering with choice A. However, only 38 percent of U.S. students answered the item correctly. They were outperformed by students in 17 other countries, including Japan, Hong Kong, Belgium, England, and the Russian Federation. In most states, children begin to plot points and draw line graphs as early as the second grade. Yet, two years later, only about one-third of the students were able to interpret this graph. As we have previously discussed, this result may be explained in part by an overemphasis on the *skill* of drawing a graph, instead of the *thinking processes* involved in interpreting such a graph.

Comparing achievements in the 26 TIMSS countries that participated in fourth-grade testing, the U.S. fourth-grade students were above the international average in mathematics. Comparing achievements in the 41 TIMSS countries that participated in the eighth-grade testing, the U.S. eighth-grade students were below the international average in mathematics. Comparing achievements in the 21 TIMSS countries that participated in the general mathematics twelfth-grade testing, the U.S. twelfth-grade students were significantly below the international average in their general knowledge of mathematics. The United States is the only country participating in the full range of TIMSS testing whose mathematics ranking fell from above

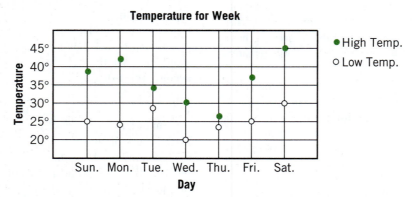

The graph shows the daily high and low temperatures for a week.

On which day is the difference between the high and low temperatures the greatest?

Ⓐ Monday

Ⓑ Thursday

Ⓒ Friday

Ⓓ Saturday

Fourth-Grade TIMSS Item from 2003

average at grade 4, to below average at grade 8, to an even more disastrous level in grade 12.

It should be noted that the TIMSS data are not necessarily an indictment of the NCTM standards reform. The TIMSS data were collected in 1995—since the initial set of standards was released in 1989, the students in that study would have had the availability (but not necessarily the opportunity) to experience a standards-based classroom for only four or five school years. A question to consider is, would this limited exposure to standards-based instruction be a cause of low performance on the part of twelfth graders who may have had a more traditional foundation in their formative elementary and middle school years? As previously stated, data from the 2007 National Center of Educational Statistics (NCES, 2007) showed that mathematics scores were higher than on all previous assessment years in grades 4 and 8.

Even though reasons for the disappointing performance on the TIMSS are difficult to isolate, attempts have been made to describe at least plausible explanations. Most often mentioned is the fact that we have no nationally defined curriculum—a characteristic of many other countries in the study. The study also found that less rigorous content makes up the bulk of our mathematics curriculum and that U.S. teachers try to cover too much material and, consequently, do so in a superficial manner—the opposite of what occurs in high-performing countries. Other reasons often cited include a weak induction process for teachers and little opportunity for professional interaction with colleagues in teaching. Perhaps you have a few theories of your own, as you think about your elementary, middle, and high school experiences. The main point to be gained from the TIMSS study is not our relative international standing, but what we can learn from others to assist us and our students in achieving higher standards. Whether the messages from TIMSS yield genuine educational reform will depend on the actions of stakeholders at the local, state, and national levels.

The National Sciences Board (NSB) report entitled *Preparing Our Children: Math and Science Education in the National Interest* (1999) urged a consensus on a core of knowledge and competency in mathematics and science. The NSB stated that it is both possible and imperative to develop standards that serve the national interest while respecting local responsibility for K–12 teaching and learning. In this report, the NSB offered four recommendations that promote student achievement. These recommendations, generated from research and analysis of best practices, include

1. More rigorous standards

2. Higher expectations that all students can meet these standards

3. Teachers well prepared in the subjects they are teaching

4. Meaningful measures of accountability

In a report to the Mathematical Sciences Education Board (MSEB), Henry Pollack of Bell Laboratories offered the findings of a study on mathematical expectations of employees in the workplace. Pollack noted that employers want people who set up and solve problems, work with others to solve problems, and believe that mathematics is valuable and important. Similar characteristics and abilities were identified in a U.S. Departments of Education and Labor Secretary's Commission on Achieving Necessary Skills paper entitled *What Work Requires of Schools: A SCANS Report for America 2000*.

Let's reflect for a moment on the difference between what industry expects of our students versus the goals of the "traditional" mathematics programs that our students experience and the questions that might be raised. For example, *The Mathematics Report Card* (1997) included children's beliefs about mathematics as a discipline. Nationally, 50% of the seventh graders either agreed or strongly agreed that learning mathematics is mostly memorization, and 83% believed that there is always a rule to follow in mathematics. If these are the perceptions of our students, then it becomes clear that they do not embrace the expectations or standards of society for a mathematically literate population.

The Identification of Standards

What does it mean to be a teacher of mathematics today? What are our goals, and how do we work toward them? How can we improve the profession? How can we provide experiences that meet the needs of our students in particular, and of society in general? Perhaps some basic principles or standards would help us decide.

A **standard** can be thought of as a benchmark or a statement against which a given item or position can be measured or compared. The Bureau of Weights and Measures, for example, has standards that define the various measures that we use. Restaurants and hotels have standards of service that they seek to uphold for their guests. As individuals, we have standards that are reflections of our personal values, philosophy, and way of life. Professions, too, have standards that mirror the vision and values of that profession.

The NCTM, with a membership of approximately 100,000 professionals, is an organization devoted to the improvement and promotion of mathematics education. Its mission is to provide vision and leadership in improving the teaching and learning of mathematics so that every student is ensured an equitable standards-based mathematics education and every teacher of mathematics is ensured an opportunity to grow professionally. The Council provides a forum to discuss new educational developments, share innovative classroom experiences, and examine changes taking place in the teaching of mathematics. In addition to publishing a wide variety of resource books, the Council publishes journals for teachers, including *Teaching Children Mathematics* (grades PreK–6), *Mathematics Teaching in the Middle School* (grades 5–9), *The Mathematics Teacher* (grades 8–12 and up), and the *Journal for Research in Mathematics Education* (PreK–16 and up), as well as an online journal titled *On-Math*.

Additional information about the NCTM, including membership information, publication catalogs, and member services/resources, can be obtained by writing NCTM, 1906 Association Drive, Reston, VA 20191–1593. You may also contact NCTM via email (nctm@nctm.org), the Web (www.nctm.org), fax (703-476-2970), or direct telephone (703-620-9840). The NCTM Web site also has information concerning student membership, NCTM administration, current issues, resources, position statements, conferences, grants, affiliated group services, and publications. Of special interest are a variety of NCTM position statements concerning issues such as calculator use, early childhood mathematics, equity, assessment, evaluation of teacher performance, mathematics for second-language learners, the achievement gap, metrication, professional development, technology, and mathematics for underrepresented groups.

The NCTM initially published its *Curriculum and Evaluation Standards for School Mathematics* in 1989. These standards were followed by the *Professional Standards for Teaching Mathematics* in 1991 and the *Assessment Standards for School Mathematics* in 1995. A major concern of all stakeholders in the education of youth was how to mesh this segregated collection of standards into a cohesive vision. As one answer, the NCTM revisited and revised the 1989, 1991, and 1995 standards into a single document entitled the NCTM *Principles and Standards for School Mathematics* (2000). This document reflects a vision of mathematical literacy necessary in a world that requires understanding and application of problem-solving and decision-making techniques. The main messages of the first three standards documents maintain their relevancy. The new standards document supports the direction and message of the original standards by refocusing, clarifying, and developing connections. The *Principles and Standards for School Mathematics* document also takes into account developments in technology that have occurred since the original standards were released and includes more examples to reinforce the intent and the spirit of the recommendations made. In 2007, the *Professional Standards for Teaching Mathematics* were revised and updated into a book entitled *Mathematics Teaching Today* (NCTM, 2007).

These standards documents are important for all mathematics teachers because they have become a primary source for evaluating and driving reforms in mathematics education. Such standards provide significant assistance in the processes of designing, implementing, and evaluating elementary and secondary mathematics programs

Principles and Standards for School Mathematics

In order to tackle the realities of today and provide for the expectations of tomorrow, it is essential that students (1) learn to value mathematics, (2) develop confidence in their ability to use mathematics, (3) become problem solvers (as opposed to simply answer finders), (4) learn to communicate mathematically, and (5) learn to reason mathematically. Societal goals for mathematics education must include the development of mathematically literate workers, lifelong learning, opportunity for all, and an informed populace. To accomplish these goals, there must be major shifts in

Curriculum—to allow a deeper study of important mathematics and its uses

Learning—to promote active student engagement with a variety of mathematical tools for solving problems

Teaching—to create a stimulating learning environment in which all students are challenged to reach their full potential

Assessment—to use assessment that is ongoing and based on many sources of evidence

The *Principles and Standards for School Mathematics* (2000) describes basic underlying assumptions regarding equity, curriculum, teaching, learning, assessment, and technology for instructional programs in mathematics. These principles endorse a view of what is necessary at the classroom, school, district, and national levels for effective mathematics education. The 1989, 1991, and 1995 standards were built on the position that all students can learn mathematics and that teachers play an essential role in helping students understand the subject. The *Principles and Standards* document goes further by spelling out six central principles that form the foundation on which the standards are built.

The six principles described in the NCTM *Principles and Standards for School Mathematics* (2000) are

- *Equity*. Excellence in mathematics education requires equity—high expectations and strong support for all students.

- *Curriculum*. A curriculum is more than a collection of activities: it must be coherent, focused on important mathematics, and well articulated across the grades.

- *Teaching*. Effective mathematics teaching requires understanding what students know and need to learn and then challenging and supporting them to learn it well.
- *Learning*. Students must learn mathematics with understanding, actively building new knowledge from experience and prior knowledge.
- *Assessment*. Assessment should support the learning of important mathematics and furnish useful information to both teachers and students.
- *Technology*. Technology is essential in teaching and learning mathematics; it influences the mathematics that is taught and enhances students' learning.

As in previous standards, the *Principles and Standards for School Mathematics* (2000) emphasizes the role of mathematical thinking—process standards—that cut across all grades. These process standards are described next.

PROBLEM SOLVING

Instructional programs from prekindergarten through grade 12 should enable all students to—

- build new mathematical knowledge through problem solving;
- solve problems that arise in mathematics and in other contexts;
- apply and adapt a variety of appropriate strategies to solve problems;
- monitor and reflect on the process of mathematical problem solving.

REASONING AND PROOF

Instructional programs from prekindergarten through grade 12 should enable all students to—

- recognize reasoning and proof as fundamental aspects of mathematics;
- make and investigate mathematical conjectures;
- develop and evaluate mathematical arguments and proofs;
- select and use various types of reasoning and methods of proof.

COMMUNICATION

Instructional programs from prekindergarten through grade 12 should enable all students to—

- organize and consolidate their mathematical thinking through communication;
- communicate their mathematical thinking coherently and clearly to peers, teachers, and others;
- analyze and evaluate the mathematical thinking and strategies of others;
- use the language of mathematics to express mathematical ideas precisely.

CONNECTIONS

Instructional programs from prekindergarten through grade 12 should enable all students to—

- recognize and use connections among mathematical ideas;
- understand how mathematical ideas interconnect and build on one another to produce a coherent whole;
- recognize and apply mathematics in contexts outside of mathematics.

MATHEMATICAL REPRESENTATION

Instructional programs from prekindergarten through grade 12 should enable all students to—

- create and use representations to organize, record, and communicate mathematical ideas;
- select, apply, and translate among mathematical representations to solve problems;
- use representations to model and interpret physical, social, and mathematical phenomena.

In addition to the five process standards, there are five content standards in the *Principles and Standards for School Mathematics* (2000) that address what a student should know. The content standards follow.

NUMBER AND OPERATIONS

Instructional programs from prekindergarten through grade 12 should enable all students to—

- understand numbers, ways of representing numbers, relationships among numbers, and number systems;
- understand meanings of operations and how they relate to one another;
- compute fluently and make reasonable estimates.

ALGEBRA

Instructional programs from prekindergarten through grade 12 should enable all students to—

- understand patterns, relations, and functions;
- represent and analyze mathematical situations and structures using algebraic symbols;
- use mathematical models to represent and understand quantitative relationships;
- analyze change in various contexts.

GEOMETRY

Instructional programs from prekindergarten through grade 12 should enable all students to—

- analyze characteristics and properties of two- and three-dimensional geometric shapes and develop mathematical arguments about geometric relationships;
- specify locations and describe spatial relationships using coordinate geometry and other representational systems;
- apply transformations and use symmetry to analyze mathematical situations;
- use visualization, spatial reasoning, and geometric modeling to solve problems.

MEASUREMENT

Instructional programs from prekindergarten through grade 12 should enable all students to—

- understand measurable attributes of objects and the units, systems, and processes of measurement;
- apply appropriate techniques, tools, and formulas to determine measurements.

DATA ANALYSIS AND PROBABILITY

Instructional programs from prekindergarten through grade 12 should enable all students to—

- formulate questions that can be addressed with data and collect, organize, and display relevant data to answer them;
- select and use appropriate statistical methods to analyze data;
- develop and evaluate inferences and predictions that are based on data;
- understand and apply basic concepts of probability.

These same 10 process and content standards are applied in each grade band to link what students should be learning across grades. Consequently, each individual standard includes an explanation and elaboration of key ideas that enable teachers to see what students should know coming to their grade band, what they should learn within that grade band, and where that will later lead. A more recent document entitled *Curriculum Focal Points for Prekindergarten Through Grade 8 Mathematics: A Quest for Coherence* (2006), describes a more detailed, grade-by-grade set of critical objectives that every student should master. This document can be

downloaded from the NCTM Web site (www.nctm.org). Perhaps most important, the *Principles and Standards for School Mathematics* includes research evidence collected since the first set of standards, which demonstrates that a long-term commitment to this vision can lead to improved mathematics teaching and learning.

According to the NCTM, the *Principles and Standards for School Mathematics* offers a vision of

1. Mathematical power for all in a technological society
2. Mathematics as something one does—solve problems, communicate, reason
3. A curriculum for all that includes a broad range of content, a variety of contexts, and deliberate connection
4. The learning of mathematics as an active, constructive process
5. Instruction based on real problems
6. Evaluation as a means of improving instruction, learning, and programs

To assist the reader, complete statements of all the standards for grades preK–2, 3–5, and 6–8 and suggested references to support each standard statement have been placed on the CD that accompanies this text.

Implementing the Process Standards

Instead of thinking of mathematics as a field of study that someone "knows," it might be more accurate to conceptualize mathematics as something that one "does"—more of a verb than a noun, if you will. NCTM defines these common process threads as problem solving, reasoning and proof, communication, and representation, as well as a connection within itself and with other subject areas. The process standards provide a philosophical base for approaching the teaching and learning of all mathematics. If we accept their importance, then they will drive the ways in which we select and organize experiences from the remaining standards.

For example, consider the case of a fourth-grade class that is learning the procedure for multiplying 16 times 25 and the instructional strategies you might use to help students make sense of the process. We could resort to a less-than-effective but all-too-common approach in which the teacher "shows and tells" the entire class how to record the algorithmic process. That is, we would write the exercise as

$$\begin{array}{r} 25 \\ \times\ 16 \\ \hline \end{array}$$

Then we would continue: "Now, multiply 6 times 5 and get 30. Write the 0 below the line under the 6, and write a small 3 above the 2 in 25."

$$\overset{3}{25}$$
$$\underline{\times\ 16}$$
$$0$$

"Next, multiply the 6 times the 2 and get 12, and add the 3 to the 12 to get 15. Write this to the left of the 0 below the line. From this point on, forget about that small 3 you wrote above the 2—you don't need it anymore."

$$25$$
$$\underline{\times\ 16}$$
$$150$$

"Now, multiply the 1 times 5, writing the answer, 5, one place to the left under the 150. Also, multiply the 1 times 2 and write that answer to the left of the 5."

$$25$$
$$\underline{\times\ 16}$$
$$150$$
$$25$$

"Finally, write the sum of the two partial products under the line, remembering to 'carry,' if necessary, when you add."

$$25$$
$$\underline{\times\ 16}$$
$$150$$
$$\underline{25\ \ }$$
$$400$$

These rote steps *can* be memorized through repetition, but the student will possess only the skill to do this particular type of problem. Transfer of this skill to other problems, even similar ones, will not necessarily occur. Under a rote procedural approach, it would be common to hear a student exclaim, "I know how to do it when they're like this one, but what do I do if a number has 'hundreds' in it?"

A more effective approach to this same computational exercise would take on a dramatically different appearance and spirit if couched in the vision of the process standards as represented by problem solving, communication, reasoning and proof, representations, and connections. In such an instance, consideration would be given to what the exercise actually represents by placing the exercise in a real-life setting. Rather than just asking for the answer to "16 times 25," we might relate it to determining the cost of purchasing 16 stickers at 25 cents each. Alternatively, we might consider the total number of stickers in an array or sheet of stickers, 16 rows with 25 stickers in each row. Suddenly, our arithmetic exercise has been transformed into a geometric context with the answer representing the area of a rectangle that has dimensions of 16 by 25.

This geometric approach might lead us, in later grades, to recognizing the connection between $(a + b)\ (c + d)$ and 16×25, both of which can be represented by the sum of four partial products. This can perhaps best be seen by rewriting 16×25 as $(10 + 6)(20 + 5)$ or as

$$\begin{array}{r} 20 + 5 \\ \underline{\times\ 10 + 6} \\ 120 + 30 \\ \underline{200 + 50\ \ \ \ \ } \\ 200 + 120 + 50 + 30 \end{array} \qquad \begin{array}{r} a + b \\ \underline{\times\ c + d} \\ ad + bd \\ \underline{ac + bc\ \ \ \ } \\ ac + ad + bc + bd \end{array}$$

Another tactic might be to emphasize a different interpretation of what "16 times 25" means; that is, "How much is 16 groups of 25?" This might lead us to think of 16 groups of 25 in an alternative form, such as 8 groups of 50 or even 4 groups of 100. In fact, if you think of "16 times 25" as "4 groups of 100," you can get the answer in your head, with no need for an algorithm (computational procedure), paper and pencil, or calculator.

Even if we chose a strictly paper-and-pencil approach to the problem, the discussion that would take place in a contemporary standards-based classroom would differ in emphasis and direction from that of a more traditional classroom. Instead of rote memorization and thoughtless reproduction of seemingly meaningless steps in the algorithm, an approach that incorporated the spirit of the standards would continually reflect not only on what was taking place, but also on why. For example, instead of taking "1 times 5 and then 1 times 2 and shifting the answer by one place" as was shown earlier, we would emphasize the multiplication of 25 by 10 to get 250.

Although the NCTM *Principles and Standards for School Mathematics* were written to be understood and translated into classroom activities and objectives, they are much more comprehensive than can possibly be conveyed here. For example, the NCTM standards also address assessment as an integral part of attaining the vision those standards represent. Assessment is, of course, measuring what students know about mathematics, but it also includes information about how they think about mathematics. Assessment is a constant part of teaching rather than a single act that occurs after teaching. Assessment goes beyond identifying right or wrong responses and requires a more comprehensive view of what is to be evaluated, including student behaviors, curricular choices, and instructional models. Effective assessment demands that we use multiple techniques (e.g., calculators, computers, manipulatives) and formats (e.g., written, oral, demonstration) for gathering data as opposed to simply using traditional paper-and-pencil methods.

Finally, assessment, as viewed through the NCTM standards, utilizes standardized achievement test results as only one of many indicators of program outcomes and student success.

Our purpose in this chapter is not to offer a detailed discussion of the NCTM *Principles and Standards for School Mathematics*. Because of the volume of material, it is impossible to do a thorough presentation here. Nevertheless, we hope that as you read this text, you will reflect on the intent and vision of mathematics that these standards represent. We urge you to familiarize yourself with this document—a document that has the potential to greatly influence the mathematics learning, teaching, and assessment procedures in our schools today and in the future. The reader is encouraged to purchase a copy of the *Principles and Standards for School Mathematics* from NCTM. The standards are also available online to members of NCTM (students can join NCTM at a reduced rate) or can be accessed online for free at http://www.nctm.org for a limited time period for nonmembers.

In Chapters 2 and 3, respectively, you will learn of two companion landmark NCTM standards projects: the *Professional Standards for Teaching Mathematics* (1991) (and its 2007 revision);— and the *Assessment Standards for School Mathematics* (1995). We will explore the many ways in which these documents reflect and support the vision of the *Principles and Standards for School Mathematics* (2000).

Describing A Contemporary Mathematics Program

As we begin to explore the elements of an effective school mathematics program, we must ask three fundamental questions: (1) What is mathematics? (2) How do students learn mathematics? (3) What mathematics should students learn?

In the past, elementary school mathematics was, at times, viewed as being synonymous with arithmetic. That is, mathematics was interpreted by many as the process of calculating numerical answers. Mathematics programs subscribing to this narrow belief were based on **rote memorization** of number facts and mindless computational drill. Contemporary programs stress a broader view of mathematics, with an emphasis on understanding fundamental mathematics concepts and the interrelationships among different topics in mathematics and other disciplines. Even the NCTM changed the title of its elementary school journal from *The Arithmetic Teacher* to *Teaching Children Mathematics* in the 1990s to reflect this important philosophical change. All students need to explore content and applications that extend beyond the solely computational aspect of the arithmetic curriculum.

Does this mean that students must no longer memorize basic facts or practice to anchor computational skills? Definitely not! It is essential that students work to develop such skills—the debate is not over "whether" they do this, but "how" they do it. Memorization and drill must be preceded by an understanding of what basic facts mean and why algorithms work. Without this understanding, the child has little chance of progressing very far in mathematics or applying the mathematics he or she knows to significant practical problems or applications. An effective school mathematics program emphasizes a marriage between the understanding of mathematical concepts and the development of skills to provide the student with true power in and over mathematics.

Now, let's address how students learn mathematics. If mathematics instruction is to develop creative, mathematical minds, then the methods of presentation and instruction must be examined. For generations, the technique of instruction in mathematics was essentially a three-step process:

1. The teacher told the students what topic they were to learn.
2. The teacher used examples to show how to solve a particular type of example or problem.
3. The students then routinely imitated the given procedure "mechanically" to find answers to a great number of similar examples.

This type of "show-and-tell" approach to teaching mathematics mainly promotes imitation and drill of seemingly meaningless facts and rules. There is not much to be gained in spending countless hours teaching a student how to do something that an inexpensive calculator can do more efficiently. This method of instruction reveals little or nothing of the meaning behind the process that the student is imitating. Thousands of people "borrow" and "carry" numbers, wonder what to do with remainders, or try to remember which of two fractions in a division exercise is the one to "invert" before multiplying. Such confusion is the natural outcome of "learning" mathematics by imitation and rote memorization. Picking the correct rule from a collection of meaningless rules should not be what mathematics learning is about.

Rather than a passive method of mathematics instruction, a contemporary program promotes an active learning process—mentally, physically, visually, and emotionally. In this active, **guided discovery method**, a skilled teacher places students in situations in which each student's actions reveal the extent of his or her reasoning and comprehension of the concepts, definitions, techniques, and processes being explored. Students who "think through" mathematics in this way gain more confidence through their own discoveries and observations than by trying to recall imposed memorized rules. They comprehend the reasoning underlying mathematical operations and processes and can apply them in new situations—a true definition of what it means to actually "learn" something.

Using this active interpretation of teaching, children still need to memorize basic facts and develop proficiency in fundamental algorithms for calculation. Also, children still need some well-designed practice and drill to anchor skills. Systematic reinforcement should be part of any effective mathematics program. However, such reinforcement must be based on the notion that the student has developed sufficient understanding of the concept prior to practice and, thus, can avoid the purely mechanical application of rules and procedures.

A guided discovery approach (sometimes referred to as *inquiry*) relies heavily on **inductive reasoning** (specific examples leading to general rules) rather than **deductive reasoning** (general rules applied to specific examples). For the inductive method, children are asked to solve some examples extending previously learned techniques and then to formulate general statements based on patterns they observe. In effect, students develop their own versions of rules or generalizations (with the teacher's guidance) and then use these to solve other examples. The teacher provides a focus for the children's active discussion, rather than simply showing them which procedure to use in a given situation. Many examples of this type of instruction will be presented throughout this textbook.

One great advantage to using an inductive approach is the freedom children experience in looking for ways to solve mathematical examples. Without teacher-imposed rules to condition or limit their thinking, children are free to find that a given example can be solved in various ways. Thus, children discover through their own experience one of the major features of contemporary mathematics: there is often more than a single way to arrive at a solution. A simple example of this can be illustrated by thinking of a classroom of second graders being asked to add two, 2-digit numbers for the first time (such as $36 + 18$). Experienced teachers know that if children are not *told* to add 6 to 8 and "carry," most children naturally add 30 to 10 (40), followed by adding 6 to 8 (14), for a total of 54. Why? Because children read from left to right, so they naturally want to work addition problems in the same way. When we ask them to begin by adding 6 to 8, we are forcing them to think in a way that is the opposite of how their minds work. Children need to be given the freedom to think creatively and to apply previous knowledge to new problem situations.

Students also quickly learn that some problems have more than one correct solution, whereas others have no solution at all. When children are allowed this freedom and are encouraged to use their imaginations without being tied to arbitrary rules and rigid steps, they will learn to seek ways to solve any problem—not just the teacher's way. Even students who struggle with mathematics, when guided by a careful and patient teacher, can appreciate the fact that a problem does not necessarily have just one way of being solved. This may, in fact, be a great encouragement to the less imaginative student, who would no longer be baffled and discouraged by trying to remember half-understood rules.

Levels of Abstraction

The issue of different levels of abstraction must also be considered when discussing a guided discovery approach. It is highly unlikely that, when encountering $126 \div 3$, a student will "discover" the standard abstract algorithm for division, but it is quite likely that the same student will "discover" a means of dividing 126 physical objects into 3 equivalent groups (or dividing 126 objects into groups of 3). The difference, of course, is that the latter is a physical representation of the abstract process. This process of examining concepts at the physical or manipulative level prior to the establishment of abstract procedures or algorithms allows the student (and the teacher) to build knowledge by constructing a bridge between the two.

Consider the following odd scenario to help you understand the importance of levels of abstraction. Suppose you were visited by a creature from another planet, and it became important for you to convey the notion of what a tree is. You would not succeed in communicating any significant meaning to this creature by *writing the word* TREE on a piece of paper. You'd have to try something other than the abstract word itself. Your success might improve somewhat if you tried *drawing a picture* of a tree. The stranger would then have a better idea of what a tree actually is, but that understanding would be severely limited by your ability to draw. In any case, even a photograph would leave some misunderstanding about the nature of trees. If you really want to give the stranger a solid foundation for understanding what a tree is, then it would be best to take the stranger outside to *see and touch an actual tree*.

This is a good analogy for the **levels of abstraction** found in the teaching of mathematics. If you want to teach children about division, you would have little success simply stating a rote rule or procedure. A picture of what takes place when you divide would certainly be more beneficial, but it would still be less effective than actually using physical objects to illustrate the process of dividing a set or collection into equivalent groups. Students are not prepared to learn a concept at the **abstract** or **symbolic level** until they have had sufficient experiences with the concept at the **concrete** or **manipulative level** or, at the very least, at the **representative** or **pictorial level**.

In most cases, a student's approach to an exercise or a problem will be conditioned by his or her own experience. The student may not choose the best or most efficient method to solve a problem if prior experience has not included relevant knowledge.

For example, if a student does not understand place value and is called on to complete an addition sentence such as $23 + 41 = \square$, an effective approach would probably be to use counters as a model. In other words, it would be appropriate to count out 23 counters, count out 41 counters, and then combine the two sets and count to determine a total of 64 counters.

Another student might recognize that 23 counters are needed at the start and, beginning with 23, count 41 more counters to arrive at a total of 64. The second method could be considered slightly more sophisticated than the first.

A third student might recognize 23 on the number line and begin counting from that point. Beginning at 23, this student would count 41 units and arrive at a point named 64.

Another student, familiar with place value, might react in this fashion: "Add the tens: $40 + 20 = 60$; add the ones: $1 + 3 = 4$; $60 + 4 = 64$; therefore, my answer is 64."

Still another child might arrange the addends vertically, thinking "$3 + 1 = 4$" and write the 4; "$20 + 40 = 60$" and write 60 under the 4; and "$4 + 60 = 64$" and write 64 for the answer.

$$
\begin{array}{r}
23 \\
+41 \\
\hline
4 \\
+60 \\
\hline
64
\end{array}
\quad \text{or} \quad
\begin{array}{r}
23 \\
+41 \\
\hline
60 \\
+\ 4 \\
\hline
64
\end{array}
$$

So we have illustrated five different methods for completing the addition sentence $23 + 41 = \square$. How many more can you think of? (You can count on your students to show you many other approaches!) In each of the cases we've shown, the student has had the opportunity to think about the exercise on a personal level. In this example, each student used the same basic concepts, but at different levels of comprehension and abstraction.

It is not our purpose to keep children operating at a primitive level but, rather, to assist them through appropriate experiences to more efficient levels of operation. We can better accomplish this if we structure increasingly abstract connections to already understood concrete and pictorial representations.

Problem-solving activities should be varied and taken from real-life situations so that students do not get the idea that mathematics problems exist only in textbooks. Research in learning theory suggests that the frequent use of physical objects is essential for developing abstract concepts. Children need to manipulate and experiment with models that represent the concept being studied. "Hands-on" and "minds-on" experiences are an important part of developing both skill and understanding in solving practical mathematical problems. Thus, it is no surprise that there is increasing interest in learning center and cooperative learning activities, as well as the use of concrete, manipulative materials for the mathematics classroom.

Learning center activities can be used for a variety of purposes—to build readiness for abstract concepts, to provide motivation, to develop problem-solving skills, and to present significant applications of mathematics to practical problems. **Students at all levels of ability can profit from learning center experiences, and a folder of instructional activities, such as those found in each of the various content chapters of this text and on the accompanying CD, can be an invaluable aid for the classroom teacher.**

Teachers should strive to keep students from developing the idea that problem solving is simply a matter of thrashing about aimlessly until one stumbles on a solution (or gives up the search). A systematic, well-thought-out approach should be selected by applying reasoning and understanding. Students should realize, however, that even with careful selection, the "best" method is not always chosen the first time, and they should be encouraged to take various approaches to a given problem when a solution is not readily apparent.

Teachers and pupils should spend time together seeking solutions to problems, rather than the student always attempting to solve problems similar to the ones that the teacher has already solved for them. Students need to recognize the importance of communicating not only their solutions to others, but also the method of arriving at a solution. They should be aware that scientists and mathematicians do not have a magical "instant" solution to every problem. It is good for them to realize that people solve problems, check them, and then go back and look for other approaches when their results indicate that something is wrong. The word *problem* itself indicates that often a solution is not readily apparent—if a solution is readily apparent, then it would no longer be a problem.

Theoretical Foundations for a Contemporary Mathematics Program

Education has developed and grown as a profession through the application and refinement of learning theory. Let's briefly examine some of the major

RESEARCH SNAPSHOT

What are some of the results of allowing students to construct their own solutions?

Kamii has found that second graders who have been encouraged to do their own thinking since kindergarten are able to invent their own procedures for adding multiplace numbers. They are able to invent procedures for problems such as 35 + 27 written horizontally, vertically, or in any other form on the chalkboard.

In a study in which a fourth-grade teacher taught algorithms and then allowed students to invent their own strategies the next year, the students were much more successful when they used invented strategies (Kamii, 1998).[1] Fifteen of the 18 students who used invented procedures correctly answered 6 + 53 + 185, while the previous year, only 3 of the 16 students who used the conventional algorithm gave the correct answer.

Do you think the conventional algorithm is more efficient than students' invented solutions? When a child uses the algorithm to solve a problem correctly, what do you know that the child understands?

[1] Kamii, C., & Dominick, A. (1998). The harmful effects of algorithms in grades 1–4. In L. Morrow & M. Kenney (Eds.), *The teaching and learning of algorithms in school mathematics* (pp. 130–140). Reston, VA: National Council of Teachers of Mathematics.
For additional research briefs, "ERIC Digests" lets you search more than 2000 short syntheses of research on a range of education topics. The syntheses were produced by the Educational Resources Information Center (ERIC). Check http://www.ericfacility.net/ericdigests/index/.

theories that influence school mathematics programs and discuss ideas for implementing these theories in your classroom.

It is possible to generalize that a majority of learning theories fall into one of two major categories—the behaviorists and the cognitivists. Any attempt to summarize these positions runs the risk of oversimplification, and this discussion is certainly not intended to be comprehensive. Nevertheless, certain fundamental characteristics can be cited that may assist you in imagining how taking a particular position on any one of these issues can affect the instructional decisions you make as a teacher.

Behaviorists

In general, behaviorists believe that

- Learning is considered to be segmented and linear. Bits and pieces of knowledge and skill are acquired sequentially and in a certain order.

- Instruction is designed to increase competence in terms of goals defined by others (e.g., teachers, administrators, local and state education agencies).

- Assessment is conducted for the purpose of identifying deficiencies and frequently occurs by means of normative instruments such as standardized tests, which interrupt instruction.

Cognitivists

In general, cognitivists believe that

- Learning is viewed as the processes of incorporating and restructuring. Knowledge and skills are acquired through experiences that add to, interrelate, and change existing perceptions.

- Instruction is a means of facilitating change in the individual. It is designed to assist learners in restructuring goals and the ways in which they interpret their environment.

- Assessment is conducted to determine the learner's perceptions, strengths, and weaknesses and is designed to serve as part of instruction, not as an interruption to it.

As you might imagine from the differences in these broad statements, it is possible to set up a form of continuum that has "pure" behaviorists on one end and "pure" cognitivists on the other. The variety of learning theories discussed here have not been identified specifically as predominantly falling into either the behaviorist or the cognitivist camp—in fact, very few existing theories lie solely in one camp or the other but are eclectic variations. As you read the descriptions of each of these theories, give some thought as to where you would place each on this continuum and how the acceptance of a particular theory would affect the climate and demeanor of a mathematics classroom.

Jean Piaget

An influential theory for interpreting mathematical learning has been that of the Swiss psychologist Jean Piaget (1896–1980). Piaget made significant use of observation of children at play to determine a theory of how they learned. He considered the concept of "operation" as fundamental to the development of knowledge (Piaget, 1954).[1] An *operation* requires that the student carry out an action on an object and be aware of the consequence of that action. A student, according to Piaget, has performed an operation only if he or she can reason about that operation. An example would be when a child decides to arrange a set of blocks in order from heaviest to lightest and recognizes this feat as an accomplishment of a goal. The action must be internalized and reversible. That is, the child must not merely be repeating someone else's prompting, and the child must recognize that there is a way to return the objects to their original state.

Piaget postulated that children construct new knowledge as they move through cognitive stages, building on what they already know. He identified four stages in a learner's development of knowledge—the sensorimotor, preoperational, concrete operational, and formal operational stages.

The sensorimotor stage generally occurs from birth to about age 2, a preverbal and presymbolic stage in which intelligence is defined as the ability to accomplish some task (e.g., to obtain a toy that is lying on a blanket by pulling the blanket). At this stage, the child solves problematic situations by experimentation and action rather than by a purely mental process.

In the preoperational stage, which begins at about the age of 2 and continues until about age 7, language is acquired, and the child begins to understand signs and symbols as representations of the real world. The world of "pretend" becomes a source of play. A table draped with a tablecloth can be just a table, but it can also be a cave or hideout. However, the child still does not develop knowledge of conservation, the concept that essential properties of things do not change when superficial properties are changed. A classical example of conservation involves two rows of counters, each row spaced differently. A child is asked if the rows contain the same number of objects, fewer objects, or more objects (see the following example).

Begin with

[1]Piaget, J. (1954). *The construction of reality in the child.* New York: Basic Books.

Change to

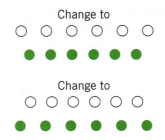

Change to

In the first example, the child at the preoperational stage will typically say that there are the same number of counters. In the second, he or she will often say that there are more unshaded counters. In the third, the response will usually be that there are more shaded ones. The child at the preoperational stage will display the same sort of faulty reasoning when confronted with other conservation tasks (e.g., number, length, area, volume).

At the concrete operational stage, stage three of Piaget's theory of development, the child develops logical thought. This stage begins at approximately age 7 (sometimes earlier, sometimes as late as age 9 or 10). At this stage, children can manipulate objects and show logical thinking—they understand conservation and simple logical processes and begin to appreciate that there are other points of view besides their own.

Finally, at stage four, the formal operational stage, children develop the ability to think abstractly, understand cause and effect, and make hypotheses. This stage begins at about age 11 or 12—the age of many fifth or sixth graders (although not even all *adults* function at this formal operations stage).

Three important aspects of Piaget's theory of learning are the notions of *disequilibrium, accommodation,* and *assimilation.* When an individual encounters information that is either new or contrary to prior knowledge, he or she experiences a discord that needs to be resolved. One way of accomplishing this resolution is to incorporate that information as part of that person's view of the world. The individual makes adjustments in the way he or she views the information and its relationship to what he or she already knows by means of accommodation. When successful, the information becomes internalized or assimilated. One might argue that learning could be defined as the recognition of personal disequilibrium, followed by the processes of accommodation and assimilation. Acceptance of such a definition of learning would have a dramatic effect on the nature and design of a child's classroom experience.

Additional research is still needed with respect to Piaget's work. Even now, there is some question as to whether the rate of progress through the four stages can be accelerated or impeded and, if so, how this could be accomplished. Piaget's theories do, however, suggest important messages for teachers. If most students at the elementary school level have not yet attained the formal operational stage, then we must provide opportunities to explore concepts at manipulative levels and aid in the transition from these models to abstractions. The child must be actively involved in the learning process—physically, visually, mentally, and emotionally. Listening to definitions read by an authority will not lead to the same outcoomes as forming and reforming a definition through observations. Teachers should strive to provide a stimulating environment for children and encourage them to interact, to experiment, to discover mathematical patterns, to question mathematical processes, and to explore mathematical thinking for themselves.

Lev Vygotsky

Lev Semenovich Vygotsky (1896–1934) was a Russian child psychologist who completed most of his work on *social constructivist theory* in the area of language and thought. Like Piaget, he believed that a child learned through sociocultural activity, but Vygotsky did not integrate biological development with cognitive development. He argued, instead, that children transform experiences into knowledge by using prior knowledge—that is, the individual's experience and the history of the culture in which the individual is raised both positively and negatively influence the child's cognitive abilities (Vygotsky, 1962).[2]

Vygotsky suggested that social play mediates learning—that play is a risk-free environment, rich in mathematics, science, and language that allows a child the liberty to make mistakes and provides the motivation to learn from others. An important concept to Vygotskian theory is the notion of two stages of development, the *zone of actual development* and the *zone of proximal development*. The child's zone of actual development is defined as the stage of development that the child has already achieved, while the zone of proximal development represents the potential developmental level of a child—the point at which a child is capable of participating in guided activities with others. Vygotsky believed that this potential was not revealed by traditional tests, but that the guiding questions of a facilitative instructor or more capable peers would bring about new levels of knowledge.

Another of Vygotsky's main concerns was that of culturally devised tools. He was intrigued that culture provides us with ways of dealing effectively with the problems we face through the use of devices as "navigational" equipment. It was his position that not only do these tools make life easier, but that we also increase our intellectual capabilities through their use. Today,

Vygotsky would undoubtedly appreciate the huge potential that calculators and computers have as aids to learning. To a Vygotskian, appropriate interaction with a calculator doesn't destroy the mind—it enriches it.

Vygotsky also championed the role of collaborative learning. He identified a process he labeled as *scaffolding*, in which the teacher builds learning experiences from a child's cognitive and social development. If a child is challenged, then it is likely that the child will learn more working with a peer or guiding authority than he or she would if the challenge were examined in isolation. With such exposure, the individual will be able to apply this learning to other situations.

It is unlikely that you can examine contemporary writings on the subject of learning theories in mathematics (or science) education without encountering a philosophy referred to as *constructivism*, sometimes described as an outgrowth of research initiated by Piaget and Vygotsky. In brief, a basic tenet of constructivism is that learners construct their own meaning through continuous and active interaction with their environment. Errors are an important part of this constructive process. Misconceptions are refined and reworked to become alternate conceptions. The idea of a structured controversy becomes a critical factor in the way the learner gains knowledge.

Von Glaserfeld (1991)[3] describes the constructivist viewpoint as having roots that stretch far back in educational history. Socrates is remembered for, among other things, a method of questioning designed to give the student's thoughts and experiences a central role in determining the direction of learning. John Dewey (1859–1952) commented on the folly of trying to learn by being told. Dewey wrote:

> No thought, no idea, can possibly be conveyed as an idea from one person to another. When it is told, it is to the one to whom it is told, another fact, not an idea. . . . Only by wrestling with the conditions of the problem at first hand, seeking and finding his own way out, does he think.[4]

Jean Piaget showed constructivist leanings when he emphasized the important role of discovery and free investigation in the learning process. According to Piaget, learning based on the transmission of knowledge from one person to another is psychologically archaic, and the goal of intellectual education is not to know

[2]Vygotsky, L. S. (1962). *Thought and language*. Cambridge, MA: M.I.T. Press.

[3]Von Glaserfeld, E. (Ed.). (1991). *Radical constructivism in mathematics education*. Dordrecht, The Netherlands: Kluwer Academic Publishers.

[4]Dewey, J. (1974). The child and the curriculum. In R. D. Archambault (Ed.), *John Dewey on education*. Chicago: The University of Chicago Press.

how to repeat or retain readymade truths. For Piaget, knowledge is constructed as students organize their experiences in a manner consistent with prior learning. This fits with the Piagetian notion of disequilibrium, in which competing ideas are refined and revised to be consistent with what the learner knows to be true.

George M. Bodner, in *Constructivism: A Theory of Knowledge* (1986),[5] capsulizes an important defining characteristic of constructivist thought:

> There is no conduit from one brain to another. All teachers can do is disturb the environment. Effective instruction depends on our ability to understand how students make sense of our "disturbances" (stimuli) rather than how we [the teachers] make sense of these stimuli ourselves. Knowledge is constructed by the learner.

An approach to implementing constructivist views in classroom instruction has been described in a model commonly known as the *learning cycle*. This model provides both teacher and learner access to ways to

1. Engage and access prior knowledge
2. Investigate problems via hands-on and minds-on activities
3. Develop, clarify, and construct meaningful explanations
4. Expand and apply new understandings
5. Use authentic assessment to judge the new understandings

Using such a model requires careful planning on the part of the teacher and conscious efforts to avoid being too restrictive in the control of the directions a lesson might take. To avoid lessons that degenerate into "what should we learn now?" a teacher must design an organized but flexible set of investigations that anticipate the various ways that students will perceive the results.

Jerome Bruner

An American psychologist and learning theorist who has received a great deal of attention is Jerome Bruner (1915–). An important idea that he espouses, which can have a significant impact on how children learn, is that a child passes through three levels of understanding: *enactive, iconic,* and *symbolic* (Bruner, 1968).[6]

At the enactive level, the child manipulates objects and in the process develops the ability to conceptualize.

At the iconic level, the child can reason without manipulating objects and may use pictures rather than physical objects to think through a situation. At the symbolic level, the child becomes capable of manipulating symbols, rather than using objects or pictures of objects, and of translating experience into language.

Bruner's theory suggests that children begin by actively manipulating concrete, or tangible, objects; generalize a concept or idea based on the manipulation of these materials; and then move to expressing the concept in symbolic form. By means of manipulative models, concepts that might be considered out of reach if dealt with only abstractly can be explored at the student's level of understanding. The guided discovery method of teaching is based on Bruner's theory, in which process is often described as more important than product.

Pierre van Hiele and Dina van Hiele-Geldof

In the late 1950s, Dutch educators Pierre van Hiele and Dina van Hiele-Geldof described a theory of geometry learning that is referred to as the van Hiele model (van Hiele, 1986).[7] This theory identified five levels of thinking in geometry. In brief, a learner is presented with appropriate instructional experiences that aid in the progress from one level to the next, with a learner able to achieve a level only by passing through the previous one(s). First, students are able to recognize shapes (level 0), then they can discover basic properties of shapes (level 1), and then they can reason informally about the properties of these shapes (level 2). In levels 3 and 4, the learner is able to work with more formal and axiomatic geometric reasoning involving proof. More specifically, the five levels are

> *Level 0.* The student is able to identify and name geometric figures and shapes such as squares, circles, angles, and line segments based on visual models. For example, if a child is asked why a figure is a square, he or she is likely to say, "because it's square" at this level but may not be able to communicate that it has four sides or "square" corners.
>
> *Level 1.* The student is able to analyze relationships among various figures and shapes based on component parts, and he or she can discover properties of a set of shapes through hands-on

[5]Bodner, G. M. (1986). *Constructivism: A theory of knowledge.* New York: Wiley.
[6]Bruner, J. S. (1968). *Toward a theory of instruction.* New York: W.W. Norton.
[7]van Hiele, P. M. (1986). *Structure and insight.* Orlando, FL: Academic Press.

actions such as direct measurement, paper folding, and picture drawing. A child functioning at this level is likely to recognize that a rhombus has four congruent sides but would have difficulty recognizing that a square is a specific type of rhombus because this requires making connections between the characteristics of two different shapes.

Level 2. The student is able to make logical, but informal, arguments that demonstrate connections between properties discovered in levels 0 and 1.

Level 3. The student is able to prove theorems using deductive reasoning and to identify relationships among groups of theorems.

Level 4. The student is able to compare and contrast theorems founded on different basic premises.

You may notice that the van Hiele model of thinking in geometry also seems to use the notion of concrete—representative—abstract stages of development that are so common to other theories. Level 0 clearly reflects a manipulative level that also requires an initial effort of verbal description that becomes more defined as the student passes into level 1. For levels 1 and 2, the student focuses on representative or pictorial models to visualize properties, while in levels 3 and 4, the student has reached a stage at which abstract, symbolic reasoning is the common strategy. Students pass from one level to the next based on developmentally appropriate learning experiences designed by the teacher. The teacher needs to assess student backgrounds to appropriately design lessons that match the level at which the students are functioning.

Theory into Practice

Translating learning theories into successful classroom practice requires a skillful blending of teaching techniques, content development, and sensitivity to student-learning characteristics. We all want to create an environment that is conducive to learning. The problem is, what is conducive? For that matter, what is learning?

The listing of students' previous experiences and the identification of targets for a given grade level provide an important frame of reference for planning the year's instruction. However, they may also mask the challenging variation in student understanding, learning styles, interests, and needs. Within any classroom, there is likely to be a range of intellectual capabilities and interests, as well as an uneven landscape of concept formation, attitudes, and learning habits. Our curriculum should *not* serve to excuse us from addressing these differences through "teaching to the middle third."

Some students will have acquired their mathematical skills through memorization, others by example and visualization. Part of the class may have a firm grasp of concepts but still be weak on skill application. The rest of the class may have the opposite problem. Some individuals will demonstrate a facility for learning new ideas and will readily explore new topics with confidence. Other individuals will be hesitant about new concepts, will be reluctant to pose questions, and will exhibit doubt and misgivings about their aptitudes for mathematics.

Diverse student backgrounds and learning needs call for multiple approaches in developing new ideas and reviewing those concepts previously studied. Some students will understand a particular concept after introduction to a model of that concept. Other students will require multiple examples and/or counterexamples, and still others will need a formal definition before they fully understand the concept.

For example, some students will distinguish between prime and composite numbers by recognizing that a composite number can be represented by at least two distinct rectangular arrays of dots, while a prime number can be represented by only one distinct rectangular array.

Composite (12)

Prime (13)

Other students may more readily understand the concept of a prime number by identifying what it is NOT and comparing this to what it is (by counterexample). Still others will be uncomfortable with the concept until they can apply a definition of a prime number as "a whole number greater than 1 with only itself and 1 as factors."

Many elementary school children are at the point at which they begin to appreciate mathematics as a process and a way of thinking rather than as merely the application of rules and formulas. Some students have sufficient mental maturity to begin to question the why and how of techniques and procedures they may have taken for granted in earlier work. The teacher's task is to encourage this type of thinking at all levels by skillful questioning and by setting an atmosphere of intellectual curiosity.

Students are innately interested in learning new things. By capitalizing on students' expanding interests and growing cognitive abilities, teachers can create situations ripe for hypothesizing and generalizing. Manipulatives, games, calculators, computers, and learning centers offer students opportunities to explore and hone their emerging thinking skills. Problem-solving experiences provide students with the means to learn how to organize information, identify patterns, apply deductive and inductive thinking, and make and check hypotheses.

Activities that do not restrict students' avenues of success to a single route are the key to devising learning experiences that encourage thinking. Students' approaches to and reasoning through learning situations should be as diverse as the students themselves. All students have reached their current levels of achievement by different routes in developing the skills they possess, the attitudes they have acquired, and the modes of thinking on which they rely. The study of mathematics should be a stimulating endeavor that enables students to build from sets of individual experience and that expands their abilities to think mathematically.

Student's perceptions of mathematics and the teacher's ability to correctly read these perceptions play a significant role in instruction. Students who have had difficulty with mathematics in the past will most likely tend to view the subject as a barrier. Efforts to review material with them at the beginning of the school year may meet with resistance and may encourage self-deprecating attitudes. Other students are at the opposite end of this spectrum. Tired of review, these students hunger for new experiences. They may also view mathematics as a wall, of sorts, but for them it is a challenge to get around or over rather than an obstacle blocking their way. For two different reasons, attempts to review at the beginning of the year frequently backfire with both types of students. A teacher who chooses to review rather than explore new topics may find one group of students threatened and the other group bored. Thus, a viable option is the combination of review and extension. The teacher can check competencies and diagnose capabilities with prior content, while also exploring alternative approaches to familiar work. Even simple tasks take on renewed importance if couched in the right situation and explored in an appropriate, sometimes novel, manner.

The building blocks of mathematical understanding are concepts (e.g., comparison, division by distributing equally, and percent as part of a whole). Concepts enable students to bring sense to the operations they perform and provide a framework within which skills are learned and retained. They supply students with the insights necessary to apply and adapt what they know. Students who have a sound conceptual background are capable of thinking and acting mathematically. Students poorly grounded in concepts are often forced to resort to memorization and superficial guesswork when confronting mathematical tasks.

In this respect, teaching mathematics is very much a team activity. Seldom are concepts fully developed during one year of instruction. Students progress through stages (concrete, representative, and abstract) in acquiring a full understanding of a concept. Instruction at each successive grade level must build on the

ideas previously developed. Assessment of student understanding at any particular grade often reflects the culmination of the efforts of teachers over several grades in building a particular idea. However, instruction conducted by a teacher during the year may receive relatively little assessment emphasis, even though that instruction may eventually be crucial to whether students comprehend subsequent material.

For these reasons, communication between teachers at all grade levels is essential to the success of the total program. Teachers must appreciate how their efforts combine and contribute to the success of the program as a whole. A student's image of what mathematics is, how it is best learned, and how it relates to his or her world is not formed within a given school year—it develops over time. The teachers in a school can aid in this development by presenting a shared and valued perspective only possible through cross-grade communication.

Closure

In this chapter, we introduced you to several aspects of mathematics in contemporary elementary schools. Mathematics education is bringing together new learning theories and materials for creative teachers to use in developing exciting classroom environments. **The CD that accompanies this text includes a summary of *Fundamental Concepts and Critical Ideas* for each grade level, preK–8.** Embedded in the discussion of each grade level is an outline of the important ideas of five content strands identified by the NCTM in the national mathematics standards. These content strands are number concepts and operations; patterns, relations, and functions; geometry; algebra; measurement; and data analysis and probability. Readers are also encouraged to examine the CD for additional information on how students learn mathematics. You will also discover three other extremely useful resources for any teacher. Specifically, the CD includes (1) a hierarchically arranged *Checklist of Mathematical Concepts*, (2) a thorough collection of *Thematic Mathematics Activities* that reflects the NCTM *Principles and Standards* in various real-life venues, and (3) a *Classroom Vignette* supporting the integration of the three NCTM standards documents. Reviewing this material on the CD at this point will help prepare you for what is to come in the rest of this text.

With this in mind, we are ready to consider an in-depth study on how these mathematics skills are developed with elementary/middle school children. Whether you have excelled or struggled with mathematics in your own schooling, *Today's Mathematics* is designed to aid you now and in the future. The contents of this book will help you rethink how and why mathematics is taught in schools and promote the vision of mathematics learning and teaching begun in this chapter.

TEACHING COMPETENCIES AND SELF-ASSESSMENT TASKS

1. Locate a copy of the NCTM *Principles and Standards for School Mathematics*. Reflect on the need for the standards and goals discussed in this chapter by considering your own mathematics experiences in the past.

2. Describe what you believe are the defining characteristics of an effective mathematics program.

3. Select a topic from elementary/middle school mathematics and describe activities for that topic at the concrete (manipulative), representative (pictorial), and abstract (symbolic) levels.

4. Describe the importance of having children work with proper materials so that they can discover and generalize about mathematical concepts.

5. Describe a teaching situation that can be used to compare and contrast various teaching methods such as inductive/deductive or guided discovery/lecture.

6. Select two theories of learning. Compare and contrast them as they relate to the teaching and learning of elementary/middle school mathematics. How can you apply these theories to planning lessons in your classroom?

7. Locate a copy of the NCTM *Principles and Standards for School Mathematics*. Compare and contrast the set of standards identified for grades preK–2 with those for grades 3–5 and grades 6–8.

8. Discuss what role YOU can play in implementing the NCTM standards.

chapter 2

Teaching Mathematics

TEACHING COMPETENCIES

Upon completing this chapter, you will be able to:

- Describe the vision of mathematics teaching put forth in the NCTM teaching standards entitled *Mathematics Teaching Today* and its relationship to the vision presented in the NCTM *Principles and Standards for School Mathematics*.

- State the characteristics of a positive mathematics classroom environment.

- Identify appropriate objectives for mathematics lessons.

- Suggest appropriate lesson organizations and structures for a given mathematics topic.

- Describe types of student participation in a mathematics lesson.

- Write sample lesson plans for a set of specific objectives in mathematics.

Steve sat down at his desk after a long day of teaching in his fourth-grade classroom. He reached into the top drawer of the desk and pulled out a spiral notebook that he had been using as a reflective journal. After tapping his pen on the desk a few times, he began to write:

> I just can't understand why today's math lesson was so difficult for the students. I asked them to identify right, acute, and obtuse triangles, and they acted like they had never seen a triangle before. The definitions seem so simple to me, but something went wrong. In hindsight, I wish I had used the Smart Board in my classroom to show them a dozen triangles or so and asked them to drag the icons and drop them into categories based on angle measures. We could have even used a virtual carpenter's square or a virtual protractor to discuss whether the angles were right, less than right, or greater than right. Instead, I rushed it by having them draw a few pictures in their notebooks. Tomorrow, I will need to reteach the topic but make some important changes based on what I learned. I learn more about them and myself every day.

Steve's experience is very real, as it is not unusual for a mathematics teacher to plan a lesson that goes over the heads of the students or, conversely, to devise an activity that is so simple that students catch on right away and are bored or even disruptive. It has been said that lessons need to present just the right level of difficulty—challenging enough to be interesting but not so deep that students believe that they will never understand the concept and give up. You have probably experienced classes on both ends of the spectrum, and behind those classes were teachers who were trying to meet the needs of all the students in the classroom but may have gotten through to only a small fraction of them.

In the best of all possible worlds, there is peace and prosperity for all. In the best of all possible worlds, the sun seems always to shine, and, even when it doesn't, there is a refreshing pleasantness to the rain. The "natural order" of things is seldom disturbed, and, when the occasional unexpected event does arise, it is often viewed as a welcome surprise or opportunity. In this, the best of all possible worlds, your car always starts, your bank account always balances, and the students in your class learn everything that you have taught them. But this idyllic description does not reflect the true nature of the day-to-day world in which we live. Much of what we enjoy and sometimes take for granted still needs our frequent attention. The car won't start unless we keep it serviced. The bank account won't

balance unless we keep accurate records. And children won't recall ALL that they have been taught, despite our best intentions and efforts. We live in a real rather than an ideal world, with mathematics teaching that requires flexibility and ongoing, reflective adjustments similar to those Steve demonstrated in the vignette to achieve a degree of success. Our world also begs for standards with which to measure our successes.

The NCTM Principles and Standards for School Mathematics

Following the success of its initial standards efforts to set meaningful and achievable standards, the National Council of Teachers of Mathematics (NCTM) released *Principles and Standards for School Mathematics* in 2000. The intent was to make it clear that curriculum, teaching, and assessment were intertwined to a degree greater than might have been interpreted by readers of previous NCTM standards documents.

As outlined in Chapter 1 of this text, the word *principles* as used in *Principles and Standards for School Mathematics* describes six basic underlying assumptions regarding equity, curriculum, learning, teaching, assessment, and technology for instructional programs in mathematics. These six principles endorse a view of what is necessary at the classroom, school, district, and national levels for effective mathematics education. The impact of these principles on the teaching process is so vital that they are repeated here for emphasis. **Interested readers should refer to the CD accompanying this text and visit http://www.nctm.org for further information.**

- *Equity Principle.* Mathematics instructional programs should promote the learning of mathematics by all students.

- *Curriculum Principle.* Mathematics instructional programs should emphasize important and meaningful mathematics through curricula that are coherent and comprehensive.

- *Learning Principle.* Mathematics instructional programs should enable all students to understand and use mathematics.

- *Teaching Principle.* Mathematics instructional programs depend on competent and caring teachers who teach all students to understand and use mathematics.

- *Assessment Principle.* Mathematics instructional programs should include assessment to monitor, enhance, and evaluate the mathematics learning of all students and to inform teaching.

- *Technology Principle.* Mathematics instructional programs should use technology to help all students understand mathematics and should prepare them to use mathematics in an increasingly technological world.

Although each of these six principles deserve elaboration and integration, the scope of this particular chapter requires that we devote our attention to the standards for teaching mathematics.

The NCTM Professional Teaching Standards: *Mathematics Teaching Today*

In 1991, the NCTM issued a publication entitled *Professional Standards for Teaching Mathematics* as a companion document to the previously issued *Curriculum and Evaluation Standards for School Mathematics* (1989). The second edition of this 1991 document, entitled *Mathematics Teaching Today*, was released in 2007 and supports the more recent *Principles and Standards for School Mathematics* (2000). *Mathematics Teaching Today* represents a set of guidelines designed to address the various aspects of professional mathematics teaching. These standards are grouped into three major categories—Standards for Teaching and Learning Mathematics; Standards for the Observation, Supervision, and Improvement of Mathematics Teaching; and Standards for the Education and Continued Professional Growth of Teachers of Mathematics.

Section one, Standards for Teaching and Learning Mathematics, deals with a vision that illuminates, supports, and assists the implementation of *Principles and Standards for School Mathematics*. Section two, Standards for the Observation, Supervision, and Improvement of Mathematics Teaching, describes the nature and purposes of supervising and reflection on teaching and the roles that should be played by those involved in those processes. The final section, Standards for the Education and Continued Professional Growth of Teachers of Mathematics, focuses on the long-term professional development of mathematics teachers. Readers who seek a more comprehensive discussion of the full set of teaching standards are encouraged to purchase a copy of *Mathematics Teaching Today* from the NCTM, 1906 Association Drive, Reston, VA 20191 (www.nctm.org).

There are seven teaching standards described in *Mathematics Teaching Today*:

- Knowledge of Mathematics and General Pedagogy
- Knowledge of Student Mathematical Learning
- Worthwhile Mathematical Tasks
- Learning Environment
- Discourse
- Reflection on Student Learning
- Reflection on Teaching Practice

Three of these standards—focusing on tasks, environment, and discourse—are referred to as the *implementation* standards since they address the kinds of daily decisions a teacher makes relative to instruction. **Tasks** are the activities in which a student engages during his or her mathematical development. These might include projects, exercises, constructions, and applications of mathematical content. **Learning environment** encompasses the setting for learning. It is the context, both physical and mental, in which the tasks and the discourse come together. **Discourse** is the manner in which teachers and students communicate during tasks—the ways of representing, thinking, and talking about tasks. In addition, the last two standards are the *analysis* standards (Reflection on Student Learning and Reflection on Teaching Practice) since they refer to the action of contemplating the interplay of tasks, environment, and discourse. They represent the identification and evaluation of the effectiveness, efficiency, and appropriateness of what the teacher is doing and what the student is learning.

The five standards described in NCTM's *Mathematics Teaching Today* that refer specifically to the teaching process are described in the following sections.

STANDARD 3
Worthwhile Mathematical Tasks

The teacher of mathematics should design learning experiences and pose tasks that are based on sound and significant mathematics and that—

- engage students' intellect;
- develop mathematical understandings and skills
- stimulate students to make connections and develop a coherent framework for mathematical ideas;
- call for problem formulation, problem solving and mathematical reasoning;
- promote communication about mathematics;
- represent mathematics as an ongoing human activity; and display sensitivity to, and draw on, students' diverse background experiences and dispositions. (NCTM, 2007, pp. 32–33)

STANDARD 4
Learning Environment

The teacher of mathematics should create a learning environment that provides—

- the time necessary to explore sound mathematics and deal with significant ideas and problems;

- a physical space and appropriate materials that facilitate students' learning of mathematics;

- access and encouragement to use appropriate technology;

- a context that encourages the development of mathematical skill and proficiency;

- an atmosphere of respect and value for students' ideas and ways of thinking;

- an opportunity to work independently or collaboratively to make sense of mathematics;

- a climate for students to take intellectual risks in raising questions and formulating conjectures; and

- encouragement for the student to display a sense of mathematical competence by validating and supporting ideas with a mathematical argument. (NCTM, 2007, pp. 39–40)

STANDARD 5
Discourse

The teacher of mathematics should orchestrate discourse by—

- posing questions and tasks that elicit, engage, and challenge each student's thinking;

- listening carefully to students' ideas and deciding what to pursue in depth from among the ideas that students generate during a discussion;

- asking students to clarify and justify their ideas orally and in writing and by accepting a variety of presentation modes;

- deciding when and how to attach mathematical notation and language to students' ideas;

- encouraging and accepting the use of multiple representations;

- making available tools for exploration and analysis;

- deciding when to provide information, when to clarify an issue, when to model, when to lead, and when to let students wrestle with a difficulty;

- monitoring students' participation in discussions and deciding when and how to encourage each student to participate. (NCTM, 2007, p. 45)

STANDARD 6
Reflection on Student Learning

The teacher of mathematics should engage in ongoing analysis of students' learning by—

- observing, listening to, and gathering information about students to assess what they are learning

So as to—

- ensure that every student is learning sound and significant mathematics and is developing a positive disposition toward mathematics;

- challenge and extend students' ideas;

- adapt or change activities while teaching;

- describe and comment on each student's learning to parents and administrators; and

- provide regular feedback to the students themselves. (NCTM, 2007, p. 55)

STANDARD 7
Reflection on Teaching Practice

The teacher of mathematics should engage in ongoing analysis of teaching by—

- reflecting regularly on what and how they teach;

- examining effects of the task, discourse, and learning environments on the students' mathematical knowledge, skills, and dispositions;

- seeking to improve their teaching and practice by participating in learning communities beyond their classroom;

- analyzing and using assessment data to make reasoned decisions about necessary changes in curriculum; and

- collaborating with colleagues to develop plans to improve instructional programs. (NCTM, 2007, p. 60)

In the NCTM document, *Mathematics Teaching Today,* each of these standards is followed by an elaboration of the bulleted statements made here, but, perhaps more illustratively, these standards are laced with vignettes, or short scenarios, designed to model various aspects of specific standards. These often take the form of a lesson in which comments reflecting important points from the standards are included as margin notes. A sample vignette showing the integration of curriculum, teaching, and assessment has been reproduced here, with permission from NCTM.

AN EXAMPLE OF A TEACHING STANDARD

The NCTM publication, *Mathematics Teaching Today*, includes 18 standards of teaching, supervision of teaching, and professional development of teachers. Chapter 2 of this text listed the five standards that focus on teaching mathematics.

The following is a sample complete standard from that section, including one of the vignettes that supports the section. Readers who wish more information are directed to NCTM.

Elaboration

The Process Standards, most particularly the Communication Standard and the Proof and Reasoning Standard, make explicit reference to the role of discourse in the mathematics classroom (NCTM 2000). The discourse of a classroom—the ways of representing, thinking, talking, agreeing, and disagreeing—is central to what and how students learn about mathematics. Discourse represents both what the ideas entail and the ways ideas are exchanged: Who talks? About what? In what ways? What do people write? What do they record, and why? What questions are important? How do ideas change? Whose ideas and ways of thinking are valued? Who determines when to end a discussion? The discourse is shaped by the tasks in which students engage and the nature of the learning environment. The teacher's role is to initiate and orchestrate discourse and to use it skillfully to foster students' learning.

> The discourse of a classroom—the ways of representing, thinking, talking, agreeing, and disagreeing—is central to what and how students learn about mathematics.

Like a piece of music, the classroom discourse has themes that are synthesized into a whole that has meaning. The teacher has a central role in orchestrating oral and written discourse in ways that contribute to students' understanding of mathematics. Students must be given opportunities to engage in making conjectures, to share their ideas and understandings, to propose approaches and solutions to problems, and to argue about the validity of particular claims; they must recognize that mathematical reasoning and evidence are the bases for discourse (NCTM 2000).

To effectively orchestrate mathematical discourse, teachers must do more listening, and students must do more reasoning. Because many more ideas often come up than are fruitful to pursue at a given moment, teachers must filter and direct the students explorations by picking up on some points and by leaving others behind. Doing so prevents student discourse from becoming too diffuse and unfocused. Such decisions depend on teachers' understandings of mathematics and of their students. In particular, teachers must make judgments about when students can figure things out individually or collectively and when they require additional input.

> To effectively orchestrate mathematical discourse, teachers must do more listening, and students must do more reasoning.

Knowledge of mathematics, knowledge of the curriculum, and knowledge of students should guide the teacher's decisions about the nature and the path of the discourse. Beyond asking clarifying or provocative questions, teachers should also, at times, provide information and lead students. Decisions about when to let students work to make sense of an idea or a problem without direct teacher input, when to ask leading questions, and when to tell students something directly are crucial to orchestrating productive mathematical discourse the classroom. Above all, the discourse should be focused on making sense of mathematical ideas and on using mathematical ideas sensibly in setting up and solving problems (Hiebert et al. 1997).

But how can teachers both stimulate and manage classroom discourse? Here are several suggestions:

1. Provoke students' reasoning about mathematics. Teachers do so through the tasks they provide and the questions they ask. For example, teachers should regularly follow students' statements with "Why?" or "How do you know?" Doing so consistently, irrespective of the correctness of students' statements, is an important part of establishing a discourse centered on mathematical reasoning. In particular, when students are allowed to examine and critique incorrect solutions or strategies, counterexamples and logical inconsistencies can naturally surface. This process of analyzing solutions instead of relying on teachers to validate them can enhance students' abilities to think critically from a mathematical perspective.

   Tasks and questions that stimulate discussion not only encourage active participation by students but also provide the teacher with ongoing assessment information.

Cultivating a tone of interest when asking a student to explain or elaborate on an idea helps establish norms of civility and respect rather than criticism and doubt. The teacher must create an environment in which everyone's thinking is respected and in which reasoning and arguing about mathematical meanings is the norm.

2. Encourage the use of a variety of representations as well as explorations of how various representations are alike and different. Require students to write explanations for their solutions and to provide justifications for their ideas. Students should learn to verify, revise, and discard claims on the basis of mathematical evidence. Although students should learn to use and appreciate the conventional symbols that facilitate mathematical communication, teachers must value and encourage the use of a variety of tools and representations as students are learning to communicate their ideas. Various means for communicating about mathematics should be accepted, including drawings, diagrams, invented symbols, and analogies. The teacher should introduce conventional notation when students are ready to formalize their ideas and in a manner that helps students understand that using agreed-on terms and notations helps promote clear communication.

   As described in the Technology Principle, teachers should also help students learn to use calculators, computers, Internet resources, and other technological devices as tools for mathematical discourse. Given the range of mathematical tools available, teachers should often allow and encourage students to select the means they find most useful for working on or discussing a particular mathematical problem.

3. Monitor and organize students' participation. Teachers must be committed to engaging every student in contributing to the overall thinking of the class. Teachers must judge when students should work and talk in small groups and when the whole group is the most useful context. They must make sensitive decisions about how opportunities to speak are shared in the large group—for example, whom to call on, when, and whether to call on particular students who do not volunteer. Substantively, if discourse is to focus on making sense of mathematics, teachers must refrain from calling only on students who seem to have right answers or valid ideas to allow a broader spectrum of thinking to be explored in the discourse. By modeling respect for students' thinking and con-veying the assumption that students make sense, teachers can encourage students to participate within a norm that expects group members to justify their ideas.

   To facilitate learning by all students, teachers must also be perceptive and skill-ful in analyzing the culture of the classroom, looking out for patterns of inequality, dominance, and low expectations that are primary causes of non-participation by many students. Engaging every student in the discourse of the class requires consid-erable skill as well as an appreciation of, and respect for, students' diversity.

4. Encourage students to talk with one another as well as in response to the teacher. Whether working in small or large groups, students should be the audience for one another's comments—that is, they should speak to one another, aiming to convince or to question their peers. When the teacher talks most, the flow of ideas and knowl-edge is primarily from teacher to student. When students make public conjectures and reason with others about mathematics, ideas and knowledge are developed col-laboratively, revealing mathematics as constructed by human beings within an in-tellectual community. Students, who are accustomed to the teacher's doing most of the talking while they remain passive, need guidance and encouragement to partic-ipate actively in the discourse of a collaborative community. Some students, partic-ularly those who have been successful in more traditional mathematics classrooms, may be resistant to talking, writing, and reasoning together about mathematics. Time and patience are required to cultivate a student-centered environment for discourse. Eventually, the payoff in student participation and learning is worth the investment.

Engaging every student in the discourse of the class requires considerable skill as well as an appreciation of, and respect for, students' diversity.

Eventually, the payoff in student participation and learning is worth the investment.

STANDARD 5: DISCOURSE

In the first vignette, the teacher facilitates a discussion about counting with young children. The choice of task creates an opportunity for reasoning and problem solving. The teacher's consistent urging of students to explain and to justify their answers invites many students into the conversation and encourages the sharing of a variety of solution methods.

5.1—Only the Nose Knows, but the Children Can Reason!

Ms. Nakamura has done a lot of number work with her kindergarten class this year, and she is pleased with the results. Now, near the end of the year, the class has been investigating patterns in the number of various body parts in the classroom—how many noses or eyes, for example, are present among the children in the class.

Earlier that week, each child had made a nose out of clay. Ms. Nakamura opens the discussion by revisiting that project. She asks, "And how many noses did we make?"

Becky (points to her nostrils): Two of these.

Teacher: But how many actual noses?

Anne: Twenty-nine.

Teacher: Why? Why were there twenty-nine noses?

Adam: Because every kid in the class made one clay nose, and that is the same number as kids in the class.

Teacher (pointing to her nostrils): Now Becky just said—remember what these are called?

Children: Nostrils!

Teacher: So were there twenty-nine nostrils?

Pat: No, there were more.

Gwen: Fifty-eight! We had fifty-eight nostrils!

Teacher: Why fifty-eight?

Gwen: I counted.

Felice: If we had thirty kids, we would be sixty. So it is fifty-nine 'cause it should be one less.

Teacher: Can you explain that again?

The teacher probes Felice's answer even though her approach goes beyond what many of the children are trying to do at this point.

Felice: It's fifty-nine because we don't have thirty kids, we have twenty-nine, so it is one less than sixty.

Teacher: What does anyone else think?

Adam: I think it is fifty-eight. Each kid has two nostrils. So if sixty would be for thirty kids, then it has to be two less: fifty-eight.

The teacher solicits other students' reactions instead of showing them the right answer. Her tone of voice and her questions show the students that she values their thinking.

Lawrence: But Felice says thirty kids makes sixty . . .

Felice: No! Adam makes sense. Fifty-eight.

The teacher moves on, asking, "What else do you think we have on our bodies that would be more than twenty-nine?"

The teacher's question challenges students to think it is open-ended; more than one right answer exists.

Graham: More than twenty-nine fingers.

Teacher: More than twenty-nine fingers? Why do you think so?

Graham: Because each kid, we have ten fingers.

Ricky: More than twenty-nine shoes.

Teacher: More than twenty-nine shoes. And what are those shoes covering?

Ricky: Your feet.

Sarah: Ears.

Beth: More than twenty-nine legs.

Ms. Nakamura tells the children, "You did some good thinking today!" The teacher chooses to comment on the children's thinking instead of their behavior.

Ms. Nakamura tells the children that they now are to work on a picture: "Choose some body part, and draw a picture of how many of those we have in our class and how you know that." She directs the children back to their tables, where she has laid out paper and cans of crayons.

In the following vignette, the teacher encourages the use of multiple representations to help students construct understandings. The students use objects and symbols to help convey their meaning. The teacher eventually introduces standard notation and helps students make connections between their own and other representations.

5.2—Making the Transition from Student-Invented to Standard Representations

Mr. Johnson has presented his first-grade class with several pairs of numbers and asked them to decide which number in each pair is greater and to justify their responses. He has also been encouraging them to find ways to write their comparisons. The students know that the teacher expects not just answers but also reasons.

Ben: I think 5 is greater than 3 because [walks to the board and sticks five magnets up and then carefully sticks three magnets in another row]).

Mr. Johnson asks whether that explanation makes sense to other people. The children nod. He asks whether anyone wants to show how you would write Ben's idea down. The teacher encourages students to use symbols to represent and communicate about ideas.

Kevin, up at the board, writes this expression:

Next, Betsy writes the following:

Mr. Johnson: Can you explain what you were thinking? Kevin?

Kevin explains that his arrow shows that 5 is more than 3 because the bigger number "can point at" the smaller one.

Mr. Johnson asks Betsy to explain hers, and she says that she thinks you should just circle the smaller one.

The teacher accepts more than one way of representing the idea of comparing numbers by using symbols; both are nonstandard but sensible. However, Mr. Johnson challenges his students by posing a question that requires students to invent a means of recording an idea.

Mr. Johnson: What if the two numbers you were comparing were 6 and 6? What would you do? How would you use your symbols for comparing numbers to write that?

Several seconds pass. The teacher gives students time to think before responding. He doesn't repeat the question or call on children; he is patient and silent. Eventually, Ruth shoots her hand in the air. Several others also have their hands up.

Ruth: You could draw an arrow to both of them.

Annie: You could circle both of them because they are the same.

Jimmy: You shouldn't mark either one, either way. They are not greater or less. They are the same.

Mr. Johnson nods at their suggestions. He writes an equals sign (=) on the board and explains that this is a symbol that people have invented for the ideas the children have been talking about.

The teacher connects the students' approaches and reasoning with the conventional notation. Because the students have thought about what it means for two numbers to be equal, they are ready to learn how that relationship is conventionally represented. In this situation, the notation follows the development of the concept in a meaningful context.

Rashida: That's like what Ruth said.

Ruth beams, and Annie calls out, "It's like mine, too."

Reprinted with permission from *Mathematics Teaching Today*, copyright 2007 by the National Council of Teachers of Mathematics.

Lesson Planning Processes and Purposes

The textbook is not the centerpiece of a lesson; the students and the blending of content and activities should be the focus. The teacher's task is to masterfully orchestrate learning experiences for children, not to simply guide the students through the material in a book. The latter may be less threatening and easier to accomplish, but the former is the essence of teaching.

Students learn when they are actively involved in tasks that they view as purposeful and interesting. Students learn when we expect them to analyze and communicate their sense-making attempts. Students learn when they are in an environment offering feedback and encouragement. Students learn when they feel comfortable with, and responsible for, taking intellectual risks and when their actions provide input regarding the direction of the lesson. How do we ensure these characteristics in a classroom? A good start is through careful planning for instruction.

Most weddings are carefully planned from the event to the reception, photography, food, and decorations. For a bride and groom to simply ask their friends to show up without having detailed the sequence of events and the materials that will be needed would be a recipe for disaster. Similarly, for a teacher to walk into a classroom with a mathematical concept in mind, such as finding the percent of a number, but to have no specific plans on how to get the idea across to children and to connect the material to their past (and future) learning experiences would be inexcusable. The point here is that all successful lessons require planning. The reasons are many and varied. Planning allows the teacher to think through the expected events, make decisions on sequence and timing, anticipate potential trouble spots, prepare alternative approaches, design appropriate assessments, and orchestrate the entire instructional process.

Not all lessons require the same type of planning. Teachers need to develop some idea of how to structure lessons for different situations. Different "types" of lessons require different types of lesson plans. Exploratory, developmental, transitional, and review are four possible types, although the list could easily be expanded.

Exploratory lessons typically provide opportunities to introduce concepts in ways that allow the student to construct meaning and respond to experiences through his or her level of understanding. Such lessons frequently have an open structure with opportunities for students to make and test conjectures. An example might be a lesson in which students experiment with rolls of Life Savers to see if all variety pack Life Savers are the same. What, in fact, does "the same" mean in this context? Do all, for example, contain the same colors? In the same quantity? In the same order? Students might demonstrate the information they gather by using graphs and/or written observations.

Developmental lessons take students from the discovery stage through the stage in which they recognize a pattern, make a generalization, or describe a rule regarding a particular concept. Our example of an exploratory lesson could be extended to one in which the students were involved in determining the answer to questions such as "Is there a pattern in the sequence in which the individual pieces are arranged?" "Is it true that if there is a green Life Saver, then it is followed by a red one?" "Is it always possible to predict which color will come out of a roll next?"

Transitional lessons connect knowledge at the concrete or representative level to an abstract level of understanding. An example would be a lesson in which students use a manipulative material, such as Cuisenaire rods, to show that the white rod is one-half of the red rod and that the red rod is one-half of the purple rod, so the white rod is one-fourth of the purple rod. This would then be connected to the abstraction that $\frac{1}{2}$ of $\frac{1}{2}$ is $\frac{1}{4}$, or $\frac{1}{2} \times \frac{1}{2} = \frac{1}{4}$.

Review lessons provide the student with opportunities to revisit a mathematical idea, typically with the intent of anchoring knowledge. Students may be exposed to a variety of exercises and applications of a concept or a definition in which practice, rather than extension, is generally the goal.

Whatever we call these lessons, it is clear that we need to identify at least three types of plans—one representing a teacher's initial attempt to introduce a "new" topic, another to serve as a bridge to extend the topic, and the last to provide a worthwhile "review" of the topic. Whenever feasible and appropriate, lessons should emphasize references to suitable children's literature, applications of technology, opportunities for cooperative learning, incorporation of standard and "homemade" manipulatives, and emphasis on connections to other disciplines. Keep in mind that the five mathematical processes—Problem Solving, Reasoning and Proof, Communication, Connections, and Representation—should be addressed in virtually every mathematics lesson that we design. Finally, we also need to be sure that the lessons incorporate opportunities for verbal and written discourse on the part of the students, perhaps making use of a "math log question" for each lesson or student-created bulletin boards. Individual lessons should also reinforce extended projects that take the topic at hand beyond the parameters of a single day.

Lesson Plan Content

It is reasonable to expect that many lessons will be developmental in nature—that is, lessons that focus on the introduction or further development of concepts, as opposed to lessons with a primary emphasis on review of previously explored material. It is also likely that guided discovery and inquiry will be integral parts of such lessons.

The format used to record plans, anticipations, and alternatives is typically not as important as the content of the plan. Consequently, you are likely to encounter a number of different lesson-planning formats if you run Internet searches or leaf through various books and resources on lesson planning. Don't let this variety of planning designs confuse you—remember that the plan is simply intended to communicate what and how you will conduct a lesson on a particular topic. Keep in mind that the intended *reader* of a lesson plan is usually someone other than you (e.g., a substitute teacher, a supervisor, or, perhaps, a professor). Consequently, teachers need to be certain that this reader can make sense of the ideas and that sufficient detail is present to communicate each step. Just the same, each teacher needs to develop an approach to record planning in a manner that is most comfortable for the individual teacher.

There are, however, common components that should be featured in every good lesson. It is often expected that these will be present in some fashion.

I. General Goal(s)

Goals are simple, concise statements of the concepts to be explored and broad statements of attainment. An example of a general goal is "The lesson will introduce the students to the process of relating patterns to describing functions. They will be involved in the discussion of concrete, representative, and abstract examples." Often, this goal is connected to a particular national or state content standard, and that standard is cited in the goal statement.

II. Specific Objectives

Objectives differ from the goal statements in that they are much more refined and specific in scope. They should be student centered; they should focus on observable and measurable actions; they should be specific in reference to content and method, and they should be complete and independent of other objectives. In some cases, a given state's standards document includes these specific statements for each grade level, so the teacher need only quote and cite the standard that is being addressed in the lesson. In addition, most school districts adopt a course of study that communicates the objectives that students are intended to learn at each grade level, so again, the course of study can simply be quoted. The teacher does not need to write his or her own objectives.

If you do need to write your own objectives (or serve on a committee that writes a course of study), the following caution is offered here: Be wary of the difference between a statement that is an objective and a statement that merely describes an activity designed to meet an objective. Rather than referring to page numbers in objective statements, focus instead on the content found on those pages. Another caution is to clearly differentiate between a prerequisite for the lesson and an objective of the lesson (i.e., what the student is supposed to know prior to the lesson versus what the student will learn as a result of participating in the lesson). A final caution: *instructional objectives* have an assumed attainment criteria of 100% (no teacher enters a lesson with the intention of teaching students to perform at a 75% level). *Evaluation objectives* should state criteria that are meaningful. (Don't ask students to define "prime number" with 90% accuracy!) Here is an example of a well-written objective: Given a sequence of numbers, the students will continue the sequence and verbally describe a rule that describes and generalizes the sequence.

III. Prerequisite Learning and/or Experiences

It is important that every teacher give serious consideration to the knowledge, skills, and experiences that are necessary for the effective presentation of any lesson. This section of a lesson plan should list or describe such preaddressed items of direct consequence to this lesson. Here is an example of a prerequisite statement: The students must know the distinction between arithmetic and geometric progressions.

IV. Materials

A complete description of the materials necessary for the presentation of the lesson must be included. When appropriate, reference should also be made to location of the materials and how many are required per class, per group, or per student. Here is an example of a materials description: 15 pegboards (one for each group of two students), pattern worksheet for each student (copy attached).

V. Procedure

This section should relate the content and methods of the lesson. It is essential that the procedure section describes the teaching process—not only what will be taught, but also how it will be taught. Detailed instructions should reflect a combination of what the *student* and what the *teacher* will do at each point in the lesson.

It is critical that lessons begin with a motivation designed to capture both the attention and interest of the students. The motivation must give the students a reason to explore the content of the lesson. Avoid beginning a lesson with either "Today we're going to learn about ..." or "Who remembers what we did in math class yesterday?" While these statements may motivate something, it isn't learning. Often, the motivational part of the lesson (often referred to as the springboard, engagement, or readiness activity) is the most difficult part of the lesson to write. But it may also be the most important component of the plan. Whether the students are engaged and excited to learn for the rest of the class period often depends on how the first five minutes of class are conducted.

It is important that lessons reflect flexibility and the acknowledgment that students are a vibrant part of the flow of a lesson. The procedure should not be a rigid scriptlike document that reads like a TV guide (i.e., first, I'll do ..., then I'll ..., and after that I'll ...). Plans should also reflect anticipation of likely occurrences and the teacher's potential reaction. In a sense, this means that every good plan probably has the words "if the students ..." and "then I'll ..." sprinkled throughout.

Notes that are designed to remind the teacher (or substitute teacher) of special emphasis, major points to make, side stories to tell, and so on should be present. This means that every good lesson plan includes variations of the words "be certain to mention" and "make sure students can" sprinkled throughout. Finally, the lesson should be as specific as possible. Avoid using expressions such as, "Show the children several examples of fraction addition problems." Instead, specify *how* they will be "shown" the examples (on the whiteboard, students making presentations, class discussion, small group work, etc.) and *which* examples you intend to explore with the class, including the order in which you plan to sequence the problems.

The plan should not end abruptly. There should be a graceful wrap-up, a culminating discussion, or some other means of assessing student attainment of the objectives of the lesson. Often, this lesson closure includes one final problem to solve, a journal entry to write, or a discussion that includes pointed questions that assess student understanding. Sometimes, the closing portion of a lesson refers back to a comment made, an example shown, or a problem posed at the very beginning of the lesson. The point here is that a statement such as "It looks like our time is up" or "Your homework for tonight will be ..." are not sufficient to adequately close a lesson.

Finally, children often pick up on the main idea of a lesson more quickly than we might have anticipated and are in need of a further challenge. Therefore, an important addition to any lesson is the consideration of extensions that reach beyond the immediate bounds of the lesson to higher-level thinking and/or applications. These extensions might take many forms. For example, an extension might be a simple question or additional problem or example that calls for a connection to a previous (or a future) concept, an interactive bulletin board or collection of math center activities that expand the concept under study, or a project that involves the class in a long-term exploration centered on the concepts of the lesson.

VI. Evaluation

Following every lesson, the teacher must reflect on that lesson. This evaluation should be insightful and go far beyond superficial analysis and generalization. Specific identification of successful and less than successful aspects of the lesson must be considered. Reasons for these successes and failures should be determined. Here is an example of specific reflective comment:

> The students had some difficulty setting up the table of differences. The biggest problem seemed to be one of neatness. One group had all the correct values but couldn't make sense of them because they were scattered all over their record paper. I could have given them a sample, but I didn't want them to simply copy my lead. Next time, I'll emphasize the importance of discussing methods with other groups as they collect and organize data.

Lesson Plan Evaluation

You may want to use the following form to assess your planning abilities both before and after a lesson is taught.

(1—UNACCEPTABLE   4—EXCEPTIONAL)

Objectives

1. Clarity: Are the objectives clear and understandable?
       1   2   3   4
2. Are the objectives developmentally appropriate?
       1   2   3   4
3. Are the objectives assessed in some way within the plan?
       1   2   3   4

Materials

1. Is the materials list appropriate?
       1   2   3   4
2. Is there enough detail for a substitute to gather the needed materials before the lesson?
       1   2   3   4

Motivation

1. Does the motivation capture both attention and interest?
       1   2   3   4
2. Does it prepare students for the lesson content?
       1   2   3   4

Procedures

1. Are the procedures clear and organized?
       1   2   3   4
2. Is the content of the lesson fully described and specific?
       1   2   3   4
3. Are the methods of teaching the content fully described?
       1   2   3   4
4. Is anticipation of potential difficulties evident?
       1   2   3   4
5. Does the lesson have an effective and nonabrupt closure?
       1   2   3   4
6. Are extensions for follow-up included?
       1   2   3   4
7. Has an appropriate means of assessment been identified?
       1   2   3   4

Self-Evaluation

1. To what degree were the identified objectives achieved?
       1   2   3   4
2. What specific examples of successes can be cited? Why were these examples successful?
3. What specific events suggest the need for reteaching? Why?
4. In what specific ways could the lesson be improved?

Chapters 4 through 17 of this text each include a complete primary-level and a complete intermediate-level mathematics lesson plan. **These plans are found on the CD that accompanies this text so that you can print them out and modify them to meet your needs.** These plans can prove to be valuable resources during and following this course for "field testing" your abilities to implement as well as modify existing lesson plans.

List of Sample Lesson Plans from Chapters 4 – 17 on the Accompanying CD

Chapter	Lesson	Level	Type
4. Technology Tools	Shoe Sorts and Graphs	Primary	Developmental
	Wipe Out	Intermediate	Review
5. Problem Solving	Attribute Baseball	Primary	Review
	Yummy Fraction Problem	Intermediate	Developmental
6. Number Sense	I'm a Ten	Primary	Review
	People Counting	Intermediate	Devel./Direct
7. Addition/Subtraction	Regrouping Up/Down	Primary	Review/Direct
	Alternate Algorithms	Intermediate	Devel./Direct
8. Multiplication/Division	Double Bubble	Primary	Developmental
	Remainder Reminder	Intermediate	Review/Application
9. Number Theory	The Even/Odd Debate	Primary	Developmental
	Ringo, Tingo, Lingo, Bingo	Intermediate	Developmental
10. Algebra	Calendar Number Patterns	Primary	Devel./Direct
	The Search for Patterns	Intermediate	Devel./Direct
11. Fractions	Fraction Attraction	Primary	Direct
	The Pizza Slice Decision	Intermediate	Developmental
12. Fraction Operations	Cookie Fractions	Primary	Developmental
	Sweet Fractions	Intermediate	Developmental
13. Decimals	The "Just So" Tower	Primary	Direct
	The Decimal Quest	Intermediate	Devel./Direct
14. Data Analysis	Penny Probability	Primary	Developmental
	Colorful M&Ms	Intermediate	Developmental
15. Measurement	Decimeter Scavenger Hunt	Primary	Developmental
	"Weigh" to Count	Intermediate	Direct
16. Geometry	Opposite Day in Math	Primary	Developmental
	Pentomino Adventure	Intermediate	Developmental
17. Geometry	Container Geometry	Primary	Developmental
	Puppy Polygons	Intermediate	Developmental

Issues in Designing Mathematics Lessons

Sometimes we characterize our efforts to provide an effective and efficient mathematics program as an attempt to reach an ideal—as aiming high or "reaching for the moon." Expanding this analogy, a vast number of "impact craters" influence the shape and the nature of this "moon" we're trying to reach. It is most important that we recognize the control we have over which craters we hit, and how hard. Our choice of the approach to a given topic, the role of the textbook, the terminology and language used, the amount of active involvement, and the use of technology and manipulatives are but a few of the factors that require our attention as we plan learning experiences for unique learners.

A lesson is the vehicle we use to convey the knowledge, skills, concepts, and values we wish to instill in students. A lesson is a planned learning experience designed (but not necessarily led) by a teacher with input from a variety of resources that takes many forms and occurs in diverse settings. A lesson might be an informal discussion involving the entire class, or it might be an experiment performed by small groups of students to collect data for analysis and debate. A lesson might occur in the classroom or outside on the school grounds—or at home, at the mall, in the car, or on a family outing.

Its nature and location aside, every lesson should be designed, implemented, and evaluated in a careful and thoughtful manner. Let's take a look at some of the aspects of lesson preparation that should become a recurring part of the planning process.

In designing a lesson, it is important to research the topic. It is not sufficient to believe that because you are capable of "doing the mathematics" called for in the lesson, you are also capable of "teaching the mathematics"—especially the meaning underlying the mathematics concepts. (Most of us have had a teacher at one time or another who was intelligent but seemed unable to get the ideas across to others!) Close examination of the content, possible different approaches, and potential methods of presentation are all central to the planning process. The teacher, whenever feasible, should not rely solely on the direction and organization suggested by the student's text. The teacher's edition, including those from textbook series other than the one used by the students, may prove to be valuable sources of alternative teaching ideas. Books such as this one, written for the preparation of teachers, are rich resources for ideas on alternative curricular, instructional, and assessment approaches. Additional resource materials and activity books published by support companies and independent authors also provide a wealth of ideas to enliven textbook lessons. Subject-specific professional organizations, such as the NCTM, the School Science and Mathematics Association (SSMA), the Research Council on Mathematics Learning (RCML), and the Association of Mathematics Teacher Educators (AMTE), as well as state-level affiliated groups and generalist organizations such as the Association for Supervision and Curriculum Development (ASCD), produce curricular and instructional materials designed to supplement ideas the classroom teacher has gleaned from other sources. **(See the CD that accompanies this text for a list of names, addresses, and telephone numbers of suppliers of mathematics instruction resource materials.)**

One of the most important aspects of the planning process centers on the teacher's ability to *anticipate*—to anticipate the need for materials or models that could help the children meet the objectives of the lesson, to anticipate the questions that children might have but not state, and to anticipate the parts of the lesson that may be the most challenging to teach or the most difficult to understand. Surely, experience has a lot to do with successful anticipation, but this talent is not reserved exclusively for those who have taught for several years.

The ability to anticipate is most heavily influenced by the quality and quantity of objective, reflective thought that goes into the planning process, not how many years a person has taught.

Teachers must be able to make use of the knowledge they have, but they must also develop the talent of standing aside from their knowledge and examining the content from a naive point of view. Being too close to the content can cause you to miss some important nuances that might help you identify and comprehend the difficulties that a less-experienced student might encounter in the lesson. For example, most adults give little or no thought to the process of finding the value of a collection of pennies and dimes in which like coins might be grouped and then to add two separate subtotals to arrive at the total value. How many children recognize the connection between this activity and the process of adding rational numbers expressed as decimals? How many, when questioned how to add decimal numbers, offer a meaningless rule such as "line up the decimal points," when they might just as easily have referred to either the money model emphasizing like coins or a place-value model emphasizing like places? Successful teachers of mathematics combine the thoughts of a child with the thoughts of an adult—successful teachers are adults who have nurtured the ability to observe the world of mathematics through the eyes of a child.

Although school districts and state agencies may provide a mandated course of study—topics that must be studied and the grades or courses in which they are to be included—the sequence in which those topics are presented is generally decided by individual schools or, in some cases, by individual teachers. Many teachers simply follow the sequence provided by the adopted textbook, beginning the year with page 1 and vainly attempting to reach the end of the book before they reach the end of the school year. Successful teachers of mathematics are capable of determining whether the textbook's sequence is appropriate for their teaching style, their course of study, and their students' prerequisite skills and experiences. And, if it is not, they should be capable of rearranging the order into one that is more appropriate to the needs of their students. Changing the sequence of topics may even provide opportunities to view mathematics not as a collection of unrelated concepts but as a structured, connected body of ideas.

Consider, for example, a fifth-grade teacher planning the start of a new school year who recognizes that many of the students in her incoming class appear to have had little or no instruction in geometry beyond the identification and naming of two- and three-dimensional shapes. Unfortunately, many units on geometry tend to be relegated to the last chapter of a school textbook, implying that the topic is less important than others.

If a previous teacher, in turn, de-emphasized the topic, the students with strong spatial abilities may have been slighted. This year's teacher wonders whether looking at other mathematics topics through a geometric lens would be beneficial to her students. Since the first few weeks of a new academic year are commonly spent reviewing previously taught concepts, she begins to look at the content presented during these weeks to determine how she could use geometry to cover these topics. For example, addition and multiplication could be reviewed while exploring concepts of perimeter, area, and volume. Fractions might be revisited through the use of tangrams, emphasizing geometric properties related to part-whole concepts. Problem-solving skills might be developed through a number of hands-on activities involving challenges and investigations in geometry. Having decided to present her curriculum by emphasizing geometric concepts, she skips the often regimented and repetitive nature of the first few chapters in her text and moves right into a review couched in the "new" setting of geometry.

After spending a couple of weeks using geometry as a context for review, this year's teacher may notice that several students who had been low achievers in previous grades are performing quite well, while some students who had been good mathematics students are now experiencing levels of frustration they had not previously encountered. Therefore, an emphasis on geometry as an organizer in this year's class may have changed the "pecking order" in her class. If this is indeed the case, it may be that those students who had had trouble in previous grades may have been more attuned to "spatial" topics than they were to "number" concepts. Their lack of readiness for the arithmetic in earlier grades may have accounted for what might have been labeled as their poor overall achievement.

In addition to the differences in student achievements, the teacher may notice a difference in students' questioning behavior. In the past, many students may have tended to avoid asking questions during mathematics instruction, simply indicating their lack of understanding by saying, "I don't get it." However, under the scenario previously described, this teacher might notice that students are actually asking questions—and the questions are coming from all the students. It may be that when those who have had an easy time in mathematics encounter topics that are more difficult for them, they are more willing to ask questions than are the low achievers or are more aware of where they need help and can formulate appropriate questions. When the lower-achieving students see the strong mathematics students asking questions, this can become a more socially accepted behavior. The teacher then becomes more excited when this willingness to ask questions

invades more traditional topics, such as place value and number theory.

A teacher who attempts to connect the topics of mathematics lessons with other content areas is one who demonstrates a loyalty to the course of study while, at the same time, displaying the ability to creatively design a meaningful learning experience. It is only natural for such a teacher to wonder what lessons might look like if, for example, probability and statistics was used as a theme—a lens—through which to explore other topics.

Mathematics Objectives

When organizing objectives for lessons, teachers must keep in mind the reasons for having objectives—most notably, to use them as guides *throughout* the planning/teaching/learning/evaluation process. Teachers can use well-conceived, clearly stated objectives in the planning stages to identify, select, and organize experiences designed to ensure attainment of appropriate outcomes. They can then use these same objectives during the teaching of the lesson to maintain a consistent focus and direction for these experiences. Finally, the lesson objectives form a sound basis for judging the effectiveness of both the planning and the teaching, as well as the attainment of the learning sought. Meaningful objectives are the glue that holds a lesson together. Without them, the smooth transition from planning to implementation to reflection is lost. In fact, without objectives, a teacher is merely passing time with students, hoping that something worthwhile will occur. If you don't know what you're doing, and why you're doing it, does it make any sense to try to do it?

The objectives of a lesson must be determined with a critical eye toward prerequisite skills and experiences central to the success of a lesson. Teachers must closely examine the content and activities of proposed lessons to determine whether any "assumed learnings" have been clearly identified. For example, an introductory lesson on percents assumes a familiarity with concepts such as ratio, proportion, and decimals, to name a few. The teacher must carefully analyze what is to be taught and how it is to be taught rather than simply relying on the textbook approach or on personal familiarity with the content. For a lesson to reach its full potential, the teacher has to attend to the knowledge, skills, experiences, attitudes, and values that the children must possess (and to what level or degree they possess them) prior to exposure to the lesson. By not doing so, the teacher runs the risk of introducing material or ideas into the lesson that only confound or increase the children's confusion and difficulties. **(See the CD that accompanies this text for a list of Concept Clusters arranged in a hierarchical fashion to help you identify prerequisites for the concepts listed.)**

Some teachers choose to include a level of performance or criterion as part of the objective by tacking on a phrase such as "with 80% or better accuracy" or "correctly at least four out of five times." Such additions to objectives are acceptable, but remember that in many instances they are markedly artificial. Why was 80% chosen? Why not 85% or 89%? Are the reasons for selecting a particular percent cutoff identifiable and rational, or is it just an arbitrary figure deemed to be "high enough"? We suggest that the debate on the level of performance or criterion be resolved by noting that there is a significant difference between an *instructional* objective and an *evaluation* objective. Instructional objectives for a mathematics lesson should focus on the student, not on the teacher. It is essential that a teacher begin any instructional opportunity with the conviction that all students are capable of learning the material. It is never acceptable to *begin* the teaching process with a stated objective that calls for less than 100% attainment. Isn't it *always* your goal to reach every student? Or do you start out with the notion that you'll be happy if you reach 8 out of 10 students? A teacher must strive for the ideal in each lesson—every student has the potential to comprehend and succeed. An evaluation objective, on the other hand, refers to an "acceptable level" of performance on an assessment *after* the lesson. In this case, an evaluation objective focuses attention on the real, rather than the ideal. It is not the case that one form of objective is better than the other, but rather that instructional and evaluation objectives take different forms because they serve different purposes and play their roles at different times of the teaching/learning process.

The Role of Motivation and Follow-Up

In addition to having meaningful objectives, a lesson plan must also include attention to motivation. The motivation for a particular lesson is so much more than simply a beginning or introductory activity. For example, a teacher could start a lesson by calling for quiet and asking the children to open their books to page 123. This opening may get their attention, but it certainly does nothing to attract their interest in what is about to occur. Alternatively, the teacher could begin a lesson on graphing by simply asking the students to guess how far a toy car would roll down a given ramp. After they guess, the teacher has them try it. Then the teacher moves the ramp to another height, and the students try again. Do the students have an idea about the "best" height for the greatest distance? Can they identify a connection between the height and the distance? Is it always true that a higher ramp yields a greater distance?

How could they see this more clearly? At this point, the teacher would be well into the lesson on graphing in an enjoyable and less teacher-oriented manner. Rather than the teacher telling them, "Today, we will do a lesson on graphing" and then continuing with a lecture-based format, the teacher with the motivation just described has captured both attention and interest and has the class considering important questions as a first step to exploring graphing.

In addition to capturing the attention and the interest of the students, an effective motivation should also provide a reason for exploring the topic of the lesson and should be tied directly to the lesson's content in such a way that the transition from the motivation to the lesson is nearly seamless. An unrelated game serves little motivational use if it captures attention and interest but does not transfer to the topic at hand. Playing a game as an introductory activity is not a motivation for a lesson unless the game can be directly tied to the objective of the day.

The conclusion of a lesson deserves as much attention as the motivation. All too often teachers end a mathematics lesson by simply asking the children to "do page 123, exercises 2 through 20, even." Every mathematics lesson should conclude with some attempt to determine the students' level of understanding of the material presented. It is essential that the teacher collect some immediate information regarding the students' understanding of the lesson. It is useless, however, to seek this information by asking, "Does anyone have any questions?" or "Does everyone understand?" Instead, the collection of information about student understanding may best be accomplished by leading a discussion of points central to the day's objective. For example, how do the children respond to both general and specific questions about the activities? How do the children use their own words, orally and in writing, to describe the processes discussed in the lesson? Can the children respond to questions about why the material is important or useful? In addition, the teacher should, whenever feasible, tie the lesson to what was done yesterday and what will be done tomorrow. Both a look back and a look ahead can help us better understand the present. Note, however, that one of the least effective ways to look back is by opening a lesson with "Who remembers what we did in math class yesterday?" This question is far removed from the concept of motivation!

Finally, returning to the issue of "do page 123, exercises 2 through 20, even," it is important to recognize that practice plays an essential role in learning mathematics. Once students have developed a foundation for practice—that is, once they have a meaningful grasp of the concept—they should work on fully developing the skill. However, the teacher must do more than blindly assign homework or seatwork exercises for the children to complete. At the very least, a teacher should closely examine the textbook exercises one by one to select those that are most appropriate, based on the lesson as taught and the sort of practice the teacher deems necessary. Each and every assignment should be selected with an eye toward student differences in learning styles. Students may learn best through a variety of formats, such as individual assignments, learning centers, peer instruction, and cooperative groups. It may be appropriate for some students to practice using concrete manipulatives to illustrate the concepts of the lesson. Others may be ready for more representative models such as pictures or diagrams. Still others may be functioning at the abstract level with numerals and symbols. It cannot be assumed, as is the case when sweeping page assignments are made, that all children are at the same level and have the same needs.

The Assessment of Learning and Teaching

Assessment is one of the most important aspects of a teacher's responsibilities. At any given point in time, a student has either learned or not learned a particular intended learning outcome. Even though there may be such a thing as "partial credit," there is no such thing as "sorta-learned." How can a teacher determine in which category a student falls for each objective?

A first step in determining the answer to this question lies in knowing what is to be taught—having a clearly identified, specific statement of what the student should learn. Vague objectives beget fuzzy assessments. If objectives are too general, then it is more likely that a teacher will experience difficulty in determining the level of understanding of a given student.

If objectives are clear, the assessment process can be directed toward those specifics. We don't mean to imply that there is no such a thing as partial, or incomplete, learning, but if a student has partially learned something, then, by definition, he or she has not yet learned it. Assessment items based on specific competencies will provide evidence of the degree of student learning.

Methods commonly employed to evaluate students include publisher-provided and similar standardized tests. Although these instruments frequently offer data for comparing students, these data are typically not beneficial in identifying individual strengths and weaknesses. To gather diagnostic and/or achievement data, teacher-made assessment tools must be woven into the assessment scheme. This type of assessment should, for example, seek information on different kinds of mathematical thinking and present concepts and procedures in varied settings and contexts.

Paper-and-pencil tests often represent an efficient way of getting the job done. However, some of the critical outcomes in a mathematics program do not easily lend themselves to this form of assessment. Evaluation procedures should reflect this need, matching both teacher purpose and student experiences. For example, the ability to think mathematically can be demonstrated through actions such as being able to approach a problem situation independently by displaying confidence and persistence—that is, a positive disposition toward mathematics. This pattern of behavior can be assessed through direct observation to determine if the student (1) makes second and third attempts at solving problems, (2) is motivated to learn, (3) knows when an answer is reasonable, and (4) can determine and communicate methods of solving problems.

Teachers are sometimes reluctant to place weight on observations as an assessment strategy because they believe that observations are subjective, hard to quantify, and difficult to defend. However, observations are a primary means of providing the basis for monitoring and adjusting instruction. Observation can also be a professional evaluation skill when used to assess individuals relative to particular objectives. Evaluative data collected through informal observations are often some of the most fruitful. Follow-up questions that probe student understanding are invaluable in formulating judgments. When compared to anticipated learning objectives, this type of subjective evaluation plays an important role in completing the overall evaluation picture.

The importance of measuring the full range of learning outcomes cannot be overemphasized. It is essential to assess entry-level knowledge and understanding, including the identification of the small steps necessary for content leaps. Assessment in mathematics must also include an attempt to measure outcomes in terms of student attitudes, values, and other affective aspects. As a generalization, it sometimes seems that those outcomes that are most important to a student's mathematical understanding and growth are the ones most difficult to assess. A mathematics program that assesses only the most easily measured outcomes will usually find only those outcomes emphasized in the classroom. Sadly, the illusion of success on easily measured outcomes may obscure subsequent difficulties students may experience for lack of sound conceptual learning.

Evaluation issues are discussed more fully in Chapter 3, Assessing Mathematics, which includes information from the *Principles and Standards for School Mathematics* (2000) and the *Assessment Standards for School Mathematics* (1995), the third volume in the trilogy of original standards documents issued by NCTM.

What does research say about the effects of cooperative learning?

Slavin, Hurley, and Chamberlain (2003) stated "Research on cooperative learning is one of the greatest success stories in the history of educational research" (p. 177). Slavin (1995) reviewed 64 studies that provided group rewards that were based on the learning of individual members. Fifty out of the 64 studies found significant positive effects of learning; none of the 64 studies found a negative effect of cooperative learning. Slavin also found that interventions that focused on social cohesion and did not provide rewards based on learning were no more effective than traditional instruction. Cooperative learning has been demonstrated to increase self-esteem (self-confidence) as a learner and to foster intergroup relations including cross-group friendships.

Some of the problems that teachers and students expressed about cooperative learning in mathematics were concerns about covering enough math material, initial problems in forming effective groups, barriers to fostering cooperation among students, and handling the shift in the roles of teacher and student.

How do you think you will organize your groups? What do you think the effect of using small groups in your classroom will be on your high-achieving students? Do you think your high-achieving students will benefit from working in small groups?

Slavin, R. E. (1995). *Cooperative learning: Theory, research and practice* (2nd ed.). Boston: Allyn & Bacon.

Slavin, R. E., Hurley, E. A., & Chamberlin, A. M. (2003). Cooperative learning and achievement. In W. M. Reynolds & G. J. Miller (Eds.), *Handbook of psychology*: Vol. 7, *Educational psychology* (pp. 177–198). Hoboken, NJ: Wiley.

For additional research briefs, "ERIC Digests" lets you search more than 2000 short syntheses of research on a range of education topics. The syntheses were produced by the Educational Resources Information Center (ERIC). Check http://www.ericfacility.net/ericdigests/index/.

Adjusting Instruction to Meet Individual Needs

The process of intervention is often defined as the identification of alternatives or supplemental action designed to remediate, reinforce, or support student learning relative to specified performance objectives. Simply stated, when some planned educational experience does not lead to a student's reaching a desired competency level, then intervention is appropriate. Intervention, then, is based on diagnosis and offers a prescriptive action. Intervention can take the form of different approaches to a topic, which may include strategies such as (1) the incorporation of manipulatives that were not present during initial instruction, (2) the use of technology to focus attention on the desired result, (3) different or unusual drill and practice, or (4) learning center opportunities.

The decision to intervene may occur, for example, in the middle of a lesson that doesn't seem to be proceeding on track. A lesson plan is not like a book, in which the print is fixed and unchangeable. Instead, it should allow for, and be receptive to, improvisation to meet "teachable moments" that might arise. Even though there is a general plan and an outline, changes can be made as dictated by "audience reaction." Intervention may be triggered by your observation of students' actions or

reactions as you teach. Intervention may also occur after the fact, as patterns on homework or tests suggest the need to approach the topic from another perspective.

Successful classrooms are classrooms in which a variety of lesson types are utilized. Every lesson, whether it focuses on introducing a new topic or concept, practicing a skill, or reviewing prior knowledge, should contain some aspect of problem solving and decision making. Exploration and manipulation can be used to encourage discovery. This discovery can be guided by the teacher through the careful selection of tasks and subsequent focusing questions. Teacher- and student-led demonstrations can provide material for both open and directed discussions. Writing activities and those that involve collecting, organizing, and recording information can be invaluable in exposing children to mathematics as it is used outside the classroom walls.

Lecture methods and lessons focusing solely on the textbook are typically not appropriate for most students. Teachers must draw from students' past experiences; continuity is important for both motivation and confidence. There is always need for exploration and further investigation through simulations, manipulatives, models, calculators, and computers. The final product of a series of lessons must be proficiency with understanding.

Teachers often find that games, calculators, computers, and learning centers allow individual students to go beyond textbook learning to discover special areas of interest in mathematics. A variety of exploration activities that go beyond arithmetic computation can help students expand their understandings of and interests in the processes of mathematics.

For example, reasoning requires interaction, and discussion plays an important role in achieving problem-solving expertise. Therefore, whole-class and small-group settings are important. The teacher must be enthusiastic, motivational, inspirational, supportive of persistent attitudes, nonthreatening, analytical, and able to summarize. Questioning is an all-important art that helps the teacher communicate, focus, direct, and suggest.

Rather than using large-group lectures or discussions exclusively, incorporate other formats such as a small-group cooperative learning environment. Activities should be designed to require the children to work together to reach a desired outcome. Tasks can be shared or decided in such a way that teamwork is encouraged or essential. These alternative approaches to instructional events should be mixed and matched in a fashion that exemplifies the varied nature of the learners, the learning process, and mathematics itself.

Classroom Instructional Aids

The use of classroom aids as part of instruction is essential for promoting understanding and skill. Meaningful instruction as well as motivational drill and practice require sound **teaching aids** and **review aids**. The names used to describe these two types of aids are descriptive of their purpose and use. A teaching aid is used to assist in the teaching of a concept. A review aid is effective in reviewing a concept. A review aid is usually a game or an activity focusing on a concept that has already been introduced and is at least partially understood. The word *review* implies that students already have some degree of competency with the concept but that additional work is necessary to maintain efficiency in associated skills. A review aid can be a learning center activity that students use by themselves or in a small group. It can also be an aid the teacher uses in front of the class to reinforce a concept. A specific example of a review aid might be a board game based on a popular television quiz show such as *Jeopardy* in which the students must state a question that fits a given answer.

The primary purpose of a teaching aid, on the other hand, is to assist in introducing or explaining a concept. Whereas a review aid focuses on instilling or maintaining a skill, a teaching aid focuses on the meaning or understanding of a concept. A teaching aid seldom takes the form of a game, because games typically require at least basal understanding of the concept being explored. A teaching aid can be used by the teacher for large-group instruction, or it can be a learning center device for individuals or small groups of children. A teaching aid can often be used again at a later date as a review aid. An example of a teaching aid is a set of fractioned circles, perhaps designed to represent pizza slices. These pieces can be used to help a student understand why $\frac{3}{4}$ is equivalent to $\frac{6}{8}$ by showing that three of four equal pieces can represent the same amount of pizza as six of eight equal pieces (as long as the pizzas are the same size).

Individual differences in learning styles dictate various teaching styles and approaches. Models and manipulatives often convey understanding in situations in which words are not appropriate or sufficient. Manipulatives—so important in the early grades—play an equally critical role throughout the entire preK–12 curriculum (and beyond!). Students should manipulate and explore, using concrete aids (e.g., base 10 blocks, fraction pieces, and geoboards) and representative models (e.g., number lines, drawings, charts, and diagrams). Readers are directed to various resources described throughout this text for a wealth of ideas on using specific manipulatives mentioned here and elsewhere.

Many different manipulative and pictorial aids can be effectively used to illustrate mathematical concepts typically found in a contemporary elementary school mathematics program. Examples of commercially available aids are Cuisenaire rods, pattern blocks, base 10 blocks, geoboards, balances, counting blocks, and attribute blocks. Many everyday items, such as spoons, milk cartons, pasta, bread slices, and sponge cubes, can also be used effectively to model concepts and processes. Remember, when introducing concepts, it is important to begin meaningfully at the concrete manipulative level and then, once the foundation is firm, work toward more efficient methods and processes.

The rates at which students progress from a concrete to an abstract level of understanding differ greatly. Students should continue to use concrete materials as they associate their actions with a manipulative to the corresponding steps of a paper-pencil-and-algorithm. When students have achieved this level of understanding, they should be able to verbalize their thoughts and write symbolic statements. Without sufficient experiences at the concrete and representative levels, students acquire, at best, only partially understood abstractions. It is easy for a teacher to remind the class of an earlier hands-on exploration when students get confused about a particular concept. But if the physical model was never used in the first place, the students have nowhere to return to if they get lost. The manipulative experiences build the foundation for later abstractions and serve as reference points for intervention if the students need additional help.

By their modeling and their expectations, teachers lead students to recognize the importance of being able to communicate and demonstrate deep understanding of mathematical ideas. By building this awareness, teachers of older students may overcome the students' resistance to manipulatives that is sometimes expressed in the form of "That's kid stuff."

It is also common to see some resistance to using the calculator as a classroom tool. Rather than "That's kid stuff," some have believed that calculators are "adult stuff!" That is, they should be used ONLY when you've demonstrated certain abilities without the calculator. In many cases, teachers simply use calculators as a means for children to check their answers once they have solved problems by hand. Similarly, we often see computers used as rewards for students who finish their worksheets ahead of the rest of the class. However, calculators and computers, when used properly, can provide excellent support for problem-solving experiences and can meaningfully aid in the development of concepts.

In fact, calculators and computers can provide access to mathematics that students would not otherwise be able to explore. Calculators can provide the means to examine problems that involve arithmetic that is too complex or too time consuming to be carried out in class with paper and pencil. These kinds of problems may involve numbers from real life ($1.36, $\frac{9}{10}$ gallon, 3 for $0.87, 15.46% interest) or may be whimsical problem situations, such as "How many years old will you be on your billionth (in seconds) birthday?" "Are there more square inches in a square mile or seconds in a century?" or "Which is taller, the Empire State Building or a stack of one million pennies?" The value of such whimsical questions often lies in the fact that the student, not the calculator, must determine which procedures are necessary to arrive at an answer. Calculators, when used properly, can stimulate, encourage, and help students achieve success in mathematics. They can also help teachers become better at what they do.

Among a wealth of other applications, computers are excellent tools for carrying out repetitive tasks. They can quickly provide the output for thousands of trials in a simulation, or they can generate a table of data, enabling the class to check conjectures and search for patterns. Many simulation programs are readily available, whether for rolling dice or identifying the number of cereal boxes needed to gain a set of prizes. Some students may even benefit from the experience of using the random number–generation capabilities of a computer and the simple programs to study problems of this kind.

Calculators and computers are not substitutes for learning to think mathematically. Nevertheless, many benefits are derived from using technology appropriately to aid learning. Research that has consistently provided overwhelming evidence of the benefits of calculator and computer use has been accompanied by little evidence of loss of computational skill. Calculators and computers enable students to overcome apprehensions about mathematics, to build self-esteem and confidence, and to learn how to solve problems independently. For these and other sound reasons, teachers are obligated to adjust their instructional styles and patterns to integrate this technology into their classes.

Rather than exploring the role of calculators and computers in the elementary classroom more fully at this time, we ask you to consider the material in Chapter 4 and the references throughout the text to suggested uses and applications of calculators and computers.

Closure

Before leaving this chapter, let us return, briefly, to the NCTM standards. Basic assumptions central to these standards are well worth remembering:

1. *Principles and Standards for School Mathematics* furnishes the basis for a curriculum in which problem solving, reasoning and proof, communication, connections, and representation are central.

2. *What* students learn is fundamentally connected with *how* they learn it.

3. All students can learn to think mathematically.

4. Teaching is a complex practice. (NCTM, 2007, pp. 17–18)

As you continue through this text and as you develop as a teacher of mathematics, the recognition of, and attention to, the importance of these basic assumptions will keep you focused on your goals.

Readers are also encouraged to examine the CD that accompanies this text for additional information on teaching mathematics, including a grade-by-grade scope and sequence, a concept cluster checklist, a collection of thematic activities across the common topic strands of elementary/middle school mathematics, and a vignette that demonstrates the integration of curriculum, teaching, and assessment.

TEACHING COMPETENCIES AND SELF-ASSESSMENT TASKS

1. The NCTM *Principals and Standards for School Mathematics* offers many promises and challenges for teachers and students of mathematics. Identify and describe what you believe may be the greatest barriers to implementing the vision of this document.

2. What are the major characteristics that you would ascribe to "a positive classroom environment"? Which of these do you, as the teacher, have direct control over? Which are dependent on your students? On the administration? Which are shared responsibilities?

3. Locate a local course of study or set of state-level standards. In small groups, discuss the outcomes for a given grade level in terms of clarity and usefulness in planning lessons.

4. Select a mathematics concept to be taught and discuss what you think is the most effective presentation to use for children at different grade levels.

5. Identify a specific mathematics concept and discuss how provisions can be made for individual differences in a teacher's approach to that concept. Include in your discussion techniques that will elicit various forms of student participation.

6. Select a specific mathematics concept and examine how several different elementary school textbooks develop the concept. Discuss what you think are the positive and negative aspects of each presentation.

3

Assessing Mathematics

TEACHING COMPETENCIES

Upon completing this chapter, you will be able to:

- Describe the vision of mathematics assessment put forth in the NCTM *Principles and Standards for School Mathematics* and the NCTM *Assessment Standards for School Mathematics*.

- State characteristics of worthwhile assessment tasks and techniques.

- State multiple purposes of assessing student progress in elementary and middle school mathematics.

- Compare and contrast standardized and nonstandardized tests that are commonly a part of assessment in elementary/middle schools.

- Describe strategies available for teachers to use in assessing student work and student attitudes and dispositions.

- Design assessment tasks for a given set of objectives in mathematics.

Anne, a middle school student, was asked to simplify the fraction $\frac{16}{64}$. She immediately answered, "That's easy; you just cancel and get $\frac{1}{4}$." The teacher smiled at this correct response, having heard Anne give evidence that she had successfully learned how to "cancel" when simplifying a fraction. After class, the teacher complimented the student on having successfully rewritten the fraction. Anne responded by saying, "Thanks. Really, it was easy—I remember that you told us to *cancel* and all you have to do is to cancel the 6 on the top with the 6 on the bottom, and you have the answer." The teacher probed a little further and asked, "What if the fraction had been $\frac{36}{64}$?" The student replied, "Then, we would still cancel the 6s, so it would be $\frac{3}{4}$." The teacher then asked, "So, does $\frac{36}{64} = \frac{3}{4}$?" When Anne answered, "Yes, of course it does because that's how you told us to do these," the smile of satisfaction left the teacher's face.

We must acknowledge that what *we* believe students have learned is not always the same as what *they* have actually learned. Often students are able to come up with answers that may appear to be carrect on the surface but do not necessarily imply or reflect conceptual understanding.

Debates have raged as to whether students should simply memorize procedures and be graded on their final answers or whether teachers should emphasize understanding and assign grades based on process as well as final products. Maybe the best answer is to combine these two positions. Research has indicated that allowing students to construct their own understandings of mathematics initially takes more time but pays much greater dividends in the future.

If we agree that teaching involves paying attention to student understanding of the mathematical processes (Problem Solving, Reasoning and Proof, Communication, Connections, and Representation), then obtaining a picture of what students know becomes a much more complex process than simply asking 10 questions on a quiz and grading the answers as right or wrong. If we are to implement the vision of curriculum and teaching addressed in Chapters 1 and 2 of this text, then it is clear that we must also change our assessments—the ways that we determine how well a student understands the mathematical concepts we are exploring.

Assessment can be described as the process of gathering information about student understanding of mathematical concepts, as well as determining the attitudes and beliefs that the student has about mathematics. These attitudes and beliefs, along with a general student willingness to do mathematics, are referred to by the National Council of Teachers of Mathematics (NCTM) as a student's *disposition* toward mathematics. Assessment information is then used to determine student progress for a number of purposes, as discussed later in this chapter.

Following the success of their initial standards-setting efforts, the NCTM released the *Principles and Standards for School Mathematics* (2000), a revision of its earlier curriculum, teaching, and assessment standards into one document. One intent was to make it clear that curriculum, teaching, and assessment are intertwined to a degree greater than that suggested by three separate sets of standards. These new standards were not intended as a replacement of the earlier works, but as an extension of the spirit and vision of mathematics so well reflected in the original standards documents.

As we discussed in Chapter 1 of this text, *Principles and Standards for School Mathematics* places emphasis on the integration of six major principles—Equity, Curriculum, Learning, Teaching, Assessment, and Technology. To assist teachers and other educators in designing a worthwhile assessment system, these principles provide a framework for decisions that need to be made and issues that must be considered in the process of assessment. Although each of the three original NCTM standards publications deserves elaboration and integration with regard to assessment issues, the scope of this particular chapter requires that we devote our attention to focusing on standards for assessing mathematics.

NCTM Assessment Standards for School Mathematics

In 1995, the NCTM issued a publication entitled *Assessment Standards for School Mathematics*. This document was written as a third companion document to the previously issued *Curriculum and Evaluation Standards for School Mathematics* (1989) and *Professional Standards for Teaching Mathematics* (1991). The assessment document presents a set of guidelines or benchmarks that assist teachers and other educational decision makers in the development of a meaningful system of assessing student competencies and dispositions. The assessment standards document is divided into two main sections: "Mathematics Assessment Standards" and "Use of the Assessment Standards for Different Purposes."

The first section, "Mathematics Assessment Standards," presents a set of six guidelines regarding the design of assessment programs and techniques. The second section, "Use of the Assessment Standards for Different Purposes," outlines four categories of uses for the results of student assessment and dispositions. The document concludes with a short reflection on what it takes to reform assessment practices in mathematics.

Each section of the assessment standards document is important for educators to explore, but for the purposes of this book, we will examine the six assessment standards in particular. For additional information on the assessment standards, contact NCTM, 1906 Association Drive, Reston, VA 20191 (www.nctm.org).

The NCTM assessment standards present a

criteria for judging the quality of mathematics assessments. They are statements about what is valued. Together, they reflect a vision of exemplary mathematics assessment.... The Assessment Standards promote the dynamic and ongoing process of improving mathematics curricula, mathematics teaching, and mathematics assessment. The process involves everyone concerned with mathematics education. These standards for assessment contribute to, and are affected by, the standards for curriculum and the standards for teaching. (NCTM, 1995, p. 9)

The six standards outlined in the NCTM *Assessment Standards for School Mathematics* (1995) are

- Mathematics Standard
- Learning Standard
- Equity Standard
- Openness Standard
- Inferences Standard
- Coherence Standard

The *Mathematics Standard* refers to the actual mathematical content that should be assessed in an effective system. The *Learning Standard* refers to the need for assessment to be more than simply gathering data for the purpose of assigning grades. Instead, an effective assessment system is one in which educators use the information to improve classroom instruction and conduct assessments as part of the classroom routine. The *Equity Standard* refers to the importance of placing high standards of achievement on all students and the need for each student to be given an opportunity to demonstrate mathematical understanding. The *Openness Standard* calls for the sharing of details of assessment by all stakeholders. The *Inferences Standard* discusses the inferences, or conclusions, that can be drawn from the analysis of data gathered in assessment procedures. Finally, the *Coherence Standard* refers to the idea that assessment processes should be appropriate for the situation. That is, in the example described at the beginning of this chapter, if the teacher had wanted to assess Anne's understanding of the concept of simplifying fractions, then simply asking for the answer to a fraction-simplifying question would not have been sufficient.

The six assessment standards in in the NCTM document that can be used to judge the quality of an assessment system are described next.[1]

STANDARD 1
The Mathematics Standard

Assessment should reflect the mathematics that all students need to know and be able to do.... To determine how well an assessment reflects mathematics that students need to know and be able to do, ask questions such as the following:

- What mathematics is reflected in the assessment?
- What efforts are made to ensure that the mathematics is significant and correct?
- How does the assessment engage students in realistic and worthwhile mathematical activities?
- How does the assessment elicit the use of mathematics that is important to know and be able to do?
- How does the assessment fit within a framework of mathematics to be assessed?
- What inferences about students' mathematical knowledge, understanding, thinking processes, and dispositions can be made from the assessment?

STANDARD 2
The Learning Standard

Assessment should enhance mathematics learning.... To determine how well an assessment enhances learning, ask questions such as these:

- How does the assessment contribute to each student's learning of mathematics?
- How does the assessment relate to instruction?
- How does the assessment allow students to demonstrate what they know and what they can do in novel situations?
- How does the assessment engage students in relevant, purposeful work on worthwhile mathematical activities?
- How does the assessment build on each student's understanding, interests, and experiences?

[1] Reprinted with permission from the *Assessment Standards for School Mathematics*, copyright 1995 by the National Council of Teachers of Mathematics.

- How does the assessment involve students in selecting activities, applying performance criteria, and using results?
- How does the assessment provide opportunities for students to evaluate, reflect on, and improve their own work—that is, to become independent learners?

STANDARD 3
The Equity Standard

Assessment should promote equity.... To determine how well an assessment promotes equity, ask questions such as the following:

- What opportunities has each student had to learn the mathematics being assessed?
- How does the assessment provide alternative activities or modes of response that invite each student to engage in the mathematics being assessed?
- How does the design of the assessment enable all students to exhibit what they know and can do?
- How do the conditions under which the assessment is administered enable all students to exhibit what they know and can do?
- How does the assessment help students demonstrate their best work?
- How is the role of students' backgrounds and experiences recognized in judging their responses to the assessment?
- How do scoring guides accommodate unanticipated but reasonable responses?
- How have the effects of bias been minimized throughout the assessment?
- To what sources can differences in performance be attributed?

STANDARD 4
The Openness Standard

Assessment should be an open process.... To determine how open an assessment is, ask questions such as these:

- How do students become familiar with the assessment process and with the purposes, performance criteria, and consequences of the assessment?
- How are teachers and students involved in choosing tasks, setting criteria, and interpreting results?
- How is the public involved in the assessment process?
- What access do those affected by the assessment have to tasks, scoring goals, performance

criteria, and samples of students' work that have been scored and discussed?
- How is the assessment process itself open to evaluation and modification?

STANDARD 5
The Inferences Standard

Assessment should promote valid inferences about mathematics learning.... To determine how well an assessment promotes valid inferences, ask questions such as the following:

- What evidence about learning does the assessment provide?
- How is professional judgment used in making inferences about learning?
- How sensitive is the assessor to the demands the assessment makes and to unexpected responses?
- How is bias minimized in making inferences about learning?
- What efforts are made to ensure that scoring is consistent across students, scorers, and activities?
- What multiple sources of evidence are used for making inferences, and how is the evidence used?
- What is the value of the evidence for each use?

STANDARD 6
The Coherence Standard

Assessment should be a coherent process.... To determine how coherent an assessment process is, ask questions such as these:

- How is professional judgment used to ensure that the various parts of the assessment process form a coherent whole?
- How do students view the connection between instruction and assessment?
- How does the assessment match its purposes with its uses?
- How does the assessment match the curriculum and instructional practice?
- How can assessment practice inform teachers as they make curriculum decisions and determine their instructional practices?

In the NCTM *Principles and Standards for School Mathematics*, the standards and their purposes are elaborated, often through the use of classroom vignettes or actual samples of student work. These examples are intended to provide a snapshot of what effective assessment looks like, to assist in guiding educators toward the vision of the standards.

AN EXAMPLE OF AN ASSESSMENT STANDARD

To provide an indication of the format and style of the NCTM *Assessment Standards for School Mathematics*, a complete statement of Standard 6 and one of the vignettes from the publication is reproduced here.

STANDARD 6: THE COHERENCE STANDARD: ASSESSMENT SHOULD BE A COHERENT PROCESS

Coherence in assessment involves three types of agreement. First, the assessment process forms a coherent whole; the phases fit together. Second, the assessment matches the purposes for which it is being done. When the design, evidence-gathering, evidence-interpreting, and action phases of the assessment process are consistent with one another and with the purposes of the assessment, it has educational value. Third, the assessment is aligned with the curriculum and with instruction. Students' learning connects with their assessment experiences.

A coherent mathematics assessment system assures that assessors will develop activities and performance criteria tailored to the purposes of each assessment. An assessment framework is useful in judging whether all parts of the process are in harmony, from the design stage to the stage of reporting and using results. The assessment process then unfolds as a logical and coherent whole.

The Coherence Standard has several implications. Just as no single instrument section makes a great orchestra, a coherent mathematics assessment system cannot be based on paper-and-pencil tests alone. Instead, a balance among appropriate and diverse assessment activities can help all students learn.

A coherent mathematics assessment system requires that activities be chosen that are appropriate to the purpose at hand. A teacher would not use a test on linear equations to assess students' knowledge of quadratic equations, or a test of procedural skills to indicate students' conceptual knowledge, or a computation test to assess problem-solving performance.

Coherence in assessment, however, raises broader issues than simply selecting an appropriate test or activity. Coherence relates to all aspects of the assessment process.

External assessment programs are moving away from an extensive reliance on machine-scored multiple-choice items to a greater use of performance tasks and to the use of multiple sources of information. Assessment activities for such programs, however, can be expensive to develop, administer, and score. The programs may entail costs in the form of instructional time taken away from other activities if they are not integrated into instruction. Greater investments of time and funding may be required, which means that people may expect more information from the assessments. As assessment programs change, the pressure to make a single assessment serve multiple purposes is likely to increase. Consequently, special vigilance may be needed to assure that all the uses to which assessment information is being put are in harmony with the purposes of the assessment.

Mathematics teachers organize, conduct, and interpret assessments as part of their ongoing mathematics instruction. When mathematics assessment is a coherent process, teachers and students benefit because they are not confronted by conflicting demands. Attention to coherence underscores the principle that assessment needs to be in step with instruction. When assessment fits the curriculum, students can see that assessment activities not only are related to the mathematics they have learned but also serve clear goals. As students understand how assessment is connected to what they are learning, an increase can be expected in the number of students who will choose to continue their study of mathematics.

Assessment developers in local and provincial or state agencies play a vital role in making sure that the assessments of students' mathematics learning form a harmonious whole as they progress through school. A single assessment touches only a part of the mathematics that students know and can use, but the totality of the assessments students encounter provides a comprehensive picture of their knowledge, skill, and understanding.

To determine how coherent an assessment process is, ask questions such as these:

- How is professional judgment used to ensure that the various parts of the assessment process form a coherent whole?
- How do students view the connection between instruction and assessment?
- How does the assessment match its purposes with its uses?
- How does the assessment match the curriculum and instructional practice?
- How can assessment practice inform teachers as they make curriculum decisions and determine their instructional practices?

Reprinted with permission from the *Assessment Standards for School Mathematics*, copyright 1995 by the National Council of Teachers of Mathematics.

A CLASSROOM ASSESSMENT VIGNETTE

INSIDE, OUT, AND ALL ABOUT

Janna McKnight perched on the edge of her desk at the back of the classroom. Her sixth-grade students were elbowing each other and chatting while parading to the front of the room to place their yellow stickies on a bar chart. They had been finding the area of a salt marsh on a map, a rather irregular shape. Each stickie represented the area (in thousands of square meters) determined by one student.

The portion of the chart from about 85 to 95 was beginning to look like the New York City skyline, with highrise towers huddled close together. Close in, to the left and right of the city, were several lower towers. Off to the right at 196 was one lonely stickie with the initials TP, and down to the left were two other stickies at 55 with the initials BT and AK.

Ms. McKnight called the class to order. "All right, let's see what you've found. Who'd like to make some observations about our data?"

"Ninety-two thousand square meters got the most, but 87 was a close second," Jeremy answered. "It seems like lots of people got answers between 86 and 94."

"The lowest answer was 55—two people got that—and the highest was 196. Those people must have done it wrong, because those answers are, like, too different to be true," Angel offered.

"Bernice, is the 55 with BT on it yours?" Wallace blurted.

"The 196 is mine, and it isn't wrong!" Tyler offered in a defensive tone.

Anthony interrupted, "Bernice and I worked together, but I think our calculator gave us the wrong answer. I just added it up again, and ours should be 85 instead of 55."

"Tyler, would you like to explain how you found 196 as the area of the marsh?"

"Well, you remember how we put string around those circles the other day? You didn't give us any string today. But my sweatshirt has a string in the hood, so I pulled it out and wrapped it around the marsh. Then I straightened it out into a square on top of the plastic, and it was about 14 units long and 14 wide. So its area was about 196. The square wasn't exactly 14, but it was pretty close!"

"So, Tyler found the area of a square he built from reshaping a string that fit around the perimeter of the marsh. I noticed most of the rest of you doing something quite different. Amy?"

Amy explained that her group had put clear plastic graph paper on top of the marsh and counted squares. Dyanne explained how her group counted partial squares as halves or fourths for more accuracy.

"Did anyone approach the problem differently? What do you think about Tyler's procedure?"

"I think it's a lot better," said Richard, "because Tyler didn't have to do all that counting. I wish I'd thought of making it into an easier shape. It would have saved a lot of work."

"But why is Tyler's answer so much bigger?" asked Nancy. "I don't know why it's wrong, but Tyler's answer is way too big."

"If the distance around the marsh is a lot, then the area is a lot—wouldn't that be right? Like when one is big, the other is big?" asked Cindy. Numerous heads nodded in agreement, amid a few dissenting frowns.

Pointing to the bulletin board, where dotpaper records of a geoboard activity from the previous week were displayed, Dyanne reminded the class that shapes with equal perimeters could have very different areas.

"All right," said Ms. McKnight, glancing at the clock over the chalkboard. "We're not going to have time today to get to the bottom of this mystery. Let's just write Tyler's conjecture on the board and see whether we can investigate it further tomorrow. Who can use some good mathematical language to say what Tyler's been thinking?"

Janna McKnight wisely did not dismiss Tyler's answer as wrong but probed to discover the source of his confusion. In doing so, she uncovered a common misconception about area and perimeter and made some decisions to adjust her instruction.

What will Ms. McKnight do tomorrow in class? The decisions that she made today have led her to a point where she will have to revise her short-range plans for tomorrow's lesson. She will need to think about ways to follow up on Tyler's conjecture. One of her goals now is to help her students explore the conjecture and decide its validity for themselves, so she wants to plan an activity to make that happen. One idea would be to have them measure the area and perimeter of their own handprints (with fingers spread and with fingers together) and explore the relationship, hoping they will begin to understand why Tyler's conjecture is false. This short range plan also fits some of her long range goals for the class. She wants her students to have a sense of what it really means to do mathematics, and she intends to communicate the principle that making conjectures and testing them for validity are important components of mathematical power.

Janna McKnight's understanding of the importance of conjecture and verification in doing mathematics helps her recognize the value of exploring Tyler's conjecture rather than quickly pointing out his error. Teachers are more effective in assessing students' understanding of mathematical ideas when they are knowledgeable about performance standards, familiar with the "big ideas" of mathematics (such as number sense, proportion, and equivalence), confident of their abilities to deal with important mathematical processes (such as problem solving, reasoning, communication, and making connections), and convinced of the importance of dispositions (such as motivation and confidence). Ongoing professional development activities—attending conferences, reading professional journals, and collaborating with other educators—help teachers become aware of, and confident in, their understanding of effective ways to help all students become mathematically powerful.

The preceeding vignette illustrates how the interactive nature of assessment and instruction in the classroom can enhance learning. In this story, a sixth-grade student made the incorrect conjecture that all shapes with equal perimeters have equal areas. His teacher decided the misconception was worth exploring in class and changed her lesson plan accordingly.

Reprinted with permission from the *Assessment Standards for School Mathematics*, copyright 1995 by the National Council of Teachers of Mathematics.

Using this sample standard as a foundation for understanding the vision of the *Assessment Standards for School Mathematics*, let's consider some of the more general characteristics of effective assessment programs.

Purposes for Assessment

Too many educators, and too many in the general public, believe that assessment is conducted for the sole purpose of yielding data for determining student grades. However, tracking individual student progress in the form of assigning grades is an extremely narrow view of assessment and only one of several purposes for gathering assessment information. In the *Principles and Standards for School Mathematics* document, the NCTM describes four purposes for gathering the information: (1) monitoring students' progress as compared with objectives outlined in the mathematics program, (2) making instructional decisions to ensure that lessons meet the needs of learners, (3) evaluating students' achievement

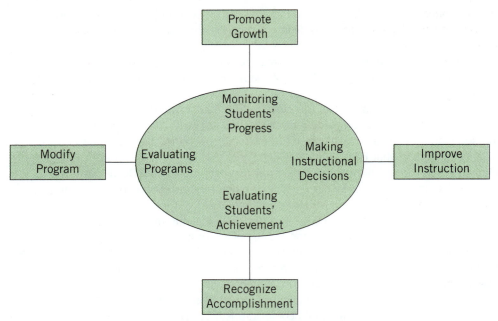

Four purposes of assessment and their results

to validate the progress made by individual students, and (4) evaluating programs to determine if changes in the mathematics program are needed.

This vision of assessment is one in which educators gather information about what students know, what they can do, and what they believe about mathematics for reasons that go beyond giving grades. The graphic on the following page illustrates the various purposes of assessment and their results.[2]

Assessments conducted by the teacher must also be used to directly improve the instructional process. There should always be a close connection between collected assessment data and classroom teaching. The teacher who uses a variety of methods to gather information about the students' knowledge and dispositions can use these data to influence future lessons. Assessment procedures may be as informal as the teacher listening in on a small-group problem-solving experience or as formal as an extended paper-and-pencil examination. However, whether formal or informal, the data gathered should be used for improving instruction.

For example, suppose that a mathematics teacher asks students to write a short entry in a mathematics journal after class each day. After collecting the journals at the end of the week, the teacher discovers that several students have a common misconception about

one of the mathematical processes explored that week. The teacher might choose to make use of the faulty reasoning that appears in the student journals to redirect the class on Monday morning. Since the class may not have asked many questions that week, without the journal information the teacher may not have known that they needed help in a particular area until after a poor performance on a test. In this case, the journal entries were not being written strictly for assigning grades. Instead, they were being used as a method of learning more about what the students think and understand as well as to determine how well they communicate their ideas and what misconceptions, if any, they might hold. Use of an ongoing assessment, such as writing journal entries, is often referred to as *formative assessment* because it is assessment that is conducted "along the way," helping both the teacher and the student set goals and refine the teaching and learning processes.

In addition to teacher-collected data for instructional and grading purposes, assessment is often conducted by outside sources, such as school districts issuing competency or standardized tests, states mandating proficiency or achievement tests, or commercial/institutional testing services offering examinations for scholarships or college placement. In general, **criterion-referenced tests**, such as local competency and state achievement examinations, are tests that are tied directly to a specified curriculum. The student score on a criterion-referenced test is "absolute" in that it may be used to determine whether a student has mastered some set of objectives, rather than to compare the student to others. In

[2]Reprinted with permission from the *Assessment Standards for School Mathematics*, copyright 1995 by the National Council of Teachers of Mathematics.

contrast, **a norm-referenced test** is an examination that compares student scores to a sample of other students across the country at the same grade level (if grade level is the norming factor used). Scores on norm-referenced tests are "relative" because student progress is compared with the achievement of other students as opposed to the attainment of certain objectives.

Proficiency tests (some are referred to as "exit exams") are generally examinations that test baseline knowledge that every student in a state, district, or school must possess at a particular grade level. Proficiency tests are often seen as accountability tools for local districts to demonstrate that they are meeting the educational expectations of some governing body at the district, county, state, or even national level. In many cases, passing scores on these types of achievement tests are required for promotion from one grade level to the next or for graduation from high school.

Proficiency exams might be either norm referenced or criterion based—depending on the purpose the exam is designed to serve. Whereas criterion-referenced competency tests are useful for measuring the effectiveness of a local program, the norm-referenced test can be used to give a national comparison of a local program to others at the same grade level. Each type of test has its own strengths and weaknesses and serves a different purpose. These types of assessments are called *summative* because they indicate a level of performance at the end of some instructional sequence (as opposed to formative assessments collected along the way).

Most of these types of tests are external in that someone other than the teacher has developed, scored, and, in many cases, interpreted them. Consequently, educators need to use caution when using the data collected from various tests. Teachers should no sooner give a grade to a student based on performance on a norm-referenced test than a school district should believe that its program is successful merely because a large number of students are earning A's in their classes. It is, after all, relatively easy to design a set of questions that everyone can answer—just as easy as it is to design a test that few can answer. There's nothing inherently meaningful or mystical about a percent score—it is merely a reflection of the ratio of correct answers to questions asked; it is not an indicator of the difficulty or the challenge found in the question selection, nor is it necessarily a good indicator of a student's depth of knowledge and understanding.

Teachers must use standardized test scores with caution because of the nature of the questions that are often asked on such tests. It is important to scrutinize any standardized test by asking, "Does this really measure the teaching that I do in my classroom?" For example, a

study by Romberg and Wilson (1989)[3] showed that the six most commonly used national standardized achievement tests for eighth graders required problem solving on an average of only 1% of the questions. In the same study, it was noted that 77% of the items centered on computation and estimation skills. If the teacher of the class that took such an exam was creating a classroom environment as described in the *Principles and Standards for School Mathematics*, then it is likely that the class emphasized worthwhile problem-solving tasks and the importance of number and computation sense. Consequently, the standardized test did not reflect or measure the full extent of what the teacher and the students spent the year trying to develop! In short, teachers should recognize that standardized test scores are only one of many possible measures of student progress and need to be interpreted in the context of the "bigger picture."

We have seen that an effective assessment system must emphasize important mathematics, enhance learning, assure equity, be open, allow for valid inferences to be made, and be coherent. We have also discussed the different purposes for assessment and the fact that some assessment data are gathered by teachers for assigning grades and improving classroom instruction, while other assessment data are gathered by a local school district, state, or national testing company for purposes of measuring program effectiveness or providing accountability measures for the public. Now, we turn our attention to specific strategies that teachers can use to gain a broad and multidimensional picture of what their students can do and what their students believe about mathematics.

Assessment Strategies

Let's take some time to challenge a traditional view of assessment as synonymous with grading. In light of the previous discussion of the standards for judging the quality of an assessment, think about what might be missed by making use of the following grading procedure.

Suppose that a teacher has just completed a set of lessons in which the students have been working with the area and perimeter of various polygons. At the conclusion of these lessons, the teacher issues a 20-question test in which the student is given 10 polygons that require the calculation of area and 10 other polygons for which the perimeter must be determined. The 20 answers are to be written on 20 blanks on an

[3] Romberg, T. A., & Wilson, L. (1989). *The alignment of six standardized tests with the NCTM standards*. Unpublished manuscript, University of Wisconsin–Madison.

answer sheet. The teacher scores the 20 answers and assigns a percent grade to each student, based on the number of correct answers given. Is the grade that the student receives truly indicative of what the student knows about the concepts of area and perimeter? What does a grade of 75% truly represent (other than the fact that the student answered 15 of the 20 questions correctly)? Which 15? Was it 5 of the area questions and all 10 of the perimeter questions? Do we have *any* other information by looking at the percent score? Will this grading process really help the teacher learn about how the students think and where their misconceptions about mathematics lie so that instruction can be improved? Although this grading process is rather typical of traditional testing procedures, it is not consistent with the vision in the standards and the contemporary view of assessment.

On the 20-question test on area and perimeter, is it possible that the student could have a deep understanding of what it means to determine area and perimeter but make several calculation errors and, therefore, receive a grade of 75%? Conversely, is it conceivable that the student could have memorized a list of formulas for calculating area and perimeter, cranked out a list of 20 correct answers, but never really had any firm understanding of what the concepts of area and perimeter are all about? The answer to both of these questions is a resounding YES! In this case, unfortunately, the assessment tool issued at the end of the lessons did not attempt to measure understanding. Instead, it focused solely on students' ability to use a formula and find correct numerical answers.

Meaningful assessment tools offer students the opportunity to demonstrate conceptual knowledge that goes well beyond simply putting right answers on blanks on a test paper. Perhaps a more insightful assessment of student learning from these lessons would have been to ask the student to draw a picture of a rectangle that has an area of 20 square centimeters and a perimeter of 24 centimeters. This alternate item would have required the student to relate the concepts of area and perimeter and would have given the teacher a much clearer picture of what the student thought and was able to do.

A student who knows that the teacher will be grading only the 20 answers on the blanks has also learned something about what the teacher values—correct answers. The same 20-question test described earlier could be greatly enhanced by eliminating the answer blanks and requiring students to explain their responses in writing. This format gives students the message that the teacher values the process that the student used to obtain an answer *and* the answer, not just the answer alone. Knowledge of the process that the student used will be more effective in making inferences about what a student can do than looking at only their final numerical

answers. Consequently, assessment procedures need to be judged on their effectiveness in determining what a student actually knows about the important mathematics. As a result, conceptual understanding becomes the emphasis, and the teacher becomes much more knowledgeable about what the students really know and how they came to know it.

One strategy that can be used effectively in any assessment system is the use of **open-ended** (also called free-response or extended-response) questions. With this type of question, the student is asked to respond by explaining, describing, showing, drawing, or verifying. A variety of student responses are expected, and no two answers in a class will necessarily be exactly alike. Traditional exam items can be rewritten as open-ended questions with some practice. For example, on a third-grade test, a traditional item may have been:

Compute: 7×12

Instead, the question could be written as follows:

A student has completed the multiplication exercise below:

$$\begin{array}{r} 12 \\ \times\ \ 7 \\ \hline 714 \end{array}$$

Explain the error that the student made and draw a picture that shows that you understand what it *means* to multiply 7 by 12.

Worded this way, the student must demonstrate a firm grasp of the *concept* of multiplication in order to address the question. In the traditional version of the item, only a procedural knowledge of regrouping (sometimes referred to as "carrying") would be required to obtain a correct answer. Furthermore, whether a student uses a calculator on the test becomes a nonissue when the emphasis of the questions is on understanding, rather than procedure. For the open-ended version of this question, the use of a calculator does not put one student at an advantage over another.

Since open-ended questions may have multiple solutions or several reasonable ways in which to reach a solution, their use can be extremely powerful in assessing what the student is thinking. However, there are two related issues that must be considered. First, an open-ended question, by definition, is open to many different responses. It is assumed that the teacher has the mathematical expertise to distinguish a good answer from a bluff. Some students are very skilled at writing long, verbose responses, but a careful analysis of the answers may indicate little, if any, mathematical understanding. Simply put, the scoring of open-ended

RESEARCH SNAPSHOT

Are there research programs that relate assessment to instruction?

In Wiliam's (2007) chapter on classroom assessment, he describes programs that integrate assessment and instruction. These programs are based on research about the development of mathematical knowledge.

Cognitively Guided Instruction (CGI) (Carpenter, Fennema, Peterson, Chiang, & Loef, 1989) requires teachers to assess their students' thinking by asking their students to explain how they figure out their answers. The student responses are related to a research-based framework of students' strategies. Based on responses to specific items, the teacher is able to determine a range of problems that the students can solve. In CGI, the instruction is based on the information provided by the assessment.

Bergan, Sladeczek, Schwarz, and Smith's (1991) measurement-and-planning system (MAPS) compared the performance of kindergarten students from districts with considerable socio-economic disadvantages. In the MAPS program, teachers were trained to interpret assessments and were provided with materials that helped them individualize instruction based on students' performance on the assessments. In their study, students in the control group were 14 times more likely to be placed in special education programs than were students taught by teachers in the MAPS program.

How will you balance assessment with instruction? When you spend time assessing your students' knowledge of facts, what do you know about what they understand about mathematics?

Wiliam, D. (2007). Keeping learning on track: Classroom assessment and the regulation of learning. In F. K. Lester (Ed.), *Second handbook of research on mathematics teaching and learning: A project of the National Council of Teachers of Mathematics* (pp. 1053–1098). Charlotte, NC: Information Age Publishing.

Carpenter, T. P., Fennema, E., Peterson, P. L., Chiang, C. P., & Loef, M. (1989). Using knowledge of children's mathematics thinking in classroom teaching: An experimental study. *American Educational Research Journal*, 26(4), 499–531.

Bergan, J. R., Sladeczek, I. E., Schwarz, R. D., & Smith, A. N. (1991). Effects of a measurement and planning system on kindergarteners' cognitive development and educational programming. *American Educational Research Journal*, 28(3), 683–714.

For additional research briefs, "ERIC Digests" lets you search more than 2000 short syntheses of research on a range of education topics. The syntheses were produced by the Educational Resources Information Center (ERIC). Check http://www.ericfacility.net/ericdigests/index/.

---

questions is not as easy as the right or wrong nature of closed questions and requires that the teacher possess a strong conceptual understanding of what is being assessed.

The second issue that is inherent to open-ended questions is the decision of how to score student solutions. If a student assessment is conducted through the use of a worthwhile, perhaps multidimensional, open-ended question, as opposed to 20 fill-in-the-blank questions, then the grading of the response is going to be much different. As a result, many teachers use a rubric for scoring student responses to open-ended questions. A **rubric** is a generalized grading scale that is used for assessing student writing on an open-ended item. Many different rubrics are used by individuals and school districts across the country. In some areas, all the teachers in district are using the same rubric for scoring student work. Some prefer a simple scoring rubric of 0 (no understanding shown or left blank), 1 (partial answer for which the work is on track, but the answer is incorrect), or 2 (a correct response). Others use more fine-grained rubrics that have several performance levels. An example of one school district's six-level rubric for scoring student responses to open-ended questions follows.

4 Complete and Competent

- A full and correct response to the question has been given.

- Illustrates excellent problem-solving, reasoning, and communication skills.

- The "answers" are all correct.

- Work is clearly shown and/or explained.

- A minor error, such as incorrect units or rounding, may be present.

3 Basic Competency

- A correct response to the question has been given.
- Illustrates good problem-solving, reasoning, and communication skills.
- Most of the "answers" are correct.
- Work is shown/explained.
- Some minor mathematical errors or errors in reasoning may be present.

2 Partial Answer

- Some of the response to the question may have been omitted.
- Illustrates fair problem-solving, reasoning, and communication skills.
- A lack of higher-level thinking is evident.
- Conclusions drawn may not be accurate.
- Some limited understanding of mathematical concepts is demonstrated.
- Several mathematical errors or errors in reasoning may be present.

1 Attempted Answer

- Problem is copied over, but mathematical ideas are never developed.
- Problem-solving, reasoning, and/or communication skills are lacking.
- Several incorrect calculations may be present.
- There is little, if any, mathematical understanding illustrated.
- The student has merely made an attempt of some kind.

0 Off-Task or No Response

- The response is totally off-task and/or inappropriate.
- No evidence of problem-solving, reasoning, or communication skills is shown.
- No mathematical understanding is demonstrated at all.
- Attempts at "bluffing" may be evident.
- No response may have been given at all.

Using this rubric scale, a student response to a question can earn a score from 0 to 4, depending on the strength of the response. Distinctions between scores are not cut and dried and as well defined as they appear to be on a true-false examination. Also, note that scores on a rubric do not necessarily correspond to the traditional notion of "partial credit," in which half of the points are awarded to an answer that is half finished or half correct.

Instead, papers are scored holistically—by looking at the total piece of student work and determining where the response lies on a continuum from, for example, 0 to 4.

Furthermore, a score of 3 using this rubric does *not* mean 75% correct. Instead, it is a numerical indicator on a four-point scale of what the student knows and can do in the problem situation. Would you say that a normal person's temperature was 98.6%? How about a person's golf score as a 78%? These, also, are merely numerical performance indicators, in these cases of general health or specific ability—they are *not* intended to be interpreted as percentages.

Other rubrics teachers may use incorporate a scale from from 0 to 6, or even a scale from 0 to 10. An example of a quite simple rubric was used by the Mathematical Sciences Education Board (1993) in conducting a pilot of fourth-grade open-ended responses that grouped student answers as high, medium, or low.

Let's take a look at actual student responses to an open-ended question. Students in this third-grade sample were asked to produce a calendar for the month of February, with the first of the month falling on a Sunday, as shown:

S	M	T	W	R	F	S
1	2	3	4	5	6	7
8	9	10	11	12	13	14
15	16	17	18	19	20	21
22	23	24	25	26	27	28

Then, they were to use the calendar to determine how many days make up $\frac{3}{4}$ of the month and to explain how they got their answers. Six samples of actual student responses are displayed on the next page.

Is it possible to score each of these responses as "right" or "wrong"? Are there any samples in which the student got the correct response of 21 but did not appear to understand the concept of taking $\frac{3}{4}$ of a number? Are there any responses in which the student seems to have grasped the concept of taking $\frac{3}{4}$ of a number but produced an incorrect numerical answer? Which students do not understand the concept of $\frac{3}{4}$ at all? If you were using the sample rubric of 0 to 4 described earlier, which scores would you give these papers?

Teachers in a school that use a rubric such as the one presented here need to be instructed on how to use it effectively to increase the consistency of scoring student work. Nevertheless, open-ended questions give the teacher considerably more information about how the student thinks than is available from traditional test items. It takes more effort and experience to learn to score these types of responses, but the payoff in the long run outweighs the cost, because the teacher gains a clearer picture of each student's reasoning abilities.

How many days make up $\frac{3}{4}$ of the month?___21___

Explain how you know this answer.

I looked aT iT and said ThaT $\frac{3}{4}$ is more Than halE oE iT so ThaT is how.

(a)

How many days make up $\frac{3}{4}$ of the month?___1___

Explain how you know this answer.

I took 3 - 4 and the dacer was 1

(b)

How many days make up $\frac{3}{4}$ of the month?___21___

Explain how you know this answer.

There are 4 weeks on thiscalender. Each week has 7 days. So I knew that if therewere4 weeks, $\frac{3}{4}$ would be 3 of them.So I started at the 1st and counted 3 weeks down.Then I went to the end of the 3rd Week,and it was the 21st

(c)

How many days make up $\frac{3}{4}$ of the month? *12 days*

Explain how you know this answer.

I looked at the first four numbers and that was $\frac{1}{4}$ and I did that two more times.

(d)

How many days make up $\frac{3}{4}$ of the month? *3 days*

Explain how you know this answer.

because if you had a pie and you could only eat $\frac{3}{4}$ of the pie your taking three pieces out of four that s my answer

(e)

How many days make up $\frac{3}{4}$ of the month? ___24___

Explain how you know this answer.

I counted 3 rows on the callender and then I counted how many days were in that 3 rows.

(f)

Another strategy that can be used for the assessment of student knowledge, attitudes, and dispositions is a project or investigation. **Projects** and **investigations** are, by nature, long-term activities and often involve teams of students working together on a multifaceted task. Because our world requires workers that are able to serve as members of teams, this type of assessment task is a realistic and authentic measure of how well students can help one another attain a common goal.

Here is an example of such a project:

City planners have been considering installing a new traffic light at the corner of Elm and Front streets. To make the decision, information is needed about the typical traffic patterns for that intersection. In a team of four students, gather data on typical use of the intersection at various times of the day and week. Then, create a graph or series of graphs on poster board and make a presentation to the class on your results. Include a recommendation for the city planners, based on your results.

The traffic investigation is a real-world project that models an actual process used by professionals to determine the feasibility of installing a new traffic light at an intersection. Students have to determine, with the assistance of the teacher, times and means in which to gather sample data about traffic patterns. Students may choose to count cars going through the intersection before school, at lunch, after school, and on Saturday or Sunday afternoon for several weeks. They may also choose to subdivide the traffic counts into the direction in which the cars are typically traveling and so on. The task of presenting a report to the class is open-ended enough to allow for a variety of possible student responses and conclusions. Students are not necessarily graded for their answers or their recommendations. Instead, they are assessed on their ability to work together, to gather data effectively, and, perhaps most important, to demonstrate an understanding of how to use the data to make an argument.

The teacher's job of assessing a project or investigation is indeed more complex than simply assigning a numerical score to the task based on correct answers. Instead, the teacher may devise a form or checklist on which to record information about student work. Such a form may include a space in which to make anecdotal notes on observations of the ability to work together, the strengths/weaknesses of plans to gather the data, the depth of understanding of the key mathematical concepts, the reasonableness of the team's conclusions and recommendations, and the strengths/weaknesses of the student presentations. After all the areas have been assessed, with notes made over a period of time, a final evaluative report that includes comments and a grade for each student can be issued.

Teachers can also gain powerful information about student understandings by conducting *informal* or *formal interviews* with the students or by *observing* the students in teamwork situations. The method of conducting individual interviews, as needed, can be particularly useful for assessment in the primary grades, in which the student is likely to be verbal but may, as yet, have limited writing skills.

In the interview, the teacher presents a task and asks the student to restate the task and to solve it, explaining by thinking out loud as the student works. The teacher can ask questions such as "What do you think the problem is asking?" "Do you see a pattern here?" "Have you seen something like this before? When?" and "What do you think would happen if we used a different number here?" Much can be learned by allowing a student to explain a process and answer these types of questions in a one-on-one setting. An anecdotal description of the student's understandings can be written by the teacher and placed in the student file.

Observations of students working individually or in teams can be recorded and used in the assessment of student understandings and dispositions. A teacher can use observation strategies to see if students are actively involved, attempting to help others, asking questions, working well with other people, and making effective use of technology and manipulatives. The teacher can also gather information about student dispositions by noting evidence of confidence, flexibility, perseverance, curiosity, reflection, and valuing and appreciating mathematics.

Another useful technique that can be used to assess student understandings and dispositions is *student writing*. Students can be asked to maintain a mathematics *journal* and make entries on a regular basis. For the entries, teachers may wish to give a specific prompt to which students are to respond, or the students may simply be asked to write a reaction to, or a summary of, the important aspects of the day's lesson. The student may wish to comment on a missed homework problem or discuss an example from class that was not clear a few days ago but seems to make sense today.

By regularly collecting the journals, the teacher can gain a broad sense of what the student thinks about mathematics on an individual basis, while also determining whether there are classwide misconceptions that need to be addressed. The power of journaling in mathematics not only lies in helping students address their understanding and communication skills, but that it also positively affects instructional decisions made by the teacher.

A teacher in the middle grades was recently about to begin teaching a series of lessons on probability. Students were asked to think about the following problem:

> Suppose that you were to hold a paper cup at arm's length and let go of it, allowing it to drop to the floor. What is the likelihood or probability that the cup will land on its top, on its bottom, or on its side?

Students were asked to think about the question and to comment on it in their journals that evening. The next morning, as the teacher gave the class a short quiz on material that was currently under discussion, the journals were collected and briefly scanned by the teacher. Shown here are three samples of actual student entries in response to the paper cup question. What are some of the misconceptions about probability that some students in the class appear to have? Which types of reasoning are illustrated in these sample responses? How might the teacher use these data to plan a beginning lesson involving a discussion of what probability means? Notice that the writing of journal entries was assigned as a means of collecting diagnostic data on what the students knew before a formal discussion occurred, rather than serving as a grading tool. Journal and log entries can be very powerful in terms of providing the teacher with information about student understanding and the need for specific intervention strategies.

Algebra

Jenny

The probability would be 1/3 because for each throw of the cup it has 3 different ways of landing, upright, down, or on its side. You could also say that it had a 33 1/3% chance.

(a)

Algebra

Nora

15	65	115
25	75	125
35	85	135
45	95	145
55	105	155

I flipped The cup 15 Times + iT always landed on iTs side, so I guess There s a 1 00% probability ThaT The cup will land on iTs side

(b)

Algebra

Jason

# of times out of 200 that landed on side=
IIII • IIII IIII • IIII IIII • IIII IIII • IIII IIII • IIII IIII •
IIII IIII • IIII IIII • IIII IIII • IIII IIII • IIII IIII • IIII IIII • IIII
IIII • IIII   IIII • IIII   IIII • IIII   IIII • IIII   IIII • IIII   IIII

# of times out of 200 that landed on
bottom = II
# of times out of 200 that landed on
top = IIII • IIII IIII • IIII IIII
Probability of landing on side = 87%
Probability of landing on bottom = 1 %
Probability of landing on top = 12%

(c)

Students may also be asked to react to a prompt in writing several days each week. For example, a fifth-grade teacher asked her class to "write about which topic you liked the most in mathematics class this week and why you liked it." Another teacher asked his class, "If math was an animal, what would it be and why?" One student responded, "Math is like a snake. While most people are scared of snakes, the fact is that most are not poisonous and can't hurt you. In the same way, lots of my friends are afraid of math, but it's really not that hard if you get into it and try. It just *looks* scary to some people." This type of analogy writing exercise can help the teacher see another side of the students than can be observed in a classroom setting. The teacher can also ask the students to complete a statement such as, "One thing I still don't understand in mathematics is. . ." These types of questions allow students to reflect on their own learning, while also serving as data for the teacher to use in determining the direction of future lessons.

The last assessment technique we discuss here is the use of a *portfolio* of student work. A portfolio is a carefully selected collection of samples of student work, including projects, writings, tests, reports, and so on. Portfolios are used to demonstrate the broad range of understanding of mathematics that a student possesses and to indicate growth in understanding and disposition over time. As a collection of items, the portfolio is much more effective in showing what a student knows and can do than any paper-and-pencil test could possibly show on its own. Portfolios have been used effectively in other subject areas, such as art and language arts, for many years, and their use in mathematics has been shown to be equally powerful.

The contents of a portfolio collection are often determined by the students. After all, who is in a better position to know what they consider to be evidence of their best work than the students themselves? Also, the teacher and student can discuss the contents, as can the student with his or her parents.

The portfolio is more than a random collection of work. Instead, it is a thoughtful selection of work that represents the range of abilities that the student possesses. Teachers who use portfolios in mathematics have commented on the strength of being able to show the actual student work to parents and administrators, over simply being able to show a gradebook filled with numbers. The portfolio, containing items such as photocopies of journal pages, sample tests, a picture of a student project, and an answer to an open-ended question, can visually present evidence of what the student knows, can do, and believes about mathematics.

The evaluation of a student portfolio is not a simple task because no two portfolios will ever look exactly alike. Learning a skill such as word processing is not necessarily an easy task either, but if we recognize the long-term benefits of developing the skill, then we can more readily commit ourselves to learning the technique. With the use of a rubric for scoring portfolios, teachers and students can work together to indicate what the collection should contain. The teacher can search the portfolio for evidence of problem-solving strategies, clear communication, thinking and reflection, proper use of terminology and notation, connections to real-world situations, and positive dispositions about mathematics. The teacher can then use the predetermined criteria for determining a holistic grade, if needed. Like the scoring of open-ended questions, a holistic score from a rubric can be assigned, with supporting written comments included as part of the total assessment of the portfolio.

One of the major reasons for making use of portfolios is to help students become better at assessing their own progress, strengths, and weaknesses. In an ideal situation, students should develop such a strong sense of what they understand and what they do not understand that they are aware of their limitations and of areas in which improvement is needed without having to be told by a teacher. Consequently, student self-assessment and reflection should be a part of any assessment program. The self-assessment may take the form of journal or log entries, or it may involve students completing checklists or questionnaires that ask questions such as "How well do you think you contributed to the team effort in your cooperative group this week?" Student self-analysis can then become part of the portfolio to serve as evidence of the student's ability to reflect on his or her own progress.

Closure

The vision of assessment presented in this chapter is broad in that it takes in many different methods for gathering information and is not limited to paper-and-pencil tests. The contemporary view of assessment is not simply a method of collecting data on which to base grades for individual students in the classroom. Instead, the process involves the gathering of information through multiple methods for a variety of educational purposes. The data can be useful to the teacher in making instructional decisions. Also, the information may be useful to other parties, such as a principal, school board, or state board of education, in measuring the effectiveness of a program or in holding educators and students accountable for their learning.

The contemporary view of assessment is also one of an ongoing, continual process. If the teacher's system of assessing student progress is limited to a Friday afternoon paper-and-pencil test, then that teacher is gaining only a very limited "snapshot" of what the students know, can do, and believe. This traditional form of testing also gives the students a message about what is important in mathematics that appears contrary to our contemporary view of the discipline. Instead, assessment must take place on an ongoing basis, including both formal and informal techniques. The teacher needs to assess student work and attitudes every day to achieve the vision of curriculum and instruction as outlined in the *Principles and Standards for School Mathematics*.

In conclusion, we revisit the *Assessment Standards for School Mathematics* (1995). The following remarks in the introduction to the document are important keep in mind:

> Instead of assuming that the purpose of assessment is to rank students on a particular trait, the new approach assumes that high public expectations can be set that every student can strive for and achieve, that different performances can and will meet agreed-on expectations, and that teachers can be fair and consistent judges of diverse student performances. Setting high expectations and striving to achieve them are quite different from comparing students with one another and indicating where each student ranks. A constant theme of [the assessment standards] document is that decisions regarding students' achievement should be made on the basis of a convergence of information from a variety of balanced and equitable sources. Furthermore, much of the information needs to be derived by teachers during the process of instruction. Teachers are the persons who are in the best position to judge the development of students' progress and, hence, must be considered the primary assessors of students. However, depending on the purpose, there are other assessors, such as learners who assess their own progress. (NCTM, 1995, p. 1)

As you read the remainder of this text, try to think of assessment strategies that can be used to gather information about what students know, can do, and believe about each of the areas of content we discuss. Reviewing the remarks from this chapter will help you reach and maintain a vision of class assessment that is consistent with the standards documents.

TEACHING COMPETENCIES
AND SELF-ASSESSMENT TASKS

1. Discuss how implementation of the NCTM *Principles and Standards for School Mathematics* will help support the vision of the three previous standards documents for curriculum, instruction, and assessment.

2. Examine several elementary school mathematics textbooks and their ancillary materials for teachers. Determine the degree to which the textbooks on the market meet the criteria for effective assessment, as outlined by the NCTM.

3. Why assess? What benefits accrue from a well-thought-out assessment program? What are the advantages and disadvantages of having a consistent or uniform schoolwide assessment framework?

4. Discuss the advantages and disadvantages of using norm-referenced versus criterion-referenced tests. When is one more appropriate than the other?

5. Obtain a set of student responses to an open-ended question. Use the rubric from 0 to 4 presented in this chapter, and give the papers a score based on the stated criteria. In small groups, discuss the difficulties you encountered in scoring the papers. What are some of the instructional implications of the results of analyzing these student samples of work?

6. Several different techniques for assessing student progress are described in this chapter. However, most school districts still require teachers to assign a letter grade to a student, based on the student's total performance. Discuss how you might use multiple methods of collecting evidence of student progress but still be able to assign a letter grade for the students in your class.

7. In a small group, write several performance tasks and open-ended questions that would be appropriate for primary, intermediate, and upper elementary/junior high students.

chapter 4

Technology in K–8 Mathematics

TEACHING COMPETENCIES

Upon completing this chapter, you will be able to:

- Describe the role played by calculators and computers in a contemporary elementary and middle school mathematics classroom as envisioned by the NCTM *Principles and Standards for School Mathematics* and the NCTM Position Statements on Calculators and Computers.

- Describe appropriate uses of calculators and computers in the problem-solving process, including the use of Calculator-Based Laboratories and Calculator-Based Rangers.

- Describe features and functions available on calculators commonly used in the elementary and middle school.

- Identify and describe a variety of purposes of educational software and applications software.

- Explore the promise of incorporating computer-based virtual manipulatives in the instructional and assessment processes at the elementary and middle school levels.

- Incorporate contemporary thought on integrating multimedia and the Internet in classroom instruction.

- State examples of ways the Internet can be used in educational settings to locate information of value in everyday life.

VIRTUAL MANIPULATIVES

Upon completing this chapter, you will be able to use the accompanying CD to:

- Explore the nature and characteristics of a virtual manipulative using *Base Ten Blocks* as an example. **(VM 4.1)**

- Explore the nature and characteristics of a virtual manipulative using *Circle-0* as an example. **(VM 4.2)**

- Explore the nature and various characteristics of a virtual manipulative using *Tangrams* as an example. **(VM 4.3)**

Alyssa, a fourth-grade teacher, was designing a lesson on finding equivalent fractions. On a Thursday evening, as she finalized her lesson plan for the following day, she was looking for an effective visual example to use with her students. She sat at her home computer, connected to the Internet, and ran a Web search for "equivalent fractions." At a popular search engine Web site, she located more than 2 million hits within a couple of seconds and was able to find an excellent activity to discuss with her students. With a click of the mouse, she downloaded a PDF file from a mathematics Web site and printed a handout to copy for her students. She then dragged the PDF file onto another document and created an interactive work page that could be projected onto her SMART Board (interactive whiteboard) in the classroom so that students could come up and draw on the projected form. Within 10 minutes, she had the lesson planned and all of the materials prepared.

Oddly enough, hundreds, if not thousands, of teachers engage in this type of scenario every day. Teaching ideas that are available at our fingertips by way of the Internet would have taken hours to find (if locatable at all!) in paper resource books just a few years ago. Take a minute to think about the technology involved in Alyssa's 10 minutes of planning and teaching: using a computer, searching the Internet, downloading a file, creating an interactive file, and using a SMART Board. These are skills that we often take for granted but have become almost essential in the teaching and learning of mathematics today. Children in our classes have grown up with this technology, and society's expectation is that we will make the best use of these resources in the planning, teaching, and assessment processes.

The National Council of Teachers of Mathematics (NCTM) *Principles and Standards for School Mathematics* acknowledges the important role that technology should play in mathematics education. One fundamental assumption of these standards, the Technology Principle, states that mathematics instructional programs should use technology to help all students *understand* mathematics and should prepare them to use mathematics in an increasingly technological world (NCTM, 2000). Research and experience have clearly demonstrated the potential of calculators and computers to enhance students' learning in mathematics. The cognitive gain in number sense, conceptual development, and visualization can empower and motivate students to engage in true mathematical problem solving at a level previously denied to all but the most talented. In many real-life situations, we commonly make use of technology to perform tedious computations that often develop when working with real data in problem situations.

Technology can provide a focus on problem-solving processes, thereby allowing students to gain access to mathematical ideas and experiences that go beyond levels limited by traditional paper-and-pencil computation. Furthermore, teachers can use technology in the planning and implementation of meaningful mathematics lessons at all developmental stages.

Let's begin our exploration of how we can use technology by looking at how technology has affected mathematics education in the past.

A Brief History of Technology's Influence on Education

Attempts to use technology to improve mathematics instruction are probably as old as mathematics instruction itself. For example, here is an illustration of a nineteenth-century "manipulative," the numeral frame, used for arithmetic instruction.

NUMERAL FRAME

In this section, we will review how different technologies have (or have not) influenced educational practices in the twentieth century. Such a perspective may provide some insight into how our latest digital technology may influence mathematics education.

In 1913, Thomas Edison once predicted, "Books will soon be obsolete in the schools. . . . It is possible to teach every branch of human knowledge with the motion picture. Our school system will be completely changed in the next ten years" (cited in Reiser, 2001, p. 55). Thomas Edison was a brilliant scientist, inventor, and businessman whose works include the development of the electric light bulb, the electronic power distribution system, the phonograph, and the motion picture. He held more than 1000 U.S. patents. Yet, Thomas Edison's prediction that the motion picture technology would revolutionize educational practices "in the next ten years" appears to have been quite inaccurate.

Edison was not, however, the only one to have overestimated how new technologies would impact educational practices. In the 1930s, many hailed radio as the technology that would revolutionize education. As we can now see, the impact of radio on our educational system has been modest at best. In the 1950s, television began to become popular. Once again, there were those who believed that educational broadcasting would revolutionize education. In fact, a number of large-scale educational projects to harness television technology were attempted. In a Maryland school system, closed-circuit television was used to deliver instruction in all major subject areas at all grade levels. In a junior college in Chicago, curriculum was presented via public television. However, our interest in television as an instructional delivery medium has all but diminished.

This pattern of overenthusiasm followed by disappointment with the advent of each new technology suggests that we should be cautious about our own enthusiasm for digital technology. Our past experiences cause us to ask, "Will our interest in digital technology for educational purposes fade in time as it did with radio and television?" "How does digital technology differ from radio and television with respect to its potential impact on mathematics education?"

Let's begin by exploring the use of calculators in the mathematics classroom.

Calculators and Exploration of Mathematical Concepts

A fifth grader named Michael asked his teacher what the "squiggly thing" (the square root button) on his calculator was used for. The teacher gave him a set of square color tiles and asked him to make a square out of 25 of them. He arranged them as shown:

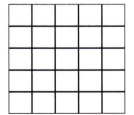

His teacher then asked him to type "25" and press the square root button ($\sqrt{\ }$) button on the calculator and to tell her what the answer had to do with the picture he had just formed with the tiles. Michael noted that the answer was 5 and that the square measured 5 units on

each side. In turn, she asked him to remove 9 of the tiles and to form a square with the remaining tiles. With the 16 remaining pieces, he formed the following square:

She asked him what problem he could enter into his calculator that would be represented by this picture. Michael answered that if he entered 16 and pressed the square root button ($\sqrt{\ }$) button, the answer would be 4 because it takes 16 tiles to form the square, and the square measures 4 units on each side. Finally, his teacher asked him what would happen if we had only 10 color tiles out of which to build the shape. Michael struggled for a few minutes and then concluded that he could not form a square with 10 tiles. His teacher asked him what would happen if he entered 10 and pressed the square root symbol on the calculator, and his response was, "Well, it doesn't work out evenly. It will be a number bigger than 3 because it takes more than 9 tiles, but it would be less than 4." Of course, his calculator displayed that $\sqrt{10}$ was approximately 3.16—a value between 3 and 4, as Michael had predicted.

The scenario of Michael is a true story that happened one day when children were exploring another problem when using calculators. It is an example of the type of mathematical reasoning that can be promoted when technology is used in a mathematics lesson. Interestingly, square roots were not the focus of the day's lesson, but the calculators motivated a discussion on the topic. A student who explores square root in the fashion described here will have an intuitive, meaningful base from which to build. The chances are dramatically increased that this student will have a better understanding of the underlying concept of square root than someone who merely memorizes without such experiences. Similarly, children often discover fundamental aspects of fractions, negative numbers, and numerous patterns when exploring problems on their calculators. So often, we hear parents (and teachers) bemoan the fact that "we didn't have calculators in our day, and we did fine" or that "a calculator is nothing but a crutch that replaces thinking." However, this is a narrow view of the use of calculators. When we think about the use of technology in the mathematics classroom, we are not implying that technology should replace everything that we used to memorize, such as addition facts. Instead, we conceptualize the use of calculators and computers to allow for deep exploration of problems and to promote mathematical reasoning.

It is also important to note that the experts are not suggesting that all computational procedures be de-emphasized because of calculators. In fact, some manual skills have become more important because of calculators. To illustrate this point, suppose that you just computed 1.234 × 2.345 using a calculator. How can you check that the answer you got with the calculator is a reasonable one?

The conventional wisdom is that it is good practice to check our computations because errors are always possible. There are two points note about error checking at this time. The first is that verifying our computation takes time and effort. Therefore, ideally, we want our verification process to be simple and easy. We also want it to be effective. That is, we want our verification process to actually catch errors, if there are any.

Second, the kinds of errors that we typically make using calculators are different from the kinds that we typically make with traditional paper-and-pencil techniques. Much more so than with manual techniques, errors that we tend to make with electronic devices produce results that are grossly incorrect. For example, the solution to 1.234 × 2.345 is around 3, but the calculator might have said 6.6. The reason the calculator produced 6.6 in our case is that while entering 2.345, the 5 key was mistakenly pressed instead of the 2 key. Therefore, the calculator produced the result for 1.234 × 5.345. This type of an error is called a *data entry error*. One of the more common errors that we make with electronic devices are data entry errors. As in our example, when data entry errors

are introduced in computational procedures, the final results are often wildly different from the correct answer.

Because a large proportion of erroneous results generated with calculators are grossly inaccurate, comparing calculator-generated results with close approximations of the actual results is an effective method for their verification. From this perspective, mental estimation is an ideal technique to verify calculator-generated results. Once mastered, students can perform mental estimates quickly and easily. Also, for reasons discussed earlier, estimates are an effective technique for catching a large proportion of errors with calculators.

The main point of the present discussion is that the calculator has an uneven influence on the significance of manual computational skills. For operations such as long division that the calculator can perform, mastery of manual techniques becomes less valuable to students. However, for other computational skills, such as mental estimations that complement the use of calculators, they become more important in our students' overall mathematical repertoire.

Reys and Arbaugh (2001) noted four aspects of calculator use: (1) calculators are inexpensive and are common in homes and schools, (2) calculators are frequently used in the workplace, (3) teachers often do not understand how to use calculators most effectively as a tool in the classroom, and (4) children often believe that using a calculator is "cheating." Not surprisingly, appropriate calculator use has been the focus of considerable discussion among mathematics educators, parents,

RESEARCH SNAPSHOT

What is the effect of using calculators on children's learning of number concepts and skills?

Groves and Stacey (1998) reported the results of a study of third and fourth graders in the Calculators in Primary Mathematics project, which took place in Australia. Each year, approximately 500 children participated in the three-year project.

The students with long-term experience with calculators performed better than the students without the calculator experience on a wide range of items, including decimals, negative numbers, and place value in large numbers. They also performed better in mental computation, made more appropriate choices of calculating devices, and were better able to interpret their answers when using a calculator.

Why do you think the students in this study who used calculators did better on noncalculator tasks than those students who relied on paper-and-pencil techniques? How much time in the school curriculum do you think we should devote to paper-and-pencil algorithms?

Groves, S., & Stacey, K. (1998). Calculators in primary mathematics: Exploring number before teaching algorithms. In L. Morrow & M. Kenney (Eds.), *The teaching and learning of algorithms in school mathematics* (pp. 120–129). Reston, VA: National Council of Teachers of Mathematics.

For additional research briefs, "ERIC Digests" lets you search more than 2000 short syntheses of research on a range of education topics. The syntheses were produced by the Educational Resources Information Center (ERIC). Check http://www.ericfacility.net/ericdigests/index/.

representatives of the workplace, and others. Of course, some extreme viewpoints have been represented along with more frequently stated moderate opinions. Some have argued that the calculator should not be used in an elementary school classroom until after the basic facts have been mastered. Others, citing research that shows the calculator does not pose a threat to skill mastery, suggest that there is no harm—in fact, a considerable amount of good—in introducing the calculator at *any* point in the curriculum.

Instruction with calculators will extend the understanding of mathematics and allow all students access to rich, problem-solving experiences, such as the one involving Michael and the square root button. This instruction must develop students' ability to know how and when to use a calculator. Skill in estimation and the ability to decide if the solution to a problem is reasonable are essential components to the effective use of the calculator.

The aggressiveness of the debate over calculator use with children has subsided in recent years. Now, the most commonly accepted position is that, *when used appropriately*, the calculator can be effective at all levels of instruction, including the primary grades. For example, a study of more than 800 teachers in a large school district showed that regardless of the grade level, teachers universally believed that students would understand mathematics more deeply and would find the subject more interesting if calculators were used. However, the research also indicated that the higher the grade level of the teacher, the more strongly the teacher tended to believe that students could carry out a calculation with technology without understanding what is really going on (Brown et al., 2007). Consequently, we need to think about what it means to use a calculator appropriately, and this implies that technology should be used for more than simply checking answers to seatwork or on homework papers. The calculator can be incorporated into instruction so that it serves as an aid to student understanding of concepts.

The NCTM has prepared a position paper on the use of calculators in the mathematics classroom. The full text of that paper is reproduced here with the permission of NCTM.

Computation, Calculators, and Common Sense

Question: Is there a place for both computation and calculators in the math classroom?

Position: School mathematics programs should provide students with a range of knowledge, skills, and tools. Students need an understanding of number and operations, including the use of computational procedures, estimation, mental mathematics, and the appropriate use of the calculator. A balanced mathematics program develops students' confidence and understanding of when and how to use these skills and tools. Students need to develop their basic mathematical understandings to solve problems both in and out of school.

Technology pervades the world outside school. There is no question that students will be expected to use calculators in other settings; this technology is now part of our culture. More important, when calculators are used effectively in the classroom, they can enhance students' understanding and use of numbers and operations. Teachers can capitalize on the appropriate use of this technology to expand students' mathematical understanding, not to replace it.

Written mathematical procedures—computational procedures in the elementary grades and more symbolic algebraic procedures as students move into the secondary level—continue to be an important focus of school math programs. All students should develop proficiency in performing efficient and accurate pencil-and-paper procedures. At the same time, students no longer have the same need to perform these procedures with large numbers or lengthy expressions that they might have had in the past without ready access to technology. Furthermore, computation should not exist in isolation. Measurement, geometry, and the analysis of data represent important mathematical content and provide useful contexts as students develop their numerical abilities.

Even more important than performing computational procedures or using calculators is the greater facility that students need—more than ever before—with estimation and mental math. These skills are essential for both understanding numbers and recognizing their usefulness outside school. Students should have a solid understanding of what addition, subtraction, multiplication, and division mean and how they work so that they can identify what operation(s) can help them solve a problem they encounter in math class, in another subject, or outside school. As they develop number sense, students acquire abilities to estimate and perform mental calculations quickly and proficiently. Students should become proficient at using mental math shortcuts, performing basic computations mentally, and generating reasonable estimates for situations involving size, distance, and magnitude.

A skillful teacher knows how to help students develop these abilities in a balanced program that focuses on mathematical understanding, proficiency, and thinking. The teacher should help students learn when to use a calculator and when not to, when to use pencil and paper, and when to do something in their heads. Students should become fluent in making decisions about which approach to use for different situations and proficient in using their chosen method to solve a wide range of problems.[1]

The calculator should be considered an essential tool for all students of mathematics and an integral part of the mathematics curriculum, not just an appendage for checking calculations already performed. The effective use of calculators in the classroom depends largely on the skill, knowledge, and ingenuity of the individual classroom teacher. In the classroom of a thoughtful and talented teacher, the calculator can be especially useful in developing understanding of place value, reversibility, relationships among numbers, operations, decimals, metric measure, prime factoring, composites, changing fractions to decimals, and percentages, as well as making mathematical estimates. Other uses become apparent as we develop a curriculum that encourages calculator use during instruction.

Calculator Features and Functions

Many different types and brands of calculators are available for classroom use. Unfortunately (or, perhaps, fortunately—when used for exploration and discovery), these various calculators do not all function in exactly the same manner. There are some important differences in available keys and the ways in which operations are handled that make it worthwhile for you to become familiar with the characteristics of the individual calculators being used by your students. Ideally, a classroom set of calculators will alleviate many of these concerns.

For most elementary or middle school use, the calculator chosen should be based on **algebraic logic**—that is, the calculator should follow the **order of operation rules** for computation. The calculator should be inexpensive, durable, and accessible to the students and should have multiple uses. The keyboard should be of reasonable size, preferably with keys that "click" when they are pressed (some sort of auditory feedback of an input is helpful for many children). The display should be bright, easily readable, and easily seen from different angles since several children may share the same calculator. Solar-powered calculators are the most popular and are less expensive than battery-powered models in the long run—in fact, it is a challenge today to find a calculator that is not solar powered.

Children must learn correct procedures for using the calculator. Proper development of a good foundation will help avoid confusion at later grade levels. (Proper classroom management of the calculators should also

be established early.) Right from the beginning, help children develop appropriate techniques for using the calculator. Teaching calculator use strategies is particularly important when working with students with learning disabilities who may have difficulty keeping track of which buttons to press (Steele, 2007). For example, students should be taught to watch the display panel and assess the reasonableness of the values that appear on it. Also, when batteries are weak or the calculator is broken (even solar-powered calculators use batteries as backups for memory), wrong answers can appear on the display panel. Have children practice operating the calculator with the opposite hand from the one they use to write. This will allow students to hold a pencil and record results from the calculations with one hand while using the calculator with the other. Begin each calculator example by pressing the CLEAR (C) or CLEAR ENTRY (CE) key twice. This will prevent extraneous numbers already entered from interfering with the results of the current operation.

Encourage children to learn how to operate the calculator and understand when it would be beneficial to a task and when it would not be helpful. The calculator will do only what it is told to do—students must learn to decide which situations require a calculator and how to use the calculator in those situations. Impress on the students that a calculator is only a supplemental tool. It is still important for the students to be able to solve some mathematics problems and examples involving calculation without the benefit of a calculator (and to understand how to transfer their skill with these problems to using a calculator for the more complicated ones).

Examples of Effective Calculator Use

Promoting mathematical reasoning and using a calculator appear, on the surface, to be at odds with each other. However, as described in the situation with the child exploring square roots, creative teachers will use calculators as a tool to promote problem solving and mathematical reasoning skills. The following are examples of problems and activities that make use of calculators in mathematics instruction.

The Game of 21

Have two students share a calculator to play this game. The first child keys in a number between 1 and 5. The second child then adds a number between 1 and 5 to the number that is displayed. So, for example, if the first student entered 3, then the second student would enter (+) 1, 2, 3, 4, or 5, and press the (=) button to display a sum between 4 and 8, passing the calculator back to the first student. In turn, the first student would add another

[1]NCTM Position Statement on Computation, Calculators, and Common Sense, 2005.

number between 1 and 5 to the current display. This process continues until one of the students is able to add a number to the previous display to make a sum of exactly 21. Whichever player obtains the sum of 21 is declared the winner.

When playing this game, children are trying to determine a strategy while, at the same time, practicing their addition facts. As a child sees, for example, the number 12 displayed, he or she might be thinking of strategies such as "if I add 4, that will give a sum of 16, but then she could add 5 and would win. If I add 3, the sum would be 15, and nothing she can add will give her 21. Even if she only adds 1, I can still win on the next move," and so forth. Likewise, children who have been learning their subtraction facts can play the game in reverse. They begin by keying in the number 21 and *subtract* a number between 1 and 5 each time, with the winner being the person who gets to 0 first. Of course, the target number can also be raised to 50 or 100, as can the range of numbers being added or subtracted each time, depending on the developmental needs of the students.

Turn Out the Lights

A simple game can be played by two students who are exploring place value of numbers. In the game of "Turn Out the Lights," a number is keyed into the calculator to begin the game, such as

31782654

Notice that all of the digits of the number must be different. The starting number can have anywhere from three to nine digits, depending on the developmental level of the students. The object is to "turn out" each of the digits in order, starting with the place value of the number 1, by subtracting a number that causes that digit to be replaced by a 0. So, the first student would announce, "Subtract one million" and would press −1000000 in the calculator. In turn, the new display would read:

30782654

The second player, in turn, needs to turn out the 2 and would say, "Subtract two thousand," keying in −2000 to produce the following display:

30780654

The next child would need to turn off the 3, and so forth, until the original number is reduced to 0 and all of the lights have been turned off.

When playing this game, it is essential that the child verbally states the number that will be subtracted, as this is how the concept of place value is built. The student may not simply say, "Subtract one, zero, zero, zero, zero," as this would be considered an illegal move. A point is scored each time the number to be subtracted is correctly named and the light is turned out. Whichever player has the most points at the end of the game is the winner.

Calculators Used as a Personal Feedback Device

The calculator can be used as a means to provide children with feedback, as illustrated in the following addition example:

Round the following numbers to the nearest hundred. After rounding each one, enter the result into your calculator, and press the addition (+) key. When you finish, the number in the display should be 59100.

6137, 13490, 2856, 9720, 26882

In this simple example, the objective is to round numbers to the nearest hundred. The student, not the calculator, must satisfy this objective. That is, the calculator does not perform the task; it merely serves as a self-checking device for the student's effort and thought. If the student does not get a result of 59100 at the end of this exercise, then an error must have occurred, and the student will be made aware of this immediately through feedback. In turn, the student can go back and try to track down where the mistake was made.

Note, however, that the calculator does not provide information about where the error occurred. This is beneficial in this case: the student who has not mastered the objective must now check each number—not too daunting since there are only five numbers—rather than simply going to the one number that is marked wrong.

Recognizing Patterns on a Calculator

When children are first learning their multiplication facts or are learning to skip count (these skills, of course, are directly related), they can use a calculator to help them memorize the sequence of products (or sums). Suppose that they are working on the 7's table for multiplication. On the calculator, if 7 is keyed in, followed by +7 and the (=), (=), (=), every time the equals button is pressed, the calculator will display the previous sum with another 7 added to it. Therefore, the calculator will generate the sequence of 7, 14, 21, 28, 35, and so forth, serving as a flash card of sorts for children to use to review the facts.

Similarly, children can be challenged to investigate patterns when solving various other types of problems. For example, have children key in the following multiplication problems:

$$11 \times 11 = 121$$
$$111 \times 111 = 12321$$
$$1111 \times 1111 = 1234321$$

Have the children predict what will happen if we multiply 11111×11111. What patterns do they see? Why is this pattern occurring? What other patterns might we recognize when we multiply numbers together (e.g., younger children will notice that multiplying by a number ending with a 5 will always produce a result that ends in 0 or 5).

The point here is that a variety of additive and multiplicative patterns can be explored on a calculator, allowing children to describe what they see and to make predictions. This process can be a powerful strategy for developing basic algebraic reasoning skills, described in more detail in Chapter 10.

Problems That Encourage Calculator Use

Some mathematical problems are interesting to explore but can be tedious, if not impossible, to solve without the use of a calculator. Instead of the emphasis being placed on the computation skills, use of the calculator frees up children to think deeply about the problem itself. Following are three problems that were posed in an article featured in the NCTM journal *Mathematics Teaching in the Middle School* (Moss & Grover, 2007):

- *Ask each student, "How many seconds old are you?" given a specific ending time.*

- *If you could walk a million strides, how many strides would you walk in three miles? In three kilometers? Suppose you walked 3 miles per hour (mph) and could walk 8 hours a day, how long would it take you to walk 1 million strides?*

- *If the federal debt is 7.92 trillion dollars, how could you express this value in terms that an average citizen could understand? What denomination of bill would you need to use to lay a path from the earth to the moon that would use all 7.92 trillion dollars?* (pp. 270–271)

These and other related problems are generally interesting to children and well worth the time to investigate them in a mathematics class. Yet, to attempt to solve them without a calculator would be like attempting to walk 20 miles to work—you *could* do it, but you might spend so much energy and time doing the walking that you wouldn't have anything left by the time you got to work!

Graphing Calculator Explorations

The use of graphing calculators has become fairly common in the middle grades, generally beginning at about the sixth or seventh grade. A graphing calculator can generate tables of values, allow for comparison of linear graphs, construct box-and-whisker plots, and calculate the mean and median for large data sets, to name but a few of its functions. As is the case with the type of problems presented in the last two sections, some mathematics problems that emphasize patterning and reasoning can be explored on a graphing calculator that would be unrealistic to investigate without technology. For example, middle school children can be given a sequence of equations, such as $y = 2x + 5$, $y = 2x + 2$, $y = 2x$, $y = 2x - 3$, and $y = 2x - 7$ and asked to sketch the graphs on the calculator and determine how the lines are similar and how they are different. What do we notice about all five of these lines? What happens if we change the linear coefficient to -2 and graph the lines $y = -2x + 5$, $y = -2x + 2$, and so forth? In this investigation, children can focus on the geometry of the problem and on finding patterns, rather than spending the class (or homework) time plotting points and drawing lines by hand.

Tools for Measuring Motion

Another powerful use of technology is to attach peripheral devices such as motion detectors to graphing calculators and use them for data collection and analysis. With the availability and ease of use of motion detectors, teachers are able to lead middle school students to an understanding of function and the interpretion of continuous graphs. A motion detector has been available for use with the **Calculator-Based Laboratory (CBL)** for a number of years. The CBL is a data-gathering device that can be used with several probes to collect different types of data. A CBL with appropriate probes can measure temperature, heart rate, light intensity, and motion, to name just a few of the possibilities.

A perceived complexity of the CBLs use has deterred middle school teachers from including the CBL in their repertoire of tools. The **Calculator-Based Ranger (CBR)** was developed in response to teachers' hesitation to use the CBL. The CBR measures motion exclusively. It can be attached to a TI-73 (a middle school graphing calculator) or to many other graphing calculators. The CBR collects motion data and sends that data to the calculator to be displayed as a graph or table. A powerful activity that is designed to help students explore functions and interpret continuous graphs is to have students match the graph. Students are given a graph of distance as a function of time. The graph is displayed on the graphing calculator. With a CBR connection to a viewscreen panel for the overhead projector (or on a SMART Board), the entire class can see the same graph simultaneously. A student is then directed to match the graph by walking in front of the CBR motion detector. The student's movement is graphed on the same graph as the original target graph so that the student and the class can compare his or her attempt to match the target. Students should be encouraged to redo their graphs after they discuss with the class how they might walk a more closely related graph. By having students actually "become" or act out a graph, the students gain a different and perhaps deeper understanding of the functional relationship of distance and time.

CBRs are designed to capture motion data with minimum of fuss. However, other graphing calculator attachments are designed to make different kinds of measurements such as temperature, heart rate, and light intensity. These devices fall under the more general category of CBLs. As mentioned, some CBL devices may be a bit more complex to use than the CBR, but they also offer wider possibilities for exploring mathematical concepts using real-time, real-world data.

Calculators are common and widely used at home and in the workplace. As the price of calculators continues to decline, many more children now have access to them than in the past. Obviously, the calculator is a phenomenon that schools cannot ignore. Calculators are not a passing fad. Educators must accept this and provide for instruction in mathematics that makes full use of the potential of the calculator as a teaching tool. Increased use of calculators in school will ensure that students' experiences in mathematics will match the realities of everyday life, develop their reasoning skills, and promote the understanding and application of mathematics.

Much of our discussion on calculators is applicable to computers. Indeed, a calculator is but a special kind of a computer. Most of us have seen computer programs that function (and even look) exactly like handheld calculators. Whereas calculators are designed for a specific purpose (e.g., to perform mathematical operations), computers are general purpose in that they can perform different functions depending on the software that is executed.

Computers and Mathematics Instruction

Preparing children to function successfully in the real world is one of the primary goals of mathematics instruction. Since technology is an ever-growing part of our world, school systems and teachers have a responsibility and an obligation to teach children how to use that technology to solve problems they face:

> Some mathematics becomes more important because technology REQUIRES it; some mathematics becomes less important because technology REPLACES it; and some mathematics becomes possible because technology ALLOWS it. (NCTM, 1998)

The responsibility for teaching children to understand and use computers rests almost entirely on the teachers and administrators in our school systems. Unfortunately, some teachers are unprepared to handle the planning and teaching of computer use and application to children. In some extreme cases, we are asking computer-illiterate teachers to help students become computer literate at a functional level.

The continued placement of computers in classrooms is supported by school administrators, teachers, and parents. If we agree with the assumption that technology is a viable tool for mathematics instruction, then the issue arises as to *when* computers should be introduced into the instructional program. Should technology use in mathematics be introduced in the primary grades or should we wait until students have mastered certain basic mathematics concepts and skills? Should computers be an integral part of classroom instruction or should they be reserved for special uses? The range of opinion concerning these and other related questions is indeed broad.

The NCTM has prepared a position paper on the role of computer technology in the mathematics classroom. The NCTM position reflects the importance of teachers being prepared to serve as knowledgeable decision makers in determining when and how their students can use these tools most effectively. How will you make these decisions? What principles will guide you? The full text of that paper is reproduced here with the permission of NCTM.

The Role of Technology in the Teaching and Learning of Mathematics

Question: What is the role of technology in the teaching and learning of mathematics?

Position: Technology is an essential tool for learning mathematics in the 21st century, and all schools must ensure that all their students have access to technology. Effective teachers maximize the potential of technology to develop students' understanding, stimulate their interest, and increase their proficiency in mathematics. When technology is used strategically, it can provide access to mathematics for all students.

Calculators and other technological tools, such as computer algebra systems, interactive geometry software, applets, spreadsheets, and interactive presentation devices, are vital components of a high-quality mathematics education. With guidance from effective mathematics teachers, students at different levels can use these tools to support and extend mathematical reasoning and sense making, gain access to mathematical content and problem-solving contexts, and enhance computational fluency. In a well-articulated mathematics program, students can use these tools for computation, construction, and representation as they explore problems. The use of technology also contributes to mathematical reflection, problem identification, and decision-making.

The use of technology cannot replace conceptual understanding, computational fluency, or problem-solving skills. In a balanced mathematics program, the strategic use of technology enhances mathematics teaching and learning. Teachers must be knowledgeable decision makers in determining when and how their students can use technology most effectively. All schools and mathematics programs should provide students and teachers with access to instructional technology, including appropriate calculators, computers with mathematical software, Internet connectivity, handheld data-collection devices, and sensing probes. Curricula and courses of study should incorporate instructional technology in learning outcomes, lesson plans, and assessments of students' progress.

Programs in teacher education and professional development must continually update practitioners' knowledge of technology and its classroom applications. Such programs should include the development of mathematics lessons that take advantage of technology-rich environments and the integration of technology in day-to-day instruction, instilling an appreciation for the power of technological tools and their potential impact on students' learning and use of mathematics. All teachers must remain open to learning new technologies, implementing them effectively in a coherent and balanced instructional program. These tools, including those used specifically for teaching and learning mathematics, not only complement mathematics teaching and learning but also prepare all students for their future lives, which technology will influence every day.[2]

This position emphasizes that the use of the tools of technology is integral to the learning and teaching of mathematics and that continual improvement is needed in mathematics curricula, instructional and assessment methods, access to hardware and software, and teacher education.

Although the nature of mathematics and societal needs influences the curriculum, the opportunities that technology presents must be reflected in the content of school mathematics. Curricular revisions allow for the de-emphasis of topics that are no longer as important as they once were, the addition of topics that have acquired new importance, and the retention of topics that remain important. With the implementation of revised curricula, time and emphasis should be allocated to topics according to their importance in an age of increased access to technology. Instructional materials

that capitalize on the power of technology must be given a high priority. The thoughtful, creative, and appropriate use of technology can greatly improve both the quality of the curriculum and the quality of students' learning.

Teachers should plan for students' use of technology in both learning and doing mathematics. The development of ideas should be made with the transition from concrete experiences to abstract mathematical ideas, focusing on the exploration and discovery of new mathematical concepts and problem-solving processes.

Students should learn how to use technology as a tool for processing information, visualizing and solving problems, exploring and testing conjectures, accessing data, and verifying their solutions. Students' ability to recognize when and how to use technology effectively is dependent on their continued study of appropriate mathematics content.

In a mathematics setting, technology must be an instructional tool that is integrated into daily teaching practices, including the assessment of what students know and are able to do. In a mathematics class, technology ought not be the object of instruction but rather a tool for instruction. This is an extremely important point, as teachers have been known to create units on "using the calculator," which runs counter to the notion that technology should be incorporated as a *tool* that helps children learn about a given mathematical topic—not as an end in itself.

The preparation of teachers of mathematics requires an ability to design technology-integrated classroom and laboratory lessons that promote interaction among students, technology, and teachers. The selection, evaluation, and use of technology for a variety of activities such as simulation, the generation and analysis of data, problem solving, graphical analysis, and geometric constructions depend on the teacher. Therefore, the availability of ongoing in-service programs is necessary to help teachers take full advantage of the unique power of technology as a tool for mathematics classrooms. Keeping pace with the advances in technology is a necessity for the entire mathematics community, particularly for teachers who are responsible for designing day-to-day instructional experiences for students.

In 1981, only 18% of U.S. public schools had even a single computer for instructional uses. By 2004, 99% of U.S. schools had computers—a total of more than 12 million machines, three times as many as in 1995. Today, the level is much closer to 100% than to 99%.

The rapid growth in the number of computers in the schools has placed pressure on teachers to become knowledgeable about computers. The vast majority, if not all, of teacher education programs require some structured experience with computers. Teachers must be afforded the time to become familiar with, and develop a degree of confidence with, computers and their uses

---

[2]NCTM Position Statement on The Role of Technology in the Teaching and Learning of Mathematics, 2008.

in the classroom before we can expect technology to be seamlessly integrated with instruction.

Instructional Software in the Mathematics Classroom

In many cases, the focus of the debate over technology in the classroom has switched from the calculator to the computer. Many of the same arguments have been presented, although the amount of opposition is considerably reduced. In fact, most schools are actively seeking ways to incorporate the computer into their curricula in all subject areas. The debate that remains does not center on whether to use computers but rather on identifying appropriate and effective educational uses.

Teachers can begin using computers as part of the school mathematics program by exploring commercial software packages. A computer work area has the potential to become an important learning center in every school classroom by using classroom computers for educational purposes. This can be accomplished by providing students with software that is appropriate for their needs and the teacher's instructional goals and objectives.

If your intent is to drill students in basic facts, then choose software that will do just that. If your intent is for students to journal about topics in mathematics, then direct students to use word-processing software. If the computer is to be used as a discovery tool, then encourage students to explore a particular topic using software designed for this application.

Develop a good filing system to allow easy access to programs needed for particular purposes. Individualizing computer use for mathematics instruction will become easier as teachers learn how to change and create programs addressed to specific student needs. The computer can become a record keeper for each child and free the teacher from the tedium of paperwork.

Various types of software programs have been developed and are available to teachers for classroom use. These include, but are not limited to, the following categories:

- drill and practice
- educational games
- simulation tutorials
- problem solving
- exploration tools
- records management
- material generation

These software types are not mutually exclusive. Most software packages address more than one of these purposes, but the majority of available computer programs do tend to focus more heavily on one of the listed applications. It is important for teachers to distinguish between these uses in order to judge the effectiveness and efficiency of a given program.

For example, we might examine a program dealing with basic multiplication facts couched in an arcade-like setting and easily categorize this as an educational game. Actually, such a program might be better classified as drill and practice, since the concepts involved are to be memorized and subject to immediate recall.

Similarly, a program that involves estimating various lengths and angles (couched in a golf or artillery game) could be classified as drill and practice, although it should really be considered an educational game. In this instance, the game format is used not to drill knowledge-level material, but rather to assist the students in developing estimation skills not subject to immediate recall.

Commercial software that emphasizes the tutorial mode can sometimes be effectively used to provide instruction. The purpose of tutorial software is to assist in the teaching of concepts, although such packages often also include a drill-and-practice component to check on progress toward a goal. Tutorial software is frequently used to introduce (or reintroduce) a topic. A student who is new to a school, or one who has been absent for several days, might make good use of a tutorial package to catch up.

Simulation, problem solving, and exploration tool software packages may be the most valuable of all. These packages are designed to establish an environment for generating and testing hypotheses and looking for patterns. Frequently, the setting is one that is not easily attained in the classroom without the use of a computer. As an example, consider a software package that allows students to "travel" from one planet to the next, collecting data about atmospheres, gravity, surface temperatures, and so on. The student is then free to make conjectures about life on those planets. Exploration tool software might allow a student to look for patterns between the sum of the measures of the angles in triangles. The software could provide far more examples to use to look for patterns than would be encountered by simply drawing triangles using paper, pencil, and a straightedge.

Teachers must become effective software evaluators on a personal level. Just as teachers must be able to critically analyze the textbooks they are using, so must they be prepared to analyze the software they are planning to use in instruction. Software evaluation techniques and forms are readily available in the literature. First, teachers should isolate the purpose of the program. Then they should compare the intended purpose with the features of the program with respect to grade level, validity of content, correlation with curriculum, preview options, and instructional design features. Also, expert opinion software reviews are often included as monthly columns in mathematics education journals such as NTCM's *Teaching Children Mathematics* and *Mathematics Teaching in the Middle School*. Check out those columns for reviews of software that might be of use to you and your students.

Drill and practice is too often the major (and sometimes the only) use of computers in the classroom, relegating it to the role of serving as an expensive electronic worksheet for children. However, more computer-assisted instruction programs are available for classroom use. **Computer-assisted instruction (CAI)** describes an individualized instructional situation in which the student is presented with material by the computer in an interactive mode with systematic evaluation and basic record keeping as integral parts of the software.

Teachers are also using computers for computer-managed instruction. **Computer-managed instruction (CMI)** provides the classroom teacher with computer technology to keep records, store test information, and provide prescriptive information to meet individual student needs.

Each teacher needs to experiment with the computer and its uses in the mathematics curriculum in order to develop more effective and efficient techniques. The computer has great educational potential, but we must first learn to use its unique characteristics to increase the efficiency and effectiveness of mathematics teaching.

Application Software in the Mathematics Classroom

Four common and practical tool computer applications are found in programs that make use of word processing, databases, spreadsheets, and graphics. A word processor, through its editing features, helps students develop confidence in communication by providing a forum for recording ideas that is removed from the restrictions of linear and rigid thinking. A database, through its searching capabilities, gives students access to patterns and trends in large amounts of data. A spreadsheet, through its formula features, allows students to hypothesize and examine the effect of changing one variable in a multivariable situation. A graphics program, through its drawing capabilities, gives students a vehicle for creative modeling of abstract concepts and geometric principles. All four programs assist students in formulating real-life situations, exploring problem-solving strategies, identifying and verifying hypotheses, communicating findings, and valuing sound decision-making processes.

The various application programs available and frequently used by teachers have individual distinctions that make a generic discussion of their operation difficult, at best. Instead of focusing on their idiosyncrasies, let's consider sample activities that make use of the power of these applications as tools for problem solving and patterning.

Word-processing programs offer more than the capabilities of a typewriter (a what??—it's hard to find a typewriter these days). The flexible formatting options of a word processor allow you to move letters, words, phrases, sentences, and paragraphs around easily. Spell-check, find-and-replace, and automatic outline features make this a valuable tool for both students and teachers. Teachers, especially, can make excellent use of the cut-and-paste feature of a word processor in preparing lesson plans. The ability to save files for future modification and use is also a real plus. Many word-processing programs can incorporate enhancement options such as graphics and different fonts and styles.

Consider the following example of an activity that engages students in the use of a word processor: Have students create a story problem—not the common form of two sentences and a question mark so often found in textbooks, but a *real* story problem. Using a word processor, the students can refine and extend their creations into actual stories. Word processors designed for use by children often provide easily accessible graphics that can enhance their stories and make them more understandable to beginning readers. Students can seek advice from others to improve the story and the need to help the characters solve their problem(s). Perhaps students can even work together in creating a story by taking turns writing sentences. When complete, changes and different versions can easily be saved for later discussion. Printouts can form an interactive bulletin board on which students are expected to solve the problems they read about. Kid Pix and Kidspiration are examples of application software packages that could readily be used for this purpose.

Database application programs have the advantage of storing a considerable amount of information in a form that makes searching, sorting, and retrieving data an easy process. Teachers can, of course, use a database to store relevant information about their students, such as home address and phone numbers, important notes about health or diet, or records of assignment completion. Teachers can also use databases to send personalized letters home to parents and students by merging the database with a word-processing document. Students can make use of the sorting ability to explore categories and attributes. For example, the teacher can create a database file for each student that includes the number of pets owned, the type of pets, the names of pets, the color of pets, who feeds the pets, and so on. Students can then search the files of all classmates to discover the most common pet type, pet name, and so on. This information can then be translated to a graph. Tabletop Jr. or Tabletop are examples of database software packages that could be used for this activity.

A **spreadsheet** is often thought of as an electronic accounting pad. Indeed, its greatest power may well lie in calculation features. Originally designed for business use as a standard ledger, spreadsheets have become much more flexible and, consequently, more widely used in schools. A teacher can, of course, incorporate the more traditional aspects of a spreadsheet by using it to record and average student grades, with, for example, weighted scores and/or percentage grades. The teacher can make graphs using these data to chart students' performance over time or in relation to other students' performances on the same assignments. One of the most valuable components to a spreadsheet program is the ability to change numbers or formulas quickly and easily to answer the question, "What if?" An interesting activity that demonstrates this feature is to set up on the spreadsheet a restaurant menu with columns for item names, how many of each item is ordered, price per item, and the total price. Students can then change the number of items ordered and see the effect of different permutations on the bill. Many integrated software packages, such as Microsoft Office and Appleworks, incorporate spreadsheets. Many spreadsheet programs have automatic transfer of data to a graph with the push of a button. Students can compare the way data are displayed in a picture graph and a bar graph using graphing software such as The Graph Club. Another commercial program dedicated to spreadsheet and data-graphing explorations is The Cruncher.

A **graphics** and/or **drawing** program is also often part of the word-processing program, the database, and/or the spreadsheet. Graphics programs can be used to create banners and signs for bulletin boards, greeting cards for special occasions, or enhancements to other documents. Students can use drawing programs to explore perspective, the two-dimensional/three-dimensional connection, and geometric properties of various shapes. Students can use drawing programs to create a series of graphic images that illustrate a repetitive pattern, such as images of a house, tree, tree, house, tree, and so on. Other students can be asked to determine the pattern and to continue it. Kid Pix Deluxe could provide the environment for this activity. A dynamic drawing program could be used to perform transformations such as reflections and then students can move the location of the mirror line to see how it affects the reflected image. Images can also be dilated, translated (slid), and rotated (turned) using this type of software. The Geometer's Sketchpad and Cabri Junior (easily downloaded onto a graphing calculator) are other software packages that can be used for this type of activity.

Virtual Manipulatives

Learning and understanding mathematics, at every level, requires student engagement. Mathematics is not a spectator sport. Learning problems occur if too much instruction fails to actively involve students. One way to address this problem is through the use of *manipulatives*, objects that help students visualize relationships and applications. But the use of physical manipulatives *could* bring a host of new potential problems and concerns, not the least of which are the finances to purchase them and facilities to manage and store them.

Fortunately, there are numerous, high-quality, **virtual manipulatives** (computer-based mathematical manipulatives or learning tools) that can be used at the elementary and middle school levels with a considerable amount of interactivity. We can use computers to create virtual learning environments to address the same goals as do physical manipulatives with, perhaps, less hassle.

The National Library of Virtual Manipulatives is a National Science Foundation–supported project that develops and disseminates a library of uniquely interactive, Web-based virtual manipulatives, mostly in the form of Java applets, for mathematics instruction. The Utah State University–based team is building Java-based mathematical tools and editors that allow the creation of exciting new approaches to interactive mathematical instruction.

The following screen shot shows a typical exercise with the base 10 blocks virtual manipulative:

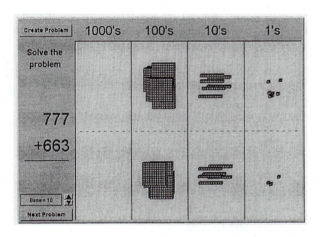

Here, the object of the manipulative is to (1) combine 10 pieces in one place into a single piece in the next higher place and (2) place each piece in the column to which it belongs. The solution of this screen shot follows:

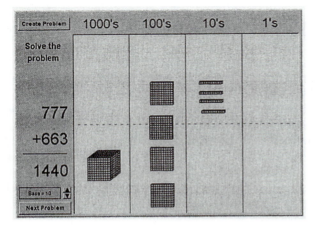

A different example is the Circle-0 virtual manipulative shown here.

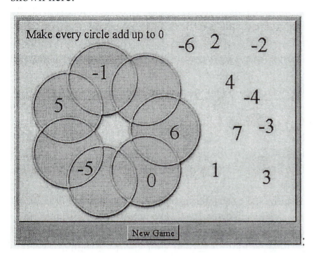

The object of Circle-0 is to place all the numbers (using the drag-and-drop technique with the computer cursor and mouse) within the circles so as to make each circle add up to 0. The following screen shot is an example of a completed Circle-0 problem:

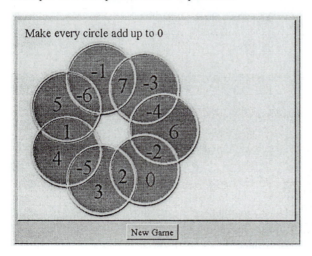

One other type of virtual manipulative is exemplified by Tangrams:

The object of the tangram puzzle is to place (using flipping, rotation, and translation) all the simple geometric shapes to completely, without any overlap, fill a more complex one, as shown here:

At the conclusion of work with the virtual manipulatives, students may be asked to submit a written description of their experiences.

Such virtual manipulatives are of importance for the mathematical training of both in-service and pre-service elementary teachers. Consequently, the virtual manipulatives on the CD that accompanies this edition of *Today's Mathematics* represents an important portion of this development, creating a resource from which teachers may freely draw to enrich their mathematics classrooms.

Design Issues and Advantages of Virtual Manipulatives

The virtual environment offers potential for substantial enhancements over similar physical manipulatives and tools, and the state of student interaction with virtual manipulatives can be printed or saved for future work.

Other advantages of virtual manipulatives include the following:

- increased access to relevant data and educational experiences at school or home
- capability to make manipulatives accessible to special-needs populations, through such means as enlarged print for sight-impaired users or voice activation for hearing-impaired users
- users' ability to individualize the information or materials to suit their own needs or creativity
- teachers' ability for quick re-creation or review of students' work
- reduced classroom management concerns (virtual manipulatives do not need to be distributed, collected, and reorganized, and lost parts don't need to be replaced)
- reduced challenges in structuring, monitoring, and assessing students' work (the software is capable of specifying goals and providing hints and feedback)

The mathlets in the National Library are designed as teaching/learning tools. As such, their use should be determined by the teacher, not by the library designers or programmers or authors. A virtual manipulative tool such as Geoboard or Pattern Blocks may be just the tool to accomplish a particular goal in a particular lesson plan, in ways that perhaps no other teacher has considered. The virtual manipulative Geoboard, for example, can be used to support instruction at every grade level, from the creation of interesting patterns and shapes and colors in the early grades through fraction concepts in the middle grades to sophisticated exploration of area, perimeter, and slopes of lines in geometry or pre-calculus courses. Accordingly, any organization of National Library materials is arbitrary and should be used only as a rough guide to help locate the most useful support.

Classification Attributes for Virtual Manipulatives

The organization of applets on the home page of the Web site http://nlvm.usu.edu is based on the NCTM Content Standards (down the left-hand column) and by grade bands (across the top), so that selection can be made from the matrix, shown at the bottom of the page.

In addition to the organization by NCTM Content Standards, each individual applet has a link (a button on the top tool bar) that goes immediately to an appropriate reference in the NCTM *Principles and Standards for School Mathematics*, making connections with the five NCTM Process Standards: Problem Solving, Reasoning and Proof, Communication, Connections, and Representation.

Virtual manipulatives, for our purposes, can thus be classified by a number of *classification attributes* (and each manipulative may belong to several classifications).

Goals

Levels—based on established grade bands

Standards—based on established standards

Content Standards—procedural, conceptual (listed in the matrix)

Process Standards (listed in the matrix)

Methods

Games—goal-driven (single-path [procedural], multipath [free play])

Visualizations—provide a visual representation of a concept

Data Generators—provide system-generated data (e.g., random selection) based on student-specified parameters

Index	Pre-K — 2	3 — 5	6 — 8	9 — 12
Number & Operations				
Algebra				
Geometry				
Measurement				
Data Analysis & Probability				

Simulations—provide a virtual reality to conduct "experiments"

Computational Devices—provide a scheme for generating solutions based on student-specified parameters.

Features

Feedback

Submission Check—{final, stepwise} × {auto, manual} Show Solution

Hint—none, upon incorrect entry, upon request

Progression

Automatic, manual (reset)

Capsule Descriptions of the National Library of Virtual Manipulatives

Abacus—an electronic version of abacus. Move beads or stacks of beads by clicking on a bead.

Algebra Tiles—a virtual implementation of the physical manipulative in which tiles represent units and variables (x, x^2, y, y^2, and xy) that can actually be varied by sliders, useful as an introduction to the array representation of multiplication and division.

Attribute Blocks—blocks in the work space have attributes: Size (Large, Small), Shape (Circle, Triangle, Square, Rectangle, Pentagon), and Color (Red, Yellow, Blue, Green). Users sort a collection of blocks that share a common attribute. The task is to identify (mentally) the common attribute and then to move into the central oval (click and drag) all pictured blocks sharing the given attribute.

Attribute Trains—practice completing a given pattern train (a sequence of blocks with shape, number, or color attributes).

Balance Beam Algebra—allows the user to solve simple linear equations through the use of a balance beam. Unit blocks (representing 1's) and X boxes (for the unknown, X) are placed on the pans of a balance beam.

Bar Chart—students create their own bar charts (by counting and recording data) with as many as 12 columns with up to 20 entries in each and can enter their own labels for each.

Base Blocks Addition and Base Blocks Subtraction (*See Multiple Base Blocks*)—allows students to practice addition and subtraction skills in different bases, with both preprogrammed problems sets or problems created by the user.

Base Blocks Decimals (*See Multiple Base Blocks*)—teachers and students can set the decimal place as desired so that any of the pieces (cubes, longs, flats, or blocks) can serve as the unit for the chosen base.

Box Model—one of the most versatile of all probability tools. Virtually the only limitation is the imagination of the user. To model a simple probability question such as tossing a coin or rolling a die, the user simply puts into the box some appropriate collection of numbers and allows the simulation to proceed by drawing from the box.

Box Plot (Histogram)—used to summarize data graphically. To construct a box plot, first find the minimum data value, the lower quartile, the median, the upper quartile, and the maximum data value. These five statistics are then marked on a number line with a box drawn from the lower quartile to the upper quartile. The median is marked inside the box. The same data can be explored in histogram form by clicking a button.

Chip Abacus—illustrates and reinforces the ideas of exchange or borrowing in place values, as in five pennies can be exchanged for a nickel (base 5) or 10 dimes for a dollar (base 10).

Circle-0 (and Circle-21, Circle-3, Circle-99)—an addition game that encourages some logical analysis as well as addition skills, in which the user drags numbers into regions of circles to make the numbers in every circle reach the desired total. The Circle-0 game uses positive and negative integers; Circle-99 uses larger numbers, with a target sum of 99; Circle-3 requires the addition of one-place decimals, and Circle-21 combines positive whole numbers.

Cob Web Plot—one of several manipulatives that illustrates "sensitive dependence on initial conditions," one of the defining characteristics of chaos and fractals. Two different shapes of curves are available, either a "tent" or a "logistic" curve (part of a parabola). The cob web plot or "Verhulst diagram" is the path starting at the initial point, moving vertically until the point hits the curve (blue), then horizontally right or left onto the $y = x$ line, and then repeating the process (black line, vertically to blue graph, horizontally to black line, and repeat).

Coin Problem—an electronic version of a classic puzzle, in which the challenge is to find the counterfeit coin (light or heavy) in a set of identical-appearing coins by successive weighings on a balance scale.

Coin Tossing (and Heads in a Row)—a simulation of tossing a coin, allowing the user to explore a random process. If a coin is tossed 100 times, how many heads should we expect? How often does the experiment come up with exactly the expected number? How many tosses does it take to get a string of five successive heads?

Color Chip Addition and Subtraction—two different manipulatives that lead the student through the processes of adding and subtracting signed numbers, including two different ways to visualize the subtraction of a negative number.

Color Patterns—the user is expected to look at a pattern of colored dots and extend the pattern by clicking on appropriate color buttons.

Congruent Triangles—a manipulative that illustrates the conditions for congruence (SSS, SAS, ASA, and the ambiguous case). The user is given matching sets of data (as three sides) and asked to construct two triangles, to see that there is essentially only one triangle determined (or in the ambiguous case, two).

Convert Units—allows the user to convert from one set of units to another (as miles per hour to feet per second), using either calculator-generated problems or some created by the user.

Conway's Game of Life—an electronic version of the remarkable game invented by John Horton Conway. It was named "Life" because of simplified analogies to living organisms. In this case, the rules for living and dying depend solely on the number of neighbors. It is played on a square grid, so that each cell has eight neighboring cells, those sharing an edge or a corner point. The game consists of observing what happens to a given pattern of cells through successive generations.

Factor Tree—a virtual manipulative with which students can explore the prime factorization of numbers and use the factorizations of a pair of numbers to find their greatest common factor (GCF) and their least common multiple (LCM).

Fill 'n Pour—disguises some useful number theory in puzzle form. With two containers of specified volumes, the user has to end up with exactly a target volume of juice in one of the containers. The user can fill or empty either container as often as desired and can pour juice from either container into the other; the applet keeps track of the amount of juice in each container after each action and recognizes a correct solution.

Fractals—a family of applets all based on computer-generated images illustrating the creation of a number of different fractal constructions. The Mandelbrot and Julia Sets explore some of the best-known and most beautiful of all fractal images, and the user can zoom in to staggering degrees of magnification.

Fraction Pieces—an electronic version of a common physical manipulative incorporating all of the options commonly available. The user can choose among pieces that represent fractional portions of either a circular or square region. For the circle version, the fraction pieces are all wedges, representing $\frac{1}{2}$, $\frac{1}{3}$, $\frac{1}{4}$, $\frac{1}{5}$, $\frac{1}{6}$, $\frac{1}{8}$, $\frac{1}{9}$, $\frac{1}{10}$, and $\frac{1}{12}$ of the whole; using a square, there are two shapes of size $\frac{1}{2}$, two of size $\frac{1}{4}$, and two of size $\frac{1}{8}$, and a trapezoid of size $\frac{3}{8}$, as well as pieces representing $\frac{1}{3}$, $\frac{1}{5}$, $\frac{1}{6}$, $\frac{1}{10}$, and $\frac{1}{12}$

Fractions–Adding—designed to help students experience the need for (and to practice with) common denominators.

Fractions–Comparing—after getting common denominators for two fractions, the user locates the fractions on a number line and can find fractions that lie between the given pair.

Fractions–Equivalent—allows the user to find other (equivalent) names for given fractions.

Fractions–Naming—understanding the names of fractions as numbers of parts of a whole.

Fractions–Parts of a Whole—making fractions by dividing a shaped whole into the desired number of pieces (denominator) and then selecting (in color) the number of parts (numerator).

Fractions–Rectangle Multiplication (Proper and Improper)—illustrating, in rectangular form, the product of two fractions, such as $\frac{2}{3}$ of $\frac{4}{5}$, or $\frac{4}{3}$ times $\frac{6}{7}$; the user may choose to work with either proper or improper fractions (less than 2).

Fractions–Visualizing—visually showing a specified fraction as the appropriate number of shaded pieces of a given whole.

Function Machine—animation to help students understand the function concept through the "machine" metaphor. Domain elements (input) are dragged into the machine, which then uses one of several functions (not seen) and spits out the range element corresponding to the input. Results are also displayed in tabular form.

Geoboard (and Circular and Isometric and Coordinate Geoboards)—virtual implementations, modeled on the ubiquitous physical geoboard made with nails. The virtual forms offer a variety of sizes and shapes, and interiors of regions can be colored. Measures of area and perimeter are available, as well as slopes of lines, on the coordinate geoboard.

Golden Rectangle—or Golden Ratio (the ratio of the long side to the short side of a Golden Rectangle) arises in many different contexts, in nature and art as well as mathematics. This virtual manipulative allows students to observe some properties of Golden Rectangles.

Grapher—a versatile graphing tool that shows many kinds of functional behavior, including the effects of parameters on the graph of a function. Users can graph as many as three functions simultaneously, allowing the exploration of, for example, function composition or reciprocals or sums and products of functions.

Histogram—(*See* Box Plot)

How High—illustrates the conservation of volume when a liquid is poured from one container into another of the same shape family, but also invites the user to compute and predict the height resulting when the liquid is poured, a substantial challenge for conical containers.

Ladybug Leaf and Ladybug Maze—a very simple programming environment similar to that in Logo that allows the user to create, try out, and revise plans (programs) by entering a sequence of steps and turns to hide the ladybug under a leaf or to negotiate a maze. In a cleared work space, many other tasks are possible.

Mastermind—a version of the classic Mastermind game of logic. Win the game by discovering the colors of the four-peg solution. You have eight chances to correctly guess the colors and sequence. After each guess, you receive feedback regarding correct colors and placement of pegs.

Multiple Base Blocks—intended to provide maximum flexibility for the teacher in explaining place naming in different bases and different numbers of decimal places. User can change the default setting of base 10 (to any of the bases 2, 3, 4, 5, or back to 10). There is an automatic grouping-ungrouping feature that exchanges, for example, an appropriate number of "longs" for a "flat," or vice versa.

Number Line Arithmetic—uses arrows on a number line to visualize whole number arithmetic operations.

Number Line Bars—uses adjustable colorable bars to illustrate whole-number arithmetic operations on the number line as in Number Line Arithmetic, laying out bars to represent integers, but here the user retains control of the number (and color) and placement of bars and can change the length or direction of each bar at will.

Number Line Bars–Fractions—colored bars illustrate arithmetic operations of fractions on the number line (which has an adjustable scale). The user determines the size (the desired fraction, positive or negative) of bars and can place them side by side or stack them to visualize addition, subtraction, multiplication, and division.

Number Puzzles—a collection of different arrangements in which the student drags numbers into spots in diagrams to obtain specified sums.

Pascal's Triangle—allows the student to study and explore patterns and relationships in this array of binomial coefficients.

Pattern Blocks—a virtual implementation of one of the most popular and versatile physical manipulatives. The electronic version can be used in at least as many ways as its physical predecessor, with some useful additions, including free coloring, grouping of blocks, rotation of single or grouped blocks, and a clone button that allows the user to make copies of constructions.

Peg Puzzle—an electronic implementation of a familiar puzzle, with the same kind of challenge features. As with any such puzzle, children learn from talking through their experiences, trying to see what sorts of moves lead to dead ends, why certain forms make it impossible to move further. Users can choose a four-, six-, or eight-peg version.

Pentominoes—all 12 possible shapes that can be made from five adjoining squares. Pieces can be rotated, flipped, and colored as desired, and the user can use any number of pieces of the same shape or differing sets of shapes.

Percentages—allows a student to enter any two of the three quantities involved in any percentage computation, *the whole, a part*, or *the percent* (which is the number of hundredths when dividing the part by the whole), leading to profitable discussions of relations among fractions, decimals, ratios, and percentages. With the displayed equation as a starting point, students can see that a percentage is always a fraction, a ratio, the first two places of the decimal form. With a little guidance, any of the forms (fractions, decimals, ratios, or percentages) can be expressed in terms of the whole/part/percentage format of the applet.

Pie Chart—creates a pie chart for any set of specified categories with numbers of items in each. Chart is displayed in colors with percentages for each slice.

Platonic Solids (and Duals and Slicing)—a set of related manipulatives that show the five Platonic Solids in three-dimensional renderings; the user can rotate and interact with the images. In the first, solids may be viewed in solid or wire-frame mode, and the user can selectively fill in faces, edges, and vertices to illustrate Euler's formula. In Duals, the dual of each solid can be seen, either in wire frame or colored; in Slicing Solids, the intersection of a vertical plane is shown, and the solid can be rotated and the plane moved forward or backward relative to the viewer.

Polyominoes—one of the simplest and most basic of the virtual manipulatives in the National Library with use as an instructional tool limited only by imagination. At the earliest level, children can just enjoy making patterns, dragging squares into the work space, grouping and rotating them, changing colors, and changing the appearance with the zoom slider. With more experience, there are endless opportunities for challenges and exploration.

Pythagorean Theorem—a dynamic illustration of the Pythagorean Theorem, that the square on the hypotenuse of a right triangle is equal to the sum of the squares on the other two sides. This proof, by dissection, is only one of literally hundreds.

Rectangle Division—helps students visualize division as separating a given number into groups of a set size. The user can set the dividend and the divisor separately, and the rectangular array dynamically shows the quotient and remainder as part of the rectangular array and in standard multiplication form.

Rectangle Multiplication (Grouping and Lattice and Common)—offers dynamic visualization of three different algorithms for multiplication, each illustrated by a rectangular array.

Scatterplot—a tool for the visual representation of the relation between two variables. User can set appropriate scales for the data to be examined and then enter (or move, or remove) data. As data points are added to the graphical representation, descriptive statistics are updated and displayed, and the regression line is automatically shown.

Sieve of Eratosthenes—show or delete (sieve out) multiples of numbers from an array of the first 200 numbers, to find primes or look at common multiples, and so on.

Space Blocks—blocks that can be stuck together and rotated in three dimensions, to explore solids and develop spatial visualization skills.

Spinner—a virtual spinner (with freedom in setting the numbers and colors of options) that can be used for many different random processes.

Stick or Switch—play *Let's Make a Deal*, with which you choose one door of three, hoping to find the prize hidden behind one door. The computer then opens one of the other doors to reveal a loser. Should you stick with your first choice, or switch doors? Multiple games and discussion of strategies are available.

Tangrams—the classic tangram pieces that can be slid, rotated, and flipped to make any of the hundreds of designs that have been studied for centuries, with color options added. Twenty outline designs are available, with hints for some, and additional activities.

Tessellations—equilateral triangles, squares, and regular hexagons, octagons, and dodecagons (12 sides) can be arranged (translated and rotated) to explore regular and semi-regular tessellations (tilings) of the plane.

Towers of Hanoi—determine how many moves are required to move two (or three or more) disks from one of two pegs onto another, when a disk can be moved only to an empty peg or onto a larger disk. A traditional, and challenging, puzzle.

Transformations (Translations, Rotations, Reflections, and Dilations)—four different virtual manipulatives that permit the user to construct objects from pattern block pieces and explore each of the named transformations by dynamically changing the slide arrow, or the center and angle of turning, or the location and angle of the mirror line, or the center and scale of the dilation.

Transformations–Composition—allows the user to experiment with what happens when two of the four transformations are applied in sequence.

Triominoes—a set of triangles, each with three colored dots that snap together when the color dots match. The triangles can be grouped, rotated, and flipped.

Turtle Geometry—a slightly more sophisticated programming experience than the Lady Bug. The user can program paths that set steps of varying lengths and angles of different sizes. Activities include matching geometric shape outlines or following mazes or avoiding rocks to reach a goal.

Turtle Rectangles—helps the user explore the consequences of incrementing parameter changes in simple programming loops to draw sequences of rectangles

Venn Diagrams—contrasting shadings can fill in various regions of a Venn diagram with three sets and complements; checkable exercises identify different subsets to be shaded.

The **virtual manipuatives and tools on the CD that accompanies this text were either created especially for this text or drawn from the National Library of Virtual Manipulatives (NLVM)**, http://nlvm.usu.edu. The NLVM has worked closely with the NCTM and the *Principles and Standards for School Mathematics* (2000). For that reason, several of the site's virtual manipulatives are also embedded in NCTM's *e-Standards* and *Illuminations* available online at http://www.nctm.org.

The developers of the virtual manipulatives on the accompanying CD incorporated several specific design considerations in each applet, including the following:

- **Simplicity**. Each applet has a tightly designed focus and a clean, intuitive interface. The mathematics underlying the functionality is often very sophisticated; what the user sees and does is very simple.

- **Interactivity**. There is a certain degree of interactivity in every applet. Users must think about a specific task, formulate a strategy to achieve a specific goal, engage in some physical action, and observe (and, perhaps, describe) consequences of the action. They must make decisions that let them observe consequences and help them understand how and why certain things work mathematically.

- **User control**. Nothing happens until the user takes action, and an activity can be repeated until there is satisfaction; the computer never tires of repetition.

- **Increased conceptual understanding** of mathematical content.

- **Content linkage**. Activities are linked to companion content instruction for parents and teachers. Virtual manipulatives directly link representational-pictorial and abstract-symbolic notations and highlight specific instructional content.

RESEARCH SNAPSHOT

Can the use of computer-based manipulatives improve student learning?

In *Principles and Standards for School Mathematics* (NCTM, 2000), the NCTM states that electronic technologies are essential tools for teaching, learning, and doing mathematics. More specifically, NCTM suggests that work with virtual manipulatives allows young children to extend physical experience and develop an initial understanding of sophisticated ideas such as the use of algorithms.

Studies suggest that students who use virtual manipulatives experience higher achievement or conceptual understanding in mathematics than those using associated physical manipulatives or no manipulatives (Kieran & Hillel, 1990; Thompson, 1992). Other studies suggest that students who use both virtual *and* physical manipulatives show an increase in conceptual understanding (Ball, 1988; Izydorczak, 2003; Olson, 1988). Still other studies found no statistically significant differences in achievement for students using physical manipulatives, virtual manipulatives, a combination of both physical and virtual manipulatives, or no manipulatives (Drickey, 2001; Kim, 1993).

While research into the use of emerging technologies continues, there are some variables to consider when using or measuring the effects of virtual manipulative use. Research design, sampling characteristics, and the type of manipulative used may influence achievement. For example, studies that show evidence of increased achievement were administered when classroom teachers believed they fit in with the natural flow of the curriculum. Studies with no noticeable increase in student achievement were administered at times that interrupted the normal curriculum. Studies that used computer-simulated base10 blocks, two-color counters, and fraction strips produced positive results. Other variables that may influence the effectiveness of using virtual or physical manipulatives include previous experience with computers, grade level, mathematics topic, treatment length, student attitudes toward mathematics, and computer-to-student ratios.

Ball, S. (1988). Computers, concrete materials and teaching fractions. *School Science and Mathematics, 88,* 470–475.

Drickey, N. A. (2001). A comparison of virtual and physical manipulatives in teaching visualization and spatial reasoning to middle school mathematics students. Unpublished doctoral dissertation, Utah State University, 2001.

Izydorczak, A. (2003). A study of virtual manipulatives for elementary mathematics. Unpublished doctoral dissertation, State University of New York–Buffalo, 2003.

Kieran, C., & Hillel, J. (1990). "It's tough when you have to make the triangles angle": Insights from a computer-based geometry environment. *Journal of Mathematical Behavior, 9,* 99–127.

Kim, S. (1993). The relative effectiveness of hands-on and computer-simulated manipulatives in teaching seriation, classification, geometric, and arithmetic concepts to kindergarten children. Doctoral dissertation, University of Oregon, 1993. *Dissertation Abstracts International, 54*(9), 3319

Olson, J. K. (1988). *Microcomputers make manipulatives meaningful*. Budapest, Hungary: International Congress of Mathematics Education.

Thompson, P. W. (1992). Notations, conventions, and constraints: Contributions to effective uses of concrete materials in elementary mathematics. *Journal for Research in Mathematics Education, 23,* 123–147.

For additional research briefs, "ERIC Digests" lets you search more than 2000 short syntheses of research on a range of education topics. The syntheses were produced by the Educational Resources Information Center (ERIC). Check http://www.ericfacility.net/ericdigests/index/.

Multimedia in the Mathematics Classroom

Multimedia refers to the combination of visual and auditory information controlled by the computer. It can incorporate text, graphics, animation, photography, video, music, and sound. Both the potential of the medium and the applications are diverse. The power of multimedia is the visual image that goes beyond spoken or written words. One embodiment of multimedia is called **hypermedia**.

Historically, the most common organizational structure for the preservation and presentation of information has been a linear mode. For example, books are typically read from cover to cover, and TV programs are normally viewed from beginning to end. Information can be cross-referenced in a book, but the general layout is still linear (front to back) and, as such, is confining and access is restrictive. Hypermedia provides an escape from the linear presentation of information. Electronic links allow the user to quickly connect to other points of information by clicking on words or graphics, thereby providing a means of making information interactive. One reason MP3 and compact disc players have replaced vinyl record albums and cassette tapes is this capability of immediately "jumping" to preferred sections of a playlist, rather than having to run through the entire record or cassette to get to the desired piece.

CD/DVD discs, similar to music CDs, store vast amounts of information in digital form that can be readily accessed by computer. A single CD/DVD holds about 700 megabytes of data (equivalent to more than 400 of the previously used high-density floppy disks). Reference CD/DVD titles such as Grolier's Multimedia Encyclopedia or Microsoft's Encarta offer photographs and video clips in addition to text information. The 3-D Atlas CD/DVD provides outstanding visuals and vast amounts of statistical data on ecology, population, and economics, as well as many other categories. Numerous educational software packages offer a multitude of sample lessons, many taken from curriculum programs indexed to the NCTM standards. Each of these resources can be effectively used by both students and teachers as research materials in problem solving and project-based inquiries or investigations.

Photography has reached the computer age with the development and proliferation of **digital cameras**. These cameras are available from a variety of computer and other manufacturers. When a digital camera is used, the images are captured on a disk, memory chip, or memory card and later downloaded to the computer using preloaded software that allows images to be viewed and used immediately. Once downloaded, images can be modified or enhanced and inserted into, for example, a word-processing document or Web page.

A variety of school applications can be identified for digital photography. As one example, a group of elementary students might be challenged to use the digital camera to take pictures of their environment that reflect the use of patterns, or measurement, or certain aspects of geometry. These images could then be downloaded to lead a discussion of mathematics in our world. The World Wide Web is a valuable resource for ideas concerning school-based use of digital cameras in the classroom.

A multimedia learning environment requires a teacher who is comfortable with technology and able to integrate that technology into the curriculum. Hypermedia tools can be used by teachers to create classroom applications, but they can also be used by students as productivity tools. Students involved in designing their own hypermedia projects, or in using hypermedia programs designed by peers, become actively involved in learning at many levels. A great deal of planning goes into organizing and linking information in meaningful ways. One of the key elements in asking students to develop hypermedia projects is to engage them in peer collaboration during the planning stages of the project.

Microsoft Office's PowerPoint and Apple's Keynote software are used as **presentation tools** in many mathematics classrooms. A student can, for example, create a visual presentation to support a unit on quadrilaterals by generating a series of slides that demonstrates the categorization of quadrilaterals. The first slide might show a "family tree" for quadrilaterals. In turn, the tree could be followed by other pages that provide justifications for polygons' placements in the tree. Also, students can take digital photographs, or even digital video footage, and incorporate these images into the presentation as links from a given page. So, for example, photographs of a door, a ceiling tile, and a store's logo on a sign might be used to illustrate a rectangle, a square, and a rhombus. Most elementary and middle school children have grown up with this type of technology, so it makes sense to utilize the tools with which they are familiar in the classroom setting.

A teacher can also use a hypermedia tool to showcase collections of students' computer work or scanned paperwork. The teacher can link the work by topic and/or student name and use the stack for a presentation to other teachers or at an open house.

In addition to curriculum-based topics, hypermedia tools can be used to develop electronic portfolios. This assessment strategy allows for much more information than the paper-based format. Student success can be documented with pictures, sound, video, and work samples. Ideally, the electronic portfolio should include student input when selections are made.

The Internet in the Mathematics Classroom

Imagine a giant web covering the globe, connecting thousands of networks of computers and allowing millions of users to access and share information! The Internet brings people and information together in a digital world unbounded by time and space. Commonly referred to as the "network of networks," the **Internet** is composed of thousands of computer networks interconnected around the globe, including many sites located at educational institutions. The Internet began in the 1960s when the U.S. Department of Defense directed the Advanced Research Projects Agency (ARPA) to design a means of preserving communication in the event of a nuclear attack. If all communications were issued from a centralized location, they could be destroyed, so a decentralized network of interconnected computers was designed. Researchers in various universities and laboratories found that they could make use of the online communications as a means of sharing information and research findings. Gradually, colleges, universities, and organizations began connecting their computers to the network and, most important, allowed others to access research information and data stored in their computers.

The Internet is often used for communicating with people (one-on-one or groups), gathering information, and, more recently, conducting business. Teachers can use the Internet as a vast resource for lesson plans and information, and as a means of collaboration and communication. Students also benefit through learning how to gather and share information online. As a research tool, the Internet offers databases of information in the form of encyclopedias, magazines, and museums. Unlike traditional materials in text form, digital information on the Internet can be updated at any time. In addition, many electronic references offer picture documents, sound bytes, and video clips as well as text information. There are also a huge number of Web sites devoted to lesson plan ideas and activities. Among the most notable are Illuminations (http://illuminations.nctm.org), Teach-Net (http://www.teachnet.com), Hotchalk's (http://www.lessonplanspage.com/Math.htm), Awesome Library (http://www.awesomelibrary.org/math.html), and Mathline (http://www.pbs.org/mathline).

Electronic mail (email) is one of the most popular uses of the Internet, as is **text** or **instant messaging** (TM or IM). Communicating with a person in another country is as easy (or easier) as communicating with a person in the same building. Using email requires access to the Internet, software, and an address for the recipient of the message. Messages can be addressed to one person or to a group of people. An email account also allows the user to subscribe to listervs, which are group discussions or interest groups. Classroom-to-classroom connections can be formed through subscribing to mailing lists designed to connect with people around the globe. Collaboration ideas can be posted through special interest groups or forums. A project idea typically has a "Call for Collaboration" subject heading and a brief description. Existing online projects can be found in many locations through education forums.

The **World Wide Web (WWW)** is a hypertext-based means of accessing and publishing information on the Internet. Web documents, referred to as Web pages, can combine text, graphics, sound, and video and often contain links to related resources. Links can be words in color text, underlined words, or pictures. Because the Web is composed of digital information, it is constantly evolving and changing. For this reason, Web locations can change or disappear without warning. Also, caution should be taken when using the Web since information available on the Web is not necessarily correct or appropriate for classroom use. The Web is not currently policed for accuracy or content by any external agent.

A **search engine** is used to locate particular topics on the Web. For instance, if you are interested in locating Web sites that focus on travel, you might use a search engine and type in "travel." The search engine would search the Web for travel sites. You would be provided with a list of Web addresses with short descriptions of what you could expect to find at those sites. You could then use the descriptions to choose the sites that might provide information to help your students plan a theoretical trip using a predetermined budget. The broader your topic, the more sites you will likely be given. You could have searched under "travel" + "Bahamas" to narrow your results. Another benefit of search engines is that you can look up specific companies such as a particular airline company to find prices of tickets to given locations. Some commonly used search engines are Google and Yahoo!

To access a particular Web page, enter the address or location of the page. A **URL (uniform resource locator)** is the form of the address. For example, http://education.nasa.gov/ is the URL for NASA Education Programs, and entering that particular URL brings its home page into view.

An invaluable resource for teachers, "Educator's Reference Desk" (formerly known as AskERIC), can be found by using http://www.eduref.org/. Key areas include ERIC's Lesson Plans, ERIC's Resource Guides, Question Archives, and the ERIC Database. The ERIC Digest database can also be accessed via http://www.ericfacility.net/ericdigests/index/. Another relevant site for mathematics educators is NCTM's home page at http://www.nctm.org/. This Web site has access to summaries of the *Principles and Standards for School Mathematics* document, information on upcoming meetings, and NCTM educational products and resources.

Other valuable WWW sites for teachers and others include the following:

Geometry Center
http://www.geom.umn.edu

e-Tutor Center
http://www.e-tutor.com/et100/index.html

Mathematics Virtual Library
http://www.math.fsu.edu/Virtual/

Scholastic Central (Scholastic Network)
http://www.scholastic.com/

PBS TeacherSource
http://www.pbs.org/teachersource/math/

TERC—Technical Education Research Center
http://www.terc.edu/

U.S. Department of Education Online Library
http://www.ed.gov/

Access to online databases provides entire libraries of information at the user's fingertips. Unfortunately, information does not equal knowledge. Finding ways to organize, use, and share information is vital. For example, students can use statistical data such as that found in the CIA *World Fact Book*, https://www.cia.gov/library/publications/the-world-factbook/, to create graphs, make comparisons, and predict trends. Challenge problems and other related bits of mathematics history can be found in various locations such as the Kid's Zone at the National Center for Educational Statistics at http://nces.ed.gov/nceskids/CRUNCH/.

Several versions of grocery list comparisons, such as a Global Grocery List found at, http://www.gsn.org/gsh/Roger/, have provided opportunities for collaboration and data analysis in a meaningful way for students. A "Let's Compare Prices" activity is repeated on a regular basis. A portion of this formerly posted Web investigation is described as follows.

Roger Williams told us the amount he paid for some items when he shopped in Japan. Roger sent these prices of things from Japan.

- 1.5 liter bottle of Coke is $3.60
- 1 gallon diesel is $3.30
- 2 liters of oil for truck is $16.00
- A hotel room in Tokyo is $250 per night.
- A Big Mac with medium Coke and small fries is $7.00.
- A Big Mac Value Meal costs $9.00.

Classes from around the world investigated prices for similar products in their locale and reported these through the Internet to other participants. Results were then shared electronically. Classes compared their information with others and, in the process, discovered the variations in currency and economic influences.

WebQuests, similar to, but often much more detailed than the activity just outlined, provide a framework for inquiry-based learning on the Web. They often involve having groups of students address engaging problems, using Web sites suggested by the teacher or sites students have themselves discovered to be relevant to the solution of the problem. They can be created for any curriculum area or grade level. Each WebQuest consists of the following elements:

- An introduction, which sets the stage and provides some background information on the problem
- A task, which defines the problem-solving goal; resources that identify preselected information sites on the Web
- A process, which provides guidelines for solving the problem; guidance, which poses questions and provides directions on how best to use time, resources, and information
- A conclusion, which provides closure, evaluation, and a review of the concepts learned

More information on WebQuests—what they are, how to construct them, samples at various grade levels, and other frequently asked questions—can be found at http://webquest.sdsu.edu/.

Without knowing any Web programming language, you can create a Web-based course site that brings learning materials, class discussions, and even tests online. Novice users can add online components to their classes by making use of Web sites such as Blackboard.com (http://www.blackboard.com/us/index.bbb) and TopClass (http://www.wbtsystems.com/).

Benefits of the Internet and multimedia to teaching and learning become obvious with use. As we expand our use and the way we apply technology, we will explore new ways to develop and deliver educational content. The greatest impact of these technologies may well be the knocking down of classroom walls, thereby enabling students and teachers to become part of the global community of learners.

Programming Computers and Calculators

When lower-cost computers first became available to the education arena, it was common for schools to focus on how to write programs for them. In their infancy, computers did not come bundled with the wealth of software choices that we now encounter. Instead, it was important, at that time, to learn to "talk" to the computer and make it function the way the user wanted. In school, this need to command the computer was translated into experiences in teaching children to write and run simple computer programs, most often in a language called BASIC (Beginners All-purpose Symbolic Instruction Code). The intent was not so much to teach children how to program a computer as it was to learn what the nature of programming entailed and the problem solving that accompanied programming. For example, the process of interpreting the nuances in a BASIC program was used to provide insight into aspects of robotics and how machines follow rules to make decisions.

Similarly, Logo—a computer language that was initially designed to promote problem-solving abilities using a computer—found some favor in the school curriculum. Logo is a graphic language that can be used for calculations, manipulations of words, writing music, and so forth, as well as for graphics. In elementary and middle schools, the graphics mode can be explored. The graphics component of Logo is an effective tool for exploring geometric concepts and principles. This aspect of Logo involves immediate reinforcement through the movement of a symbol, referred to as the *turtle*. Orders are given to the turtle through commands, called *primitives*, such as FD 50, RT 90, BK 30, and LT 45, in which the letters represent a directive to the turtle; the number refers to a quantity for that directive (e.g., FD 50 might be used to move the turtle forward 50 units). Many different age-appropriate versions of Logo are available. Each version is supported by its own set of primitives, but these differ only slightly in form and use. Once a version of Logo is mastered, other versions are not difficult to learn. **The Logo-based virtual manipulatives Ladybug Leaf, Ladybug Maze, and Turtle Tracks can be explored on the CD that accompanies this text.**

Use of such virtual manipulatives has the potential to help students become better reasoners and problem solvers—not programmers—by analytically examining a series of algorithmic steps. The real benefit is in providing children with an environment in which they can learn to hypothesize how a computer deals with data by making changes in program code and examining the results. Seymour Papert, a mathematician and student of Piaget, was the person most responsible for the development of Logo. His vision was to make the computer an object to think with a mental tool for learning based on personal experience. This vision can be realized, especially if we don't teach programming for programming's sake, but instead examine programs for valuable problem-solving experiences.

HTML, hypertext markup language, is a computer language that is employed to create Web pages on the Internet. Today, constructing your own simple Web page with text and graphics has evolved into an extremely easy task using tools that automatically translate word-processed documents into HTML code. An example would be to use Microsoft Word to create a document and then simply save it under the "Save as a Web Page. . ." option found under the MS Word file menu.

As stated earlier, it is not necessary to learn any HTML code if you instead choose to make use of an HTML Editor such as

Dreamweaver
http://www.adobe.com/products/dreamweaver/

Netscape Composer
http://www.csulb.edu/~jvancamp/composer.html

Microsoft Word
http://www.microsoft.com/word/

These WYSIWYG (What You See Is What You Get) editors make creating a Web page no more challenging than creating a word-processing document. With these, the user simply types in what is wanted, and the appropriate HTML code is automatically applied.

A final example of programming experiences that are readily available to many students is the programming function on a graphing calculator. In most cases, middle school students simply use applications software that came prepackaged on their graphing calculators or download it from a Web site (see, for example, http://education.ti.com). However, some students are interested in writing their own simple programs to tell the calculator what to do. Again, analysis of a prewritten program, or the development of a program of their own, can help children think about how a carefully sequenced set of instructions can be used to carry out a routine procedure. Although most students will never have to write programs in the workplace (instead, they will be expected to *use* programs written by someone else), the exploration of programming on a computer or a calculator can enhance the student's problem solving and reasoning abilities.

Closure

This chapter has exposed you to effective methods and procedures for using technology in teaching children. Sometimes, technology's role is as a tool, sometimes as a tutor, and sometimes as a tutee. Remember that the calculator and the computer are not "topics" in and of themselves, within the field of mathematics. Instead, they are devices—tools—that aid understanding, increase quickness, achieve a high degree of accuracy, or provide a window into reasoning. Yes, a calculator (or computer) is still useful for simply getting an answer, but if that is its sole purpose in a mathematics program, then we are vastly underestimating its potential to assist both teacher and student in significant learning experiences.

Compare how mathematics was taught when you were in school to the techniques suggested in this chapter. Concentrated attention should be given to activities and the question of how children may make *appropriate* use of technology. What mathematics become "less important" because of technology? What mathematics is necessary because of technology? And what are possible because of technology? Perhaps, most important, how might a calculator or computer be used to enhance understanding and skills—not just to provide an answer?

The use of technology should be initiated with primary-age children and extended each year. For example, a young child can learn some basic keyboarding on either the calculator or computer and apply this to writing one- and two-place numbers. Middle elementary school children can use technology to discover, extend, and create patterns through a series of repeated key strokes, and older elementary and middle school children can make use of technology to explore graphs and their properties.

Calculators and computers can become tools of exploration—not replacements for skill—to enhance understanding. In this light, technology can be used to assist in choosing the most effective and efficient strategy for solving a problem, to simplify mathematical expressions by making use of order of operations or parentheses, to develop a working description of squaring a number and approximating a square root, to understand the meaning of overflow errors and the benefits of scientific notation, to examine the nature of a limit and a reason for not dividing by zero through dividing a constant by a progressively smaller value, and so on.

Calculators are an invaluable tool in the mathematics classroom. The NCTM and the National Council of Supervisors of Mathematics, among other forward-thinking professional organizations, support the use of calculators in every classroom and at every level of teaching mathematics.

The widespread impact of technology on nearly every aspect of our lives requires changes in the content and nature of school mathematics programs. In keeping with these changes, students should be able to use calculators and computers to investigate mathematical concepts and increase their mathematical understanding (NCTM, 1989).

We've introduced you to several applications of technology for the elementary and middle school classrooms. This chapter includes lesson plans that demonstrate the integration of calculators and computers in mathematics instruction. **Lesson plans are located on the CD that accompanies this text so that you may print them out and modify them. The CD also describes instructional and assessment activities for technology in grades preK–2, 3–5, and 6–8. The CD also contains a list of computer software suppliers and summaries of several different software packages and their applications to common content strands of elementary/middle school mathematics. Additional activities involving calculators and computers can be found in each of the other content chapters in the text and on the CD.**

The influences of technology on the teaching and learning of mathematics are far-reaching. As you read the remainder of this text, think of how you might use computers and/or calculators to lead students to deeper understandings of mathematical concepts. Strive to develop an indication of, and a healthy respect for, what and how technology can increase your instructional options as well as your students' learning.

TEACHING COMPETENCIES AND SELF-ASSESSMENT TASKS

1. Locate the standards related to the use of calculators and computers in the NCTM *Principles and Standards for School Mathematics*. Discuss examples of how calculators and computers might be used within a contemporary elementary/middle school mathematics classroom to meet each of the standards.

2. Locate at least three elementary or middle school problem-solving activities that incorporate the use of a calculator in the exploration process. Complete the activities and discuss how the calculator enhances each activity.

3. Use the Calculator-Based Ranger's program for matching a graph of distance as a function of time. Try to match the graph you are given by walking in front of the graph. After several attempts, write a short story that describes a child moving from one place to another with stops and other changes in speed and direction. Sketch a graph to match your story.

4. Locate and examine at least two different examples of problem-solving or exploration software. Describe how each might fit within a contemporary elementary or middle school curriculum.

5. Locate at least two different elementary or middle school–level calculators (one calculator should be a four-function calculator and the other should be a fraction calculator), and explore the features and functions available on each. Write a comparison of the calculators and their uses. For the upper grades, also examine a graphing calculator and its uses.

6. Identify at least one piece of software for each of the software types and applications listed in the chapter. State which software fits with which category and provide a justification for your choice. Examples of software types are drill and practice, tutorial, and simulation. Examples of applications are spreadsheets, databases, and word processors.

7. Locate recent articles on incorporating multimedia in elementary or middle school mathematics instruction. Report on the ways in which multimedia was used.

8. Locate a dynamic Web site that contains rich data and design an elementary or middle school–level activity incorporating the data that will require student interpretation and use.

9. Locate and examine at least two Web sites that contain lesson plans for elementary or middle school mathematics. Examine those lessons and modify them to make them appropriate for use in a classroom in which you might be the teacher.

10. Browse the Web in search of information related to your personal hobbies. Once you have found at least one relevant site, explore the links from that site to other sites. If none are given, use a search engine to generate a list of related sites. Then, use PowerPoint, Keynote, or a similar presentation tool to create a short presentation about your hobby.

chapter 5

Problem Solving and Mathematical Language

TEACHING COMPETENCIES

Upon completing this chapter, you will be able to:

- Describe the nature of a "problem" and the problem-solving process.
- State and effectively use a variety of strategies in solving problems.
- Incorporate contemporary thought on integrating problem solving into classroom instruction.
- Describe the role played by logic and reasoning in a contemporary elementary and middle school mathematics classrooms.
- State examples of inductive and deductive reasoning that commonly occur in everyday life.
- Plan and implement lessons for elementary and middle school students that incorporate problem solving, reasoning, communication, connections, and representations.

VIRTUAL MANIPULATIVES

Upon completing this chapter, you will be able to use virtual manipulatives on the accompanying CD to:

- Explore common characteristics and patterns using *Attribute Blocks*. **(VM 5.1)**
- Compare and contrast representations of patterns using *Attribute Trains*. **(VM 5.2)**
- Examine conjunctions, disjunctions, and negations using *Attribute Baseball*. **(VM 5.3)**
- Duplicate, extend, and create patterns using *Color Patterns*. **(VM 5.4)**
- Duplicate, extend, and create patterns using *Number Patterns*. **(VM 5.5)**
- Use strategies to problem solve using *Counterfeit Coins*. **(VM 5.6)**
- Use patterns and the strategy of using a simpler problem to solve a problem using *Towers of Hanoi*. **(VM 5.7)**
- Use trial and success along with observation to make predictions using *Fill and Pour*. **(VM 5.8)**
- Demonstrate persistence and a problem-solving attitude using *Number Puzzles*. **(VM 5.9)**
- Demonstrate persistence and a problem-solving attitude using *Circle-21, Circle-99, Circle-0*, and *Circle-3*. **(VM 5.10)**

Numbered CD icons throughout the chapter refer to the virtual manipulatives in this list.

There is an old adage that states, "In our lives, there is nothing certain but death and taxes." Although there may be a degree of truth in that statement, we all face many other certainties. For example, we can all be certain that we will encounter problems that influence our lives and that require us to make decisions to solve those problems. The ability to solve problems is a necessary function in our lives that includes so much decision making. Yet ongoing studies such as the National Assessment of Educational Progress as well as the Trends in International Mathematics and Science Study continue to indicate that the problem-solving abilities of children are sadly inadequate. Also, teachers often express a feeling of inadequacy when attempting to teach problem-solving techniques to children. Perhaps if we concentrate on methods of developing our own problem-solving strategies, then our efforts to assist children in improving their performances when they are faced with such tasks will not only increase but also be more effective. After all, how many times have you heard someone say that, "I was pretty good in math, but I could never solve those story problems"? But the fact is that if we can't solve real-life problems, then we really don't *know* the math. To *know* the math implies that we are able to *use* it in applied situations.

The National Council of Teachers of Mathematics (NCTM) *Principles and Standards for School Mathematics* (2000) identifies five standards that it refers to as "process" standards:

- Problem Solving
- Reasoning and Proof
- Communication
- Connections
- Representations

These process standards reflect major aspects of competency that are essential to increased sophistication of an individual's power over mathematics:

> As students learn mathematics, they will develop an increasing repertoire of problem-solving skills, a wide range of mathematical "habits of mind," and increasing sophistication in mathematical argument. Also, students should become proficient at expressing themselves mathematically, both orally and in writing, gain fluency in the language of mathematics and be able to make connections within mathematics and from mathematics to other disciplines. (NCTM, 1998, p. 46)

As you study this chapter on solving problems and using mathematical language, consider the foundation it presents and how this impacts your perspective of the material presented throughout the rest of this book.

The Nature of Problem Solving

Before continuing further, it is essential that we describe what we mean by *problem solving*. In mathematics, we sometimes equate problem solving with word or story problems that we might remember from elementary school textbooks. Although word or story problems do encompass a portion of the world of problem solving, they represent only a very small portion. As it is commonly defined in contemporary mathematics education, **problem solving** describes the process an individual uses to respond to and overcome obstacles or barriers when a solution or method of solution to a problem is not immediately obvious. Given this context, problem solving is very much an interdisciplinary activity and should not be restricted to a single unit or topic in mathematics. Throughout this book, you will spot applications of problem solving in all topic areas and suggestions for activities across many disciplines.

You may have heard statements such as "3 + 5 = □ " referred to as problems. In reality, for most this does not represent a problem, but is more aptly termed an *exercise*. This distinction is much more than a case of semantics. An **exercise** is typically solved by a collection of prescribed steps, commonly called an *algorithm*, which leads to a solution. A ***problem***, on the other hand, requires greater insight and analysis before an approach to a solution is offered. An example of a problem for a child might be, "How many sheets of paper would we need to total a weight equal to 2 pounds?" Certainly, an exercise for some people is a problem for others not because the answer is unknown, but rather because a method of determining the answer is unknown. Solving problems requires that the learner be involved in decision making, whereas answering exercises involves applying an algorithm or a set of structured step-by-step procedures. This is an important point for teachers to keep in mind, as many of the problems included in textbooks are really not problems at all; they are simply exercises that require the student to practice a skill over and over.

To clarify the nature of a problem, consider these four examples. First, a traditional textbook word problem:

> Billy has three apples and Margie has five apples. How many more apples does Margie have than Billy?

Second, a multistep textbook word problem:

> Ryan has a square garden bordered by a 36-foot fence.

If Ryan wishes to use that same fence to border a 4-foot by 9-foot rectangular garden, will he have enough fence? How much fence will be left over?

Third, a nontraditional word problem:

Marilyn and Ginny are taking turns in a game of darts on the board shown.

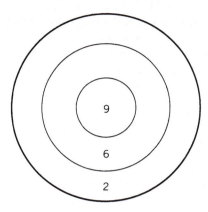

If a game is won with an exact score of 34, what is the fewest number of darts that can be thrown before a winner is declared?

Fourth, a problem situation that you may recognize from your life:

How much carpet should Jeff purchase to cover the floor?

The first two examples illustrate the important point made about problems in the previous paragraph: What is considered a problem for some may simply be an exercise for others. Although many children will quickly recognize that the first example can be solved by subtraction, others will not. Some younger children may even think that the answer is simply "yes," believing that all that was requested was a yes or no answer to the question, "Does Margie have more apples?" The second example, however, is more likely to be a problem since an immediate solution or a method of solution is not necessarily evident. Should we divide the 36 by the 4? Should we multiply the 4 and the 9 and see what we get for a product? Even though the problem makes use of knowledge of shape and perimeter, it is not a straightforward application of an algorithm. We must analyze the situation more carefully if we wish to arrive at a meaningful method of answering the question.

In the third example, still another aspect of the nature of a problem is revealed. In this case, not only must we analyze the situation carefully, but we must also be willing to create a method of attack. There is no formula that we can fit—we must apply critical reasoning if we

are to succeed without resorting to blind guessing. In this case, even when we discover that 6 is the fewest number of darts that yields a total of 34 (two 9s, two 6s, and two 2s), we must also note that the players are taking turns. Thus, a total of 11 darts is the fewest that could be thrown before a winner is declared.

The fourth example is, perhaps, one of the purest forms of a problem. How is this fourth example different from the others? In the first three, the information needed to solve the problem was present in the setting. The problem solver was asked to read the information and then decide if, when, and how to use it. In the fourth case, however, the information needed to solve the problem is not present. In fact, part of the problem is deciding what information is important when attempting to find an answer. For example, how many rooms do we wish to carpet? Does that include the hallway or entryway? Is money a factor in this decision? Is color? Is availability? These represent only a few of the real-life concerns that we may need to address as we seek a solution. In this last example, as in real life, the question came first, followed by the identification of important information, which, in turn, was followed by the collection and analysis of information and the application of information to isolate a potential solution.

It is commonly acknowledged that problem solving is a critical aspect of the education (mathematical and otherwise) of our populace and that more emphasis must be placed on developing problem-solving strategies and integrating their application across the curriculum and through the life experiences of children. The NCTM has long called for increased attention to problem solving. Nevertheless, an analysis of problem solving as presented in many elementary and middle school textbooks indicates that present attention to problem solving is woefully inadequate.

Many mathematics textbooks and, consequently, some teachers mistakenly overemphasize the role of traditional word problems in the development of problem-solving abilities. Some shortcomings common to school mathematics textbooks may include the following:

- Word problems are relegated to a single section at the end of a unit, rather than being a constant presence throughout that unit.

- Word problems are used that seem only to require the concepts studied in a particular unit rather than integrating topics from different units and different subjects.

- Word problems tend to focus on one specific interpretation of an operation, such as only "takeaway" subtraction, thereby narrowing the child's perspective of how the operation can be interpreted in different ways.

- Word problems are wr itten in such a way that children are conditioned to look for key words to interpret what to do, rather than focusing on context clues in the action that provide the real context clues in the problem.

- Word problems often oversimplify and trivialize the applications they are intended to demonstrate.

All these observations suggest that we must reexamine the ways in which we approach problem solving if we are to truly nurture thinking about mathematics. The last point in the preceding list, although not necessarily more important than the others, is of particular concern. In fact, if we attend to it effectively, we lessen the possibilities that the other weak points will occur.

Applications play a critically important role in the mathematics curriculum. Children need to see and comprehend applications of the concepts they study. Everyday uses of estimation, fractions, percents, decimals, ratios and proportions, geometry, measurement, statistics, and probability should receive at least as much attention as the concepts themselves. Applications provide a context in which a given set of skills may be practiced, as well as an opportunity to demonstrate, during motivations and follow-ups, situations in which skills are meaningfully and purposefully used. However, if these applications are presented in one- or two-sentence word problems, they are removed from everyday life and become artificial. The very aspects that make applications interesting in the first place are stripped away.

A word problem that can be solved by simply applying the mathematical operation that is currently being studied in class is not really a problem at all. A word problem that only includes information necessary for its solution is not really a challenge at all. A word problem that requires the child to copy a procedure demonstrated at the top of the page is not really a test of the child's ability to solve a problem at all. Perhaps we need to direct much of our attention away from how to solve word problems, as such, and focus more on the true nature of problem solving instead.

In life, problems do not come to us with labels and algorithms in place. We cannot count on all of Tuesday's problems to be solvable by dividing, since division is what we talked about in class on Monday. In life, we don't get advance organizers for problem solving. Instead, we begin with the question and then collect the information we believe we may need to solve the problem. We then sort out the data that are relevant to the problem, abandoning some information and, perhaps, gathering more. The approach to a solution is not necessarily well formulated; in fact, it may be quite different from the one we used to solve the last problem

we considered. It may even be a procedure that we have never tried before.

Careful selection of problems is critical to nurturing successful problem-solving abilities in children. Challenging students to think about mathematics can be difficult. Some students have simply not had to actually think about mathematics in the past, particularly if their teachers lectured and spent class time showing examples to the students. Mark Twain once said that "the lecture method of teaching is the only way I know of to get information from the teacher's notes into the students' notebook without passing through a brain!" Instead of encouraging a narrow view of problems, consider presenting problems in one or more of the following ways:

- with pictures
- without numbers
- involving manipulatives
- with more than one solution
- with real-world applications
- with no easily identifiable answer
- requiring more time to solve than one mathematics period
- requiring the collection of data
- requiring the following of specific directions
- requiring interpretation of tables and graphs
- requiring a drawing to be made
- with no solution
- with extraneous information
- requiring use of a formula
- involving logic and inference
- requiring inductive or deductive reasoning

Focusing on problem solving helps us assist the student in making generalizations. A child's innate curiosity causes him or her to pose questions such as "Why?" "When?" and "How?" Unfortunately, these questions, as common as they may be in the child's mind, often remain there, unstated—perhaps not verbalized because a previous attempt went unrewarded by the teacher. By exploring problem-solving situations, we encounter many opportunities for hypothesizing—for saying "What if?" and examining the consequences. These opportunities are too valuable to miss.

Ideas are like clay. If you want them to reflect something new and different, you must mold and shape them. It may be necessary to look at things from a new perspective—perhaps inside out or upside down. Hunch playing becomes a valued friend as you learn to try things that you suspect may not lead anywhere, but that seem to at least have a shot at progress toward a solution.

The Fill and Pour virtual manipulative located on the CD that accompanies this text provides students with the opportunity to explore the Piagetian task of conservation of volume in a manner that encourages making observations and conjectures about the influence of changing variables. Interest should be placed on how the learner approaches the problem. Does a student simply begin by apparent random guessing? Are the results obtained on each try incorporated into new solutions? Does the student comment on the relationship between the height of the liquid and the diameter of the container? For older students, is there any attempt to connect the reality of the various attempts to a more general function of height and diameter?

VM 5.8

You break rules and make rules to eventually reach conclusions that are sound. Unfortunately, students too often perceive rules—which are really no more than generalizations—as merely ways to get to a correct answer. Without proper guidance, students will neither recognize nor appreciate the role of generalizations in understanding mathematics.

Mathematical thinking is nurtured through problem-solving experiences that do not restrict a child's avenues of success to a single route. Problem solving should be systematic but not rule bound. Reliance on one method can create difficulty rather than lessen it—instead of trying to solve the problem, the student may simply try to find the "right" way to solve the problem.

By definition, divergence in approach can lead to delightful open-mindedness for alternative solutions. Fascinating discussions can result from considering what is meant by a question and how it might be answered. For example:

- How might a glass be dropped from a height of 10 feet and not break?

- How could we find out how many fish are in a lake?

- What might we need for our trip to the amusement park, and why do we need it?

- What price do we need to charge for the school spaghetti dinner to cover our expenses?

When confronting a problem, some see a challenge and some see a wall. It's the level of anxiety, blended with individual personality traits, that determines the next move. Sometimes just getting started creates a level of frustration that becomes more of a problem than the problem itself (similar to the feeling we get when we know that our room needs cleaning—the work itself isn't that difficult, but gearing up to get it done can create the anxiety). Some students fail to realize that problems are not like exercises—problems are neither straightforward nor quickly answered. Often, problems do not lend themselves to algorithms or prescribed procedures. They require novel approaches and risk

taking—the willingness to be wrong during the search for what is right.

Students require three sets of skills to solve problems: (1) skills such as computation and measuring (empirical skills), (2) skills to handle common situations (application skills), and (3) skills required to work through unfamiliar situations (thinking skills). A student's ability to solve a problem depends on many factors, such as conceptual style, organizational ability, techniques of processing information, mathematical background, desire for a solution, and confidence in the ability to tackle the problem. Students who seek a rule to follow or an algorithm to use or the key words that tell them what to do will not become proficient problem solvers. To gain power in solving problems, a student must be willing to invest in understanding the problem and learn to unravel the problem before trying to state an answer.

Children need to learn how strategies can help them work through any problem they encounter, including traditional and nontraditional word problems. If textbook word problems are too narrow in scope to require or encourage student thinking, teachers must supplement assignments with problems and investigations that incorporate several strategies in the quest to identify possible solutions. Let's explore some of the more commonly used problem-solving strategies that we should consider developing in our students.

Problem-Solving Strategies

If an appliance breaks, we may go to the storeroom or garage and retrieve a toolbox. In that box might be a screwdriver, a hammer, a wrench, a utility knife, a pair of pliers, and several other tools. As we begin the work, we may determine that a loose wire caused the problem, and a simple tightening of a screw is all that is needed to fix the problem. Or we might determine that we need to strip a wire with our utility knife before tightening it, and so forth. When the job is finished, we close the toolbox, without having used most of the tools in the kit. One could argue, at this point, that the hammer is

VM 5.10

The Circle-0 virtual manipulative on the CD that accompanies this text provides the student with a challenge that often requires a persistence and a willingness to backtrack—that is, a willingness to give up some of the gains seemingly achieved in order to reach a solution. The object of Circle-0 is to place all the numbers (using the drag-and-drop technique with the mouse) within the circles so as to make each circle to add up to 0. Some students seem to get "stuck" in the search space when things seem to be working and then fail. The level of challenge represented by the need to throw out apparently good answers in order to complete a task may be counterproductive to some students. The screen shot below is an example. Here, 5 out of 7 circles (shaded) have met the criteria: They add up to 0. There are two numbers left (−2 and −4) that must be placed in the two remaining spots (between 7 and 6) so that the remaining two circles also add up to 0. It is easy to see that neither of the two combinations of placing the remaining numbers produces the solution. Therefore, in order to reach the solution in which all the circles add up to 0, the partial solution generated so far must be sacrificed. In other words, the student must take out at least some of the numbers in the shaded circles, that is, the circles that already add up to 0.

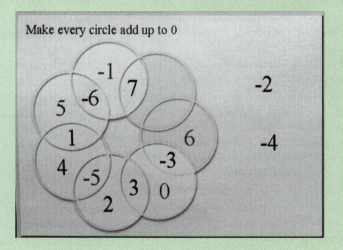

The next screen shot provides an even more dramatic example of the need to backtrack from seemingly sound answers.

In this example, all the numbers have been positioned; however, only 6 out of 7 circles add up to 0.

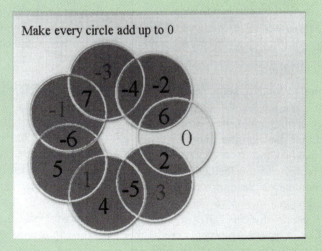

The situation can be, it seems, rather perplexing to the student. The question remains as to whether such perplexity is conducive or counterproductive to learning. What do you think?

A classic problem called the Towers of Hanoi, found in virtual manipulative form on the CD that accompanies this text, provides a good environment for a challenge that causes the student to analyze conditions and fulfill requirements necessary to complete a task. The student is presented with three towers with a certain number of disks of increasing radius stacked on one of the towers. The task is to move all the disks, one at a time, from one tower to another. The condition that must be met is that no smaller disk can be placed on top of a larger disk. Students may begin this with a trial-and-error technique but usually quickly recognize that there are some moves that are important to continued progress toward the goal. A few will notice a pattern that will assist in finding the solution no matter how many disks are used at the start.

useless because it had nothing to do with this repair job. But don't tell the homeowner that, as the very next thing to go wrong could be a loose board on the deck that needs nailing back down. The point here is that we often don't know which tool we are going to need to do a home repair, so we try to be as prepared as possible by having a full kit available to us at all times. The same is true when solving mathematics problems: We develop a "toolkit" of strategies, out of which we can pull the appropriate method for a problem that we have encountered. The richer our set of strategies is, the better we will be at addressing different types of problems when they arise.

Here are four suggestions that may help you to meet the challenge of solving problems:

1. Problem solving should be approached with the attitude of meeting an intellectual challenge rather than finishing a menial task.

2. An open-minded, initial examination of the problem helps avoid a tunnel-vision approach to the solution. Be prepared to try unusual ideas and take some risks that might lead to a dead end—often, you'll find that they don't.

3. Persistence, with thought, is often a major ally in problem solving. Take your bearings frequently. Remind yourself of where you are in the problem and what you need to do. Problem solving is not a race with a stopwatch. At times, it pays dividends to stand back and reflect.

4. reflection should not only occur during the problem-solving process, but after it as well. Look back at the problem and the solution and see if they match. Too often, we end up with a solution that doesn't answer the question asked.

RESEARCH SNAPSHOT

What are the perspectives of children on what it means to do mathematics in problem-solving classrooms?

Franke and Carey (1997) studied 36 first graders from classrooms that reflected the spirit of the reform movement in mathematics education. The children viewed mathematics as a problem-solving endeavor in which communicating mathematical thinking was an integral part of the task. They assumed a shared responsibility with the teacher for their mathematics learning. The students also explained, justified, and accepted a variety of solution strategies, valuing all solutions equally.

Are these perspectives in line with what you hope your students believe about mathematics? If the students value all solution strategies equally, what will motivate them to progress to more sophisticated strategies?

Franke, M. L., & Carey, D. A. (1997). Young children's perceptions of mathematics in problem solving environments. *Journal for Research in Mathematics Education, 28,* 8–25.

For additional research briefs, "ERIC Digests" lets you search more than 2000 short syntheses of researchon a range of education topics. The syntheses were produced by the Educational Resources InformationCenter (ERIC). Check http://www.ericfacility.net/ericdigests/index/.

Now, let's carefully examine some of those strategies we that encourage students to use to help them develop problem-solving techniques. Traditionally, a four- or five-step process has been taught to help students approach solving problems: (1) read the problem, (2) determine what is given, (3) decide what is to be found, and then (4) solve and (5) check. These steps *are* the steps that a person usually goes through in the problem-solving process, but simply recognizing these steps does not really help children solve problems.

To use an analogy, it is true that these steps to problem solving do represent the route to a solution, but they do not represent a map that will guide us along the route. That is, to solve a problem, we must go through these steps, but how do we go through them? Assuming appropriate reading skill and ability, we can all read the problem, but how do we identify what is given (especially if either too much or not enough is given)? How do we decide what is to be found? And how do we solve the problem? These are the real questions that, if answered, will provide the map for the route. The same can be said for the scientific method. Often, school science classes teach children to state a hypothesis and then design an experiment and collect data. However, in the real world of science, researchers often collect data first and then *use the data* as a basis for making a hypothesis. So, the sequence in which we go through steps—whether solving a problem or conducting research—will vary, depending on the situation.

As useful as the problem-solving process described here might be, we still need to arm the students with strategies that actually help them solve the problem. That is, what tools can students turn to when they think that they don't know what to do next? Rather than encourage them to ask the teacher or some other authority what to do next, let's teach them to recognize and apply potentially effective strategies on their own. What are some of these problem-solving strategies that we can teach children to apply?

Identifying Patterns

Children who have a background in using Attribute Blocks, classifying, looking for patterns, and extending patterns are definitely ready for solving problems by looking for and applying patterns. This problem-solving

strategy often begins in kindergarten and can be extended to all other grade levels.

If we charge $.25 for a ticket for the play, how much should we charge for 2 or 3 tickets? A pattern is developed: If 1 ticket costs $.25, then 2 tickets will cost $.25 + $.25. Three tickets will sell for $.25 + $.25 + $.25. This is a pattern. Now we can put the data into a table, as shown.

Number of tickets	1	2	3	4	5	6
Price to charge	$.25	$.50	$.75	$1.00	$1.25	$1.50

This example of looking for patterns is often coupled with the next strategy to be developed—creating tables and charts.

Creating Tables and Charts

Learning to organize data into tables and charts can help children solve problems. Consider this: I want to build a rectangular dog pen. There is a roll of fencing in the garage that I will use; it is 36 meters long. What should be the dimensions of the pen for the dog to have as much play area as possible? Children should think about the data involved in the problem and organize the information into a table. The pertinent ideas involved are perimeter, length, width, and area. Let's make a table for the problem by systematically entering data into the table. (Other types of tables would also be acceptable.)

Perimeter (in meters)	Length (in meters)	Width (in meters)	Area (in square meters)
36	17	1	17
36	16	2	32
36	15	3	45
36	14	4	56
36	13	5	65
36	12	6	72
36	11	7	77
36	10	8	80
36	9	9	81
36	8	10	80

Four virtual manipulatives Attribute Blocks, Attribute Trains, Color Patterns, and Number Patterns, located on the CD that accompanies this text, can be effectively used to provide opportunities for children to explore patterns.

After the children have made a table, discuss it with them by asking questions such as "Why does the area start to increase?" and "At what point will the area begin to decrease?" The children should discover that the greatest area is obtained when the length and width are the same. The children should generalize that a square will have more area than related rectangles with the same perimeter.

Note that, at this point, the focus should be on the *existing concepts and relationships* rather than the *answer* to the problem. Organizing data and using tables are important mathematics problem-solving strategies. The problem begins with a question, and then a technique for solving the problem is developed by using a table. Many examples that require the use of many different operations and processes should be used so that children will see the benefits of this problem-solving strategy.

Dramatization (Acting It Out)

For many years, dramatization has been used to help children understand lessons in reading, and it represents another strategy that can be effectively applied to problem solving. How many apples are in Tom's box now if Tom began with an empty box and Mary put in 3 apples and George put in 4 apples? Using dramatization, have children take the parts of Tom, Mary, and George and act out the problem.

Three apples

Four apples

If the children are functioning at the appropriate level of abstraction, ask them to write a mathematical sentence for what they observed: $3 + 4 = \square$. Which number correctly completes this number sentence? (7) What is the answer to the problem? (Tom now has 7 apples in his box.)

Make the problems gradually more complicated. All children could participate at once by providing them

with coins and challenging them to find out how many different ways they can make 10 cents.

One dime

Two nickels

One nickel
Five pennies

Ten pennies

When developmentally appropriate, children should be encouraged to write mathematical sentences to express the problem-solving situation and to use a complete sentence to answer. This practice will cut down on the careless mistakes that some students make.

Make a Drawing or Diagram

Another technique to help children solve mathematical problems is to make a drawing or diagram. Encourage children to make sketches to help them visualize spatial relationships. How many tiles will be needed to place a new floor in a given room? Draw a sketch of the room, and then draw squares to represent the tiles. This will help the children comprehend the concept and develop a technique for solving fundamental area problems. Of course, this technique should be used to develop understanding of the concept of area for figures of all shapes.

A diagram is also helpful in problems dealing with measurement situations such as "It is twice as far from city A to city B as it is from city B to city C. If all three cities are connected by roads, and if city A is 10 miles from city B, what is the shortest distance possible from city A to city C?" Of course, making a diagram can be utilized in problem-solving situations besides geometry and measurement.

Guess and Check

Another effective problem-solving strategy that can be taught to children is to guess an answer and then check the appropriateness of this guess. Children should be encouraged to make reasonable guesses and not just select a random number. For instance, ask them which single number can be used to make $4 \times \square + \square = 30$? Which number belongs in the boxes? Take a guess and then check it. Will the number 4 make the sentence true? Check: $4 \times 4 + 4 = 20$. No. Discuss with the children what they have learned. Why doesn't 4 make the sentence true? (Because using 4 gives an answer that is too small.) Then what should we try? Do you want to try 5? $4 \times 5 + 5 = 25$. Discuss the guess again. Is the value 5 closer to the correct number? How do you know? Which number do you want to try now? Should we try 10? (That would be too much.) Why? Should we try 6? $4 \times 6 + 6 = 30$. This checks out, so 6 is the number that fits into the box. It's important to note that "guess and check" is really more like "guess, check, and revise your guess based on what you've learned."

Estimation

Estimation is a tool that has always had a significant application in problem solving. It may be true in everyday life that we use estimation more frequently than we perform exact computations. Estimation often provides an answer that is sufficient for the question asked. Estimation can also be an effective tool when the numbers are too "messy" to compute an exact answer. Estimation is, at times, the only way to get any answer at all. Estimation also provides a means of determining whether an answer is a reasonable or unreasonable one. The technological age places new emphasis on estimation in the mathematics program. Calculators and computers can calculate much more quickly and efficiently than we can. However, occasional malfunctions of equipment and poorly selected or incorrectly entered data are but a few reasons we might arrive at absurd responses from the technological devices we use. Estimation should be used to verify that such computations are, at least, reasonable answers to the problem as we understand it.

For example, suppose that it is late in the evening on the last night of the school play and we wish to know how much money we collected. We're certain that we did well; in fact, we know we sold 321 tickets, but we don't want to take time to count the receipts until morning. If we sold 294 adult tickets at $7.50 each and 27 youth tickets at $4.00 each, how much money was received? Using a calculator, we come up with a total of $1378.50. Does this amount seem reasonable? We can check by using approximately 300 adult tickets at $7.00 ($2100.00), and we quickly see that a mistake must have been made with the calculator. (Determine what that mistake might have been.)

Let's consider the same problem and the same question, but apply a slightly different interpretation of estimation to help us. As before, we wish to determine about how much we collected, but a calculator is not readily available. Instead, we elect to use numbers that approximate the real situation. That means, for example, that we sold about 300 adult tickets for about $7.00 and about 30 youth tickets for $4.00. Thus we should have about $2220.00 ($2100.00 plus $120.00) when we count the receipts in the morning.

When we approximate numbers, we sometimes use a specific method frequently referred to as *rounding*. This method can take many forms but is most commonly stated as "Five or more, round up; less than five, round down." If, for instance, we strictly followed this rule in our school play problem, we might have rounded the 294 adult tickets to 290 (if rounding to the nearest 10) or to 300 (if rounding to the nearest 100). We would round the youth tickets to 30 (to the nearest 10) or to 0 (to the nearest 100).

It is not difficult to imagine how following a specific rounding rule might lead to less-than-desirable approximations. Consider the task that a bank might face in rounding all of its average daily balances to the nearest dollar. Of course, the bank wants to ensure that it does not lose money because of this rounding process. If the computer is programmed to use the "five or more, round up" method, then it is possible that the estimate of total deposits will be more than they actually are. In this case, the bank would end up paying more interest than it is required to pay.

To illustrate this, consider a hypothetical bank that had only four accounts—$16, $28, $45, and $37. If the

The Number Puzzle virtual manipulative on the CD that accompanies this text provides the student with a challenge that often requires a guess-and-check approach that benefits from revision based on the results obtained from an initial guess. For example, if numbers are tried that yield an answer greater than required, an adjustment in the guess is made by choosing as the next guess one that is less by some reasonable amount. It is important for the student to reflect on what has happened in previous trials before making a new conjecture.

VM 5.9

interest were computed by rounding to the nearest $10, then the bank would be figuring interest on $20, $30, $50, and $40 (a total of $140) instead of on the actual amount of $126. This may not seem like much in this case, but imagine the losses a bank would incur if it followed this procedure for thousands of accounts with thousands of dollars in each account!

A more appropriate alternative rounding rule to use in this case might be, "If the amount is even, round up—if odd, round down." This means that roughly half of all accounts will be rounded up, and half down. In our simple example, the rounded total would be $120—a closer estimate to the actual amount. Some computers are even programmed to round down when the digit is 0 to 4, round up when the digit is 6 to 9, and if the digit is 5, round down if the digit before it is odd and up if the previous digit is even. In this case, 45 would round to 50, but 75 would round to 70. What other possible rounding rules can you create, and in which situations might they be most appropriate or effective?

Another common rounding strategy is often referred to as *front-end estimation*. This method is frequently employed when a range of answers is all that is needed. For example, if we wanted a rough idea of the total cost to repair a car that had $437 damage to the front fender, $223 damage to the side mirror, and $589 to the left side, then we could use front-end estimation to get a low total of $400 + $200 + $500 ($1100) or a high total of $500 + $300 + $600 ($1400).

Solve a Simpler Problem

Our last example in the previous section shows another aspect of estimating in problem solving: Sometimes it makes sense to solve a simpler, related problem when searching for a solution to a more complex problem. In a sense, this strategy involves turning a problem into an exercise (a distinction made earlier in this chapter). In our example, it would have been much more difficult to show the effects of a different rounding technique if we had used real figures from a real bank's files. There would have been too many accounts and too many different dollar and cent amounts to deal with easily. The point being made and the reasoning behind it were better explained by creating a simpler situation

that mirrored the more challenging real life one. Often, the use of a simpler, but related, problem will point the way to a method of finding a solution that can be applied to the original problem.

For example, consider the following problem: A person should drink about $2\frac{3}{4}$ liters of water every day. How much water should 5 people take on a $6\frac{1}{2}$ day camping trip? If there is some confusion as to how to approach this, change the figures to 3 liters of water, 5 people, and 6 days, and restate the problem. The use of less-intimidating numbers may lighten the perceived level of difficulty of the problem. You may even want to temporarily eliminate some of the additional considerations as you search for a solution method. In this case, for example, how would you find out how much water was needed for just one person?

The discussion of the techniques of estimating to solve a problem gives rise to another important concern. Sometimes approximations of an answer are all that we can reasonably expect to achieve. Some problem-solving situations do not lend themselves to exact answers. Children need experience with problem situations in which approximations are an appropriate answer. For example, how many jellybeans are in a gallon container? Children could count the number of jellybeans they can place into a half-pint jar and then multiply to approximate the number of jellybeans in a gallon container. If a half-pint container is not available, any small container may be used. Count the number of jellybeans in one small full container, and then count the number of times that the container must be filled to fill the gallon container. Similar estimating techniques can be used to estimate the number of blades of grass on a football field, the number of windows in a skyscraper, or the area of a playground.

Working Backward

Another strategy that can lead us to a solution to a problem is to look at it from another perspective—working backward. The dart game problem we referred to earlier in this chapter offers one example of this technique. Recall that we needed an exact total of 34 to win on this dartboard, and that we wanted the fewest number of tosses.

Sometimes it makes sense to solve a simpler, related problem when searching for a solution to a more complex problem. This is certainly the case with examples from the Counterfeit Coin virtual manipulative, found on the CD that accompanies this text. The Eight-Coin problem is quite easy to solve and leads to the strategy of comparing weights of undetermined coins with known good coins. The Challenge problem is famous and appropriately named. Good Luck!

VM 5.6

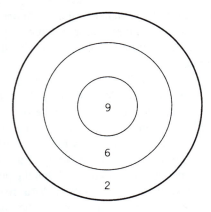

We can begin at the end, that is, with our total of 34 and then subtract the largest amount possible on a toss, 9, to get 25. Is there a way to get 25 that uses another 9? Yes, for example, one 9 and four 4s. Subtract another 9 to get 16. Is there a way to get 16 that uses another 9? No, one 9 means we need 7 more, which we can't get with just 6s and 2s. Therefore, we can throw two darts and get a total of 18 points. Thus we need 16 more points made up of just 6s and 2s. So the fewest number of darts, by one person, to get exactly 34 is two 9s, two 6s, and two 2s.

Working backward can also be used as an effective strategy in many logic problems. Consider a game in which the loser has to double each opponent's chips. After three rounds of the game, you know that each player has 8 chips. You also know that player A lost the first round, player B lost the next round, and player C lost the third round. How many chips did each player have at the start of the game? We begin with the end; that is, we know each player had 8 chips after the third round and that player C lost that round. Thus players A and B must have each had 4 chips at the end of round 2, while player C must have had 16. Since player B lost round 2, we know that before that, player A must have had 2 chips and player C had 8, with B having 14. Finally, since player A lost the first round, we know that the game must have begun with player B having 7 chips, player C having 4, and player A having 13. Now, to check our solution, we play the game as described.

As we hope you have noted by now, you will certainly have greater success in problem solving by mixing and matching problem-solving strategies to serve your needs. In the chip problem, it might be beneficial to your understanding if you not only work backward but also use objects or a diagram to act it out. This leads us back to perhaps the most effective problem-solving approach of all—open-minded brainstorming and divergent thinking on the part of the problem solver. If we broaden our focus, we are much more likely to identify given and needed information, check for hidden assumptions, and account for all possible answers.

As children develop problem-solving abilities, the teacher must constantly remind them to apply basic ideas in the process of solving problems, as follows:

1. Read the problem several times and restate it to make sure you understand the problem.

2. Think about the relationship between the information given in the problem and what is being asked.

3. Translate the problem, if appropriate, into a mathematical sentence that expresses this relationship.

4. Check the mathematical sentence with the original problem.

5. Find the solution of the mathematical sentence.

6. Write a sentence that translates the mathematics back into English.

Approaching Word Problems Effectively

For children to develop successful problem-solving techniques, instruction must begin early and be constantly nurtured as each new mathematical concept is introduced and developed. The establishment of problem-solving techniques must begin in the primary grades: First, discuss everyday situations that require mathematics, such as "How many cups will be needed for the children at two tables if there are four children at one table and five at another?" In this way, children will begin to relate mathematics to real-life situations.

As children begin to learn to read, they can be given problems using rebuses. A *rebus* is a picture that is substituted for a word. Study the example:

I have 2 🪁

You have 1 🪁

How many 🪁 in all?

This example should be answered in a complete sentence. A child might print and use a rebus such as:

There are 3 🪁 in all.

Make sure that the picture used for a rebus can be easily drawn by children. Do not use animals or other objects that are difficult for children to draw. Stickers may also be used as rebuses.

In these first steps to solving word problems, have the children develop good habits right from the beginning. Children should read and reread an example before beginning work on paper. If appropriate, ask that an equation be written for each example (even if the word problem is easily solved), and accept only complete answers. You are teaching a technique as well as how to obtain correct answers. For instance, consider this example:

Do not accept only a written "3" for the solution to this example. The full equation $2 + 1 =$ should be written, and the solution should be given as "There are 3 in all." Use of this procedure encourages children to think about the reasonableness of their solution. Each solution is a complete spoken or written sentence that must make sense in response to the question the children are trying to answer.

The following examples suggest how mathematical sentences may be written for other word problems:

Bob has 32 marbles. He wins 17 more marbles in a game.

How many marbles does Bob have now?

We can represent the problem as a mathematical sentence this way:

To solve the problem, we must find a solution—in this case another way to say $32 + 17$, since our mathematical sentence is an equation:

$$32 + 17 = 49$$

Bob has 49 marbles.

Now look at another example:

Bob has a certain number of marbles. He won 23 marbles in a game today. He now has 47 marbles. How many marbles did Bob have before?

What kind of mathematical sentence can we use to represent this story problem? Some children might write addition sentences, and others might write subtraction sentences.

$$\Box + 23 = 47$$
$$47 - 23 = \Box$$
$$\Box = 47 - 23$$
$$23 + \Box = 47$$

Although the first sentence listed best fits the language and action of the problem statement, each of these mathematical sentences is an acceptable representation of the story problem. Examples such as this show the flexibility of thinking and interpretation and the variety of approaches to any problem that contemporary mathematics emphasizes. Students should be challenged to come up with more than one mathematical sentence for an example.

Here are two more problems to consider:

How many eggs are there in 3 dozen? How many different mathematical sentences can you write for this problem?

$$3 \times 12 = \Box$$
$$12 \times 3 = \Box$$

If each of 32 children in a class has a desk, and the desks are arranged in rows with 8 children in each row, how many rows of desks are there in the classroom? How many different mathematical sentences may be written for this problem?

$$32 \div 8 = \Box$$
$$32 \div \Box = 8$$
$$8 \times \Box = 32$$
$$\Box \times 8 = 32$$

As children learn to represent word problems as mathematical sentences, the teacher should check their work carefully. Sometimes children have difficulty reading and comprehending the problems, and this difficulty may incorrectly be assumed to be a lack of mathematical ability.

There are many different types of problems for which we must learn to write mathematical sentences. Let's look at more examples. Compare the position of the unknown part in each of the following mathematical sentences and its relation to the action suggested in the English sentence.

1. Jon had three football cards. Lila gave Jon her four football cards. How many football cards does Jon have in all?

Mathematical sentence: $3 + 4 = \square$

● Answer: Jon has seven football cards in all.

2. Bonnie collects seashells. After Sally gave Bonnie two shells, Bonnie then had eight shells. How many shells did Bonnie have at the beginning?

Mathematical sentence: $\square + 2 = 8$

● Answer: Bonnie had six shells at the start.

3. Joy had three pencils. George gave Joy the pencils he owed her, and now Joy has eight pencils. How many pencils did George owe Joy?

Mathematical sentence: $3 + \square = 8$

● Answer: George owed Joy five pencils.

4. Millie had five rings. She gave three of the rings to Sue. How many rings does Millie have left?

Mathematical sentence: $5 - 3 = \square$

● Answer: Millie has two rings left.

5. Karen had seven pictures made of her teacher. Karen gave some of the pictures to other classmates. When Karen counted the number of pictures she had left, she found three. How many pictures did Karen give away?

Mathematical sentence: $7 - \square = 3$

● Answer: Karen gave away four pictures of her teacher.

6. Mike had some Matchbox cars. He gave five of the cars to Jon. Mike had four Matchbox cars left. How many Matchbox cars did Mike have at the beginning?

Mathematical sentence: $\square - 5 = 4$

● Answer: Mike had nine Matchbox cars at the beginning.

7. How many eggs are in four dozen eggs?

Mathematical sentence: $4 \times 12 = \square$

● Answer: There are forty-eight eggs in four dozen.

8. Ted will need twenty-four balloons for his birthday party. If eight balloons are in a package, how many packages of balloons will Ted need to buy?

Mathematical sentence: $24 = \square \times 8$

● Answer: Ted will need to buy three packages of balloons.

9. There are thirty-six chairs set up for a play in our classroom. There are four rows of chairs. How many chairs are in each row?

Mathematical sentence: $36 = 4 \times \square$

● Answer: There are nine chairs in each row.

10. Hank's mother gave him twelve cookies. If Hank shares the cookies equally with two other friends, how many cookies will each of the three boys have?

Mathematical sentence: $12 \div 3 = \square$

● Answer: Hank and his friends will receive four cookies each.

There are still other types of problems that children must learn to solve. In many cases, textbooks provide skill-based exercises first and then follow these questions with applied word problems later in the section, at the end of the unit, or in a separate chapter on "applications." Rather than waiting for the end of a unit of instruction (or a separate unit altogether), provide children with opportunities to solve problems *each day* so that they will begin to develop techniques in solving problems and will maintain those skills.

Another technique that has proven successful is to write a story at the top of a page and then ask a series of questions about the story at the bottom of the page. In such cases, a "story" problem lives up to its billing—it really is a story, rather than just a sentence or two with a question mark at the end. In that sense, these story problems are closer to what we actually face in everyday life. For example:

Martha is planning her twelfth birthday party. She will be 15 years old that day. She wants to invite nine of her friends to share the party with her. Of course, she will want to include her three younger brothers, her mother, and her father. Martha would like to give each child three balloons. They will play games at the party. Two teams will be formed to play the peanut relay game, and there will be four teams formed to play Twister. Help Martha plan her birthday party by answering the following questions. Remember to write a mathematical sentence for each example and to write a complete sentence to answer each question.

1. If all of those invited attend the birthday party, how many will be at the party?

2. How many children will attend the party?

3. How many balloons will Martha need?

4. How many children will be on each team when they play the peanut relay game?

5. How many children will be on each team when Twister is played?

6. How many years did Martha not have a birthday party?

7. How tall will Martha be on her fifteenth birthday?

8. How many boys will be at the birthday party?

Note that there are not sufficient data for the children to answer all of the questions: Questions 7 and 8 cannot be answered from the information given.

Logic and Reasoning

Problem solving and decision making go very much hand-in-hand. The analysis of information and the weighing of affecting factors help us decide to take one course of action over another. As the student progresses in mathematics, logic will become increasingly important in his or her mathematical thinking. The student will wonder how one can be sure that a given statement is always true (or false) and will become more and more critical of the reasons that are offered as justification for mathematical statements. Eventually, this will lead to the exploration of the notion of proof, both formal proof and proof by counterexample.

As our society evolves, we need more insight and understanding to comprehend, for instance, statements made by politicians and advertisers. Knowledge of the nature of logical reasoning will provide a sound base for children to analyze claims critically.

From an early age, children are exposed to television commercials that use reasoning in their presentations. Consumers must carefully analyze the logic employed in these commercials and other sales pitches to ascertain whether fallacious reasoning is being used to sell the product or convince them of its value. For example, students at a young age can be sensitized to the truth or falsity of quantified statements such as "All of the blocks are red" or "Some of the chairs are being used." As their use of language grows, they can explore the negation of simple statements such as the negation of "blue" is "not blue." With increased sophistication, they can realize that the negation, or opposite, of "All horses run" is not "No horses run," but instead is "Some horses do not run."

The use of computers has brought about renewed interest in the study of logic as well, as computer programs require logical, step-by-step reasoning. However, logic is usually not studied as a separate topic in elementary or middle school. Rather, logic is treated as a tool for helping children understand other concepts such as data analysis. In the same spirit, symbolic logic is seldom studied formally, but the underlying principles are explored—at a low level of abstraction.

Logic is implicit in the structural approach used in contemporary mathematics programs. Children use logical reasoning more and more as they progress from the primary grades through the intermediate grades and into high school. At the intermediate level, children are more conscious of the way in which statements are related to one another, and they become more clearly aware of how they reason their way to solutions of problems.

The Language of Logic

In everyday speaking and writing, we make frequent use of compound statements by joining two simple statements with a connective. **Simple statements** are statements such as the following:

1. The sky is clear.

2. It is cold.

3. Grass is green.

4. It is cloudy.

5. It is raining.

Each of these statements contains a noun phrase and a verb phrase.

We can use connectives such as *and; or; if...*, *then...*; and so on, to form compound statements from simple statements. For example, we can use these connectives and the simple statements just listed to form the following **compound statements**:

The sky is clear, and it is cold.

It is cold, or it is raining.

If it is raining, then it is cloudy.

These are examples taken from our everyday language. We also have simple statements and compound statements in mathematics. For example, consider these statements:

$$2 < 3 \text{ and } 3 < 4$$
$$2 < \pi \text{ or } 4 < \pi$$
$$\text{If } 7 > x, \text{ then } 8 > x.$$

A compound statement formed by joining two simple sentences with the connective *and* is called a **conjunction**. A conjunction is true if both of its components are true. If either component (or both) is false, the conjunction is considered false.

Consider the compound statement

$$5 + 4 = 9 \text{ and } 6 - 2 = 5$$

Is this statement true or false? Although the first sentence is true, the entire statement is false; the connective *and* requires that both of the statements involved be true for the entire statement to be true. What can we say about the following compound statement?

Rectangles have four sides, and triangles have three angles.

This statement is true, since both of its component statements are true.

A compound statement formed by joining two simple statements with the connective *or* is called a **disjunction**. In everyday speaking and writing, the connective *or* is sometimes used to mean "one or the other, but not both." When *or* is used in this way, it is being used in the exclusive sense. In mathematics, the word *or* is always used in the inclusive sense to mean "either or both." If either (or both) of the components of a disjunction is true, the disjunction is true; otherwise, the disjunction is false.

Consider these mathematical statements:

$$6 + 22 = 28 \text{ or } 1 - 1 = 1$$

$$5 > 4 \text{ or } 2 > 2$$

$$\frac{4}{8} = \frac{2}{4} \text{ or } \frac{1}{3} > \frac{1}{5}$$

Each of these disjunctions is true, since in each case one or both of the components are true. The following disjunction is false, since neither of its components is true:

Triangles are squares or $5 = 6$.

One simple way to teach children about the proper use of *and* and *or* is to have the class seated and ask them to stand up if "you are 10 years old *or* if you are a girl." After sitting back down, ask them to stand up if "you are 10 years old *and* you are a girl." Children will quickly see that they must fall into both categories—10 years old and be a girl—to stand up in the latter example, while they need to meet only one of the qualifications to stand up in the first instance. An interesting discussion can follow, in which children talk about the fact that they could be both 10 years old *and* a girl but still stand up in the first case.

The next kind of compound statement we consider is the conditional statement. Conditional statements are fundamental to mathematics since they provide the language and the logic to evaluate conjectures or hypotheses. An example of a conditional statement is, "If it is raining, then it is cloudy." In general, a **conditional statement** is a statement of the form "If P, then Q," where P and Q are used to stand for component statements.

To discover how conditional statements are judged true or false, let us consider the following promise that one friend might make to another:

If it rains, then I will drive you home.

Think of a promise that is kept as a true statement and of a promise that is broken as a false statement. Let us consider the possible cases. Suppose it does indeed rain and the person who made the promise does drive his friend home. In this case the promise has clearly been kept. (The statement is true.)

Next, suppose it rains and the person does not drive his friend home. Has the promise been kept or broken? Clearly, it has been broken. (The statement is false.)

Now suppose it does not rain, but the person drives his friend home anyway. Certainly the promise has not been broken, so we may as well say that it was kept. (The statement is true.)

One more possibility remains—the case in which it does not rain and the friend doesn't get driven home. It would not be fair to say that the original promise was broken. (The statement is true.)

Notice that the promise was broken only when the first statement was true and the second statement was false. Thus, we can say that a conditional statement is false only when the first statement (sometimes called the *antecedent*) is true and the second statement (sometimes called the *consequent*) is false. In all other cases, it is true.

Conditional statements (sometimes called *implications*) are quite significant; they form the basis for structured reasoning and cause-and-effect arguments. If–then statements also play an important role in geometry. For example, "If the base angles of a triangle are equal, then the sides opposite those angles are equal."

All the connectives we have examined are used to join two single statements to form a new, compound statement. The word *not* is also used to obtain one statement from another, called the statement's **negation**. When the word *not* is used for this purpose, it is frequently expressed by using the symbol $\sim$ and written in front of the statement to which it applies. Thus we could write, "It is not raining" as

$$\sim (\text{It is raining})$$

Notice that some familiar mathematical statements could also be written in a different form with this symbol. Thus, "3 is not less than 2" could be written as

$$\sim (3 < 2)$$

Words such as *some, all*, and *none* are examples of logical **quantifiers**. Quantifiers help us express ideas of quantity clearly. The quantifiers *all* and *none* are used to make sweeping statements to the effect that such and such a thing is true of every number or geometric figure. The quantifier *some* is used when we wish to claim the existence of at least one thing of a given sort. ("Some real number is equal to its own square" is an example of such a statement.)

A main purpose of logic is judging the validity of arguments. By *argument*, we mean a chain of reasoning designed to show that if certain statements called *premises* are true, then a final statement called the *conclusion* of the argument is necessarily true. We say that an argument is *valid* if there is no way for the premises to be true and the conclusion false. If the truth of the conclusion is not guaranteed by the truth of the premises, the argument is said to be *invalid*.

Consider this argument:

If it is snowing, then it is cold.

It is snowing.

_____

Therefore, it is cold.

This argument has two premises (the two statements written above the line). The conclusion of the argument is the statement written below the line. Is it possible for the premises to be true but the conclusion false? (No.) Therefore, the argument is a valid argument. As a matter of fact, every argument similar to this one is valid. That is, arguments of the form

If *P*, then *Q*

P

_____

Therefore, *Q*

are valid no matter which statements we may put in place of the letters *P* and *Q*.

Now consider this example. Is this a valid argument?

All dogs are animals.

Bambi is an animal.

_____

Therefore, Bambi is a dog.

Our everyday experience refutes this argument. Since the truth of both premises does not guarantee the truth of the conclusion, we know that the argument is invalid.

What role should logic play in the elementary and/or middle grades mathematics program? Mathematical logic is a field of study in its own right. It should be obvious that a child age 4 can speak grammatically correct sentences even though he or she has not studied English grammar. The child will occasionally make mistakes and will need correction, but, eventually, the child will become familiar with grammar. This will include inventing sentences, some of them rather complex. Nevertheless, the child will need to know how to make communication clear and consistent with standard English usage.

The analogy of the development of language with the development of logic should be easy to see. A careful teacher can do much to develop a child's capacity for logical reasoning. The child needs many experiences to discover how to avoid faulty reasoning. The teacher may find that some children in grades 5 or 6 are ready for an elementary discussion of compound sentences and quantifiers. Many children will not be ready to consider these abstract concepts explicitly. As always, it is the teacher's job to assess the needs of individual students and give sensitive guidance based on awareness of these needs.

The Language of Mathematics

Let's close this chapter by expanding on the notion that logic and logical reasoning are intertwined with mathematics and problem solving to assist us in communicating decisions we make. One of the most important ways in which we communicate with each other is through language. In language arts, children learn to construct complete, meaningful English sentences. We learn that to be complete, a sentence must express at least one complete idea. To convey ideas, we learn to use particular patterns of words to form complete sentences.

Mathematics, too, is a form of language and in some respects can be compared with the English language. In English, we express ideas by symbols called *words*, which are arranged in patterns to form sentences. In mathematics, we express ideas by mathematical symbols, arranged in meaningful patterns called **mathematical sentences**. Just as we observe certain conventions in writing sentences in English, we follow certain rules in constructing sentences in mathematics, too.

In general, the language of mathematics uses four categories of symbols: symbols for ideas (numbers and elements), symbols for relations (which indicate how ideas are connected or related to one another), symbols for operations (which indicate what is done with the ideas), and symbols for punctuation (which indicate the order in which the mathematics is to be completed).

To express a complete thought, a declarative English sentence requires, as a minimum, a noun phrase and a verb phrase. Consider the sentence "The girl is running." This sentence has both a noun phrase ("The girl") and a verb phrase ("is running"). If we had just said, "The girl," this would not have been a complete sentence, because we would not have been expressing a complete thought (no verb phrase). Similarly, "is running" is not a complete sentence because these words by themselves do not express a complete thought (no noun phrase).

Mathematical sentences, too, require a particular structure. An examination of various mathematical sentences should suggest ideas about the structure of mathematical sentences in general. Examine the following mathematical sentences carefully:

$$2 + 4 > 5$$

$$\square \div 7 = 2$$

$$\frac{1}{2} + \frac{1}{4} = \frac{3}{4}$$

$$3 \times (n + 4) = (3 \times n) + (3 \times 4)$$

First we examine how these mathematical sentences should be read; then we will study the common characteristics of mathematical sentences.

$2 + 4 > 5$ is read, "Two add four is greater than five."

$\square \div 7 = 2$ is read, "What number divided by seven is equal to two?"

$\frac{1}{2} + \frac{1}{4} = \frac{3}{4}$ is read, "One-half add one-fourth is equal to three-fourths."

$3 \times (n + 4) = (3 \times n) + (3 \times 4)$ is read, "Three times the quantity n add 4 is equal to three times n added to three times four."

Is there some common characteristic of these sentences? It should become clear through comparison that each sentence has a particular pattern. Each sentence consists of two or more names for numbers joined together by a relation symbol.

Consider the mathematical sentence "$2 + 4 = 6$." This sentence contains number symbols on the left (an expression composed of two number symbols and an operation symbol, $2 + 4$) and a number symbol on the right, 6, joined by a relation symbol ($=$). But none of these three symbols or expressions forms a sentence by itself, just as neither "John" nor "runs" forms a sentence by itself. However, the expression "$2 + 4 = 6$" is a mathematical sentence, just as "John runs" is an English sentence, because it expresses a complete thought.

The English sentence "There are seven days in a week" would be classified as true. The sentence "There are 29 days in a week" would be classified as false. In the same way, mathematical sentences can be classified as true or false. The mathematical sentence "$7 < 3$" would be called false. The sentence "$4 = 3 + 1$" would be called true.

Suppose someone wrote, "He was president of the United States." This is a complete sentence, but we cannot judge it to be true or false until we know who "he" is. What about the following sentences?

1. Theodore Roosevelt was president of the United States.

2. Mickey Mouse was president of the United States.

Both are complete sentences, and both contain enough information to be judged true or false, since in both sentences a name has been substituted for "he." Thus we can judge sentence (1) to be true and sentence (2) to be false.

Now look at these mathematical sentences:

1. $\square + 7 = 13$

2. $6 + 7 = 13$

3. $14 + 7 = 13$

Sentence (3) is a complete mathematical sentence, that is, two number expressions joined by a relation symbol. But we cannot judge the sentence to be true or false until we know what number the placeholder represents. In sentence (4) the number 6 has replaced the placeholder. Thus we have enough information to judge (4) to be true. Sentence (5) is clearly false.

Mathematical sentences that cannot be judged true or false, such as $\square + 7 = 13$, are called **open sentences**. Sentences such as (4) or (5), which contain enough information to be judged true or false, are called **mathematical statements** (or **closed sentences**).

When we write an open mathematical sentence, it is necessary to indicate in some way that a numeral is missing. Very often a frame or placeholder is used to show that one or more numerals are missing. The following are some typical placeholders used in elementary programs:

$$\triangledown \quad \triangle \quad \bigcirc \quad \square \quad \pentagon$$

The idea of using figures such as these to hold the place of missing symbols in mathematical sentences is developed early in the primary grades and is an important underpinning for a more formal study of algebra. As an introduction to this idea, the teacher can write a simple sentence on a sheet of construction paper:

$$\boxed{2 + 3 = 5}$$

After children have seen this sentence, the teacher cuts out one of the numerals, leaving a box-shaped opening:

$$\boxed{2 + \square = 5}$$

Children can see that numbers (on box-shaped pieces of paper) can be placed in the box to complete the sentence. Sentences such as the following can provide computational drill and familiarize children with placeholders in mathematical sentences:

$\square + 3 = 8$	$7 - 3 = \triangle$
$\bigcirc + 5 = 12$	$8 \div \bigcirc = 4$
$3 + \square = 10$	$3 \times \diamondsuit = 27$

Later, children can examine sentences with missing relation symbols and supply the missing symbols:

$$3 + 2 \bigcirc 4 + 1 \qquad \oslash \text{ or } \ominus \text{ or } \oslash$$
$$14 \div 7 \bigcirc 10 \div 1 \qquad \oslash \text{ or } \oslash \text{ or } \oslash$$
$$3 \times 7 \bigcirc 2 \times 9 \qquad \oslash \text{ or } \oslash \text{ or } \oslash$$

Missing operation signs can be supplied in the same way:

$$8 \bigcirc 2 = 10 \qquad \oplus$$
$$9 - 7 = 10 \triangle 5 \qquad \triangle$$
$$6 = 9 \triangle 3 \qquad \triangle$$
$$18 \triangle 2 = 12 \triangle 3 \qquad \triangle$$

Such exercises provide vital reinforcement of computational skills while teaching the meaning of operations and relations.

As children become familiar with sentences that contain frames, they can be led to see that letters can also be used as placeholders. Letters that are used in this way are called *variables*; for example, $3 + n = 8$. What numeral can replace n to make the sentence a true statement? (5) As children develop a more sophisticated concept of placeholders, they should understand that when a particular placeholder is used more than once in the same sentence, it represents the same value each time. For example, the open sentence

$$\Box + \Box = 8$$

indicates that the same numeral is to be used in both boxes:

$$\boxed{4} + \boxed{4} = 8$$

This same concept is also valid in algebra. A given letter represents the same value wherever it occurs in any one problem.

Some traditional elementary arithmetic programs tend to disregard all mathematical sentences except those using the relation symbol (=), "is equal to." Consider, for example, a typical simple story problem:

If John is 45 inches tall and Jim is 48 inches tall, how much taller is Jim than John?

This problem would usually be solved in the following way:

$$\begin{array}{r} 48 \\ -45 \\ \hline 3 \end{array}$$

"Jim is 3 inches taller than John."

This problem, as traditionally introduced, merely involves the translation of an English sentence into a simple subtraction problem. It can be thought of, in this sense, as nothing more than a simple computation with words wrapped around it! However, in a contemporary elementary mathematics class, the variety of ways of expressing the relations involved should be emphasized. The following are some examples of true statements that can be made from the information given in the story problem:

$48 - 45 = 3$	Jim is 3 inches taller than John.
$45 + 3 = 48$	John's height plus 3 inches equals Jim's height.
$48 > 45$	Jim is taller than John.
$45 < 48$	John is shorter than Jim.
$45 \neq 48$	John is not the same height as Jim.

At this point, we can begin to classify mathematical sentences according to the relation symbols in the sentences. We have seen sentences of this type called equations. An **equation** is a mathematical sentence in which two expressions are joined by an equal sign:

$$8 - 3 = 4 + 1$$

The equal sign indicates that the expression on the left of the sign names the same number as the expression on the right. In the preceding sentence, 8–3 names the same number as $4 + 1$.

If the expression on the left names a number different from the one on the right, we can use the symbol $\neq$ ("is not equal to") to make a true mathematical sentence. For example, $9 \div 3$ is 3 and $3 \times 4 = 12$. Therefore $9 \div 3$ and 3×4 name two different numbers, and we can write

$$9 \div 3 \neq 3 \times 4$$

We can use the relation symbol $>$ (which means "is greater than") and the symbol $<$ (which means "is less than") to express the relationship with greater precision:

$$9 \div 3 < 3 \times 4$$
$$3 \times 4 > 9 \div 3$$

Sentences of this kind are examples of **inequalities**. We also call $9 \div 3 \neq 3 \times 4$ an inequality.

The inequality symbol ($\geq$) expresses "is greater than or equal to," and the inequality symbol ($\leq$) expresses "is less than or equal to."

$n \geq 5$ is read "n is greater than or equal to five."

$m \leq 10 + 15$ is read "m is less than or equal to ten add fifteen."

Other inequality symbols are the following:

$\ngtr$	is not greater than
$\nless$	is not less than
$\ngeq$	is not greater than or equal to
$\nleq$	is not less than or equal to

Here are some examples of sentences that use these symbols:

$4 \not> 5$	Four is not greater than five.
$p \not< 10$	p is not less than 10.
$q \not\geq 5$	q is not greater than or equal to five.
$10 \not\leq 4 + 5$	Ten is not less than or equal to four add five.

The symbols for the two fundamental operations of arithmetic and their inverse operations are also part of the grammar of mathematics:

+   addition

−   subtraction

×   multiplication

÷   division

These symbols indicate operations to be performed but do not, by themselves, form mathematical sentences. They indicate operations to be performed on numbers, not relations between numbers. For example, the expression

$$(4 + 3) - (6 \div 2)$$

indicates several operations to be performed. If these operations are performed, giving $7 - 3$, or 4, we see that we have renamed the original expression. Thus, another name for $(4 + 3) - (6 \div 2)$ is 4.

When several operations are to be performed but no symbols are included to indicate the order in which the operations should be accomplished, multiplication and division should be evaluated from left to right and then addition and subtraction from left to right. Children should learn this important **order of operations**. Consider this example: $2 + 3 \times 4$. If 2 is added to 3 and then multiplied by 4, the answer is 20. If 3 and 4 are multiplied first and then 2 is added, the answer becomes 14. Following the mathematical order of operations, 14 is the only correct answer. So that there can be no mistake in the order of operations, we may choose to use parentheses and write $2 + (3 \times 4)$. However, if we really intend to add 2 and 3 first and then multiply the sum by 4, we should write $(2 + 3) \times 4$; then the answer would be 20.

On a calculator, this discussion of order of operation takes on new meaning. In evaluating numerical expressions, some calculators commonly found in homes and schools make use of what is referred to as arithmetic logic whereas others employ algebraic logic. A calculator that uses **arithmetic logic** will evaluate an expression in the order in which it is entered. That is, the expression "$3 + 5 \times 6 = \square$" when keyed into an arithmetic logic calculator will be evaluated as 48 (3 plus 5 equals 8, and 8 times 6 is 48). An **algebraic logic** calculator will automatically apply the order of operations mentioned in the previous paragraph. With algebraic logic, "$3 + 5 \times 6 = \square$" will be evaluated as 33 (5 × 6 equals 30 and 3 plus 30 is 33). The algebraic calculator yields 33, the only correct response for the expression "$3 + 5 \times 6 = \square$."

Use this discussion to determine whether your calculator uses arithmetic or algebraic logic. You can often tell by just looking at your calculator keys. An algebraic logic calculator contains parentheses keys, (), so that the order of operations can be overridden when desired. That is, if you use an algebraic logic calculator with the expression "$3 + 5 \times 6 = \square$" and you wanted to add the 3 and the 5 before multiplying times 6, then you could key in the sequence $(3 + 5) \times 6 = \square$ to get 48. Similarly, if you had an arithmetic logic calculator and wanted to multiply the 5 times 6 first, then you would have to revise the expression in your mind first to be "$5 \times 6 + 3 = \square$" and then key it in that order.

Which type of calculator is preferred? It depends entirely on your intended use. Although used in different ways, both calculators can be effective as tools for teaching the order of operations. The decision depends on the approach that you wish to use to demonstrate the need to agree on an order with which to carry out operations.

When a mathematical sentence includes several numbers and several operations to be performed, it is often necessary to indicate the order (other than the usual order of operations) in which the operations are to be performed. To indicate this order, we use punctuation or grouping symbols—parentheses, brackets, and braces.

Parentheses are grouping symbols used to indicate which operations are to be performed first. You might interpret parentheses to mean "do me first." Some teachers prefer to use this expression with children. In the example $7 - 4 - 1 = \square$, we might write $(7 - 4) - 1 = \square$, which means that we are to subtract 4 from 7 and then subtract 1 from that difference:

$$(7 - 4) - 1 = \square$$
$$3 - 1 = \square$$
$$2 = \square$$

Or we might write $7 - (4 - 1) = \square$, which means that we are to first subtract 1 from 4 and then subtract that difference (3) from 7:

$$7 - (4 - 1) = \square$$
$$7 - 3 = \square$$
$$4 = \square$$

In either case, the operation to be performed first is indicated within the parentheses.

More than one set of parentheses can be used in the same equation, as in $(7 + 2)–(2 + 3) = \square$. Again, the operations indicated within the parentheses are to be performed first. The sum of $2 + 3$ is to be subtracted from the sum of $7 + 2$:

$$(7 + 2) - (2 + 3) = \square$$
$$9 - 5 = \square$$
$$4 = \square$$

Later, children will be introduced to another grouping symbol, square brackets, usually printed [ ]. These are used when one or more pairs of parentheses have already been used and another pair might result in confusion. For example, this sentence is a bit confusing to the eye:

$$\left(\frac{1}{4} \times \left(\frac{2}{3} \times 24\right)\right) \div \frac{2}{3} = \square$$

It is more clearly written as follows:

$$\left[\frac{1}{4} \times \left(\frac{2}{3} \times 24\right)\right] \div \frac{2}{3} = \square$$

The grouping symbols still indicate the order in which operations are to be performed. The operations within the parentheses are usually performed first, then the operations within the brackets.

Some teachers use "rings" or "loops" to reinforce the notion of "do me first." For example, in the following, we would do the inside loop first, then the outside:

After considerable practice, the loops are replaced by parentheses and brackets.

In even more complicated expressions, we may use parentheses, brackets, and braces as punctuation symbols. For example,

$$500 - (50 \div (2 \times (3 + 5))) =$$

is not nearly as easy to read as

$$500 - \{50 \div [2 \times (3 + 5)]\} =$$

Braces are written as { }. They are used in punctuating number expressions and in naming sets. Context always makes it clear how they are being used in any given situation. Of course, the looping method also works here.

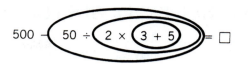

Closure

For many years, teachers have indicated that teaching problem solving to children has been a difficult task. Problem solving is more challenging because it is a more complex process than merely writing numerals in a certain manner and performing operations by using a given rule. Instead, students need to integrate their mathematical knowledge and use this information in a thought process to solve problems. Children need encouragement to help them recognize mathematics in their daily environment. Conceptual understanding is developed first, followed by the development of efficient algorithms. These skills are then applied in real-life situations.

Reading has been, and probably always will be, one of the major difficulties encountered in solving word problems. Children need specific help in reading mathematics and learning how mathematics reading differs from other kinds of reading.

Dramatization (acting out the problem) is an excellent technique to help children learn how to translate words into mathematical sentences. Encourage children to first read, then dramatize the situation into a mathematical sentence. These two intermediary steps are very often neglected. To help children accurately comprehend the meaning and interpretation of the mathematics, they should be encouraged to reply in a complete sentence that answers the original question.

The calculator can provide computing capabilities for students so that they can concentrate on the mathematics involved in solving problems. The use of calculators to solve problems is part of functioning in society today—children need to know how to use this device in real-life situations. The calculator cannot make decisions about when to add, subtract, multiply, or divide. Students must organize the data themselves and learn to use the calculator as a tool.

In this chapter, we discussed a number of concerns relative to mathematical problem solving, decision making, and using mathematical language. As you continue to explore other chapters, you will encounter many opportunities to expand on these themes. Remember, the ideas discussed in this chapter are part of the daily diet of mathematics instruction. As teachers, we must recognize and reinforce the importance of having children model and verbalize what we wish them to learn.

PRACTICE EXERCISES FOR TEACHERS

These exercises are designed for the reader of this book, not for the children whom the reader may teach. Even though some of these examples are suitable for use in the elementary or middle school classroom, they should not necessarily be assigned to children in the form presented here. Ideas appropriate for classroom activities on the concepts and ideas discussed in this chapter can be found in a later section of this chapter and on the CD that accompanies this text.

1. Decide which of the problem-solving strategies described in this chapter would be most appropriate in solving the following problem, and then use that technique to solve it: A candy factory has a warehouse full of cardboard that has been cut into rectangular regions that measure $8\frac{1}{2}$ inches by 11 inches (the size of a standard sheet of paper). You have been asked to design a box (a bottom and four sides) that will hold the most candy by removing a square from each corner of the cardboard, then folding and gluing the sides. What should the size of the square be so that the box will have the greatest volume for holding candy?

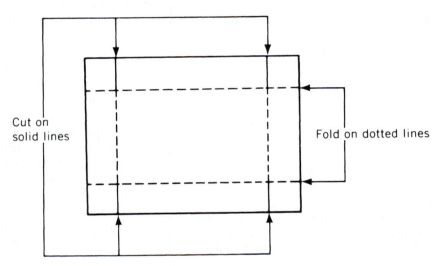

Cut on
solid lines

Fold on dotted lines

2. Find all rectangles having the same numerical value for their area and perimeter. Use only whole numbers for measurements. That is, if A = length and B = width, then for which whole number values of A and B does the following equation hold true?

$$A + A + B + B = A \times B$$

3. How many ways can six squares, each sharing at least one side with another, be drawn on a sheet of paper so that when the figure is cut out, it can be folded into a cube? One example is shown here.

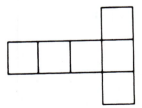

4. Label each of the following as a "true statement," "false statement," "open sentence," or "not a sentence."

a) $34 = 7$

b) $7 + 9 \neq 8 - 4$

c) $3^2 > 1 + 2^2$

d) $9 \times y \geq 7$

e) $\square + \triangle > 8$

f) $12 = [(2 \times 5) - 3] + 1$

g) $2 + \square > 6$

h) $18 \div 2 < 3^2$

i) $6 + (3 + 7) = (6 + 3) + 7$

j) $n - 3n + 2$

k) $a^2 + 1 > 2$

l) $[\lozenge \times 2] \div 5$

5. Rewrite each of the following word problems as an open mathematical sentence. Notice that each story problem may be represented in more than one way.

a) Bobby weighs fourteen pounds more than Edward. Edward weighs fifty-nine pounds. How much does Bobby weigh?

b) Yesterday there were forty-two children playing at the school playground. Today, thirteen more children are playing there. How many children are playing at the school playground today?

c) Ryan has twice as many football trading cards as Jeff. Ryan has 234 football trading cards. How many football trading cards does Jeff have?

d) Tommy Tuna weighs 130 kilograms and Barry Barracuda weighs twenty kilograms. How much more does Tommy Tuna weigh than Barry Barracuda?

6. Solve each equation.

a) $(3 + 4) \times 2 =$

b) $3 + (4 \times 2) =$

c) $(6 + 2) \div 2 =$

d) $6 + (2 \div 2) =$

e) $(3 - 2) + (7 - 1) =$

f) $(\times 2) + 3 = 15$

g) $(2 + 3) + (+7) = 12$

h) $(2\times) + (3\times) = 20$

7. Solve the following word problem. Be sure to write an appropriate mathematical sentence. Remember to translate the mathematics back into an English sentence for your answer.

Mike is three years older than Lila. The sum of their ages is twenty-nine. How old is each person?

8. Solve the following word problem.

Mary is one year older than four times Tammy's age. Kelly is three times as old as Mary. If Kelly is twenty-seven, then how old are Mary and Tammy?

9. Indicate the operation that would most commonly be used to solve each of the following problems.

a) What will six bicycles cost if one sells for $49.95?

b) If I buy a new shirt, jacket, and hat, how much will all three items cost?

c) How much change will I get back from $10.00 if I buy a pair of gloves?

d) How many balloons will go to each of seven people at my birthday party if I have twenty-eight balloons to distribute equally?

10. Write mathematical sentences for each of the following examples.

a) If each of the thirty-two students in our classroom brings a quarter for a school charity, how much money will our room contribute?

b) If we distribute six dozen cookies equally to the twenty-nine members of our class, how many cookies will each person get?

c) How much change will I receive from a dollar if I buy an ice-cream cone for eighty-seven cents?

11. Identify each of the following statements as simple or compound, and classify each compound statement as a conjunction, disjunction, conditional, or negation.

a) Jim is tall or Ray is short.

    b) Ice cream melts.

    c) If you stay, then I go.

    d) The hour is late and the air is sweet.

    e) Roses are red.

    f) Smith did it.

12. Tell whether each compound or conditional statement is true or false.

a) If $(6 < 10)$, *then* $(5 < 10)$	f) If $(\frac{1}{2} = 6/4)$, then $(0 \neq 1)$,
b) $(6 = 5)$ or $(6 > 5)$	g) $(2 < 1)$ and $(1 < 2)$
c) $(9 + 1 = 10)$ and $(8 < 7)$	h) $(2 < 1)$ or $(1 < 2)$
d) If $(7 < 5)$, then $(7 + 1 < 5 + 1)$,	i) *If* $(50 \div \backslash 2 = 25)$, then $(7 < 3)$.
e) $(6^2 = 5)$ or $(5^2 = 6)$	j) $(8 > 1)$ and $(6 > 1)$ and $(0 > 1)$

13. Rewrite each of the following as a conjunction, a disjunction, or a conditional. (Use words for the connectives.)

    a) Marilyn and Ginny are good students.

    b) I tried the car, but it wouldn't start.

    c) Cailin will succeed provided she tries.

    d) Carey or Ryan will call before noon.

14. Identify each of the following sentences as true for all integers x, for some integers x, or for no integers x.

a) $x > 0$	d) $x < x + {}^+1$,
b) $x^2 > 0$	e) $x \geq x - {}^+1$
c) $x^2 \geq 0$	f) $x^4 < {}^-1$

15. Which of the following statements are true and which are false?

    a) All isosceles triangles are equilateral triangles.

    b) All squares are rectangles.

    c) Some trapezoids are rectangles.

    d) All squares are quadrilaterals.

    e) All rectangular prisms are cubes.

    f) No triangles are rectangles.

    g) Some right triangles are equilateral triangles.

    h) All quadrilaterals are squares.

    i) No parallelograms are trapezoids.

    j) All isosceles triangles are acute triangles.

16. In the following examples, assume that the conditional statement is true.

    a) If Figure C is a square, then Figure C has four sides.

        Figure C is a square.

        What can you conclude from these statements?

    b) If Jeff plays basketball, then he will not have time to do his schoolwork.

        Jeff plays basketball.

        What can you conclude from these statements?

    c) If it rains, then we will not go on a picnic.

        It is snowing.

        What can you conclude from these statements?

d) If it snows, then we will shovel the sidewalk.

It is snowing.

What can you conclude from these statements?

17. During class you told your students, "If we finish the chapter by Wednesday, then there will be a test on Friday." In which of the following cases would you have broken this promise?

a) You finished the chapter and gave the test.

b) You finished the chapter and did not give the test.

c) You did not finish the chapter but gave the test.

d) You did not finish the chapter and did not give the test.

TEACHING COMPETENCIES AND SELF-ASSESSMENT TASKS

1. Discuss how the problem-solving strategies presented in this chapter are different from the techniques you may remember learning for solving word problems as a child.

2. Discuss the merits and deficiencies of each of the problem-solving strategies suggested in this chapter. Create sample problems to defend your position on the value and benefits of each strategy.

3. Order the strategies discussed in this chapter according to the degree in which you use them to solve the problems you face on a day-to-day basis. Which strategies do you believe you could make better use of and why?

4. Discuss the roles of the calculator and the computer in *developing* problem-solving skills.

5. Locate and examine the most recent mathematics results of the National Assessment of Educational Progress or international comparative study of mathematics achievement or performance. Report your findings on U.S. problem-solving attainment to the class.

6. Discuss the relationship that should exist between problem solving in the mathematics program and the entire elementary/middle school curriculum. Also, research the relationship between reading and problem-solving ability, and present your findings to the class.

7. Discuss the pros and cons of developing a card file of good word problems. How should such a file be organized? How should it be used in the classroom?

8. Examine at least three school mathematics textbooks, and report on the inclusion of logic—as a separate topic and/or as used within other topics.

9. Report on the appearance of logic in advertising. Locate several examples of both compound and conditional statements in advertising, and determine whether these ads have hidden implications or include fallacious reasoning.

10. Identify real-world problems from a child's perspective (or an adult's perspective) that lend themselves to the use of more than one of the strategies described in this chapter to identify a solution.

11. (Bonus Challenge) Discuss the truth or falsity of the statement "I always lie." Also, analyze the following situation: A student found a piece of paper. On one side of the paper it read, "The other side of this paper is a lie." When the paper was turned over, it read, "The other side of this paper is the truth." Could this "logically" be possible? Why or why not?

12. (Bonus Challenge) A certain island is the home of two distinct types of inhabitants. One type always tells the truth, and the other type always lies. As you travel down an unfamiliar path, you come to a fork leading in two directions. One path leads to the village, the other to the caverns. You would like to find out, from the islander standing by the road, which direction leads to the village. What is the ONE (and only one) question that you can ask to be sure of finding your way to the village on the first try?

SAMPLE INSTRUCTIONAL AND ASSESSMENT ACTIVITIES

These activities and more are available on the CD that accompanies this text.

VM 5.8

1. Children need to learn how to make tables and record data. Obtain many measuring containers, and have children compare the volumes by pouring sand from one container to another. For example, children can discover that a pint container must be filled twice in order to have as much as a quart container filled once. Use metric as well as U.S. customary measuring containers. The Fill and Pour virtual manipulative on the CD that accompanies this text will provide students with an opportunity to collect data and make predictions and conjectures based on observation.

VM 5.1

2. Obtain a set of colored blocks (or use the Attribute Blocks virtual manipulative on the CD that accompanies this text) and have the children group the blocks by color. Place all of the red blocks into a box that has been covered with red contact paper, the blue blocks into a blue box, and the yellow blocks into a yellow box. Discuss the following with the children: (a) blocks that are red, blocks that are blue, and blocks that are yellow; (b) blocks that are not red, or blocks that are not blue, or blocks that are not yellow; (c) blocks that are not red or blue, blocks that are not blue or yellow, or blocks that are not red or yellow; or (d) blocks that are not red, yellow, or blue.

VM 5.1

3. Introduce the ideas of conjunction and disjunction to the children by having them select an attribute block that is blue and circular and then a block that is red or square. This activity is also supported by the Attribute Blocks virtual manipulative that is on the CD accompanying this text.

VM 5.1

4. The quantifiers *all, some, none,* and *one* can be used with young children. If the Attribute Blocks have been sorted by color and shape, the children can be asked such questions as:

a) Are all the squares red?

b) Are all the red blocks squares?

VM 5.1

5. Provide an opportunity for the children to describe certain attribute blocks. For instance, place all the blocks on the table in front of the children. Have a child describe a piece, and have another child pick up the block described. You may also want to pick up any other blocks that might also fit the description. For example, one child might say, "a block that is blue and square." If another child picks up a large, blue, square block, you might want to pick up a small, blue, square block and then discuss how the two blocks meet the specifications. This activity is also supported by the Attribute Blocks virtual manipulative that is on the CD accompanying this text.

VM 5.2

6. Set up simple sequences of four or five blocks, and then have a child tell what the next block in the sequence should be. Have the child state the reason for selecting that particular block. What should the next block in this sequence be? This activity is also supported by the Attribute Trains virtual manipulative that is on the CD accompanying this text.

red   yellow   red   yellow

VM 5.1

7. Place two large loops of yarn on the table or floor. Ask children to place attribute blocks into the loops where they belong. In one loop, place red blocks. In the other loop, place triangles. Discuss the results of the activities. Which blocks belong in both loops (i.e., in the intersection)?

VM 5.5

8. Place the correct sign ($+$, $-$, $\times$, or $\div$) in each blank. There may be more than one possibility. See how many true statements you can make. An extension of this to a more complex exercise occurs with the Number Patterns virtual manipulative on the CD that accompanies this text. Explore the notion of a valid argument by discussing the following:

a) 10__2 = 15__3   c) 9__3 = 3__1
b) 2__5 = 10__3   d) 8__4 = 4__2

VM 5.2

9. Make a pattern that has two or three changes between each pair of blocks in a sequence. Have children take turns selecting a block that could follow in the sequence. Discuss why each block could or could not follow. Study the following example.

What block could follow?

VM 5.4

10. Create a sequence that has a predictable, changing pattern. Study the following example. This activity is also supported by the Color Pattern virtual manipulative that is on the CD accompanying this text.

VM 5.7

11. Encourage the children to play games that involve logic and reason—games such as chess, Tower of Hanoi, and Equations. The Tower of Hanoi virtual manipulative on the CD that accompanies this text provides an excellent opportunity for students to look for patterns, make conjectures, and problem solve.

chapter **6**

Number Sense, Numeration, and Place Value

TEACHING COMPETENCIES

Upon completing this chapter, you will be able to:

- State the anticipated mathematics knowledge that children possess when they enter formal schooling.
- Conceptualize and state appropriate learning experiences for children in a beginning mathematics program.
- Describe the development of number sense, beginning on the concrete level and moving through the semiconcrete, semiabstract, and abstract levels.
- Identify the fundamental features of a place-value numeration system.
- Model numbers using a place-value box and numeral expander.
- Use standard notation, expanded notation, and exponential notation to express a given number.
- Describe characteristics of several ancient numeration systems and how those systems compare to our numeration system.
- Incorporate the principles and structures of numeration and place value in lessons for elementary and/or middle school students.

VIRTUAL MANIPULATIVES

Upon completing this chapter, you will be able to use virtual manipulatives on the accompanying CD to:

- Copy, extend, and create patterns using *Pattern Blocks*. **(VM 6.1)**
- Compare and contrast sorting rules and characteristics using *Attribute Blocks*. **(VM 6.2)**
- Create patterns using *Tesselations*. **(VM 6.3)**
- Compare and contrast different arrangements using *Polyominoes*. **(VM 6.4)**
- Compare and contrast different arrangements using *Shape Patterns*. **(VM 6.5)**
- Compare and contrast different representations of number using *Base Blocks*. **(VM 6.6)**
- Represent numerical relationships using *Number Line Bars*. **(VM 6.7)**
- Compare and contrast different representations of numbers in various bases using *Multiple Base Blocks*. **(VM 6.8)**
- Compare and contrast different representations of place value using *Numeration–Abacus*. **(VM 6.9)**

Numbered CD icons throughout the chapter refer to the virtual manipulatives in this list.

Young children have creative ideas concerning mathematics and its relationship to their world. They have an inventive quality that, to them, offers a way to acknowledge their interaction with the wonders they uncover every day. Consider the following:

> A young boy used to count without shame "one, two, three, four, five, six, then sebbow."
>
> Five and a half was his age, he'd exclaim, even though his birthday was just a month ago.
>
> To push a game piece ahead a space more he'd exclaim that the square he was on is "one."
>
> When playing a girl who said her ring finger WAS four, you could count on a game that would never get done.

Even though the poetic license taken in the preceding passage could be questioned, the children described therein did use "numberness," counting, and number sense in ways that are not uncommon for children just beginning to explore such concepts. Some children invent names for numbers that make more sense to them. Some children use fraction language long before they possess any meaningful understanding of fraction concepts. Some children have difficulty with one-to-one correspondence and with matching word names for numbers to physical actions. All children, however, need a sound foundation in number sense that requires thoughtful planning and organization on the part of the teacher.

The National Council of Teachers of Mathematics (NCTM) lists Number and Operations as the first of the content standards in *Principles and Standards for School Mathematics*.

> Central to this standard is the development of number sense—the ability to decompose numbers naturally, use particular numbers like 100 or $-\frac{1}{2}$ as referents, use the relationships among arithmetic operations to solve problems, understand the baseten number system, estimate, make sense of numbers, and recognize the relative and absolute magnitude of numbers. (NCTM, 2000, p. 32)

A Foundation for Mathematics Development

The mathematics experiences of children beginning formal schooling vary tremendously, depending on a number of factors that include the education of their parents, the time the parents devote to their children's education, attendance at structured preschools, travel experiences, play materials and opportunities, family relationships (older brothers and sisters), television viewing habits, exposure to books, listening to reading by others, and a multitude of other factors. This variance helps define the first mathematical task of any classroom teacher—to assess the mathematics experiences the students have encountered in the past.

A primary mathematics program should begin with the unique mathematics experiences young children have had prior to entering school, and teachers need to isolate these types of mathematical experiences. For example, children who enter school with counting ability do not necessarily exhibit readiness for mathematics. The child may have simply memorized a series of word names and have little or no concept of the numberness involved.

An effective program should reflect the connections of mathematics to applications in the child's world and should emphasize the integration of mathematics into other subject areas. Situations that develop from the real world should be set up in the classroom. Children may have had any of the following experiences:

- using the telephone
- earning and spending their own money correctly
- setting the table for a meal
- recognizing house numbers
- playing with toys that incorporate balance and symmetry
- tuning the television to a designated channel
- playing with a calculator
- playing video games
- loading software on a computer
- using a computer or typewriter keyboard

These prior experiences, or lack of them, may form a common basis for establishing cooperative groups, setting up workstations, and developing the scope and sequence of a beginning mathematics program.

A theoretical base for an early mathematics program can be built on Piaget's learning theory, as well as learning theories from Bruner and others. However, each theorist seems, in one way or another, to support the idea that mathematics should begin in the real world with concrete materials. Children learn through doing (and, more important, discussing what they're doing), so they need many firsthand experiences manipulating, examining, verbalizing, and sharing mathematical ideas. Easily recognizable, familiar materials—such as plastic spoons, forks, paper cups, paper plates, and so forth—should be the main teaching materials. Some specialized educational materials, such as attribute blocks, Cuisenaire rods, base ten blocks, color tiles, pattern blocks, and various forms of physical counters can also be used to provide a sound base for development in mathematics.

A beginning mathematics program establishes the foundation of a solid contemporary mathematics program. At one time, mathematics focused on the ability to juggle numbers rapidly and accurately. Today's mathematics places emphasis on the development of number sense and the recognition and the study of patterns.

Students with number sense naturally decompose numbers, develop and use benchmarks as referents, use the relationships among operations and their knowledge about the base ten numeration system to solve problems, estimate a reasonable result for a problem, and have a disposition to make sense of numbers, problems, and results. (NCTM, 1998, pp. 50–51)

Patterns and Other Relationships in the Primary Curriculum

Numberness and topics related to the development of number sense do not represent the sole focus of a beginning mathematics program. The teacher must also ensure that significant opportunities are provided for interaction with other aspects of the mathematics curriculum. Children should explore concepts such as patterns, measurement, estimation, fractions, and geometry on a regular basis. Of course, this exploration should be carried out at an appropriate level of abstraction, typically at the concrete-manipulative level.

The study of patterns is central to all mathematics learning. If students have developed an appreciation for patterns and can recognize them in different contexts, then transfer of learning will proceed more smoothly. Students who understand the importance of patterns begin to look for patterns in places that others might not look. This leads eventually to reasoning by analogy—that is, a pattern evident in one setting can be used to explain a different situation.

VM 6.1

At the primary level, manipulatives such as pattern blocks, attribute blocks, and color tiles are frequently used for pattern making. Virtual manipulatives such as those on the CD that accompanies this text may also be used to explore patterns.

VM 6.2

Patterning usually begins with a teacher-generated concrete-manipulative pattern that the student is asked to duplicate. This calls for attention to the individual elements of the pattern and a recognition of the order of these elements. This is followed by requests to have the student extend a pattern. Rather than simply duplicating a pattern, the child must now determine what would

come next in order to maintain the orderly sequence. Finally, students are asked to create a pattern of their own, usually with concrete objects. At each step of the patterning process, the teacher should emphasize the role of communication and verbalization and justification in describing the pattern and the "rules" the pattern follows.

The study of measurement in the early grades should consist of a wide variety of hands-on experiences in which the children are actively involved in discovering relationships. Initially, attention should be devoted to exploring lengths (linear measure) using *nonstandard units* of measure such as used pencils or different-length strips of sturdy paper. This should initiate a discussion (with the children—not the teacher—in the lead) of the need for a unit that stays consistently the same length *(standard units)* such as chalkboard erasers or paper clips, which, in turn, should result in the realization of the need for some *commonly accepted standardized units* such as inches, feet, centimeters, and meters. Children should be given ample opportunity to use these measures to describe objects, both by direct measurement and through estimation prior to direct measurement.

The study of measurement should not be limited to linear measure and the use of a ruler. The children should also explore simple weight and capacity measurement at this stage through experiences at a sand table, for example. It is important to note, however, that memorization of equivalent measures is not an issue here. The real purpose is to explore, to experiment, and to interact with the measuring process.

Time is another aspect of measurement that deserves attention here. At the primary level, the development of time concepts frequently includes the ability to read a traditional clock to the hour, half-hour, and minute. Children are also taught to read the display of a digital clock. (See Chapter 15 for an effective and efficient way to introduce young children to reading a clock to the minute.) Days, weeks, months, seasons, and years and the use of calendars to record these aspects of time passage are also part of the primary curriculum.

One other use of measurement that receives attention in the primary grades is money. Children learn to recognize the different coins (and bills), begin to associate a particular value with each coin, compare relative values of different coins and sets of coins, and may even begin to explore forming equivalent sets of coins and making change. Readers who desire to explore further discussion of measurement topics at this point are directed to Chapter 15.

Children in the early grades have often formed a notion of fractions before they come to school for the first time. Many children have had the experience of trying to share a group of toy cars or attempting to choose half of a candy bar. Because of such real experiences in the child's life, this notion of fraction tends to reflect an idea of sharing that does not always call for equal shares. How else can we explain the child who breaks the candy bar in two pieces to show halves and then, before sharing, inspects the two pieces to see which is the "bigger half"?

The idea that a fraction represents equal portions should definitely be part of a primary mathematics program. Considerable use should be made of models, such as circular regions, cut or shaded to demonstrate halves, thirds, and fourths. The children should also discuss why certain other shadings or cuttings do not represent these fractions. However, avoid the temptation to introduce the traditional fraction symbolism at this stage—it is the concept of a fraction, not the symbol for a fraction, that must be the focus here.

Geometric concepts form an integral part of every child's life. Long before children begin formal schooling and apply number concepts to describe things, they explore the world from a geometric standpoint. Objects are thought of and described in terms of geometric traits such as round, curved, flat, pointed, sharp, straight, or crooked. Because the child lives in a three-dimensional world, and because three-dimensional objects can be held and manipulated, a discussion of the traits of three-dimensional objects such as balls, boxes, cylinders, and cones is less difficult than might be imagined. In fact, you may well encounter more difficulty with a discussion of two-dimensional shapes since any model of a two-dimensional shape that we might show a child, even a drawing, is, by its very nature, a three-dimensional model.

The computer can provide a nonthreatening environment for young children to explore fundamental geometric concepts. Software programs for primary children frequently use single keystrokes to move a "turtle" or "ladybug" (the cursor) around the display screen while leaving a trail represented by line segments. The reader is directed to the Ladybug virtual manipulative on the CD that accompanies this text. Also, check the CD for contact information for computer resource supply companies to determine the availability of similar programs in the exploration of geometry.

No matter what resources you choose to make use of, be sure to take full advantage of the child's natural curiosity and the surroundings. The geometry of the environment—shapes and curves in building interiors and exteriors, patterns and designs in sidewalks and gardens, boundaries and angles in playgrounds and games—is a familiar aspect of a child's life that can be drawn on for geometric models. This awareness of the geometry around us not only provides the teacher with a wealth of available teaching aids, but also illustrates the practical application of geometric concepts and ideas.

Algebra and data analysis are also topics that deserve attention in the primary program. The form of algebra most frequently encountered by a primary child is the algebraic logic present in the language a child uses. For example, just as an adult can express a relationship as, for example, one value is three times another value ($x = 3y$), a child might express a relationship between two objects by noting that one is above, or inside, or underneath, or next to, or heavier than, or shorter than the other. Primary children also encounter seriation (ordering) activities in which certain tasks or events occur in a certain sequence. Also, young children begin to explore the notion of consequence through real experiences with conditional events using "if–then" reasoning. Children should encounter many classroom scenarios during which they realize that "*if* this happens, *then* that will be the result."

Data analysis is yet another form of relationship that children explore. Most commonly, this analysis occurs in the creation of physical graphs used to compare data collected. For example, during a refreshment break the students might be given a choice of two different fruit drinks. When finished drinking, their choice can be recorded by placing their empty cup on the table behind signs indicating the two types. The two physical models of the bars on this concrete bar graph can then be compared. In such a setting, early explorations of data analysis mirror the kinds of experiences all children encounter as they develop number sense.

In summary, children will enter their formal schooling with a wide variety of experiences and knowledge bases. The successful teacher of the primary-age child will attempt to identify these differences and make use of them for cooperative learning, grouping, and other aspects of everyday instruction. This teacher will also emphasize the critically important role of hands-on activities and the equally important need to have children relate the mathematics to their world and to verbalize their discoveries and their understandings.

Number Sense

Children enter formal schooling from a real world in which they have handled real objects. This is the place at which a mathematics program must begin—the concrete level. Giving children tasks based on Piaget's experiments can help determine their developmental levels.

Four activities that seem vital for helping children develop number sense are

1. sorting or classifying items into groups
2. recognizing the cardinal number of a group
3. using one-to-one correspondence, which will help with counting
4. ordering or sequencing of events or ideas.

Sorting is a natural activity. Children sort toys when they place cars in garages, dishes in cupboards, dolls in doll beds, or baseball cards into teams or positions played. At more advanced levels, children must be able to sort through information to select appropriate groups. In mathematics, we sort for numbers, least common denominators, prime numbers, factors, geometric shapes, and so on.

At beginning levels, sorting leads to the development of the concept of *number sense*. A child experiences many groups with, say, three elements—three cups, three napkins, three forks, three spoons, three toys. Ultimately the child needs to conceptualize and abstract the common property of "threeness." A child might be shown a red triangle-shaped attribute block and be asked to go to the storage box and find three more triangles or to locate three more red blocks. As time progresses, children can be asked to sort out orally described groups—for example, to locate all of the red triangles or locate all of the small, thin squares.

VM 6.2 **Attribute blocks** are a commonly used manipulative that provide opportunities for children to sort, classify, and search for and develop patterns that are the basis of all mathematical thinking. Attribute blocks are a set of blocks that have varying identifying characteristics (or *attributes*). Typical attribute blocks might, for example, vary in *color*, *shape*, *size*, and *thickness*.

Color	Shape	Size	Thickness
Red	Square	Large	Thick
Blue	Rectangle	Small	Thin
Yellow	Triangle		
	Circle		

The first level of activity with any manipulative should be a free-play period. During such initial activities, attribute blocks might be randomly distributed to groups of children. The children are usually given no instructions or structuring clues at this time. After they have familiarized themselves through play with the blocks, then ask them to sort the blocks. Typically, they often select color and make piles—for example, one pile of yellow blocks, one pile of blue blocks, and one pile of red blocks. Challenge them to classify the blocks in other ways. Shape may be selected as another way to classify the blocks. Children will probably need to be encouraged to try other classifications based on less obvious attributes such as size or thickness.

VM 6.5 On the next level, start a pattern with the blocks, and allow a child to select the block that should be next. For example, lay out the following blocks and ask the child to place the next block:

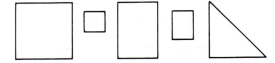

The child must carefully examine the pattern presentation and then decide which attribute block must be placed next to extend the pattern. Often, more than one block could be used to continue the pattern. Have the child verbalize the reason for selecting a particular block. (The activities found on the CD accompanying this text contain more developmental ideas.)

Cuisenaire rods are a set of wooden or plastic rods based on centimeters and varying in length and color. The rods are not scored. Consequently, length is determined by comparing a rod to the unit rod. The rods can be used to sort, classify, develop patterns, and develop numberness and to explore many other mathematical concepts.

Color	Size of Rod (in cubic centimeters)
White	1 × 1 × 1
Red	1 × 1 × 2
Light green	1 × 1 × 3
Purple	1 × 1 × 4
Yellow	1 × 1 × 5
Dark green	1 × 1 × 6
Black	1 × 1 × 7
Brown	1 × 1 × 8
Blue	1 × 1 × 9
Orange	1 × 1 × 10

Initial activities with Cuisenaire rods should center on free play, during which neither teacher-imposed structure nor formal instruction is attempted. After the children have become familiar with the color and the relative lengths of the rods, instruction can begin. The children may first organize the rods by separating them by color or by length. The same classification will result either way. Children need many experiences with relationships between the rods. How many red rods does it take to equal the length of one purple rod?

Red	Red
Purple	

How many different ways can we show a dark green rod?

W	Yellow
Dark green	

Red	Purple
Dark green	

Lt. green	Lt. green
Dark green	

Red	Red	Red
Dark green		

W	W	Red	Red
Dark green			

Children will soon learn that the length of every rod can be shown using other rods.

Note that during beginning experiences, the children are developing relationships and do not necessarily associate numbers with the rods. Because of the nature of the rods, a rod's length can be defined many different ways. In one case, the white rod could be defined as one; yet, at another time, the red rod could be defined as one. As soon as a unit length is established, a number value is automatically assigned to all other rods. Children should understand the interrelationships among the rods before they associate numberness with the rods. Relationships are developed first, followed by numberness and counting.

For additional information about using Cuisenaire rods in a beginning mathematics program, research the literature and locate teachers' manuals specifically designed to direct such a program.

Base ten blocks are another set of materials that can be used to develop fundamental number sense, most often in conjunction with the concepts of place value. As with Cuisenaire rods, the base ten blocks set has a centimeter cube that can be used to represent one unit. The set also has long blocks, much like the Cuisenaire ten rods, although color is usually not a factor in the base ten blocks set. In addition to these blocks, the base ten blocks set also includes flat blocks and large cubes.

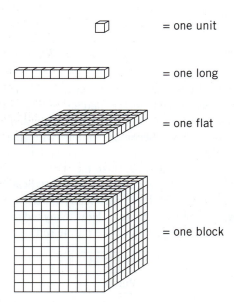

= one unit

= one long

= one flat

= one block

Similar materials are available for other number bases and are sometimes referred to as **Dienes Multibase Blocks**.

Zoltan P. Dienes, British educator and creator of the Dienes Multibase Blocks, recommends that the children have free play with the blocks and then move to structured activities from which they can abstract basic mathematical concepts; these concepts should then be examined in many different contexts. Dienes identifies four basic principles on which he structured these blocks:

1. According to the *dynamic principle*, children should be given undirected free play with the blocks before they are given structured activities.

2. According to the *constructive principle*, children develop constructive thinking intuitively before developing analytical thinking (before they can make logical judgments). For instance, children explore what a place-value system is by manipulating the base ten blocks rather than by reasoning out the connection without the benefit of manipulation. The children should realize that it takes 10 units to have as much wood as one long, that it takes 10 longs to have as much wood as one flat, and that it takes 10 flats to have as much wood as one block. This requires constructive but not analytical thinking (which, according to Dienes, is usually not developed before age 12).

For example, the following figure represents the number 134:

VM 6.6

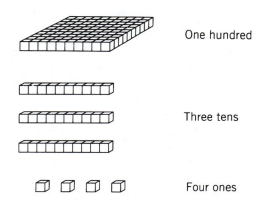

One hundred

Three tens

Four ones

3. According to the *mathematical variability principle*, the relationship among variables can remain constant, although the variables themselves are changed. Using the place-value concept exemplified with base ten blocks, you can see that 10 longs contain as much wood as one flat and that 10 units have as much wood as one long. For example, look at the following arrangement:

One long may be exchanged for 10 units. Then we have

4. According to the *perceptual variability prin-ciple*, a conceptual structure can remain un-changed when precepts are changed. We can use the same conceptual structure of base ten blocks and then substitute with base five or base three blocks. The place-value concept is the same, but the blocks are grouped by fives or by threes.

When used with Piagetian tasks and a constructivist approach to teaching and learning, materials such as attribute blocks, Cuisenaire rods, and base ten blocks will provide a firm foundation on which children can build and develop mathematical thought. The use of collections or groups of objects is a sound and logical way to develop the concept of numbers in gradual stages.

Many contemporary mathematics programs at the elementary school level include the concepts of sets, usually in some concrete/pictorial fashion. Formal set theory is typically not taught at the elementary or middle school level but is informally explored to provide techniques for introducing and describing some of the fundamental ideas of mathematics. Rather than emphasizing the formal topic of sets that was common in the New Math movement of the 1960s, most programs today emphasize set concepts by focusing on groups, or collections of objects put together for a particular purpose.

By using set concepts, we are able to describe mathematical ideas and operations more clearly and more simply than without them. Groups and grouping are used with children to develop the concept of numbers, as well as classifying, sorting, and ordering. Many educators believe that informal set concepts should be introduced very early, that they help young children form proper number concepts, and that the development of proper number concepts will make more advanced mathematics concepts easier to grasp.

What would you take with you to play golf? You would play golf with a *set of clubs*. What would you buy if you needed dishes to serve eight people? You would buy a *set of dishes*. Using these two examples, we can discuss the nature of a set. A set can be thought of as any collection or group of things or ideas that are precisely described. The things or ideas that constitute a given set are called the **elements** (or **members**) of the set.

We have often used other words to indicate a set—words such as *team, flock, herd, club,* and *family.* These items indicate that the members of such a set have some common characteristics. However, a set could be made up of elements that have almost nothing in common—a set, in mathematics, can be composed of any elements we choose to include. The only thing the elements of a set must have in common is membership in the set.

It is extremely important that the groups consist of distinguishable, well-defined objects. A set or collection is well defined when we can readily tell exactly which elements or objects belong to it. Consider this example: "all the old homes in the town of Hanover, Illinois." Would the elements of this set be clear to everyone? No, because "old" is not a precise term. One person's idea of what "old" means will not always be another person's idea. We must describe the elements of a group precisely to have a well-defined set or collection. The collection of all *daisies* in Mrs. Smith's yard at 3:00 P.M. today is well defined; while the set of all *pretty* flowers in Mrs. Smith's yard at 3:00 P.M. is not well defined.

We can usually describe a group in several different ways, using several different **levels of abstraction**. We can describe a group by taking real objects and putting them together. For example, a class party requires a decorations committee; the members appointed to that committee are Betty, Jean, and Mary. This group is composed of real elements—people. When we work with real or tangible items, we refer to this as a **concrete** situation. The use of real items on the concrete level will help children relate the mathematics they are about to learn to the real world. For instance, children have had experiences grouping with actual cookies, toys, and playmates.

A second way to describe a group is by drawing pictures. A group of three chairs could then be represented this manner:

Instead of working with real chairs, we could use drawings of the chairs to represent the real objects. We call this a **semiconcrete** situation. The semiconcrete level is a representation of a real situation but uses pictures or images of the real items rather than the items themselves.

The **semiabstract** level involves a symbolic rep-resentation of a concrete item, but the symbols or images do not look like the objects they represent. A semiabstract representation can use tallies to represent elements. A common example of such a representation for four objects is ////. A number line is also commonly used as a semiabstract model. It can picture a situation involving real objects, but the number line doesn't look like the objects it represents.

A group can also be described by using **abstract** symbols. We might use the letters *a*, *b*, and *c* to stand for the chairs. We can also describe a group by using words—for example, "all presidents of the United States."

Are words and symbols as precise as the other means of describing groups? Yes, words and symbols, if used carefully, can be just as precise. However, words and symbols are more abstract than pictures and the actual objects. However, in each case, we can clearly and precisely describe the members of a given group. Children reach the abstract level when they can understand and use numbers and numerals, without the need to refer to concrete or representative models.

ABSTRACT
(Numerals/letters)

SEMIABSTRACT
(Tally marks/number line)

SEMICONCRETE
(Pictures of objects)

CONCRETE
(Actual objects)

The initial level of number-sense development occurs at the concrete level. In kindergarten and grade 1, the idea of set (and the associated terminology used to describe real collections) is developed using real objects. A *pack* of crayons, a *box* of pencils, or a *bowl* of apples can be presented as a set. This idea can then be extended to present any collection of different real objects. For example, a pencil, a ball, and a book could be placed together on a desk and described as "the set (or group) of objects on the desk."

On another level, numberness is explored with a group of physical objects that can be represented by drawings (on chalkboard or paper). The use of drawings is more abstract than the use of the objects themselves, so we call this the semiconcrete level. The real objects presented at the concrete level would now be drawn:

At a higher level, the child is able to match tallies (tally marks or counters such as ice-cream sticks) with

the objects of a set. On this semiabstract level, we draw the student's attention away from irrelevant properties of individual elements of the given set and direct attention toward the question "How many?"

When the child performs such a matching, the emphasis is on discovering whether one group has as many elements as another, although the child is still not using numbers, as such, to make this comparison.

On the highest level, the abstract level, the child matches the elements of a given group with numbers, starting with 1.

The child comes to understand that the last counting number used in such a matching can be used to tell how many objects there are in the given group. Thus, the child can speak and write an abstract symbol (a **numeral**) to tell how many (the **number**) objects are in the given set.

Sometimes we are interested not in the objects that comprise a set but in only one particular characteristic of the objects. One such characteristic that we might want to consider is the cardinal number. The **cardinal number** of a given set or collection of objects is the number that indicates how many elements the set contains. Note that as soon as we use the cardinal number of a set, we are functioning on an abstract level. For example, consider set A:

Having matched the objects of the group with the counting numbers, we can say that the number of objects in set A is 3. This is sometimes written as $n(A) = 3$. This symbolic sentence is seldom, if ever, used with children.

When working with young children, we often simply ask, "What is the number of objects in this group?" Usually, we just write 3 beside the group.

The cardinal number of this set, represented by the numeral 3, is an expression of the number characteristic of the group—in this case, the characteristic of threeness. This aspect of number sense enables children to discuss groups in terms of number and provides a means by which they can understand the meaning of number. The characteristic of threeness is amplified through the comparison of groups. Children are now able to look at groups such as the following in a new way:

Even though these groups possess many differences, it is evident that they have something in common: the characteristic of threeness.

Sets can now be compared by comparing cardinal numbers, that is, by counting and comparing the number of objects in each collection of objects. The set of **counting numbers** (also referred to as **natural numbers**) can be written using set notation as follows:

$$\{1, 2, 3, 4, 5, \ldots\}$$

When there is no final element to a collection, an ellipsis ($\ldots$) indicates that the sequence of elements continues in the same manner, either endlessly or until a given number is reached.

When we count, we are essentially putting objects into a one-to-one correspondence with counting numbers arranged in the form

$$\{1, 2, 3, \ldots, n\}$$

where n is a counting number. In other words, we match the objects with successive counting numbers, starting with 1. Any set that is either empty (has no elements) or that can be counted in this fashion is called a **finite set**. Sets that are not finite are called **infinite sets**. You are probably already familiar with the following mathematical examples of infinite sets:

1. The counting numbers: 1, 2, 3, 4, 5, . . .
2. The whole numbers: 0, 1, 2, 3, 4, . . .
3. The even (whole) numbers: 0, 2, 4, 6, . . .
4. The odd (whole) numbers: 1, 3, 5, 7, . . .

Each of these is an infinite set (i.e., each continues on in the same fashion without end). There is no greatest element in any of these sets.

In the physical world, groups of objects are finite—in fact, it should be noted that there are no examples of infinite sets of objects in the physical world. The number of grains of sand on the earth's surface is a staggeringly large number, but these grains form a finite set. One reason we have so much difficulty comprehending the nature of an infinite set is surely because we have no real experience with such a set. When you're weeding a garden on a hot day, it seems as though there is always another weed to pull, and yet we know that the number of weeds in the garden, or in the world for that matter, is finite—not infinite!

Number Relations

A child begins at a very early age to make comparisons using terms such as *larger*, *smaller*, *more*, *less*, and so on. Even though the child may not yet be able to count, he or she can make decisions regarding the size of two groups by matching the elements one to one. By doing this, the child can say that one group has more objects than another group. Consider a child presented with two groups of lollipops:

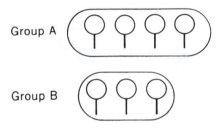

The child will probably choose the group that has more lollipops. By trying to match each object in B with only one object in A, the child sees that there is one lollipop unmatched, or left over, in A. The matching might be done mentally, but on paper it would look like this:

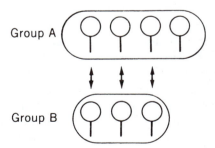

In situations such as this, we realize that children have a background of real experiences in dealing intuitively with nonequivalent sets. It seems only natural to make use of these experiences to further their mathematical knowledge to include unequal as well as equal sets.

A **one-to-one correspondence** between two groups means that each object in the first group is matched with exactly one object in the second group, and each object in the second group is matched with exactly one object in the first group. In a one-to-one correspondence between two sets, there are no elements left over, or left unmatched, in either set.

Two collections that can be placed in one-to-one correspondence are called **equivalent sets**.

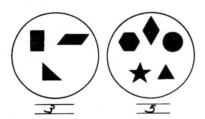

Collections A and B are equivalent, because each element in A is matched with exactly one element in B, and no element in either collection is left unmatched. Since they have the same number of elements in one-to-one correspondence, equivalent sets have the same cardinal number.

The ability to count evolves out of manipulating, observing, and conceptualizing numbers. After a strong base is established, children might then be ready to begin writing numerals. Children are usually asked to write the correct numerals under displays of that many objects.

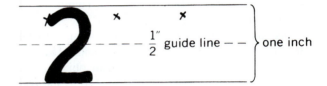

We must emphasize here that you should not rush children into writing numerals. Muscular development and fine motor skills of children vary a great deal. Some 5-year-old children will be developmentally ready to begin writing numerals, but others will need to wait until they are age 6 or even age 7. Do not ask a child to write numerals before he or she has had many opportunities to observe numerals and associate them with the appropriate word names. A child needs to have a mental image of what a numeral looks like in order to write it. Children who have not developed an accurate mental image of the numerals often write numerals in a reversed form. In fact, such numeral reversal is not an uncommon occurrence in the written work of many primary school children.

Begin teaching children to visualize numerals by using cards with numerals written on them and matching them with groups of objects. Hold the cards in your hand, and with a finger trace the numeral as if you were writing it. You may want to put a small "x" on the numeral showing children where to begin. The goal is to have the children eventually write numerals that

are legible and that communicate the intended number. The precise duplication of numeral formation is not of greatest concern. The numerals, however, should be legible and look something like these:

$$\overline{1\,2\,3\,4\,5\,6\,7\,8\,9\,0}$$

Next, have the children trace each numeral with a finger. When you think the children have the numeral configurations well in mind, they are ready to begin writing. Give the children large sheets of paper without lines. Provide a model of the numeral to be drawn, and ask the children to draw one like the model.

Primary school paper with 1-inch lines and $-\frac{1}{2}$-inch guide lines should then be used. Make small reference x's so that the child knows where to begin each numeral. Provide models so that children are less likely to write numerals backward.

As children begin to compare the cardinal numbers of groups, they are ready to expand their idea of number to discover the relations between numbers.

For the cardinal numbers of any two sets A and B, only three relations are possible:

1. A = B: The cardinal number of set A is equal to the cardinal number of set B.

2. A > B: The cardinal number of set A is greater than the cardinal number of set B.

3. A < B: The cardinal number of set A is less than the cardinal number of set B.

The number can then be compared with any other number. Given any two numbers, x and y, one and only one of the following relations will hold true:

Either $x = y$ or $x > y$ or $x < y$

This fact is sometimes called the **Law of Trichotomy**. The term *trichotomy* comes from the Greek word meaning 'threefold'.

We have presented a logical development beginning with concrete representation of sets and leading to awareness of the possible relations between any two numbers. It is hoped that children will achieve this awareness rapidly and arrive at a proper understanding of the concept of number.

Extending Numberness Concepts

Number lines can be used to reinforce and extend students' understanding of relations between numbers. A **number line** is a representation of a geometric line with an arrowhead at each end to indicate that the line continues in both directions:

We mark two points on the line. The first point we label 0, sometimes referred to as the origin, and the second point we label 1:

Now that we have marked a line segment of one unit length on the number line, we can mark off other congruent line segments (segments having the same measure) on the number line and label these points:

VM 6.7

We can establish a unit length on our number line to be any convenient length, provided that on any given number line all unit lengths are equal. Also, we can select any portion of the number line that we wish to use. For example:

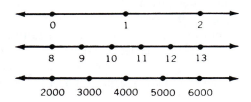

In using the horizontal number line, we agree, by conventional use, that numbers of greater value are represented to the right of numbers of lesser value. If the number line is drawn vertically, then the greater value numbers are usually on top. Children can use the number line as another means of examining relations between numbers. For example, on the following number line:

some of the evident relations are $2 > 1$, $3 > 2$, $1 < 3$, $0 < 2$, $3 > 1$, and so on.

Remember that the number line represents the semiabstract level of development. Before you introduce the number line, children should have had experiences on the concrete and semiconcrete levels of development.

Number lines will prove useful for much of a child's mathematical development. In grades 1 and 2, the number line can be used to suggest the concept of *ordinal number*. Here are two ways of representing a group that consists of a star, a square, a rhombus, a circle, and a hexagon:

In the representation on the left, the objects are jumbled. In the one on the right, they are listed in a certain order: The star is first, the square is second, the rhombus is third, and so on. The numbers we use to tell which position the elements occupy are called **ordinal numbers**. To attach an ordinal number to an element of a set, the objects must be arranged in a definite order, one after another, starting with a certain one. For example, you might ask children to line up for lunch by identifying only certain positions by name—for example, Ann first in line, Dan fourth, Mark sixth, Luke seventh, and John tenth. Allow the children to arrange themselves, with others filling in where appropriate.

Children arrive at school with different backgrounds in number concept development. The task of the teacher is to determine at which level each child is functioning. Some children will be operating on a rote counting level, others will have some comprehension of groups, others will be able to count rationally (use one-to-one correspondence in counting), and others will have a well-developed concept of numbers. Differing backgrounds raise problems that the teacher must solve by individualizing the mathematics program.

Place-Value Numeration

Any **place-value numeration system** has a grouping scheme that is unique of that system. Let's take an imaginary trip to a faraway land. The inhabitants of this place, the Quints, seem friendly enough and engage us in a spirited conversation about our home and about theirs. We soon discover that we enjoy many of the same amusements and suffer many of the same problems. In fact, the further the conversation goes, the more we realize that we live nearly parallel lives—right down to the fact that the Quints also buy their eggs by the dozen. But they claim that they don't buy 12 eggs. Their dozen, they say, is written ㉒, not 12 like ours. They have, it seems to us, an odd way of recording numbers. To write a numeral to represent they write ㉒. To count these eggs, they count 1, 2, 3, 4, 5 and draw a loop around that group, or set, and then they count another 1, 2, 3, 4, 5 and draw another loop around that group. They record this process with a 2. Then they count the elements not included in the set—1, 2—and record another 2.

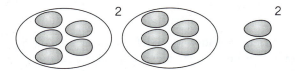

The two 2s are then looped: ㉒. This numeral represents the two sets of five elements and the leftover two elements.

Using this system, how would the citizens of this land record the following quantity?

They would count five and draw a loop enclosing that set. They would then count five more and draw a loop around that group. They would find that four elements are left over. They would record the count as ㉔. The 2 stands for two sets of five, and the 4 stands for four ones.

Upon reflection, it appears that the method of counting used in this faraway land is not as strange as it first seemed. We both use "dozens" to describe the way we buy eggs, but when we write our numeral that represents a dozen, we use tens and ones rather than fives and ones. When we count to 24, the numeral we use represents 2 tens and 4 ones, not the 2 fives and 4 ones written by the Quints. But other than the value of the places in the numerals, our system of numeration seems to be the same as the one used by the Quints. We use a decimal place-value system—a system based on grouping by tens.

Decimal Numeration

The notion of place value is an important idea that is fundamental to whole numbers, integers, and rational numbers expressed as decimals. Understanding the concept of place value is essential to comprehending the common computational algorithms we teach. The individual steps of a computational algorithm can often be conveyed meaningfully through the use of a discussion of the algorithm centered on a place-value argument. However, many teachers do not adequately emphasize place value in their teaching of algorithms. This may lead the student to believe that an algorithm is merely a blind application of seemingly arbitrary rules and may contribute to the development of an attitude that mathematics doesn't make sense. Knowledge of the principles of place value gives us power with the numeration system we use. The more students learn about the characteristics and benefits of a place-value system of numeration, the more likely they are to appreciate its superiority, in terms of ease of use, to other types of numeration systems.

Any place-value numeration system has a grouping scheme that is basic to that system. The number of symbols necessary for a particular numeration system is directly related to this basic grouping. For example, in base ten system has 10 symbols or **digits**:

$$0, 1, 2, 3, 4, 5, 6, 7, 8, 9$$

Using these digits, or a combination of these digits, any number, no matter how great or small its value, can be expressed. This is possible because the **decimal system** (or **base ten system**) uses place value and has a special symbol, the zero, for indicating "not any." Zero, as we use it in our numeration system, is a concept that makes our system unique compared to ancient numeration systems.

When we agree that ten is to be the base of a numeration system, we are saying that ten is the basis for grouping in that system. We can count from 1 to 9 and record this count in the ones column (the first column to the left of the decimal point in the base ten system) with a single digit; when we reach a count of ten, we form a group of ten and express it by a 1 in the next (tens) column to the left. A count greater than 9 but less than 100 must be expressed as a group or groups of ten, and any ones left over are recorded in the ones column.

 VM 6.6

Children need many experiences grouping and regrouping objects into groups of tens and ones. Place two sheets of paper in front of the children. On one of the sheets print the word *Ones*, and on the other sheet print the word *Tens*. To mimic the place-value arrangement that the children will later use, place the *Tens* sheet to the children's left and the *Ones* sheet to the right.

Have the children place plastic spoons on the sheet marked *Ones*. As they reach 9 ones, encourage them to think about what we might do when we get 10 ones. By focusing on the name of the *Tens* sheet, children should recognize that whenever 10 items (spoons, in this case) are on the *Ones* sheet, they should be regrouped into one 10 on the *Tens* sheet.

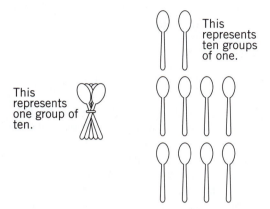

A place-value box may also be used. A place value box is any box that has compartments labeled corresponding to decimal places. For example:

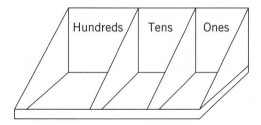

The number 23 can be shown with two groups of tens and 3 ones. In the place-value box, we would place three single spoons in the compartment labeled *Ones*, and we would place two packages of 10 spoons each into the compartment labeled *Tens*. We can also show the number 23 by placing three single spoons on a sheet of paper marked *Ones* and placing to the left two packages of 10 spoons each on a sheet labeled *Tens*:

Have the children select numeral cards and place them on the place-value sheets:

We have already said that 10 is the basis for grouping in the decimal system. Now let's examine the regular patterns inherent in this grouping. A group of 10 ones becomes 1 ten and 0 ones; a group of 10 tens becomes 1 hundred, 0 tens, and 0 ones; a group of 10 hundreds becomes 1 thousand, 0 hundreds, 0 tens, and 0 ones. This can be shown in a large grid made for the children, and they can manipulate groups of objects bundled in ones, tens, or hundreds right on the grid. The children can use a small grid such as the following by placing numeral cards on the grid or using a marking pencil on a grid covered with a clear plastic film:

Thousands	Hundreds	Tens	Ones	
		1	0	10 ones or 1 ten
	1	0	0	10 tens or 1 hundred
1	0	0	0	10 hundreds or 1 thousand

It is evident that whenever we have 10 in any group, we move one place to the left and record a one in that column (for one set of 10, one set of 100, and so on). Thus, a digit in any column represents 10 times the value of that same digit in the column to its right. For example, the numeral 1 in the thousands column represents 10 times the value of the numeral 1 in the hundreds column. We can rearrange the information in our grid to express this another way:

$10 \times 10 \times 10$	10×10	10	1
Thousands	Hundreds	Tens	Ones

This is an abstract idea—one that is often very difficult for young children to comprehend. Provide physical materials—such as Popsicle sticks and rubber bands—for children to manipulate, and systematically teach, apply, and have children practice the concept of bundling and unbundling. By noting the number of times 10 is used as a factor, we see that each column represents 10 times the value of the column to its right. By the use of **exponential notation**, we can write this in simpler fashion. We can write a numeral (called an *exponent*) above and to the right of the 10 (in this case, to indicate how many times 10 is used as a factor). We can abbreviate $10 \times 10 \times 10$ by writing 10^3, and 10×10 by writing 10^2. We read 10^3 as "ten to the third power," and we read 10^2 as "ten to the second power."

The number 10 can be written as 10^1 (ten to the first power), since 10 occurs only once and is represented simply by 10.

Study the following list of powers of 10. Do you see a pattern that indicates how the number 1 can be written as a power of 10?

$$1000 = 10^3$$
$$100 = 10^2$$
$$10 = 10^1$$
$$1 = 10^?$$

The exponents are decreasing by one as we go down the list, so the exponent that we want is 0; 1 is equal to 10 to the **zero power**: $1 = 10^0$. (In fact, any nonzero number raised to the zero power is equal to 1.) We can show the values for each column in the grid by using exponential notation:

10^3	10^2	10^1	10^0
Thousands	Hundreds	Tens	Ones

In this chart, 10 is called the *base*, and 3, 2, 1, and 0 are called *exponents*. A positive whole number exponent on a numeral can be thought of as indicating the number of times that the base is to be used as a factor:

$$\text{Base} \rightarrow 10^{2\text{(Exponent)}}$$

A number with an exponent is said to be raised to a *power;* the power is named by the exponent. The powers of 10 in the grid are as follows:

10^0 means 10 to the zero power—1. (Except for zero, any number raised to the zero power is equal to 1.)

10^1 means 10 to the first power—10. (Any number raised to the first power is the number itself; so 10^1 = 10.)

10^2 means 10 to the second power—100. (10^2 means 10 used as a factor two times: $10 \times 10 = 100$.)

10^3 means 10 to the third power—1000; and so on.

To illustrate how exponential notation and place value are related, consider the number 1314. Arrange the numerals in a grid as we did earlier:

10^3	10^2	10^1	10^0
1	3	1	4

In this grid, the place value of each digit is indicated by the power of ten at the top of the column.

$$1314 = (1 \times 10^3) + (3 \times 10^2) + (1 \times 10^1)$$
$$+ (4 \times 10^0)$$
$$= (1 \times 10 \times 10 \times 10) + (3 \times 10 \times 10)$$
$$+ (1 \times 10) + (4 \times 1)$$
$$= (1 \times 1000) + (3 \times 100)$$
$$+ (1 \times 10) + (4 \times 1)$$
$$= 1000 + 300 + 10 + 4$$
$$= 1314$$

Thus, we see the relation in our decimal system between place value and exponential notation.

The operations that children perform on numbers are often understood more easily through the use of **expanded notation**, in which numbers are thought of in particular component parts before the operations are performed. These component parts show the place values of the digits in the numerals. A numeral written in expanded notation is called an **expanded numeral**.

Consider the number 2346 written in expanded notation:

1. $2000 + 300 + 40 + 6$

By naming a number in this way, children can see at a glance the makeup of the number in terms of groups of ones, tens, hundreds, thousands, and so on. The preceding expanded notation could also be written as:

2. $(2 \times 1000) + (3 \times 100) + (4 \times 10) + (6 \times 1)$

or

3. 2 thousands, 3 hundreds, 4 tens, 6 ones

or

4. $(2 \times 10 \times 10 \times 10) + (3 \times 10 \times 10) + (4 \times 10)$
$+ (6 \times 1)$

or, using exponential notation:

5. $(2 \times 10^3) + (3 \times 10^2) + (4 \times 10^1) + (6 \times 10^0)$

Forms 1, 2, and 3 are the ones most commonly used in the elementary school, with form 3 probably the most meaningful for the elementary school child. Forms 4 and 5 tend to be too abstract at this level. Expanded notation helps the child understand the grouping process and see clearly how the original number is actually made up of groups of numbers.

Numeral expanders are excellent devices for children to manipulate and for teachers to use to demonstrate the meaning of place value. The following are two types of numeral expanders using the number 124:

Standard Notation

Expanded Notation

By "expanding" the numeral expander, we can see how the number 124 can be thought of in many different ways, as the accompanying illustration shows:

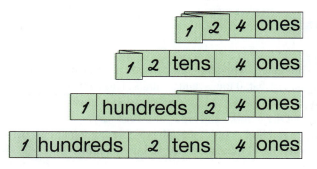

The use of a numeral expander makes it easier to discuss three aspects of numberness essential for interpreting a given numeral: the distinctions among *face value, place value,* and *total value* when reading a multiplace number. Consider 242. The 2 on the left in this numeral has a face value of 2, a place value of hundreds, and a total value of 200 (2 × 100). The 2 on the right also has a face value of 2, but its place value is ones, so the total value is 2 (2 × 1). The lesson that children need to learn is that in such a numeral, the 2s don't look different—what makes their value different is the place they occupy*

Note to the reader: Information on purchasing numeral expanders and a 24-page teachers' support manual can be obtained by contacting Dr. William Speer via email at William.Speer@unlv.edu or by writing to him in care of *Today's Mathematics,* at the publisher, John Wiley & Sons, Inc.

As may be evident from the numeral expander examples, sometimes it is less confusing for children if word names for numbers are used instead of just numerals. This seems to be particularly true when discussing subtraction. Study this example written both with words and numerals and with numerals alone:

$$
\begin{array}{r}
46 = 4 \text{ tens } 6 \text{ ones} \\
-23 = -2 \text{ tens } 3 \text{ ones} \\
\hline
2 \text{ tens } 3 \text{ ones} = 23
\end{array}
\qquad
\begin{array}{r}
46 = (40 + 6) \\
-23 = -(20 + 3) \\
\hline
20 + 9 = 29
\end{array}
$$

Children often incorrectly add the numbers in the ones place and subtract the numbers in the tens place (in this case, obtaining a wrong answer of 29).

Let's examine the organization of the base ten number system. Elementary schools in the United States most often retain the use of commas to separate the places of the base ten system into *periods.* Each period has three places; they are named, right to left, ones, tens, and hundreds. The names ones, tens, and hundreds are repeated in each period along with the period name. Each period has its own name and is used every time we read a number. The international trend in writing large numbers is to replace the commas with spaces—for example, 20 000 instead of 20,000. Since commas are not used in the metric system or in computers or calculators to separate periods within a number, children must be able to read numbers separated by spaces as well as those separated by commas.

Now let's consider the number in the "period name" display shown. (We introduce this as a curiosity and so you can note similarities with place-value names. It is neither necessary nor desirable for children—or even adults for that matter—to learn all these places.)

Each period has a name and a ones, tens, and hundreds place. Study this pattern. To read a decimal number, read the three digits in a period; then give the period name. Continue this process from left to right. Thus, the number in the figure would be read, "One hundred twenty-three decillion, four hundred fifty-six nonillion, seven hundred eighty-nine octillion, one hundred twenty-three

hundreds tens ones	hundreds tens ones	hundreds tens ones	hundreds tens ones	hundreds tens ones	hundreds tens ones	hundreds tens ones	hundreds tens ones	hundreds tens ones	hundreds tens ones	hundreds tens ones	hundreds tens ones
{1 2 3}	{4 5 6}	{7 8 9}	{1 2 3}	{4 5 6}	{7 8 9}	{1 2 3}	{4 5 6}	{7 8 9}	{1 2 3}	{4 5 6}	{7 8 9}
Decillions	Nonillions	Octillions	Septillions	Sextillions	Quintillions	Quadrillions	Trillions	Billions	Millions	Thousands	Units

Period Name

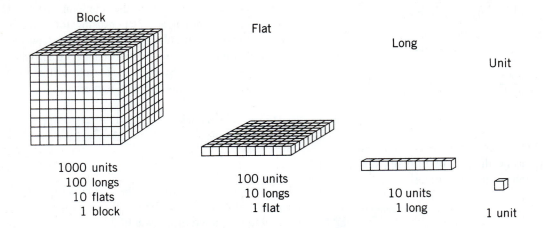

Block

1000 units
100 longs
10 flats
1 block

Flat

100 units
10 longs
1 flat

Long

10 units
1 long

Unit

1 unit

septillion, four hundred fifty-six sextillion, seven hundred eighty-nine quintillion, one hundred twenty-three quadrillion, four hundred fifty-six trillion, seven hundred eighty-nine billion, one hundred twenty-three million, four hundred fifty-six thousand, seven hundred eighty-nine." Wow! Before returning to reality, you might want to research a very large number referred to as a *googol*—the name given to a 1 with 100 trailing zeros!

As discussed previously, the materials for a base ten place-value system are composed of the units shown in the illustration above. Note the relationships that exist among these materials—units, longs, flats, and blocks.

Although not always apparent to the children using the blocks, renaming numbers using blocks involves a form of Piaget's idea of conservation of volume. Children benefit from manipulating and exchanging blocks so that they maintain the same amount of wood. For example, if a child wants to show the number 123 using base ten blocks, what is the fewest number of base ten blocks (pieces of wood) the child could have? In this case the child would have 1 flat, 2 longs, and 3 units. Have the child go to the base ten block bank and exchange one of the pieces for an equivalent amount of wood. The child might change 1 long for 10 units. Then he or she would have 1 flat, 1 long, and 13 units. If the child now exchanges 1 long at the bank so that the

amount of wood remains constant, then he or she would have 1 flat, 0 longs, and 23 units. This same process can be used so that the amount of wood is always the same but the number and types of pieces vary.

A child should see all possible combinations. All possible combinations for 123 units follow:

		123 units
	1 long,	113 units
	2 longs,	103 units
	3 longs,	93 units
	4 longs,	83 units
	5 longs,	73 units
	6 longs,	63 units
	7 longs,	53 units
	8 longs,	43 units
	9 longs,	33 units
	10 longs,	23 units
	11 longs,	13 units
	12 longs,	3 units
1 flat,	2 longs,	3 units
1 flat,	1 long,	13 units
1 flat,	0 longs,	23 units

Children should now begin to realize that in each case, there is exactly the same amount of wood. The only differences are the type and the number of pieces.

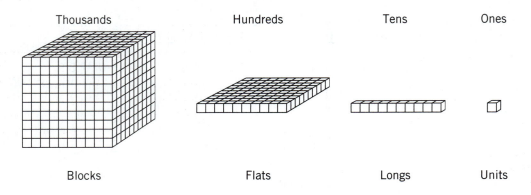

Thousands

Blocks

Hundreds

Flats

Tens

Longs

Ones

Units

Use the Base Ten Blocks virtual manipulative on the CD that accompanies this text to explore different combinations of 123 units.

What similarities and differences do you notice when converting a number from base 10 to base 5?

VM6.6

The block, flat, long, and unit can be related to the base ten place-value system. Have the children study the relationships among the blocks and the base ten place-value system.

Ones place	One is equivalent to a unit.
Tens place	Ten is equivalent to a long.
Hundreds place	Hundred is equivalent to a flat.
Thousands place	Thousand is equivalent to a block.

VM 6.9

These blocks and pictures of these blocks provide children with many experiences on the concrete, semiconcrete, and semiabstract levels. Children could have more experiences on the semiabstract and abstract levels by using an **abacus** or a **chip-trading** device. In chip trading, a chip of one color is given a value 10 times that of another color. Consequently, a collection of, say, 2 blue chips, 4 red chips, and 5 green chips might refer to the number 245, even though there are only 11 chips in all. Often, but not always, chip-trading activities incorporate a positional value for the colored chips as shown in the following figure:

Once children have learned about the base ten system, they may want to apply this knowledge to other systems. This is an appropriate time to introduce some of the features of numeration systems used in the past.

Ancient Numeration Systems

As human beings mastered their environments and developed organized societies, they found that a major necessity was a method of counting and recording numbers. From primitive one-to-one matching (perhaps notching a stick to keep a tally) to present-day computers, people have created and modified a bewildering variety of ways to count and record numbers.

We tend to take our familiar base ten (decimal) system for granted—so much so, in fact, that we usually fail to thoroughly understand the meaning of the numerals we write and the computations we perform.

A brief examination of several historical numeration systems, as well as systems using bases other than ten, might afford us all a fuller understanding of the measures of our decimal system, such as place value, the zero symbol, and the base of ten. The point here is not the memorization or even the application of other numeration systems, but, rather, an appreciation of the strengths and weaknesses of each.

Obviously we can't study all of the many different numeration systems that have been created and used over the centuries. But we can look at a few valuable examples of additive systems, multiplicative systems, and place-value systems. The ancient Egyptian numeration system is an example of an additive system; the Romans used a modified additive system; the ancient Chinese used a multiplicative system (still in use today); and the Babylonians used a place-value system, although the Babylonian system lacks some of the refinements of our base ten (decimal) system, which, of course, also uses place value.

Every **numeration system** uses some set of symbols to represent numbers. The following chart shows the symbols used by the ancient Egyptians:

Egyptian Numeral	Number Named	Meaning of Picture Symbol
l	1	stroke
∩	10	cattle hobble or oxen yoke
ℓ	100	coil of rope
↑ or ⅄	1000	lotus plant
∂ or ⌐	10,000	bent finger
⌐⌐	100,000	tadpole
⚐ or ⚐	1,000,000	a god with arms supporting the sky

The ancient Egyptians used an **additive system of numeration** in which the values of numerals were added together regardless of the order in which the numerals were written. For example, the numeral representing 13 could be written as

∩lll, lll∩, or l∩ll,

Other examples include

$$ℰ ∩ ∩ ∩ \; |||||= 135$$

$$∩∩\,∩\,∩\,∩\,∩\,∩\,∩∩ \; |||||||||| = 99$$

$$⟋\; (\; \{\; ℰ∩| = 111{,}111$$

What do you think the major difficulties would be if you had to calculate using the Egyptian system? As you study the following examples, you should begin to appreciate the advantages of calculating with a place-value system instead.

Addition:

$$ℰℰ∩∩∩∩|||+ℰ∩∩∩\,{}^{|||}_{|||}$$

$$= \;{}^{∩∩∩\;|||||}_{ℰℰℰ\;∩∩∩∩||||}$$

Subtraction:

$$ℰℰ∩∩∩|||-ℰ∩∩||||=ℰ\,{}^{||||}_{|||||}$$

Do NOT ask children to calculate in other numerations systems or in other base systems. This system is illustrated here to help students comprehend and appreciate our base ten system. Children who are weak in arithmetic or have little interest in mathematics will not profit from computational practice of this type. It would be much more advantageous to devote teaching time to the study and understanding of computation in our base ten system.

The Egyptian system was based on simple addition, but its symbols represent powers of 10. It did not have a place-value component, and it did not have a symbol for zero. Such a system becomes clumsy and difficult when greater numbers are involved.

Of all the older systems, the Roman system of numeration is probably the one most familiar to us. We still see Roman numerals used for identifying book chapters, clock numerals, formal inscriptions, and even for creating an outline. The Roman system was not a place-value system and did not have a symbol for zero. The most common Roman symbols are as follows:

Roman Numeral	Value of Numeral
I	1
V	5
X	10
L	50
C	100
D	500
M	1000

To find the value of a numeral, the Romans added the values of numerals in much the same way as the Egyptians did:

$$XVI = 10 + 5 + 1 = 16$$
$$LXVIII = 50 + 10 + 5 + 1 + 1 + 1 = 68$$

However, unlike the Egyptian system, the Roman numeration system was not based entirely on simple addition of number values represented by numerals in any order. Although the Roman system did not have place value, numerals of greater value were usually placed to the left of the numerals of lesser value:

$$CLXVI = 100 + 50 + 10 + 5 + 1 = 166$$

If a numeral of lesser value was placed to the left of (or preceding) numerals of greater value, this indicated that the lesser value was to be subtracted from the greater value. For example:

$$IX = 10 - 1 = 9$$
$$IV = 5 - 1 = 4$$
$$XCIV = (100 - 10) + (5 - 1) = 94$$

The Chinese continue to use a **multiplicative system of numeration** to indicate number value. This system has symbols to represent the numbers from 1 through 9 and separate symbols for powers of 10. The Chinese symbols and their values are shown in the accompanying table:

Chinese Symbol	Value
一	1
二	2
三	3
四	4
五	5
六	6
七	7
八	8
九	9
十	10
百	100

七十

7 x 10 = 70

Greater numbers could be written this way:

四 百 五 十 六

(4 × 100) + (5 × 10) + 6 = 456

RESEARCH SNAPSHOT

How does the Asian system of naming numbers compare to how English-speaking cultures name numbers?

The Asian system of naming numbers is a complete regular-named value system including the tens. That is, 11 is "ten one," and 21 is "two ten one." So in Asian languages, 3 + 9 is "ten two," while in English, it is "twelve." "Ten two" can be thought of as a multiunit, while "twelve" has no connotation of a 10 and a 2 (Uy, 2003).

It is frequently noted that it is more difficult for children from English-speaking countries to construct and use multiunit conceptual structures. Most English-speaking U.S. first graders, given base ten blocks (tens) and unit counters (ones), make unitary models using only the ones, while most Chinese, Japanese, and Korean first graders would use the tens and ones (Miura, Kim, Chang, & Okamoto, 1988). That is, an English-speaking child, when asked to show what the 1 means in the numeral 16, will often pick up one stick instead of the 10 sticks that it actually represents.

What are the implications of basing primary mathematics instruction on unitary models? What implications would this have for teaching multiplace operations in your classroom?

Miura, I., Kim, C. C., Chang, C., & Okamoto, Y. (1988). Effects of language characteristics on children's cognitive representation of number: Cross-national comparisons. *Child Development*, 59, 1445–1450.
Uy, F.(2003).The Chinese numeration system and place value.*Teaching Children Mathematics*,9(5),243–247.

For additional research briefs, "ERIC Digests" lets you search more than 2000 short syntheses of research on a range of education topics. The syntheses were produced by the Educational Resources Information Center (ERIC). Check http://www.ericfacility.net/ericdigests/index/.

The ancient Babylonian civilization was one of the first to develop and use a form of place-value system. The basic symbol of the Babylonians was a wedge shape. Symbols were inscribed on wet clay tablets with a stylus, and the tablets were then dried. Owing to the dry climate, many of these tablets containing Babylonian cuneiform writing and mathematical symbols have been preserved. The Babylonian place-value system was based on groupings of 60 and multiples of 60; for this reason, it is called a sexagesimal system. The Babylonian system did not have a symbol for zero until about 200 B.C.

The symbols generally used by the Babylonians were two distinctive wedge-shaped marks ◀ and ▼:

The principal values of these symbols are

◀	▼	◀	▼	◀	▼
36,000	3600	600	60	10	1

Obviously, since the same symbol could represent more than one value, there was likely to be some confusion in interpreting numerals. Apparently the Babylonians depended on the context of the numerals to indicate their values. Values from 1 through 9 were noted by the following simple repetition and addition.

Babylonian Symbol	Value	Babylonian Symbol	Value
▼	1	▼▼▼ / ▼▼▼	6
▼▼	2	▼▼▼▼ / ▼▼▼	7
▼▼▼	3	▼▼ ▼▼ / ▼▼ ▼▼	8
▼▼▼ / ▼	4	▼▼▼ / ▼▼ / ▼▼▼	9
▼▼▼▼▼	5	◀	10

Place value was indicated by the arrangement of the numerals. In the following examples, the values of the numerals are indicated.

$$(22 \times 60^2) + (15 \times 60) + 33 = 80,133$$

Since the Babylonians did not have a symbol for zero for many centuries, their place-value system was liable to be misread. For example,

could represent 21; or, if the first two symbols were read as 600 + 600, it could represent either 1201 or

1260. Similarly, the number 35 could be written as follows:

  (3 × 10) + (5 × 1)

But this could also be interpreted as 2100:

  (3 × 600) + (5 × 60)

A symbol for zero, it seems, is a necessity for an efficient place-value system.

The numeration system that we use today was invented by the Hindus and modified by the Arabs. The Hindu-Arabic system eventually spread through Europe and evolved into our modern base ten or decimal system of numeration. The efficiency of the decimal system depends on two important features—a symbol for zero and the use of place value. These two features serve to eliminate awkward notation and provide for ease in calculation.

Number Bases Other Than Ten

Many elementary and middle school mathematics programs provide an introduction to other numeration systems, including numeration systems having bases other than ten. There are several reasons for examining numeration systems in a mathematics program. First, it creates an awareness of mathematics as part of our cultural history. Also, it demonstrates the possibility of using numeration systems that differ from ours in significant ways.

Many of the basic generalizations made about the base ten system also apply to bases other than ten. Consequently, teaching students about other base systems can reinforce the meaning and underlying structure of our base ten system. Students then have an opportunity to apply what they have discovered about one place-value system to new situations. If we teach base five, for example, merely for its own sake or as a curiosity of numbers and do not reinforce the student's knowledge of mathematical structure and number relations in base ten, then we are wasting time that could be put to better use.

VM 6.8

Throughout history, various societies have developed different types of numeration systems, or ways of counting and calculating. But the idea of grouping probably first occurred when people began to work with large quantities. A basic concept for any place-value system is some method of grouping. Recall our imaginary trip to a faraway land at the beginning of this chapter. The people we visited counted in a manner similar to, but clearly different from, the way we count. These people, we discovered, were grouping by fives, not tens. Such a system is called a **base five** or **quinary numeration system**. When we calculate using base five (or any base other than base

ten), we usually write the name of the base as a subscript to avoid confusion. Thus, we could record two groups of five and four ones as 24_{five}. This is read, "two-four, base five," and means two groups of five and four ones. The reason we don't call this number "twenty-four" is that the word name "twenty-four" actually means "two tens and four ones." Examine the accompanying table, which is written in the base five, or quinary, system:

Base Five Grouping	Base Five Notation	Base Five Name
•	1	one
••	2	two
•••	3	three
••••	4	four
•••••	10_{five}	one-zero base five
••••• •	11_{five}	one-one base five
••••• ••	12_{five}	one-two base five
••••• •••	13_{five}	one-three base five
••••• ••••	14_{five}	one-four base five
••••• •••••	20_{five}	two-zero base five
••••• ••••• •	21_{five}	two-one base five
••••• ••••• ••	22_{five}	two-two base five
••••• ••••• •••	23_{five}	two-three base five
⋮	⋮	⋮
••••• ••••• ••••• ••••• ••	42_{five}	four-two base five
••••• ••••• ••••• ••••• •••	43_{five}	four-three base five
••••• ••••• ••••• ••••• ••••	44_{five}	four-four base five

Let's use these basic ideas about grouping to develop an octal numeration system. An **octal numeration system** is a system in which we group by eights. Using this system, how would you count the following elements?

Since we are grouping by eight, we would count 1, 2, 3, 4, 5, 6, 7, 8; draw a loop around this group; and record a 1 to represent one group of eight. There are two left over, so this number would be recorded as a 2. The completed numeral is 12_{eight}. The 1 stands for one group of eight, the 2 stands for two ones, and the subscript reminds us that we are grouping in base eight. How can we record the following items in base eight?

How many groups of eight are there? (Three.) How many ones? (Three.) The number, then, would be recorded as 33_{eight}. Now, examine the octal numeration table.

Octal Grouping	Octal Notation	Octal Name
•	1	one
••	2	two
•••	3	three
••••	4	four
•••• •	5	five
•••• ••	6	six
•••• •••	7	seven
•••••	10_{eight}	one-zero base eight
••••• •	11_{eight}	one-one base eight
••••• ••	12_{eight}	one-two base eight
••••• •••	13_{eight}	one-three base eight
••••• ••••	14_{eight}	one-four base eight
••••• ••••	15_{eight}	one-five base eight
••••• ••••	16_{eight}	one-six base eight
••••• ••••	17_{eight}	one-seven base eight
••••• •••••	20_{eight}	two-zero base eight

Thus, we have developed base five and base eight for one- and two-digit numerals. Now let's consider the value of the third place value. In base five, the first place-value column was used to record the number of ones, and the second column was used to record the number of groups of five. What meaning does a numeral have in the third place value? As soon as five ones are counted, they are recorded as 1 in the fives column, or the second place value. This indicates one set of five. What happens when we reach five sets of five? Five sets of five are written as 100_{five}. The third column, then, is used to record the number of sets of five-fives (i.e., twenty-fives, using our familiar decimal language).

$100_{five} = 25_{ten}$

100_{five} is equal to 1 set of 25, no sets of 5, and no sets of 1

What does 123_{five} mean? It means one group of five-fives, two groups of five, and three ones, or, translated into base ten, 38_{ten} (since $25 + 10 + 3 = 38$).

What value would the third column have in base eight? The first column is used to record the number of ones and the second column the number of groups of eight. The third column, then, would be used to record the number of groups of eight-eights (8^2 or 64). Eight groups of eight would be written 100_{eight}, which means one group of eight-eights (64s), no groups of eight, and no ones.

Sixty-fours	Eights	Ones
1	0	0

$$100_{eight} = 64_{ten}$$

Actually, we use many groupings other than 10 on a day-to-day basis; for instance:

2 dozen and 3 eggs are 27 eggs or $23_{twelve} = 27_{ten}$

3 weeks and 4 days are 25 days or $34_{seven} = 25_{ten}$

1 hour and 8 minutes are 68 minutes or $18_{sixty} = 68_{ten}$

2 quarters, 1 nickel, and 4 pennies are 59 cents or $214_{five} = 59_{ten}$

A numeration system can be developed using any method of grouping. The base of the numeration system indicates the number of items grouped together. The accompanying table indicates the notation for numeration systems based on various groupings.

Base Ten	Base Twelve	Base Eight	Base Five	Base Three	Base Two
1	1	1	1	1	1
2	2	2	2	2	10_{two}
3	3	3	3	10_{three}	11_{two}
4	4	4	4	11_{three}	100_{two}
5	5	5	10_{five}	12_{three}	101_{two}
6	6	6	11_{five}	20_{three}	110_{two}
7	7	7	12_{five}	21_{three}	111_{two}
8	8	10_{eight}	13_{five}	22_{three}	1000_{two}
9	9	11_{eight}	14_{five}	100_{three}	1001_{two}
10	T	12_{eight}	20_{five}	101_{three}	1010_{two}
11	E	13_{eight}	21_{five}	102_{three}	1011_{two}
12	10_{twelve}	14_{eight}	22_{five}	110_{three}	1100_{two}
13	11_{twelve}	15_{eight}	23_{five}	111_{three}	1101_{two}
14	12_{twelve}	16_{eight}	24_{five}	112_{three}	1110_{two}
15	13_{twelve}	17_{eight}	30_{five}	120_{three}	1111_{two}
16	14_{twelve}	20_{eight}	31_{five}	121_{three}	10000_{two}
17	15_{twelve}	21_{eight}	32_{five}	122_{three}	10001_{two}
18	16_{twelve}	22_{eight}	33_{five}	200_{three}	10010_{two}
19	17_{twelve}	23_{eight}	34_{five}	201_{three}	10011_{two}
20	18_{twelve}	24_{eight}	40_{five}	202_{three}	10100_{two}
21	19_{twelve}	25_{eight}	41_{five}	210_{three}	10101_{two}
22	$1T_{twelve}$	26_{eight}	42_{five}	211_{three}	10110_{two}
23	$1E_{twelve}$	27_{eight}	43_{five}	212_{three}	10111_{two}
24	20_{twelve}	30_{eight}	44_{five}	220_{three}	11000_{two}
25	21_{twelve}	31_{eight}	100_{five}	221_{three}	11001_{two}

Note the column for base twelve. How many numerals would be needed for a base twelve numeration system? (12) We cannot represent all 12 by using base ten numerals, because base ten has only 10 one-digit numerals. Consequently, we must invent two new symbols. In this case, as is usually the norm, we have chosen to use T and E as one-digit numerals to represent groupings of 10 and 11.

Considering the previous discussion, the numeration table, and our knowledge of the base ten system, we can make the following generalizations about the nature of place-value numeration systems using any base:

1. The first column on the right is always the ones place in any place-value base system.

2. The second column is always used to record the groupings named by the base. In base five, the second place is called the fives place; in base eight, the second place is called the eights place; in base ten, the second place is called the tens place, and so on.

3. The third column is always used to record the number of groupings named by the square of the base. In base five, the third place is for the number of groups of five-fives (5^2). In base eight, the third place is for the number of groups of eight-eights (8^2). In base ten, the third place is for the number of groups of ten-tens (10^2).

4. The numeral that records the number named by the base is always written as 10_{base}. In base five, 10_{five} stands for one group of five. In base eight, 10_{eight} stands for one group of eight.

5. The number of symbols used in any whole-number numeration system is the same as the base of the system. Base five uses five symbols, usually 0, 1, 2, 3, 4. Base eight uses eight symbols, usually 0, 1, 2, 3, 4, 5, 6, 7. Base ten uses ten symbols: 0, 1, 2, 3, 4, 5, 6, 7, 8, 9.

Using these generalizations, we can develop a base two, or **binary numeration system**. How many symbols will we need? (Two, since we are constructing a base two system.) We know that one of the symbols will have to be a 0. Why? (Because our binary system has place value and requires a symbol to represent "not any.") So let's use the symbols 0 and 1. Let's name the following set in binary notation:

First we want to record the number of ones in the ones place, so we draw a loop around groups of two:

There is 1 one left over to record in the ones column. What will we record in the next column? (The number of sets of two.) How many groups of two are there? (Two.) But the symbol "2" is not a numeral in our base two

system. What about the third column? What is recorded there? (The number of sets grouped according to the square of the base, in this case 2^2, or 4.) How many groups of four are there? (One.)

From this diagram, we see that we have one group of four, no groups of two, and one group of one. We can now write the base two numeral as 101_{two}.

In the binary system the values of the places are shown by this diagram:

Sixteens (2^4)	Eights (2^3)	Fours (2^2)	Twos (2^1)	Ones

Note that the fourth column from the right is used to record the number of groups of eight and the fifth column the number of groups of sixteen. Drawing on what we have just learned about the binary system, we can now write a table of the binary notations for the first 12 numbers:

Decimal Notation	Binary Grouping	Binary Notation
1	●	1
2	●●	10_{two}
3	●●●	11_{two}
4	●●●●	100_{two}
5	●●●●●	101_{two}
6	●●●●●●	110_{two}
7	●●●●●●●	111_{two}
8	●●●●●●●●	1000_{two}
9	●●●●●●●●●	1001_{two}
10	●●●●●●●●●●	1010_{two}
11	●●●●●●●●●●●	1011_{two}
12	●●●●●●●●●●●●	1100_{two}

Can we now develop a base four system? This time, just for a change, let's invent four new symbols instead of borrowing Hindu-Arabic symbols.

Quantity	Symbol
	◯
●	/
●●	∠
●●●	△
●●●●	/◯

In our notation, the first column on the right is used to record the number of ones, the second column to record the number of groups of four, and the third column to record the number of groups of four-fours (16).

Sixteens	Fours	Ones	Grouping
		/	•
		∠	••
		△	•••
	/	○	••••
	/	/	•••• •
	/	∠	•••• ••
	/	△	•••• •••
	∠	○	•••• / ••••
	∠	/	•••• • / ••••
	∠	∠	•••• •• / ••••
	∠	△	•••• ••• / ••••
	△	○	•••• •••• / ••••
	△	/	•••• •••• / •••• •
	△	∠	•••• •••• / •••• ••
	△	△	•••• •••• / •••• •••
/	○	○	•••• •••• / •••• ••••

Closure

Educators agree that children enter school with widely varying backgrounds. Home environment, travel experiences, stimulating toys, and human communication have had an effect on each child's personality. It is the teacher's responsibility to assess accurately each child's entrance level and provide experiences that capitalize on inherent curiosity to develop a deeper understanding of the child's environment.

The primary school teacher must constantly be aware that children may have vague and somewhat uninformed ideas about mathematics. The teacher is a "question clarifier" rather than a "question answerer." Some teachers find it difficult to comprehend that some young children have not grasped such relatively simple concepts as one-to-one correspondence. Resist the temptation to simply tell the students what you want them to know. The primary mathematics program should be geared toward how children learn mathematics and not how to listen to a teacher talk about mathematics. Thus, children should find themselves in situations that require them to discuss and use mathematics to answer their needs.

If our educational system is to prepare children for success, we must teach them to recognize mathematics in the real world. The use of attribute blocks and other manipulative materials provides a valuable vehicle for doing so. Children need numerous experiences observing, identifying, and verbalizing ideas to others. While basic mathematics concepts are being developed, the children are also developing logical thought processes in mathematics. Children will usually find the concrete-level approach to numberness and operations to be an enjoyable and logical approach to mathematics.

Because of daily contact with our base ten numeration system, it isn't long before that exposure causes us to think that our system of numeration is the only system and that it has been in existence forever. The Hindu-Arabic numeration system that we use is relatively new compared to many ancient numeration systems.

A comment often heard is, "I understand our base ten system, but I certainly do not understand any of the other bases." Comments such as this actually indicate a shallow understanding of base ten. The basic concepts of a place-value system that uses ten as a base are identical to those of a place-value system that uses any other number as a base. There seems to be little need to translate numerals from one base system to another base system. The value of exploring other bases stems primarily from the development of an in-depth understanding of place value and, to a degree, from an interest in the historical development of numbers.

The development of the concept of place value is very important, beginning in the first grade with the base ten (decimal) system. We are concerned with the structure of our place-value system—understanding, extending, expanding, and comparing what is discovered at each successive step. We should give children an opportunity to apply some of the mathematical concepts they learn to situations that will allow them to think analytically and creatively.

Children are often curious about the past and about what happened before and after a particular event. Ancient numeration systems provide a mental transition for children that should arouse not only curiosity about mathematics but curiosity about history as well. Ancient systems of numeration may be presented as part of a social studies unit that integrates mathematics and social studies. The geographical, social, and economic structure of particular societies could be analyzed so that children can compare these systems from a broader perspective and realize that our system isn't the only one, that we might well have had another system, and that we had a great deal of work done for us by ancient cultures we read about in history books.

The activities that follow focus on number sense and numbers, as well as the algorithms applied to these numerations, and place value. Children first need to understand the physical representation of groups and one-to-one correspondence and then learn to write numerals as a solid base for developing mathematics concepts. For appropriate activities on other aspects of the beginning mathematics program, please refer to the appropriate chapters and the CD that accompanies this text.

PRACTICE EXERCISES FOR TEACHERS

These exercises are designed for the reader of this book, not for the children that the reader may teach. Although some of these examples are suitable for use in the elementary or middle school classroom, they should not necessarily be given to children in the form presented here. Ideas appropriate for classroom activities on the concepts and ideas discussed in this chapter can be found in a later section of this chapter and on the CD that accompanies this text.

1. Name the level of abstraction a child is using in each of the following situations. Use the labels "concrete," "semiconcrete," "semiabstract," or "abstract."
    a) One child walks around and counts the students present by touching each on the head.
    b) A child holds up five fingers when asked how many members are in the child's family.
    c) A child cuts pictures of shoes out of a catalog and pastes them on a sheet of construction paper to represent a collection of shoes.
    d) A child forms a collection using a ball, a mitt, and a bat.
    e) A child keeps score in a spelling bee by placing tallies on the chalkboard.
    f) A child is asked how many toy cars she has and responds by saying, "five" without counting objects or referring to pictures.

2. Using objects and one-to-one correspondence, create a drawing to show that 7 is less than 9.

3. Construct a number line, and mark an *x* on the first eight counting numbers.

4. Use Cuisenaire rods to answer the following questions.
    a) How many red rods does it take to equal the length of a brown rod?
    b) How many white rods does it take to equal the length of a black rod?
    c) How many light green rods does it take to equal the length of a blue rod?
    d) How many red rods does it take to equal the length of a black rod?
    e) How many red rods does it take to equal the length of an orange rod?

5. State the number of ones, tens, and hundreds for each of the following numbers.

    a) 423   b) 79   c) 382   d) 1365   e) 37   f) 963

(Note: Some textbooks ask children how many tens are in 123 and then make the mistake of stating that the answer is 2 when it should be 12; 2 is the digit in the tens place, but there are actually 12 tens in 123.)

VM 6.6

6. Which digit is in the tens place in 578? How many tens are in the number 578?

VM 6.6

7. Which digit is in the hundreds place in 2481? How many hundreds are in the number 2481?

VM 6.6

8. Which digit is in the ones place in 386? How many ones are in the number 386?

VM 6.6

9. Using base ten blocks, state the least number of pieces necessary to represent each of the following numbers. Then identify the blocks that should be used.

    a) 214   b) 2496   c) 63   d) 563   e) 731   f) 3867

10. List four important characteristics of our base ten system.

11. Write each of the following numbers three ways, using expanded notation (using words, exponents, and digits).

    a) 197   b) 2496   c) 63

    d) 563   e) 731   f) 3060

12. State all the possible ways that base ten blocks can be used to represent the number 123.

13. Write the decimal equivalent of each of the following numerals.

a) ௧ᐟᐟ∩∩ || ||| b) = + ቲ c) ᛉ ◄ ᛉ ◄ ᛉ d) MCCLXXIX

e) ◁ (((ᚗᚗᚗᚗ ᕬᕬᕬᕬ∩∩ |||| f) ◄ ᛉᛉ ᛉᛉᛉ g) MMDCCCXLIX

14. How you would read or say each of the following numerals?

a) 35_{eight} b) 87_{nine} c) 40_{five} d) 432_{ten}

15. Explain why it would be incorrect to read 125_{twelve} as "one hundred twenty-five, base twelve."

16. Using the following base groupings, name the number represented by the tally marks.

a) _____$_{\text{eight}}$ b) _____$_{\text{twelve}}$ c) _____$_{\text{two}}$

d) _____$_{\text{five}}$ e) _____$_{\text{nine}}$ f) _____$_{\text{four}}$

17. a) If you wanted to "invent" a base sixteen numeration system, how many basic symbols would you need?

b) Develop a numeration system with a base of sixteen; then list its first 20 counting numbers.

18. In the numeral 9843, the 4 represents a value how many times the value represented by the 8?

19. Make a place-value grid showing the first five places in base three, base four, base five, base six, base seven, base eight, base nine, and base twelve. For example, a base two chart would begin with:

Base Two				
		2^2	2^1	2^0
		2		1

20. a) A system for naming numbers in which a digit receives its value from where it is placed is called a _____ system.

b) The number that indicates the number of objects that can be grouped together in a number system is called the _____.

c) Any number (except 0) to the zero power is equal to _____.

d) In any place-value system, a numeral may be written in _____ notation, _____ notation, or _____ notation.

e) In any base system, the basic symbols used to name numbers are called _____.

21. Using the symbol b for base, use exponents to write a place-value sequence that you can apply to any base system.

22. Write the next five consecutive numerals in the base indicated after each of the following numerals.

a) 21_{nine} b) 14_{five} c) 101_{two}

d) $\text{TE}_{\text{twelve}}$ e) 10055_{seven} f) 535_{eight}

g) 1088_{nine} h) 1212_{three} i) 233_{four}

23. Complete the table by writing each number in standard notation, in expanded notation, and in exponential notation.

Standard Notation	Expanded Notation	Exponential Notation
101101_{two}	—	
1234_{five}		
3765_{eight}		
_____three	$(2 \times 100)_{three} + (1 \times 10)_{three} + (2 \times 1)_{three}$	
_____seven	$(6 \times 1000)_{seven} + (4 \times 10)_{seven} + (5 \times 1)_{seven}$	
_____six		$(5 \times 10^3)_{six} + (2 \times 10^3)_{six} + (1 \times 10^1)_{six} + (4 \times 10^0)_{six}$
_____four		$(2 \times 10^2)_{four} + (1 \times 10^1)_{four} + (2 \times 10^0)_{four}$
$12TE_{twelve}$		
_____nine	$(8 \times 1000)_{nine} + (6 \times 100)_{nine} + (4 \times 10)_{nine}$	

VM 6.6

24. Complete the table (below) by counting in each base shown.

Base Ten	Base Nine	Base Eight	Base Seven	Base Six	Base Five	Base Four	Base Three	Base Two
0								
1								
2								
3								
4								
5								
6								
7								
8								
9								
10								
11								
12								
13								
14								
15								
16								
17								
18								
19								
20								
21								
22								
23								
24								
25								

25. Write in words how each of the following base ten numbers is read.

a) 3003   b) 606,060   c) 707,700

d) 345,768,231   e) 1,001,001,001,001   f) 21,478,000

VM 6.6

26. Study these numerals written in base nine and base three:

$$578_{nine} = 122122_{three}$$
$$56_{nine} = 1220_{three}$$
$$483_{nine} = 112210_{three}$$
$$3452_{nine} = 1011202_{three}$$

Search for a pattern that will permit you to convert quickly from a base nine numeration system to a base three system without changing to base ten.

TEACHING COMPETENCIES AND SELF-ASSESSMENT TASKS

1. Suggest a variety of assessment activities that can be used with young children to determine whether they are ready to begin a formal mathematics program.

2. Discuss the advantages and disadvantages of a structured mathematics program as compared with an incidental mathematics program in kindergarten.

3. Identify "at home" activities that are beneficial for children in developing number readiness.

4. Discuss how a calculator could be used to help young children recognize and discriminate among numerals.

5. Analyze elementary and/or middle school mathematics textbooks, isolating all instances where place value is used; then make a list of your findings.

6. Conduct a debate regarding which portion of an elementary or middle school mathematics program should be devoted to number systems with bases other than base ten. Defend your position.

7. Describe activities for the concrete, semiconcrete, semiabstract, and abstract levels of developing numberness.

8. Study the learning theory of a particular theorist (such as Piaget, Bruner, or Gagné), and describe the implications of adopting that theory for teaching mathematics in the primary grades.

9. Discuss the importance of developing the concept of one-to-one correspondence in a beginning mathematics program.

10. Research the names for large and small numbers in our base ten place-value system of numeration.

11. Make a list of materials that can be used for teaching place value to children. Discuss the comparative benefits and the limitations of each.

12. In this chapter, counting numbers were expressed using standard, expanded, and exponential notation. Research how these various forms of notation might be applied to decimal numbers between 0 and 1. How would these forms of notation be used for describing numbers written in bases other than ten?

13. Research an ancient numeration system not described in this book, and present your findings to the class.

14. Make a list of place-value teaching procedures for each of the four levels of development: concrete, semiconcrete, semiabstract, and abstract. Discuss the effectiveness of each procedure as a transition from one level to the next.

SAMPLE INSTRUCTIONAL AND ASSESSMENT ACTIVITIES

These activities and more are available on the CD that accompanies this text.

VM 6.7

1. Make a walk-on number line by taping a roll of shelf paper to the floor. Mark off spaces that are about the same length as a child's pace. Write the numerals so that the child views the numeral correctly as the child walks forward on the number line. Have one student direct another through commands such as, "Take three steps forward and then two steps backward" or "Move to the next greatest even number."

VM 6.6

2. Draw a loop around each group of ten. Then write a numeral in each blank that shows how many groups of ten are in that box.

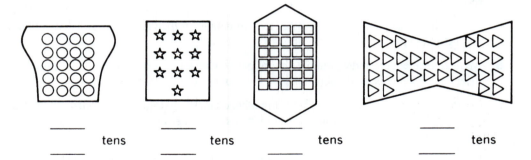

| ____ tens | ____ tens | ____ tens | ____ tens |

VM 6.6

3. Place 10 objects on a table. Have one child count the objects while another places a tally mark on the chalkboard as each object is counted. Have the children think about the various ways we would group these objects. Encourage them to express some of these ways, such as ten groups of one, two groups of five, five groups of two, and so on. Then ask them to think of these 10 objects as one group of ten. Ask how a numeral could be written to record this. Discuss the meaning of the number and the identifying numeral. Extend this kind of activity to help children understand groups of 11 through 19, 20 through 29, and so on.

4. Instruct children to loop or ring sets of 10 objects.

a) ▽ ▽ ▽ ▽ ▽ ▽ ▽ ▽ ▽ ▽

b) ○ ○ ○ ○ ○ ○ ○ ○ ○ ○ ○ ○ ○ ○

c) □

VM 6.6

5. To extend understanding of place value and the meaning of the numbers 1000 through 9999, use prepared numeral cards again—for example, 3051, 3151, 3115, 3105, 3510, and so on—in the same way they were used for the numbers 1 through 99 and 100 through 999. Always ask for the reasoning behind the selection and comparison. This will present many opportunities to discuss why one way may be more efficient than another. The students should understand that more than one way is correct, but that one way may be the most efficient for them.

6. Fill each blank with the correct numeral.

VM 6.6

a) 37 = _____ tens _____ ones

b) 70 = _____ tens _____ ones

c) 387 = _____ hundreds _____ tens _____ ones

d) 149 = _____ hundreds _____ tens _____ ones

e) 9370 = _____ thousands _____ hundreds _____ tens _____ ones

f) 3907 = _____ thousands _____ hundreds _____ tens _____ ones

Watch for these common misunderstandings of the place-value concept: 38 incorrectly written as 30 tens 8 ones, 164 incorrectly written as 100 hundreds 60 tens 4 ones, and 2728 incorrectly written as 2000 thousands 700 hundreds 20 tens 8 ones.

7. By comparing place value, determine which relation symbol (<, >, or =) should be placed in each blank. Have the children explain their reasoning for selecting the symbol.

VM 6.6

a) 76____ 67   b) 456____ 654   c) 58____ 57   d) 203____ 302

e) 357____ 357   f) 409____ 410   g) 4554____ 4544   h) 3000____ 4000

8. Base ten blocks should be used with intermediate-grade children. Have a student represent a number using base ten blocks; then have each class member write the number for the blocks. Write the number for this block representation:

VM 6.6

9. In small groups, provide each student with a place-value chart with ones and tens. Children then take turns rolling a pair of dice. At each roll of the dice, the child takes blocks from the "bank" to represent the number that was rolled and adds them to the blocks they've already collected. All players must continually turn in blocks so that each always has the least number of blocks possible. The first child to obtain a block representing 100 is the winner.

VM 6.6

10. a) Write the numeral for the greatest number that can be named with a two-digit numeral that has 7 as one of its digits.

VM 6.6

b) Write the numeral for the least number named with a two-digit numeral that has 3 as one of its digits.

c) Write the numeral for the greatest number named with a four-digit numeral that has 3 as one of its digits.

d) Write the numeral for the greatest number named with a four-digit numeral that has 4 as one of its digits.

e) Write the numeral for the least number named with a three-digit numeral that has 0 as one digit.

VM 6.8

11. The study of systems of numeration other than our own emphasizes the structure of our decimal system and the meaning of our numerals by comparison and contrast. The study of place value and the examination of the strengths and weaknesses of several systems of numeration sharpen students' interest in the history of our Hindu-Arabic numerals and the development of decimal numeration.

Hindu-Arabic	1	10	100	1000	10,000
Egyptian	I	∩	℮	⸚	⸙

a) ∩∩∩ ||| |||

b) ∩∩∩∩∩ |||| ∩∩∩∩ ||||

c) ℮℮℮ ||| ℮℮℮

d) ⸚℮℮ |||

e) ⸚℮℮℮∩|||

f) ⸙⸙⸚ |||

g) 123_____
h) 24_____
i) 1001_____
j) 1111_____
k) 223_____
l) 1214_____

VM 6.8

12. Make a counting chart to compare the symbols that are used to represent numbers in base two, base five, base eight, and base ten systems.

Can you discover any interesting patterns in this chart? How would you make a counting chart for other bases from what you have discovered by examining this chart?

Base Ten	Base Eight	Base Five	Base Two
1	1	1	1
2	2	2	
3			
4			
5			
6			
7			
8			
9			
10			
11			
12			
13			
14			
15			
16			

7

Addition and Subtraction of Whole Numbers

TEACHING COMPETENCIES

Upon completing this chapter, you will be able to:

- State and demonstrate at least two models of the addition process used to develop an understanding of addition and subtraction.

- Model at least three distinct types of subtraction examples, using groups, the number line, and inverse relationships.

- Discuss the use of basic structures and properties to aid children in developing and memorizing basic facts.

- Demonstrate regrouping in addition and subtraction using a place-value box.

- Prepare a plan for teaching a lesson involving basic facts, concepts, or procedures of addition or subtraction.

VIRTUAL MANIPULATIVES

Upon completing this chapter, you will be able to use virtual manipulatives on the accompanying CD to:

- Demonstrate the process of addition using *Modeling Addition with Objects*. **(VM 7.1)**

- Illustrate the concept of adding using *Modeling Addition on a Number Line*. **(VM 7.2)**

- Compare and contrast combinations of numbers using *Families of Numbers*. **(VM 7.3)**

- Engage in a problem-solving activity involving addition and subtraction using *Circle 21* **(VM 7.4)**.

- Explore representations of regrouping using *Regrouping in the Addition Process*. **(VM 7.5)**

- Compare and contrast different representations of subtraction using *Meaning and Models for Subtraction*. **(VM 7.6)**

- Explore basic subtraction facts using *Developing Basic Subtraction Facts*. **(VM 7.7)**

- Look for patterns and relationships among the basic addition facts using *Addition Table*. **(VM 7.8)**

- Explore representations of regrouping using *Regrouping in the Subtraction Process*. **(VM 7.9)**

Numbered CD icons throughout the chapter refer to the virtual manipulatives in this list.

A **young first-grade** boy excitedly shouted that he knew how many paper cups would be needed for refreshments for the class party. Although he wasn't exactly sure how to say it, he was so sure he knew the answer that he wrote it on the board. He knew there were 18 girls and 16 boys in the class. All he had to do was add these numbers together. The numeral that he wrote for the answer was 214. It didn't occur to him that this seemed to be an unusual number of paper cups for a class party—probably because the actual problem meant something to him, but the process he used to get an answer did not. He knew he should add 18 and 16, but when he added the 8 and the 6 he got 14 and simply wrote it down:

$$\begin{array}{r} 18 \\ +16 \\ \hline 14 \end{array}$$

Then, when he added 1 and 1 he got 2 and wrote this next to the 14:

$$\begin{array}{r} 18 \\ +16 \\ \hline 214 \end{array}$$

This gave the student the improbable answer of 214 for the sum of 16 and 18! Improbable to us, but not to a child who thoughtlessly applies rote procedures and processes without understanding the underlying concepts.

The National Council of Teachers of Mathematics (NCTM) Standards call for a balanced approach to basic computational skills. This balance is achieved by giving appropriate attention to both memorization and understanding. The original NCTM *Curriculum and Evaluation Standards* (1989) stated that students should develop both numbers sense and operation sense and explore relationships among representations of operations, as well as examine and create algorithms and procedures. This theme was expanded in the *Principles and Standards for School Mathematics*, as illustrated by the following statement:

> Knowing basic number combinations . . . is essential. Equally essential is computational fluency—having and using efficient and accurate methods for computing. Regardless of the particular method used, students should be able to explain their method, understand that many methods exist, and see the usefulness of methods that are efficient, accurate, and general. (NCTM, 2000, p. 32)

The purpose of this chapter is to help you develop a view of addition and subtraction that includes, but goes beyond, the skill of getting an answer. You should develop an appreciation of the benefits achieved by focusing attention on both skills and understanding—in other words, on mathematical power. This chapter offers you a repertoire of ideas from which to build your philosophy. How can we best ensure that both skill and understanding develop? Read on.

Creating a Sound Base for Addition and Subtraction

Previous chapters have suggested techniques for developing both numberness and place value with young children. These two basic ideas form a framework for meaningfully teaching the concepts of addition. Consequently, when teaching addition to children, we must first evaluate the children's readiness. The teacher should evaluate each child's number sense, including such specific elements as conservation of number, seriation (ordering of events), one-to-one correspondence, counting ability, recognition of numerals, and writing numerals. Also, research supports the concept that addition should proceed from the concrete level through the semiconcrete, semiabstract, and abstract levels. Two models are commonly used to help children progress through these levels as they develop an understanding of addition: groups of objects and the number line.

Objects taken directly from the child's environment should be used to concretely model number concepts and operation procedures. Teachers will also find that many commercial materials are available for use at the manipulative level—for example, Cuisenaire rods, base ten blocks, pattern blocks, attribute blocks, and number tiles—and a set of these manipulatives can easily be prepared for an overhead projector using color transparencies. This text includes information that describes some of these tools for learning, teaching, and assessing and explains selected activities that make good use of these aids. In addition, the CD that accompanies this text has a wealth of virtual manipulatives that can be used by both teachers and students alike. Check the resource manuals for each of these materials for more detailed instructions about how to use them with children.

An addition and subtraction program should begin informally in kindergarten and proceed into a more formal development in grade 1. As we begin the development of the concept of addition, our emphasis must be placed on the concepts and mathematical relationships involved and not on the rote computation aspect. Also remember that word problems and problem solving should be included in each step of addition concept development. Develop the concept first; then work on memorizing the facts and algorithms. You'll find that students will memorize them more quickly and with greater accuracy when there is a foundation of understanding in place first. In fact, many students will begin to memorize them on their own by associating an arrived-at answer with the concrete/manipulative process of getting that answer.

This chapter on teaching addition and subtraction is organized around five basic concepts that must be understood to solve any addition or subtraction example in a meaningful way. These five major organizational areas are

1. Understanding the operation
2. Basic facts
3. Place value
4. Basic structures
5. Regrouping

These areas serve as a sound foundation for organizing an addition and subtraction program and also as the basis for valuable review at each subsequent grade level.

Meaning and Models for Addition

Now let's begin our study of addition by examining two groups of real objects. Using two separate sheets of paper, place two cubes on one sheet and three cubes on the second sheet.

VM 7.1 Children have three readily available techniques to associate a number with each group. One technique is to simply count the cubes. A second technique is sometimes called *partial counting*. When using partial counting, children recognize the number of cubes in one group and then, beginning with that number, count the number of cubes in the second group. A third technique is to simply associate 2 and 3 with each group, respectively, and recognize this as a total of 5 (without actually counting). Children should be encouraged to associate a number with a small group of objects without counting, a process called *subitizing*. For groups of about seven or less, children should be able to look at, visualize, and state the total number for each group without having to resort to counting the individual objects in the group.

At this stage of development, begin to associate meaning with the addition symbol (+). Through use, children will associate the addition symbol with the physical act of putting together two (or more) groups of objects.

Ask the children to choose a card with the numeral on it that represents the number in each group. Place the numeral card under the proper group of objects. Then place an additional sheet of paper to the right of the groups, and move the two cubes to that sheet. Move the three cubes onto the new sheet, and ask the children how many cubes there are all together. Have one child choose a card with a numeral that describes this new group. It is important to stress that 2 cubes and 3 cubes put together make 5 cubes. Do not use the 2 cubes, 3 cubes, and then another, different, set of 5 cubes. Put the 2 cubes together with the 3 cubes to make a total of 5 cubes.

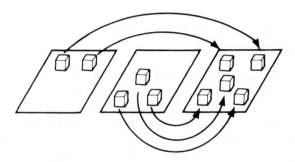

To the degree possible, discourage direct counting at this point. Children should begin to associate the numbers 2, 3, and 5 with the process. After they have had many similar experiences, you might then begin to write the addition sentence $2 + 3 = 5$ to represent what they saw with the model. Generally, teachers do not provide adequate experiences before requiring children to write numerals. Do not rush into writing abstract number sentences—the concept is more important at this stage than the abstract number sentence.

In the operation of addition, the numbers to be added are called **addends**, and the number obtained by adding the addends is called the **sum**.

$$\text{Addend} + \text{Addend} = \text{Sum}$$

or

$$\text{Sum} = \text{Addend} + \text{Addend}$$

The addition operation can be symbolized as:

$$a + b = S$$

or

$$a$$
$$\underline{+b}$$
$$S$$

where a and b are the addends and S represents the sum. The addition sentence is read, "Addend plus Addend equals Sum," or "Addend add Addend equals Sum." Addition is a binary operation because even in a series of 5 numbers to add, only two numbers can be added at any one time. The sum of 5 is obtained by adding 2 and 3 and is unique because no other sum can possibly be obtained using the addends 2 and 3.

VM 7.2 Another model that is useful in developing an understanding of addition is the number line. Recall that a number line is a representation of a geometric line, with arrows at each end to indicate that the line extends in both directions. Two points are marked on the number line, and the resulting line segment, representing one unit, is used to mark off other segments equal to one unit. These segments determine a series of points on the line, and the points are then named by placing them in one-to-one correspondence with the whole numbers.

We can use the number line to model addition examples. To illustrate how this is done, let's solve the example $2 + 3 = \Box$. When we use the number line with young children, remember that we should always begin modeling at the reference point, zero, sometimes called the *origin*. From zero, we measure a segment two units long. From that point, we measure a segment three units long and arrive at the point named 5. The number line model shows that $2 + 3 = 5$.

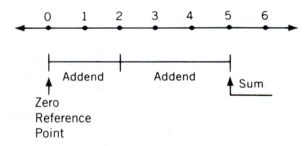

Note that we do not place arrows on the number line segments representing the whole number addends since arrows indicate a direction; direction is not a part of this model until the set of integers (directed numbers) is introduced.

Models using groups and the number line will help children develop an understanding of the addition process. Remember, each of these is a model that achieves the same results as addition but is not addition. Counting is not addition. Partial counting is not addition. Putting objects together is not addition. Then what is addition? Addition is the cardinal number of the union of two or more disjoint sets. That's a lofty phrase and shouldn't, of course, be used as stated with children. However, it efficiently describes the nature of addition and the process one might use to arrive at, or

to describe, an answer. An alternative description of addition follows:

> Addition is a binary operation performed on a pair of numbers called addends to obtain a unique sum.

To reinforce the basic structure of addition, place each of the terms and symbols for addition on separate cards.

$$\text{Addend} + \text{Addend} = \text{Sum}$$

Place the cards randomly in front of the children, and have them arrange the cards in proper order to form an addition sentence. Other cards containing numerals may be placed on the addend and sum cards to relate numbers with the addition sentence.

Developing Basic Addition Facts

A family of numbers is often used to help children extend their understanding of addition. A family of numbers, in the context of addition, includes all possible combinations of addends that will produce a given sum and should be used for both the exploration and development of addition facts but not for memorization of the basic addition facts. As you will discover later in this chapter, there are more effective means for organizing basic facts when it is time for memorization.

To model number families, place a group of cubes and two sheets of paper in front of small groups of children and ask them to make all possible combinations of two groups. The children should record each of their discoveries. For example, 7 cubes might be placed in front of the children, and they would be expected to find all possible combinations for 7. **VM 7.3**

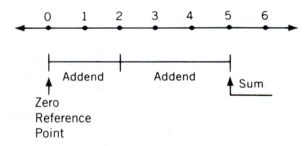

The term *number family* is usually reserved for developing and memorizing basic facts. However, some students may benefit from an activity in which the target is a number other than 0 through 18—that is, when the sum they are dealing with is, for example, 21. Consider the Circle-21 virtual manipulative on the CD that accompanies this text. The challenge is to fill each section of the circle with a number that will yield a total of 21 in each of the intersecting regions. This virtual manipulative provides an interesting combination of basic fact knowledge with problem solving.

VM 7.4

By placing all 7 cubes into two groups, children should discover and write these mathematical relationships:

$$1 + 6 = 7 \quad 6 + 1 = 7$$
$$2 + 5 = 7 \quad 5 + 2 = 7$$
$$3 + 4 = 7 \quad 4 + 3 = 7$$
$$7 + 0 = 7 \quad 0 + 7 = 7$$

This set of examples is called the addition family of seven.

Memorizing Basic Addition Facts Using Structures

The teacher should assist in the development of the children's understanding of addition by using both groups of objects and the number line as models. When the children are able to generate families of numbers, they are ready to begin memorizing the basic addition facts. Basic addition facts must be memorized. To assist children in this process, you must help them organize the facts into structures. When you help children organize the basic addition facts, you encourage thinking strategies and an understanding of relationships useful in memorizing the basic addition facts.

> Basic addition facts include all combinations of any one-place whole number (addend) added to any one-place whole number (addend) to obtain a one- or two-place sum.

Examples will range from $0 + 0 = 0$ to $9 + 9 = 18$.

Now, let us consider these two groups:

Have the children locate the numeral cards to place under the groups. The numbers that represent the two groups are 1 and 0. Under the addition operation, $1 + 0$ is another name for 1. Thus, we can say that $1 + 0 = 1$.

Now let's look at this example:

Under the addition operation, the sum of the numbers 2 and 0 is another name for 2. The sum is unique, because the sum obtained for $2 + 0$ is always 2.

Now let's consider the following set of addition examples:

$$\begin{array}{ccccccc} 2 & 5 & 0 & 0 & 7 & 9 & 0 \\ +0 & +0 & +8 & +3 & +0 & +0 & +4 \\ \hline 2 & 5 & 8 & 3 & 7 & 9 & 4 \end{array}$$

Have the children respond to these questions: "How are all these examples alike? How are the examples different?" After discussing the students' discoveries, what generalizations should children make about the operation of adding the number 0 to another number? The sum of 0 and any other number is always the other number. For this reason, zero is called the **identity element of addition**. Using this basic generalization, children can begin to construct an addition table.

> An addition table is an orderly arrangement of columns and rows in which each column and row is headed by an addend and each cell in the table contains a sum.

The following is an incomplete addition table:

Addends

+	0	1	2	3	4	5	6	7	8	9
0										
1										
2										
3										
4					Sums					
5										
6										
7										
8										
9										

(Addends — vertical label on left)

The next table shows the sums in the addition table for all basic addition facts related to the identity element of addition.

Addends

+	0	1	2	3	4	5	6	7	8	9
0	0	1	2	3	4	5	6	7	8	9
1	1									
2	2									
3	3									
4	4									
5	5				Sums					
6	6									
7	7									
8	8									
9	9									

(Addends — vertical label on left)

Note that sums related to the identity element of addition will complete the first row and the first column of the addition table.

Learning the basic addition facts is a two-step process. The first step is to *develop* the basic facts in a family of numbers, and the second step is to *memorize* the basic facts when organized in structures. From an understanding of this single generalization about the identity element, children will be able to efficiently memorize 19 basic addition facts.

Now let's carefully examine another basic structure that will help children memorize basic addition facts. We begin with another group model.

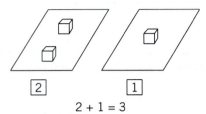

2 + 1 = 3

Now examine the same example, using the number line as a model.

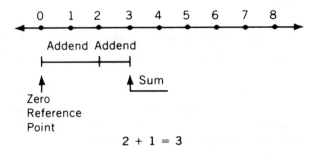

2 + 1 = 3

The expression 2 + 1 is another name for 3. Consider this set of examples:

$$
\begin{array}{cccccc}
3 & 5 & 1 & 1 & 7 & 4 \\
+1 & +1 & +8 & +6 & +1 & +1 \\
\hline
4 & 6 & 9 & 7 & 8 & 5
\end{array}
$$

After the children have solved a number of these types of examples and studied these models, ask them, "How are all these examples alike? How are the examples different?" After a discussion with the children, they should be able to generalize that the sum of any number and 1 is the next greater counting number. If children can count, they can add 1 to a number. These sums fit into the second row and second column of the addition table.

From this "counting" generalization, children should be able to quickly memorize 17 more basic addition facts. Using the two generalizations mentioned so far, the children will have already memorized a total of 36 basic addition facts. Thus, two relatively simple generalizations about adding 0 and adding 1 will help the children memorize more than one-third of the 100 basic addition facts.

Addends

+	0	1	2	3	4	5	6	7	8	9
0	0	1	2	3	4	5	6	7	8	9
1	1	2	3	4	5	6	7	8	9	10
2	2	3								
3	3	4								
4	4	5								
5	5	6			Sums					
6	6	7								
7	7	8								
8	8	9								
9	9	10								

(left side label: A d d e n d s)

The application of this process to the basic structure of our number system will help explain the use of the addition table. For example, the use of the *commutative property* of addition will almost cut in half the task of memorizing the basic addition facts. The basic structural property of commutativity for addition can be examined using groups. For example:

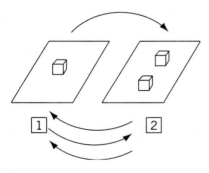

Using groups of cubes on sheets of paper, have children build the addition example $1 + 2 = 3$. Now interchange the two sheets of paper with cubes on them, and have the children write the appropriate addition sentence for the new arrangement: $2 + 1 = 3$. Give the children experience with many similar examples, using sets and number sentences.

We can also use the number line model to demonstrate the commutative property of addition. Using the same example, we can show that $1 + 2 = 2 + 1$ with the following model. The children should model many similar examples.

Discuss the two models shown on the number line, compare them to the relationship with the group model, illustrate many different examples, and then have the children generalize the commutative property of addition using words such as, "When you add two numbers, it doesn't matter in what order you add them—you'll still get the same answer."

> The commutative property of addition means that the order of two addends does not affect the sum. For example, $2 + 3 = 5$ and $3 + 2 = 5$.

Now let's return to the organization of the basic addition facts for memorization, using basic structures. Children are taught to count by twos long before they begin formal study of the addition of whole numbers. Examine this set of basic addition facts:

$$\begin{array}{ccccccc} 3 & 2 & 6 & 5 & 2 & 2 & 8 \\ +2 & +7 & +2 & +2 & +4 & +9 & +2 \\ \hline 5 & 9 & 8 & 7 & 6 & 11 & 10 \end{array}$$

Have the children examine these examples and determine how they are alike and how they are different. Some children may want to use chips or counters to help them find likenesses and differences. After a discussion with the children, they should generalize that adding 2 to a number is just like counting by twos. These sums fit into the third row and the third column of the addition table. Also reinforce the commutative property of addition, such as $2 + 5 = 5 + 2$.

From this generalization of "skip counting," the children will have memorized an additional 15 basic addition facts. With only three generalizations to remember, the children will have memorized 51 basic addition facts—more than half of the facts.

Addends

+	0	1	2	3	4	5	6	7	8	9
0	0	1	2	3	4	5	6	7	8	9
1	1	2	3	4	5	6	7	8	9	10
2	2	3	4	5	6	7	8	9	10	11
3	3	4	5							
4	4	5	6			Sums				
5	5	6	7							
6	6	7	8							
7	7	8	9							
8	8	9	10							
9	9	10	11							

(Addends — labelled on the left side.)

Children seem to have less difficulty memorizing basic facts when the two addends are the same number, perhaps because the world in which we live is full of symmetry—5 fingers on each of 2 hands, 9 tires on each side of an 18-wheeler truck, 3 legs on each side of an insect, and so on. Facts with both addends the same are called the *doubles facts*.

This set of examples is made up of doubles:

$$
\begin{array}{ccccccc}
3 & 4 & 5 & 6 & 7 & 8 & 9 \\
+3 & +4 & +5 & +6 & +7 & +8 & +9 \\
\hline
6 & 8 & 10 & 12 & 14 & 16 & 18
\end{array}
$$

This set of sums fits into the addition table on the diagonal; now the addition table will look like this:

Addends

+	0	1	2	3	4	5	6	7	8	9
0	0	1	2	3	4	5	6	7	8	9
1	1	2	3	4	5	6	7	8	9	10
2	2	3	4	5	6	7	8	9	10	11
3	3	4	5	6						
4	4	5	6		8		Sums			
5	5	6	7			10				
6	6	7	8				12			
7	7	8	9					14		
8	8	9	10						16	
9	9	10	11							18

(Addends — labelled on the left side.)

Immediately following the doubles, we have children memorize basic addition facts called *related doubles* (sometimes referred to as *near doubles*). Each double has two related doubles (except for 9 + 9).

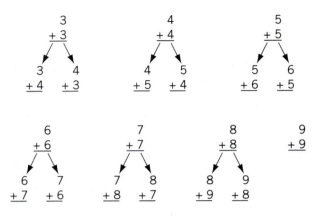

The generalizations become more abstract as we move through the basic addition facts, but the children are also becoming more sophisticated. Memorizing the seven doubles will help the children memorize the twelve related doubles. Since 3 add 4 is one more than 3 add 3, the sum of 3 add 4 will be one more than the sum of 3 add 3. The sums of all related basic facts will be one more than the corresponding double.

Following the structural approach to memorizing the basic addition facts, the students will have efficient techniques for memorizing a total of 70 basic facts. The addition table will now look like this:

Addends

+	0	1	2	3	4	5	6	7	8	9
0	0	1	2	3	4	5	6	7	8	9
1	1	2	3	4	5	6	7	8	9	10
2	2	3	4	5	6	7	8	9	10	11
3	3	4	5	6	7			Sums		
4	4	5	6	7	8	9				
5	5	6	7		9	10	11			
6	6	7	8			11	12	13		
7	7	8	9				13	14	15	
8	8	9	10					15	16	17
9	9	10	11						17	18

(Addends — labelled on the left side.)

The next set of basic facts to be introduced for memorization are the 10 facts related to "tenness." Let's examine this set of basic facts:

$$\begin{array}{ccccc} 7 & 4 & 9 & 9 & 5 \\ +9 & +9 & +6 & +3 & +9 \\ \hline 16 & 13 & 15 & 12 & 14 \end{array}$$

This set of addition facts can be related to place value and tenness. As the children have been regrouping by bundling and unbundling groups of ten, the tenness concept is related to this set of facts. For example, consider 9 + 6. Make a group of 9 blocks on the left and a group of 6 blocks on the right. Take 1 block from the group of 6 blocks (making that now a group of 5) and place it with the group of 9 blocks (making it now a group of 10). So, 9 + 6 has become 10 + 5 by "building" a 10. To build a 10, one element is taken from the group other than the group of 9 and is placed with the 9 to make a group of 10. Thus, the sum will be a group of 10 and one less than the other addend. Now we have accounted for 80 basic addition facts.

Addends

+	0	1	2	3	4	5	6	7	8	9
0	0	1	2	3	4	5	6	7	8	9
1	1	2	3	4	5	6	7	8	9	10
2	2	3	4	5	6	7	8	9	10	11
3	3	4	5	6	7					12
4	4	5	6	7	8	9	Sums			13
5	5	6	7		9	10	11			14
6	6	7	8			11	12	13		15
7	7	8	9				13	14	15	16
8	8	9	10					15	16	17
9	9	10	11	12	13	14	15	16	17	18

*(Addends label along left side)*

There are 20 basic facts yet to be memorized. By using the commutative property of addition, we can cut these remaining addition facts to the following 10 facts:

$$\begin{array}{cccccccccc} 3 & 3 & 3 & 3 & 4 & 4 & 4 & 5 & 5 & 6 \\ +5 & +6 & +7 & +8 & +6 & +7 & +8 & +7 & +8 & +8 \\ \hline 8 & 9 & 10 & 11 & 10 & 11 & 12 & 12 & 13 & 14 \end{array}$$

These facts may be the most difficult addition facts for some children to memorize. Do not rush the children into memorizing these facts, but do consider both the fact and its commuted form.

Children should memorize basic addition facts after they understand the concept of addition and the basic addition structures. However, although memorizing facts is important, it shouldn't take priority over all the other aspects of an elementary mathematics program. Children should engage in problem-solving experiences, measurement, and geometry, for example, as they continue to build their repertoire of facts.

Regular and systematic practice must be provided to help children memorize the basic addition facts. In general, have the children consider only one classification at a time. For instance, study the identity element of addition for an appropriate period of time and guide the children to realize how easy it is to memorize 19 basic facts. Have the children:

- Look at the facts.
- State the facts.
- Listen to the facts.
- Write the facts.
- Visualize the facts.
- Classify the facts.

Aids such as flash cards, calculators, computer software, games, and individual drill activities are potentially valuable in providing a variety of formats for helping children memorize the basic addition facts.

As the basic facts become more challenging, the children can make use of the *associative property* of addition, in conjunction with place value.

> The associative property of addition states that when three or more numbers are added, the way in which the addends are grouped does not affect the sum.
> For example, (3 + 6) + 4 = 13 and 3 + (6 + 4) = 13

In the operation of addition, the associative property of addition allows us to combine (or associate) addends with one another in whatever grouping we choose. That is, we can elect to operate on any two addends at a time. For example, we can add $3 + 6 + 4$ in either of two ways without changing the order of the addends:

$$(3 + 6) + 4 = 9 + 4 = 13$$
$$3 + (6 + 4) = 3 + 10 = 13$$

The parentheses tell us how to group or associate the addends. We can consider 3 and 6 and then add 4; or we can choose to associate the 6 and 4 and then add 3 to the sum. Solving the example this way, we might proceed as follows: 6 add 4 is 10, and 10 add 3 is 13. Since 10 is an easy number to build on, it may be simpler for some children to add 3 to 10 than to approach the computation as $3 + 6 = 9$ and $9 + 4 = 13$. This example may be modeled on the number line.

While children are memorizing the basic addition facts and developing an understanding of the associative property, column addition might be introduced. Column addition is the addition of three or more addends in one example. Beginning examples should include only one-place numbers, such as:

$$\begin{array}{ccc} 4 & & 6 \\ 3 & & 2 \\ \underline{+2} & \text{or} & \underline{+1} \end{array}$$

Because addition is a binary operation, the first two addends are added, and that sum is then added to the next addend. In the first example, 4 and 3 are addends; the sum 7 becomes the "unseen number." The unseen number of 7 is then added to the next addend, 2. Thus, 7 add 2 is 9. In the second example, 8 is the unseen number, and then 8 and 1 are added to obtain a sum of 9.

Children should be provided with physical models to help them comprehend the concept of column addition. Again, groups and the number line are commonly used as models. Groups of objects can be used on sheets of paper, flannel/felt boards, magnetic boards, or an overhead projector. Children should manipulate many different materials to grasp the underlying concepts of column addition.

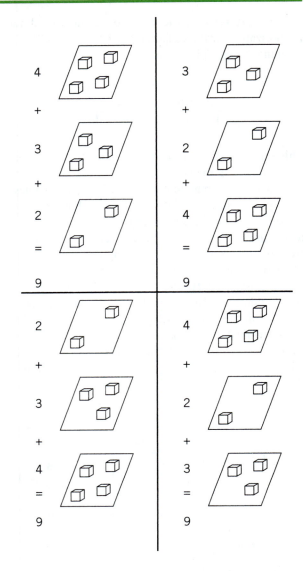

The number line may also be used to effectively show the process of column addition.

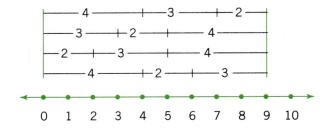

Another model that works particularly well for addition, both column and horizontal, is the use of

Cuisenaire rods. Note that the following figure shows that $4 + 3 + 2$ equals 9, regardless of the order in which the numbers are added:

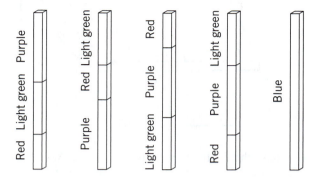

In this example, the students are applying the associative property of addition in the process of finding the sum in column addition. The concept must be extended into more places as children develop their understanding of place value. In fact, extended column addition provides an excellent opportunity to review important concepts of place value.

Extending Basic Addition Facts Using Place Value

A logical extension of the basic addition facts is to use multiples of 10. The basic fact of $2 + 3$ can easily be extended to $20 + 30$. Think $2 + 3 = 5$, and relate this basic fact to 2 tens $+$ 3 tens $=$ 5 tens. Plastic spoons can be used to model this concept. Place the following two groups on the overhead projector, and ask the children to state a mathematical sentence that represents placing the two groups together:

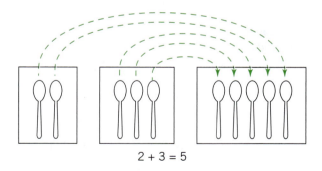

$$2 + 3 = 5$$

Hold up a package of 10 plastic spoons. Ask the children, "How many plastic spoons?" Ask the children to watch you carefully as you exchange each plastic spoon in this set with a package of 10 plastic spoons.

Children are now bringing together the concept of place value and the concept of addition. After examining many examples, children should generalize that the basic addition facts are the same regardless of their place value. That is, just as 3 *cows* add 4 *cows* gives a total of 7 *cows*, so does 3 *tens* add 4 *tens* give a total of 7 *tens*.

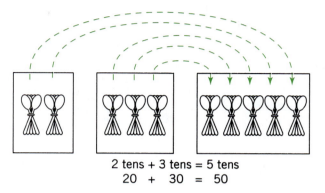

$$2 \text{ tens} + 3 \text{ tens} = 5 \text{ tens}$$
$$20 \quad + \quad 30 \quad = \quad 50$$

Expanded notation provides an efficient method for introducing the addition of numbers having two or more digits. In expanded notation, a number is separated into its component place-value parts (hundreds, tens, ones, and so forth). Written this way, children can better see the structure of the numbers and are better able to rename the numbers in a more convenient form.

$$35 = 3 \text{ tens } 5 \text{ ones}$$
$$\underline{+21 = 2 \text{ tens } 1 \text{ one}}$$
$$5 \text{ tens } 6 \text{ ones} = 56$$

Children have studied the basic facts $2 + 3 = 5$ and $1 + 5 = 6$. Their understanding of the basic fact $2 + 3 = 5$ has been extended to 2 tens $+$ 3 tens $=$ 5 tens, which can be written $20 + 30 = 50$.

Traditional Worksheet

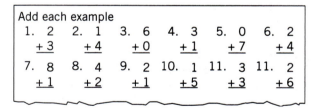

Add each example
1. 2	2. 1	3. 6	4. 3	5. 0	6. 2
+3	+4	+0	+1	+7	+4
7. 8	8. 4	9. 2	10. 1	11. 3	11. 2
+1	+2	+1	+5	+3	+6

Alternative Approach

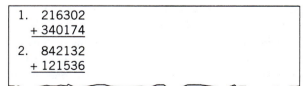

1. 216302
    + 340174
2. 842132
    + 121536

When children have memorized the basic addition facts and understand place value, these two concepts can be brought together to provide the children with the ability to think through examples such as 21 + 35. The same approach may be used as children move into addition examples with more decimal places.

Now let's examine a three-place addition example, using expanded basic facts and place value.

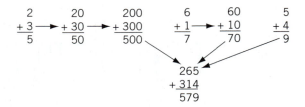

Children need to understand that the basic facts are the cornerstones of success in addition, regardless of the place values involved. Understanding place value and memorizing the basic addition facts are the prerequisites needed to extend the addition concept. Children with a solid foundation in the concept of addition, the basic addition facts, and place value have a great deal of power with addition.

Regrouping in the Addition Process

One major concept of addition remains to be developed: *regrouping*. If regrouping is introduced on an abstract level, children will often have difficulty with place value when writing the sum. Consider the following example:

$$\begin{array}{r} 37 \\ +25 \\ \hline \end{array}$$

Children will sometimes obtain a sum of 512—that is, $7 + 5 = 12$ and $3 + 2 = 5$, so $37 + 25 = 512$. Presenting the example on the concrete level or requiring children to write partial sums will go a long way to prevent this error. Preventive action *during* instruction is better than corrective action *after* instruction.

VM 7.5   Using the place-value box, place 7 single straws in the ones place and three packages of 10 in the tens place. On a sheet of paper in front of the ones place, place 5 single straws; in front of the tens place (on a different sheet of paper), place two packages of 10 straws.

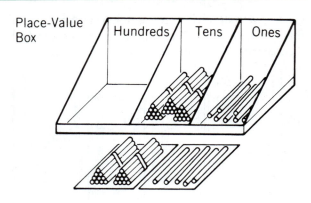

Place-Value Box   Hundreds   Tens   Ones

Combine the 5 straws with the 7 straws. Ask these questions: "How many straws are now in the ones place? What do you do if you have more than 9 straws in the ones place?" The 12 straws are regrouped into one 10 and two 1s. Place the 2 straws into the ones place. Place a rubber band around the 10 straws to make one group of 10. You have now regrouped 10 ones into one new group of 10. Place the one new group of 10 straws into the tens place; this now makes four groups of 10 straws in the tens place. Then place the two groups of 10 straws on the sheet of paper with the group of 4 tens. There are now six packages of 10 straws in the tens place. Thus we have 62 straws in the place-value box.

Since words alone can be difficult in such contexts, relate the manipulation of tens and ones as in the previous example while recording the numbers on the chalkboard or overhead projector: 7 and 5 is 12. What did we do with the 12 when we manipulated the straws? The 12 was regrouped as one 10 and two 1s. The 2 is written in the ones place:

$$\begin{array}{r} 37 \\ +25 \\ \hline 2 \end{array}$$

Now combine the tens: the one regrouped ten is combined with the 3 tens and the 2 tens, to obtain a total sum of 6 tens. The 6 is written in the tens place:

$$\begin{array}{r} 37 \\ +25 \\ \hline 62 \end{array}$$

If partial sums are recorded, the example would be:

$$\begin{array}{r} 37 \\ +25 \\ \hline 12 \\ 50 \\ \hline 62 \end{array}$$

When teaching children, teachers generally do not encourage enough examples using partial sums so that students can fully comprehend the process this reveals. Provide children with many opportunities for manipulating materials at this point, and have them record these manipulations using partial sums.

The preceding example indicates the sequence of thought that children might follow in learning the operation of regrouping. Much practice will be necessary before the children should begin to take shortcuts suggested by the teacher. Mastery of the process using concrete models should come first. Based on their understanding of these models, some students will invent their own procedures, such as adding the tens first, then the ones. The constructive nature so common in children can yield many inviting opportunities for the teacher to engage the children in explaining their thinking. Once the children understand the meaning of addition, they can lessen the emphasis on the manipulative steps and write the examples in more abbreviated forms. However, do not rush the children through this process. Developing a good foundation will save them time and frustration in the future.

Here is an abbreviated form that children can discover and use:

$$\begin{array}{r} {}^{1}37 \\ +25 \\ \hline 62 \end{array}$$

These are the familiar forms of the addition algorithm. The term *algorithm* refers to the steps and the form of writing we use to solve an exercise. Even though calculators play a much larger role in everyday computation than they once did, children should still demonstrate a high degree of competence with the familiar algorithm. This is not to suggest that we should expend considerable time and effort teaching children to do things that can be and are easily done with a calculator. Rather, students should be able to explain their reasoning during any computation exercise, whether it be paper and pencil, mental computation, or calculator based. When feasible, discourage children from writing the regrouped number above the example so that such "crutches" aren't applied mindlessly. After all, some students don't require a visual little number to remember to regroup.

The familiar short form algorithm for addition with regrouping is written:

$$\begin{array}{r} 37 \\ +25 \\ \hline 62 \end{array}$$

The regrouping concept needs to be extended into more place values. Regrouping in addition should first be explored from the ones place to the tens place followed by regrouping from the tens place to the hundreds place.

As children become proficient with single regrouping, they are ready for double regrouping. Double regrouping includes regrouping from ones to tens and from tens to hundreds within one exercise.

Meaning and Models for Subtraction

The development of subtraction should stress the relationship between addition and subtraction. If one operation undoes what another operation does, the undoing operation is called the *inverse operation* of the first. Familiar actions and their inverse actions include unlacing our shoes and then lacing them, buttoning our shirts and then unbuttoning them, or covering our eyes and then uncovering them. Similarly, we can add and then "unadd" or subtract. That is, subtraction is the inverse operation of addition.

$$\text{Addend} + \text{Addend} = \text{Sum}$$

becomes

$$\text{Sum} - \text{Addend} = \text{Addend}$$

The process of addition involves finding a missing sum; in subtraction, we find a missing addend.

Addition	Subtraction	
$a + b = \square$	$a + \square = S$	$\square + b = S$

$$\begin{array}{r} a \\ +b \\ \hline \square \end{array} \qquad \begin{array}{r} S \\ -a \\ \hline \square \end{array} \qquad \begin{array}{r} S \\ -b \\ \hline \square \end{array}$$

Understanding addition helps prepare children for subtraction, but many elementary textbooks introduce addition and subtraction at approximately the same time. Research concerning an optimum time to introduce subtraction has been inconclusive. However, introducing addition and subtraction simultaneously may well lead to confusion. On the other hand, waiting for children to master addition unnecessarily delays the exploration of fundamental subtraction concepts.

Readiness for subtraction includes knowledge of numberness, conservation of number, place value; a beginning understanding of the addition concept; and reversibility. The inverse relationship between addition and subtraction is beneficial in teaching subtraction. Since subtraction is the inverse of addition, reversibility concepts (as defined by Piaget) may be one of the most important prerequisites. Children should be tested by using Piagetian tasks to determine their readiness to begin the study of subtraction.

With children, the subtraction concept must be developed from the concrete level with continual

RESEARCH SNAPSHOT

What does the research tell us about the consequences of having students solve multiplace addition examples followed by multiplace subtraction examples?

In Fuson et al.'s (1997) examination of four research projects with a problem-solving approach to teaching and learning multiplace number concepts and operations, the results from two projects suggested that it may be beneficial to intermix multiplace addition and subtraction problems early in instruction.

In the Problem Centered Mathematics Project (PCMP), some children developed an incorrect generalization of an addition solution method to subtraction: They subtracted the tens and then subtracted both ones. In the Children in the Conceptually Based Instruction (CBI) project, students had trouble devising a written method for subtraction because their addition solution method did not generalize to subtraction.

What real-world problem contexts might you use in your classroom if you wanted to teach addition and subtraction examples simultaneously?

Fuson, K. C., Wearne, D., Hiebert, J. C., Murray, H. G., Human, P. G., Olivier, A. I., Carpenter, T. P., & Fennema, E. (1997). Children's conceptual structures for multidigit numbers and methods of multidigit addition and subtraction. *Journal for Research in Mathematics Education, 28*, 130–162.

For additional research briefs, "ERIC Digests" lets you search more than 2000 short syntheses of research on a range of education topics. The syntheses were produced by the Educational Resources Information Center (ERIC). Check http://www.ericfacility.net/ericdigests/index/.

---

progress to the abstract level. As in addition, models used to introduce subtraction concepts frequently include groups of objects and the number line. However, subtraction may prove to be more difficult to teach and to learn because there are at least three different types of subtraction situations to consider.

Some elementary school mathematics textbooks (and teachers) emphasize only one type of subtraction, the "take-away" model. If the other types of subtraction situations are not explored with children, they will experience difficulty when they encounter examples such as $4 + \square = 7$. For this equation, the child seems to ask, "What do I need to add to 4 to get to 7?" In a child's mind, that hardly seems to be a take-away situation!

VM 7.6

Let's first examine this most common conceptualization of subtraction, take-away subtraction. If we have 7 spoons and we take away 3 spoons, how many spoons will be left? If children count the 4 spoons that are left, they are not subtracting: they are counting! To prevent counting, you might show the 7 spoons on the overhead projector and then turn the projector off. Have the children watch as you remove some *announced* quantity of spoons, say, 3. Then, without turning the overhead back on, ask the question, "How many spoons are still on the overhead projector?" After the children have subtracted, turn on the projector and check their response.

Initially, children see the 7 spoons, and then they see 3 spoons physically removed; then they must subtract. They can readily check to see whether they are correct.

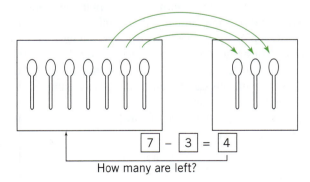

How many are left?

Although this may be the most familiar form of subtraction, children still need to model many take-away subtraction examples and record each step of the inverse operation in writing. Relate addition with subtraction by combining the two groups of objects that were separated and having children write the addition sentence. Discuss how 3, 4, and 7 are related by addition and subtraction.

Another type of subtraction is *comparison* subtraction. Consider the following two groups:

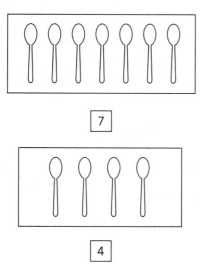

One set has 7 spoons, and the other has 4 spoons. The teacher can ask either, "How many more spoons does the first group have than the second?" or "How many fewer spoons does the second group have than the first?" One-to-one correspondence can be used to compare the two groups. There is no take-away action in solving this type of subtraction.

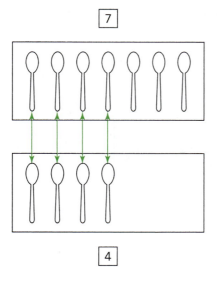

The difference between the two groups, 7 and 4, is 3, because 3 of the spoons in one set cannot be paired with 3 spoons in the other group. We write $7 - 4 = 3$. Comparison subtraction is often seen as more difficult than take-away subtraction because the student must think about two different groups at once and then compare the two groups by using one-to-one correspondence.

The third type of subtraction is frequently referred to as *add-on* or, sometimes, as *missing addend* subtraction.

Look at the following group and ask, "How many more spoons are needed to have 7 spoons in all?"

This may be difficult for children because they must think of the number 7 and compare the 4 spoons that they see with the number 7. The missing addend can also be obtained by counting beginning with 5 and, as spoons are placed, counting 6 and 7. Three spoons were added: $4 + 3 = 7$ or $7 - 4 = 3$.

Children need many experiences on the concrete level with each type of subtraction. Some teachers choose to teach only one type of subtraction at a time, believing that after children become effective with one type of subtraction, then they are ready to move on to the next type. After the various types of subtraction have been taught and the children can function effectively with each type, teachers then provide mixed practice with all types. Other teachers may elect to expose the children to all types from the onset, with emphasis on the real-world action that accompanies each type of subtraction. That is, these teachers would engage the children in problem situations in which the particular type of subtraction would be called for by the action needed to solve the problem.

Here are examples: take-away—if you have 7 cookies and you eat 4 of them, how many do you have left?; comparison—if you have 7 cookies and I have 4 cookies, how many more do you have than I have?; and missing addend—if you have 4 cookies, how many more do you need to have 7 cookies? Each of these problems has a known addend and a sum and is seeking a missing addend—the context of the problem determines which type of subtraction is appropriate. The most important consideration, however, is that the children have ample experiences in acting out all types of subtraction using manipulative models. This forces acknowledgment that the process of subtraction may require different interpretations of the same abstract subtraction sentence.

Using these interpretations of subtraction, children are then ready to understand a working definition for subtraction. Remember that subtraction is not counting either forward or backward. Remember that take away is not synonymous with subtraction, but only one of the possible forms subtraction may take. Then what is subtraction?

Subtraction is an operation performed on a sum and one addend to obtain a missing addend.

Developing Basic Subtraction Facts

The children are now ready to use the same addend and sum cards for subtraction sentences that they used with addition sentences. To help children recognize the reversibility of addition and subtraction, they should have many experiences relating an addition sentence to a subtraction sentence and relating a subtraction sentence to an addition sentence.

VM 7.7　Many elementary school mathematics programs successfully use the number line as a model for developing an understanding of all types of subtraction. Consider the example $7 - 4 = \square$. Because 7 is the sum and 4 is an addend, we can write $4 + \square = 7$. Then subtraction is modeled in much the same way as addition was modeled. Children know that modeling addition on the number line should begin at the reference point, zero. Draw a line segment from 0 to 4 for the known addend. Then, locate the point on the number line that corresponds to 7, the sum. Now use a dotted line and draw a line segment from 4 to 7. This dotted-line segment represents the missing addend. How long is the dotted-line segment? It is three units long.

This way we can use the number line to identify the missing addend as 3. Therefore we see that $4 + 3 = 7$, so $7 - 4 = 3$.

At this stage of development, children should be able to look at two groups and write four related mathematical sentences. For example:

$4 + 5 = 9$　　　　　　$9 - 4 = 5$
$5 + 4 = 9$　　　　　　$9 - 5 = 4$

If children have memorized the basic addition facts, then they also know, or at least have a good jump on, the basic subtraction facts. What is a basic subtraction fact?

> A basic subtraction fact is a one- or two-place sum subtract a one-place addend to obtain another one-place addend.

For example, if children have memorized $4 + 5 = 9$ and if they understand the inverse relationship between addition and subtraction, then they should see the solution to $4 + \square = 9$ is 5. Identify another way to express this inverse relationship.

$$9 - 4 = \square \quad \text{or} \quad \begin{array}{r} 9 \\ -4 \\ \hline \square \end{array} \quad \text{or} \quad \begin{array}{r} 4 \\ +\square \\ \hline 9 \end{array}$$

The table of basic addition facts can be used to solve subtraction exercises. Consider $7 - 4 = \square$. In this **VM 7.8** example, 7 is the sum, 4 is the known addend, and the box indicates the missing addend. In the addition table, the addends are located in the top row and in the left-hand column. Locate the known addend 4 in the top row, and look down the column until you come to the sum 7. Now look to the left along the row containing 7 until you come to the missing addend, 3, in the left-hand column. Clearly, $7 - 4 = 3$.

Addends

+	0	1	2	3	4	5	6	7	8	9
0	0	1	2	3	4	5	6	7	8	9
1	1	2	3	4	5	6	7	8	9	10
2	2	3	4	5	6	7	8	9	10	11
3	3	4	5	6	7	8	9	10	11	12
4	4	5	6	7	8	9	10	11	12	13
5	5	6	7	8	9	10	11	12	13	14
6	6	7	8	9	10	11	12	13	14	15
7	7	8	9	10	11	12	13	14	15	16
8	8	9	10	11	12	13	14	15	16	17
9	9	10	11	12	13	14	15	16	17	18

(left-hand column labeled vertically: Addends)

Sometimes children need a guide to help them locate a specific example in the addition table. Make a guide by cutting two strips from a sheet of transparent acetate.

Use rubber cement to connect the two strips at a 90° angle. Cut a square for the product where the two strips overlap. When placed on a basic fact table, the answer will be displayed through the cutout square.

Glue together.

Cut out rectangle.

The basic subtraction facts must be developed, organized into a table, and then memorized. This sequential procedure for teaching subtraction is much like that for addition. Teachers report that organizing basic subtraction facts into a structural or conceptual approach that children understand (much like we did for addition) is helpful to students trying to memorize the basic subtraction facts.

Memorizing Basic Subtraction Facts Using Structures

Now let's begin by considering this set of basic subtraction facts:

0	1	2	3	4	5	6	7	8	9
−0	−1	−2	−3	−4	−5	−6	−7	−8	−9
0	0	0	0	0	0	0	0	0	0

Students should again look for likenesses and differences in these examples. They should generalize much as they did when learning addition and note that when a number is subtracted from itself, the missing addend (the answer to a subtraction exercise) is 0. With this conclusion, children will have memorized 10 of the 100 basic subtraction facts.

Examine this set of basic subtraction examples:

1	2	3	4	5	6	7	8	9
−0	−0	−0	−0	−0	−0	−0	−0	−0
1	2	3	4	5	6	7	8	9

Following an observation-based procedure, the children should be encouraged to examine these examples for likenesses and differences. Children should notice that when 0 is subtracted from a number, the other number is the same as the missing addend (the answer). Another 9 basic facts have now been memorized. Thus, using only two basic structure ideas,

children can effectively memorize 19 basic subtraction facts.

As numberness and number sequencing were developed with the children, we noted which number comes after a certain number and which number comes before a certain number. What number is just before 6? Children can use the number line as a model to help them. This idea will help them memorize this set of basic subtraction facts:

2	3	4	5	6	7	8	9	10
−1	−1	−1	−1	−1	−1	−1	−1	−1
1	2	3	4	5	6	7	8	9

These examples can be considered neighbors, as the children look for likenesses and differences. When 1 is subtracted from a number, the number that precedes it is the missing addend (the answer). Nine more basic facts have been memorized for a total of 28. More than one-fourth of the basic subtraction facts have now been memorized by using three simple observations.

Extending the idea of neighbors a little further, we can consider this set of examples:

3	4	5	6	7	8	9	10
−2	−3	−4	−5	−6	−7	−8	−9
1	1	1	1	1	1	1	1

Again, after the children have studied the examples, encourage them to conclude that when a number just before a given number is subtracted, the missing addend (the answer) is 1. Eight more basic subtraction facts have been memorized, making a total of 36 that have been memorized (more than one-third of all basic subtraction facts).

Now review counting by twos with the children. This concept will help them memorize this set of basic subtraction facts:

4	5	6	7	8	9	10	11
−2	−2	−2	−2	−2	−2	−2	−2
2	3	4	5	6	7	8	9

Using the number line, the children can realize that subtracting 2 yields the same result as skip-counting backward by two on the number line. This is the third row of the subtraction and addition table. These 8 examples along with the 36 already memorized make a total of 44 basic subtraction facts that have been memorized.

Related to the previous set of subtraction facts is the following set of facts:

5	6	7	8	9	10	11
−3	−4	−5	−6	−7	−8	−9
2	2	2	2	2	2	2

These numbers are two apart on the number line, so the missing addend (the answer) is 2. This will help children memorize 7 more basic facts. Now 51 basic subtraction facts have been memorized.

The children have studied the doubles with respect to basic addition facts. Now relate the doubles to the subtraction facts. This set of facts is:

$$
\begin{array}{ccccccc}
6 & 8 & 10 & 12 & 14 & 16 & 18 \\
-3 & -4 & -5 & -6 & -7 & -8 & -9 \\
\hline
3 & 4 & 5 & 6 & 7 & 8 & 9
\end{array}
$$

After careful examination, the children should see that the given addend is the same as the missing addend (the answer). Using this idea of the inverse of the addition doubles, seven more basic subtraction facts have been memorized, for a total of 58.

The next set of subtraction facts to consider is the following:

$$
\begin{array}{cccccc}
12 & 13 & 14 & 15 & 16 & 17 \\
-9 & -9 & -9 & -9 & -9 & -9 \\
\hline
3 & 4 & 5 & 6 & 7 & 8
\end{array}
$$

After studying these examples, the children should discover that the missing addend is one greater than the number in the ones place of the sum. This generalization will help the children memorize 6 more basic facts, for a total of 64.

Consider this set of facts with a difference of 9:

$$
\begin{array}{cccccc}
12 & 13 & 14 & 15 & 16 & 17 \\
-3 & -4 & -5 & -6 & -7 & -8 \\
\hline
9 & 9 & 9 & 9 & 9 & 9
\end{array}
$$

In subtraction, when the numbers in the ones place are neighbors and the lesser number is on top, the missing addend is 9. This makes another 6 basic subtraction facts, so at this point the children should have 70 basic facts memorized. Encourage the children to examine carefully the last 30 basic subtraction facts that must be memorized and to use whatever they discover will help them. All children do not need the same methods to help them memorize the facts. The basic subtraction facts remaining to be memorized are:

$$
\begin{array}{ccccccccc}
7 & 8 & 9 & 10 & 11 & 9 & 10 & 11 & 12 \\
-3 & -3 & -3 & -3 & -3 & -4 & -4 & -4 & -4 \\
\hline
4 & 5 & 6 & 7 & 8 & 5 & 6 & 7 & 8
\end{array}
$$

$$
\begin{array}{ccccccccc}
11 & 12 & 13 & 13 & 14 & 15 & 7 & 8 & 9 \\
-5 & -5 & -5 & -6 & -6 & -7 & -4 & -5 & -5 \\
\hline
6 & 7 & 8 & 7 & 8 & 8 & 3 & 3 & 4
\end{array}
$$

$$
\begin{array}{ccccccccc}
9 & 10 & 11 & 10 & 11 & 12 & 13 & 11 & 12 \\
-6 & -6 & -6 & -7 & -7 & -7 & -7 & -8 & -8 \\
\hline
3 & 4 & 5 & 3 & 4 & 5 & 6 & 3 & 4
\end{array}
$$

$$
\begin{array}{ccc}
13 & 14 & 15 \\
-8 & -8 & -8 \\
\hline
5 & 6 & 7
\end{array}
$$

This last set of 30 basic facts is often more challenging for children. Give them 1 or 2 of these basic facts to memorize at a time. Teachers sometimes tend to require too much memorization too rapidly. The organization suggested in this chapter has proved successful, even with children with certain severe learning difficulties.

Extending Basic Subtraction Facts Using Place Value

After understanding place value, subtraction as the inverse of addition, and the basic subtraction facts, children should be ready to extend the basic subtraction facts. Help the children relate the following two examples, much as we did for addition:

Write 4 – 1 = 3   Write 40 – 10 = 30

Children should generalize that the basic subtraction facts still apply, regardless of the decimal place. Children who understand place value and who have memorized basic facts can apply this knowledge to successfully solve two-place subtraction examples.

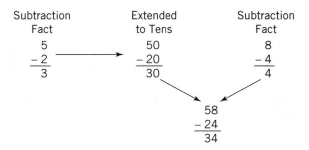

Subtraction examples can also be written in another form:

$$
\begin{aligned}
64 &= \quad 6 \text{ tens } 4 \text{ ones} \\
-12 &= -1 \text{ ten } \ 2 \text{ ones} \\
&\hphantom{=} \ \ 5 \text{ tens } 2 \text{ ones} = 52
\end{aligned}
$$

$$
\begin{aligned}
57 &= \quad 5 \text{ tens } 7 \text{ ones} \\
-23 &= -2 \text{ tens } 3 \text{ ones} \\
&\hphantom{=} \ \ 3 \text{ tens } 4 \text{ ones} = 34
\end{aligned}
$$

$$
\begin{aligned}
45 &= \quad 4 \text{ tens } 5 \text{ ones} \\
-31 &= -3 \text{ tens } 2 \text{ ones} \\
&\hphantom{=} \ \ 1 \text{ ten } \ 4 \text{ ones} = 14
\end{aligned}
$$

Do not write the examples like this:

$$64 = 60 + 4$$
$$\underline{-12 = -10 + 2}$$

If we do, children may subtract the number in the tens place and then add the number in the ones place, because they see the addition sign in the middle of the subtraction example. This is a poor teaching procedure that, potentially, will cause the children to subtract only the 10 and not the 2. Instead, use place-value names until children internalize them. That is, the expanded form might be read as "6 tens and 4 ones subtract 1 ten and 2 ones." Even a correct abstract form using parentheses, shown here,

$$64 = 60 + 4$$
$$\underline{-12 = -(10 + 2)}$$

will likely cause confusion about what should be added and what should be subtracted.

The notion of inverse operation is an important aspect of basic mathematical structure; it is essential to understanding elementary arithmetic. Also, the basic properties of subtraction should be examined. Using manipulative materials, children can explore the ideas of basic structures and generalize that

1. Subtraction is not commutative: $8 - 6 \neq 6 - 8$
2. Subtraction is not associative: $(8 - 4) - 2 \neq 8 - (4 - 2)$
3. Subtraction does not have an identity element: Even though $7 - 0 = 7$, it is not true that $0 - 7 = 7$

Regrouping in the Subtraction Process

The trend in contemporary classrooms is to use the term *regroup* to describe the process that has previously been called *carry and borrow*. The word *regroup* seems more descriptive of the process that we are trying to delineate. The manipulation and concept are the same for addition and subtraction: 10 ones are changed (or regrouped) to be one group of 10, and one group of 10 is changed (or regrouped) to be 10 ones. The terminology will help relate the two ideas, but it is only a process of regrouping taught as one reversible concept, not as two separate concepts.

Before introducing subtraction examples that require regrouping, it is a good idea to review expanded notation

and the concept that a number can be named in many ways. The children should use some type of counter, such as ice-cream sticks or tongue depressors, and demonstrate each name for a number. The number 372, for example, can be written as

3 hundreds	7 tens	2 ones
or		
2 hundreds	17 tens	2 ones
or		
2 hundreds	16 tens	12 ones
or		
2 hundreds	15 tens	22 ones

and so on.

The use of numeral expanders, as described in Chapter 6, will assist greatly here.

When beginning subtraction with regrouping, children will often subtract the lesser value from the greater value, regardless of the position of the digits in the example. For instance, children might think that

$$\begin{array}{r} 71 \\ -28 \\ \hline 57 \end{array}$$

Since 8 cannot be subtracted from 1, children will often resort to subtracting 1 from 8. This type of response indicates that the children do not really understand the meaning of subtraction and that they were likely told how to regroup on the abstract level. If children are encouraged to explore on the concrete level, they will not be as likely to make this type of error. It is better to anticipate the children's difficulties and prevent them from occurring than to try to correct the misconceptions later.

Now, let's carefully examine the regrouping process in subtraction. How would a child subtract 27 from 53, **VM 7.9** beginning on the concrete level? Using a place-value box and the take-away model, start with 53 counters and have the students remove 27 counters.

To remove 7 ones, the student must regroup one pack of 10. A student cannot remove 7 counters from the ones place without regrouping 1 ten to 10 ones. This is the same way a child must think in order to understand regrouping in the written algorithm for subtraction. Children need many concrete examples before they can begin to record their ideas using the algorithm.

Next, have the students use place value to rewrite this example:

$$53 = \quad 5 \text{ tens } 3 \text{ ones}$$
$$-27 = -2 \text{ tens } 7 \text{ ones}$$

The children should see that they can't subtract *yet*, since the number of ones in the first line of the example is less than the number of ones in the second line. Continually relate to the concrete model, using the place-value box as we have pictured. To overcome the difficulty, 5 tens 3 ones can be regrouped as 4 tens 13 ones:

$$53 = \quad 4 \text{ tens } 13 \text{ ones}$$
$$-27 = -2 \text{ tens } 7 \text{ ones}$$
$$ 2 \text{ tens } 6 \text{ ones} = 26$$

Children need to model and record the results of many examples.

Children who have been taught regrouping from the concrete level to the abstract level will be able to apply the concept to more places and manipulate counters to understand the regrouping.

$$323 = \quad 3 \text{ hundreds } 2 \text{ tens } 3 \text{ ones}$$
$$-156 = -1 \text{ hundred } 5 \text{ tens } 6 \text{ ones}$$
$$ = \quad 2 \text{ hundreds } 11 \text{ tens } 13 \text{ ones}$$
$$ = -1 \text{ hundred } 5 \text{ tens } 6 \text{ ones}$$

Place value and expanded notation can be used to develop an understanding of regrouping. After children understand regrouping, it should be easy for them to see the relationship of these concepts to the mental processes involved in using the short subtraction algorithm with which we wish them to become familiar:

$$323$$
$$-156$$
$$\overline{167}$$

Children who have been taught this way will not need to write regrouped numbers above the examples. Children who understand the concept will not need these crutches; children with a weak or poorly developed understanding may, however, need additional help.

Children who have a sound understanding of regrouping will also have little difficulty with zeros in subtraction. Consider the example 700–256.

Traditionally, this type of example required double regrouping:

$$\begin{array}{ccc} {}^{6}\cancel{7} & {}^{9}\cancel{0} & {}^{1}0 \\ -2 & 5 & 6 \\ \hline 4 & 4 & 4 \end{array}$$

If we think of the number 700 as 70 tens and 0 ones, we need only one regrouping. Study this example. Note that no markings are placed above the example.

$$700 = 70 \text{ tens } 0 \text{ ones} = 69 \text{ tens } 10 \text{ ones}$$
$$-256 = 25 \text{ tens } 6 \text{ ones} = 25 \text{ tens } 6 \text{ ones}$$
$$\overline{44 \text{ tens } 4 \text{ ones}}$$
$$= 4 \text{ hundreds } 4 \text{ tens } 4 \text{ ones} = 444$$

Other children might approach this exercise by subtracting the 200 from the 700 and then deal with how to take away the remaining 56. As stated earlier, many invented mental strategies can and should be explored along with the more common, traditional algorithms.

It is of historical interest that many other algorithms have been used for addition and subtraction. Many of these alternative algorithms are interesting and motivating for students. You may wish to research the Austrian method and the method of complementary subtraction. Consider what might be probable advantages and disadvantages of these other algorithms.

Closure

Your familiarity with many of the topics of this chapter may lead you to overlook some important details in the teaching/learning process as it relates to addition and subtraction. Compare how mathematics was taught when you were in elementary school to the techniques as suggested here. Concentrated effort should be devoted to the question of how children develop the necessary understanding and skills. Become well versed in the concepts, the materials used in teaching the concepts, and the methodology used in teaching.

This chapter has exposed you to effective methods and procedures for teaching children, for helping them discover ideas and generalizations, and for developing skills. When you have concluded the study of this chapter, you should have an intuitive understanding of and a formal definition for addition and its inverse operation, subtraction. The basic properties of addition for whole numbers should be understood and functional.

Addition and subtraction should be initiated with primary-age children and be reviewed and extended every year in the elementary school. For example, the

6-year-old child can learn what addition is and apply it to one- and two-place numbers. The 7-year-old child should memorize the basic facts and extend addition to three-, four-, and five-place numbers. The 8-year-old child might extend the concept of addition into another number system, such as integers or rational numbers expressed as fractions. The 9-year-old child should review addition of whole numbers and extend the idea to any number of places and/or extend the idea of addition to another system of numbers. The spiral curriculum approach can be extended through the child's various age levels. A systematic, cyclic approach to concept and skill development is essential. The activities for this chapter follow a consistent pattern of presentation and reinforcement.

As children develop and become more complex individuals, the problems that they encounter also become more complex. We suggest starting the mathematics program for each grade level with new concepts and ideas and then reinforcing the operations when the need arises. Children quickly become bored when each grade level is begun with a reexamination of addition, subtraction, multiplication, and division.

Children need practice and drill to maintain skills and concepts that they have previously developed. However, practice and drill need not be boring. Positive results can be obtained in many interesting and unique ways. Experiences for children should progress from the concrete through the semiconcrete and from the semiabstract to the abstract. Remember that many types of materials are available and should be used in developing children's concepts of addition and subtraction. Materials that should be explored at this time include, but should not be limited to, base ten blocks, Cuisenaire rods, calculators, and computers.

The operation of addition and its inverse have always been part of the child's work in mathematics. The objective is still to identify a shorter, more effective way than counting to determine a total or a part, but the child's understanding must precede the presentation of conventional algorithms.

In summary, there are five major concepts that a student should understand to assist him or her in solving any addition example:

1. The student must understand what the process of addition means.
2. The student must understand the basic addition facts and have them memorized.
3. The student must understand place value and be able to relate place-value concepts to addition.

This allows the student to extend the basic addition facts to many-place numbers.

4. The student should understand the basic structures or properties (e.g., the commutative property and the identity element) as applied to addition.
5. The student must understand the concept of regrouping and be able to relate the regrouping concept to addition.

There are also five major concepts that a student should comprehend to assist him or her in solving any subtraction example:

1. The student must understand the various interpretations of subtraction.
2. The student must comprehend the basic subtraction facts and have them memorized.
3. The student must understand place value and relate place-value concepts to the inverse operation of subtraction.
4. The student must understand that the basic structures or properties of addition (e.g., commutativity) do not apply to subtraction.
5. The student must understand the concept of regrouping as it applies to the subtraction process.

The major concepts of addition and subtraction have been organized into the following convenient table:

	Addition	**Subtraction**
Understanding the operation	$A + A = S$	$S - A = A$
Basic facts	100 basic facts	100 basic facts
Place value	Same as for subtraction	Same as for addition
Structures	Commutative property, associative property, identity element of addition, and so on	Properties do not apply to subtraction.
Regrouping	Change ones to tens, and so on.	Change tens to ones, and so on.

PRACTICE EXERCISES FOR TEACHERS

These exercises are designed for the reader of this book, not for the children that the reader may teach. Although some of these examples are suitable for use in the elementary or middle school classroom, they should not necessarily be given to children in the form presented here. Ideas appropriate for classroom activities on the concepts and ideas discussed in this chapter can be found in a later section of this chapter and the CD that accompanies this text.

1. Create a number line diagram to solve these examples. Label the addends and sum for each.

    a) $5 + 4 = \square$ b) $3 + 2 = \square$ c) $1 + 6 = \square$ d) $8 + 7 = \square$

    e) $9 - 4 = \square$ f) $7 + \square = 11$ g) $8 - 2 = \square$ h) $15 - 9 = \square$

2. Use the addition operation and its inverse to write four related sentences using each of the given numbers.

    a) 4, 7, 11   b) 9, 2, 7   c) 6, 13, 7   d) 31, 75, 44

3. Write two subtraction sentences suggested by each of these addition sentences.

    a) $8 + 9 = \square$ b) $4 + 9 = \square$ c) $\square = 53 + 39$ d) $7 + 6 = \square$

4. Name the two basic facts and the expanded basic fact that will help children solve each of the following two-place addition examples:

    a) $18 + 31 = \square$ b) $26 + 31 = \square$ c) $73 + 15 = \square$ d) $52 + 45 = \square$

5. Rewrite each of the following examples in expanded notation and solve.

    a) 18   b) 247   c) 73   d) 364
       $+41$ $+532$ $+25$ $+213$

VM 7.5

6. Solve each of the following examples with regrouping. Show each step of the regrouping process using either the short form or longer form.

    a) 37   b) 61   c) 73   d) 219   e) 378
       $+49$ $+54$ $+88$ $+486$ $+154$

    f) 56   g) 346   h) 459   i) 521   j) 832
       $+29$ -83 -272 -146 -398

7. Use expanded notation to calculate each of the following sums. Show your work in horizontal form, and name the property of addition that justifies each step. (The purpose of this exercise is to help teachers understand the mathematics properties underlying the algorithm. Do not ask children to solve examples in this manner.)

    a) 37   b) 276   c) 48
       $+28$ $+49$ $+75$

VM 7.9

8. Solve each subtraction example, using renaming and only one regrouping and with no borrow marks written above the example.

    a) 500   b) 802   c) 900
       $+273$ -367 $+258$

9. Using the words *addend* and *sum*, write four related addition and subtraction sentences.

10. Describe how the subtraction example shown below might be solved using take-away, comparison, and missing addend models.

$$54 - 18 = \square$$

TEACHING COMPETENCIES
AND SELF-ASSESSMENT TASKS

1. Which prerequisite skills and concepts are needed for the development of the *concept* of addition? The subtraction *concept?*

2. According to Piagetian theory, when is it likely that a child will be ready to comprehend subtraction?

3. Discuss how Cuisenaire rods and base ten blocks can be used in developing the concepts of addition and subtraction.

4. Discuss the pros and cons for each model used in this chapter to develop an understanding of the addition and subtraction processes.

5. Research the literature, and then discuss effective techniques for encouraging children to memorize the basic addition and subtraction facts.

6. Discuss the likenesses and differences between how addition and subtraction are presented in this chapter and how you remember learning these as a child.

7. Which types of materials can be used with children to develop the concepts of addition and subtraction?

8. Research the literature for alternative ways to add and subtract, and then compare and contrast the different methods (e.g., low-stress algorithms, Austrian method of subtraction, and the equal additions method).

9. Some textbooks suggest that addition and subtraction should be taught simultaneously; others recommend that subtraction be taught after addition. Take a stand on this debate and support your position.

SAMPLE INSTRUCTIONAL AND ASSESSMENT ACTIVITIES

These activities and more are available on the CD that accompanies this text.

VM 7.1

1. Use many concrete situations in teaching the understanding of the concepts and processes of addition and its inverse, subtraction, at this level: counting sticks, plastic spoons, plastic forks, paper cups, flannel/felt board, cutout shapes, and anything available from the child's everyday world. For example:

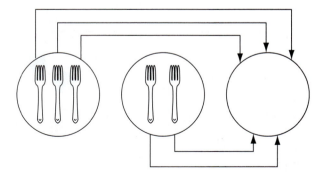

Place plastic forks on a table and encircle them with yarn to indicate groups. Use another piece of yarn to make the outline of another set. Move the three forks and the two forks into the new group. This is a model for the concept $3 + 2 = 5$. A group of three elements joined with a group of two other elements forms a new group of five elements. Many of these experiences with groups should be used to teach the children what actually happens when two groups are joined. Then introduce the sign of operation (+) and the relation symbol (=) in developing mathematical sentences.

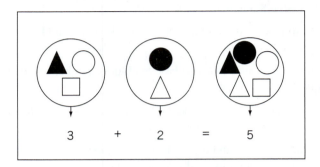

2. On a set of cards about 2 inches by 3 inches, write the numerals 0 through 9. Place the cards facedown, and draw two cards to use as addends. Model the addition example on the number line. Exercises of this type provide practice in addition facts by using number line diagrams.

Children can label the addends and the sum. For this example, they can write the addition sentence $3 + 1 = 4$.
Model $1 + 4$ on the number line.

3. Use the flannel/felt board to display two disjoint groups with different cardinal numbers. Discuss how the two groups are different. Use yarn to connect the objects in the two disjoint groups to show one-to-one correspondence. Write a comparison subtraction sentence. Discuss the subtraction sentence that can be written. Then place a numeral for the cardinal number of the group under that group.

$6 - 4 = \square$

VM 7.2

4. Have the children model addition and subtraction examples on the number line. Then have them write number sentences from number line models.

5. Children in the early grades can learn to add a constant using the calculator. When adding a constant, you can add the same number to many numbers without reentering the constant number. For instance, if the constant number is 3 and you want to add 3 to many different numbers, you would use the following procedure:

ANY NUMBER		ENTER THE CONSTANT		DISPLAY READS
1	+	3	=	4

The calculator is now set up to add the constant 3 to any number that is entered. If you press the 2 key and the equal key, the display will show 5. You can now enter any number and then hit the equal key, and the calculator will add 3 to the entered number and display the new sum.

EXAMPLE	KEYS PUSHED	DISPLAY SHOWS
7 + 3 =	7 =	10
12 + 3 =	1 2 =	15
37 + 3 =	3 7 =	40

VM 7.5

6. Have the children use base ten blocks to demonstrate the concept of regrouping in addition. The children may work in small groups; one member is the banker, and the children must exchange the blocks at the bank.

7. For the following activity, you will need a deck of cards with the face cards removed. Before the game begins, a sum is chosen (such as 10). Deal each student five cards. Turn four cards face up, with the remainder of the deck placed in the middle (see the illustration). The students take turns playing their cards on one of the four cards face up to obtain the predetermined sum. If a student does not have a card to play, he or she draws from the deck to see if that card can be played; this is continued until a play can be made. In the following example, proper plays would be 7, 9, 2, and 6, respectively:

Changing the sum is one of many ways of varying this activity.

8. In the following activity, 81 cards are used, each 6 centimeters by 3 centimeters or 2 inches by 3 inches. Each set of 9 cards should be composed of the numbers 1 through 9. Shuffle the entire deck and place the cards facedown. A sum greater than 9 is chosen before the beginning of the game. Each player draws 15 cards. The first puts down 2 or more cards to add up to the predetermined sum. The following players place their cards in such a way that the sum of the cards is equal to the predetermined sum. The play continues until one of the players is out of cards or until no other play can be made. In the latter case, the player with the lowest sum on the cards in his or her hand is declared the winner. In the following illustration, a sum of 12 is used:

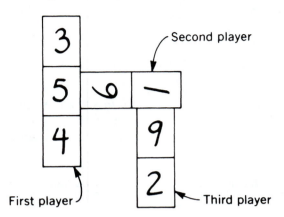

First player   Third player

9. A "diffy board" is an excellent device to use for subtraction practice.

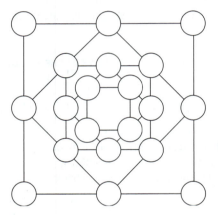

With the diffy board, place any number in each of the four corners. Subtract the smaller number from the larger on any one line, and write the difference between the two in the loop between the two numbers. Continue the process as you work toward the center of the square. Use the diffy board with whole numbers, fractions, decimals, money amounts, measurements of the same type (e.g., linear, capacity), or any numbers that can be compared by subtraction.

10. This is a game played by two children using one calculator. The children take turns by passing the calculator back and forth. The rules of the game define a set of one-place numbers to be used with the operation of addition. The winner of the game is the player who causes a preselected sum to appear on the display. For example, in this game, children will use addition and the digits 1, 2, 3, 4, 5, 6, and 7. The winner must display the sum of 31. Suppose that the first player enters the digit 3 and passes the calculator to the second player. The second player enters the operation (+) and a selected digit such as 7; 10 will appear on the display. The calculator is then passed back to the first player. For the second turn, the child presses (+) and a selected digit such as 4; 14 will appear on the display. This process continues until the preselected number (31 in this case) appears on the display.

8

Multiplication and Division of Whole Numbers

TEACHING COMPETENCIES

Upon completing this chapter, you will be able to:

- State and physically demonstrate at least four different models that can be used to develop an understanding of the process of multiplication.

- Use at least four different models to demonstrate and describe two types of division (measurement and partition).

- Use a model that represents multiplication or division, and demonstrate regrouping with multiplication and division using a place-value box.

- Write examples to demonstrate the basic properties of multiplication.

- Develop an effective teaching sequence for basic facts, concepts, and processes of multiplication and division.

VIRTUAL MANIPULATIVES

Upon completing this chapter, you will be able to use virtual manipulatives on the accompanying CD to:

- Compare and contrast different representations of multiplication using groups with *Modeling Multiplication with Groups—1* and *Modeling Multiplication with Groups—2.*
  (VM 8.1a; VM 8.1b)

- Compare and contrast different representations of multiplication using arrays with *Modeling Multiplication with Arrays—1* and *Modeling Multiplication with Arrays—2.* **(VM 8.2a; VM 8.2b)**

- Examine properties of multiplication using *Commutative Property of Multiplication—1* and *Commutative Property of Multiplication—2.*
  (VM 8.3a; VM 8.3b)

- Explore the relationship between skip counting and multiplication using *Skip Counting.* **(VM 8.4)**

- Examine the multiplication algorithm using *Modeling Regrouping in Multiplication.* **(VM 8.5)**

- Compare and contrast two common interpretations of the division process using *Measurement Division* and *Partition Division.*
  (VM 8.6a; VM 8.6b)

- Explore the interpretations of "remainder" in the division process using *Division with a Remainder on a Number Line.* **(VM 8.7)**

- Examine the role of place value in the division process using *Expanding Basic Division Facts Through Place Value.* **(VM 8.8)**

Numbered CD icons throughout the chapter refer to the virtual manipulatives in this list.

Children encounter multiplication and division concepts in their real-life experiences long before they begin the formal study of such notions in school. A kindergarten child might be asked to share a box of 18 crayons with two other friends so that all three children have the same number of crayons. A first grader might begin a hide-and-seek game by closing his or her eyes and skip-counting by fives: 5, 10, 15, 20, . . . (or by twos or by tens). A group of second graders might want to determine how many cans of food they will collect for the holiday food drive if each of the 25 children in the class brings in 4 cans. A third grader might notice the pattern in the arrangement of floor or ceiling tiles in the classroom and wonder how many tiles there are in all. In each of these cases, a child has an opportunity to explore a practical application of multiplication and/or division concepts. In each situation, the child can determine the answer in a way that lends meaning to the concept, rather than shrouding the concept in rules and rote procedures. The National Council of Teachers of Mathematics (NCTM) has responded to the call for reform in the teaching and learning of mathematics by publishing the *Principles and Standards for School Mathematics* (2000). This chapter on multiplication and division incorporates both the organization and the spirit suggested by these NCTM standards. Although purposeful practice and the anchoring of certain fundamental skills are important, even more emphasis must be placed on development of understanding and thinking skills applied to computation. The calculator and computer should receive greater emphasis as our culture moves forward in a knowledge-centered society. Teachers must be willing to experiment with new techniques and media to accomplish more effective mathematics teaching. Chapter 7 carefully examined the teaching of addition and its inverse operation, subtraction, to children. In this chapter, we examine the operation of multiplication and its inverse operation, division. The basic organizational structure for teaching multiplication and division is similar to that used for teaching addition and subtraction.

Meaning and Models for Multiplication

Readiness for multiplication and division includes an understanding of numberness to at least into the thousands; place value of at least ones, tens, and hundreds; conservation of number; reversibility; and addition and subtraction as inverse operations. This readiness has been developed in Chapters 5, 6, and 7, so

we can now develop an understanding of the operation of multiplication and its inverse operation, division.

> Multiplication is a binary operation performed on two numbers to obtain a unique result. The numbers we multiply are called factors, and the result of the multiplication is called a product.

For example, in the mathematical sentence

$$3 \times 4 = 12$$

the numbers 3 and 4 are called the **factors**, and 12 is called the **product**.

$$\text{Factor} \times \text{Factor} = \text{Product}$$
$$3 \times 4 = 12$$

Now, let's carefully examine how to introduce children to the concept of multiplication. The first step in teaching multiplication to children is to develop an understanding of the operation. An understanding of the operation is developed from the concrete-manipulative level to the abstract-symbolic level using a variety of models. We will make use of five models to develop an understanding of the concept of multiplication—*groups of objects, arrays, number lines, repeated addition,* and *Cartesian product.* Let's begin to develop an understanding by examining each multiplication model as we would develop them with children.

The approach to multiplication using groups resembles the approach we used for addition. Suppose we want to find the product that is associated with three groups of 4. The children should be asked to make three separate groups with 4 items in each group. To illustrate this idea, select three distinct groups with 4 objects in each. For example:

In most U.S. curricular programs, the first factor, 3, tells us the number of groups; the second factor, 4, tells us how many objects should be in each group. The product, 12, is the total number of objects. This model would be read, "Three groups of four is twelve." The mathematical sentence $3 \times 4 = 12$ may then be related to the model, and the reading of "three groups of four is twelve" is related to reading the sentence as "three times four is twelve." One difference between addition and multiplication is that in multiplication, each group must have the same number of items. The multiplication symbol, ($\times$), should be related to "groups of " in the mathematical sentence.

VM 8.1a

Since children have already studied addition, the model of successive addition can be introduced to help them realize why three groups of four is twelve. We can obtain the same results by placing the three groups together into one group much as we did in addition. We can think of 3×4 in terms of addition, but remember that repeated addition is not the same thing as multiplication—repeated addition is merely a model to help children develop an understanding of one interpretation of multiplication.

Therefore, we can think of this example as $4 + 4 + 4 = 12$, or 3 groups of 4 is 12, or $3 \times 4 = 12$. Using multiplication, we write $3 \times 4 = 12$ (most often read, "Three times four is equal to twelve").

Similarly, we can identify the product of 4×5.

Here we have four groups with 5 objects in each group. We can read this, "Four groups of five equals twenty." The repeated addition sentence that helps explain that 4×5 equals 20 is $5 + 5 + 5 + 5 = 20$. Remember that if a child adds 4 fives, the child is adding, not multiplying. This does, however, help the child realize that four groups of 5 is really twenty by using the familiar operation of addition. The multiplication sentence, $4 \times 5 = 20$, is read, "Four times five equals twenty."

Now, let's examine another useful model for multiplication: the array. A child's real-life experiences include many examples of objects arranged in an orderly array format—for example, the desks in many elementary and middle school classrooms, the seats in many movie theaters, the tiles used on many floors or ceilings, the individual partitions in an egg carton, or the individual blocks of candy in a certain chocolate bars.

> An array is an arrangement of objects or symbols into orderly rows and columns.
> ```
> *   *   *   *   *
> *   *   *   *   *
> *   *   *   *   *
> ```

This array is most frequently called a 3-by-5 array. The child should use the eye movement developed in learning to read and begin at the upper left-hand corner. The child's eye moves across, visualizing one group of five down to two groups of five, and then down to three groups of five. Thus a child should think of and read this array as "three groups of five." The product of the number of rows and the number of columns in an array is always equal to the number of objects or symbols in the array. Thus, to discover that $3 \times 5 = 15$, the child can count the objects or symbols in a 3-by-5 array or use successive addition ($5 + 5 + 5$) to obtain the product.

Arrays can be helpful for developing the basic facts and the properties for multiplication. For example, a 2-by-4 array can be turned on its end to form a 4-by-2 array. This can be done to show that $2 \times 4 = 4 \times 2$.

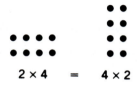

This example illustrates that the multiplication of whole numbers is commutative. This certainly seems reasonable, since multiplication of whole numbers can be considered in terms of repeated addition (i.e., addition of equal addends), and we know that addition is commutative.

As another example of commutativity, consider that $3 \times 2 = 6$ could be interpreted as $2 + 2 + 2 = 6$. It is easy to illustrate the commutative property of multiplication by simply turning an array on its end. In the array pictured here, the total number of objects is six in both cases:

The grouping or physical arrangement appears different, but the product is the same. Whether two groups of three or three groups of two are used, the total number involved is six. This is the commutative property of multiplication.

> The commutative property of multiplication means that the order of two factors does not affect the product.
>
> For example, $2 \times 3 = 6$ and $3 \times 2 = 6$,
> or $a \times b = c$ and $b \times a = c$

It is important to emphasize that under the commutative property of multiplication, it is the product that is the same, not the grouping. For example, if you work 3 hours for $10 per hour, you will earn $30 ($3 \times 10 = 30$). Note that if you work 10 hours for $3 per hour, you will still earn $30 ($10 \times 3 = 30$). BUT, are the two jobs the same? Which job would you choose if they involved the same amount of skill and effort? The product in each case is $30, but the multiplication situations are different. Many more examples of the commutative property of multiplication that yield the same product but involve commuted factors should be presented to children in the same fashion.

VM 8.3b

Multiplication can also be examined by using the number line. Let's look at the example $3 \times 4 = 12$ and show it by modeling on the number line, using repeated addition.

We begin to model multiplication at the origin, zero, and mark off four units, which puts us at the point named by 4. From this point, we mark off another four units; and from that point, named by 8, we mark off four more units. This puts us at the point labeled 12. Therefore, $4 + 4 + 4 = 12$ and $3 \times 4 = 12$. The same procedure, of course, can be used to show that $4 \times 3 = 12$, thus illustrating again the commutative property of multiplication.

When using the number line with young children, always begin modeling at the origin, zero. In this example, we mark off three units, starting at zero, which puts us at the point named 3. From that point, we mark off another three units; from that point (6), we mark off three more units; and from that point (labeled 9), we mark off another three units. Now we have arrived at the product of 12. Thus this model illustrates that four groups of three modeled on the number line is $4 \times 3 = 12$. You should provide children with many experiences modeling multiplication on the number line. This should also serve to reinforce the meaning of the commutative property of multiplication.

The Cartesian product can also be used by middle school students as a model for multiplication; however, it is usually not recommended for elementary school children unless you make use of concrete objects or

pictorial representations. This model is more difficult for students to comprehend at the abstract level, so a symbolic approach should be reserved for more developmentally mature students.

As an example of Cartesian product, consider one group of 2 sweaters and one group of 3 pairs of pants. How many combinations of sweaters and pants into outfits are possible?

red   yellow

blue   green   tan

The red sweater, r, may be worn with each pair of pants to give the following color combinations:

$$(r, b) \quad (r, g) \quad (r, t)$$

The yellow sweater, y, may also be worn with each pair of pants. Thus we have three more possible combinations:

$$(y, b) \quad (y, g) \quad (y, t)$$

The group of all color combinations is shown in the following table:

	Sweaters	
	red	yellow
Pants		
blue	(r, b)	(y, b)
green	(r, g)	(y, g)
tan	(r, t)	(y, t)

Each time we match a sweater with pants, we obtain an ordered pair representing an outfit. For example, (r, t) is the outfit ordered pair obtained by matching the red sweater with the tan pants. The set of all ordered pairs obtained by matching the elements of sweaters with the elements of pants is called the Cartesian product of the set of sweaters and the set of pants. This set of ordered pairs is denoted by A × B (read, "the Cartesian product of A and B" or sometimes read as "A cross B"). Note that when we create a table to display the possible combinations of 2 sweaters and 3 pairs of pants, an array is generated. In this case we have a 3-by-2 array that provides six different combinations.

We have identified five models that can be used for multiplication: groups of objects, arrays, number lines, repeated addition, and Cartesian products. These models can help children discover and develop an understanding of multiplication. None of these models is likely to solve all a student's difficulties in understanding the concept of multiplication. The teacher should be flexible and sensitive and must vary the models to suit the needs of the children in each class.

Developing and Memorizing Basic Multiplication Facts

How are these models used to help children understand and use multiplication? Let's deal with groups as an example of a model. Place three sheets of paper on a desk; on each sheet of paper place 2 cubes, small toys, or plastic eating utensils.

Then ask these questions:

How many groups are there?

How many items are in each group?

How many items are there all together?

In this case, there are three groups with 2 items in each group, so there are 6 items all together. Thus we can say that three groups of two is six.

$$3 \text{ groups of } 2 = 6$$
$$3 \times 2 = 6$$

Children need to view many groups of materials and to say, discuss, and write multiplication sentences. The overhead projector is an excellent tool for presenting groups and arrays to children. Use small rectangles of colored plastic on an overhead projector for each group, and place plastic spoons or forks as items on each group. Arrays can be made on overhead transparencies by pasting circular disks in columns and rows. Stickers also work well on worksheets. Use base ten blocks, Cuisenaire rods, attribute blocks, pattern blocks, and other materials to model multiplication in many ways. Check the Instructional and Assessment Activites sections of this book or consult the specific manuals designed to help teachers use each of these materials.

Teachers can make demonstration multiplication arrays on sheets of paper, using gummed dots as shown

here. Roll up the sheets of paper. As the students unroll each array, they can develop the multiples for any given number. When first modeling multiplication, do not begin with two groups of 2, since 2 times 2 yields the same result as 2 add 2.

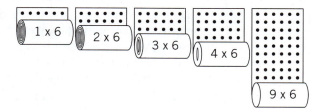

> Multiples of a given number include all products obtained by multiplying the set of whole numbers by a given factor.

For example, the multiples of 4 are obtained by multiplying 4 by 0, 1, 2, 3, 4, 5, . . . So, the multiples of 4 are 0, 4, 8, 12, 16, 20, . . .

Now children can begin to generate the multiples of a number by using groups as models. Generating the multiples of 2 using groups as models is illustrated here as an example:

	1 group of 2	1 x 2 = 2
	2 groups of 2	2 x 2 = 4
	3 groups of 2	3 x 2 = 6
	4 groups of 2	4 x 2 = 8
	5 groups of 2	5 x 2 = 10
	6 groups of 2	6 x 2 = 12
	7 groups of 2	7 x 2 = 14
	8 groups of 2	8 x 2 = 16
	9 groups of 2	9 x 2 = 18

Children need many experiences generating multiples of a given number. Skip-counting is one method of helping children learn the multiples of a number. Practice counting by twos, then by fives. Try having the children skip-count by threes while they are looking at a number line. Use a calculator with automatic memory to practice skip-counting by fours by punching the 4 key followed by the (+) key and then punch the (=) key several times in a row. Use this method to practice skip-counting by many different numbers.

The **Sieve of Eratosthenes virtual manipulative** that can be found on the CD that accompanies this text can be effectively used to present students with a visual base for the process of skip-counting. The traditional image of the Sieve is usually an array of the numbers 0–99 or 1–100 written in 10 horizontal rows of 10. If students choose any given single digit number to mark on the Sieve and then mark off the multiples of that number, various patterns will emerge. For example, if you begin with 2 and mark off the multiples of 2, you will get 5 vertical "bars" of marked numbers. If, instead, you begin with 3 and mark off the multiples of 3, you'll get a diagonal pattern of marked numbers. What other patterns occur for other multiples? What happens if you change the arrangement of the original Sieve from 10 × 10 to, say, a 5 × 20 arrangement or an arrangement that has only six numbers per row?

Remember that a multiple is a product obtained by multiplying a whole number by a given factor. Applying this definition to a given factor of 6, we multiply 6 by 0, 1, 2, 3, 4, . . . This procedure must be followed very carefully. Note that the first factor changes but the second factor remains constant. In this example, we continually add another group of 6 and generate the multiples for 6.

Whole Numbers as Factors	Factor	Multiples
0	6	0
1	6	6
2	6	12
3	6	18
4	6	24
5	6	30
6	6	36
7	6	42
8	6	48
9	6	54
10	6	60
⋮	⋮	⋮

By using appropriate models, children should be able to develop the basic facts of multiplication and organize them into a multiplication table. Ten 1-digit factors are written on the horizontal axis and on the vertical axis. The products associated with these factors are placed within the table. Consequently, there are 10 × 10 or 100 possible pairs of one-place factors and 100 possible products in the table.

Factors

×	0	1	2	3	4	5	6	7	8	9
0										
1										
2										
3										
4										
5										
6										
7										
8										
9										

Factors (vertical axis label)

The children must memorize 100 basic multiplication facts in order to develop power with computation. Two things must be done: The basic multiplication facts must be developed and then memorized.

The basic multiplication facts include all one-place factors multiplied by all one-place factors to obtain a one- or two-place product.

Prior to focusing on techniques to use to *memorize* basic facts, we should address the techniques for the *development* of the basic multiplication facts. We begin with those facts that do not involve zero as a factor, because if we do elect to begin with zero as one of the factors, then we are stuck in a dilemma of how to show zero groups of three on the concrete level. (It may also be just as difficult for the children to comprehend three groups of zero as a beginning example.)

The children can use groups of objects, successive addition, arrays, and the number line to discover facts such as $2 \times 3 = 6$, $3 \times 2 = 6$, $4 \times 2 = 8$, $2 \times 4 = 8$, $3 \times 4 = 12$, and $4 \times 3 = 12$. As the children discover basic facts, be certain to help them become aware of the basic structure of multiplication. (Commutativity is especially helpful in both the development and memorization stages.) Arrays, as we have already mentioned, can be convincing models for illustrating the commutative property of multiplication.

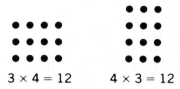

$3 \times 4 = 12$ $4 \times 3 = 12$

When the students have had sufficient experience with nonzero factors, they should then begin the exploration of exercises that have zero as the second factor. Groups may perhaps be the most useful model for introducing multiplication facts such as $2 \times 0 = 0$ and $4 \times 0 = 0$. Two empty boxes would be one acceptable model for two $2 \times 0 = 0$; four empty boxes could be used to model $4 \times 0 = 0$.

$4 \times 0 = 0 + 0 + 0 + 0 = 0$

When the children have used arrays or other models to discover the commutative property of multiplication, then they can use this property to discover that

$$0 \times 2 = 0$$
$$0 \times 3 = 0$$
$$0 \times 4 = 0$$
and so on

The children need to generalize that the product of 0 and any other factor is 0. This is known as the **zero property of multiplication**. For all numbers n:

$$n \times 0 = 0$$
$$0 \times n = 0$$

This generalization allows the completion of one entire row and one entire column of the multiplication table:

Factors

×	0	1	2	3	4	5	6	7	8	9
0	0	0	0	0	0	0	0	0	0	0
1	0									
2	0									
3	0									
4	0									
5	0									
6	0									
7	0									
8	0									
9	0									

(Factors — left side label)

A similar approach can be used to develop the identity element for multiplication. Three groups of 1 can be modeled with three boxes and one block in each box.

By applying the basic property of commutativity, we see that $1 \times 3 = 3$. Successive addition will also help children understand the relationship between addition and multiplication and the commutative property.

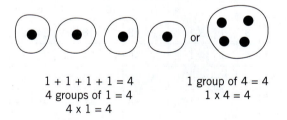

$1 + 1 + 1 + 1 = 4$ 1 group of 4 = 4
4 groups of 1 = 4 $1 \times 4 = 4$
$4 \times 1 = 4$

Again, by applying the basic property of commutativity, we see that $1 \times 4 = 4$. The children can now make the generalization that the product of 1 and any other factor is equal to the other factor. The number 1 is thus defined as the identity element of multiplication. The **identity property for multiplication** states that for any number a,

$$a \times 1 = a$$
$$1 \times a = a$$

The basic facts that represent the identity property have been inserted in the table that follows:

Factors

×	0	1	2	3	4	5	6	7	8	9
0	0	0	0	0	0	0	0	0	0	0
1	0	1	2	3	4	5	6	7	8	9
2	0	2								
3	0	3								
4	0	4								
5	0	5								
6	0	6								
7	0	7								
8	0	8								
9	0	9								

(F a c t o r s — row label on left)

The children need to generate the multiples for 2, 3, 4, 5, 6, 7, 8, and 9 and enter the products into the multiplication table. The children will eventually be able to construct the entire multiplication table of basic facts. When the students have memorized 55 of the basic multiplication facts in the table, they will know the remaining 45 facts because of the commutative property of multiplication. (The symmetry resulting from the commutative property is indicated by shading.)

Factors

x	0	1	2	3	4	5	6	7	8	9
0	0	0	0	0	0	0	0	0	0	0
1	0	1	2	3	4	5	6	7	8	9
2	0	2	4	6	8	10	12	14	16	18
3	0	3	6	9	12	15	18	21	24	27
4	0	4	8	12	16	20	24	28	32	36
5	0	5	10	15	20	25	30	35	40	45
6	0	6	12	18	24	30	36	42	48	54
7	0	7	14	21	28	35	42	49	56	63
8	0	8	16	24	32	40	48	56	64	72
9	0	9	18	27	36	45	54	63	72	81

(F a c t o r s — row label on left)

Expanding Basic Multiplication Facts Through Place Value

As soon as children understand place value and the operation of multiplication, they can solve a great number of related examples. For instance, if they understand that $3 \times 2 = 6$, then they should be able to solve these related examples by relating multiplication and place-value concepts. Two groups of 3 can be modeled as follows:

$$\begin{array}{r} 3 \\ \times\, 2 \\ \hline 6 \end{array}$$

Now exchange each element in each group with a package of ten. The model now becomes

$$\begin{array}{r} 3 \text{ tens} \\ \times\, 2 \\ \hline 6 \text{ tens} \end{array}$$

Children can easily count to verify that two groups of 3 is 6 and two groups of 3 tens is 6 tens (or two groups of 30 is 60). From many of these related models, children should generalize what happens in each case. The basic fact is the same in both examples: $2 \times 3 = 6$. The only difference is the place value. This concept is known as *expanding the basic facts.* By using place value, we expand the basic fact of $2 \times 3 = 6$ into $2 \times 30 = 60$. Children should generalize that the basic facts are the same regardless of place value.

$$\begin{array}{r} 3 \\ \times\, 2 \\ \hline 6 \end{array} \qquad \begin{array}{r} 30 \\ \times\, 2 \\ \hline 60 \end{array}$$

You might want to review place-value names and concepts with the children before developing this lesson.

The multiplication table could be expanded to include an indefinite number of products, but it would then become large, awkward, and difficult to use. Instead, given an understanding of the properties of multiplication and the basic multiplication facts, a multiplication algorithm can be developed for solving multiplication examples that involve greater values.

Before we continue the development of multiplication with children, let's examine some other properties of this operation. We have already studied the commutative property of multiplication. Now, let's consider the associative property of multiplication. Multiplication is a binary operation; this means that it can be performed on only two numbers at one time. This gives us the freedom to associate factors in different ways for greater ease in computation. Consider the associative property of multiplication, and note its effective application in this example:

$$(29 \times 25) \times 4 = 29 \times (25 \times 4)$$

The parentheses tell us how to associate the factors. Obviously, the student who does not learn to explore for shortcuts will multiply 29×25 and then multiply the product by 4.

$$
\begin{array}{r}
29 \\
\times\ 25 \\
\hline
145 \\
58 \\
\hline
725
\end{array}
\qquad
\begin{array}{r}
725 \\
\times\ 4 \\
\hline
2900
\end{array}
$$

However, an observant student who understands and knows how to use the associative property of multiplication will rethink the example $(29 \times 25) \times 4$ as $29 \times (25 \times 4)$ and, consequently, reason that $25 \times 4 = 100$, and then that $29 \times 100 = 2900$. Using the associative property of multiplication to look at an example this way, we can see the kind of efficiency and understanding that a good mathematics program stresses.

In this example, we used a specific instance of the associative property:

$$(29 \times 25) \times 4 = 29 \times (25 \times 4)$$

In general:

> The associative property of multiplication means that when three or more factors are to be multiplied, the grouping of the factors does not affect the product.
>
> For example, $(8 \times 2) \times 5 = 8 \times (2 \times 5)$,
> or $(a \times b) \times c = a \times (b \times c)$

Let's look at an example that uses both the commutative and associative properties of multiplication:

$$
\begin{aligned}
60 \times 21 \times 5 &= (60 \times 21) \times 5 \\
&= 60 \times (21 \times 5)\ \text{Associative property} \\
&= 60 \times (5 \times 21)\ \text{Commutative property} \\
&= (60 \times 5) \times 21\ \text{Associative property} \\
&= 300 \times 21\ \text{Multiplication(renaming)} \\
&= 6300
\end{aligned}
$$

Do *not* ask children to label each statement of an exercise such as this; we have done so here only to illustrate the properties being used. Children should examine many exercises before they begin to calculate. If they can see that a property will help them simplify an exercise, they should use that property. In this case, the use of two properties has simplified the mental steps to an answer (although not the way you write out the steps).

Use of basic structural properties to arrive at an answer to a computation exercise achieves another worthwhile objective: It keeps children from believing that there is only one way to solve an exercise. Since

mathematics uses a highly disciplined approach to problem solving and since there is often (but not always) only one answer to a given problem, it is easy for children to believe that there is only one approach to a correct solution. This mistaken belief is one of the greatest enemies of insight, creativity, and intelligence in problem solving. Students must learn to seek from the many possible paths the best approach for a given situation. They must be released from narrowly channeled patterns of thought and allowed to develop their own critical and analytical abilities.

Another fundamental property of operations on whole numbers is the distributive property of multiplication over addition. This simply means that an example such as 3×23 can be thought of as $3 \times (20 + 3)$ and can be written as $(3 \times 20) + (3 \times 3)$. The steps in the calculation are then much simplified:

$$
\begin{aligned}
3 \times 23 &= 3 \times (20 + 3) \\
&= (3 \times 20) + (3 \times 3) \\
&= 60 + 9 \\
&= 69
\end{aligned}
$$

Inspection of this statement reveals that this multiplication algorithm depends on the distributive property of multiplication over addition. Essentially, in multiplication we express one of the factors as the sum (or difference) of two or more numbers. For instance, in the example, 3×23, we rename 23 as $(20 + 3)$. We then find the partial products and the final product by applying the distributive property, just as we did in the previous example.

> The distributive property of multiplication over addition means that the product of a number and a sum can be expressed as a sum of two products.
>
> For example, $4 \times (20 + 3) = (4 \times 20) + (4 \times 3)$,
> or $a \times (b + c) = (a \times b) + (a \times c)$

Many school mathematics textbooks inappropriately introduce the distributive property of multiplication over addition using 2 one-place numbers such as 2×8. For example, 2×8 can be rewritten as $2 \times (2 + 6) = (2 \times 2) + (2 \times 6) = 4 + 12 = 16$. The distributive property is applied here, but the students will see no need for this property, since we would have expected them to have memorized the product of 2×8 (a basic fact). So, do not introduce the distributive property of multiplication over addition until the children are ready to multiply a two-place number by a one-place number, where the application of the distributive property actually plays a useful role.

Now consider another exercise: $2 \times 42 = \square$. In this case, we can set up our multiplication as follows:

$$
\begin{array}{r}
42 \\
\times\ 2 \\
\hline
4 \rightarrow (2 \times 2) \\
+80 \rightarrow (2 \times 40) \\
\hline
84 \rightarrow (2 \times 42)
\end{array}
$$

Here we are renaming the number 42 as groups of tens and groups of ones. Then we can state the example as $2 \times (40 + 2)$. The distributive property allows us to express this multiplication in the form $(2 \times 40) + (2 \times 2)$. Carrying out these operations gives us $80 + 4$, or 84. The product is the same as that obtained by using the multiplication algorithm.

Showing the multiplication step-by-step in expanded notation can be helpful for guiding children to a clear understanding of the operation.

$$
\begin{array}{ccccc}
\begin{array}{r} 42 \\ \times\ 2 \end{array} & \Rightarrow &
\begin{array}{r} 40+2 \\ \times\quad 2 \end{array} & \Rightarrow &
\begin{array}{r} 40+2 \\ \times\quad 2 \\ \hline 80+4=84 \end{array} \\
\\
\begin{array}{r} 42 \\ \times\ 2 \end{array} & \Rightarrow &
\begin{array}{r} 42 \\ \times\ 2 \\ \hline 4 \\ 80 \end{array} & \Rightarrow &
\begin{array}{r} 42 \\ \times\ 2 \\ \hline 4 \\ 80 \\ \hline 84 \end{array}
\end{array}
$$

Our numeration system is a place-value system. Thus the shorter algorithm (the standard algorithm) represents a brief and accurate method of performing the operation. In other words, multiplying 2 ones by 2 in the ones place gives us 4 ones, which is recorded in the ones column. Then, multiplying 4 tens by the 2 in the ones place gives us 8 tens. The 8 is written in the tens column to the left of the 4 in the ones column. The alignment of the numbers in the vertical algorithm is efficient because of our place-value numeration system and the distribution of multiplication over addition.

Suppose a child wants to multiply 4×28. Using the distributive property, the child can make the example easier to solve by breaking up one of the factors into another grouping. Considering our decimal system of numeration, the child might write $4 \times (20 + 8)$. This is grouped in terms of tens and ones. (This is not necessarily the most efficient rearrangement, however.) The child would then think $(4 \times 20) + (4 \times 8) = 80 + 32 = 112$. Or the child might group in this manner: $4 \times 28 = 4 \times (25 + 3)$. In this case the child would think $(4 \times 25) + (4 \times 3) = 100 + 12 = 112$. Adding to the number 100 is clearly a simple matter; it is also clear that 4×25 is 100. Familiarity with our money system (a decimal system) makes it easier for children to multiply such combinations.

The concepts of the zero property of multiplication and the identity element of multiplication can be put together to help children multiply by 1, 10, 100, and so on. After working many examples, children should generalize that multiplying by 10 changes the place value by one place. In other words, we move the numeral one place to the left, and place a zero in the ones place. Study these examples:

$$
\begin{array}{ll}
2 \times 10 = 20 & \quad 10 \times 2 = 20 \\
10 \times 7 = 70 & \quad 7 \times 10 = 70 \\
10 \times 4 = 40 & \quad 4 \times 10 = 40
\end{array}
$$

Children should be given much oral practice in multiplying by 10. Then the teacher should extend the idea into more places, and multiply two- and three-place numbers by 10.

$$
\begin{array}{l}
1 \times 5 = 5 \\
10 \times 5 = 50 \\
1 \times 12 = 12 \\
10 \times 12 = 120 \\
10 \times 234 = 2340
\end{array}
$$

Apply the same two concepts to numbers multiplied by 100: $1 \times 5 = 5$, $10 \times 5 = 50$, $100 \times 5 = 500$. After doing numerous examples, children can generalize that multiplying by 100 changes the place value by moving the numeral two places to the left, and zeros are placed in the tens and ones places.

For a sound understanding of multiplication involving factors with two or more digits, the children will need to be familiar with the distributive property of multiplication over addition. Arrays are another excellent device for helping children to discover this property.

$$
3 \times 12 \qquad\qquad (3 \times 10) \quad + (3 \times 2)
$$

Introduce the distributive property of multiplication over addition as the class begins to study multiplication of a two-place number by a one-place number.

Consider this example: $3 \times 13 = \square$. The number 13 can be named in many ways. In this case, let's use $(10 + 3)$ because place value is useful in the multiplication algorithm. If the distributive property is used, children can apply basic multiplication facts to find the product:

$$
\begin{array}{rll}
3 \times 13 &= 3 \times (10 + 3) & \text{Renaming} \\
&= (3 \times 10) + (3 \times 3) & \text{Distributive property} \\
&= 30 + 9 & \text{Multiplication (renaming)} \\
&= 39 & \text{Addition (renaming)}
\end{array}
$$

The solution to this example can best be written as follows:

$$
\begin{array}{c} 13 \\ \times\ 3 \end{array}
\quad\blacktriangleright\quad
\begin{array}{r} 1\ \text{ten}\ 3\ \text{ones} \\ \times\qquad 3 \\ \hline 3\ \text{tens}\ 9\ \text{ones} = 39 \end{array}
\quad\blacktriangleright\quad
\begin{array}{r} 13 \\ \times\ 3 \\ \hline 39 \end{array}
$$

Encourage children to look for the relationships that exist within the examples. For instance, the preceding example can be thought of as follows:

Basic Fact	Extended Basic Fact	Basic Fact
1	10	3
× 3	× 3	× 3
	30	9

$$
\begin{array}{r} 13 \\ \times\ 3 \\ \hline 39 \end{array}
$$

The children have memorized the basic multiplication facts, so they should know the basic facts in this example: 3 × 1 and 3 × 3. The basic fact 3 × 1 has been expanded to 3 × 10. The two examples 3 × 10 and 3 × 3 are put together using the concept of place value to get the example 3 × 13.

Consider the example 3 × 23 = □. The number 23 can also be named as (20 + 3). Again, the students can apply the distributive property:

$$
\begin{array}{c} 23 \\ \times\ 3 \end{array}
\quad\blacktriangleright\quad
\begin{array}{r} 2\ \text{ten}\ 3\ \text{ones} \\ \times\qquad 3 \\ \hline 6\ \text{tens}\ 9\ \text{ones} = 69 \end{array}
\quad\blacktriangleright\quad
\begin{array}{r} 23 \\ \times\ 3 \\ \hline 69 \end{array}
$$

Renaming using expanded notation can also help develop the concept of multiplication with three-place factors:

$$
\begin{array}{l} 124 = \\ \times\ 2 = \end{array}
\quad\blacktriangleright\quad
\begin{array}{r} 1\ \text{hundred}\ 2\ \text{tens}\ 4\ \text{ones} \\ \times\qquad\qquad 2 \\ \hline 2\ \text{hundreds}\ 4\ \text{tens}\ 8\ \text{ones} = 248 \end{array}
\quad\blacktriangleright\quad
\begin{array}{r} 124 \\ \times\ 2 \\ \hline 248 \end{array}
$$

Another form of algorithm can be used when an understanding of multiplication has been developed through expanded notation.

$$
\begin{array}{r}
121 \\
\times 3 \\
\hline
3 \\
60 \\
300 \\
\hline
363
\end{array}
\begin{array}{l}
\\
\\
\rightarrow (3 \times\ \ \ 1) \\
\rightarrow (3 \times\ \ 20) \\
\rightarrow (3 \times 100) \\
\\
\end{array}
$$

Use the longer forms of the multiplication algorithm to develop understanding. When the children are ready to develop the skill, use the short algorithm. Children should have the opportunity to apply their knowledge of basic structure and of the algorithm to two-place multiplication.

A good beginning example might involve an even ten (10, 20, 30, and so on). Consider the example 10 × 12 = □. The identity element of multiplication has been developed:

$$
\begin{array}{c} 3 \\ \times\ 1 \end{array}
\qquad\qquad
\begin{array}{c} 4 \\ \times\ 1 \end{array}
$$

The basic facts have been expanded into

$$
\begin{array}{c} 30 \\ \times\ \ \ 1 \end{array}
\qquad\qquad
\begin{array}{c} 40 \\ \times\ \ \ 1 \end{array}
$$

Spend time with the children now to help them understand the place-value concepts involved at this point.

$$
\text{If}\quad
\begin{array}{r} 12 \\ \times 1 \\ \hline 12 \end{array}
\quad\text{Then}\quad
\begin{array}{r} 12 \\ \times 10 \\ \hline 120 \end{array}
$$

$$
\text{If}\quad
\begin{array}{r} 12 \\ \times 2 \\ \hline 24 \end{array}
\quad\text{Then}\quad
\begin{array}{r} 12 \\ \times 20 \\ \hline 240 \end{array}
$$

After the children understand the concept of multiplying by an even ten, then two examples that children can already solve may be put together. Consider the example 12 × 14 = □. The two examples prerequisite to solving 12 × 14 are 2 × 14 and 10 × 14. Both of these examples have been taught. Now you must help the students bring these two ideas together into one example:

$$
\begin{array}{r} 14 \\ \times\ 2 \\ \hline 28 \end{array}
\qquad\qquad
\begin{array}{r} 14 \\ \times\ 10 \\ \hline 140 \end{array}
$$

$$
\begin{array}{r} 14 \\ \times\ 12 \\ \hline 28 \\ 140 \\ \hline 168 \end{array}
$$

Note that in each method for solving this example, the answer has been obtained by taking the sum of four different products: (2 × 4), (2 × 10), (10 × 4), and (10 × 10). This idea must then be expanded into other decimal places. Children must be able to analyze multiplication examples and recognize all the different basic multiplication facts that make up the examples.

Regrouping in Multiplication

There is still another major concept that must be developed to establish power with multiplication: regrouping. The term regrouping is used here because it applies to addition, subtraction, multiplication, and division; we do not need to introduce the less appropriate terms of *carrying and borrowing* as two different concepts if we introduce regrouping and use it with all the operations. The term *regrouping* is used to indicate when a number is renamed from one place value to another.

VM 8.5

The following example illustrates the development of regrouping in the multiplication algorithm:

$$\begin{array}{r} 24 \\ \times\ 3 \\ \hline \end{array}$$

A child might think and write:

$$\begin{array}{r} 24 \\ \times\ 3 \\ \hline 12 \\ 60 \\ \hline 72 \end{array}$$

In this particular case, the child thought 3×4 and wrote 12 and then thought 3×20 and wrote 60; the two partial products of 12 and 60 were then added. There is no regrouping involved in finding the sum of 12 and 60. Nevertheless, examples of this type are prerequisite to understanding the regrouping concept. Rewriting the example using tens and ones is another excellent activity:

$$\begin{array}{rcl} 24 & & 2\ \text{tens} \quad 4\ \text{ones} \\ \times\ 3 & = & \times \qquad\qquad 3 \\ \hline & & 6\ \text{tens} \quad 12\ \text{ones} \end{array}$$

This is the beginning of readiness for regrouping:

6 tens 12 ones =
6 tens (1 ten 2 ones)
= 7 tens 2 ones = 72
= 72

If the child thinks 3×4 is 12 and then thinks of 12 as 1 ten and 2 ones, the child is regrouping. Regrouping was used at the stage when 12 was regrouped as 1 ten and 2 ones and the 1 ten was regrouped with the tens.

Regrouping is also used in the following example:

$$\begin{array}{r} 48 \\ \times\ 2 \\ \hline 96 \end{array}$$

In multiplying 2×8 to get 16, we record the 6 in the ones place and regroup 1 ten. Multiply 2×40 or 2×4 tens (do not just say 2×4) to get 8 tens, add the regrouped number of 1 ten with 8 tens, and record the 9 in the tens place.

Another regrouping example is the following:

$$\begin{array}{rcl} 268 & = & 2\ \text{hundreds}\ 6\ \text{tens}\ 8\ \text{ones} \\ \times 26 & = & \times \qquad\qquad 2\ \text{tens}\ 6\ \text{ones} \\ \hline \end{array}$$

$$\begin{array}{rl} 48 & (6 \times\quad 8) \\ 360 & (6 \times\ 60) \\ 1200 & (6 \times 200) \\ 160 & (20 \times\quad 8) \\ 1200 & (20 \times\ 60) \\ 4000 & (20 \times 200) \\ \hline 6968 \end{array}$$

When multiplying 6×8 to get 48, we record 8 in the ones column and regroup the 4 (40). When multiplying 6×60 to get 360, we record 6 in the tens column and regroup the 3 (300). The carried or regrouped numbers are written in the proper place and added to the sum. Note that the regrouped figure is not written above the example. If children need to record the regrouped number as a crutch, teach them to write it below the example, where it has real meaning.

The familiar short algorithm, however, omits the extra steps that show how we regroup:

$$\begin{array}{r} 268 \\ \times\ 26 \\ \hline 1608 \\ 5360 \\ \hline 6968 \end{array}$$

When the concept of regrouping is taught, a great deal of practice must be provided. The concept should be extended so that children can multiply at least a two-place number times a three-place number with multiple regroupings. In society today, we commonly use a calculator or even a computer to multiply many-place numbers. But the consumer of mathematics must be able to understand the concept and estimate the reasonableness of the answer provided by the calculator or computer.

VM 8.5

Closely reexamine the examples discussed in the previous section and then use the Modeling Regrouping in Multiplication virtual manipulative that is on the CD accompanying this text to check your answers (click and drag the sliders to represent the problems):

3×24
2×48
26×268

Compare your steps with those shown in the virtual manipulative.

At this level of development, all the basic ideas of multiplication have been taught:

1. The student must understand what multiplication means.

2. The student must understand the basic multiplication facts and have them memorized.

3. The student must understand place value and multiplication of greater values.

4. The student must understand the structures of multiplication (the commutative property of multiplication, the associative property of multiplication, the zero property of multiplication, the identity element of multiplication, and the distributive property of multiplication over addition). There are other properties, but these are the ones usually taught and used in elementary and middle school.

5. The student must understand the concept of regrouping as it applies to multiplication.

The concepts developed must be applied to many different examples; children should practice and review them. Electronic devices can be used with children for drill and practice of these concepts. Computer software is available, but teachers must carefully evaluate the software to make sure that the practice and the feedback to that practice are appropriate for each child. Students in upper grades can write simple computer programs or programs for calculators such as the TI-73 to solve mathematics exercises.

Meaning and Models for Division

Division has the same sort of inverse relationship to multiplication that subtraction has to addition.

> Division is performed on two numbers to obtain a unique result. The number we divide is called a product, and both the number we divide by and the result of the division are called factors.

Division undoes what multiplication does; consequently, teaching the basic ideas of division should parallel the teaching those of multiplication. Traditional mathematics programs have not placed sufficient emphasis on division as the inverse operation of multiplication. The understanding of division has often been neglected, because so much emphasis has been placed on memorizing the algorithm and developing the skills of computation. Also, research tells us that division has the most difficult algorithm to teach, although it is not the most difficult operation to understand.

To develop children's understanding of division, instruction should begin on the concrete level. A mathematics program that tries to teach division on the abstract level focuses on rote calculation, and not on the meaning of division as representing an inverse relationship to multiplication. Models that might be used to introduce division include groups of objects, arrays, number lines, and successive subtraction. Let's carefully examine each of these models as we develop an understanding of division.

RESEARCH SNAPSHOT

Are there alternatives to teaching the formal multiplication algorithm?

Baek (1998) observed six classrooms in grades 3 to 5 in which teachers never taught students formal algorithms to solve multidigit multiplication problems, but instead encouraged students to solve problems in different ways and to invent algorithms.

The multiplication problems were usually given to the students as word problems. The students solved them individually or in small groups. The children then shared their invented algorithms, compared them, and discussed the mathematical meaning underlying their inventions. The invented algorithms demonstrated the students' understanding of multiples of ten and number sense. The algorithms were classified developmentally according to the main schemes that the students used to solve the problems.

How can you, as a teacher, help your students develop their own invented algorithms and how can you help them move to more sophisticated algorithms?

Baek, J. (1998). Children's invented algorithms for multidigit multiplication problems. In L. Morrow & L. M. Kenney (Eds.), *The teaching and learning of algorithms in school mathematics* (pp. 151–160). Reston, VA: National Council of Teachers of Mathematics. For additional research briefs, "ERIC Digests" lets you search more than 2000 short syntheses of research on a range of education topics. The syntheses were produced by the Educational Resources Information Center (ERIC). Check http://www.ericfacility.net/ericdigests/index/.

Consider a group of 6 plastic spoons:

We can ask the children, "How many groups of 2 spoons can we make from a group of 6 plastic spoons?"

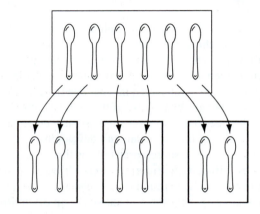

By moving the plastic spoons and making groups of 2 spoons, children see that they can make three groups. A group of 6 plastic spoons can be separated into three groups of 2. We can write:

$$
\begin{array}{r}
3 \\
2\overline{)6} \\
-6 \\
\hline
0
\end{array}
$$

We could have asked a different division question about the 6 plastic spoons: "If the 6 plastic spoons are separated into two groups, how many spoons will be in each group?" Again, children must be able to manipulate the plastic spoons into two groups.

The two illustrations here showing six spoons divided *into groups of 2* or *into 2 groups* are the two interpretations used to teach division to children. Notice that both interpretations represent a solution to the example "six divided by two," and yet these interpretations are visually and procedurally quite different.

Now, let's us consider the use of arrays in division. The following array has a total of 8 dots, but a sheet of paper is covering part of the array. We can ask, "How many dots are in each row?"

Number of rows $2\overline{)8}^{\,4}$ How many in each row?
Total amount

There are 4 dots in each row. After the children think about the example and decide that there are 4 dots in each row, they can remove the sheet of paper and check to see whether they are correct.

An array can be used in another way: Use the same procedure as in the previous example, but this time use the sheet of paper to cover part of the columns. We can ask, "How many dots are in each column?" The example will be written the same, but the labels will be different. There are 4 dots in each column. After the children have discussed the example and reached a conclusion, the sheet of paper can be removed, and the children can check to see whether they are correct. We have examined division by using both groups of objects and the array model to develop an understanding of the concept. Now let's study the number line as a model for division. We will look again at the example $2\overline{)8}$. (i.e., 8 divided by 2 or $8 \div 2$) and model this on the number line:

We might choose to begin at the point marked 8, and mark off two units to the left, which puts us at the point marked 6. From the point named 6, we mark off another two units to the left; from that point, named 4, we mark off two more units to the left. We continue marking off two-unit segments to the left until we reach 0. Now we can see that there are four segments, each two units long, in eight. Therefore $8 - 2 = 6$, $6 - 2 = 4$, $4 - 2 = 2$, and $2 - 2 = 0$ (or $8 \div 2 = 4$), because 2 has been subtracted four times from 8. Thus successive subtraction can also be used to model $8 \div 2 = 4$.

The children have learned that $4 \times 2 = 8$ and that 4 and 2 are the factors and 8 is the product. Begin with multiplication examples written on a sheet of paper; use a pair of scissors to cut out one of the factors. Now ask the question, "What number was on the piece of paper that has been cut out?"

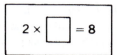

Since division is the inverse operation of multiplication, we can think of division in terms of finding a missing factor. Thus, the example $12 \div 3 = \square$ can be thought of as $3 \times \square = 12$. The example $12 \div 3 = \square$ can be (and should be) written in other equivalent forms. For example:

$$3\overline{)12} \quad \text{or} \quad \frac{12}{3} = \square \quad \text{or} \quad \frac{12}{\square} = 3$$

$$3 \times \square = 12 \quad \text{or} \quad \square \times 3 = 12$$

$$\text{or} \quad 12 = \square \times 3 \quad \text{or} \quad 12 = 3 \times \square$$

It is important for children to recognize division when it is written in any of its many different forms. Children should be able to rewrite any of these examples into a form that they can use to calculate the missing factor.

If multiplication can be thought of as an operation in which a factor times a factor equals a product, then division can be thought of as an operation in which a product is divided by a factor to equal a factor.

Factor × Factor = Product

Product ÷ Factor = Factor

Provide the students with cards that have the words *factor, factor,* and *product* and the symbols (×), (÷), and (=) printed on them. Have the students construct a multiplication sentence with the cards. Then have the students rearrange the cards into a division sentence. Children should observe the multiplication sentence being changed into an inverse division sentence, and they should notice how the product moves to the other side of the equation.

As mentioned earlier in this section, two interpretations of division must be developed with children: *measurement division* and *partition division.* The names of the two interpretations are not important for children to know, however, it is critical that students experience the meaning and modeling of each type.

VM 8.6a Measurement division seems to be more readily understood by children, so it is usually taught first. Consider the following example: If a person has 12 cookies and wishes to put them into packages of 3 cookies for sale at a bake sale, how many packages can be made?

The person can take the 12 cookies and then place 3 cookies into a first package, 3 cookies into a second package, and so on until the cookies are distributed.

Measurement division begins with a product and then asks the questions, "How many groups of a certain number can be made?" or, in this case, "How many groups of 3 can be made from 12?" This can be written as

$$3\overline{)12}^{\,4}$$

Therefore, measurement division begins with a product and the number of objects in each group. We must find the number of groups.

$$\text{Factor} \times \text{Factor} = \text{Product}$$
$$\square \quad \times \quad 3 \quad = \quad 12$$

VM 8.6b Partition division is commonly taught after measurement division has been introduced. Even though the physical act of dividing using the partitive method is easy for one- and two-place numbers—that is, physically distributing a collection of things by dealing them out one at a time to a given number of groups—is not challenging for 24 divided by 3, the extension of this process to situations involving greater values can literally be exhausting.

Let's consider a simple example just to make a point. If a person has 12 cookies and wishes to put them into 3 packages with the same number in each package, how many cookies will each package contain?

It would not make sense to use the measurement model (or successive subtraction) to solve this type of division example. If a person has 12 cookies, he or she cannot subtract 3 "packages." Instead, it does make sense to put the 12 cookies into 3 packages by dealing them out to the each of the packages one at a time.

Therefore, partition division begins with a product and the number of groups. We must find the number of items in each group.

$$\text{Factor} \times \text{Factor} = \text{Product}$$
$$3 \quad \times \quad \square \quad = \quad 12$$

Children need many experiences with models of group separation, arrays, number lines, and successive subtraction to develop an understanding of division. Both measurement and partition division must be modeled and developed. The terms *dividend, divisor,* and *quotient* also need to be taught because of their relatively common use in the classroom, on tests, and, sometimes, in real-life situations.

$$\overset{\text{Factor}}{\text{Factor}\overline{)\text{Product}}} \qquad \overset{\text{Quotient}}{\text{Divisor}\overline{)\text{Dividend}}}$$

Developing and Memorizing Basic Division Facts

Basic division facts exist—just as basic addition, subtraction, and multiplication facts do. However, when children thoroughly understand multiplication and the inverse relationship, then they already know all basic division facts.

The multiplication table should also be used for the basic division facts. Locate the given factor in the top row; then move down that column until you locate the product. Move to the left in that row; the first number is the missing factor. To use the table with the example $6 \div 2 = \square$, find the factor 2 in the top row of the table. Move down the 2 column until the product 6 is located. Now move to the left, and you will find the missing factor, 3.

Factors

	x	0	1	2	3	4	5	6	7	8	9
	0	0	0	0	0	0	0	0	0	0	0
	1	0	1	2	3	4	5	6	7	8	9
F	2	0	2	4	6	8	10	12	14	16	18
a	3	0	3	6	9	12	15	18	21	24	27
c	4	0	4	8	12	16	20	24	28	32	36
t	5	0	5	10	15	20	25	30	35	40	45
o	6	0	6	12	18	24	30	36	42	48	54
r	7	0	7	14	21	28	35	42	49	56	63
s	8	0	8	16	24	32	40	48	56	64	72
	9	0	9	18	27	36	45	54	63	72	81

Sometimes children need a guide to help them locate a specific example in the multiplication table. Make a guide by cutting two strips from a sheet of transparent acetate. Use rubber cement to connect the two strips at a 90° angle. Cut a square hole for the product where the two strips overlap. When placed on a basic fact table, the answer will be displayed through the cut square.

Glue together.

Cut out rectangle.

Difficulties arise if we attempt to divide by zero. Consider the sentence $5 \div 0 = \square$. If we rewrite this sentence as a multiplication sentence with a missing factor, we obtain:

$$0 \times \square = 5$$

There is no whole number that we can use in the box to make the sentence true. Regardless of which whole number we put in the $\square$, the product will be 0, so the resulting sentence will be false.

An even stranger situation results when we attempt to divide zero by itself. The sentence $0 \div 0 = \square$ could be rewritten as $0 \times \square = 0$. Which whole number will make this sentence true? Any whole number! There is no unique number that can be considered the quotient for $0 \div 0 = \square$. Each time we attempt to divide by zero, we encounter this dilemma. Teachers must be careful not to tell children that *any* number divided by itself equals 1. Zero divided by zero is an exception to this statement. Therefore, at the elementary level, we either leave division by zero undefined or else we say that division by zero is not possible.

After acquiring an understanding of division, children should be given ample practice to anchor the basic division facts and to learn to calculate efficiently. Again, you might want to obtain software practice programs for your computer to provide the necessary practice of the basic division facts. Many examples similar to the following should be provided for practice:

$$6 \times \square = 24 \qquad 2 \times \square = 4 \qquad \square \times 3 = 12$$
$$\square \div 6 = 3 \qquad 8 \div 2 = \square \qquad 10 \div \square = 2$$
$$2\overline{)6} \qquad\qquad 5\overline{)15} \qquad\qquad 3\overline{)9}$$

Remainders in Division

Now, let's consider the notion of remainders in division. What is the missing factor in the following example?

$$2\overline{)7}$$

Three different answers might be given, and all could be considered correct under specific circumstances. For instance:

1. If the example refers to 2 sticks of gum that sell for 7 cents, how much will 1 stick of gum cost? This example of 7 divided by 2 has an answer of 4. At the store, the child will pay 4 cents per stick of gum. There is no remainder in this case. One-half is not a remainder, because the child can't pay in half cents.

2. If the example refers to 7 children forming 2 teams, with the same number of children on each team, how many children will be on each team? This example of 7 divided by 2 is 3; there will be 3 children on each team and one person left over to referee the game.

3. If the example refers to 7 candy bars to be equally shared by 2 children, the question becomes, "How much candy will each child receive?" In this case, the answer is $3\frac{1}{2}$ candy bars for each child; there is no remainder.

Children need to understand that remainders are handled in different ways, depending on the situation. We do not really know what the solution to

$$2\overline{)7}$$

is until the example has been placed in context. From the context of an example, we choose one of three ways to handle a remainder:

1. Drop the leftover part.
2. Raise the answer to the next number.
3. Place the leftover part as a fraction of the missing factor.

We do not recommend that children be taught to write a missing factor as "3 r 1." What is the meaning of "r 1" to a child? This is only a mechanical way to write a response so that the student's paper will be easier for the teacher to check the answer. The real meaning of a remainder is not apparent to the child if "r 1" is used. Instead, expose children to the three types of situations that give rise to a remainder in real-life situations and have the children label or describe any existing

remainder in a way that emphasizes an interpretation appropriate to their reasoning.

After solving examples of this type, the teacher can introduce an example involving division with a remainder using the method of successive subtraction. For example, $19 \div 4 = \square$:

$$
\begin{array}{r}
19 \\
\underline{-4} \quad (1) \\
15 \\
\underline{-4} \quad (2) \\
11 \\
\underline{-4} \quad (3) \\
7 \\
\underline{-4} \quad (4) \\
3
\end{array}
$$

We can see that there are 4 fours in 19, with a remainder of 3. This example can also be shown using the number line as a model:

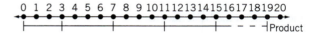

Beginning at 19, we mark off successive segments of four units each to the left and then recognize that there are three units left over. In fact, the number line is an excellent way to introduce the notion of remainder interpreted as a fraction. In this example, we were successively subtracting groups of 4. On our last step, we would be able to subtract only a part of a group of 4, namely 3 of 4. Another way to write this leftover as a part of a group of 4 would be as a ratio of 3 parts to 4 total, or $\frac{3}{4}$.

Expanding Basic Division Facts Through Place Value

After studying the basic facts and solving a number of simple examples such as these, the children will be ready to extend the basic division facts. Using $6 \div 2$ and groups, we can think of 6 objects separated into groups of 2. How many groups of 2 can we make from one group of 6?

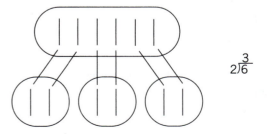

Six elements can be separated into three groups of 2.

Using the same example but substituting bundles of ten for each object, we can ask, "How many groups of 2 can we make from a group of 6 bundles (6 tens)?"

$$\frac{3 \text{ tens}}{2)6 \text{ tens}} \quad \text{or} \quad \frac{30}{2)60}$$

Six bundles of 10 can be separated into two groups of 3 bundles of 10. Thus, just as 6 elements can be separated into two groups of 3, 60 elements can be separated into two groups of 30. Children should be given many such examples extending the basic division facts.

VM 8.8 After extending the basic division facts, children are ready to study division of a two-place number by a one-place number. Consider 69 divided by 3. The children have solved:

$$\frac{2}{3)6}$$
$$\frac{-6}{0}$$

and extended the basic fact to

$$\frac{20}{3)60}$$
$$\frac{-60}{0}$$

They have also solved:

$$\frac{3}{3)9}$$
$$\frac{-9}{0}$$

Now these two examples can be put together so that the children can solve 3)69. Addition, multiplication, and subtraction examples are solved by beginning on the righthand side; children need to know that the standard division algorithm is begun on the left-hand side. First give them simple examples that they already know how to solve.

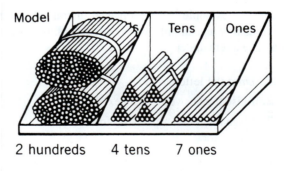

Children should then solve each of the following examples:

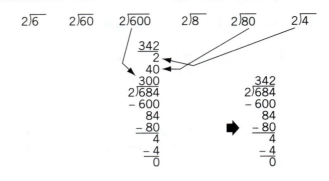

Again, children must learn to analyze division examples so that they can see the simple examples that they know how to solve within the more complex examples. After solving division examples of a two-place number divided by a one-place number, the teacher must help the students extend the division concept into two-place or many-place products divided by one-place factors. Examples with and without remainders should be considered.

The division algorithm and techniques of estimating quotients must be developed with students. Let's examine the example 7)247 and develop the algorithm using the partition division model. In this model, 247 objects would be "shared" or partitioned equally in 7 groups. How many would be in each group? The task of using manipulatives to answer this question would be a bit overwhelming, but it would be beneficial to go through the process at least once to impress the need for a quicker, more efficient algorithm.

Using a place-value box and the partition model, we would begin the example with the following arrangement:

Model   Tens   Ones

2 hundreds   4 tens   7 ones

To share these equally among 7 groups, it would be useful to rearrange them (regroup them) as 24 tens and 7 ones.

Change hundreds to tens.

24 groups of ten   7 ones

Now, the 24 tens can be put into 7 groups with 3 tens in each group and 37 (3 tens and 7 ones) left over. Consequently, we have 3 tens as part of our answer to the original question, but we must deal with the remaining 37 objects.

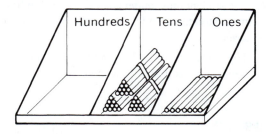

These can be remaned as 37 ones.

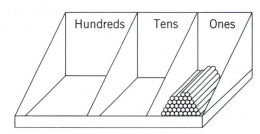

Thus, we need to partition these 37 leftovers into 7 groups. We are able to do so by putting 5 in each group and having 2 left over. To complete our answer, we note that we were able to share the 247 objects evenly in seven groups with 3 tens and 5 ones (35) in each group with 2 left over.

Children need a great deal of practice using tangible materials and relating them to the development of the division algorithm. Mastery of one-digit division is essential before beginning two-digit division.

Now consider this example:

$$15\overline{)349}$$

Outside the four walls of the classroom and away from the practice worksheets, division is couched in a real setting. The answer to whether a problem represents a partition or measurement situation is easily determined by context of that situation. However, when presented as purely abstract division exercises—a reality only common in the school setting—such examples are more easily understood using the measurement model. That is, how many groups of 15 can be made from 349? Estimation and mental mathematics can help us find appropriate trial quotients.

In the exercise of $349 \div 15$, we need to know how many multiples of 15 can be subtracted from 349. Can 100 fifteens be subtracted from 349? No, because $100 \times 15 = 1500$, which cannot be subtracted from 349. Can 10 fifteens be subtracted from 349? Yes, because $10 \times 15 = 150$, which can be subtracted from 349. Can a greater multiple be subtracted? Yes; 20 fifteens can be subtracted: $20 \times 15 = 300$.

$$
\begin{array}{r}
20 \\
15\overline{)349} \\
-300 \quad (20 \times 15) \\
\hline
49
\end{array}
$$

How many fifteens can be subtracted from 49? We try 3:

$$
\begin{array}{r}
23 \\
\hline
3 \\
20 \\
15\overline{)349} \\
-300 \quad (20 \times 15) \\
\hline
49 \\
-45 \quad (3 \times 15) \\
\hline
4
\end{array}
\qquad or \qquad
\begin{array}{r}
23 \\
15\overline{)349} \\
-300 \\
\hline
49 \\
-45 \\
\hline
4
\end{array}
$$

$$349 = (23 \times 15) + 4$$

Thus we see that there are 23 fifteens in 349, with a remainder of 4.

Consider another example: $34\overline{)856}$. How many groups of 34 can be made from 856 things?

Can one group be made? Yes. $1 \times 34 = 34$
Can ten groups be made? Yes. $10 \times 34 = 340$
Can one hundred groups be made? No. $100 \times 34 = 3400$, too much since we have only 856

Thus the first estimate of the quotient must be in the tens place. How many tens are in 856? Compare 34 with 85. The first estimate would be 2, so that is placed in the tens place, representing 20.

$$\begin{array}{r} 2 \\ 34\overline{)856} \\ -68 \\ \hline 176 \end{array}$$

How many groups of 3 can be made out of 176 things?

Can one group be made? Yes. $1 \times 34 = 34$
Can ten groups be made? No. $10 \times 34 = 340$

Therefore this estimate must be placed in the ones place. Comparing 3 with 17, the best estimate is 5.

$$\begin{array}{r} 25 \\ 34\overline{)856} \\ -68 \\ \hline 176 \\ -170 \\ \hline 6 \end{array}$$

The more accurately a child estimates the trial quotient, the shorter the actual computation will be. For instance, inaccurate estimates make the following example unnecessarily long:

$$\begin{array}{r} 25 \\ 1 \\ 4 \\ 10 \\ 10 \\ 27\overline{)691} \\ -270 \quad (10 \times 27) \\ \hline 421 \\ -270 \quad (10 \times 27) \\ \hline 151 \\ -108 \quad (4 \times 27) \\ \hline 43 \\ -27 \quad (1 \times 27) \\ \hline 16 \end{array}$$

Now the same example is shown with more accurate estimates:

$$\begin{array}{r} 25 \\ 5 \\ 20 \\ 27\overline{)691} \\ -540 \quad (20 \times 27) \\ \hline 151 \\ -135 \quad (5 \times 27) \\ \hline 16 \end{array} \quad \text{or} \quad \begin{array}{r} 25 \\ 27\overline{)691} \\ -540 \\ \hline 151 \\ -135 \\ \hline 16 \end{array}$$

These examples are provided to help teachers visualize the steps through which children progress as they learn to divide. It is not suggested that children write out each step as shown here.

Children's comprehension of division begins with real-world experiences from which we assist them visualize, understand, and record. The basic facts of division must be memorized to contribute to a student's power with computation. Establishing place value and then making the estimate of a trial quotient are aids for children in dividing. Much practice of division is necessary as children explore, progress, and learn new concepts.

As we carefully examine the teaching of division to children, we note again that there are five major ideas that students must understand to solve any division example:

1. The student must understand what division is.

2. The student must understand the basic division facts and have them memorized.

3. The student must understand place value and be able to relate the place-value concept to division.

4. The student must understand that division has no basic structures, in that it is not commutative or associative.

5. The student must understand the concept of regrouping as it applies to division.

Closure

Multiplication and division are fundamental tools of mathematics. Many children (and some adults) are able to perform these functions mechanically but have little or no understanding of the underlying concepts. Students exploring multiplication and division need to pay particular attention to appropriate readiness activities, various models for developing meaning, basic properties, and traditional and nontraditional algorithms. Because of different entrance levels, considerable variance in ability and understanding will likely be apparent among the students. Irrespective of the prerequisites the students possess, the exit level of comprehension must emphasize correct use of the mathematical language, appropriate symbolic representation, and an understanding of the uses of multiplication and division in real-world situations.

Multiplication can be thought of as an efficient way of counting or adding; yet it has uniqueness as an operation on a number of equal-sized sets. Division has two distinctly different meanings that must be developed. Division is modeled by separating a given number of elements into equal-sized groups, or it can mean the separation of a given number of elements into a certain number of groups.

Students should receive multiplication and division development at each grade level. Readiness activities must begin with the preschooler and then be extended each year thereafter. By the end of elementary school, children should be able to function successfully with both multiplication and division. During that period of time, children must develop a sound understanding of multiplication and division, master the basic facts of multiplication and division, apply the principles of place value, understand the interrelatedness of the basic structures, and understand and apply the basic ideas of regrouping.

As with addition and subtraction, the concepts of multiplication and division are not new, but the methods that we use to teach these concepts to children have been reexamined. Manipulating concrete objects from the real world, using the number line, and studying illustrations all allow children to build an understanding of the computational process before conventional algorithms are presented. Understanding must precede skill; when understanding and skill are properly developed, children will have a great deal of power in mathematics. When skill precedes understanding, too often the reasons why a particular process works are lost along with a potential loss of transfer to related processes.

Students should be introduced to multiplication and division with concrete materials from the real world. They should see these concepts in many different modes to help them think about the meanings of multiplication and division. Children should memorize the basic multiplication facts and become acquainted with the distributive property of multiplication over addition and its use in solving multiplication examples. At the intermediate level, the meaning of division should be developed and the children should memorize many division facts. The study of the division process is expanded in the upper elementary levels.

The nature and role of computation are rapidly changing in our technological world. The form and frequency of our encounters with computation are influenced by the ways in which we process information in our society. Even though it is hard to imagine a world in which computation is unimportant, it is not hard to imagine one in which it is important to know when (or whether) to use alternative means of determining an answer to a computational exercise. It's not hard to imagine such a world because we live, work, and play in that world now. The calculator, as one example, is an integral part of day-to-day life and cannot be (nor should it be) ignored as one of the tools for computation. Estimation, as another example, is something that we do on a daily basis, often without stopping to acknowledge the value of our abilities to estimate length, amount, capacity, weight, and so on. Students need to explore and determine the appropriate time to use paper-and-pencil algorithms, mental computation, estimation and rounding, and calculators. Instruction in computation must make allowances for that.

PRACTICE EXERCISES FOR TEACHERS

These exercises are designed for the reader of this book, not for the children that the reader may teach. Although some of these examples are suitable for use in the elementary or middle school classroom, they should not necessarily be given to children in the form presented here. Ideas appropriate for classroom activities on the concepts and ideas discussed in this chapter can be found in a later section of this chapter and the CD that accompanies this text.

1. Use the multiplication example $3 \times 4 = \square$ to sketch a model using

    a) groups of objects   b) arrays   c) number line
    d) ordered pairs   e) successive addition

VM 8.2a

2. Draw an array for each of the following examples.

    a) $4 \times 2 = 8$ b) $3 \times 6 = 18$ c) $2 \times 3 = 6$ d) $5 \times 3 = 15$

3. Draw arrays to show a model for $3 \times 6 = 6 \times 3$.

VM 8.3a

4. Write a multiplication sentence for each of the following arrays.

5. Model 6×4 on a number line.

6. Show how successive addition can verify that $4 \times 5 = 20$.

7. Write a multiplication sentence for each given example; then write a related inverse sentence.

a)   b)

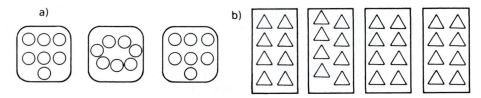

8. Use a number line model to show each of the following division examples.

a) $18 \div 3 = \square$ b) $12 \div 4 = \square$ c) $16 \div 8 = \square$ d) $11 \div 3 = \square$

9. Write two inverse sentences for each given sentence.

a) $7 \times 8 = \square$ b) $72 \div 9 = \square$ c) $108 \div 9 = 12$

d) $8 \times 23 = 184$ e) $221 \div 17 = 13$ f) $124 \times 9 = 1116$

10. Solve each of the following sets of examples.

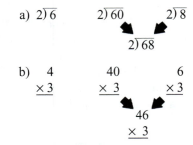

11. We have used the distributive property of multiplication over addition. We can also use the distributive property of multiplication over subtraction. Study the general statement; then solve the following examples by using the general statement as a guide:

$$a \times (b - c) = (a \times b) - (a \times c)$$

a) 6×97 b) 7×48 c) 4×98 d) 3×1998

12. Show how successive subtraction can verify that $48 \div 6 = 8$.

13. On a sheet of graph paper 24 squares wide and 36 squares long, demonstrate that 24×36 is 864; use the distributive property of multiplication over addition to explain your model.

14. Using graph paper, demonstrate how you can verify that the answer to $448 \div 14$ is 32.

VM 8.2b

TEACHING COMPETENCIES
AND SELF-ASSESSMENT TASKS

1. Discuss the prerequisite knowledge that is necessary to understand and model multiplication and division.

2. Discuss reasons that might be offered to explain why division is the more difficult operation for children to learn.

3. Create word problems to demonstrate the distinction between measurement and partition division.

4. Research the work of John Napier, and make a report on the use of "Napier's bones" in teaching multiplication.

5. Research three methods of estimating quotients to two-place division examples, and discuss the merits and disadvantages of each. These methods are often referred to as the apparent method, the increase-by-one method, and the round-off method.

6. Discuss the notion of remainder in division and the advantages and disadvantages of expressing the remainder in various ways.

7. Discuss objections to writing the zero to the right of the ones place when multiplying a number by another number having a zero in the ones place. For example:

$$
\begin{array}{r} 23 \\ \times\ 40 \\ \hline \end{array}
\quad \text{or} \quad
\begin{array}{r} 23 \\ \times\ 40 \\ \hline \end{array}
$$

8. Demonstrate why it is impossible to divide by zero.

9. Discuss how the calculator can be integrated into the teaching of multiplication and/or division.

10. Locate the results of the most recent International Mathematics and Science Study or a recent National Assessment of Educational Progress in Mathematics report related to multiplication and division. Discuss the implications of these results.

11. Discuss the similarities and differences between teaching multiplication and division.

SAMPLE INSTRUCTIONAL AND ASSESSMENT ACTIVITIES

These activities and more are available on the CD that accompanies this text.

1. Multiplication and division activities for primary school children are readiness activities; teaching of abstract concepts does not take place until the intermediate grades. However, many situations that are indicative of multiplication can be shared with first-grade children. For instance, if you have four tables and six children are sitting at each table, the children can count to find out how many are seated in all. Make use of occasions when children line up in pairs or by threes or fours, and again discuss the multiplication situation.

2. In primary grades, the number line provides a natural readiness activity for children. Run a strip of masking tape the length of the classroom. Place small strips of masking tape perpendicular to the strip, about one child's pace apart. Write numerals on the cross-strips to make a number line. Have the children walk on the number line and say, for example, the number that the right foot steps on—2, 4, 6, 8, 10, and so on. These numbers are the multiples of two.

VM 8.1a

3. Give the children a group of counters and 15-centimeter by 25-centimeter (or 5-inch by 8-inch) cards. Have the children model physical representations of many multiplication facts.

VM 8.3b

4. Model each example on a number line.

a) $2+2+2+2=$ b) $4 \times 2 =$ c) $3+3+3+3=$ d) $4 \times 3 =$

VM 8.4

5. Fill in the missing numerals in each sequence.

a) 2, 4, 6, 8, _____, _____, _____, _____, _____, _____.

b) 5, 10, 15, _____, _____, _____, _____, _____, _____, _____.

c) 3, 6, 9, _____, _____, _____, _____, _____, _____, _____,

VM 8.5

6. Use concrete materials for children to see how regrouping in multiplication works. They may need to use expanded notation before becoming familiar with the algorithm and being able to use the conventional short form. Base ten blocks could be put to excellent use here.

a)   23   b)   36   c)   48   d)   426
      $\times\ 4$ $\times\ 2$ $\times\ 3$ $\times\ 5$

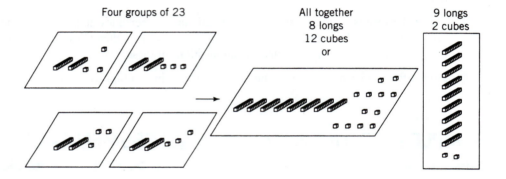

Four groups of 23   All together / 8 longs / 12 cubes / or   9 longs / 2 cubes

VM 8.8

7. The place-value box is an excellent device to use for beginning division because it can be used to model as many as three place holders in the dividend.

$3\overline{)6}$ Hundreds   Tens   Ones

Three sheets of paper

If six things are separated into three groups, how many things go into each group?

8. Use short, relatively simple word problems to give students practice in translating problem situations into mathematical sentences. Write an equation for each problem; then find the solution.

a) Thirty-eight books on each shelf. Five shelves. How many books?

b) Ten pairs of socks on each section of the clothesline. Four sections of clothesline. How many socks?

c) Nine players on each team. Eight teams in the league. How many players in the league?

d) Five school days in each week. How many school days in four weeks?

e) Eight hot dogs in each plastic pack. Twelve packs. How many hot dogs?

f) Twenty-four hamburger buns. Eight in a package. How many packages?

g) Sixteen scouts. Four scouts per boat. How many boats will be needed?

9. The multiples of any given number can be generated using a constant. For instance, to generate the multiples of 4, set up the calculator with the constant 4. By entering the set of whole numbers one at a time and striking the equal key each time, the multiples of 4 will be displayed.

EXAMPLE	KEYS STRUCK	DISPLAY WILL GENERATE THE MULTIPLES OF 4
0×4	$\boxed{0}\ \boxed{=}$	0
1×4	$\boxed{1}\ \boxed{=}$	4
2×4	$\boxed{2}\ \boxed{=}$	8
3×4	$\boxed{3}\ \boxed{=}$	12
4×4	$\boxed{4}\ \boxed{=}$	16
5×4	$\boxed{5}\ \boxed{=}$	20
6×4	$\boxed{6}\ \boxed{=}$	24
7×4	$\boxed{7}\ \boxed{=}$	28
and so on		

Have the children explore by generating sets of multiples for any given number.

10. Pretend that most of the calculator keys are broken. Using only the operation keys and the digit keys 7 and 2, make the calculator display screen show 93 with the least number of key punches.

chapter

9

Number Theory and Number Systems

Let's begin this chapter with a number riddle. Play along by following each direction as you go. Ready?

Choose any whole number between 1 and 10.

Add 3 to that number.

Multiply the resulting sum by 9.

Find the sum of the individual digits of this product.

If the sum is greater than 10, then find the sum of these digits.

Subtract 5 from the resulting sum.

Now, continue by following these steps.

Translate your final number above into a letter of the alphabet using this code: A = 1, B = 2, C = 3, D = 4, and so on.

Write down the name of a country in Western Europe that begins with that letter.

Write down the name of an animal that begins with the letter that ends the country name.

Write down the name of a color that begins with the letter that ends the animal name.

At this point, turn to page 226 and look at the print at the bottom of that page.

It is quite likely that the authors of this book were able to predict the color, animal, and country that you came up—without knowing which number you originally chose. How is this possible? After all, you chose the number at random to start this off. You might have picked the number 4, or 7, or 9. Perhaps you should go back to the start of this series of steps and choose a different number and see how it works out this time. We'll wait. . . .

How did you do this time? Same answer? Was it just chance that following the arithmetic steps led you to the answer "4," which translates to the English letter "D," and hence leads you to the country of Denmark (since Denmark is the only country in Western Europe that begins with "D")?

A close examination of the arithmetic steps reveals that in the third step you multiplied a number by 9. You may recall (or you can easily verify) that when you multiply any whole number by 9, the sum of the digits of the resulting product will always be some multiple of 9. If you got a multidigit multiple of 9, say 36, you were then asked to add those digits together. Eventually you will get a sum of just 9. Then, when you subtract 5, you will always get 4—the number that you were asked to translate into a letter. Since everyone gets a 4, everyone must use D. After exhausting your

knowledge of the names of Western European countries and settling for Denmark, you almost surely will choose kangaroo (or, perhaps, koala) as the animal that begins with "k"—there just aren't that many animals beginning with "k" that come quickly to mind. The selection of kangaroo leads to the color orange, while the selection of koala might likely lead to aqua.

So, some things that first appear to be unlikely are not always so unlikely when mathematics is applied. Surprising results can be explained with mathematics and, perhaps, even appreciated more for their elegance. Try this riddle with others and amaze your friends with mathematics!

In this chapter, we look more closely at several aspects of a structured approach to teaching mathematics. Mathematical structures provide a solid foundation for building real power with mathematics—not just the ability to process algorithms. Here we consider some of the most efficient approaches to understanding numbers and their factors.

The National Council of Teachers of Mathematics (NCTM) *Principles and Standards for School Mathematics* (2000) embeds the discussion of number theory and number systems within the process standards (Problem Solving, Reasoning and Proof, Communication, Connections, and Representations) and, most notably, in the content standards for Number and Operation and Algebra.

The content standard for Number and Operations in grades preK–12 states the following:

Instructional programs from prekindergarten

through grade 12 should enable all students to—

Understand numbers, ways of representing numbers, relationships among numbers, and number systems

Understand meanings of operations and how they relate to one another

Compute fluently and make reasonable estimates

The content standard for Algebra in grades preK–12 states the following:

Instructional programs from prekindergarten

through grade 12 should enable all students to—

Understand patterns, relations, and functions

Represent and analyze mathematical situations and structures using algebraic symbols

Use mathematical models to represent and understand quantitative relationships

Analyze change in various contexts

We hope that as a result of the examination of number structure as presented in this chapter, each teacher will recognize the importance of a thorough understanding of operations on whole numbers, integers, and fractional numbers (a term commonly reserved for fractions greater than zero). The information in this chapter is essential background for every elementary or middle school classroom teacher—not solely for those who teach these concepts at a given grade level.

The Language of Number Theory

Before delving into the main subject of this chapter, let's review some of the language commonly used in discussing multiplication of whole numbers as presented in many mathematics programs today. (See Chapter 8 for further details.) Let's begin by naming the parts of a mathematical sentence involving multiplication:

$$2 \times 3 = 6$$

In this sentence the 2 and the 3 are both called **factors**, and the 6 is called the **product**. We also say that

2 is a *factor* of 6

3 is a *factor* of 6

6 is the *product* of the *factors* 2 and 3

6 is a *multiple* of 3

6 is a *multiple* of 2

When we say that 6 is a multiple of 2, we mean that we can multiply 2 by some whole number factor to get 6 as a product. Each time we multiply 2 by a whole number, we get a multiple of 2. Thus, the multiples of 2 are 0, 2, 4, 6, 8, 10, and so on. The multiples of 5 are 0, 5, 10, 15, 20, 25, and so on. In the primary grades, we often have children count by 2s, by 3s, by 5s, and by 10s, a practice often referred to as skip-counting. When children do this, they are naming multiples of 2, multiples of 3, multiples of 5, and multiples of 10. This experience provides a foundation for developmentally appropriate skill building that will later assist the children in the understanding and memorization of basic multiplication facts.

As early as the primary grades, a child learns that a number such as 7 can be named in many ways. For example, usually beginning with addition, children learn that $2 + 5 = 7$ and $3 + 4 = 7$. Later, they note that $9 - 2 = 7$ and $12 - 5 = 7$. Still later, they begin to recognize that each of the following is another name for 12:

$$11 + 1 \qquad 2 \times 6$$
$$15 - 3 \qquad 24 \div 2$$
$$3 \times 4 \qquad 36 \div 3$$

We use the words **product expression** to talk about names, such as 3×4 and 2×6, that involve multiplication (or finding a product). In other words, 3×4 and 2×6 are product expressions for 12.

As we saw in Chapter 8, a product expression with two factors can be pictured by a rectangular array. For example, we can picture the product expression 3×4 as this array:

We call this a 3-by-4 array. The first number tells how many rows (3), and the second number tells how many columns (4).

We can use any of several different product expressions to represent the number 12. Some examples are

     1 x 12   2 x 6   3 x 4

Each of these product expressions for the number 12 has been expressed here as a rectangular array. This means that they can be expressed as an orderly arrangement of one or more rows and columns. Any whole number can be represented by a rectangular array having only one row. That is, the number 7 could be represented by a 1-by-7 array.

In the case of the number 6, there are two product expressions containing two factors (plus two more that are omitted because of the commutative property):

       1 x 6   2 x 3

We have formed rectangular arrays with 12 objects (1×12, 2×6, and 3×4) and with 6 objects (1×6 and 2×3). Now, let's consider other numbers:

Number	Product Expression	Array
14	1 × 14	• • • • • • • • • • • • • •
	2 × 7	• • • • • • • • • • • • • •
20	1 × 20	• • • • • • • • • • • • • • • • • • • •
	2 × 10	• • • • • • • • • • • • • • • • • • • •
	4 × 5	• • • • • • • • • • • • • • • • • • • •

But, what happens in the case of the number 13? With 13 objects or symbols, we can form only a rectangular array of a single row (1 × 13) or a single column (13 × 1).

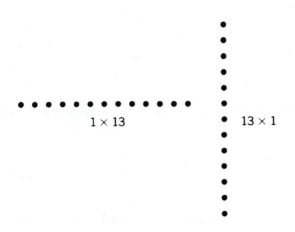

1×13 13×1

Which other numbers can be represented only by a rectangular array of a single row or column?

Examining the following table, we find that 2, 3, 5, 7, and 11 also can be represented only by single rows or single columns.

Number	Product Expression	Array
2	1 × 2	••
3	1 × 3	•••
4	1 × 4	••••
4	2 × 2	•• ••
5	1 × 5	•••••
6	1 × 6	••••••
6	2 × 3	••• •••
7	1 × 7	•••••••
8	1 × 8	••••••••
8	2 × 4	•••• ••••
9	1 × 9	•••••••••
9	3 × 3	••• ••• •••
10	1 × 10	••••••••••
10	2 × 5	••••• •••••
11	1 × 11	•••••••••••

What about a greater number—for example, 30?

1 x 30

2 x 15

3 x 10

5 x 6

From this brief examination, we can draw several conclusions:

1. A product expression for a number is another name for the number itself. For example, product expressions for 12—that is, 1 × 12, 12 × 1, 2 × 6, 6 × 2, 3 × 4, and 4 × 3—are different ways of naming 12.

2. Every whole number greater than 1 can be named by at least one product expression: 1 times the number itself (and, by using the commutative property, the number itself times 1).

3. Many numbers can be named by more than one product expression. For example, 4, 6, 8, 9, 10, 12, 14, 20, and 30 can all be named by more than one product expression.

From our review of the language of multiplication, we know that the numbers making up a product expression are called factors. We know that many of the numbers we've discussed have more than two factors. For example, we can name the set of all factors of 12: {1, 2, 3, 4, 6, 12}. But many numbers have only two factors: 1 and the number itself. The only factors of 11, for example, are 1 and 11.

The Sieve of Eratosthenes

Another way of examining numbers in light of their factors comes to us from ancient Greece. Eratosthenes, a famous geographer of the third century B.C., first devised a method that has come to be called the *Sieve of*

VM 9.1

Eratosthenes. The following arrangement of numerals is one example of a pattern for a sieve:

	2	3	4	5	6	7	8	9	10
11	12	13	14	15	16	17	18	19	20
21	22	23	24	25	26	27	28	29	30
31	32	33	34	35	36	37	38	39	40
41	42	43	44	45	46	47	48	49	50
51	52	53	54	55	56	57	58	59	60
61	62	63	64	65	66	67	68	69	70
71	72	73	74	75	76	77	78	79	80
81	82	83	84	85	86	87	88	89	90
91	92	93	94	95	96	97	98	99	100

To begin our examination of the sieve, recall our discussion of rectangular arrays. The number 2 can be represented by a rectangular array of a single row or column only. The product expression for 2 is 1×2, but every multiple of 2 (other than 2 itself) can be represented by rectangular arrays with more than a single row or column.

$$2 \times 2 = 4$$
$$3 \times 2 = 6$$
$$4 \times 2 = 8$$
$$5 \times 2 = 10$$

Now, referring to the table, or sieve, draw a loop around the numeral 2, and cross out all of the other multiples of 2 (i.e., 4, 6, 8, 10, . . . , 100).

Next, consider 3. You will recall that 3 can be represented by only a single row or column array: the only factors of 3 are 1 and 3. All of the multiples of 3 (other than 3 itself), however, can be represented by rectangular arrays with 3 rows or 3 columns. On the sieve, draw a loop around the 3, and then cross out all of the other multiples of 3 (6, 9, 12, 15, 18, . . . , 99). You will notice that many of the multiples of 3 have already been crossed out, because some multiples of 3 are also multiples of 2—for example, 6, 12, 18, and so on.

The next consecutive numeral not already looped or crossed out is 5. Draw a loop around the 5, and cross out all of the other multiples of 5 (10, 15, 20, 25, . . . , 100). Again, you will notice that many of the multiples of 5 have already been crossed out, because some of the multiples of 5 are also multiples of 2 or 3—for example, 30, 60, 90, and so on.

The next numeral not crossed out is 7. Draw a loop around the 7, and cross out all other multiples of 7 (14, 21, 28, . . . , 98).

The next numeral not crossed out is 11. Draw a loop around the 11, and cross out all other multiples of 11 (22,

33, 44, . . . , 99). You will observe that all the multiples of 11 (other than 11 itself) have already been crossed out.

⑪	②	③	4̶	⑤	6̶	7̶	⑦	8̶	9̶	1̶0̶
⑪	1̶2̶	13	1̶4̶	1̶5̶	1̶6̶	17	1̶8̶	19	2̶0̶
2̶1̶	22	23	2̶4̶	2̶5̶	2̶6̶	2̶7̶	2̶8̶	29	3̶0̶
31	3̶2̶	3̶3̶	3̶4̶	3̶5̶	3̶6̶	37	3̶8̶	3̶9̶	4̶0̶
41	4̶2̶	43	4̶4̶	4̶5̶	4̶6̶	47	4̶8̶	4̶9̶	5̶0̶
5̶1̶	5̶2̶	53	5̶4̶	5̶5̶	5̶6̶	5̶7̶	5̶8̶	59	6̶0̶
61	6̶2̶	6̶3̶	6̶4̶	6̶5̶	6̶6̶	67	6̶8̶	6̶9̶	7̶0̶
71	7̶2̶	73	7̶4̶	7̶5̶	7̶6̶	7̶7̶	7̶8̶	79	8̶0̶
8̶1̶	8̶2̶	83	8̶4̶	8̶5̶	8̶6̶	8̶7̶	8̶8̶	89	9̶0̶
9̶1̶	9̶2̶	9̶3̶	9̶4̶	9̶5̶	9̶6̶	97	9̶8̶	9̶9̶	1̶0̶0̶

At this point, what generalizations could you make about the multiples of 13? (All multiples of 13, other than 13 itself, have already been crossed out.)

You will notice that there are still some numerals on the chart that have not been crossed out. What generalization could you make about the arrays that illustrate these numbers? (In each case, the array consists of either a single row or a single column. We cannot form any other rectangular arrays for these numbers.) For each of these numbers, what are the only factors? (For each number, the only factors are 1 and the number itself.) Make a list of the numerals on the chart that are not crossed out (2, 3, 5, 7, 11, 13, 17, 19, 23, 29, 31, 37, 41, 43, 47, 53, 59, 61, 67, 71, 73, 79, 83, 89, and 97). These whole numbers are greater than 1 and have only 1 and themselves as factors; they are called **prime numbers**. Whole numbers greater than 1 that have whole number factors other than 1 and themselves are called **composite numbers**.

What do you notice that is common to all prime numbers except 2? (They are all odd.) This is true because every even number has 2 as a factor, so every even number greater than 2 must have a factor other than itself and 1. Note, however, that not all odd numbers are prime. For example, 23 is a prime number, but 33 is not.

We have now examined the structure of certain numbers in two ways—by making arrays of physical objects or symbols and by marking off multiples of certain numbers on a chart or sieve.

We have not included the number 1 in this discussion because the number 1 is unique. It is a factor of every number ($2 = 1 \times 2$, $3 = 1 \times 3$, $15 = 1 \times 15$, $189 = 1 \times 189$, and so on) and, consequently, 1 is called the *identity element for multiplication*. To say that 1 is a factor of a number, then, does not really tell us much about the number. By definition, the number 1 is neither prime nor composite. (It is sometimes called a *generator*.)

Remember that any number greater than 1 that has only 1 and the number itself as factors is a prime number.

Any whole number greater than 1 must, therefore, be either prime or composite (nonprime). Using arrays and the Sieve of Eratosthenes, we have sorted the set of whole numbers between 2 and 100 inclusive into prime and composite numbers. A further remark on the work of Eratosthenes explains the term *sieve*. Working with numerals arranged on a parchment sheet, it is said that Eratosthenes physically punched out all the multiples of 2, except for 2 itself, leaving holes in the parchment. The multiples of 3, except for 3 itself, were cut from the sheet in the same way; then the multiples of 5, and so on. The result was a sheet on which only the prime numbers remained. This parchment filled with holes where the composite numbers had dropped through closely resembled a sieve.

We can discover interesting patterns in number charts by placing varying amounts of numbers in the rows or columns. Let's look at the pattern that develops when the numbers are placed into a chart with six columns.

1	②	③	4	⑤	6
⑦	8	9	10	⑪	12
⑬	14	15	16	⑰	18
⑲	20	21	22	㉓	24
25	26	27	28	㉙	30
㉛	32	33	34	35	36
㊲	38	39	40	㊶	42
㊸	44	45	46	㊼	48
49	50	51	52	㊾	54
55	56	57	58	㊾	60
�61	62	63	64	65	66
㊻	68	69	70	㉑	72
㊴	74	75	76	77	78
㊴	80	81	82	㊳	84
85	86	87	88	㊾	90
91	92	93	94	95	96
㊴	98	99	100	⑩1	102

Where are the prime numbers located? Will a prime number ever appear in the column headed by 4 or 6? Why? Encourage students to study this table further. Where are the multiples of two located? the multiples of three? the multiples of five? of seven? of eleven? Look for patterns and improve communication skills by describing these patterns to others.

Factor Trees

We have found that every composite number can be renamed as a product expression other than 1 times the number. For instance, 24 can be renamed using any of the following product expressions:

$$2 \times 12$$
$$3 \times 8$$
$$4 \times 6$$

This can also be shown in another way:

Example (a):　　Example (b):　　Example (c):

In example (a), we know that 12 can be renamed as 2 × 6 or as 3 × 4, so example (a) can be extended in two possible ways:

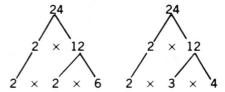

We can see in these two cases that 6 and 4 are both composite numbers, but each can be factored in only one way (excluding 1 as a factor):

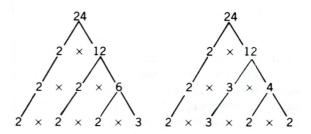

We see now that every number named in the last row is a prime number. Because of the shape of these particular diagrams, they are sometimes referred to as *factor trees*.

In example (b), we know that 8 can be expressed only as 2 × 4. Hence we have the following factor tree:

VM 9.2

Examining the last row of this factor tree, we find the composite number 4, which can be named by the product expression 2 × 2:

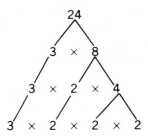

By examination, we see that every number named in the last row is now a prime number.

In example (c), both 4 and 6 are composite numbers and can be shown by the product expressions 2 × 2 and 2 × 3, respectively. The following factor tree results:

Since every number named in the last row is a prime number, the factor tree is complete.

Now examine the last row of each of the factor trees:

Example (a):	2 × 2 × 2 × 3 or
	2 × 3 × 2 × 2
Example (b):	3 × 2 × 2 × 2
Example (c):	2 × 2 × 2 × 3

You will notice that in each example the final result is a product expression for 24 in which each factor is a prime number. Furthermore, each product expression uses the same set of factors. The fact that they are arranged in a different order is not important because of the commutative property of multiplication.

Now examine another number, 18, and its appropriate factor trees:

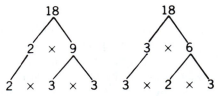

Notice that whether we use 2 × 9 or 3 × 6 as the first product expression, the last product expression in each factor tree is composed of the same set of factors.

Factor trees for the number 36 look like these:

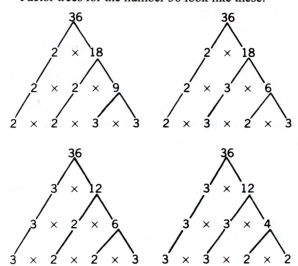

We see that these factor trees appear to be a bit different from each other. Nevertheless, the same set of factors is found in the last product expression of each of these trees. Will there ever be more than one set of factors in the last row of the factor trees for a given number? (No.) This important conclusion is formally known as the **Fundamental Theorem of Arithmetic**.

VM 9.2

> The Fundamental Theorem of Arithmetic states that except for the order of the factors, a composite number can be expressed as a product of prime numbers in one and only one way.

You may wish to use the Factor Tree Virtual Manipulative on the accompanying CD to create a series of examples of the Fundamental Theorem of Arithmetic by factoring a number in many different ways. This is not a proof, but it does provide an illustration of the meaning of the theorem.

Prime Factorization

When a composite number is expressed as a product of prime numbers, we often refer to this as **prime factorization**, or complete factorization. The following are some examples of prime factorization:

VM 9.2

$45 = 3 \times 15$	$42 = 2 \times 21$
$= 3 \times 3 \times 5$	$= 2 \times 3 \times 7$
$50 = 2 \times 25$	$56 = 2 \times 28$
$= 2 \times 5 \times 5$	$= 2 \times 2 \times 14$
	$= 2 \times 2 \times 2 \times 7$

$$72 = 2 \times 36$$
$$= 2 \times 2 \times 18$$
$$= 2 \times 2 \times 2 \times 9$$
$$= 2 \times 2 \times 2 \times 3 \times 3$$

Notice that the prime factorization of a number is complete when each factor in the final product expression is a prime number.

Now let's investigate some of the practical applications of prime factors. Many times, in different mathematical contexts, it is helpful to factor numbers into primes. For example, we can use prime factorizations when we write fractions in simplest form and when we find least common denominators (see Chapters 11 and 12). Thus we may choose to use prime factorization to factor a number in the most efficient manner.

To decide whether any given number is prime or factorable, we apply a successive division test. First we attempt to divide the given number by the least prime number, 2; then we try successively greater prime divisors. For example, let's test 92:

$$2\overline{)92}$$
$$2\overline{)46}$$
$$23$$

By starting with the divisor 2, it quickly becomes evident that 92 can be factored by 2, since we obtain a quotient and a zero remainder. That is, 92 divided by 2 is 46. Now, 46 is also divisible by 2. Remember, in testing each quotient we always begin with the least prime number, 2, as the divisor. The next quotient, 23, we find is not divisible by 2, or by 3, 5, 7, 11, 13, or 19. It is a prime number, so our factoring is complete. The prime factorization of 92 is thus shown to be $2 \times 2 \times 23$.

Now try a number with more factors, 468:

$$2\overline{)468}$$
$$2\overline{)234}$$
$$3\overline{)117}$$
$$3\overline{)39}$$
$$13$$

In this case, the divisor 2 is effective in the first two steps, but the quotient, 117, can't be divided by 2. Our next step, then, is to see if 117 is divisible by the next prime number, 3. It is, so the division is performed, and the new quotient obtained is 39. Obviously, 39 is not divisible by 2, since it is an odd number. However, it is again divisible by the prime number, 3. Since the quotient 13 is prime, this is as far as our prime factoring can be carried. The prime factorization is a combination of all the divisors and the final quotient. (Divisors are, of course, also factors.) The following expression shows the prime factorization of 468:

$$2 \times 2 \times 3 \times 3 \times 13$$

Because some greater numbers are prime, much time can be wasted attempting to find divisors for greater numbers that are, in fact, prime. However, there is an aid that can save us some time. We should try only divisors that are not greater than the square root of the number being tested. The *square root* of a given number is the number that when multiplied times itself yields that given number. For example, 5 is the square root of 25, because $5 \times 5 = 25$. In general, N is called the square root of P if, and only if $N \times N = P$.

Let's consider the number 97 and test it for factorization, beginning with the least prime number as a divisor. The number 97 is obviously not divisible by 2, because 97 is not an even number. It is also not divisible by 3. Next we try the divisors 5 and 7, still unsuccessfully. There is no reason to try any greater primes as divisors of 97. We know that the square root of 97 is less than 10 (since $10 \times 10 = 100$), and 7 is the greatest prime divisor that isn't greater than this square root. If we bothered to test the next prime number greater than 7 (11), the square would be 121 (11×11) or greater than 97. Consequently, checking for divisibility by 2, 3, 5, and 7 is sufficient for us to conclude that 97 must be prime.

Students should understand the reasons we do not attempt to use divisors greater than the square root of the number involved, but do not ask children to merely apply this as a rote rule. To illustrate the reasoning, let's consider what happens when a divisor is selected. For example:

$$2\overline{)24}$$
$$12$$

We see that factors appear in pairs. As soon as one number is used as a divisor, a second number appears as a quotient. When 24 is divided by 2, another factor, 12, appears automatically. For a moment, let's consider all pairs of factors of 24: 1×24, 2×12, 3×8, and 4×6. Notice that in each case, a greater factor is paired with a lesser factor.

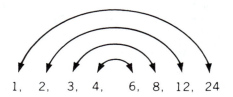

1,   2,   3,   4,   6,   8,   12,   24

Clearly, if no lesser number (other than those listed) is a factor of 24, then no greater number is a factor either. We see that 4 is the greatest factor we need to divide into 24 to list all the factors of 24 (if we have already divided by 1, 2, and 3). Hence, generalizing from the example of 24 to all whole numbers, we need to consider only the lesser numbers as divisors—that is, numbers that aren't greater than the square root of the number under consideration.

Note that the square root of 24 lies between the square root of 16 and the square root of 25:

$$\sqrt{25} = 5 \qquad 5 \times 5 = 25$$
$$\sqrt{16} = 4 \qquad 4 \times 4 = 16$$

Because 25 > 24, we do not need to test any divisors greater than 4 to obtain all the factors of 24.

Consider the number 100.

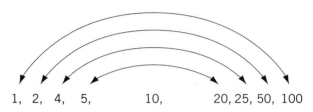

1, 2, 4, 5,   10,   20, 25, 50, 100

If we divide 100 only by factors of 100 up to and including the square root of 100 (10), we will obtain all the factors of 100. What is our procedure for finding the prime factorization of 100?

1. Begin by trying the least prime number, 2, as a divisor:

$$2)\underline{100}$$
$$50$$

2. We can divide by 2 again, since the quotient, 50, is an even number:

$$2)\underline{100}$$
$$2)\underline{50}$$
$$25$$

3. This quotient is not divisible by 2 or by the next prime, 3; but it is divisible by the prime number 5:

$$2)\underline{100}$$
$$2)\underline{50}$$
$$5)\underline{25}$$
$$5$$

4. Our prime factorization of 100 is now complete, since the quotient 5 is prime:

$$2 \times 2 \times 5 \times 5$$

VM 9.2

With greater numbers, it is extremely helpful to use only prime number divisors that are less than the square root of the dividend. For example, consider the number 469. Is this a prime number? If not, what is its prime factorization?

Our first step is to determine the greatest prime number that we need to try as a divisor. To determine this, we need to find only the square root, or the approximate square root, of 469. We know that 20 × 20 = 400. What are the prime numbers closest to 20? They are 19 and 23. Since 23 × 23 = 529 (and 529 >

469), we know that 19 is the greatest prime number we need to try as a divisor.

Dividing 469 by primes (beginning, as always, with 2), we find that 2, 3, and 5 will not divide 469 evenly. The next prime number is 7, which does divide 469 evenly:

$$7)\underline{469}$$
$$67$$

Because 469 is not a multiple of 2, 3, or 5, neither can the number 67 be a multiple of 2, 3, or 5. By trying 7, 11, 13, 17, and 19 as divisors, we find that 67 is prime. Or, because the square root of 67 is approximately 8, we find that we have tested as far as is necessary with a divisor of 7. In either case, 67 is prime, and the prime factorization of 469 is 7 × 67.

Now let's test 73. We know that the square root of 73 lies somewhere between 8 and 9, because 8 × 8 = 64 and 9 × 9 = 81. The greatest prime divisor to test, then, is 7.

Is 73 divisible by 2? (No)

Is 73 divisible by 3? (No)

Is 73 divisible by 5? (No)

Is 73 divisible by 7? (No)

Any attempt to go further in division is unnecessary, because the next prime, 11, is greater than the square root of 73. The number 73, then, is prime.

To factor numbers completely and efficiently:

1. We should understand prime factors.

2. We should have a systematic approach to factorization.

3. We should have some simple rules for determining whether or not a number is divisible by the most common prime numbers.

Divisibility "Rules"

The sieve we discussed earlier in this chapter can be used to help children derive simple tests of divisibility for the numbers 2, 3, and 5. By inspecting the multiples of 2, 3, and 5, children can discover the structural peculiarities of any number divisible by 2, 3, or 5. First, by examining several multiples of 2, children can see that the digit in the ones place of these multiples is always either 0, 2, 4, 6, or 8. Only whole numbers ending in one of these digits are divisible by 2. In other words, only even numbers are multiples of 2 (i.e., divisible by 2). Next children should inspect the multiples of 3. A more complex observation may become apparent here. After inspection of various multiples of 3, and, with some guidance, it may be noticed that any number divisible by 3 is a number whose individual digits add up to be a number that is divisible by 3. For example, consider the following:

Number	Sum of Digits	Factors of Numbers
12	$1 + 2 = 3$	3×4
15	$1 + 5 = 6$	3×5
18	$1 + 8 = 9$	3×6
21	$2 + 1 = 3$	3×7
24	$2 + 4 = 6$	3×8
27	$2 + 7 = 9$	3×9
96	$9 + 6 = 15$	3×32
168	$1 + 6 + 8 = 15$	3×56
4035	$4 + 0 + 3 + 5 = 12$	3×1345

In each case, the sum of the digits is divisible by 3 and the original number is also divisible by 3. On the other hand, any number whose digits do not sum to a multiple of 3 will not be divisible by 3. This can be verified by examining numbers such as 11, 13, 14, 76, and 371.

Finally, children should inspect the multiples of 5. Every number that is divisible by 5 contains 0 or 5 in the ones place:

$$2 \times 5 = 10$$
$$3 \times 5 = 15$$
$$4 \times 5 = 20$$
$$5 \times 5 = 25$$
$$6 \times 5 = 30$$
$$7 \times 5 = 35$$
$$8 \times 5 = 40$$
$$9 \times 5 = 45$$
$$10 \times 5 = 50$$
and so on.

Any whole number that doesn't end with 0 or 5 is not divisible by 5—for example, 11, 17, and 134.

These simple rules of divisibility can be very helpful. Students learn more about number sense and number structure by applying such tests than by going through the more cumbersome and time-consuming process of checking for factors by trial and error.

To become proficient at certain aspects of mental mathematics and estimation, it is often helpful to be able to recognize certain patterns and structures in numbers. For instance, it can be helpful to be able to determine whether one number is a factor of another without the use of potentially lengthy or time-consuming computation. If a calculator is handy, this would be an excellent time to put it to use, but what can be done if a calculator is not readily available?

Children should be able to determine rather quickly if a given number is divisible by another number. Children need a great deal of guidance and focus as they discover and use divisibility rules. Examples need to be carefully examined, and children should discuss how the examples are alike and how they are different.

Let's summarize divisibility. When we say that a given counting number is *divisible*, we mean that it can be divided by a counting number divisor so that there is a zero remainder. Look at the following examples. We say that 9 is divisible by 3 because we obtain a zero remainder:

$$\begin{array}{r} 3 \\ 3\overline{)9} \\ \underline{-9} \\ 0 \end{array}$$

In the following example:

$$\begin{array}{r} 2 \\ 3\overline{)9} \\ \underline{-6} \\ 1 \end{array}$$

we say that 7 is not divisible by 3 because when 7 is divided by 3 we have a nonzero remainder—in this case, 1.

Now let's summarize the divisibility rules. We have already systematically explored divisibility by 2, 3, and 5. To develop other divisibility rules, use the following procedure: Use a calculator to identify numbers that are multiples of (and thus divisible by) 9. Find at least 10 such numbers and list them. Examine the list, looking for some common pattern or trait that the numbers share. With focused attention, you may note that in each case, the sum of the digits of the number is divisible by 9. Check this with many other examples. A similar procedure can be used to discover other divisibility rules for 4, 6, and 8. Use this procedure, and have the children check a sample of numbers so that they can justify the following divisibility rules:

1. Any even number is divisible by 2. Two is a factor of any even number, and 0 is obtained as a remainder.

2. A number is divisible by 3 if the sum of the digits is a multiple of 3. We know that 144 is divisible by 3 because by adding the digits 1, 4, and 4, we obtain a sum of 9, and 9 is divisible by 3.

3. A number is divisible by 4 if the last two digits, taken together as a number, are evenly divisible by 4. The number 328 is divisible by 4 because 28 is divisible by 4; therefore, 328 is divisible by 4.

4. A number is divisible by 5 if there is either a 0 or a 5 in the ones place.

5. A number is divisible by 6 if the number is divisible by both 2 and 3. The number 546

RESEARCH SNAPSHOT

What are the consequences of memorizing the divisibility rules without conceptually understanding them?

In a study of 21 preservice elementary school teachers, Zazkis and Campbell (1996) found that many of the teachers were procedurally oriented and considered the divisibility rules procedurally as well.

In the absence of conceptual understanding, many of the teachers misapplied and overgeneralized the divisibility rules when they did not have rules to use. The results suggest that for these teachers, insufficient emphasis has been placed on a meaningful understanding of divisibility.

What could you do in your classroom to promote the development of a conceptual understanding of divisibility?

Zazkis, R., & Campbell, S. (1996). Divisibility and multiplicative structure of natural numbers: Preservice teachers' understanding. *Journal for Research in Mathematics Education, 27*, 540–563.

For additional research briefs, "ERIC Digests" lets you search more than 2000 short syntheses of research on a range of education topics. The syntheses were produced by the Educational Resources Information Center (ERIC). Check http://www.ericfacility.net/ericdigests/index/.

is even; therefore it is divisible by 2. It is divisible by 3 because $5 + 4 + 6 = 15$, and 15 is divisible by 3. Therefore 546 is divisible by 6 because it is divisible by both 2 and 3.

6. A number is divisible by 8 if the last three digits, taken together as a number, are divisible by 8; 9864 is divisible by 8 because 864 is divisible by 8.

7. A number is divisible by 9 if the sum of the digits is divisible by 9. The number 756 is divisible by 9 because $7 + 5 + 6 = 18$, and 18 is divisible by 9.

8. A number is divisible by 10 if there is a 0 in the ones place.

Note that these are not rules in the sense that they must be committed to memory. In fact, some teachers ask students to memorize them in a rote manner, and, consequently, the children forget them and lose the point of what divisibility is all about. The divisibility rules should instead be treated as interesting investigations. They are useful observations of number structure and applications of number sense.

Least Common Multiples and Greatest Common Factors

Every composite number has been shown to have a unique prime factorization. We can use this fact to help us find other information about numbers. For example, it is often useful to know the greatest common factor (GCF) of two numbers.

GCF and LCM (least common multiple) are used extensively to develop concepts about operations on fractional numbers. They are mentioned in this chapter because of their relation to prime factors. The practical applications shown in subsequent chapters will be of interest to the teacher and of great importance throughout the study of rational numbers.

Let's first examine the concept of **greatest common factor (GCF)**.

> The greatest common factor (GCF) of two or more given numbers is the greatest number that will divide evenly into the numbers.

Consider the numbers 24 and 36. What is the greatest common factor of these two numbers?
VM 9.3

Perhaps the easiest way to approach this question is to break the question down into three parts:

1. What are the factors of 24 and the factors of 36?

2. What are the common factors of 24 and 36?

3. Which is the greatest of the common factors of 24 and 36?

What are the factors of 24? (1, 2, 3, 4, 6, 8, 12, and 24) What are the factors of 36? (1, 2, 3, 4, 6, 9, 12, 18, and 36) The common factors of 24 and 36 are 1, 2, 3, 4, 6, and 12. Twelve is the greatest factor common to both 24 and 36.

We can also find the greatest common factor of 24 and 36 by using prime factorization. To do this, we first write prime factorizations for 36 and 24:

$$36 = 2 \times 2 \times 3 \times 3$$
$$24 = 2 \times 2 \times 2 \times 3$$

By inspecting these factorizations, we can select each factor that is common to both numbers. Clearly, 2 × 2 × 3 appears in both sets of factors. Since each number is "built" with these factors, each of the numbers is divisible by these factors. Thus, the greatest common factor (GCF) of 36 and 24 is 2 × 2 × 3, or 12.

The previous development of prime factorization and factor trees should clarify why the method described here leads to the determination of the GCF. You will recall that a number can be factored (with factor trees) into successive product expressions until the prime factorization is reached. For example:

Note that any factor or combination of factors expressed in the last line of the preceding factor tree is a divisor of 36. From this list of factors (2, 2, 3, 3), we can take any two, three, or four factors and multiply them together to find another factor, one that is greater than any of the single factors listed. In this case, we discover the following factors:

$$2$$
$$3$$
$$2 \times 2 = 4$$
$$2 \times 3 = 6$$
$$3 \times 3 = 9$$
$$2 \times 2 \times 3 = 12$$
$$2 \times 3 \times 3 = 18$$
$$2 \times 2 \times 3 \times 3 = 36$$

By drawing a factor tree to discover the prime factorization, we found that 24 = 2 × 2 × 2 × 3. From the list of factors (2, 2, 2, 3), we can take any two, three, or four factors and multiply them together to find other factors that are greater than the single factors listed. Thus we discover the following factors:

$$2$$
$$3$$
$$2 \times 2 = 4$$
$$2 \times 3 = 6$$
$$2 \times 2 \times 2 = 8$$
$$2 \times 2 \times 3 = 12$$
$$2 \times 2 \times 2 \times 3 = 24$$

By comparing the set of factors of 36 and the set of factors of 24, we can see that the greatest number that is a factor of both 36 and 24 is 12 (or 2 × 2 × 3).

As well as finding the greatest common factor of two numbers, we can also find the **least common multiple (LCM)** of two numbers. What do we mean by least common multiple? First, we know that a multiple of any number is evenly divisible by that number. For instance, the multiples of 2 (0, 2, 4, 6, 8, 10, . . .) can all be divided evenly by 2. Second, when we say "common multiple," we are speaking of a number that is a multiple for each of at least two numbers. For example, 24 is a common multiple of 12 and 8 because it can be divided evenly by either 12 or 8. Third, when we speak of the least common multiple, we mean the least nonzero number that is a multiple of all the numbers being considered.

> The least common multiple (LCM) of two or more given numbers is the least nonzero number that is a multiple of each of the given numbers.

Now let's find the least common multiple of 24 and 36. We can begin by listing multiples of each number until we find a common multiple. The multiples of 24 are:

$$0, 24, 48, 72, 96, 120, 144,$$
$$168, 192, 216, \text{ and so on}$$

The multiples of 36 are:

$$0, 36, 72, 108, 144, 180,$$
$$216, 252, \text{ and so on}$$

By careful examination of the multiples of these two numbers, we find that some of the common multiples of 24 and 36 are

$$0, 72, 144, \text{ and } 216$$

Thus the least common nonzero multiple of 24 and 36 is 72.

Another method for finding the least common multiple for two (or more) numbers is to use Cuisenaire rods as a concrete, manipulative model. To find the LCM for 6 and 9, make two separate rod trains, one of multiples of 6 and the other of multiples of 9. Compare these trains and make note when the two trains are of equal length.

For example, the figure shows that the two trains match at 18. The least common multiple of 6 and 9 is 18.

Now let's find the least common multiple for 24 and 36 by using the more abstract method of prime factorization:

$$36 = 2 \times 2 \times 3 \times 3$$
$$24 = 2 \times 2 \times 2 \times 3$$

Since a multiple of a number must contain that number, it must also contain the prime factorization of that number. This stands to reason, since the prime factorization is the basic structure or composition of the number. Hence we can conclude that a multiple of a number must, at the very least, include the prime factorization of that number. Now we want to construct a multiple of both 36 and 24. This must contain the prime factorizations of both 36 and 24 to be a common multiple:

$$36 = 2 \times 2 \times 3 \times 3$$
$$24 = 2 \times 2 \times 2 \times 3$$

The LCM must contain $2 \times 2 \times 3 \times 3$ to accommodate 36, and it must contain $2 \times 2 \times 2 \times 3$ to accommodate 24. By comparing the two product expressions, we see that in addition to the factors in the product expression for 36 ($2 \times 2 \times 3 \times 3$), we need an additional 2 to make sure that the prime factorization of 24 is included. Clearly, then, the least common multiple of 24 and 36 must be $2 \times 2 \times 3 \times 3 \times 2$, or 72.

Notice that the least common multiple contains the prime factorizations of both 36 and 24 ($2 \times 2 \times 3 \times 3$) $\times$ ($2 \times 2 \times 2 \times 3$), but it is not simply the product of 36 and 24. If a factor appears in both numbers, then it must appear in the LCM only as often as it appears in the number (of the two numbers) in which it appears more often. For example, the factor 2 appears twice in 36 ($2 \times 2 \times 3 \times 3$), and three times in 24 ($2 \times 2 \times 2 \times 3$); therefore, it must appear exactly three times in the LCM. In the same way, the factor 3 appears once in 24 ($2 \times 2 \times 2 \times 3$) and twice in 36 ($2 \times 2 \times 3 \times 3$); therefore, it must appear exactly twice in the LCM. Clearly, 72 ($2 \times 2 \times 2 \times 3 \times 3$) is the least number that contains three 2s and two 3s as factors.

The relationship between LCM and GCF can be more clearly seen in the following diagram:

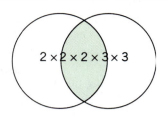

The loop on the left encircles the factors of 24, while the loop on the right contains the factors of 36. Examination of the intersection of these two circles (i.e., the factors they have in common) yields the GCF, while the union of the two circles is the LCM.

In this chapter, we have examined only number theory applicable to the elementary or middle school mathematics program. Some children will become interested in number theory and will want to do additional study on their own. There are many other aspects of number theory that children might find interesting. These include topics such as figurate numbers, perfect numbers, amicable numbers, Pythagorean triples, and Fibonacci numbers, to name but a few. Look for information on these in subsequent chapters of this text, on the CD that accompanies this text, and in other teacher resources.

Number Systems

In previous chapters, we've examined various aspects of our number system. We began with numberness associated with concrete objects; then, we moved to the study of abstract numbers. After that, we looked at some of the various sets of numbers that make up our mathematics system.

Numberness in the elementary and middle school mathematics program is based on a logical organization that begins with the numbers we call the *counting numbers* or the *natural numbers*. You should recall that **counting numbers (natural numbers)** begin with 1 and continue with 2, 3, 4, 5, and so forth, in that pattern. We symbolize the set of counting numbers as {1, 2, 3, 4, 5, . . .}.

The next logical extension of numbers we consider is the set of **whole numbers**—that is, the counting numbers with the inclusion of 0. The whole numbers are symbolized by {0, 1, 2, 3, 4, 5, . . .}. Note that one new element, 0, has been included to expand the set of counting numbers to the system of whole numbers.

Use the **Factor Tree virtual manipulative** on the accompanying CD to compare the factors of a pair of numbers. Try this with several pairs. Will the GCF always be the product of the numbers listed in the Common Factors region? Why or why not? Will the LCM always be the product of the number listed in the three regions. Why or why not?

VM 9.2

The following diagram illustrates the subset relation between counting numbers and whole numbers:

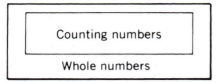

This figure shows that whole numbers include all counting numbers.

Another set of numbers we will examine in this chapter is the set of *integers*. Counting numbers and whole numbers are included in the set of integers. We can now show the relationship of the counting numbers to the positive integers $\{^+1, ^+2, ^+3, ^+4, ^+5, \ldots\}$. Zero is also included as an integer but is considered neither positive nor negative. By extending the number line to the left, we see that there is a logical need for negative numbers. So, we can name three sets of numbers that make up the integers: counting numbers, negative numbers (i.e., the opposites of the positive numbers), and zero. (Negative numbers will be explained in more detail later.) We can show the relationship among the numbers with the following diagram:

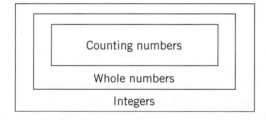

The system of numbers can now be extended to include *rational numbers*. Rational numbers are commonly written in two different forms—fractions and decimals. Since counting numbers, whole numbers, and integers are all examples of rational numbers, we can extend the diagram of the number system as follows:

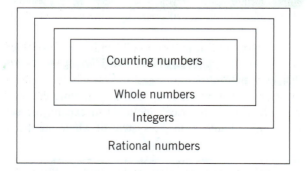

In this chapter we will also briefly examine *irrational numbers*. We will show that **irrational numbers** (for example, $\sqrt{5}$ or π) are not part of the counting numbers, whole numbers, integers, or rational numbers, so they are set off to one side in the diagram.

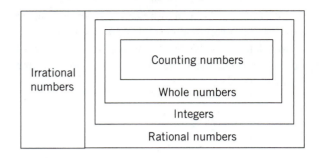

All of these systems of numbers make up the **real number system**, as shown in the following figure:

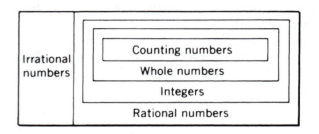

Let's consider the system of integers and some approaches that might be used to convey important aspects of this system to elementary or middle school children.

As we worked with whole numbers, we found that the sum of any two whole numbers is a whole number, but sometimes the difference between two whole numbers is not a whole number. Consider, for example, $3 - 4 = \square$. There is no whole number that satisfies this equation. Thus we need a different type of number to solve examples such as this.

The call for a number system that includes numbers less than zero is answered by the use of negative numbers. Many children are familiar with real-life situations that can be represented by integers such as above/below sea level and upper floors/subbasements in buildings. To explore this concept, let's take a look at a familiar number line that we all use in our everyday lives—a thermometer.

Essentially, a thermometer is a number line with equivalent divisions on both sides of the zero point.

We see that zero is the reference point (origin) on this thermometer and that numerals are marked at regular (equal) intervals to indicate temperature. Many of us are familiar with readings such as 25°, 32°, 59°, and 89°. But what about midwinter readings in cold climates, or the readings on a deep-freeze thermometer, such as 10 below zero or 15 below zero? Temperatures below zero, when recorded in the newspaper, are often written as −10° and −15° and, technically, should be read, "negative 10 degrees" or "15 below zero." Although you will frequently hear it on the TV weather, you should not refer to temperature below zero as "minus 10 degrees" since "minus" refers to the operation of subtraction, not to a relative position on a number line.

Can we, on our number line, mark and label points to show the part of the number line that corresponds to the below-zero readings of a thermometer?

Obviously we must use symbols to distinguish between the numerals written on the negative side of the zero and those written on the positive side. One way of doing this is to place a negative sign (−) in front of any numeral written on the negative side of 0 to indicate that it represents a number less than zero:

A number represented by a numeral with this sign is called a *negative number*, and the sign (−), sometimes written in a "raised" fashion ($^-$) is called a *negative sign*. The numerals written on the positive side of the zero represent positive numbers, and a positive number is sometimes written with a positive sign (+ or $^+$) placed in front of it (for example, $^+10$ or $^+20$). Later, children will recognize that positive numbers can sometimes be written with the $^+$ sign implied. That is, numerals written without signs are understood to represent positive numbers. The number zero is neither positive nor negative. Numbers that are named by numerals with signs to indicate that the numbers named are positive ($^+$) or negative ($^-$) are called *directed numbers*.

When positive and negative numbers are first introduced to children, it is best to place the raised ($^+$) and ($^-$) signs with every number under discussion. Otherwise, children may become confused over the relationships between "positive" and "addition" and between "negative" and "subtraction." Some individuals read $^-2$ as "minus two" and $^+2$ as "plus two." When the terms *minus* and *plus* are associated with positive and negative numbers, children confuse the concept of

integers with the operations of addition (plus, +) and subtraction (minus, −). This is why, in Chapter 7, we suggested reading the (+) sign as "add"; now with integers we will read the raised ($^+$) sign as "positive." The raised sign ($^-$) with integers will be read as "negative." The difficulties that children experience in developing an understanding of integers are usually caused by confusion over the language used for reading the signs.

Examine the following number line diagram:

Notice that the points labeled $^+20$ and $^-20$ are the same distance from zero, but that one is to the right of zero, while the other is to the left of zero. In general, if two points are the same distance from the zero point, but on opposite sides of the zero point, the numbers that correspond to these points are called **opposites** or **additive inverses**. Thus, $^+10$ and $^-10$ are opposites, as are $^+5$ and $^-5$, $^+3$ and $^-3$, and so on. So that every number will have an opposite, it is customary to say that zero is its own opposite.

A number is an **integer** if it can be represented by a whole number or the opposite of a whole number. We can indicate the integers as follows:

$$\{\ldots, ^-4, ^-3, ^-2, ^-1, 0, ^+1, ^+2, ^+3, ^+4, \ldots\}$$

The integers that are greater than zero form the positive integers:

$$\{^+1, ^+2, ^+3, ^+4, ^+5, \ldots\}$$

The integers that are less than zero form the negative integers:

$$\{^-1, ^-2, ^-3, ^-4, ^-5, \ldots\}$$

The number 0 is an integer, but it is considered to be neither positive nor negative.

We have seen that we can represent the integers on the number line. On the following number line, locate the point named by $^+5$. As we have just seen, the 5 indicates how many unit lengths the number is from zero, and the ($^+$) indicates the direction.

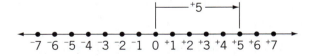

Considering the line segment that begins at zero on the number line, the arrow indicates the direction (the sign of the number), and the length indicates the number of unit lengths from zero (the value of the number regardless of its sign). This line segment stands for the value $^+5$.

Consider the value $^-2$. The negative sign indicates direction, and the 2 indicates magnitude. **Magnitude (or absolute value)** refers to the length of the line segment in unit lengths—that is, the distance the point is from zero. Note that distance is always positive; thus, absolute value is always positive. The absolute value of a number x is symbolized by $|x|$. The absolute value of $^+5$ is 5 ($|^+5| = 5$) and the absolute value of $^-2$ is 2 ($|^-2| = 2$).

This line segment represents $^-2$ because it is two units long and has a negative direction. Remember, to represent a given integer we move left from zero to indicate negative numbers, and right from zero to indicate positive numbers. The point $^-2$, however, has an absolute value of 2 because it is a distance of two units from zero.

Using the number line, children have learned number relations in whole numbers and in fractional numbers. They have found that beginning with zero, numbers increase in value to the right on the traditional horizontal number line. This, of course, is still valid when the negative integers are located on the number line.

Since children have already learned relations such as $4 > 2$, $5 < 7$, $3 > 0$, and so on, it is not difficult to extend this concept to include negative integers. Any number on a horizontal number line is greater than any number to its left, as we have seen. So, on the preceding number line, we see that $^-1 > ^-2$, $^-3 > ^-7$, $0 > ^-1$, $^-2 > ^-3$, $^-1 > ^-10$, and so on. This extension of students' knowledge of relations on the number line is consistent and logical. The evident truth of statements such as $^+1 > ^-7$, as seen on the number line, will help students understand the meaning of negative integers. A number is still greater than any number named to its left on the horizontal number line. However, zero is not a beginning point (as it was for whole numbers), but a point of reference between positive and negative numbers. The set of integers extends endlessly to both the right and the left of zero.

To further clarify the meaning of $^-8 < ^+1$, for example, the familiar analogy of being in debt could be mentioned. If Mr. Stiff owes $8 and Ms. Friedlund has $1, who has more money? Ms. Friedlund does because Mr. Stiff is $8 in debt or has $^-8$ dollars, while Ms.

Friedlund has $^+1$ dollar. That is, Mr. Stiff has less money than Ms. Friedlund ($^-8 < ^+1$).

The addition (and subtraction) of integers can be modeled effectively using chips of two different colors. For example, let's say that red chips are used to represent positive numbers and blue chips are used to represent negative numbers. Then, $^-5 + ^+6 = \square$ can be shown as a pile of 5 blue chips and a pile of 6 red chips. To find the sum, combine the two piles into one. To interpret the value of this new pile, match blue and red chips in pairs until you can no longer do so. These pairs represent zeros (according to the property of opposites). In this exercise, one red chip would be left, representing $^+1$, the answer to $^-5 + ^+6 = \square$.

It may be beneficial to look at this color chip approach in terms of a subtraction of integers exercise. Consider, for example, $^+6 - ^-3 = \square$. Begin with a pile of 6 red chips to represent $^+6$. To subtract $^-3$, you would need to remove 3 blue chips from this pile. Since there currently aren't any blue chips in this pile, you can put some in by putting in a total of 3 blue and 3 red (i.e., add 0 to the pile in the form of $^-3 + ^+3$). Now the pile contains 3 blue chips that can be removed, leaving a total of 9 red. These 9 red chips represent $^+9$, the answer to $^+6 - ^-3 = \square$.

Now let's look at some examples of addition of integers modeled on the number line. In each of the following examples, find the indicated sum.

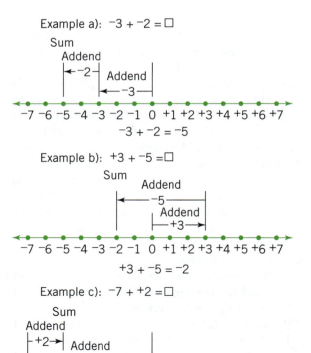

In each example, all the arrows are drawn according to the magnitude and direction indicated in the equation. Generalizing from these examples, we see that if we wish to represent sums of positive and negative numbers as moves on the number line, we can observe the following procedure:

1. Starting at zero on the number line, draw an arrow so that its length in unit lengths equals the first addend to be added. The direction in which the arrow is drawn corresponds to the sign of the number (left for $^-$ and right for $^+$).

2. Starting from the end of the first arrow (and just above it), draw an arrow so that its length in unit lengths equals the second addend to be added. The direction in which the arrow is drawn corresponds to the sign of the number.

3. The point on the number line where the second addend ends names the sum. The resultant is always the sum of an addition example, and it is read from the end of the arrow that names the second addend. It is named by a point on the number line.

VM 9.4

You will readily see that if we add two integers that are opposites, we get zero for the sum. For example, $^+4 + {}^-4 = 0$:

The arrow for the first addend ($^+4$) takes us to $^+4$, and the arrow for the second addend ($^-4$) brings us back to zero. If we read the point at the end of the second arrow, we find the sum to be zero. Nevertheless, it should be clear from the diagram that $^+4 + {}^-4 = 0$. Similarly, the sum of any two opposites is zero:

Addend		Addend		Sum
$^+7$	$+$	$^-7$	$=$	0
$^-9$	$+$	$^+9$	$=$	0
$^+12$	$+$	$^-12$	$=$	0
		and so on		

The fact that any two opposites have a sum of zero is often referred to as the **additive inverse property**.

Besides the additive inverse property, which other properties exist for addition of integers? Using number line models, it is easy to see that addition of integers has all the basic properties that we found for whole numbers and fractional numbers:

1. Addition of integers is commutative.

2. Addition of integers is associative.

3. Zero (0) is the additive identity element for the operation of addition on the integers.

At this point, we will leave it to you to draw number line models to convince yourself that these properties do indeed hold true.

From the number line diagrams, it is easy to see that the sum of two positive integers must be positive: $^+3 + {}^+5 = {}^+8$, $^+6 + {}^+7 = {}^+13$, and so on. It is equally clear that the sum of two negative integers must be negative: $^-2 + {}^-3 = 5$, $^-7 + {}^-1 = 8$, and so on. What about the sum of a positive integer and a negative integer?

Consider this example: $^+8 + {}^-4 = \square$. The property of opposite numbers tells us that $^+4 + {}^-4 = 0$. We can use the concept of opposites and the number line to find a solution:

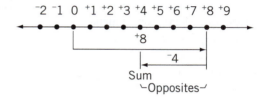

Let us look at another example: $^+3 + {}^-9 = \square$.

Another example: $^+10 + {}^-7 = \square$

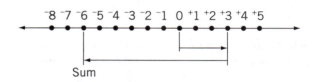

Add another: $^-17 + {}^+19 = \square$

Locate where the opposites are apparent in each example.

Notice that integers, like other numbers, can be renamed in different ways. For example, we can rename 12 as $11 + 1$, $10 + 2$, $9 + 3$, and so on. In a similar manner, we can rename $^-12$ in several different ways: $^-11 + {}^-1$, $^-10 + {}^-2$, $^-9 + {}^-3$, and so on. We could also rename $^-12$ as $^-13 + {}^+1$.

Now, let's look at the inverse operation of subtraction in relation to the set of integers. Subtraction, we know, is the inverse operation of addition.

Addend		Addend		Sum
6	+	8	=	14
Sum		Addend		Addend
14	−	6	=	8
or 14	−	8	=	6

Let's examine the way in which the inverse operation of subtraction is performed using the number line. Consider $^+4 - {}^+2 = \square$. We can rewrite the example in the form $^+2 + \square = {}^+4$. Draw an arrow that is two units long and points to the right (the positive direction) to represent the first addend. The arrow for the second addend, which is the missing addend, must go from the tip of the first arrow to the point representing $^+4$ (the sum). Draw this arrow, using a dotted line to indicate that it represents the missing addend.

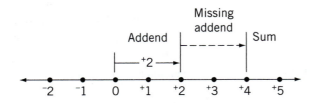

which integer does the dotted arrow represent? Since it is two units long and points in the positive direction, it represents $^+2$. The missing addend is therefore $^+2$. Thus:

Sum		Addend		Addend
$^+4$	−	$^+2$	=	$^+2$

Consider this example: $^-5 - {}^+3 = \square$. This example can be rewritten in the form $^+3 + \square = {}^-5$. It can also be modeled on the number line by beginning at the reference point, 0, and pointing the arrow of the addend $^+3$ in a positive direction. Next locate the point $^-5$, which is the sum. We know that the missing addend must begin at the end of the first addend and end at the sum. The number line model can be drawn in the following way:

The diagram shows that $\square = {}^-8$. Therefore: $^-5 - {}^+3 = {}^-8$ Look at the following subtraction examples,

which have been rewritten and solved:

Subtraction	Rewritten	Solution
$^+4 - {}^+2 = \square$	$^+2 + \square = {}^+4$	$\square = {}^+2$
$^+4 - {}^+1 = \square$	$^+1 + \square = {}^+4$	$\square = {}^+3$
$^+4 - 0 = \square$	$0 + \square = {}^+4$	$\square = {}^+4$
$^+4 - {}^-1 = \square$	$^-1 + \square = {}^+4$	$\square = {}^+5$
$^+4 - {}^-2 = \square$	$^-2 + \square = {}^+4$	$\square = {}^+6$

These five examples have been rewritten to illustrate the generalization that subtracting a number gives the same result as adding its opposite. However, do not push this generalization as a rule to be rotely remembered and repeated by children. It should be viewed as merely an observation that they might discover and make:

$^+4 - {}^+2 = \square$	$^+4 + {}^-2 = \square$	$\square = {}^+2$
$^+4 - {}^+1 = \square$	$^+4 + {}^-1 = \square$	$\square = {}^+3$
$^+4 - 0 = \square$	$^+4 + 0 = \square$	$\square = {}^+4$
$^+4 - {}^-1 = \square$	$^+4 + {}^+1 = \square$	$\square = {}^+5$
$^+4 - {}^-2 = \square$	$^+4 + {}^+2 = \square$	$\square = {}^+6$

The concept of subtracting integers closely parallels subtraction of whole numbers. The number line has been used as a model to help develop an understanding. Inverse sentences have been used to help children comprehend the existing relationships. After the children have had many experiences with subtraction as related to integers, they should begin to look for patterns to help them generalize. Teachers should not rush the children by pushing them into generalizing prematurely. Generalizations should be based on patterns observed through the exploration of a wide variety of examples.

We mentioned earlier that addition of integers retains all the properties of addition of whole numbers and fractional numbers. Which properties does subtraction of integers possess? When we studied subtraction of whole numbers, we found that it was neither commutative nor associative. The same is true for subtraction of integers. For example, $^+2 - {}^+4 = {}^-2$ but $^+4 - {}^+2 = {}^+2$, therefore $^+2 - {}^+4 \neq {}^+4 - {}^+2$. One counterexample is enough to show that subtraction is not commutative. Can you devise a counterexample to show that subtraction is not associative?

So far we have found two properties that subtraction of integers does not possess. (Subtraction of whole numbers did not have these properties, either.) **Closure** is an important property that subtraction of integers does possess—that is, for any integers a and b, $a - b$ is always an integer. Within the system of whole numbers, there is no way to subtract a greater number from a lesser one, but in the system of integers, this is possible.

Let's turn our attention now to multiplication of integers. The process used to multiply two nonnegative integers is the same as the process used to multiply whole numbers. For instance:

Factor		Factor		Product
$^+3$	$\times$	$^+2$	$=$	$^+6$
0	$\times$	$^+5$	$=$	0
$^+6$	$\times$	$^+7$	$=$	$^+42$
$^+1$	$\times$	$^+8$	$=$	$^+8$

and so on

Multiplication examples such as 2×4 can be interpreted to mean "two sets of four." We can model the example on the number line:

If we interpret $^+2 \times {}^+4$ as two jumps of $^+4$ in a positive direction, we arrive at $^+8$. Following the same logic, we can interpret $^+2 \times {}^-4$ as two jumps of $^-4$ in the negative direction. Thus we see that $^+2 \times {}^-4 = {}^-8$.

Using the commutative property of multiplication, we can change $^+2 \times {}^-4 = {}^-8$ to $^-4 \times {}^+2 = {}^-8$.

Statements such as $^+3 \times {}^+5 = {}^+15$ and $^+3 \times {}^-5 = {}^-15$ can be illustrated on the number line if we use the idea of repeated addition.

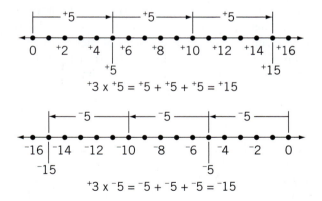

$^+3 \times {}^+5 = {}^+5 + {}^+5 + {}^+5 = {}^+15$

$^+3 \times {}^-5 = {}^-5 + {}^-5 + {}^-5 = {}^-15$

However, a number line approach to multiplication examples in which both factors are negative is awkward, at best. The movement on the number line is not as natural and easily interpreted as it was in the preceding examples. Instead, one of the most effective approaches is to use a combination of patterns and generalizations.

Patterns are helpful for students to justify the results of multiplication of integers. Now let's look at the operation of multiplication using negative numbers and

looking for patterns. Consider the following examples:

Factor		Factor		Product
$^+3$	$\times$	$^+5$	$=$	$^+15$
$^+2$	$\times$	$^+5$	$=$	$^+10$
$^+1$	$\times$	$^+5$	$=$	$^+5$
0	$\times$	$^+5$	$=$	0
$^-1$	$\times$	$^+5$	$=$	?
$^-2$	$\times$	$^+5$	$=$	?
$^-3$	$\times$	$^+5$	$=$	?

Examining the pattern found here, we discover that the product becomes five less every time the first factor becomes one less. If this pattern is extended to include the last three examples in the previous series, we get negative products:

$$^-1 \times {}^+5 = {}^-5$$
$$^-2 \times {}^+5 = {}^-10$$
$$^-3 \times {}^+5 = {}^-15$$

A similar approach can be used to discover how to define multiplication when the second factor is negative and the first factor is positive. Look for the pattern in these examples:

Factor		Factor		Product
$^+5$	$\times$	$^+3$	$=$	$^+15$
$^+5$	$\times$	$^+2$	$=$	$^+10$
$^+5$	$\times$	$^+1$	$=$	$^+5$
$^+5$	$\times$	0	$=$	0
$^+5$	$\times$	$^-1$	$=$	?
$^+5$	$\times$	$^-2$	$=$	?
$^+5$	$\times$	$^-3$	$=$	?

Examining the pattern, we see that the first factor is the same in all the examples. The second factor is decreasing by one, and the product is decreasing by five. If this pattern continues, the last three examples will give negative products:

$$^+5 \times {}^-1 = {}^-5$$
$$^+5 \times {}^-2 = {}^-10$$
$$^+5 \times {}^-3 = {}^-15$$

We can generalize from these examples by saying that the product of a positive integer and a negative integer is the same as the product of two positive integers, except that the sign of the product is negative.

Now consider the following examples:

Factor		Factor	$=$	Product
$^-4$	$\times$	$^+3$	$=$	$^-12$
$^-4$	$\times$	$^+2$	$=$	$^-8$
$^-4$	$\times$	$^+1$	$=$	$^-4$
$^-4$	$\times$	0	$=$	0
$^-4$	$\times$	$^-1$	$=$	?
$^-4$	$\times$	$^-2$	$=$	?
$^-4$	$\times$	$^-3$	$=$	?

We can discover a pattern here: Every time the second factor becomes one less, the product becomes four greater. Extending this pattern to include the last three examples in the series, we get positive products:

$$^-4 \times {}^-1 = {}^+4$$
$$^-4 \times {}^-2 = {}^+8$$
$$^-4 \times {}^-3 = {}^+12$$

We can generalize from these examples by saying that the product of two negative numbers is the same as the product of two positive numbers.

This examination of the multiplication of negative numbers has revealed that the product of a negative number and a positive number is negative, and that the product of two negative numbers is positive. Of course, the product of two positive numbers is positive. Therefore, we can observe the following steps in the multiplication of signed numbers:

1. Determine the value of the product, regardless of its sign, by multiplying the two factors as though they were both positive.

2. Determine the sign of the product. If the factors have identical signs (both positive or both negative), the sign of the product is positive. If the factors have different signs (one positive and the other negative), the sign of the product is negative.

Multiplication of integers, like multiplication of whole numbers, is a binary operation. Multiplication of integers has the same basic properties that we found for multiplication of whole numbers: Multiplication of integers is commutative, associative, and distributive over addition. The number $^+1$ is the identity element for multiplication of integers.

Now, let's examine the operation of division with respect to integers. Consider the following multiplication examples and the division examples that have been derived from them:

Factor		Factor		Product	Product		Factor		Factor
$^+3$	$\times$	$^+4$	$=$	$^+12$	$^+12$	$\div\ ^+4 =$	$^+3$		
$^-3$	$\times$	$^+4$	$=$	$^-12$	$^-12$	$\div\ ^-3 =$	$^+4$		
					$^-12$	$\div\ ^+4 =$	$^-3$		
$^-3$	$\times$	$^-4$	$=$	$^+12$	$^+12$	$\div\ ^-4 =$	$^-3$		

We know that the multiplication examples are correct, because we have just examined multiplication with integers. We also know that the division examples are correct, because we discovered in Chapter 8 that the operation of division may be interpreted as the inverse operation of multiplication. Examining the division examples and generalizing from them, we see that we can observe the following steps when dividing one number by another:

1. Determine the value of the quotient, regardless of its sign, by performing the indicated division as though both the divisor and the dividend were positive.

2. Determine the sign of the quotient. If the divisor and dividend have the same signs (both positive or both negative), the sign of the quotient is positive. If the divisor and dividend have different signs (one positive and the other negative), the sign of the quotient is negative.

Division with negative numbers can also be modeled on the number line. However, this is considerably more complex than the development of multiplication and would not prove useful to an elementary-level child.

The system of integers was formed as an extension of the system of whole numbers. For each whole number greater than zero, we include the opposite negative number. By including numbers less than zero with our system, we were able to describe an infinite set of points to the left of zero on the number line.

Now let's consider the system of fractional numbers and form a larger system by including the opposites of all the fractional numbers. When we do this, we obtain a system of numbers that includes not only $\frac{1}{2}$, $\frac{3}{7}$, $\frac{4}{5}$, $\frac{9}{8}$, and so on, but also numbers such as $-\left(\frac{1}{2}\right)$, $-\left(\frac{3}{7}\right)$, $-\left(\frac{4}{5}\right)$, $-\left(\frac{9}{8}\right)$, and so on. This larger system of numbers, consisting of all the fractional numbers and their opposites, is called the system of rational numbers. The **rational numbers** can be thought of as all quotients $\frac{a}{b}$, where a is any integer and b is any nonzero integer. Notice the similarity between this last statement and the definition of a **fractional number** as the quotient $\frac{a}{b}$ where a is any whole number and b is any counting number. The system of numbers called rational numbers is most frequently written in one of two different forms—as fractions or decimals.

Let's look at a number line on which some of the points have been labeled with rational numbers expressed as fractions.

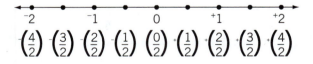

We know that the point halfway between 0 and $^+1$ is $^+\left(\frac{1}{2}\right)$. Then, from our knowledge of opposites, the point halfway between 0 and $^-1$ is $^-\left(\frac{1}{2}\right)$. The point named $^+1$ could be named as $^+\left(\frac{1}{1}\right)$, $^+\left(\frac{2}{2}\right)$, and so on. Then, in the same way, we could rename $^-1$ as $^-\left(\frac{1}{1}\right)$, $^-\left(\frac{2}{2}\right)$, and so on. So, it should be clear that every rational number has an opposite. That is, $^+\left(\frac{1}{2}\right) + ^-\left(\frac{1}{2}\right) = 0$, $^+\left(\frac{2}{3}\right) + ^-\left(\frac{2}{3}\right) = 0$, and so on.

Operations with signed rational numbers follow the same patterns that we discovered among the integers.

$$^+2 +^+ 3 = ^+5 \qquad ^+\left(\tfrac{1}{2}\right) + ^+\left(\tfrac{1}{3}\right) = ^+\left(\tfrac{5}{6}\right)$$
$$^-3 \times^- 2 = ^+6 \qquad ^-\left(\tfrac{1}{2}\right) \times ^-\left(\tfrac{1}{4}\right) = ^+\left(\tfrac{1}{8}\right)$$
$$^+8 \div^- 2 = ^-4 \qquad ^+\left(\tfrac{1}{2}\right) \div ^-2 = ^-\left(\tfrac{1}{4}\right)$$
$$^+2 -^+ 5 = ^-3 \qquad ^+\left(\tfrac{1}{8}\right) - ^+\left(\tfrac{3}{8}\right) = ^-\left(\tfrac{1}{4}\right)$$

Of course, rational numbers can be named in many ways. For example:

$$^+\left(\tfrac{1}{4}\right) =^+\left(\tfrac{2}{8}\right) =^+\left(\tfrac{3}{12}\right) =^+\left(\tfrac{4}{16}\right) \text{ and so on}$$

Also:

$$^+\left(\tfrac{1}{4}\right) = \tfrac{^+1}{^-4} = \tfrac{^-1}{^-4} = \tfrac{^-2}{^-8} \text{ and so on}$$

Similarly:

$$^-\left(\tfrac{2}{3}\right) = \tfrac{^-2}{^+3} = \tfrac{^+2}{^-3} = \tfrac{^+10}{^-15} \text{ and so on}$$

A full discussion of all the fundamental operations as they apply to rational numbers is presented in Chapters 11, 12, and 13. It will probably come as no surprise that within the system of rational numbers, these fundamental operations possess all the properties that they had in the systems studied earlier. You will perhaps find it helpful to convince yourself of this fact by testing each property with specific examples.

We have now extended our number line in the negative direction, thus increasing the number of points with which we are familiar. If we take any two points on the number line that represent rational numbers, there is always another point between them that represents another rational number. This third number is necessarily greater than one of the first two numbers and less than the other; that is, the third number is necessarily intermediate in value between the first two. Consider, for example, the points labeled 0 and 4. Between them we find points labeled 1, 2, and 3, to name just a few. Consider the points labeled 0 and 1. Between them we find points labeled $\tfrac{1}{2}$, $\tfrac{1}{4}$, and $\tfrac{5}{8}$, again naming just a few.

We can also perform this process without benefit of the number line. For example, between the rational numbers $\tfrac{1}{4}$ and $\tfrac{3}{4}$, we find other rational numbers such as $\tfrac{1}{2}$ and $\tfrac{5}{8}$. The fact that we can always perform this process is due to the **property of density for rational numbers**.

> The Property of Density for Rational Numbers states that between any two rational numbers there exists a third rational number of intermediate value.

Not all number systems possess this density property. Whole numbers, for example, do not possess density. By way of illustration, consider the whole numbers 11 and 12; there is no third whole number that falls in between 11 and 12. The rational numbers, however, do possess the property of density. Given any two rational numbers, we can always find a third rational number between them. Another way of illustrating this property is to add the two given numbers and divide the sum by 2. For example, given $\tfrac{1}{5}$ and $\tfrac{2}{5}$, we know that $\tfrac{3}{10}$ is between them:

$$\tfrac{1}{5} + \tfrac{2}{5} = \tfrac{3}{5} \text{ Adding the two numbers}$$
$$\tfrac{3}{5} \div 2 = \tfrac{3}{10} \text{ Dividing the sum by 2}$$

Of course, there are also many other rational numbers between $\tfrac{1}{5}$ and $\tfrac{2}{5}$.

If you divide some integer by any other nonzero integer, your result will always be a member of the rational number system. That is, any rational number can always be rewritten as the quotient of two integers. There are, however, some numbers that cannot be written as the quotient of two integers. These are called *irrational numbers*, and, of course, they are not part of the rational number system. Examples include decimal numbers that neither terminate in a fixed number of places nor repeat a set of digits endlessly. For example, .25, .34, and .666666 . . . are rational numbers because their decimal form either terminates or repeats. However, consider, for example, .12112111211112111112 . . . This is an irrational number because it is a nonterminating, nonrepeating decimal. It is nonrepeating because each successive 2 has one more 1 immediately preceding it than the preceding 2. Another example of an irrational number is the square root of 2, the number that when multiplied by itself equals 2. At one point in history, all numbers were thought to be rational. The Greek mathematician Pythagoras, or, as some believe, his followers, proved some 2400 years ago that the square root of 2 is not a rational number. There are also negative irrational numbers; for example, the opposite of the square root of 2, which we write as $-\sqrt{2}$, is an irrational number.

Putting together the rational numbers and the irrational numbers gives us a system called the set of **real numbers**. One of our goals has been to show how number systems are expanded step-by-step and how each move to a larger system allows us to incorporate new numbers and, in many cases, new properties to the previous number system. This development of numberness evolved from practical applications and continues in the fields of pure and applied mathematics. As one example, the extension of the real number system to include a set of numbers called imaginary numbers occurred *BEFORE* there was an application for them in the real world. Only later was it determined that imaginary numbers behave in a manner suitable for describing alternating current in electricity.

Closure

In this chapter, we considered several different kinds of points on the number line. The easiest method for developing the relationships between the different systems of numbers that we have considered is to draw a diagram, as was shown earlier in the chapter and repeated here. This diagram depicts the set of real numbers (the most comprehensive of the systems we have considered) broken down successively into the different kinds of numbers that make up the systems of numbers.

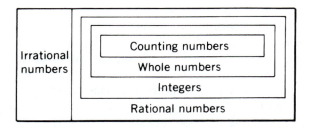

The teaching of the structure of the real number system is begun in grade 1 with the concept of number developed from the real world and leading into the counting numbers. Children are gradually introduced to different number systems through extension of those already encountered. It is not uncommon for children to have explored up to and including the system of real numbers by the time they complete grade 8.

Elementary number theory is a valuable tool to help children develop understanding and meaning as they learn mathematics. Knowledge of prime numbers and factorization provides a tool for the children to use in developing number sense, especially in finding common denominators and rewriting fractions in simplest form. This study of prime numbers and factorization can also introduce children to the exciting topic of number theory. The Fundamental Theorem of Arithmetic (FTA) is an important foundation for further work. This chapter provides a solid base on which an understanding of mathematics may be built.

The student of mathematics may want to research some of the historical aspects of the material found in this chapter. The history of the Sieve of Eratosthenes is interesting for some, as is the study of some prominent ancient mathematicians such as Pythagoras and Archimedes. Long an intriguing topic to mathematicians and nonmathematicians alike, the study of number lore can be a motivating topic for children to consider. For example, in Greek numerology, two was considered a "female number," while three was considered "male." Did you know that some numbers have been given supernatural connotations? Check out how people have historically reacted to 7 or 13—you might get lucky. According St. Augustine, God created the world in six days because six is a perfect number (i.e., six is the sum of all its divisors except itself, $6 = 1 + 2 + 3$). Research into this subject can be fascinating—you never know what you'll find along the way!

PRACTICE EXERCISES FOR TEACHERS

These exercises are designed for the reader of this book, not for the children the reader may teach. Although some of these examples are suitable for use in the elementary or middle school classroom, they should not necessarily be given to children in the form presented here. Ideas appropriate for classroom activities on the concepts and ideas discussed in this chapter can be found in a later section of this chapter and on the CD that accompanies this text.

1. List all of the whole number factors for each of the following numbers.

a) 8   b) 17   c) 24   d) 100   e) 10

2. List all possible product expressions containing exactly two factors for each of the following numbers.

a) 12   b) 27   c) 48   d) 100   e) 10

3. Draw all the possible rectangular arrays for each of the following numbers.

a) 9   b) 11   c) 10   d) 4

4. List the prime factors for each of the following composite numbers.

VM 9.2

a) 8   b) 14   c) 36   d) 80   e) 41

5. Factor each of the following composite numbers completely (into prime factors).

    a) 28   b) 78   c) 38   d) 92   e) 110

VM 9.2

6. Use the principles of divisibility to determine whether each of the following numbers is divisible by 2, 3, or 5.

    a) 99   b) 831   c) 615   d) 118,590   e) 458

7. Twin primes are two prime numbers that have exactly one composite number between them. For example, 3 and 5 are considered to be twin primes. Name all the twin primes between 4 and 100.

8. Determine the greatest common factor for each of the following pairs of numbers.

    a) 372 and 390   b) 168 and 714   c) 340 and 390   d) 80 and 84

VM 9.3

9. Determine the least common multiple for each of the following pairs of numbers.

    a) 36 and 60   b) 20 and 42   c) 8 and 14   d) 9 and 15

VM 9.3

10. Study the following number sentences:

$$4 = 2 + 2$$
$$6 = 3 + 3$$
$$8 = 5 + 3$$
$$10 = 7 + 3 = 5 + 5$$
$$12 = 7 + 5$$

Which kind of numbers do the numerals on the left side of the equal signs represent? Are the addends on the right side of the equal signs prime numbers? Formulate a statement that relates this information in the form of a general conjecture.

11. Study the following.

$$2^2 = 4, \text{ which has divisors } 1, 2, 4$$
$$3^2 = 9, \text{ which has divisors } 1, 3, 9$$
$$5^2 = 25, \text{ which has divisors } 1, 5, 25$$
$$7^2 = 49, \text{ which has divisors } 1, 7, 49$$
$$11^2 = 121, \text{ which has divisors } 1, 11, 121$$

Devise a general formula that summarizes the apparent pattern here. Use your formula to determine the divisors of 169.

12. As mentioned in this chapter, a number is called *perfect* if it is the sum of all the numbers (except itself) that evenly divide it. For example, 6 is a perfect number because $6 = 1 + 2 + 3$, where 1, 2, and 3 are divisors of 6. Find another perfect number between 6 and 35. Use the Factor Tree VM to assist you in finding this perfect number.

VM 9.2

13. Name six different number systems, and list several subsets of each.

14. Name the opposite of each of the following numbers.

    a) $^+2$ b) $^-3$ c) 0

    d) $^-\left(\frac{1}{4}\right)$ e) $^-\left(\frac{2}{3}\right)$ f) $^+217$

    g) $^-43$ h) $^-47$ i) $^+73$

    j) $^-49$ k) $^-\left(\frac{7}{8}\right)$ l) $^-\left(\frac{14}{23}\right)$

VM 9.4

15. Draw a number line model for each of the following examples, and name the sum.

a) $^+3 + ^-2 = \square$ b) $^-5 + ^+2 = \square$

c) $^-4 + ^-5 = \square$ d) $^+7 + ^-3 = \square$

e) $^+6 + ^+2 = \square$ f) $^-8 + ^+5 = \square$

g) $^-2 + ^-4 = \square$ h) $^+1 + ^-6 = \square$

16. Solve each of the following addition examples.

a) $^-43 + ^+17 = \square$ b) $^-57 + ^-78 = \square$ c) $^+61 + ^-56 = \square$

d) $^-83 + ^+69 = \square$ e) $^+47 + ^+34 = \square$ f) $^-92 + ^-89 = \square$

g) $^-68 + ^+73 = \square$ h) $^-37 + ^-53 = \square$ i) $^+48 + ^-84 = \square$

17. Draw a number line model for each of the following examples, and name the missing addend.

a) $^+7 - ^-8 = \square$ b) $^-4 - ^-3 = \square$ c) $^-6 - ^+2 = \square$

d) $^-9 - ^+3 = \square$ e) $^-1 - ^-8 = \square$ f) $^+4 - ^-7 = \square$

18. Solve each of the following subtraction examples.

a) $^-24 - ^-42 = \square$ b) $^-51 - ^+68 = \square$ c) $^+23 - ^-19 = \square$

d) $^-73 - ^+91 = \square$ e) $^+86 - ^-27 = \square$ f) $^+39 - ^+93 = \square$

19. Using the rules for multiplying integers, solve each of the following examples.

a) $^+7 \times ^-9 = \square$ b) $^-8 \times ^+6 = \square$ c) $^-9 \times ^-6 = \square$

d) $^-43 \times ^-17 = \square$ e) $^-32 \times ^-23 = \square$ f) $^-47 \times ^-18 = \square$

g) $^-68 \times ^+42 = \square$ h) $^+53 \times ^+65 = \square$ i) $^-85 \times ^-19 = \square$

j) $^-39 \times ^+17 = \square$ k) $^+74 \times ^-51 = \square$ l) $^-67 \times ^+37 = \square$

20. Solve each of the following division examples.

a) $^-48 \div ^+6 = \square$ b) $^+72 \div ^+9 = \square$ c) $^-63 \div ^-7 = \square$

d) $^-42 \div ^-7 = \square$ e) $^-69 \div ^-3 = \square$ f) $^-144 \div ^+6 = \square$

g) $^-72 \div ^-4 = \square$ h) $^+84 \div ^-12 = \square$ i) $^+98 \div ^-14 = \square$

j) $^-204 \div ^-34 = \square$ k) $^-208 \div ^+26 = \square$ l) $^+378 \div ^-42 = \square$

VM 9.4

21. Solve the following examples selected from the system of real numbers.

a) $^+\left(-\frac{3}{4}\right) \times ^-\left(-\frac{7}{8}\right) = \square$ b) $^-\left(-\frac{5}{6}\right) \div ^-\left(-\frac{2}{3}\right) = \square$ c) $^-.8 \times ^-.06 = \square$

d) $^-.96 \div ^+1.2 = \square$ e) $^-\left(-\frac{3}{5}\right) + ^-\left(-\frac{5}{9}\right) = \square$ f) $^+7.8 - ^-.21 = \square$

g) $^+\left(-\frac{7}{8}\right) - ^+\left(-\frac{2}{3}\right) = \square$ h) $^-3.41 + ^+2.9 = \square$ i) $^-\left(-\frac{5}{8}\right) \times ^-\left(-\frac{4}{15}\right) = \square$

j) $^-1.84 \div ^+2.3 = \square$ k) $^+2.03 - ^+1.45 = \square$ l) $^+\left(-\frac{3}{19}\right) + ^-\left(-\frac{2}{7}\right) = \square$

22. Suppose that we use letters to designate the following systems of numbers we have studied.

A = counting numbers   E = rational numbers
B = whole numbers   F = irrational numbers
C = integers   G = real numbers
D = fractional numbers

a) Which of these contain all of the others in the list?

b) Which of these does not contain group A?

c) Which of these contain group E?

d) Which of these are contained in group E?

e) Which of these have $^-\left(-\frac{2}{3}\right)$ as an element?

f) In which group is division by zero possible?

TEACHING COMPETENCIES AND SELF-ASSESSMENT TASKS

1. Draw a picture using arrays to show why 21 is not considered to be a prime number but 13 is prime. Relate the argument using arrays to the abstract definition of a prime number as "a number greater than 1 with only 1 and itself as factors."

2. Discuss why 1 is not a prime number.

3. Identify at least two methods of convincing students that zero is an even number.

4. Discuss how a student might be able to predict whether a sum will be even or odd without actually adding the addends.

5. Discuss the collection of numbers having an odd number of factors. Make a generalization about these numbers.

6. A child has some blocks with values of either 2, 3, 5, or 7 written on them. You don't know how many blocks the child has, but you do know that the product of the values of the blocks is 126. What are the values of the individual blocks? How many blocks does the child have?

7. Describe the relationship between least common multiple (LCM) and least common denominator (LCD). How is this relationship similar to the relationship between greatest common divisor (GCD) and greatest common factor (GCF)? How is it different?

8. A student excitedly states that there is a relationship between the least common multiple (LCM) and greatest common factor (GCF) of two numbers and the two numbers themselves. If you multiply the LCM and GCF of two numbers, you get the same product as when you multiply the two numbers. Does this always work? How would you explain this?

9. What is the least (smallest) whole number that is divisible by 1, 2, 3, 4, 5, 6, 7, 8, and 9? How do you verify this?

10. If you have determined that 35,694 is divisible by 9, how can you quickly tell if 49,653 is divisible by 9? What about 96,534? 56,349? 69,345? 6345?

11. Use both the number line and the chip-matching method to illustrate addition and subtraction of integers. Compare the advantages and disadvantages of these two methods of modeling integer operations.

12. Describe the relationship of the integers to the operation of subtraction. What problems are encountered by using the take-away model of subtraction for integers on a number line? Does the missing addends model suggested in this chapter work for whole numbers? Discuss the advantages and disadvantages of using only one approach to modeling subtraction for all number systems.

13. Using a reference book or the Internet, locate the height of the tallest mountain in the world (Mt. Everest) and the depth of the deepest ocean (Pacific Ocean—Marianas Trench). Which of these varies most from sea level? Relate the discussion to integers.

14. Locate a copy of Dr. Marijane Werner's booklet, *Teaching the Set of Integers to Elementary School Children*. Discuss the variety of suggested teaching techniques.

15. Some mathematics educators suggest that following the structures of mathematics, integers should be taught before rational numbers. Each member of the class should take a stand either supporting or rejecting this statement and debate the question in class.

16. Examine standardized achievement tests for children. Itemize the number of examples related to each system of numbers defined in this chapter. Discuss the appropriateness of the distribution of examples.

17. Discuss the points on the number line in relation to rational numbers, irrational numbers, and integers.

18. Define the terms *integers*, *rational numbers*, and real *numbers*.

19. Locate and describe materials that can be used for the concrete development of number theory.

20. Examine elementary school mathematics textbooks. How and when are integers introduced? Have a class discussion on the merits of teaching integers in the elementary classroom.

21. Research the literature, and provide evidence to support teaching integers to elementary school children.

22. Discuss the dot pictures that can be drawn for square numbers and triangular numbers and the relationships between these dot pictures and the patterns they represent.

23. Locate and study Goldbach's Conjecture about prime numbers; then present your findings to the class.

SAMPLE INSTRUCTIONAL AND ASSESSMENT ACTIVITIES

These activities and more are available on the CD that accompanies this text

1. Number theory and number systems activities for primary school children are readiness activities; abstract teaching should not take place until the intermediate grades. However, many situations that open the door to number theory can be discussed with first-grade children. For instance, make use of occasions when children line up in pairs, or by threes, or fours, and again discuss the relationship between skip-counting and multiplication in this situation.

2. Have children stack 10 cubes into two stacks, alternating between the stacks. Then have them stack seven cubes in the same manner. If the two stacks of cubes are the same height, the number is even. If the two stacks of cubes are uneven, then the number of cubes is odd.

Ten is even.

Seven is odd.

Using the same procedure, have the children examine the sum of two even numbers, the sum of two odd numbers, and the sum of one even and one odd number.

3. When we look at a thermometer and observe that the temperature has dropped below zero, we begin to see the need for negative numbers. Using integers to describe concrete situations in mathematical terms allows you to introduce them easily in the intermediate grades. To lay a good foundation, it is important to draw on situations in which children can see a real need or use for integers.

4. You will need wooden or plastic tiles and a sheet of paper with the headings Numeral, Dimensions of Rectangle, and Number of Rectangles for this activity. Beginning with one tile, the student records the numeral 1 under the Numeral column, records the dimensions of the rectangle (1×1) formed by the tile, and records the number of rectangles formed (1). Have the children record the numbers with only two rectangles, the numbers with more than two rectangles, and the numbers with less than two rectangles. Continue recording information until children have enough information to make a generalization.

Numeral	Dimensions of Rectangle	Number of Rectangles
1	1×1	1
2	$1 \times 2, 2 \times 1$	2
.	.	.
.	.	.
.	.	.
6	$1 \times 6, 6 \times 1, 2 \times 3, 3 \times 2$	4
.	.	.
.	.	.
.	.	.

5. One game for finding prime factors is called "Prime Spin." Cut out a large (approximately 24-inch diameter) cardboard circular region and mark it into sections as shown. Mount a cardboard arrow in the middle with a brass fastener.

To play the game, separate the class into two teams. Have each team member alternately spin the wheel. A member of the rival team must then provide the prime factors of the number spun. If this student is correct, then the team scores the number that has been spun. If the same number is spun twice, another spin should be performed so that new numbers will be factored. The team with the highest point total is declared the winner.

For more efficient use, cover the region with clear Contact paper so that numerals could be written with a grease pencil and then erased. This would provide greater variety to the game.

VM 9.1

6. Use the Sieve of Eratosthenes VM on the accompanying CD to name the prime numbers between 1 and 200.

VM 9.3

7. Write the set of factors for each number in the pairs below—if you'd like, use the Sieve of Eratosthenes VM on the accompanying CD. Then write the set of common factors of the given numbers.

a) 14 and 20   b) 36 and 24   c) 15 and 25   d) 40 and 16   e) 18 and 36

VM 9.3

8. Use the GCF/LCM VM on the accompanying CD to find the greatest common factor (GCF) of each pair of numbers in Activity 16.

VM 9.2

9. Use the Factor Tree VM on the accompanying CD to write each number as the product of primes.

a) 90   b) 144   c) 220   d) 420   e) 275

VM 9.4

10. Model each integer addition example on the number line. If you prefer, use the Number Line VM on the accompanying CD.

a) Begin with examples of like signs of direction.

$$^+3 +\, ^+7 = \square \quad\quad ^-4 +\, ^-5 = \square$$

b) Follow like signs of direction in examples with examples of unlike signs of direction.

$$^-3 +\, ^+4 = \square \quad\quad ^+6 +\, ^-9 = \square \quad\quad ^+5 +\, ^-3 = \square$$

After many integer addition examples have been solved, have the students study them and look for patterns. Through guided discovery, they should develop some generalizations about how to add integers.

AN ORANGE KANGAROO IN DENMARK
(OR, PERHAPS, AN AQUA KOALA IN DENMARK)
See the riddle at the beginning of this chapter on
page 200.

10

Algebraic Reasoning: Generalizing Patterns and Relationships

TEACHING COMPETENCIES

Upon completing this chapter, you will be able to:

- Formulate a definition of algebraic reasoning and describe several purposes for the need to develop algebraic reasoning in elementary school mathematics programs.

- Outline the major algebra concepts that are developed throughout a child's elementary school experiences.

- Give examples of the types of experiences that children in elementary school might have that will help them develop algebraic thinking.

- Explain how early explorations of patterns can lay a foundation for the study of more abstract algebra concepts.

- Demonstrate how to use concrete materials to illustrate equation-solving and expression-simplifying processes.

- Explain the rule for a pattern by using multiple representations, including a verbal pattern, a table, a graph, or an algebraic expression or equation.

- Describe the development of the use of variables in elementary school mathematics programs.

- Design instructional activities that promote algebraic thinking in ways appropriate for elementary school children.

VIRTUAL MANIPULATIVES

Upon completing this chapter, you will be able to use virtual manipulatives on the accompanying CD to:

- Analyze patterns and functions using *Function Machine*. **(VM 10.1)**

- Explore equations and expressions using *Algebra Tiles*. **(VM 10.2)**

- Examine numerical patterns and functions using *Number Patterns*. **(VM 10.3)**

- Explore patterns and sequences using *Color Patterns*. **(VM 10.4)**

Numbered CD icons throughout the chapter refer to the virtual manipulatives in this list.

One train leaves New York for Chicago at 3:30 P.M. and another leaves Chicago for New York at 4:15 P.M. If the first train is traveling at a speed of 55 mph … Had enough yet? Think back to your experiences with learning algebra. What do you remember? Many adults recall taking an algebra course in high school that included solving equations and inequalities, factoring, and working with complicated symbolic expressions. It may have also involved the solving of different types of word problems, from age and coin and mixture problems to questions about trains (or cars or airplanes) traveling in different directions at different speeds. From a contemporary view of elementary and middle school mathematics, the development of algebraic thought should be a meaningful and gradual process, requiring exposure to a variety of algebra-related problems each and every year that a child is in school. If we believe that the development of number sense is important enough to include in the curriculum every year in order to develop it over time, then algebraic reasoning should also be included in the curriculum every year to develop it over time. The key is to present activities to children that are developmentally appropriate as they construct an understanding of algebra and algebraic thinking.

The Content of Algebra

Algebra may be thought of as the process of generalizing, abstracting, and representing functions and relationships. Algebra can also be viewed as the study of mathematical structure and as a language for conveying and applying that structure. Algebra can further be thought of as a language that explores unknowns, placeholders, formulas, relationships, and generalizations.

The National Council of Teachers of Mathematics (NCTM) *Principles and Standards for School Mathematics* (2000) describes a vision of algebra that should be developed for all children in grades preK–8 as follows:

Instructional programs from prekindergarten through grade 12 should enable all students to—

- understand patterns, relations, and functions;
- represent and analyze mathematical situations and structures using algebraic symbols;
- use mathematical models to represent and understand quantitative relationships;
- analyze change in various contexts.[1]

---

[1]Reprinted with permission from the *Principles and Standards for School Mathematics*, copyright 2000 by the National Council of Teachers of Mathematics.

This algebra standard acknowledges the importance of students' exploring patterns and relationships as a foundation for algebraic thinking. The fundamental elements of the algebra standard are reflected in the following expectations for the grade levels of pre–K to 2, 3 to 5, and 6 to 8.

ALGEBRA STANDARD

PreK–2 Expectations

In prekindergarten through grade 2 all students should—

- sort, classify, and order objects by size, number, and other properties;
- recognize, describe, and extend patterns such as sequences of sounds and shapes or simple numeric patterns and translate from one representation to another;
- analyze how both repeating and growing patterns are generated;
- illustrate general principles and properties of operations, such as commutativity, using specific numbers;
- use concrete, pictorial, and verbal representations to develop an understanding of invented and conventional symbolic notations;
- model situations that involve the addition and subtraction of whole numbers, using objects, pictures, and symbols;
- describe qualitative change, such as a student's growing taller;
- describe quantitative change, such as a student's growing two inches in one year.

Grades 3–5 Expectations

In grades 3–5 all students should—

- describe, extend, and make generalizations about geometric and numeric patterns;
- represent and analyze patterns and functions, using words, tables, and graphs;
- identify such properties as commutativity, associativity, and distributivity and use them to compute with whole numbers;
- represent the idea of a variable as an unknown quantity using a letter or a symbol;
- express mathematical relationships using equations;
- model problem situations with objects and use representations such as graphs, tables, and equations to draw conclusions;

RESEARCH SNAPSHOT

What does research say about the experiences of teachers who follow NCTM reform documents and focus the teaching of algebra on conceptual understanding, using functions to develop the concept of variables?

In a case study of a ninth-grade teacher of introductory algebra, Haimes (1996) found that the actions of the teacher in the implementation of the "function" curriculum did not reflect the intended teaching approach of the curriculum. The intended curriculum emphasized conceptual understanding and process skills, the promotion of problem solving, applications, and the use of student-centered activities. The teacher focused on curriculum content coverage and emphasized rules and procedures using teacher-centered pedagogy.

The teacher's beliefs about algebra and teaching algebra were the most powerful influences on her teaching. Her own prior experiences as a student and a teacher reinforced the importance of methods and procedures.

Do the results of this study surprise you? Would your answer change if the mathematics content area that was taught was not algebra?

Haimes, D.H. (1996). The implementation of a "function" approach to introductory algebra: A case study of teacher cognitions, teacher actions, and the intended curriculum. *Journal for Research in Mathematics Education, 27*, 582–602.

For additional research briefs, "ERIC Digests" lets you search more than 2000 short syntheses of research on a range of education topics. The syntheses were produced by the Educational Resources Information Center (ERIC). Check http://www.ericfacility.net/ericdigests/index/.

- investigate how a change in one variable relates to a change in a second variable;
- identify and describe situations with constant or varying rates of change and compare them.

Grades 6–8 Expectations

In grades 6–8 all students should—

- represent, analyze, and generalize a variety of patterns with tables, graphs, words, and, when possible, symbolic rules;
- relate and compare different forms of representation for a relationship;
- identify functions as linear or nonlinear and contrast their properties from tables, graphs, or equations;
- develop an initial conceptual understanding of different uses of variables;
- explore relationships between symbolic expressions and graphs of lines, paying particular attention to the meaning of intercept and slope;
- use symbolic algebra to represent situations and to solve problems, especially those that involve linear relationships;
- recognize and generate equivalent forms for simple algebraic expressions and solve linear equations;
- model and solve contextualized problems using various representations, such as graphs, tables, and equations;

- use graphs to analyze the nature of changes in quantities in linear relationships.

A contemporary view of algebraic thinking holds that algebra should not be relegated solely to a high school course. Instead, algebraic reasoning is a gradual process of developing the use of algebra across grade levels. The teacher should utilize activities that allow students to make connections among major aspects such as

1. patterns and models
2. variables
3. exponents
4. graphing
5. functions

At the elementary level, the use of concrete discovery should be emphasized over abstract symbolism and procedural algorithms. If prerequisite material is considered, and if the content is presented in a manner that is developmentally appropriate, then even the youngest children can grasp the underlying concepts of algebra. This thinking is not entirely new. Barber (1932),[2] for example, argued for the inclusion of algebraic topics in the elementary and middle grades more than 75 years ago!

[2] Barber, H. C. (1932). Present opportunities in junior high school algebra. In W. D. Reeve (Ed.), *The teaching of algebra*. New York. Teachers College, Columbia University.

Algebra in Problem Solving

Let's turn our attention to the types of activities that allow for the development of algebraic thinking in the elementary grades.

Consider the following problem:

> A teacher administers a 5-question, true-false quiz to a class. Suppose that a student had been absent for several days and simply guessed on each quiz item. How likely is it that the student would get all 5 questions correct?

A number of approaches can be used to solve this problem. First, each student in the class might simply take a piece of paper, number from 1 to 5, and then randomly place a T or an F by each number. By comparing student responses to the teacher's answer key, the class can count the number of times that a student answered (in this case, guessed) all of the questions correctly. This experimental approach can be used to provide a basis on which to explore the problem in a more theoretical manner.

A second approach to this problem would be for a student to make a systematic list of ALL of the possible answer keys. By taking five slips of paper with "T" written on one side and "F" written on the other, a student can arrange and rearrange them on a desk and record all of the various keys (different combinations) that could be formed. For example:

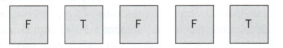

Students should determine a strategy for systematically laying out the pieces to ensure that ALL of the keys are listed. For example, they might begin by listing each of the answer keys that has only one True answer (e.g., TFFFF, FTFFF, FFTFF, FFFTF, and FFFFT) and then move on to those keys that have exactly two true answers, and so on.

A third approach to this problem might involve the use of the strategy of solving the simpler problem. In this case, the student might ask, "What if the quiz had only one question instead of five?" In this case, the quiz would have only two possible keys—T or F. If the quiz had only two questions, then a total of four keys could be formed—TT, TF, FT, or FF. A quiz with only three questions would have exactly eight keys. (Are you able to list them?) Then, noticing a pattern, a table might be constructed to represent the data collected so far:

Number of Quiz Items	Number of Answer Keys
1	2
2	4
3	8

At this point, students might notice two things: (1) the number of possible answer keys doubles with each new quiz item added and (2) the numbers in the "Number of Answer Keys" column are all powers of two. An interesting discussion should occur as students explain why the number of possible answer keys appears to double each time. Looking at this observation in a different way, each time a new item is added, the list of answer keys would include all of the previous keys with a "True" added to the end of each key AND all of the previous keys with a "False" added to the end of each key—exactly twice as many as there were at the beginning.

Using this logic and extending the pattern, students can determine that the number of possible answer keys for a 4-item quiz would be 16, and for a 5-item quiz, it would be 32. Therefore, the chances of guessing all 5 items correctly is $\frac{1}{32}$ or approximately 3% of the time.

The students could take the data and put them into a graphical form, as follows:

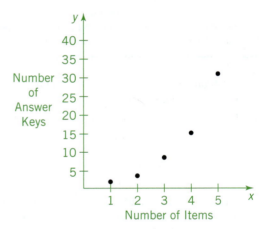

Notice that the values on the x-axis represent the number of items on the quiz, and the y-axis represents the possible number of answer keys that can be constructed. Students should recognize that the graph does not represent a linear function (the points do not lie in a straight line) and that as x-values get larger, the y-values grow larger at a greater rate each time.

This same notion is central to understanding how compound interest works: The amount of money earned from interest on an investment in the first few years may be relatively small, but after 20 or 30 years, the interest can make the initial investment grow to a surprisingly large amount. For example, an investment of $5000 at 9% interest compounded annually will earn only $450 in the first year but will grow to more than $28,000 in 20 years and more than $66,000 in 30 years. Solving problems involving compound interest is likely to be less confusing in high school if the student has had experiences with problems such as our earlier answer key problem in elementary school.

If students recognize that the "Number of Answer Keys" column is a power of two, then they may be able to generalize the formula for x items on the quiz.

Number of Quiz Items	Number of Answer Keys	Power of Two
1	2	2^1
2	4	2^2
3	8	2^3
x	y	2^x

By making this variable representation, students can quickly determine not only the solution to the original problem, but they can also generalize the solution for quizzes with even more questions. For example, the chances of guessing all 10 items correctly on a true-false quiz are less than 1 in 1000, and the chances of guessing all 20 items correctly on a true-false quiz are less than 1 in 1,000,000!

Similarly, the student can generalize the result to the following "new" (but related) problem:

> Suppose that the teacher decided to give a 5-question, multiple-choice quiz instead, with each item having 5 possible choices. How likely would it be to guess all 5 of these answers correctly?

In this case, the student could decide to simply compute 5^5 to find that there are 3125 possible answer keys. Students will see that the benefit of the algebraic solutions of graphing and writing an equation such as $y = 2^x$ is that the solutions can be used to generalize the problem and, consequently, solve other, related problems. The systematic construction of a table is often an integral part of the generalization process.

Let's consider how this problem parallels the content strands suggested previously. Solving the answer key problem called for the systematic listing of quiz items and numbers of answer keys to determine a pattern and to develop a mathematical model. When the pattern was generalized into the expression 2^x, a variable expression was developed. A **variable** is a symbol that represents a number or set of numbers in an expression or an equation. This particular problem also dealt with the proper use of exponents. Also, the data from the table was translated into a series of points that could be graphed.

Finally, the answer key problem involved a function, $y = 2^x$. A **function** is a rule that assigns one value in a set to exactly one given value in another set. In our case, for example, "2" was associated with "4," since 2 questions generate 4 answer keys. Similarly, "5" is associated to "32," in that a 5-item quiz produces 32 possible answer keys. We could say, therefore, that the number of answer keys "is a function of" the number of items on the quiz. When we describe functions, we discuss how changes in one value bring about changes in the other value, a basic concept that is fundamental to the study of algebra.

Furthermore, a function generally consists of an **independent variable** and a **dependent variable**. The value of the dependent variable "depends on" the value of the independent variable. In our example, the dependent variable would be the number of answer keys because it depends on the number of items asked on the quiz.

The answer key problem allows children to design multiple representations, including verbal ones, using a table, drawing a graph, and writing an equation with variables. In summary, a problem that is rich in mathematical content can be used to develop the type of algebraic thinking described in NCTM's *Principles and Standards for School Mathematics*.

Promoting Algebraic Thinking in the Lower Elementary Grades

In the primary grades, it is important that children develop a sense of "if this happens, then the result will be . . ." as they work toward developing basic patterning and reasoning skills. Linking literature to mathematics, teachers can make use of children's books that describe situations such as, "Cats have fur. Fluffy is a cat. So . . .," which allows children to consider a given condition and draw conclusions based on that condition.

In addition, the analysis of simple patterns is critical to the development of algebraic thinking in the early primary years. Reasoning skills are being nurtured any time a child creates a pattern that another student must extend and explain. For example, using play money, a child might lay out the following sequence on her desk:

A partner might explain, for example, that a dime might come next because the pattern of "quarter–dime–dime–quarter" seems to have been established. Not only should students become proficient at naming the next term in a sequence, but they should also be required to verbalize the pattern that has been recognized (e.g., "In this pattern, if a quarter is laid down, then two dimes always come next, so the next coin in this pattern should be a dime").

With the use of concrete materials, children can also generate patterns that connect algebra with other content areas. For example, a child has an oyster cracker that is the shape of a hexagon and lays it on the desk. The perimeter of the cracker could be described as 6 units because it has 6 equal sides exposed. Have the child then place two and then three of the crackers side-by-side so that the crackers share a side, as shown. The child should continue to determine the perimeter of the modified figure.

Students should be able to count to determine that the distance around one cracker is 6 units, but when two are joined together, the total perimeter is "only" 10 units. They should notice and be able to communicate that the perimeter is not 12 units, because two of the sides are touching one another and are no longer part of the perimeter of the shape. Taking the data from several examples and putting it into a table yields the following result:

Number of Crackers	Perimeter
1	6
2	10
3	14
4	18

The children should then be asked to predict the perimeter of a similar shape that is made up of 5 or 10 crackers. They should recognize that the "rule" being applied here is that each cracker adds 4 to the perimeter. This rule by which the "Perimeter" changes as the "Number of Crackers" changes describes a function in the problem. We would say that the perimeter is a function of the number of crackers. The number of crackers is the independent variable, and the perimeter is the dependent variable. Although it is certainly worthwhile to spend time exploring these concepts associated with functions, we would not generally use this terminology with elementary school children.

Functions can be explored in other ways in the lower grades. Have students draw a vertical line down the center of a blank piece of paper and lay cubes on each side of the line—8 cubes on the left side and 5 cubes on the right, as shown:

Children should be challenged to "compare what you see on the two sides of the line." Responses might include the following:

- The right side is three less than the left.
- The right side is the left side minus three.

- The left side is three more than the right.
- The left side is the right side plus three.
- The number of cubes on the left is greater than the number of cubes on the right.
- The number of cubes on the right is less than the number of cubes on the left.

Now ask the children to place 4 cubes on the left and 1 cube on the right. They should recognize this as another example of the same rule. Then you can ask the children to tell how many cubes would be on the right if there were, for example, 7 cubes on the left. During this exploration, children are attempting to apply an observed rule and extend it to other situations—a key concept in the study of algebra.

The data for the number of cubes can also be put into a table:

Number on the Left	Number on the Right
4	1
5	_____
6	_____
7	_____
8	5
_____	8

Children can be encouraged to identify and apply a rule to fill in the blanks in the table. Eventually, students should be encouraged to use variables to express a rule describing the relationship, such as $R = L - 3$ or $R + 3 = L$, where R is the number on the right, and L is the number on the left.

The issue of getting children comfortable with the use of variables at the lower grades is not to be taken lightly. One study showed that nearly 90% of ninth graders could solve the equation $\square - 6 = 9$. That is, find the value for $\square$. But when the problem was expressed as $x - 6 = 9$, only 50% of the same students could find the value of x! In other words, it was not the difficulty of the problem but the unfamiliarity with variable notation that scared off even high school students. Children need exposure to working with variables throughout their academic careers to avoid the development of an attitude that algebra is too difficult—especially when algebraic thinking often is not.

Algebraic thinking can also be promoted while working with basic addition facts. Suppose that a child was to be given a family of facts, such as the "7 family." All of the facts that make up the 7 family can be systematically listed: $0 + 7$, $1 + 6$, $2 + 5$, $3 + 4$, $4 + 3$, $5 + 2$, $6 + 1$, and $7 + 0$. Then each of these facts can be viewed as coordinates of points that can be graphed. The points are (0, 7), (1, 6), (2, 5), (3, 4),

(4, 3), (5, 2), (6, 1), and (7, 0). Placing these points on a coordinate grid would yield a graph similar to the one shown.

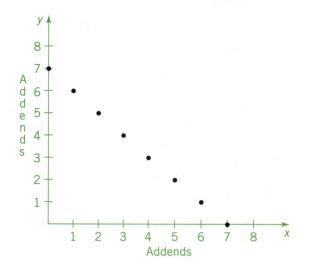

Children should be asked to describe what they see. They should note that the points are linear—that is, if connected, they form a straight line. Children can explore other fact families, such as the fact families for 5s or 12s, to list them in order and graph the facts to find out if they are also linear. They can also discuss the fact that $3 + 4$ and $4 + 3$ represent different points on the graph but yield the same result. Finally, children can make a list of the fact families and the number of facts in each family to form a table such as this:

Fact Family	Number of Facts
0	1 (0 + 0)
1	2 (1 + 0, 0 + 1)
2	3 (2 + 0, 1 + 1, 0 + 2)
3	4 (3 + 0, 2 + 1, 1 + 2, 0 + 3)
4	5 (4 + 0, 3 + 1, 2 + 2, 1 + 3, 0 + 4)

Children can use this table to predict the number of facts in, say, the 10 family and then list them to verify their conjecture. Finally, children can generalize the result to determine that for the n family, $n + 1$ facts can be listed.

Similar patterns can be explored in the upper primary grades by working with multiplication and looking at factors of given numbers. The point here is that some powerful algebraic skills can be developed in the context of exploration of what we consider to be basic facts in traditional computational mathematics. In the process, children get additional practice with basic facts and may be more likely to memorize those facts that are a challenge more effectively and efficiently. Teachers often express concern about there being too

many objectives in their local course of study, arguing that they don't have time for teaching the basic ideas of algebra. However, by using some of the examples described here, they will find that algebraic thinking can be seamlessly woven into the exploration and review of basic facts that they would have spent time on with their classes anyway.

Another technique frequently used in elementary school for the study of functions is the function machine. A function machine virtual manipulative can be found on the CD that accompanies this text. Alternatively, you can easily construct a classroom function machine by taking cardboard and cutting a circle and a square with small slits above and below each shape as shown:

Also, several strips of heavy stock paper should be made so that they can be inserted in the slits and slid behind the cut-out shapes. Then numbers should be written on the strips so that, for example, when the circle shows a "3," the square displays a "5," and when the circle shows a "6," the square displays an "8." This construction is called a function machine because it displays pairs of numbers—the one showing through the circle is the input, and the one displayed through the square is the output (or vice versa, for that matter).

The role of the student is then to explain a rule that the machine is following to make each input into an output. For the example previously described, a rule might be that "the nuber in the square is the number in the circle plus two." By using several strips, a teacher can challenge a class or small group of children to determine a rule that makes the input value into the output. The function machine helps children analyze functions and patterns and become familiar with the use of variables to describe the models.

By engaging in activities such as the ones described in this section, children in the lower elementary grades gain considerable exposure to and practice in algebraic thinking. Developmentally appropriate methods allow children to reason and communicate patterns through activities that use concrete materials. These early experiences then set the tone and lay the groundwork for more advanced algebraic reasoning problems in the upper elementary and middle grades.

Enhancing Algebraic Thinking in the Upper Elementary and Middle Grades

Now, let's turn our attention to some of the problems and teaching strategies that can be used at the upper elementary and middle school levels. In the upper elementary grades, children should explore and extend the notions of patterns, variables, exponents, graphing, and functions. Experiences should continue to emphasize the reasoning that is involved in representing problems in a variety of ways. Children should become more familiar with the use of variables and should also explore functions that are nonlinear. Simple equation-solving processes and mathematical properties should also be developed in these grades.

Consider the following problem:

Each student in the class is given a rectangular piece of paper. Ask the students, "How many rectangles do you see?" Then have them fold the paper in half, and repeat the question. Have them put one more fold in the paper, and ask the question again. Finally, have them fold the paper a third time, and ask the question one last time. Record the data in a table and predict how many rectangles you would be able to count if the paper were folded 10 times.

Of course, most of the students would note that the piece of paper with no folds forms one rectangle. After folding the paper one time, there are three rectangles—two, smaller rectangles and the original rectangle (some students may not recognize that the original large rectangle should still be counted). Folding the paper again, the sheet would look like this:

A	B	C

How many rectangles do you see? If you take each of the pieces A, B, and C by themselves, there are three rectangles. Then there is a rectangle that contains both A and B and one that contains both B and C. Finally there is the rectangle with which we started, the one made up of all three—this gives a total of six rectangles. Now suppose you add one more fold to the paper so that there are now three folds and four sections formed. You should find 10 rectangles. (Did you?)

The collected data can be placed in a table, as follows:

Number of Folds	Number of Rectangles
0	1
1	3
2	6
3	10

After putting the data in the table, allow students to predict how many rectangles would be formed after adding a fourth fold by asking them to verbalize any patterns that they see. Typically children recognize that the difference between 1 and 3 is 2; the difference between 3 and 6 is 3; and the difference between 6 and 10 is 4; so they speculate that the next number in the sequence might be 5 greater, or 15. Ask them to fold the paper once more and count the rectangles to verify their conjectures.

At this point, children should have worked with the pattern of numbers enough to be able to use a calculator to determine the number of rectangles formed when the paper has 10 folds. As discussed earlier in this chapter, students can then take the values in the table and plot them on a graph, with the x-axis representing number of folds and the y-axis representing the number of rectangles, as shown.

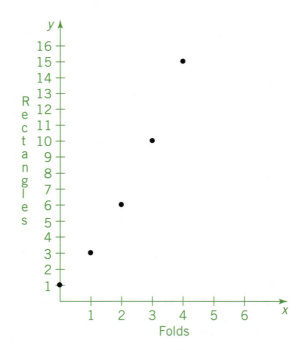

When asked to describe what they see, children should acknowledge that the graph is not linear because the y-value increases by more and more each time the x-value is increased by one. Finding the equation of a function that is nonlinear is much more challenging than it is for linear functions. At the upper grades, children should be challenged to determine the equation that relates the x- and y-values in the table and on the graph. In this case, the equation is rather complicated,

$$y = \frac{(x+1)(x+2)}{2}$$

but careful and deliberate analysis of the table or graph may lead students to it.

This paper-folding problem allows students to explore a nonlinear set of data points through a hands-on activity that is used to generate a table. Subsequent discussions can center on drawing a graph and looking for patterns to determine an equation for the function. As with the true-false quiz problem discussed earlier in this chapter, the paper-folding puzzle emphasizes the multiple representations of a function and gives students practice in going back and forth between the folded paper, raw data, a table, a graph, and an equation, all of which describe the function.

Students in the upper elementary grades should begin to develop equation-solving processes through informal means. One way to explore equation solving is to present a situation such as the following to students:

3 bags + 7   1 bag + 15

Students are told that

1. There are an equal number of cubes on each table.

2. There are an equal number of cubes in each bag.

Unfortunately, we don't know how many cubes are on each table, because we can see only those cubes that are outside of the bags. The problem is to determine how many cubes must be in each bag.

There are a number of ways in which students might solve this problem. A common approach might be to compare the stack of 7 cubes on the table on the left to the stack of 15 cubes on the table on the right and then to deduce that there are 8 more cubes showing on the table at the right. Since the rules state that each bag has the same number of cubes, the 8 extra cubes on the right must be balanced with the cubes in two of the bags on the left. We know that each bag contains the same number of cubes, so each bag must contain 4 cubes, and the problem is solved.

In symbols, this problem could have been written as:

$$3x + 7 = x + 15$$

Traditionally, in a first-year algebra course, we solve this type of problem by using a series of steps similar to that shown in the following procedure:

$3x + 7$	$= x + 15$		$3x + 7$	$= x + 15$

$$
\begin{array}{llcll}
3x + 7 & = x + 15 & & 3x + 7 & = x + 15 \\
3x + 7 - x = x + 15 - x & & & 3x + 7 - 7 = x + 15 - 7 \\
2x + 7 & = 15 & \text{OR} & 3x & = x + 8 \\
2x + 7 - 7 = 15 - 7 & & & 3x - x & = x - x + 8 \\
2x & = 8 & & 2x & = 8 \\
x & = 4 & & x & = 4
\end{array}
$$

This *symbol manipulation* method does yield a result for the number of cubes in each bag but requires a much higher level of abstraction to follow the procedure. By using the bags and cubes, children explore the processes involved with equation solving long before they actually put a pencil to paper and "solve for x" using adopted rules for symbol manipulation that may not yet be grounded in meaning.

One of the most powerful manipulatives for exploring equations and expressions is a set of **algebra tiles**. A set of algebra tiles typically contains at least three different shapes with the following dimensions and values:

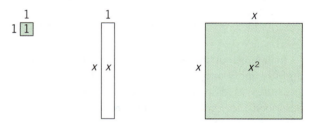

This physical representation of algebraic concepts uses an area model—the area of the small square with dimensions 1 by 1 is 1; the rectangle has dimensions 1 by x and, consequently, an area of x; and the large square has dimensions x by x and, consequently, an area of x^2. With these tiles, a number of algebraic processes can be readily illustrated.

Suppose that students were to solve the following equation:

$$4x + 5 = 3x + 9$$

They would begin by using a mat with a line drawn down the center representing the equals sign. With the algebra tiles, they would represent the quantities shown on each side of the line:

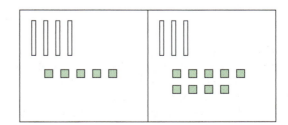

Because both sides of the paper are in balance, students may remove any tiles they wish from each side, provided that they keep both sides in balance by removing the same number from each side. In a very concrete way, they can remove 5 small squares and 3 rectangles from each side of the sheet, leaving a rectangle on the left side and 4 small squares on the right. Therefore, the x tile represented 4 tiles, and $x = 4$ is the solution to the equation.

Suppose that the problem had been the following:

$$2(x + 3) = 10$$

In this case, the students would lay out the tiles on their mats as shown:

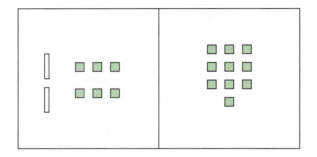

In laying out the tiles on the mat, students meaningfully apply one of the most important mathematical structures used in algebra—the distributive property, described more fully in Chapter 8. Clearly, $2(x + 3)$ means to repeat $x + 3$ twice, resulting in a total of $2x + 6$ (and children don't need to be told this as a rule in algebra—they can construct their knowledge through such experiences). After the tiles are laid out, the children can remove 6 squares from each side and complete the problem by splitting the remaining squares on the right into two piles, since they represent two x values:

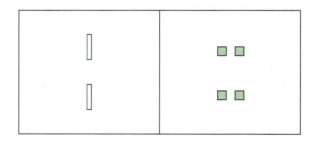

Again, if the student were to use a purely symbolic method of solving this equation for x, it would look like this:

$$2(x + 3) = 10$$
$$2x + 6 = 10$$
$$2x + 6 - 6 = 10 - 6$$
$$2x = 4$$
$$x = 2$$

But younger children who are still operating at a concrete-operational stage can solve the same problem with algebra tiles. Later, students can draw pictures of their tiles as they move from the concrete to the pictorial stage, and eventually (assuming appropriate connections have been made), the tiles can give way to pure symbolic manipulation.

More advanced students who are working with positive and negative numbers can incorporate tiles of two different colors—one to represent positives and one to represent negatives—and use similar hands-on methods to solve algebraic equations involving integers. Students can also explore equations in two variables since some sets of algebra tiles come with tiles that represent a second variable, y, as well as y^2 and xy.

When solving equations by using algebra tiles, it is extremely important that students verbalize throughout the process what they are doing and why they are doing it. They should be communicating, "I am trying to find what number the x tile equals, so, I need to get the x tile by itself on one side of the line." This focuses the student on the goal of symbolic equation manipulation before a move from the concrete level to the pictorial and the abstract level is made.

Algebra tiles can also be useful for teaching children how to multiply expressions that involve variables. An effective way to represent a multiplication fact such as 4×5 is to picture a rectangle whose height and width is 4 units by 5 units, thereby having an area of 20 square units:

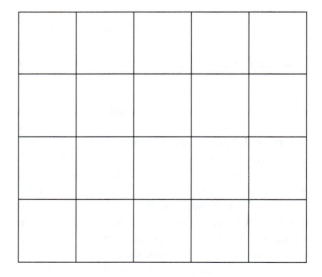

Also, children may have already had experiences with modeling the multiplication of two-digit numbers with base ten blocks. For example, the following model shows the four partial multiplications that determine the answer to 12×14:

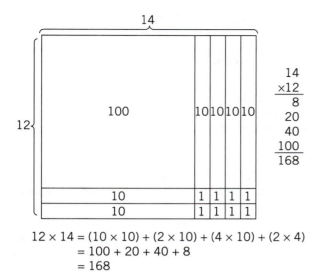

$$12 \times 14 = (10 \times 10) + (2 \times 10) + (4 \times 10) + (2 \times 4)$$
$$= 100 + 20 + 40 + 8$$
$$= 168$$

Similarly, children can explore the multiplication of polynomials by using an area model. A *polynomial* is the sum of one or more algebraic expressions that are sometimes referred to as *monomials* or *terms*. Examples of polynomials include $y + 6$, $- 7 + 3n$, $x^2 + 4x - 2$, $3x + 5y + 1$, and so on. Suppose that the child were asked to multiply $(x + 5)$ and $(x + 3)$. In this case, the tiles would be arranged so that a rectangle is formed whose height is $x + 5$ and whose length is $x + 3$, as shown:

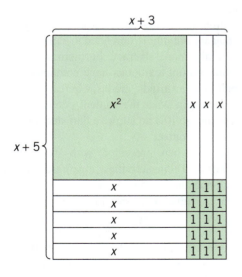

In high school algebra, many of us memorized this procedure for multiplying polynomials when the teacher asked us to use the FOIL method—*F*irst (x by x), *O*utside (x by 3), *I*nside (5 by x), and *L*ast (5 by 3)—without having any idea why the FOIL method required these four particular multiplications. By using the algebra tiles, students are able to make a connection not only to area but also to previous learning about multiplying two-digit numbers. There is no need to memorize an abstract procedure such as FOIL here because the process is NOT a new one. Instead the algebra is a logical extension and abstraction of something that children already know from the study of arithmetic multiplication.

Children can also explore number puzzles by using algebra tiles. Suppose that a teacher asks the class the following:

> Think of a number. Add 5 to that number. Double the result. Subtract 4 from this answer. Divide by 2. Subtract the number that you started with.
>
> I can read your mind—your final number is 3!

Actually, for this set of directions the final number will always be 3, and students should quickly realize this when they compare different starting numbers. But why? What is going on here? By using algebra tiles and then symbol manipulation, students can model the problem-solving process. The sequence of six steps with algebra tiles shown parallels the steps in the puzzle and illustrates why the result must be 3.

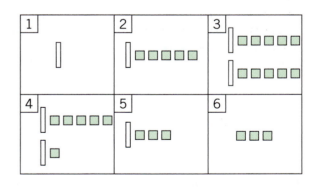

One benefit of using Algebra Tiles is to develop a sequence of structured tasks that helps the user explore and understand the concepts involved in adding, subtracting, multiplying, and dividing algebraic expressions. The Algebra Tiles virtual manipulative on the CD that accompanies this text can be used as a means of exploring the results of combining expressions and balancing equations. Use the VM to model $(x + 3)(x + 4)$ and describe the result in terms of the pieces. What happens when the expression is changed to $(x + 3)(x - 4)$? What about $(x - 3)(x - 4)$?

VM10.2

Children should realize that the puzzle can be analyzed through the use of a concrete model, and they can be challenged to design their own puzzle that will always result in a particular answer.

By dealing with greater numbers that don't lend themselves to the use of algebra tiles, students can be led to the use of symbols and pencil-and-paper algebra skills to explore them. Consider this problem:

> Write down the number of the month in which you were born. Multiply that number by 10. Add 20 to the result. Multiply this answer by 10. Add 165. Now, add your age to the result. Subtract 365. The result should be a number that contains the number of the month of your birth, followed by your age.

This is another example of a procedure that always works. Use your knowledge of algebra to determine why.

Upper-grade children should have experiences interpreting a variety of functions displayed as graphs. Real-life phenomena are often recorded as data points and graphed, and the skill of analyzing the graphical data is important to the development of algebraic thinking. Consider the graph:

In this graph, the trip of a person driving a car from his or her driveway to the grocery store is represented. The *x*-values represent the total amount of time, and the *y*-values display the distance from home.

Students should be asked to interpret the graph—that is, to explain what is going on throughout the trip. For example, they should be able to determine that horizontal line segments in the graph represent time spent without moving, perhaps at a traffic light or stopped on a congested street. They should also be able to determine that steeper line segments mean that the car traveled a given distance in less time; therefore, the car was moving faster. This discussion can lead to an informal understanding of the slope of a line

representing a rate of change. A connection can also be made to literature: Children can be asked to write a story about the trip to the grocery store that the graph represents.

A common misconception the children may have when they interpret graphs such as those discussed in the previous paragraph is that the car is "driving up hill," rather than thinking in terms of distance traveled in a given amount of time. It is a worthwhile exercise for children to begin with a graph and give examples of the coordinates of points on the graph. Often, mathematics textbooks overemphasize the conversion of sets of points into graphs and ignore the reverse process—that is, students are often given a set of points to put on a graph but are seldom given a graph and asked to interpret what it means. A student's elementary and middle school background should include a balance of both.

Closure

When asked to recall experiences with algebra, most people think back to a first-year algebra course, ordinarily studied in the first year of high school. The content of that course generally included equation solving; some graphing; and a great deal of manipulation of symbols, including variables. For many, algebra content was relegated to one or two high school courses, which often took students by surprise as they explored topics that are seemingly unrelated to elementary school and certainly more abstract. Furthermore, traditional elementary school textbooks have contained little new information in the middle grades, whereas algebra books typically contain what the student perceives to be all new material, so it is no surprise that students are often put off by the course.

However, when presented with developmentally appropriate learning activities, algebraic thinking can be developed throughout the K–8 grade range. Early experiences with algebra should include logical, "if . . . then" discussions, as well as verbalizing and extending patterns and using "more than" and "less than" to compare collections. As children explore both visual and numerical patterns, they should learn to put data into a table, graph it on a coordinate grid, and, eventually, write an equation that relates the numbers in the table. The processes of equation solving and working with variables needs to be firmly rooted in concrete activities, gradually working students toward symbolic processes typically associated with more traditional algebra courses.

In the contemporary view of the teaching and learning of mathematics, we acknowledge that algebra is a critical content strand that should be developed for all students across all grade levels. National reports have pointed out that the vast majority of jobs available today require proficiency in algebra. Consequently, the NCTM initially established standards for algebra in 1989, since reaffirmed and expanded in its *Principles and Standards for School Mathematics* (2000),[3] that emphasize the development of algebraic thinking throughout the elementary school years. NCTM has also released a series of resource books entitled the *Navigations* series that provides specific teaching ideas for developing algebra in grades preK to 2, 3 to 5, 6 to 8, and 9 to 12 (see www.nctm.org for details). Just as a topic such as number sense or geometry constitutes a part of the mathematical content at each grade level, algebra should also be explored each year. By the time a student has completed the upper elementary and middle grades, the foundation should be firmly established for a more formal study of algebra from a more symbolic standpoint.

The general consensus of the participants at a conference on Algebra for the Twenty-first Century conducted by the NCTM was that with the advance of technology and our increased understanding of how children learn, algebra cannot continue to be taught as a separate high school course, as has been the case for decades. The conference identified the following eight "big ideas" of algebra that need to be developed throughout a student's K–12 experience:

- Representation of Patterns—relationships, situations, number sequences with table/graph/matrices and the ability to explore interrelationships between representations

- Language—appreciation of symbols; precision of symbolic representations; modeling

- Sense of Symbol Use—modeling contextual cases; different meanings/uses of variables as a name, as changing quantity, as a placeholder; equivalence of expressions; formulas; write expression, sentences for various situations

[3]National Council of Teachers of Mathematics. (2000). *Principles and standards for school mathematics*. Reston, VA: Author.

(linear, quadratic, inverse, exponential, periodic)

- Graphing—exploration of/comparison of situations that produce linear, quadratic, inverse, exponential, periodic patterns/shapes; structure of number system; connection between graph and solution

- Applications of Patterns—critically analyze data, sequences, shapes; investigate graphically and symbolically

- Expressions and Equations—solving equations and inequalities; finding and recognizing equivalent functions

- Structure of Algebra—appreciation of the structure; parallelism with structure of number systems (properties)

- Proof and Logic—derivations; connections with geometry (NCTM, 1992, pp. 63–64)

Proficiency with using these big ideas demands that students have experiences with problems requiring algebraic thinking at all grade levels, preK–12. We believe that algebra is best learned through active teaching methods that involve students developing their own methods and procedures to solve problems, rather than being told how to use abstract procedures to solve equations and simplify expressions. The product of this type of active teaching and learning is not only the eventual mastery of procedures to manipulate variables, but also the development of an algebraic way of thinking about mathematics.

We use algebraic thinking any time we look at a table, a graph, or an equation and acknowledge a trend and use it to predict future events. This observation alone suggests that we need to establish a goal that every student will develop algebraic thinking. Algebra should not and cannot continue to exist as a stand-alone course for high school students. By using developmentally appropriate means, students can establish their ability to work with patterns, variables, exponents, graphing, and functions throughout their elementary school experience. Algebra is for all students, not just those enrolled in high school mathematics courses.

PRACTICE EXERCISES FOR TEACHERS

These exercises are designed for the reader of this book, not for the children the reader may teach. Although some of these examples are suitable for use in an elementary or middle school classroom, they should not necessarily be given to children in the form presented here. Ideas appropriate for classroom activities on the concepts and ideas discussed in this chapter can be found in a later section of this chapter and on the CD that accompanies this text.

1. Solve each of the following equations for x.

a) $2x - 3 = 5x + 9$

b) $4(x + 2) = -6 + 2x$

c) $1 - 5x = -14$

d) $3x + 7 - 2x + 1 = 7 - x$

e) $8 - 2(x + 5) = 3(2x - 4) + 12$

2. Find a function rule for each of the following tables and determine whether the function is linear or nonlinear.

a) x	y	b) x	y	c) x	y
3	8	2	5	0	1
5	10	4	9	2	5
6	11	7	15	4	17

VM 10.2

3. Draw a picture of algebra tiles arranged to represent each of the following equations.

a) $2x + 3 = 7$

b) $5x + 6 = 1 + 3x$

c) $3(x + 3) = x + 4$

d) $2 + 4(2x + 1) = 6$

e) $x^2 + 4x + 1 = 2x + 3$

4. In this chapter, the following puzzle was posed: "Write down the number of the month in which you were born. Multiply that number by 10. Add 20 to the result. Multiply this answer by 10. Add 165. Now, add your age to the result. Subtract 365. The result should be a number that contains the number of the month of your birth, followed by your age." Use algebra symbols to show why this "trick" always works. Explain what is happening.

VM 10.2

5. Use drawings of algebra tiles to visualize and to simplify each of the following products.

a) $(x + 3)(x + 4)$

b) $(x + 1)(x + 5)$

c) $(2x + 5)(x + 2)$

d) $(x + 1)^2$

e) $(3x + 1)(2x + 2)$

6. A tennis tournament involves 20 participants in a round-robin playoff. In other words, each participant must play the other 19 competitors exactly once.

a) How many games must be played to complete the tournament?

b) Use the strategy of solving the simpler problem to construct a table, find a pattern, and extend the pattern to find the total number of games that need to be played.

c) Write an equation that relates the number of games played to the number of competitors.

d) Which variable is independent and which variable is dependent in this problem?

7. Suppose that you invest some money in the bank and leave it there over a period of many years, allowing the interest to compound each year (i.e., both the principal and the interest earn interest). Find the amount of money in the bank for each of the following cases.

a) $1000 invested at 7% for 40 years

b) $10,000 invested at 8% for 30 years

c) $7500 invested at 6.5% for 25 years

d) $1 invested at 5% for 200 years

e) $500 invested at 10% for 18 years

8. The following graph represents the height that a projectile launched from a pad is above the ground.

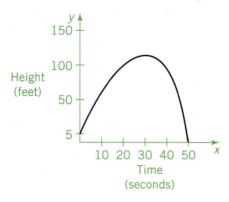

a) What is the maximum height reached by the projectile?

b) Why is the starting point at (0, 5), rather than (0, 0)?

c) How many seconds is the projectile in the air?

d) How high is the projectile after 45 seconds?

e) Write three more questions that could be asked about this graph.

9. Suppose that a new video store opens in your neighborhood. You have a choice between two plans for rental of DVDs, as follows:

Plan A: You pay an annual membership fee of $20, and each video rental costs $1.50.
Plan B: There is no annual fee, but the cost of each video rental is $2.75.

Compare the two plans. Which plan would you choose and why? How did you use algebraic thinking to answer the questions?

10. Explain a rule describing each of the following sequences of numbers.

a) 1, 3, 5, 7, 9, . . .

b) 1, 4, 9, 16, 25, . . .

c) 5, 10, 8, 13, 11, 16, 14, . . .

d) 1, 2, 3, 5, 7, 11, 13, . . .

e) 2, 7, 17, 37, 77, . . .

11. Suppose that T stands for the price of a cassette tape, and D stands for the cost of a compact disc. Write an equation relating these variables for each of the following situations.

a) A CD costs $4 more than a cassette tape.

b) A cassette tape costs $3.50 less than a CD.

c) On sale, the cost of a cassette tape is half the cost of a CD.

d) Two CDs cost $1 more than three cassette tapes.

e) Four cassette tapes and a CD cost $43 altogether.

TEACHING COMPETENCIES AND SELF-ASSESSMENT TASKS

1. Discuss the difference between the traditional view of "algebra as a one-year, high school course" and the more modern view of "algebraic thinking as an important strand of elementary school mathematics."

2. List the five content strands often associated with the study of algebra and describe an activity that would help children develop their knowledge of each strand at the lower-elementary level, the upper-elementary level, and the middle school level.

3. To what degree can equation solving be explored in the lower primary grades? Explain how you might do this.

4. When a piece of paper is folded in half, it is now two layers thick, and when folded a second time, the piece becomes four layers thick. Using a piece of paper, determine how many times it can be folded until it becomes impossible to fold it in half again. Then represent this problem as a function in three forms: a table, a graph, and an equation relating the number of folds to the number of layers. Compare the actual results with the theoretical results. Can you fold a piece of paper in half 10 times? If you could, how many layers thick would it be?

5. Examine the NCTM *Principles and Standards for School Mathematics* and/or one of the *Navigations* books on algebra. What role does pattern recognition and description play in the development of algebraic thought?

6. Locate a middle school mathematics textbook and find a chapter that deals with solving equations. Discuss the degree to which concrete methods are emphasized to assist students in learning what it means to solve an equation.

7. Explain how two-colored algebra tiles can be used to solve an equation such as

$$3(x - 4) + 5 = 8 - 2x$$

8. When children use manipulatives extensively to explore algebraic thinking, as described in this chapter, assessment in the traditional paper-and-pencil sense becomes less relevant. Explain how you might assess your middle school students' understanding of multiplying polynomials as they work with algebra tiles.

9. Research the literature to explore how children develop a sense of the use of variables. Then describe the types of experiences that children need in elementary school to prepare them to work with variable expressions with confidence.

10. Identify several real-life situations in which you use algebraic thinking. Which content strands within the area of algebra seem to be used the most in these situations?

11. Choose another content strand, such as measurement or probability. Describe how you might pose a problem or series of problems involving measurement or probability that will develop algebraic thinking in your students as they explore the problem.

12. Locate several elementary mathematics textbooks. You are likely to see entire chapters devoted to geometry or fractions but not to algebra. Page through these books and find examples—if there are any—of algebraic thinking being promoted in other contexts.

SAMPLE INSTRUCTIONAL AND ASSESSMENT ACTIVITIES

These activities and more are available on the CD that accompanies this text

VM 10.1

1. The study of functions is rooted in an understanding that changes in one variable bring about changes in another variable. Have children generate a list of real-life situations in which changes in one event bring about changes in another. For example, they might say that "The number of hours of sleep I get at night depends on what time I go to bed" or that "The number of times I get to go down the slide on the playground depends on how many children are in line to ride it."

VM 10.3

2. Present the following scenario to a class:

We are going to an ice cream store, and each person is going to buy a cone with two scoops of ice cream. We need to decide how many cones and how many scoops of ice cream will be purchased. Make a table, as shown:

No. of Children	No. of Cones	No. of Scoops
1	1	2
2	2	4
3	3	6

Ask the students to describe any patterns that they see in the table. Allow them to predict how many cones and ice cream scoops will be needed for the entire class.

VM 10.1

3. Construct an addition or subtraction function machine for use with the whole class or small groups of children seated at a learning station. To build the machine, you will need an empty half-gallon milk carton and posterboard. In the front of the milk carton, cut two slots and insert a curved, rectangular piece of posterboard on the inside of the carton that connects the two slots.

Finally, construct some cards that fit in the slots that have an input value on one side and an output value, upside down, on the other side (e.g., 2 with 3, 4 with 5, 5 with 6). Then, when a card is inserted in the slot on the top of the carton, it should slide through the machine and come out displaying the output answer on the reverse side at the bottom of the carton. The student is to decide what the machine is doing to the input value to produce the output. Encourage children to express their answers as, for example, "The function adds 1 to the input," "The output is one more than the input," and so forth.

4. Distribute sets of pattern blocks to tables of children. Ask each child to build a kite by placing a yellow hexagon and two green triangles together as shown:

The tan rhombuses represent bows on the tail of the kite. Children should generate a table of values that relates the number of bows on the tail to the total number of pattern blocks required to build the picture.

Number of Bows	Total Number of Blocks
0	3
1	4
2	5

Through analyzing the table, children should be able to address questions such as

a) What patterns do you see?

b) How many blocks will it take to build a kite that has 16 bows on its tail?

c) If a picture required 40 blocks, how many bows would the kite have in its tail?

d) Have the variable *t* represent the number of bows on the tail. Write an expression that generalizes the number of blocks required to build the picture.

VM 10.1

5. Have one child raise his or her hand and ask the rest of the children how many fingers they see. Then have a second child raise his or her hand and ask how many fingers are being held up altogether. Continue this process using several children. Then generate a table of values and a graph of the data. Finally challenge children to write a variable expression in which the number of hands is represented by *h* and to come up with a formula for determining the number of fingers (e.g., $f = 5h$).

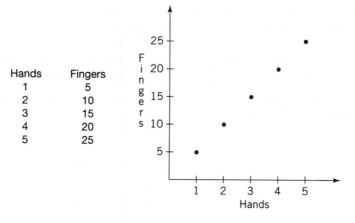

Hands	Fingers
1	5
2	10
3	15
4	20
5	25

6. Challenge children to locate a calculator that evaluates the expression below as "46" and a different calculator that evaluates the same sequence as "31." Have children predict exactly what another calculator that you provide will display as they press each button in the sequence:

$$\boxed{3}\ \boxed{+}\ \boxed{5}\ \boxed{\times}\ \boxed{6}\ \boxed{-}\ \boxed{2}\ \boxed{=}$$

Discuss the different responses and which response should be considered as the correct one according to the rules of order of operations.

7. Give each student a set of cubes, such as Unifix cubes. Then challenge the children to solve the following number puzzles by using these cubes. They should be required to explain their reasoning and to demonstrate their problem-solving process for the class.

a) I'm thinking of a number that is 5 more than 31.

b) My number, divided by 6, is 7.

c) If you double my number and add three, you get 15.

d) Three less than my number is 18.

e) If you take away 5 from half of my number, you get 1.

f) If you take my number away from 14, you get 6.

8. Algebraic thinking can be connected with probability explorations since there is often a great deal of patterning involved with finding permutations and combinations. Suppose that you were going to toss one coin. In this case, there are 2 possible outcomes—the coin could either come up heads or tails. If you toss two coins, there are 4 possible outcomes—HH, HT, TH, or TT.

a) Have students list and count all of the possible outcomes for tossing 1, 2, 3, 4, and 5 coins.

Coins Tossed	Outcomes
1	2 (H, T)
2	4 (HH,HT, TH, TT)
3	? (?)

b) Predict the number of possible outcomes when 10 coins are tossed.

c) Find the probability of tossing exactly one head when 1, 2, 3, 4, or 5 coins are tossed.

Coins Tossed	Outcomes	Probability of 1 Head
1	2	$\frac{1}{2}$ (H)
2	4	$\frac{2}{4}$ (HT or TH)
3	8	$\frac{3}{8}$ (HTT, THT, or TTH)

9. Using a scale balance, have students weigh a paper cup filled with cereal. Then have them place a second cup filled with the same type of cereal on the pan and find the total weight of the two cups. Continue this process with up to five cups of cereal and record the data in a table:

Cups of Cereal A	Total Weight
?	?

Then, repeat the process with a second brand of cereal to create a new table:

Cups of Cereal B	Total Weight
?	?

Finally, students should use a single piece of graph paper to graph the data from both tables on the same set of axes. Ask them to describe what they see. What does the steepness or the slope of the line tell us about the cereal? Which type of cereal would have a steeper graph—Grape Nuts or Cheerios? Conduct the experiment to verify your conjecture.

10. Suppose that you had an important message that you wanted every student in your school to know. Tell the message to two students on the first day and ask each of them to tell two more students the next day. Continue this process until the whole school knows the message. A table can be generated to think about what happens:

Day No.	New Students Told	Total Students Told
1	2	2
2	4	6
3	?	?
n	?	?

a) How many days would it take for the message to get around to everyone in a school of 250 students?

b) How many days would it take for the message to get around to everyone in a school of 800 students?

c) Write a variable expression that would allow you to determine the numbers of new students told and total students told if you know only the day number.

11. Present the following problem to your students:
At a local county fair, you have two choices when you go through the entrance gate. You can either pay $5 at the door and then pay $1.75 for each ride, or you can pay $17 at the door and ride all day for "free."

a) Determine which plan you would choose and defend your solution with mathematics.

b) Draw a graph in which the *x*-values represent the number of rides, and the *y*-values stand for the amount of money spent. Where do these lines intersect (cross) each other, and what does this tell you?

NOTE: It is important to give students this problem and little, if any, coaching at first. Let them deal with it in their own ways, and you may discover that some students choose to use guess and check, while others prepare an organized table, and still others may decide to draw a graph to display the options. One of the key concepts in algebra is to develop multiple representations of the same problem—sometimes an equation is better, while other times a graph is more helpful. Students need to become comfortable with working a problem using several different models.

11

Rational Numbers Expressed as Fractions: Concepts

TEACHING COMPETENCIES

Upon completing this chapter, you will be able to:

- Use at least three models to develop an understanding of nonnegative rational numbers expressed as fractions.
- Describe alternative sequences to teaching fraction concepts.
- Identify prerequisite knowledge, skills, and understandings to be achieved before the formal study of operations on rational numbers expressed as fractions.
- Demonstrate the concept of fraction in a meaningful way for elementary and middle school students.
- Develop student-centered lessons that focus on understanding various fraction concepts and terminology.

VIRTUAL MANIPULATIVES

Upon completing this chapter, you will be able to use virtual manipulatives on the accompanying CD to:

- Identify fractions using *Naming Fractions*. **(VM 11.1)**
- Develop an understanding of fractional numbers by working with groups of objects using *Fractional Portions of Sets*. **(VM 11.2)**
- Examine another model to help understand fractions using *Modeling Fractions on a Number Line*. **(VM 11.3)**
- Explore circular and rectangular regions using *Parts of a Whole*. **(VM 11.4)**
- Build the foundation of the concept of *Equivalent Fractions*. **(VM 11.5)**
- Model fractional numbers by shading appropriate regions using *Visualizing Fractions*. **(VM 11.6)**

Numbered CD icons throughout the chapter refer to the virtual manipulatives in this list.

Three children were bragging about how much pizza they had eaten at a friend's party. They each thought that they had eaten more pizza than anybody else and were determined to prove it any way they could. Jeff stated that he had eaten 4 pieces and that he knew that was more pieces than anyone else had eaten—so he should be the winner! Marge ate only 3 pieces of an 8-piece pizza, but they were bigger pieces than Jeff's—so she should be the winner! Ryan ate $\frac{1}{2}$ of a small pizza, also only 3 pieces, but $\frac{1}{2}$ of a pizza is more than $\frac{3}{8}$ of a pizza—so he should be the winner! What do *you* think? Who is the "winner"? Perhaps more important, what do you think the children might think in this situation? And why?

This story illustrates how fractional parts can be misinterpreted and how this might lead to confusion. Children often focus attention on parts to the exclusion of the whole. Students must realize that a fraction means little without reference to a whole unit associated with that fraction. For example, it may come as a surprise that a half does not always equal a half, especially if the first refers to half of a dollar and the second refers to half of a dime. Unless you have a reference to what the whole is, it is difficult, at best, to compare two or more fractions. A sound foundational understanding of important, but often overlooked, fraction concepts will provide students with a base for meaningful communication about fractions in their world.

A Fraction of the History of Fractional Numbers

In reviewing the early history of number development, we find that the growth and extension of number ideas are directly related to the increasing complexity of civilization. In much the same way that limited tallying or matching became insufficient, so eventually did whole numbers alone not satisfy human needs. It became necessary to describe parts of whole things or parts of groups of things. Fractions are often, but not exclusively, used to describe parts of a "broken" whole. The word *fraction* is derived from the Latin *frangere*, which means "to break."

Early applications of fraction concepts were, by our standards, quite challenging. Ancient Egyptians, with a few exceptions, employed only unit fractions—fractions whose numerators are one and whose denominators vary (but were never zero). To express a given nonunit fraction, the Egyptians added together the required unit fractions. For example, the fraction that was equivalent to $\frac{5}{8}$ was expressed as $\frac{1}{2} + \frac{1}{8}$, whereas $\frac{5}{6}$ would be expressed as $\frac{1}{2} + \frac{1}{3}$ and $\frac{7}{12}$ would be written as $\frac{1}{4} + \frac{1}{3}$. The difficulties involved in such a notational system are

obvious, especially when you consider that the ancient Egyptians were also hampered by cumbersome numerals (see Chapter 6). The symbol used for a fractional number was the *hieroglyph* $\bigcirc$, which was placed over a numeral that indicated the number of parts into which the whole was divided:

$$\overset{\bigcirc}{|\,|\,|\,|} = \tfrac{1}{4} \qquad \overset{\bigcirc}{\cap\cap|} = \tfrac{1}{21} \qquad \overset{\bigcirc}{?} = \tfrac{1}{100}$$

The Babylonian numeration system was vastly superior to that used by the Egyptians, which may help account, in part, for many Babylonian advances in astronomy and construction. Theirs was a sexagesimal system (i.e., it was based, like their system of whole numbers, on groupings of 60). The many possible factors of 60 (2, 3, 4, 5, 6, 10, 12, 15, 20, 30, and 60) greatly facilitated work with fractions. The denominator in a Babylonian fraction was a factor or multiple of 60, while the numerator, in contrast to the Egyptian system, was allowed to vary. As was the case for Egyptian fraction notation, the symbols used by the Babylonians for fractional numbers were extremely complicated.

In Roman society and culture, fractions were used largely in commerce. The Romans used denominators that were based on 12 and multiples of 12, and names were given to twelfths and twenty-fourths of whole things, with the parts of the whole becoming "nonfractional subunits." By using these subunits, they avoided the use of fractions in computation, much the same as we do today by choosing to use "one ounce" rather than using "one-sixteenth of a pound."

The development of our familiar representation of fractional numbers comes from Hindu mathematicians, who began the convention of writing one numeral over another. The incorporation of the **fraction bar** separating the numerator from the denominator was an Arabic device that was not generally used in the Western world until the late Middle Ages.

Today, the place of rational numbers expressed as fractions (and as decimals) and the rationale for exploring them in the curriculum are changing. Because of the increasing role of technology in our society (calculators and computers almost exclusively use decimal notation), and other factors such as an increased use of the decimal-based metric system for measurement, some elementary and middle school mathematics programs are teaching rational numbers expressed as decimals BEFORE teaching rational numbers expressed as fractions. When the teaching strategy is based on the concrete level and models, the sequences "fraction then decimal" or "decimal then fraction" can be easily interchanged. We believe that Chapters 10 to 13 in this text can be easily interchanged with only a few minor alterations.

Rational Numbers—
A Definition and Description

Rational numbers are commonly written in two different forms—as fractions or as decimals. This chapter deals with rational numbers expressed as fractions.

> A rational number is any number that may be written in the form of $\frac{b}{a}$, where a is any integer and b is any nonzero integer.

Thus, three-fourths is a **rational number**. When this number is written in fraction form, we call it a **fractional number**, and the symbol used to represent the fractional number, $\frac{3}{4}$, is called a **fraction**. Despite a perception that mathematics definitions never vary, some texts do not make a distinction between fractional numbers (positive rationals) and rational numbers (positive and negative rationals). It is always paramount that the teacher (and the student) be familiar with the definitions in the curricular materials they are using.

Parents divide candy bars or apples in half for children and introduce them to ideas underlying the concept of fractions at a very early age. Children may enter school with the mistaken notion that one-half means "one of two pieces." Sometimes, teachers use food as a device to illustrate this notion. However, we do not usually cut food items exactly in half: We tend to cut them in two similar, but not identical, pieces, and children always take the larger piece. When children say they will take the larger piece, they may be demonstrating a mistaken understanding of the notion of one-half—or, perhaps, they understand the concept well and recognize that the cutting *really* didn't produce one-half. If it did, they wouldn't care which piece they received. The task then becomes helping students develop a more refined meaning and a sound understanding of the appropriate use of rational numbers and fractions.

Fractions can be thought of as more than "part of a whole object." Fractions can also be viewed as an indicated division. For example, the fraction $\frac{3}{4}$ can be thought of as 3 divided by 4. However, indicated division is generally explored more abstractly and should not be introduced too early in a child's development.

Because whole numbers are a subset of rational numbers (i.e., all whole numbers are also rational numbers), students know a great deal about rational numbers *before* they begin formal study. Too often we don't take full advantage of the whole number knowledge base in designing and implementing approaches to teaching and learning fraction concepts. Sadly it is not too uncommon to hear the study of fraction concepts prefaced by an announcement that "we're going to do something unlike what we've done with whole numbers." Rather than giving students the impression that we're learning something "new," we should help the students realize that we're going to be *extending something we already*

RESEARCH SNAPSHOT

What knowledge about fractions do elementary school students bring to the classroom?

What do we know about the achievement of elementary school students whose instruction is based on different interpretations of understanding rational numbers?

In Susan Lamon's (2007) longitudinal study, five cohorts of students in two urban schools from different parts of the country built their understanding of rational numbers from different subconstructs of rational numbers. For four years, in grades 3 through 6, each cohort focused on a different structure: part/whole, measure, quotient, operator, and ratio.

On most days, the mathematical activity consisted of problem solving in groups, sharing, and then individually writing and revising solutions. Students were encouraged to express their thinking and no rules or operations were taught.

After four years, all five cohorts of students had developed deeper understanding of rational numbers than had the students in the control group. In computation, achievement was also greater in all five study groups.

Lamon, S. J. (2007). Rational numbers and proportional reasoning: Toward a theoretical framework for research. In F. K. Lester (Ed.), *Second handbook of research on mathematics teaching and learning: A project of the National Council of Teachers of Mathematics* (pp. 629–667.) Charlotte, NC: Information Age Publishing.   For additional research briefs, "ERIC Digests" lets you search more than 2000 short syntheses of research on a range of education topics. The syntheses were produced by the Educational Resources Information Center (ERIC). Check http://www.ericfacility.net/ericdigests/index/.

know. Relations between whole numbers and fractions should be explored, not hidden.

Fraction Models

There are basically three models that can be used to develop students' understanding of fractions: *regions, sets*, and *number lines*. Either circular and/or rectangular regions are customarily used in modeling the concept of fractions. For example:

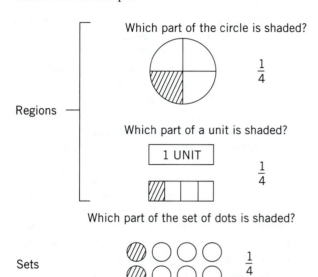

Which part of the circle is shaded?

Regions

Which part of a unit is shaded?

Which part of the set of dots is shaded?

Sets

Which part of the number line is marked?

Number line

Materials such as Cuisenaire rods, base ten blocks, pattern blocks, and fraction bars or circles are excellent tools for assisting students in understanding fundamental fraction concepts. Cuisenaire rods may be used either with or without a referencing number line that defines the unit length and shows partitions of the unit into equal pieces. Carefully examine teachers' manuals for each set of materials; these manuals give specific directions and describe effective activities for using these manipulative materials to develop fraction concepts. You will also find ideas and activities for their use in professional journals such as *Teaching Children Mathematics* and in the activities found throughout this text and on the CD that accompanies this text.

Let's carefully examine each of the three common models—regions, sets or groups of objects, and number lines—as we discuss fundamental fraction concepts.

The Regions Model for Fractional Numbers

The teacher should present the concept of fractions by having children manipulate physical models showing a whole and fractions of that whole. Most commonly, either rectangular regions or circular regions (or both) are used as physical models. Let's examine rectangular regions first. Usually we start with a *basic unit* or *unit region*, such as the region pictured, often cut from some manipulative material such as posterboard or felt that has been divided into equal parts.

BASIC UNIT OR BASIC REGION

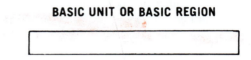

Equal parts are parts of a whole that have the same area, although not necessarily the same shape. For early examples in particular, the parts are not only the same area but also congruent. **Congruent parts** are parts that have the same area and shape. For example, consider this rectangular region:

BASIC UNIT OR UNIT REGION

If we wish to identify the shaded part of the basic unit with a fractional number, that number is one-half, which can be written $\frac{1}{2}$. In this specific case, the 2 denotes the number of equal (congruent) pieces into which the basic unit is divided. The 1 denotes how many of these two equal (congruent) pieces we are concerned with at the moment to represent this fraction.

For practice, children can be asked to recognize equal parts of regions and name the parts, or they can color appropriate physical models, In these physical models, children can, by counting, identify the part of each region that is shaded, name the appropriate fractional number, and write the corresponding fraction.

VM 11.1

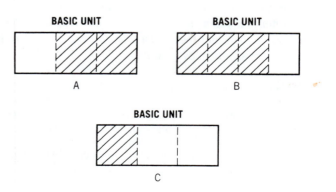

In A, two of three equal parts are shaded; the corresponding fraction is $\frac{2}{3}$. In B, three out of four equal parts are shaded; this can be represented by the fraction $\frac{3}{4}$. In C, one part out of three equal parts is shaded; the appropriate fraction is $\frac{1}{3}$.

As an extension of this activity, children can be asked to shade or color given parts of regions—for example, shade one-sixth of the following circular region:

ANSWER

Or, shade one-half of the following region:

We should emphasize that the answer to this shading task can be done in several ways; three possible ways are indicated here.

VM 11.6
These examples stress the fact that fractions can be used to indicate parts of a whole. In each of the drawings, two out of four congruent regions have been shaded. Thus we can write the fraction $\frac{2}{4}$. The 4 is the **denominator** of the fraction; in this case, it shows us into how many equal parts the whole has been separated. The name *fourth* is assigned to each of the four equal pieces. The word *denominator* comes to us from the Latin word *nomen*, which means "to name." Thus, the denominator can function as the "namer" of the number of congruent parts into which a unit has been separated.

In the fraction $\frac{2}{4}$, the 2 is the **numerator**. In the examples shown, the numerator tells us how many of these equal pieces we are considering. In this case, we have considered two of the pieces, each called *fourths*. The *numerator* of the fraction is the number that expresses how many of the equal pieces we are considering out of the total number of equal pieces. In the fraction $\frac{2}{4}$, the 2 and the 4 are called the *terms* of the fraction.

Now let's examine fractions using circular regions. The following illustration represents a unit:

Children should use a template to cut circular regions from a thicker piece of paper or thin posterboard and then subdivide these circular units into fractions—$\frac{1}{2}$, $\frac{1}{4}$, and $\frac{1}{8}$—by folding and then cutting. Since it is difficult to fold a circular region into thirds, you may want to provide a template for thirds and any other reasonable fractional parts you want the children to make. Give each child an envelope in which to place the fractions of the circular regions.

VM 11.4

At the early stages of concept development, it might be beneficial to color-code these fraction pieces for ease of sorting. It should be noted, however, that color-coding can also be a disadvantage, since it may lessen attention to the attributes of fractions that really matter—one-half isn't one-half because it's green! That is, the two $\frac{1}{2}$ pieces match, not because they are the same color, but rather because they are the same size.

Once the children have made these fraction kits, discuss how the fractional parts of the unit relate to the whole. The two equal pieces forming the unit (or whole) are called *halves*. If we consider one of the pieces, then we would call that piece *one-half*, written in fraction form as $\frac{1}{2}$. The numerator 1 tells us how many pieces we are considering, and the denominator 2 tells us the name of the pieces.

Consider a circular region separated into four equivalent pieces.

VM 11.5 **Although it is too early in the development** of fraction concepts to discuss equivalent fractions abstractly, it is not too early to begin the foundation of the concept, and an important foundation is the notion of comparing the two fractions that have a common unit region. Although we discuss equivalent fractions later in the book, this VM provides a preliminary look at them. Why might equivalent fractions be important when we encounter addition and subtraction of fractions? Envision a way in which the division of fractions might make use of equivalent fractions.

UNIT REGION

Because this unit is separated into four equal pieces, we name each piece *one-fourth*. The one piece that is shaded would be represented by the fraction $\frac{1}{4}$ because we are considering one of the four pieces. If two are shaded, we write $\frac{2}{4}$ because two of the pieces we call fourths are shaded.

Notice that the shaded region is the same size as one-half of the unit. That is, $\frac{2}{4}$ is the same size as $\frac{1}{2}$.

It is important to note that there may be advantages to using circular regions either early in the child's development of the fundamental concepts of fractions or when difficulties or misunderstandings seem to arise. When a fractional part of a circular region is displayed, the child can more readily picture or visualize a whole circular region and make a mental comparison. If a fractional part of a rectangular region is used, then there is no ready mental image of the whole for the child to reference. The child will need to refer to an actual model of the whole before comprehending. To ensure your own understanding of this observation, trace the figures, and show the circular fraction piece to a friend and ask your friend to state a fraction name for that piece. Then show the rectangular piece and ask the same question.

Most will say "one-fourth" for the circular piece. For the rectangular fraction piece, most will say that they can't name it yet—that they need to know how big the original unit is before they can give an answer. Note that they assumed that the first piece was part of a circle even though it may actually have been part of a semicircle or some other unit. If it actually represented part of a semicircle, then it would represent one-half, not one-fourth. Until we know for certain what the unit or whole is, we run the risk of falling victim to assumption.

Once children have had many experiences using both rectangular and circular regions to help them understand fractions, then introduce fractional parts of other shapes. For example, $\frac{1}{2}$ of this region is shaded:

and $\frac{3}{4}$ of this region is shaded:

Emphasize that the *shape of a region* does not influence the fraction—the number of equal pieces into which that region is divided does.

The Groups of Objects Model for Fractional Numbers

Children should also have an opportunity to develop an understanding of fractional numbers by also working with groups of objects, the second model we will use to give meaning to fraction concepts. To establish a complete experience and firm understanding of fundamental fraction concepts, children must actually manipulate materials. When these manipulatives are groups of objects, fractions can be used to name parts of the groups. **VM 11.2**

Consider the following group of six objects:

By separating the group into two equal subgroups and considering one of those subgroups, we can show one-half of the original group. A loop can be drawn around one-half of the group, or one-half of the objects can be colored or shaded, to indicate the fractional number $\frac{1}{2}$.

Many other fractional numbers can be represented in the same way:

In the first picture on the left, we can separate the 12 dots into four equal subgroups by considering only columns of dots. Then by drawing a loop around one of the columns, we represent the fractional number $\frac{1}{4}$. In the middle picture, we can separate the 8 dots into four equal subgroups by considering only rows of dots. Then if we enclose one of the rows with a loop, the number $\frac{1}{4}$ is again represented. Similarly, the picture on the right illustrates $\frac{1}{3}$.

Suppose that now, however, we consider the dots individually, not as rows or columns. Again taking the preceding group of 12 dots, let's consider the dots independently of the column that was enclosed. We can do this by enclosing each of the dots of that column individually:

In this way, we illustrate the number $\frac{3}{12}$, since there are 12 dots and we are separately considering 3 of them. Notice that in both cases exactly 3 dots out of the 12 are under consideration, but that in one case we are illustrating the number $\frac{1}{4}$ (one of four equal parts), while in the other we are illustrating $\frac{3}{12}$ (three of twelve equal

parts). Evidently, $\frac{1}{4}$ and $\frac{3}{12}$ are equivalent fractions. Why? Compare these two figures:

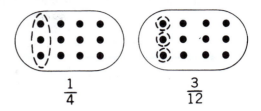

In a similar fashion, we can demonstrate that $\frac{1}{4} = \frac{2}{8}$ and that $\frac{1}{3} = \frac{3}{9}$.

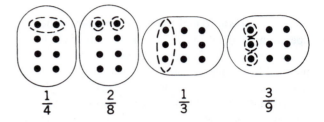

It is very important to emphasize that the unit here is the entire group by drawing a loop around it. Otherwise, children may focus their attention on each of the individual elements of the group rather than the entire group itself. Without this attention, a student might easily believe that $\frac{4}{8}$ is "bigger" than $\frac{3}{6}$ instead of correctly interpreting that $\frac{4}{8}$ of one unit may be more than $\frac{3}{6}$ of a *different* unit.

Children should make a number of representations to help them identify two distinct concepts:

1. A fraction may represent part of a whole.

2. A fraction may represent part of a group.

The Number Line Model for Fractional Numbers

Now let's reiterate that a fraction is a number that can be written in the form $\frac{a}{b}$ in which a and b are integers, and b is not zero. Of course, fractions can also be written as decimals—for example, .1 and $\frac{1}{10}$ represent the same number—one-tenth.

Along with regions and set models, a third model may be used to help us understand fractions: the number line. We can ask, "How do fractions fit in with the numbers we have already studied on the number line?" So far we have matched equally spaced points on the number line with whole numbers (the numbers 0, 1, 2, 3, . . .):

VM 11.3

But what about points that are located between the whole number points? Are there numbers to match with these points? We will find that many of these "in-between" points can be matched with fractional numbers.

When we considered the whole numbers under the operation of division, we found that division is not closed for this set. That is, when you divide one whole number by another, you don't always get a whole number as an answer. We discovered division examples in which the missing factor could not be expressed as a whole number. By way of illustration, consider $4 \div 5 = \square$. This example indicates the need for another set of numbers besides whole numbers if we are to find answers for examples such as this—there is no whole number that fits for $4 \div 5 = \square$.

We may note another indication of the need for fractional numbers as we attempt to express some of our measurements more precisely. Using a ruler in a practical application, we seldom, if ever, arrive at a measurement of an exact number of inches. A method of expressing measurements that includes parts of inches, parts of feet, parts of cups, and parts of pounds is provided by using the set of fractional numbers.

As we continue to adopt and use the metric system of measurement, there is less need for common fractions in measurement since the metric system is based on a decimal relationship. Measurements in the metric system are recorded most commonly in decimal form—for example, in tenths, hundredths, or thousandths (.1, .01, or .001). There will, however, always be a place for reference to simple fractions in measurement settings, such as $\frac{1}{2}$, $\frac{3}{4}$, $\frac{2}{3}$, and even $\frac{5}{12}$ and $\frac{3}{16}$, but the need for and advantages of considering fractions such as $\frac{3}{29}$ or $\frac{15}{37}$ have all but disappeared. If application is one test of the usefulness of fractions, then these awkward fractions can easily be replaced by those that are more commonly encountered—after all, the procedures used to compare or compute would be identical.

Before developing fractional numbers on the number line, children should be familiar with the way we illustrate basic operations with whole numbers on the number line. Draw a number line and indicate a reference point on it. Let's label that point the origin, "0," calling it zero. Now select another point, anywhere on the line

(most commonly to the right of zero), and label that point "1." Using this segment from 0 to 1 as a standard unit, mark off additional line segments equal in length to the standard unit. Each point should be matched with one of the whole numbers.

Now, let's play a game and pretend that we are at the point named 0. If we make a jump of one unit to the right, where do we land? We land at the point named 1. If we make another jump of one unit to the right, where do we land this time? We land at the point named 2. Now, starting at 2, if we take a jump of one unit to the left, where do we land? We land back at 1.

But suppose that we are now getting tired and, when we jump to the left, we do not make it all the way back to 0 but land at the point labeled "A."

How can we name the point where we have landed? Every point on the number line that we have seen so far has had a name. What do you think the name of this point should be? We have found that point A is equidistant from 0 and 1. The length of the line segment between 0 and A is the same as the length of the line segment between A and 1. The segment that we have defined as one unit for this particular number line has been divided by point A into two segments of equal length. How can we express this idea? We can express it by the notation $\frac{1}{2}$. Of the two equal segments between 0 and 1, we are one of the two segments away from 0. The notation $\frac{1}{2}$ expresses this fact. Another name for point A, therefore, is $\frac{1}{2}$.

Now suppose that we are at the point named by $\frac{1}{2}$ and jump to the point named by 1. How far are we then from the starting point 0? How many one-half units separate us from 0? Clearly, we are 2 one-half units from the starting point. This is expressed by the fraction $\frac{2}{2}$. We divide the whole into two equivalent parts and consider them both:

If we now start at 1 and jump another one-half unit to the right, where do we land? (Halfway between 1 and 2.)

How many one-half units are we away from 0? (Three.) We can express this fact by the fraction $\frac{3}{2}$, which can be interpreted to mean that if we divide each unit length into two equivalent parts, we are considering three of the resulting one-half-unit segments.

We can continue in this way, naming each whole number and each point halfway between any pair of whole numbers. The resulting collection of points names the set of halves.

What is another name for 1? Two halves, $\frac{2}{2}$, is another name for 1, because $\frac{2}{2}$ and 1 name the same point on the number line. What is another name for 2? Four halves, $\frac{4}{2}$, is another name, because $\frac{4}{2}$ and 2 name the same point.

Knowledge and Understandings Prior to Operations on Rational Numbers Expressed as Fractions

There are a number of experiences focusing on foundational skills and understandings of rational numbers expressed as fractions that must be an integral part of instruction BEFORE students are introduced to the formal study of the addition, subtraction, multiplication, and division of rational numbers expressed as fractions. A teacher who adjusts instruction to emphasize these prerequisites will provide an excellent base for expansion later. Students need to understand the meaning of fractions, model fractions in several ways, generate equivalent fractions, simplify fractions, compare fractions, and order fractions. Once students have these prerequisites in hand, the study of operations on fractions becomes a matter of applying these understandings rather than searching, often aimlessly, for the correct rule to apply when adding, subtracting, multiplying, or dividing.

To fully explore the conceptual base for fractions, some common terminology is essential for communicating ideas. At this point, it is not necessary that this terminology be either formal or definitional. You'll find that children often invent language that conveys meaning better than the words that we use as adults. For example, "bottom-nator" is certainly a more vividly descriptive term than *denominator*, although, of course, *not* preferred. If you accept this child-developed, personalized language and complement it with the more widely accepted terminology, you'll find that students will begin to adopt the appropriate words they read and hear in correct use.

A **proper fraction** is one in which the numerator is less than the denominator. Examples of proper fractions are $\frac{2}{3}$, $\frac{4}{5}$, $\frac{3}{8}$, and $\frac{24}{25}$. A fraction, such as $\frac{3}{2}$, in which the numerator is greater than or equal to the denominator, is called an **improper fraction**. Thus, $\frac{3}{2}$, $\frac{7}{5}$, $\frac{6}{6}$, and $\frac{13}{8}$ are improper fractions. Rather than risk giving children the impression that there is something "wrong" with fractions that have been labeled as "improper," some programs have initially made use of children's invented language, such as "top-heavy," to describe improper fractions, followed by the more formal term at a later date. Again, although the concept is more critical, be careful to not let the invented language get in the way of the development of correct terminology.

There are many names for any point on the number line. For the number 1, we have written the symbols 1 and $\frac{2}{2}$; for the number 2, we have written 2 and $\frac{4}{2}$. Is there another way we can write $\frac{3}{2}$, $\frac{5}{2}$, and other fractional numbers in which the numerator is greater than the denominator? Consider the point labeled $\frac{3}{2}$. This point is one-half unit ($\frac{1}{2}$) to the right of 1, so another way to indicate $\frac{3}{2}$ is $1 + \frac{1}{2}$, or $1\frac{1}{2}$. If the expression $1 + \frac{1}{2}$ is rewritten as $\frac{2}{2} + \frac{1}{2}$, which clearly equals $\frac{3}{2}$, it becomes obvious that $1 + \frac{1}{2}$ and $\frac{3}{2}$ are different names for the same number.

Now consider the fraction $\frac{5}{2}$. By looking at the number line, we find that the point named by $\frac{5}{2}$ is one-half unit ($\frac{1}{2}$) to the right of 2. This point, therefore, can be indicated by $2 + \frac{1}{2}$, or $2\frac{1}{2}$. If $2 + \frac{1}{2}$ is rewritten as $\frac{4}{2} + \frac{1}{2}$, which is clearly equal to $\frac{5}{2}$, it becomes evident that the symbols $\frac{5}{2}$ and $2\frac{1}{2}$ (or $2 + \frac{1}{2}$) are merely different names for the same number. Numerals such as $1\frac{1}{2}$, $3\frac{1}{2}$, and $6\frac{1}{2}$ (for $\frac{3}{2}$, $\frac{7}{2}$, and $\frac{13}{2}$, respectively) are called **mixed numerals**. In this form, we combine, or mix, a numeral naming a counting number and a numeral naming a fraction.

Circular regions should also be used to develop the concept of mixed numerals. Consider three of the pieces that we have named half of a circle:

We can use $\frac{3}{2}$ as a fraction for these regions. By rearranging the regions, we can easily see that we have one whole and one-half circular regions.

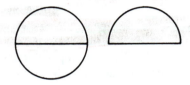

Children need many experiences in manipulating regions that they have cut from thicker paper and included in their fraction kits. They also must be put into situations that require them to verbalize the relationships shown by these fraction pieces. The language and terms the students use in communicating about fractions are not, at this early stage, as critical as the awareness and identification of important fraction concepts.

We can also develop the concept of mixed numerals using rectangular regions:

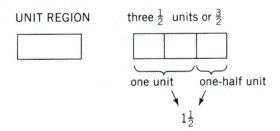

Children can rearrange the pieces to see why $\frac{3}{2}$ and $1\frac{1}{2}$ are names for the same number. Children should be given the opportunity to discover relations between the set of halves and other numbers on the number line. They may make the generalization that when we add parts by moving to the right on the number line, the denominators remain the same and the numerators are added the way whole numbers are added. Children have had experience in counting by ones, fives, and tens. Now the opportunity is provided for them to count by halves: $\frac{1}{2}, \frac{2}{2}, \frac{3}{2}, \frac{4}{2}, \frac{5}{2}$, and so on). The patterns in counting the set of halves should become clear.

Now let's develop the set of fourths, again using a number line. Each unit-long line segment is divided into four segments of equal length.

If the segment between 0 and 1 is divided into four equivalent parts, what should we name one of these parts? We name it *one-fourth*. Thus we can label the first point to the right of zero on the number line as $\frac{1}{4}$, or one-fourth. Similarly, we can label the second point $\frac{2}{4}$, or two-fourths; the third point $\frac{3}{4}$, or three-fourths; and the fourth point $\frac{4}{4}$, or four-fourths. Thus:

We can continue in this manner indefinitely, naming the set of fourths:

It is evident now that another name for 1 is $\frac{4}{4}$. Similarly, another name for 2 is $\frac{8}{4}$. We can also use other names to designate the points on the number line that represent fractional numbers greater than 1; we can use mixed numerals to designate these points. For example, the point labeled $\frac{5}{4}$ can be renamed with the mixed numeral $1\frac{1}{4}$, and the next point can be designated $1\frac{2}{4}$ instead of $\frac{6}{4}$.

Now let's represent the set of halves and the set of fourths on the same number line. We should encourage children to discover as many relations as possible.

What are some other names for 1? ($\frac{2}{2}$ and $\frac{4}{4}$.) After children have examined the point named by 1, they should be able to make the generalization that when any counting number (1, 2, 3, 4, and so on) appears as both numerator and denominator, the resulting fraction is another way to name 1. Thus there are an infinite number of fraction names for 1.

$$\frac{1}{1}, \frac{2}{2}, \frac{3}{3}, \frac{4}{4} \cdots$$

The point named by 1 can be indicated by either $\frac{1}{1}$ or $\frac{2}{2}$ because these are merely different names for the same point ($\frac{1}{1} = \frac{2}{2}$). Children should then be shown that $\left(\frac{1\times2}{1\times2} = \frac{2}{2}\right)$ and $\frac{1\times3}{1\times3} = \frac{3}{3}$. The important thing for children to recognize here is that in each example, the same factor is used in the numerator and in the denominator. Moreover, $\frac{1}{2}$ and $\frac{2}{4}$ name the same number ($\frac{1}{2} = \frac{2}{4}$), and the relation $\frac{2\times1}{2\times2} = \frac{2}{4}$ is thus valid. We call fractions that name the same number **equivalent fractions**.

Despite the appearance of the abstract notation, emphasis should be placed on the notion of actually multiplying a fraction by 1, written in the form $\frac{a}{a}$ (where $a \neq 0$), rather than using the wording, "Multiply both the top and the bottom by the same number." This wording certainly does yield a correct answer, but children tend to see it as only an arbitrary rule with no foundation in their prior knowledge of the result of applying the identity principle for multiplication—that is, multiplication by 1 in the form $\frac{a}{a}$ (where $a \neq 0$) does not change the value of the fraction, only its appearance.

The concept of equivalent fractions can also be presented by using regions. For example:

This basic unit is divided into thirds and has also been divided into sixths. The shaded part of the unit region is $\frac{2}{6}$ of the entire region (two parts out of a total of six). But the shaded part is also $\frac{1}{3}$ of the entire unit region. When $\frac{2}{6}$ is renamed as $\frac{1}{3}$, we say that it is in simplest form. A fraction is in **simplest form** if the numerator and the denominator have no common factors other than 1. For example, we have seen that $\frac{2}{6} = \frac{1}{3}$.

$$\begin{aligned} \frac{2}{6} &= \frac{1\times2}{3\times2} \\ &= \frac{1}{3} \times \frac{2}{2} \\ &= \frac{1}{3} \times 1 \\ &= \frac{1}{3} \end{aligned}$$

We use the phrase *simplest form* rather than the more traditional *reduce to lowest terms*. To children, the term *reduce* means "to make smaller," but the fraction is really still the same size and represents the same amount. We are actually writing a fraction in a form that is easier to comprehend. Students are not just mechanically following an algorithm: They are developing the concept of renaming fractions. In the

fraction $\frac{2}{6}$, the numerator and the denominator have the factor 2 in common; therefore $\frac{2}{6}$ is not in simplest form. The fraction $\frac{1}{3}$, however, is expressed in simplest form because the numerator and the denominator share no common factors except 1.

The number line can also be used to model equivalent fractions. For instance, we can show the truth of the statement $\frac{1}{2} = \frac{2}{4}$ by using the number line. In the following illustration, the unit segment is divided into two segments of equal length:

Similarly, the segment between 0 and $\frac{1}{2}$ is separated into two equivalent parts, and the segment between $\frac{1}{2}$ and 1 is also divided into two equivalent parts. Thus, the unit segment has been separated into four equivalent parts, and the point $\frac{1}{2}$ (or $\frac{2}{4}$) is two of the $\frac{1}{4}$ units from 0.

Notice that $\frac{1}{2}$ and $\frac{2}{4}$ each name the same point and that $\frac{1\times2}{2\times2} = \frac{2}{4}$. This is an application of the identity element for multiplication, which states that any number multiplied by 1 is the number itself, $a \times 1 = a$. Of course, we can substitute any equivalent name for 1—for example, $\frac{2}{2}$ or $\frac{3}{3}$. If $a = \frac{1}{2}$ in the mathematical sentence $a \times 1 = 1$, then we write $\frac{1}{2} \times 1 = \frac{1}{2}$. Also, because $\frac{2}{2}$ is another name for 1, we can write $\frac{1}{2} \times \frac{2}{2} = \frac{1}{2}$ or $\frac{1\times2}{2\times2} = \frac{2}{4} = \frac{1}{2}$. Similarly, because $\frac{3}{3}$ is another name for 1, we can also write $\frac{1}{2} \times \frac{3}{3} = \frac{1}{2}$ or $\frac{1\times3}{2\times3} = \frac{3}{6} = \frac{1}{2}$. By using the identity element this way, we can find many different names for any point on the number line.

$$\begin{aligned} \frac{1}{4} &= \frac{1}{4} \times \frac{2}{2} = \frac{1\times2}{4\times2} = \frac{2}{8} \\ \frac{1}{4} &= \frac{1}{4} \times \frac{3}{3} = \frac{1\times3}{4\times3} = \frac{3}{12} \\ \frac{1}{4} &= \frac{1}{4} \times \frac{5}{5} = \frac{1\times5}{4\times5} = \frac{5}{20} \end{aligned}$$

The authors realize that children have not yet formally studied multiplication of fractions. However, we believe that they can explore relationships among the fractions to justify that fractions can be renamed by means of the identity element of multiplication. Students should have an opportunity to discover many names for any point on the number line. They will want to expand their concept of fractions to include other fractions such as thirds, sixths, and eighths.

Combining regions to form a chart is another excellent way to develop students' concept of equivalent fractions and the relationships among fractional numbers. Children can discover visually that any fraction has many names. For example, we know that $\frac{1}{2} = \frac{2}{4} = \frac{4}{8}$. A child can discover this by manipulating materials or using a fraction tower chart such as this one:

Unit	1							
Halves	$\frac{1}{2}$				$\frac{1}{2}$			
Fourths	$\frac{1}{4}$		$\frac{1}{4}$		$\frac{1}{4}$		$\frac{1}{4}$	
Eighths	$\frac{1}{8}$	$\frac{1}{8}$	$\frac{1}{8}$	$\frac{1}{8}$	$\frac{1}{8}$	$\frac{1}{8}$	$\frac{1}{8}$	$\frac{1}{8}$

Unit	1											
Thirds	$\frac{1}{3}$				$\frac{1}{3}$				$\frac{1}{3}$			
Sixths	$\frac{1}{6}$		$\frac{1}{6}$		$\frac{1}{6}$		$\frac{1}{6}$		$\frac{1}{6}$		$\frac{1}{6}$	
Twelfths	$\frac{1}{12}$	$\frac{1}{12}$	$\frac{1}{12}$	$\frac{1}{12}$	$\frac{1}{12}$	$\frac{1}{12}$	$\frac{1}{12}$	$\frac{1}{12}$	$\frac{1}{12}$	$\frac{1}{12}$	$\frac{1}{12}$	$\frac{1}{12}$

In this chart, the unit interval is represented in four different ways: At the top, it is represented by a single rectangular region, labeled 1 because it spans the entire interval. Below this, the unit interval is represented by two rectangular regions; these are labeled $\frac{1}{2}$ because each region spans only one-half of the interval. Next the unit interval is represented by four rectangular regions, each labeled $\frac{1}{4}$ to indicate that it spans only one-fourth of the interval. Finally, there are eight congruent rectangular regions, each labeled $\frac{1}{8}$.

By shading some of the regions on the chart, children can see that fractional numbers can be renamed in various ways:

Unit	1							
Halves	$\frac{1}{2}$				$\frac{1}{2}$			
Fourths	$\frac{1}{4}$		$\frac{1}{4}$		$\frac{1}{4}$		$\frac{1}{4}$	
Eighths	$\frac{1}{8}$	$\frac{1}{8}$	$\frac{1}{8}$	$\frac{1}{8}$	$\frac{1}{8}$	$\frac{1}{8}$	$\frac{1}{8}$	$\frac{1}{8}$

For example, in this chart, there are eight rectangular regions labeled $\frac{1}{8}$. Four of these have been shaded. This fact can be indicated by the fraction $\frac{4}{8}$, the denominator, 8, indicating the total number of regions, and the numerator, 4, indicating the number of these regions that are shaded. Considering the rectangular regions labeled $\frac{1}{4}$, we see that an equal area has been shaded. There are four regions labeled $\frac{1}{4}$, two of which have been shaded. This fact is indicated by the fraction $\frac{2}{4}$. Clearly, $\frac{4}{8}$ and $\frac{2}{4}$ are equivalent fractions. Now considering the rectangular regions labeled $\frac{1}{2}$, we see that an equal area has again been shaded. There are two regions labeled $\frac{1}{2}$, only one of which has been shaded. The fraction $\frac{1}{2}$ indicates this fact. Obviously, $\frac{1}{2}$ is equivalent to $\frac{2}{4}$ and $\frac{4}{8}$ ($\frac{1}{2} = \frac{2}{4} = \frac{4}{8}$). Other charts can be made that illustrate equivalent fractions. For example, the following chart illustrates the equivalence of $\frac{1}{3}$, $\frac{2}{6}$ and $\frac{4}{12}$ ($\frac{1}{3} = \frac{2}{6} = \frac{4}{12}$).

Practice with these charts to help clarify the meaning of equivalent fractions and to build a foundation for examining methods of finding equivalent fractions. Let's construct a chart that includes all denominators from 2 to 10. A chart such as the one that follows emphasizes the fact that increasing the value of the denominator, while leaving the numerator unchanged, reduces the value of the fraction.

1 Unit									
$\frac{1}{2}$									
$\frac{1}{3}$									
$\frac{1}{4}$									
$\frac{1}{5}$									
$\frac{1}{6}$									
$\frac{1}{7}$									
$\frac{1}{8}$									
$\frac{1}{9}$									
$\frac{1}{10}$									

On such a chart, equivalent fractions can be found and comparisons can be made among fractions of different values. For example, we see that $\frac{1}{2} = \frac{2}{4} = \frac{4}{8}$. In this way, rows of equivalent fractions can be determined:

$$\frac{1}{2} = \frac{2}{4} = \frac{3}{6} = \frac{4}{8} = \frac{5}{10}$$

$$\frac{2}{3} = \frac{4}{6} = \frac{6}{9}$$

Furthermore, the relation between fractional numbers such as $\frac{1}{3}$ and $\frac{1}{7}$ can readily be seen:

$$\frac{1}{3} > \frac{1}{7} \ \text{or} \ \frac{1}{7} < \frac{1}{3}$$

A concrete version of this chart can be made using the manipulatives known as Cuisenaire rods. In this case, use the orange rod and two white rods end-to-end to form the unit length. Now, for this arrangement, $\frac{1}{2}$ would be represented by a dark green rod, $\frac{1}{3}$ by a purple rod, $\frac{1}{4}$ by a light green rod, $\frac{1}{6}$ by a red rod, and $\frac{1}{12}$ by a white rod ($\frac{1}{5}$, $\frac{1}{7}$, $\frac{1}{8}$, and $\frac{1}{10}$ cannot be shown for this size unit because no existing rod or combination of rods represents these fractional parts of a unit made up of 12 subsections).

The number line is an excellent device for developing the order of fractions. Children should discover that the numerators of the set of halves follow the same pattern as the counting numbers; that the denominators are the same, 2, in every case; and that any fraction named on a traditional number line is greater than ($>$) each fraction to its left and is less than ($<$) each fraction to its right. When two fractions are compared, one of three possible relations between them will hold true: One fraction is equal to ($=$), is greater than ($>$), or is less than ($<$) the other. Using the number line, children can begin to see relationships among fractions that do not name the same number.

When several sets of related fractions appear on one number line, children can readily tell which one of any two fractional numbers is greater. They should acquire experience in writing statements such as $\frac{1}{2} < \frac{3}{4}$. This statement is read, "One-half is less than three-fourths." The statement $\frac{1}{2} > \frac{1}{3}$ is read, "One-half is greater than one-third."

As discussed earlier, mathematicians read the symbol ($<$) as "is less than" and read the symbol ($>$) as "is greater than." With young children the phrase "is more than" may be clearer at first than "is greater than"; children have experienced situations in which one child has more marbles or more pieces of candy than another. In any case, always avoid referring to one fraction as being "smaller than" another fraction because it is possible that $\frac{1}{2}$ is, in reality, smaller than $\frac{1}{4}$, if the two fractions refer to different unit sizes.

Teachers should introduce the correct terminology in its proper place, and children will come to understand this terminology by using it. In working with whole numbers, children learn that as they move to the right on the traditional number line, the numbers become greater, and as they move to the left, the numbers become less. Fractional numbers, of course, follow the same pattern. Teachers should provide many opportunities for children to show the relation between two fractional numbers by placing the proper sign between them. Using

placeholders between fractions as shown, have children fill in the correct relation symbol:

$$\frac{1}{4} \bigcirc \frac{3}{4} \qquad \frac{1}{4} \ominus \frac{3}{4}$$
$$\frac{1}{8} \bigcirc \frac{2}{4} \qquad \frac{1}{8} \ominus \frac{2}{4}$$
$$\frac{3}{4} \bigcirc \frac{7}{8} \qquad \frac{3}{4} \ominus \frac{7}{8}$$
$$\frac{3}{2} \bigcirc \frac{11}{8} \qquad \frac{3}{2} \oplus \frac{11}{8}$$

If you prefer not using symbols, a blank line can be used between the two fractions, and the student can be asked to fill in the correct word phrase: "is greater than," "is less than," or "is equal to."

Another way to look at a fraction is as a number obtained when an integer is divided by an integer other than zero. No rational number is named by $\frac{2}{0}$ (or $\frac{3}{0}$, $\frac{4}{0}$, and so on), because $\frac{2}{0}$ indicates division by zero. Zero, however, can be renamed by a fraction. Zero divided by any counting number is zero; $\frac{0}{2} = 0$, $\frac{0}{3} = 0$, $\frac{0}{27} = 0$, and so on.

Every whole number is a part of the set of fractional numbers, since every whole number can be considered the result of dividing some whole number by a counting number. For example, every whole number is equal to itself (a whole number) divided by one (a counting number). Look at the following examples:

$$2 = 4 \div 2 \text{ or } 2 = \frac{4}{2}$$

But not every fraction is an element of the set of whole numbers—for example, $\frac{1}{3}$, $\frac{3}{12}$, and $\frac{5}{14}$.

All mixed numerals name fractions because all whole numbers can be written as fractions. For example:

$$\begin{aligned}
2\tfrac{1}{7} &= 2 + \tfrac{1}{7} \\
&= (1 + 1) + \tfrac{1}{7} \\
&= (\tfrac{7}{7} + \tfrac{7}{7}) + \tfrac{1}{7} \\
&= \tfrac{14}{7} + \tfrac{1}{7} \\
&= \tfrac{15}{7}
\end{aligned}$$

A number line showing equivalent fractions is a useful aid in preparing to develop the four basic operations with respect to fractional numbers.

Children can be asked to begin at zero and move a jump of $\frac{2}{4}$ to the right. An additional jump of $\frac{1}{4}$ will end at $\frac{3}{4}$. Thus, we conclude that $\frac{2}{4}$ add $\frac{1}{4}$ is $\frac{3}{4}$, or $\frac{1}{2}$ add $\frac{1}{4}$ is $\frac{3}{4}$.

Regions can also be used to introduce children to the foundations of adding and subtracting fractions. First, discuss the use of regions to model equivalent fractions. Have the children lay out one-half of a circular region and find how many fourths can be placed on top to completely and exactly cover half the region.

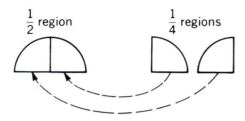

How many $\frac{1}{8}$ circular regions can be placed on top of the $\frac{1}{2}$ region? Continue this process until children realize that $\frac{1}{2} = \frac{2}{4} = \frac{4}{8} = \frac{5}{10}$, and so forth.

Next, instead of having the children place one region on top of the other, have them place it adjacent to the other. The following examples show that $\frac{1}{2} + \frac{1}{4} = \frac{3}{4}$ and $\frac{1}{6} + \frac{2}{6} = \frac{3}{6}$:

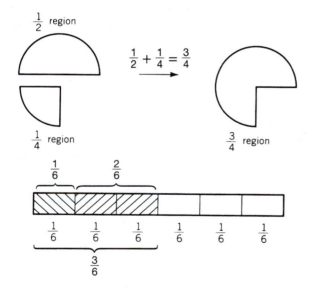

Closure

Students should be exposed to fundamental fraction concepts at each grade level. The primary grade teacher should concentrate on providing an intuitive approach to fractional numbers involving explorations with continuous and discrete models. Groups of objects, number lines, and regions are three models that should be used to develop an understanding of fractional numbers. Greater emphasis needs to be placed on a basic understanding of the concept of fractions. If done effectively, this will result in a lesser need to devote time to the operations on fractions. Many elementary school teachers begin teaching operations on fractional numbers before children have internalized the prerequisite fraction concepts. It is important to remember that concrete and semiconcrete experiences and demonstrations should be used frequently to provide a background of understanding necessary for working with the more abstract concepts later.

The contemporary approach to elementary school mathematics provides a consistent pattern of experiences designed to extend the child's understanding of concepts with each successive step. A basic understanding of fraction concepts beginning in the primary grades not only meets the mathematical needs of the child, but also gives the child a proper perspective of number structure. The child who is introduced to concepts of fractional numbers at the primary grades sees their relation to whole numbers at an advantageous time. When the child reaches the point of studying operations with fractional numbers, he or she does not think of these operations as something completely new and different.

Since so many children want the "biggest half of the candy bar," there is a need to provide many situations that will help children understand the meaning of the denominator and the numerator in a fraction. This understanding must precede any computation with fractional numbers. Manipulation of real objects, demonstrations on the felt board with regions separated into fractional parts, and simple exercises involving folding and cutting paper not only will increase understanding of fractional parts but will also introduce computational skills as well. Cuisenaire rods, base ten blocks, pattern blocks, and fraction bars are all useful tools in presenting the concept of fractions.

Home-made fraction kits can be valuable supplements to instruction. Using transparent colored plastic, cut out circular regions about 8 centimeters in diameter. Using a different color for each set of fractions, make five circular regions of each color. Cut one set of five circular regions into halves, and cut the remaining sets into thirds, fourths, fifths, sixths, sevenths, eighths, ninths, tenths, and twelfths. Keep each set in a small envelope marked to indicate the type of pieces inside. You and your students can easily manipulate the pieces on the overhead projector or Elmo®, and students can readily see the relationships among the pieces.

At the primary grade levels, it is particularly important to establish visual perception of the concept of fractional parts. Use of the number line will help in establishing the idea of $\frac{1}{2}$, $\frac{1}{4}$, and so on, and the fact that a fractional number has many names.

Use the whiteboard or pictures of articles to give children opportunities to talk about fractions. For example:

Jimmy and Johnny were playing together at Johnny's house. Johnny's sister came home with a candy bar for Johnny. She didn't know that Jimmy was going to be there, too. She cut the candy bar into two pieces so that Jimmy and Johnny could each have one-half.

Have a child come to the whiteboard and point out the candy bar that is cut into halves (or point to the proper picture, if pictures are used).

Using this same kind of activity, have children make up stories about the pictures. Encourage them to write sentences that describe the fractional parts represented by the objects in the picture. This activity can be extended to include one-fourth, one-third, and so on.

Make the following models to demonstrate the relationships between fractions and equivalent fractions. Using heavy cardboard or posterboard, make a fraction chart similar to the one shown.

1 Unit				
$\frac{1}{2}$			$\frac{1}{2}$	
$\frac{1}{3}$		$\frac{1}{3}$		$\frac{1}{3}$
$\frac{1}{4}$		$\frac{1}{4}$	$\frac{1}{4}$	$\frac{1}{4}$
$\frac{1}{5}$	$\frac{1}{5}$	$\frac{1}{5}$	$\frac{1}{5}$	$\frac{1}{5}$

End view · Front view · Cards cut into fractional parts

Narrow strips of cardboard

Plywood

Wider strips of cardboard

Cardboard is stapled with staple gun to plywood

Stapled strips

1 Unit	
$\frac{1}{2}$	$\frac{1}{2}$

$2 - \frac{1}{2}$

$\frac{1}{3}$ $\frac{1}{3}$ $\frac{1}{3}$ — $3 - \frac{1}{3}$

$\frac{1}{4}$ $\frac{1}{4}$ $\frac{1}{4}$ $\frac{1}{4}$ — $4 - \frac{1}{4}$

$\frac{1}{5}$ $\frac{1}{5}$ $\frac{1}{5}$ $\frac{1}{5}$ $\frac{1}{5}$ — $5 - \frac{1}{5}$

$\frac{1}{6}$ $\frac{1}{6}$ $\frac{1}{6}$ $\frac{1}{6}$ $\frac{1}{6}$ $\frac{1}{6}$ — $6 - \frac{1}{6}$

$\frac{1}{7}$ $\frac{1}{7}$ $\frac{1}{7}$ $\frac{1}{7}$ $\frac{1}{7}$ $\frac{1}{7}$ $\frac{1}{7}$ — $7 - \frac{1}{7}$

$\frac{1}{8}$ $\frac{1}{8}$ $\frac{1}{8}$ $\frac{1}{8}$ $\frac{1}{8}$ $\frac{1}{8}$ $\frac{1}{8}$ $\frac{1}{8}$ — $8 - \frac{1}{8}$

$\frac{1}{9}$ $\frac{1}{9}$ $\frac{1}{9}$ $\frac{1}{9}$ $\frac{1}{9}$ $\frac{1}{9}$ $\frac{1}{9}$ $\frac{1}{9}$ $\frac{1}{9}$ — $9 - \frac{1}{9}$

$\frac{1}{10}$ $\frac{1}{10}$ $\frac{1}{10}$ $\frac{1}{10}$ $\frac{1}{10}$ $\frac{1}{10}$ $\frac{1}{10}$ $\frac{1}{10}$ $\frac{1}{10}$ $\frac{1}{10}$ — $10 - \frac{1}{10}$

$\frac{1}{12}$ $\frac{1}{12}$ $\frac{1}{12}$ $\frac{1}{12}$ $\frac{1}{12}$ $\frac{1}{12}$ $\frac{1}{12}$ $\frac{1}{12}$ $\frac{1}{12}$ $\frac{1}{12}$ $\frac{1}{12}$ $\frac{1}{12}$ — $12 - \frac{1}{12}$

Make the same type of fraction model on plywood. Construct a frame from a piece of plywood on which narrow strips of wood are nailed or glued. Construct rectangles of plywood so that the rectangles will fit between the wooden strips. Cut each rectangle into different fractional parts.

Attach a long string (the length of the fraction board) to a thumbtack. The children can see which fractions are related by placing the thumbtack on the top edge of the fraction board and drawing the string taut. For instance, place the thumbtack in the top of the fraction board directly above the split between the 2 one-half pieces. Tighten the string down the center of the board so that the children can see that 2 one-fourths, 3 one-sixths, 4 one-eighths, 5 one-tenths, and 6 one-twelfths are the same in length as one-half. Thus, one-half is equivalent to two-fourths, three-sixths, four-eighths, five-tenths, and six-twelfths. A similar procedure can be used with the other fractional parts.

To construct a circular fraction kit, trace 16 large circles on construction paper (or use paper plates if available). Cut them as follows: three regions intact (units), two regions in two parts (halves), two regions in three parts (thirds), two regions in four parts (fourths), two regions in five parts (fifths), two regions in six parts (sixths), two regions in eight parts (eighths), and one region in twelve parts (twelfths). You may want to make a fraction kit out of colored transparencies to use on an overhead projector.

Before beginning a more rigorous or formal study of operations on fractions, a child must have a solid grasp, as measured by both action and word, of the many foundational concepts discussed in this chapter. Careful and deliberate attention to the prerequisite knowledge, skills, understandings, and experiences described here will result in significant benefits in later instruction. With such a foundation, as we will see in the next chapter, the learning of operations on rational numbers is greatly aided, and the time spent attaining understanding and skill greatly lessened.

PRACTICE EXERCISES FOR TEACHERS

These exercises are designed for the reader of this book not for the children the reader may teach. Although some of these examples are suitable for use in the elementary or middle school classroom, they should not necessarily be given to children in the form presented here. Ideas appropriate for classroom activities on the concepts and ideas discussed in this chapter can be found in a later section of this chapter and on the CD that accompanies this text.

VM 11.4

1. Shade part of each of the following regions as suggested by the given fraction.

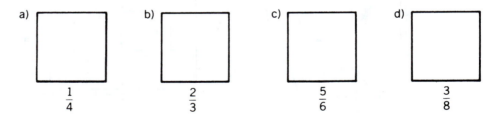

VM 11.2

2. Shade part of each of the following groups as indicated by the given fraction.

VM 11.4

3. Shade part of each of the following regions as suggested by the given fraction.

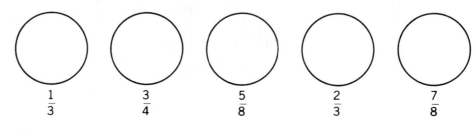

4. Make a number line from 0 to 2; locate and label each of the following fractions.

$$0, 1, 2, \tfrac{1}{2}, \tfrac{1}{3}, \tfrac{1}{4}, \tfrac{2}{3}, \tfrac{3}{4}, \tfrac{2}{2}, \tfrac{4}{2}, \tfrac{2}{4}, \tfrac{1}{6}, \tfrac{2}{6}, \tfrac{4}{6}, \tfrac{3}{6}, \tfrac{5}{6}, \tfrac{4}{3}, 1\tfrac{1}{2}, 1\tfrac{1}{3}, \tfrac{5}{3}, 1\tfrac{2}{3}$$

5. Place each of the following groups of fractions in order from least to greatest.

a) $\tfrac{1}{6}, \tfrac{1}{2}, \tfrac{1}{4}, \tfrac{1}{5}, \tfrac{1}{3}, \tfrac{1}{7}, \tfrac{1}{9}, \tfrac{1}{8}$

b) $\tfrac{3}{5}, \tfrac{1}{5}, \tfrac{2}{5}, \tfrac{5}{5}, \tfrac{4}{5}, \tfrac{6}{5}$

c) $\tfrac{3}{6}, \tfrac{1}{3}, \tfrac{6}{4}, \tfrac{1}{6}, \tfrac{5}{6}, \tfrac{3}{3}$

d) $\tfrac{5}{8}, \tfrac{1}{3}, \tfrac{3}{8}, \tfrac{2}{3}, \tfrac{3}{4}, \tfrac{1}{4}, \tfrac{1}{8}, \tfrac{4}{4}$

6. Place the correct relation symbol ($<, =$, and $>$) or phrase ("is less than," "is equal to," and "is greater than") between each of the following pairs of fractions to make a true statement.

a) $\tfrac{1}{10}$ ____ $\tfrac{2}{10}$ b) $\tfrac{3}{4}$ ____ $\tfrac{3}{8}$ c) $\tfrac{3}{8}$ ____ $\tfrac{2}{3}$ d) $\tfrac{1}{2}$ ____ $\tfrac{5}{12}$

e) $\tfrac{2}{3}$ ____ $\tfrac{5}{6}$ f) $\tfrac{11}{3}$ ____ $\tfrac{5}{4}$ g) $\tfrac{5}{8}$ ____ $\tfrac{3}{4}$ h) $\tfrac{3}{14}$ ____ $\tfrac{6}{28}$

7. Write each of the following as a fraction in simplest form.

a) $\tfrac{8}{12}$ b) $\tfrac{4}{16}$ c) $\tfrac{18}{32}$ d) $\tfrac{15}{18}$

e) $\tfrac{16}{24}$ f) $\tfrac{125}{5}$ g) $\tfrac{91}{161}$ h) $\tfrac{34}{51}$

8. Write each of the following mixed numerals as a fraction.

a) $3\tfrac{3}{5}$ b) $5\tfrac{3}{10}$ c) $1\tfrac{7}{8}$ d) $3\tfrac{1}{7}$

e) $4\tfrac{1}{2}$ f) $16\tfrac{3}{8}$ g) $5\tfrac{2}{5}$ h) $7\tfrac{1}{7}$

VM 11.1

9. Fill in the blanks in the following lists of equivalent fractions. Keep the denominators in increasing order.

a) $\tfrac{1}{2}$, _____, _____, $\tfrac{4}{8}$, _____, _____, _____

b) $\tfrac{3}{8}, \tfrac{6}{16}$, _____, _____, _____, _____, _____

c) $\tfrac{5}{7}$, _____, $\tfrac{15}{21}$, _____, _____, _____, _____

10. Complete the following explanation of why the fraction $\tfrac{3}{5}$ is equivalent to $\tfrac{21}{35}$.

If a rectangular region is divided into 5 regions of the same size, we can shade_____ (how many?) of these regions to represent $\tfrac{3}{5}$. If each of the 5 regions into which the original region is divided is itself divided into 7 equivalent regions, then the original rectangular region will have been divided into 5 × _____ equivalent regions. The portion that was shaded will then consist of _____ × 7 of these smaller regions. Thus the portion of the original rectangular region that is shaded can also be represented by the fraction $\tfrac{21}{35}$. Since $\tfrac{21}{35}$ and $\tfrac{3}{5}$ both indicate that portion of the original region is shaded, we can conclude that $\tfrac{21}{35}$ and $\tfrac{3}{5}$ are_____ fractions.

11. Use reasoning similar to that in Exercise 10 to argue that $\tfrac{4}{7}$ is equivalent to $\tfrac{400}{700}$.

12. Write each of the following improper fractions as a mixed numeral.

a) $\tfrac{29}{5}$ b) $\tfrac{17}{4}$ c) $\tfrac{37}{7}$ d) $\tfrac{29}{4}$ e) $\tfrac{43}{12}$

f) $\tfrac{31}{4}$ g) $\tfrac{49}{9}$ h) $\tfrac{19}{5}$ i) $\tfrac{25}{13}$ j) $\tfrac{44}{9}$

13. Mark each of the following statements true or false.

a) The number represented by $1\frac{2}{7}$ can be named with a proper fraction.

b) It is incorrect to call $2\frac{2}{3}$ a fractional number, because it is the sum of a whole number and a fractional number.

c) Every improper fraction names a number that is either greater than or equal to 1.

d) Every mixed numeral can be rewritten as an improper fraction.

e) The number $\frac{10}{5}$ is a fraction but not a whole number.

f) Every proper fraction names a number greater than 0.

g) Every proper fraction names a number less than 1.

h) An infinite number of fraction names are possible for the number 1.

TEACHING COMPETENCIES AND SELF-ASSESSMENT TASKS

1. Set up an experiment to compare the use of circular regions versus rectangular regions in exploring a fraction concept. What are the advantages and disadvantages of one over the other? How do other shapes fit into this discussion?

2. Make a set of number line overlays for the overhead projector, each illustrating different fractions marked on a number line. Demonstrate the use of the number line transparencies to your class.

3. Research the use of the following materials to introduce fraction concepts in the elementary grades. Present your findings to the class.

a) Cuisenaire rods   b) pattern blocks   c) base ten blocks   d) graph paper

4. Examine the fraction curriculum scope and sequence found in several elementary school textbooks and discuss with your peers the similarities and differences among the content, sequence, and approaches found in these programs.

5. In preparation for a discussion on which notation should be taught first (rational numbers expressed as decimals or rational numbers expressed as fractions), separate a page into columns. In one column, list the advantages and disadvantages of teaching decimals first, and in the second column, list the advantages and disadvantages of teaching fractions first. Compare the lists and debate the findings.

6. Discuss how pure discovery and guided discovery can be effectively used in introducing fractions to children.

7. Prepare a collection of readiness activities that can be used in the elementary grades, especially at the primary level, as a foundation for the formal introduction of fractions.

8. When fractional parts of a group are being considered, is it necessary that the number of objects in the group always be some multiple of the denominator of the fraction being considered? For example, if you wish to find one-fifth of a group of objects, must the number of objects in the group be a multiple of five? Is it possible to find one-third of a group of five? Can this be shown on the following group?

How about on this group?

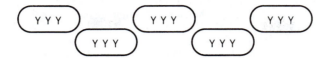

What difficulties arise from such a discussion in a classroom, and how do you overcome them?

9. Fractions should be introduced on the concrete level and then carried through the semiconcrete, semiabstract, and abstract levels. Discuss manipulative materials, commercial and teacher/student-made, that can be used at various levels of student development.

10. Identify and discuss situations that a teacher can create in the primary classroom to involve children with fractions from their real-world experiences.

11. Discuss how problem solving would be incorporated into the study of fractions. How might the notion of communication be incorporated? reasoning? connections? Describe examples of each in the preK to 2, 3 to 5, and 6 to 8 curriculum.

SAMPLE INSTRUCTIONAL AND ASSESSMENT ACTIVITIES

These activities and more are available on the CD that accompanies this text.

1. Open a manila file folder and write the fraction $\frac{1}{2}$ on one side; on the other, write the fraction $\frac{1}{4}$. Cut out a number of geometric shapes, and color either $\frac{1}{2}$ or $\frac{1}{4}$ of each. Children can sort the shapes by placing them on the proper side of the folder. (Note: Two of the figures that follow might be used to determine if a child is ignoring the requirement that the parts be equal parts. Which two?)

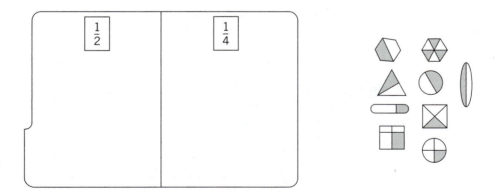

2. Give each child two congruent circles of different colors cut from construction paper. Instruct the children to fold one circle in half and cut with scissors along the fold. Fit both halves over the other circle. Have the children trade halves with another student to see if two halves still make a whole. Use a third circle with a larger diameter than that of the other two. Fold it in half; have the children discuss why this half doesn't match the halves from the other circles. This is an important activity to emphasize the attention that must be paid to unit size.

VM 11.6

3. Use the Visualizing Fractions VM on the CD that accompanies this text to show the given fraction on the shape by dividing it and selecting the correct number of divisions.

VM 11.1

4. Use the Naming Fractions VM on the CD that accompanies this text to name the fraction shown by the shape.

VM 11.5

5. Use the Equivalent Fractions VM on the CD that accompanies this text to find an equivalent fraction for the given fraction.

6. Give a student two yellow buttons, eight blue buttons, and five cards. Ask the student to tell what fraction of the buttons is yellow ($\frac{2}{10}$) and what fraction is blue ($\frac{8}{10}$). Have the student place two buttons on each card, making sure they put the two yellow ones together. Now ask which fraction of the cards with buttons is yellow ($\frac{1}{5}$) and which is blue ($\frac{4}{5}$). Variations of this activity can be done by changing the number of buttons and cards.

7. For this activity, cardboard cutouts of circles, squares, rectangles, triangles, and rhombuses are cut into halves, thirds, and fourths. Construct a die with the fractions $\frac{1}{2}$, $\frac{1}{3}$, and $\frac{1}{4}$. Roll the die. The person with the largest fraction rolls first. Roll the die in turn, and select a corresponding region to match the die. With the cardboard cutout regions, try to form one whole figure. The first person to form one whole figure can be declared the winner, or you can keep score and play the game for a certain period of time. The high scorer is the winner. Vary this game by trying to form one of each of the shapes.

8. Most calculators do not display fractions on the screen, but calculators can be used to change fractions to decimal form, if fractions are interpreted as division. The numerator divided by the denominator will produce a decimal on the display screen. An interesting discussion can arise from comparing the indicated division (e.g., $\frac{1}{3}$ or 1 divided by 3) to the decimal display (.33333333) and the fraction it represents ($\frac{33333333}{100000000}$). Does this fraction *equal* $\frac{1}{3}$?

9. Construct a deck of about 60 cards. Write a fraction on each card. You may start by using fractions with the denominators of 2, 3, 4, 6, and 8. Deal five cards to each player and place them faceup in front of the player in the order in which they are dealt. For example:

Each player draws a card or takes a discard from the pile in order. The first person to have five fractions in order from least to greatest is the winner. For instance, the player's first draw is, $\frac{2}{3}$ so he or she discards $\frac{1}{8}$.

The fraction $\frac{5}{8}$ must be replaced by some fraction less than $\frac{1}{4}$, and $\frac{5}{6}$ must be replaced by some fraction more than $\frac{1}{4}$ and less than $\frac{2}{3}$ for the player to win.

10. The following activity can be used to reinforce the students' understanding of equivalent fractions. Construct a deck of 42 cards with the following sets of fractions: halves, thirds, fourths, fifths, sixths, eighths, and tenths. One card should also be constructed for each of the whole numbers 1, 2, 3, and 4. The cards are

$$\frac{1}{2}, \frac{2}{2}, \frac{1}{3}, \frac{2}{3}, \frac{3}{3}, \frac{1}{4}, \frac{2}{4}, \frac{3}{4}, \frac{4}{4}, \frac{1}{5}, \frac{2}{5}, \frac{3}{5}, \frac{4}{5}, \frac{5}{5}, \frac{1}{6}, \frac{2}{6}, \frac{3}{6}, \frac{4}{6}, \frac{5}{6}, \frac{6}{6}, \frac{1}{8}, \frac{2}{8}, \frac{3}{8}, \frac{4}{8}, \frac{5}{8}, \frac{6}{8}, \frac{7}{8}, \frac{8}{8},$$
$$\frac{1}{10}, \frac{2}{10}, \frac{3}{10}, \frac{4}{10}, \frac{5}{10}, \frac{6}{10}, \frac{7}{10}, \frac{8}{10}, \frac{9}{10}, \frac{10}{10}, 1, 2, 3, 4.$$

Deal each player seven cards. Place the deck in the middle of the playing area, and turn a card from the deck faceup. Players take turns playing their cards. A card with the same denominator or a card with an equivalent fraction is discarded on top of the card that is faceup, on the discard pile. If a player has a card with a whole number, he or she can play the card and change the denominator to be played next. If a player does not have a card that can be played, he or she must draw from the deck and lose a turn. The game ends when one player gets rid of all of his or her cards.

12

Rational Numbers Expressed as Fractions: Operations

TEACHING COMPETENCIES

Upon completing this chapter, you will be able to:

- Use regions, groups, number lines, and other appropriate models to develop an understanding of addition, subtraction, multiplication, and division of fractions.

- Describe an efficient and effective instructional sequence for addition, subtraction, multiplication, and division of fractions.

- Use commonly employed algorithms for addition, subtraction, multiplication, and division of fractions.

- Use the least common denominator and the greatest common factor, as well as fundamental numerical properties, as tools in calculating with fractions.

- Design lessons for children that incorporate meaningful models for exploring operations on rational numbers expressed as fractions.

VIRTUAL MANIPULATIVES

Upon completing this chapter, you will be able to use virtual manipulatives on the accompanying CD to:

- Model the addition of fractions using *Fraction Bar Addition—1, 2, 3, and 4, Finding a Common Denominator*, and *Adding Fractions with Unlike Denominators*. **(VM 12.1a; VM 12.1b; VM12.1c)**

- Model the subtraction of fractions using *Fraction Bar Subtraction—1 and 2, Fraction Bar Subtraction—Missing Addend Form*, and *Subtracting Fractions with Mixed Numerals— 1 and 2*. **(VM 12.2a; VM 12.2b; VM 12.2c)**

- Model the multiplication of fractions using *Fraction Bar Multiplication—1 and 2* and *Rectangle Multiplication of Fractions*. **(VM 12.3a and VM 12.3b)**

- Model the division of fractions using *Fraction Bar Division—1, 2, 3, and 4* and *Parts of a Whole*. **(VM 12.4a and VM 12.4b)**

Numbered CD icons throughout the chapter refer to the virtual manipulatives in this list.

Consider the following drawing of an arrangement of Cuisenaire rods that uses the dark green rod to represent one unit. What does the picture reveal to you? What fraction concepts can be seen in this picture? What relationships between the rods can you find?

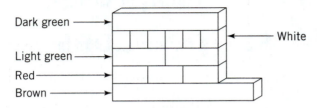

Dark green
Light green
Red
Brown
White

See if you can use relationships shown in the drawing to make some specific statements about the many names for 1, equivalent fractions, comparing fractions, mixed numerals, improper fractions, and even adding and subtracting fractions with unlike denominators! Ready? Look closely before reading on.

Examination of the picture should reveal that

● One UNIT (the dark green rod, in this case) can be represented by $\frac{6}{6}$, $\frac{2}{2}$, and $\frac{3}{3}$.

● $\frac{2}{6}$ (two of the white rods) equals $\frac{1}{3}$ (one of the red rods) showing that $\frac{2}{6} = \frac{1}{3}$.

● $\frac{2}{3}$ (two of the red rods) is more than $\frac{1}{2}$ (one of the light green rods) showing that $\frac{2}{3} > \frac{1}{2}$.

● The brown rod is clearly more than one unit—in fact, it is $\frac{8}{6}$ (the same length as eight of the white rods), or $\frac{4}{3}$ (the same as four of the red rods), or $1\frac{1}{3}$ (the same as one dark green and one red) showing that $\frac{8}{6} = \frac{4}{3} = 1\frac{1}{3}$. And, finally,

● $\frac{2}{3}$ (two red rods) is more than $\frac{1}{2}$ (one light green rod). How much more? That is, how much of a difference in length is there between $\frac{2}{3}$ and $\frac{1}{2}$ as shown by the drawing? Do you see that the difference is one white rod (i.e., $\frac{1}{6}$)? So, $\frac{2}{3} - \frac{1}{2} = \frac{1}{6}$.

RESEARCH SNAPSHOT

If children are encouraged to create their own ways to solve problems, can they invent their own algorithms for operations with fractions?

Along with two fifth-grade teachers, Huinker (1998) investigated this question. Rather than directly teaching algorithms as presented in the textbooks, the research team focused the class on developing meaning for fractions operations. They began with word problems to give their students a context in which to use objects and pictures to make sense of fraction concepts and operations. Students were encouraged to share their solution strategies with one another while the teachers would focus on making connections between the various representations.

The students were able to invent algorithms for adding, subtracting, multiplying, and dividing fractions, and there were many positive results in allowing students to invent their own algorithms. Some of them include that

The students were interested in solving and posing word problems with fractions.

They were flexible in their choice of strategy for solving both fraction word problems and computation exercises.

They were more accustomed to discussing their mathematical thinking and reasoning.

How will you make use of fraction models in support of allowing your students to create their own representations?

Huinker, D. (1998). Letting fraction algorithms emerge through problem solving. In L. Morrow & L. M. Kenney (Eds.), *The teaching and learning of algorithms in school mathematics* (pp. 170–182). Reston, VA: National Council of Teachers of Mathematics.

For additional research briefs, "ERIC Digests" lets you search more than 2000 short syntheses of research on a range of education topics. The syntheses were produced by the Educational Resources Information Center (ERIC). Check http://ed.gov/databases/ERIC_Digests/index/.

Quite a fraction feast from such a small drawing! Imagine what might be illustrated using other arrangements of Cuisenaire rods! (Try this by making a similar arrangement using one orange rod, ten white rods, five red rods, and two yellow rods.)

Approaches using regions, groups, and number lines, as well as Cuisenaire rods, base ten blocks, pattern blocks, and other manipulative materials, can help develop students' understanding of operations on fractions. Locate and study teachers' manuals and support books and articles that will provide assistance as you instruct children using such materials.

In Chapter 11, we used models of regions, groups, and number lines as techniques to help students develop an understanding of rational numbers written in fraction form. After the children have developed this understanding, as reflected by their grasp of the topics discussed in the previous chapter, they are ready to address the operations of addition, subtraction, multiplication, and division as applied to fractions. A strong understanding of whole numbers and operations with whole numbers forms a base for developing operations with fractions. Many of the previously learned concepts and structures of whole numbers can be directly applied to operations on fractional numbers.

The binary operations of addition and multiplication and the inverse operations of subtraction and division can be extended to fractions so that fundamental numerical properties are preserved. Addition and multiplication retain the **commutative** and **associative** properties; multiplication is still **distributive** over addition and subtraction; and 0 and 1 continue to be the **identity elements** for addition and multiplication, respectively. Once children grasp the idea that the operations and structure already studied extend naturally to fractions, they have learned a great deal about the system of rational numbers. This recognition of shared properties also helps children see the connections and relationships between things too often incorrectly viewed as having little or nothing to do with one another—operations on whole numbers and operations on rational numbers.

Addition of Fractional Numbers

Let's begin our study of computing with fractional numbers by examining addition. The following figures illustrate the use of rectangular regions in modeling addition of fractional numbers. We choose to begin with fractions with like denominators because the addition process involving such fractions most closely resembles the process of addition with whole numbers and it's always a good idea to tie what we are trying to learn to what we already know. A fraction chart (as illustrated in Chapter 11) is an excellent device for children to use in exploring addition. For example:

$$\frac{3}{4} + \frac{2}{4} = \frac{5}{4} = 1\frac{1}{4}$$

The two unit regions are both divided into fourths. Each smaller subregion therefore represents $\frac{1}{4}$.

Suppose we want to add $\frac{3}{4}$ and $\frac{2}{4}$. To represent $\frac{3}{4}$ in the diagram, we shade 3 of the smaller subregions; to represent $\frac{2}{4}$, we shade 2 more subregions. This gives us a total of 5 subregions that are shaded, each one representing $\frac{1}{4}$. We can indicate 4 of these regions as $\frac{4}{4}$, which equals 1 unit. Since the subregion remaining represents $\frac{1}{4}$, we can represent the sum of the 5 shaded regions by the numeral $\frac{5}{4}$—that is, $\frac{4}{4} + \frac{1}{4}$ or $1\frac{1}{4}$. (Note that this example presents an opportunity to reinforce the equivalency of the improper and mixed numeral forms of writing a given fraction greater than 1.)

VM 12.1a

Regions that are circular shaped should also be used as models of units to illustrate addition of fractions. Consider the previous example using equal circular regions as unit models instead of rectangular regions. Using fraction kits, each child should model the example:

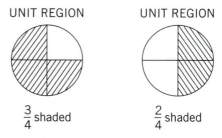

$\frac{3}{4}$ shaded $\frac{2}{4}$ shaded

The 2 circular unit regions shown here have been separated into fourths. Each small region then represents $\frac{1}{4}$ of the circular unit region. If we wish to add $\frac{3}{4}$ and $\frac{2}{4}$, we shade $\frac{3}{4}$ of one circular unit region and $\frac{2}{4}$ of a second circular unit region; then we combine the shaded regions.

$$\frac{3}{4} + \frac{2}{4}$$

$$\left(\frac{3}{4} + \frac{1}{4}\right) + \frac{1}{4}$$

$$\left(\frac{4}{4}\right) + \frac{1}{4}$$

$$1 + \frac{1}{4} = 1\frac{1}{4}$$

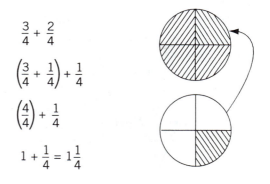

Note that by moving one of the fourths to the first region, we can form one complete unit, and $\frac{1}{4}$ of a unit is left over. So the result of adding $\frac{3}{4}$ and $\frac{2}{4}$ must be $1\frac{1}{4}$. (A point made in Chapter 11 is worth repeating here: When we use circular units, a student's ability to visualize the completion of a whole unit is much more obvious, especially compared to the use of rectangular units.)

The same example can also be illustrated with sets or groups of objects as follows:

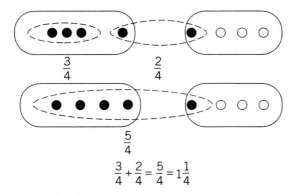

$$\frac{3}{4} + \frac{2}{4} = \frac{5}{4} = 1\frac{1}{4}$$

In this case, each group of 4 dots represents a unit, and each individual dot represents $\frac{1}{4}$. To represent $\frac{3}{4}$, we draw a loop around 3 dots, and to represent $\frac{2}{4}$, we draw a loop around 2 more dots. This gives us a total of 5 dots that have been enclosed with each dot representing $\frac{1}{4}$, indicating a value of $\frac{5}{4}$ or $1\frac{1}{4}$. We can represent this by drawing a loop around all 5 dots, as shown.

We have used rectangular regions, circular regions, and sets or groups to model addition of fractions; we can also use the number line. Remember that children have already modeled addition on the number line using whole numbers. We can use this prior experience with the number line to develop children's understanding of addition of fractions. Consider $\frac{3}{4} + \frac{1}{4} = \square$, for example.

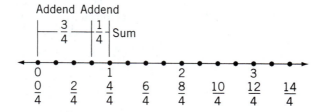

Children should have no difficulty finding the point on the number line that names $\frac{3}{4}$ and, since this is addition, then jumping one-fourth of a unit to the right. To start at $\frac{3}{4}$ and then jump $\frac{1}{4}$ of a unit to the right puts us at the point labeled $\frac{4}{4}$. We know, of course, that $\frac{4}{4}$ is another name for 1. Therefore:

$$\frac{3}{4} + \frac{1}{4} = \frac{4}{4} = 1$$

Some children may wonder about the example $\frac{1}{4} + \frac{3}{4} = \square$. To answer this, they will start at $\frac{1}{4}$ and then jump $\frac{3}{4}$ of a unit to the right.

These children will write:

$$\frac{1}{4} + \frac{3}{4} = \frac{4}{4} = 1$$

From these two examples, some children might conclude that since

$$\frac{3}{4} + \frac{1}{4} = 1 \text{ and } \frac{1}{4} + \frac{3}{4} = 1, \text{ then } \frac{3}{4} + \frac{1}{4} = \frac{1}{4} + \frac{3}{4}$$

This example hints at the existence of the commutative property for addition of fractional numbers. Here is an excellent chance for children to apply the basic structure that they have previously learned for whole numbers to test a hypothesis for rational numbers.

Consider this example: $\frac{3}{8} + \frac{7}{8} = \square$.

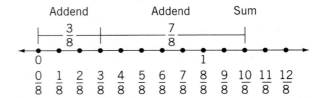

Locate $\frac{3}{8}$ on the number line; then jump, or count, $\frac{7}{8}$ unit (seven-eighths of a unit) to the right. This puts us at $\frac{10}{8}$. But $\frac{10}{8}$ has another name. We have passed the point named by 1 and moved another $\frac{2}{8}$ unit (two-eighths of a unit) to the right. Another name for $\frac{10}{8}$, then, is $1\frac{2}{8}$. Since $\frac{2}{8}$ can also be renamed in simplest form as $\frac{1}{4}$, another name for $\frac{10}{8}$ is $1\frac{1}{4}$.

$$\frac{3}{8} + \frac{7}{8} = \frac{10}{8} = \frac{8}{8} + \frac{2}{8}$$
$$= 1 + \frac{2}{8}$$
$$= 1 + \frac{1}{4}$$
$$= 1\frac{1}{4}$$

(Children are usually not asked to record each of these steps in this manner since it can become tedious and may detract from the focus on what is being learned. The steps are shown here for the teacher's benefit to aid the discussion of the underlying process.)

After exploring and examining many examples, children should be able to generalize: To add fractional numbers with like denominators, we add the numerators as we would add any pair of whole numbers and keep the same denominator. We may want, as in the preceding example, to express the sum as a mixed numeral and to write it in simplest form (e.g., $\frac{2}{8} = \frac{1}{4}$) for greater clarity.

Children can discover how to add using mixed numerals while they are learning to add fractional numbers with like denominators. Consider the example $\frac{4}{3} + \frac{5}{3} = \square$.

Locate $\frac{4}{3}$ on the number line; from this point, jump $\frac{5}{3}$ units to the right. This puts us at the point named $\frac{9}{3}$, so $\frac{4}{3} + \frac{5}{3} = \frac{9}{3}$. This can also be expressed with mixed numerals: $1\frac{1}{3} + 1\frac{2}{3} = 3$, since $\frac{4}{3} = 1\frac{1}{3}$ and $\frac{5}{3} = 1\frac{2}{3}$ and $\frac{9}{3} = 3$. Therefore, if we were given the example $1\frac{1}{3} + 1\frac{2}{3} =$, we COULD approach it by first translating it into improper fraction form, then solving it, and finally translating it back into mixed numeral form.

There is, however, a more direct, perhaps more efficient, method for solving examples written in mixed numeral form. We know that $1\frac{1}{3}$ can be expressed as $1 + \frac{1}{3}$ and that $1\frac{2}{3}$ can be expressed as $1 + \frac{2}{3}$. Thus $1\frac{1}{3} + 1\frac{2}{3} = \square$ can be rewritten as $(1 + \frac{1}{3}) + (1 + \frac{2}{3}) = \square$. We can then solve the example as follows:

$$
\begin{aligned}
1\tfrac{1}{3} + 1\tfrac{2}{3} &= (1 + \tfrac{1}{3}) + (1 + \tfrac{2}{3}) && \text{Renaming} \\
&= (1 + 1) + (\tfrac{1}{3} + \tfrac{2}{3}) && \text{Commutative} \\
& && \text{and associative} \\
&= 2 + \tfrac{3}{3} && \text{Renaming} \\
&= 2 + 1 && \text{Renaming} \\
&= 3 && \text{Renaming}
\end{aligned}
$$

Remember: This drawn-out written form illustrates how we want children to mentally manipulate examples. It is not recommended that you require children to write out each of these steps. That is, we want children to recognize that we can add mixed numerals by adding their whole number parts separately ($1 + 1 = 2$), then adding their fractional parts separately ($\frac{1}{3} + \frac{2}{3} = \frac{3}{3}$), and, if necessary, rewriting the sum ($2 + \frac{3}{3} = 3$).

Regions can also be used as models to help children understand how to add numbers expressed as mixed numerals. You can see that 3 one-thirds equals 1 unit, that $\frac{4}{3}$ is $\frac{1}{3}$ more than a unit, and that $\frac{5}{3}$ is $\frac{2}{3}$ more than 1 unit. When we put them together, there are 2 and $\frac{3}{3}$ or a total of 3 units.

1 unit			1 unit			1 unit		
$\frac{1}{3}$	$\frac{1}{3}$	$\frac{1}{3}$	$\frac{1}{3}$	$\frac{1}{3}$	$\frac{1}{3}$	$\frac{1}{3}$	$\frac{1}{3}$	$\frac{1}{3}$

$$\frac{4}{3} \qquad + \qquad \frac{5}{3} \qquad = \frac{9}{3} = 3$$

Experiment using circular regions as a model or using Cuisenaire rods, pattern blocks, or any other appropriate manipulative material as models. Children should be encouraged to experiment with a number of different models to assist them as they generalize concepts.

Children often have little difficulty adding fractions with *like* denominators. Addition of fractions with *unlike* denominators, however, may prove to be more of a challenge (depending on how the topic is approached). Gradually move into unlike denominators by beginning with examples that have *unlike but related denominators*. Examples of these would include $\frac{1}{3} + \frac{1}{6}$. In this case, one of the denominators of the given fractions turns out to be the common denominator for the two fractions. After children become proficient with unlike but related denominators, move on to examples with *unlike and unrelated* denominators, such as $\frac{1}{3} + \frac{1}{4}$. Note that in this case, neither of the given denominators is the common denominator for the two fractions. Next, examples such as $\frac{1}{4} + \frac{1}{6}$ may be studied. In this case, the two denominators do share a common factor (2), but neither denominator is the common denominator.

How can we add fractions when the denominators of the addends are unlike? Consider the example $\frac{1}{3} + \frac{5}{6} = \square$.

VM 12.1a

Let's use a number line model:

Locate $\frac{1}{3}$ on the number line. We can see that $\frac{1}{3}$ has another name, $\frac{2}{6}$. After locating $\frac{1}{3}$ (or $\frac{2}{6}$), we can add $\frac{5}{6}$ by moving $\frac{5}{6}$ units (five-sixths of a unit) to the right, which brings us to the point named by $\frac{7}{6}$. The fact that $\frac{1}{3}$ can be rewritten as $\frac{2}{6}$, which has the same denominator as $\frac{5}{6}$, should suggest another way of obtaining the sum $\frac{7}{6}$.

$$
\begin{aligned}
\tfrac{1}{3} + \tfrac{5}{6} &= \tfrac{2}{6} + \tfrac{5}{6} \\
&= \tfrac{7}{6} \text{ or } 1\tfrac{1}{6}
\end{aligned}
$$

Note that, as emphasized in Chapter 11, the child who is well versed in the prerequisite skill of writing equivalent fractions should encounter little or no difficulty here.

The example $\frac{1}{3} + \frac{5}{6} = \square$ may also be modeled using rectangular regions.

1 unit		
$\frac{1}{3}$	$\frac{1}{3}$	$\frac{1}{3}$

$\frac{1}{6}$	$\frac{1}{6}$	$\frac{1}{6}$	$\frac{1}{6}$	$\frac{1}{6}$	$\frac{1}{6}$

Separate the region into thirds and sixths, since those are the denominators of the two fractions to be added. The student can easily see that $\frac{2}{6}$ is another name for $\frac{1}{3}$. When $\frac{1}{3}$ is put with $\frac{5}{6}$, we see that we have $\frac{1}{6}$ more than 1; thus, we have $\frac{7}{6}$.

1 unit					
$\frac{1}{3}$	$\frac{1}{6}$	$\frac{1}{6}$	$\frac{1}{6}$	$\frac{1}{6}$	$\frac{1}{6}$

$$\frac{1}{3} \quad + \quad \frac{5}{6} \quad = \frac{7}{6} = 1\frac{1}{6}$$

This will be a relatively simple step for many children if models have first been used to develop a basic understanding of what abstract rational numbers expressed as fractions really represent in model form. An understanding of how to generate sets of equivalent fractions and renaming fractions is also necessary. We cannot stress too often the importance of developing an understanding through models. If more emphasis is placed on developing an understanding of fraction concepts, less time (and less effort) will be needed to develop an understanding of addition, subtraction, multiplication, and division with fractions.

After studying equivalent fractions, children should not have difficulty with addition of fractions having unlike denominators. They can apply knowledge they already have to find equivalent fractions with common denominators. In general, if two fractional addends have unlike denominators, we can rename one (or both) of the addends so that the denominators are the same; then we find the sum of these fractions in the usual manner. Consider $\frac{1}{3} + \frac{1}{6} = \square$: $\frac{1}{3} + \frac{1}{6} = \frac{2}{6} + \frac{1}{6}$ (since $\frac{1}{3} \times \frac{2}{2} = \frac{2}{6}$). We may prefer to express our answer, $\frac{3}{6}$, in simplest form, usually the most convenient way to name

fractions. Reviewing simplest form briefly, we know from number line models that $\frac{3}{6} = \frac{1}{2}$. At this point of the children's development, you may wish to review simplifying fractions and renaming fractions using the identity element of multiplication. We can multiply any fraction by 1 without affecting the value of the fraction.

$$\frac{1}{2} \times 1 = \frac{1}{2} \times \frac{3}{3}$$
$$= \frac{1 \times 3}{2 \times 3}$$
$$= \frac{3}{6}$$

The inverse of this is also true. We can divide any fraction by 1 without changing the value of the fraction. Thus:

$$\frac{3}{6} = \frac{3 \div 3}{6 \div 3} = \frac{1}{2}$$

Now let's consider addition of unlike and unrelated fractions—that is, fractions whose denominators are different and which don't share a common factor. How can we add $\frac{1}{4}$ and $\frac{1}{3}$? Begin with models to help children understand why a common denominator is important and how a common denominator can be found. If circular regions are used as models, we can place $\frac{1}{4}$ of a unit circle together with $\frac{1}{3}$ of a unit circle, but the children probably do not know which fraction name to use to describe this new region.

By placing other parts of circular regions on top of these 2 regions, children should discover that seven-twelfths would cover the new region exactly. After much experimentation, children should develop a systematic technique to solve examples of this type.

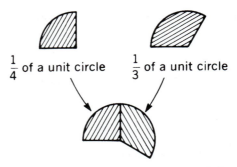

$\frac{1}{4}$ of a unit circle $\frac{1}{3}$ of a unit circle

What part of a circular region is this?

VM 12.1a

The virtual manipulative *Fraction Bars 12.1a* provides a technological opportunity to use rectangular regions and number lines to model addition of fractional numbers.

Use the *Fraction Bars* virtual manipulative on the accompanying CD to illustrate $\frac{1}{4} + \frac{3}{4}$. Model $\frac{3}{4} + \frac{2}{4}$. Add a new bar of $\frac{1}{1}$.

What does the denominator of the answer represent?

How do we use the virtual manipulative to add fractions when the denominators are not the same as in $\frac{2}{3} + \frac{5}{6}$? As a hint, first use the virtual manipulative to model equivalent fractions such as $\frac{2}{3}$ and $\frac{4}{6}$.

Before fractional numbers such as $\frac{1}{4}$ and $\frac{1}{3}$ can be added (or subtracted), a common denominator must be found that is divisible by each of the two original denominators—alternatively, it must be a multiple of each of the denominators. In the case of $\frac{1}{4} + \frac{1}{3} = \square$, the collection of possible common denominators includes 12, 24, 36, 48, or, for that matter, any nonzero multiple of 12. Any one of these common denominators could be used in adding the two fractional numbers; however, it is typically most convenient to use the least common denominator (12, in this case).

Finding the **least common denominator (LCD)** is actually an extension of the process of finding the **least common multiple (LCM)** of the denominators. In fact, a student who knows how to find the LCM can readily make the connection to finding a LCD—the multiples found in the LCM process are simply used as denominators in the LCD process. When the least common multiple is used as the common denominator, it is usually easier for us to express our answer in simplest form.

Consider the example suggested earlier: $\frac{1}{4} + \frac{1}{3}$. One common method of identifying the least common multiple (i.e., the denominator) is to break the process into three steps:

1. List several of the multiples of each of the numbers in order:

Multiples (nonzero) of 4: 4, 8, 12, 16, 20, 24, 28, . . .

Multiples (nonzero) of 3: 3, 6, 9, 12, 15, 18, 21, 24, . . .

2. Find those multiples that are common to both lists:

4, 8, ⑫ 16, 20, ㉔ 28, . . .
3, 6, 9, ⑫ 15, 18, 21, ㉔ . . .

3. Simply select the least of these common multiples. This choice will be the least common multiple, and when expressed as a denominator, it will be the least common denominator.

Another method of determining the LCM is by factoring the denominators completely—that is, by factoring them into prime factors:

$$\frac{1}{4} = \frac{1}{2 \times 2}$$
$$\frac{1}{3} = \frac{1}{3}$$

The LCM can be constructed from the prime factorizations of the denominators. First, the LCM must have 2×2 as a factor in order for it to be a multiple of 4:

$$\text{LCM} = 2 \times 2 \times ?$$

The 2×2 ensures that the LCM is divisible by 4, and the question mark indicates that there may be other factors. Next, we know that the LCM must contain the factor 3 in order to be divisible by 3:

$$\text{LCM} = 2 \times 2 \times 3$$

Now it is apparent that the LCM we have constructed is divisible by both 4 and 3. So, $2 \times 2 \times 3$, or 12, is the least common multiple of 3 and 4 and, hence, the least common denominator of thirds and fourths.

The least common multiple can always be built by factoring the denominators into prime factors and then identifying the least number that is a multiple of both denominators. Let's consider another example:

$$\frac{1}{6} + \frac{1}{8} + \frac{1}{3} = \square$$

Factor the denominators completely:

$$\frac{1}{6} = \frac{1}{2 \times 3} \qquad \frac{1}{8} = \frac{1}{2 \times 2 \times 2} \qquad \frac{1}{3} = \frac{1}{3}$$

Now build the least common multiple of 6, 8, and 3. The LCM must contain 2×3 in order to be divisible by 6:

$$\text{LCM} = 2 \times 3 \times ?$$

It must also contain $2 \times 2 \times 2$ to be divisible by 8. That is, the LCM must contain 2 as a factor three times. But since we have already recorded 2 as a factor once (LCM $= 2 \times 3 \times ?$), it is necessary to record it only twice more for the LCM to accommodate divisibility by 8:

$$\text{LCM} = 2 \times 3 \times 2 \times 2 \times ?$$

Finally, the LCM must contain the factor 3 so that it can be divided by 3. But 3 has already been indicated as a factor (LCM $= 2 \times 3 \times 2 \times 2 \times ?$), so it shouldn't be recorded again. Thus we have identified the LCM as

$$2 \times 3 \times 2 \times 2 = 24$$

The basic structure that we have studied shows that multiplying a number by the **identity element for multiplication**, 1, does not change the value of the number ($a \times 1 = a$). We have also learned how to name 1 by using fractions such as $\frac{2}{2}, \frac{3}{3}, \frac{4}{4}, \frac{5}{5}$, and $\frac{6}{6}$. Therefore, any fraction can be multiplied by an equivalent value of 1 (any fraction whose numerator and denominator are identical, other than 0) without changing the value of the fraction. With this in mind, let's return to our original example and find the sum.

$$\frac{1}{6} + \frac{1}{8} + \frac{1}{3} = \square$$

$$\frac{1}{6} = \frac{\square}{24} \rightarrow \frac{1 \times \square}{6 \times \square} = \frac{\square}{24} \rightarrow \frac{1 \times 4}{6 \times 4} = \frac{4}{24}$$

$$\frac{1}{8} = \frac{\square}{24} \rightarrow \frac{1 \times \square}{8 \times \square} = \frac{\square}{24} \rightarrow \frac{1 \times 3}{8 \times 3} = \frac{3}{24}$$

$$\frac{1}{3} = \frac{\square}{24} \rightarrow \frac{1 \times \square}{3 \times \square} = \frac{\square}{24} \rightarrow \frac{1 \times 8}{3 \times 8} = \frac{8}{24}$$

We have now found equivalent fractions for each fraction in the original example. Since these new fractions have a common denominator, we can easily find the sum by adding their numerators.

$$\frac{4}{24} + \frac{3}{24} + \frac{8}{24} = \frac{15}{24}$$
$$\frac{15}{24} = \frac{15 \div 3}{24 \div 3} = \frac{5}{8}$$

Now let's consider another example: $\frac{3}{8} + \frac{5}{6} = \square$. First we must find the least common denominator for $\frac{3}{8}$ and $\frac{5}{6}$—that is, the least common multiple of 8 and 6.

$$\frac{3}{8} = \frac{3}{2 \times 2 \times 2}$$
$$\frac{5}{6} = \frac{5}{2 \times 3}$$

$LCM = 2 \times 2 \times 2 \times ?$ (The LCM is divisible by 8)
$\quad\quad\; = 2 \times 2 \times 2 \times 3$ (The LCM is also divisible by 6)
$\quad\quad\; = 24$

Then we must rename $\frac{3}{8}$ and $\frac{5}{6}$ as fractions having the common denominator of 24.

$$\frac{3}{8} = \frac{\square}{24}$$
$$\frac{3}{8} \times 1 = \frac{\square}{24}$$

Which equivalent fraction can we use for 1 in this example? Since $\frac{3}{8} \times \frac{3}{3} = \frac{9}{24}$, we can use $\frac{3}{3}$ to make the denominator 24.

$$\frac{5}{6} = \frac{\square}{24}$$
$$\frac{5}{6} \times 1 = \frac{\square}{24}$$

Which equivalent fraction can we use to represent 1 this time? We can use $\frac{4}{4}$ to make the denominator 24.

$$\frac{5}{6} \times \frac{4}{4} = \frac{20}{24}$$

Now we can use these conversions to add:

$$\frac{3}{8} + \frac{5}{6} = \frac{9}{24} + \frac{20}{24}$$
$$= \frac{29}{24}$$
$$= \left(\frac{24}{24} + \frac{5}{24}\right)$$
$$= 1 + \frac{5}{24}$$
$$= 1\frac{5}{24}$$

The concept of finding common denominators must be extended to the addition of numbers expressed as mixed numerals. Begin with examples such as $1\frac{1}{2} + \frac{1}{3}$; then move to examples with two mixed numerals, such as $1\frac{1}{2} + 4\frac{1}{3}$. Then, move on to examples that will require renaming, such as $3\frac{4}{5} + 2\frac{3}{4}$.

Subtraction of Fractional Numbers

Subtraction of fractional numbers can be introduced shortly after beginning the exploration of addition. Regions, groups of objects, and number lines may be used as models for subtraction as well as addition. The children should manipulate the pieces in fraction kits, or pieces from a fraction chart; appropriate pattern blocks; or Cuisenaire rods before attempting to use the more abstract number line.

Let's model the example $\frac{3}{4} - \frac{1}{4} = \square$ using regions. The unit has been separated into fourths, and we begin with 3 one-fourths ($\frac{3}{4}$). One-fourth may be taken away from the $\frac{3}{4}$, leaving $\frac{2}{4}$. Another name for $\frac{2}{4}$ is $\frac{1}{2}$.

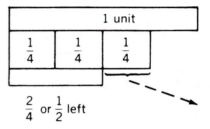

$\frac{2}{4}$ or $\frac{1}{2}$ left

Regions can also be used to model subtraction of fractions according to the missing addend (or the comparison) method first discussed in Chapter 7, "Addition and Subtraction of Whole Numbers." Rather than taking away one-fourth, we can place a region representing one-fourth on top of a region representing three-fourths. The question then becomes, "What do we need to add to the one-fourth to equal the three-fourths?"

Through use of the number line (using whole numbers), children should realize that subtraction is the inverse operation of addition and that we can use the number line to model subtraction. Consider this example:

$$\frac{3}{4} - \frac{1}{4} = \square$$

We could use the idea that subtraction is the inverse of addition and rewrite the subtraction example $\frac{3}{4} - \frac{1}{4} = \square$ as $\frac{1}{4} + \square = \frac{3}{4}$. This example can then be solved on a number line as follows:

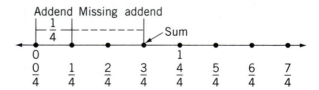

Therefore, $\square = \frac{2}{4} = \frac{1}{2}$; so $\frac{3}{4} - \frac{1}{4} = \frac{1}{2}$. Notice that $\frac{2}{4}$ is renamed as $\frac{1}{2}$. This is possible because $\frac{2}{4}$ and $\frac{1}{2}$ are equivalent fractions. We rename $\frac{2}{4}$ as $\frac{1}{2}$ to express the answer in simplest form.

After working through several examples directed to students' understanding of the process, children should be able to make some generalizations about subtraction of fractions:

1. To subtract fractional numbers, represent them by fractions having like denominators.

2. Then subtract the numerators in the same way that whole numbers are subtracted.

3. The denominator of the difference is the same as the common denominator found in step 1.

4. The answer is usually written in simplest form for convenience.

VM 12.2b

Consider another example, $\frac{5}{8} - \frac{3}{8} = \square$. Again, using the idea that subtraction is the inverse of addition, we can think of $\frac{5}{8}$ as the sum and $\frac{3}{8}$ as the known addend. What, then, is the missing addend? This example could be rewritten as $\frac{3}{8} + \square = \frac{5}{8}$ and then be modeled on a number line as follows:

We find that the missing addend is $\frac{2}{8}$. Notice that $\frac{2}{8}$ in simplest form is $\frac{1}{4}$. Therefore, $\frac{5}{8} - \frac{3}{8} = \frac{2}{8} = \frac{1}{4}$.

We can use a similar method to subtract $\frac{7}{8}$ from $\frac{19}{8}$.

Mark the known addend on the number line, $\frac{7}{8}$, and then locate the sum, $\frac{19}{8}$. The missing addend is found to

be $\frac{12}{8}$ but another name for $\frac{12}{8}$ is $\frac{3}{2}$. That is, $\frac{12}{8} \div \frac{4}{4} = \frac{3}{2}$ or $1\frac{1}{2}$.

Children should apply fundamental knowledge of addition to the subtraction of fractions to discover how a problem such as the following can be solved:

$$\frac{7}{8} - \frac{3}{4} = \square$$

They should recall that it is useful for fractions to have like denominators before addition or subtraction is performed. In this case, one of these fractions should be renamed. We can rename $\frac{3}{4}$ as $\frac{6}{8}$. The example can now be solved.

$$\frac{7}{8} - \frac{3}{4} = \frac{7}{8} - \frac{6}{8}$$
$$= \frac{1}{8}$$

This example, of course, can also be solved using the number line as a model:

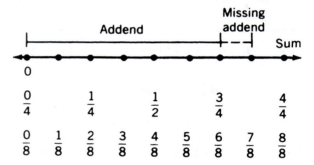

Again, the answer is clearly $\frac{1}{8}$.

Now let's consider a slightly more complex example:

$$\frac{11}{12} - \frac{5}{8} = \square$$

By applying knowledge of least common multiples, children should be able to factor both denominators and identify the LCM:

$$\frac{11}{12} = \frac{11}{2 \times 2 \times 3}$$
$$\frac{5}{8} = \frac{5}{2 \times 2 \times 2}$$

Just as we did with the addition of fractional numbers, the virtual manipulative *Fraction Bars 12.2a* provides a technological opportunity to use rectangular regions and number lines to model subtraction of fractional numbers. As before, the use of equivalent fractions before computation is an important step in understanding the process.

Subtraction can be modeled using the missing addend method first discussed in Chapter 7. For example, $\frac{5}{8} - \frac{3}{8} = \square$ may be modeled as adding an amount to $\frac{3}{8}$ to get $\frac{5}{8}$. Use the virtual manipulative *Fraction Bars* on the accompanying CD to explore the idea of "missing addend" subtraction.

VM 12.2a

The exercise $\frac{5}{8} - \frac{3}{8} = \square$ may also be viewed as adding $\frac{3}{8}$ to $\frac{3}{8}$. Create $\frac{3}{8}$ using the virtual manipulative *Fraction Bars* by adding a negative sign to either the numerator or denominator before clicking "New Bar." Explain how to use the model to show that $\frac{5}{8} - \frac{3}{8} = \frac{5}{8} + (-\frac{3}{8})$.

Then they should build the LCM by using the factors of 12 and 8. The LCD is thus $2 \times 2 \times 3 \times 2$, or 24. Finally, they should rename $\frac{11}{12}$ and $\frac{5}{8}$ and perform the indicated subtraction.

$$\frac{11}{12} = \frac{11 \times 2}{12 \times 2} = \frac{22}{24}$$

$$\frac{5}{8} = \frac{5 \times 3}{8 \times 3} = \frac{15}{24}$$

$$\frac{22}{24} - \frac{15}{24} = \frac{7}{24}$$

We can solve each of these subtraction examples by using regions or sets. Let's demonstrate the region and set approaches in solving the example $\frac{7}{8} - \frac{7}{16} = \square$. Consider the following unit region, which has been divided into 16 parts (subregions) to illustrate eighths and sixteenths:

UNIT REGION

We can represent $\frac{7}{8}$ by shading 7 of the 8 regions that illustrate eighths. We can represent $\frac{7}{16}$ by shading 7 of the 16 regions that illustrate sixteenths. To represent $\frac{7}{8} - \frac{7}{16}$ however, the shaded region indicating $\frac{7}{16}$ must be entirely contained within the shaded region indicating $\frac{7}{8}$ (because we are subtracting $\frac{7}{16}$ *from* $\frac{7}{8}$), so the regions indicating $\frac{7}{8}$ and $\frac{7}{16}$ must be shaded differently:

UNIT REGION

In this unit region, the difference between $\frac{7}{8}$ and $\frac{7}{16}$ is indicated by the part of the region shaded only once. This region contains 7 smaller regions illustrating sixteenths; therefore it represents $\frac{7}{16}$. So $\frac{7}{8} - \frac{7}{16} = \frac{7}{16}$.

Now let's approach this same example using groups instead of regions. Consider the following group of 16 dots:

If this entire group of dots represents 1 unit, then each individual dot represents $\frac{1}{16}$ of a unit, and each column of dots represents $\frac{1}{8}$. Now, if we enclose seven of the eight columns with a loop, the 14 enclosed dots illustrate

the fractional number $\frac{7}{8}$. The difference between $\frac{7}{8}$ and $\frac{7}{16}$ is indicated by all the dots enclosed by the outside dashed loop but not by the inside dashed loop. In the following figure, these dots are shaded:

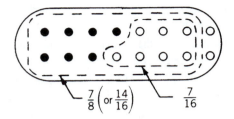

Because there are 7 dots shaded (out of a total of 16 dots in the group) and since each of the dots represents $\frac{1}{16}$, then difference between $\frac{7}{8}$ and $\frac{7}{16}$ is clearly $\frac{7}{16}$. That is, $\frac{7}{8} - \frac{7}{16} = \frac{7}{16}$.

Often we need to work with fractions in the form of mixed numerals—for example, $5\frac{7}{8} - 4\frac{5}{8} = \square$. It should not be difficult to extend our understanding of subtraction to include numbers expressed as mixed numerals. Our approach here is very similar to that used for addition with mixed numerals:

$$5\frac{7}{8} = 5 + \frac{7}{8}$$

$$-4\frac{5}{8} = \frac{-\left(4 + \frac{5}{8}\right)}{1 + \frac{2}{8}}$$

$$= 1 + \frac{1}{4}$$

$$= 1\frac{1}{4}$$

Note that the this notation introduces two extra addition symbols, the one appearing in front of the $\frac{7}{8}$ and the one in front of the $\frac{5}{8}$. Some children may be more likely to subtract the whole numbers and then add the fractions. To lessen this possibility, you may wish to replace the addition symbol with the word *and* so that instead of writing "$5 + \frac{7}{8}$," you have "5 and $\frac{7}{8}$." If, however, you think that the addition symbol is a must in this situation, then call children's attention to the parentheses, and explain that both the whole number and the fraction must be subtracted. That is, we write mixed numerals as the sum of whole numbers and fractional numbers. Then we subtract whole numbers to obtain the whole number difference and subtract the fractional numbers to obtain the fractional number difference. Notice that we write the fractional number difference in simplest form.

In subtraction with mixed numerals, it is important to develop an understanding of renaming. For instance, consider the following subtraction example:

$$3\frac{1}{4}$$

$$-2\frac{3}{4}$$

In such cases, even though the fractions already have a common denominator, we cannot simply subtract the numerators. Therefore, we must find another way of expressing $3\frac{1}{4}$ so that we can subtract $2\frac{3}{4}$ from it.

$$3\frac{1}{4} = 3 + \frac{1}{4}$$
$$= (2+1) + \frac{1}{4}$$
$$= (2 + \frac{4}{4}) + \frac{1}{4}$$
$$= 2 + (\frac{4}{4} + \frac{1}{4})$$
$$= 2 + \frac{5}{4}$$
$$= 2\frac{5}{4}$$

By renaming 3 as $2 + 1$ and expressing 1 as $\frac{4}{4}$, we can rewrite $3\frac{1}{4}$ as $2\frac{5}{4}$ and proceed with subtraction.

$$3\frac{1}{4} = 2\frac{5}{4}$$
$$\underline{-2\frac{3}{4}}$$
$$\frac{2}{4} = \frac{1}{2}$$

VM 12.2c   Note that the series of written steps shown here is usually not recorded by students in such detail. It is important, however, that these same steps be demonstrated many times through the use of physical models such as regions or number lines. The children must see that $3\frac{1}{4}$ has been renamed as $2\frac{5}{4}$. This should not be left to the abstract form only. Consider, for example, the pictorial representation of $3\frac{1}{4} - 2\frac{3}{4} = \square$.

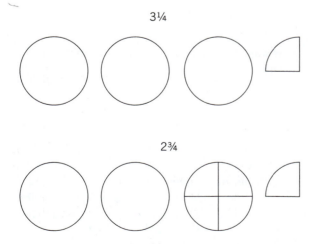

3¼

2¾

In this representation, one of the 3 units in $3\frac{1}{4}$ has been cut into fourths so that $3\frac{1}{4}$ is now represented by 2 units and a total of 5 fourths—that is, $2\frac{5}{4}$.

Another example of this kind, presented abstractly, is $8\frac{1}{6} - 3\frac{5}{6} = \square$.

$$8\frac{1}{6} = 8 + \frac{1}{6} = 7 + (\frac{6}{6} + \frac{1}{6}) \qquad = \quad 7 + \frac{7}{6}$$
$$\underline{-3\frac{5}{6} = -(3 + \frac{5}{6})} \qquad\qquad = \quad \frac{-(3 + \frac{5}{6})}{4 + \frac{2}{6}}$$
$$= \quad 4 + \frac{1}{3}$$
$$= \quad 4\frac{1}{3}$$

Now let's examine another example:

$$7\frac{3}{8}$$
$$\underline{-2\frac{3}{4}}$$

First, we should obtain a common denominator. Because $\frac{3}{4} = \frac{6}{8}$, we can rename $2\frac{3}{4}$ as $2\frac{6}{8}$.

$$7\frac{3}{8} = 7\frac{3}{8}$$
$$\underline{-2\frac{3}{4}} = \underline{-2\frac{6}{8}}$$

Now we should find another way to name $7\frac{3}{8}$ so we can easily subtract the numerators:

$$7\frac{3}{8} = 7 + \frac{3}{8}$$
$$= (6+1) + \frac{3}{8}$$
$$= (6 + \frac{8}{8}) + \frac{3}{8}$$
$$= 6 + (\frac{8}{8} + \frac{3}{8})$$
$$= 6 + \frac{11}{8}$$
$$= 6\frac{11}{8}$$

Now we can solve the example:

$$6\frac{11}{8} - 2\frac{6}{8} = 4\frac{5}{8}$$

In general, the difference between two fractions named by mixed numerals can be determined in the following way:

1. Find a common denominator for the fractional number parts, if necessary.
2. Rewrite the first mixed numeral, if necessary, so that the numerators of the fractional number parts can be subtracted.
3. Find the difference between the whole number parts of the two numbers.
4. Find the difference between the fractional number parts of the two numbers.
5. Express the difference in simplest form.

We have used the number line, physical models, and groups of objects to develop the operations of addition and subtraction with respect to fractional numbers. We must emphasize that we are extending old ideas—not teaching new ones. We are helping children discover how to apply the operations and basic structure they have previously studied and learned about whole number operations to a new situation: operations with fractional numbers.

Multiplication of Fractional Numbers

In this chapter so far, we have examined addition and subtraction with respect to fractional numbers. Now let's consider multiplication. To help establish a pattern of reasoning, we begin with examples in which a fractional number is multiplied by a whole number. As is the case with other operations, children should work with a variety of models to develop an understanding of the processes involved when multiplying fractions.

Multiplication of whole numbers, with which children at this stage of development should be quite familiar, always results in a product that is either equal to or greater than either of the original factors. When children begin to apply the operation of multiplication to fractional numbers, they will, for the first time, find that a product may be less than both factors.

Look at the number line and the example $3 \times \frac{1}{4} = \square$. In the same manner as we did for whole numbers, we may think of this example as meaning three groups with $\frac{1}{4}$ in each group.

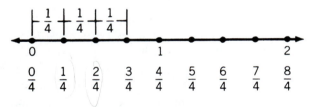

If we start at the point named 0 and make three jumps to the right, each jump $\frac{1}{4}$ of a unit in length, where do we land? We land at the point named $\frac{3}{4}$. By using the number line in this way, we can show the product, $3 \times \frac{1}{4}$, to be equal to $\frac{3}{4}$.

$$3 \times \frac{1}{4} = \frac{3}{4}$$

This example can also be written as follows:

$$\left(\frac{3}{1}\right) \times \left(\frac{1}{4}\right) = \frac{3}{4}$$

As we will discuss later, you should not be too quick to use this form of notation. Meaning is more important than symbolism at this developmental stage.

Now let's look at another example.

$$6 \times \frac{2}{3} = \square$$

On the number line, we can model $6 \times \frac{2}{3}$ with 6 line segments, each $\frac{2}{3}$ of a unit in length, placed end to end.

In doing so, we find that the resulting line segment is 4 units long. Thus, the product of 6 and $\frac{2}{3}$ is shown to be 4.

$$6 \times \frac{2}{3} = \frac{2}{3} + \frac{2}{3} + \frac{2}{3} + \frac{2}{3} + \frac{2}{3} + \frac{2}{3}$$
$$= \frac{12}{3}$$
$$= \frac{4}{1}$$
$$= 4$$

On the same number line, we can also show $\frac{2}{3} \times 6$. This can be pictured as $\frac{2}{3}$ of a line segment 6 units long. If the segment from 0 to 6 is divided into three parts, each 2 units long, $\frac{2}{3} \times 6$ is represented by two of these parts, or a total of 4 units.

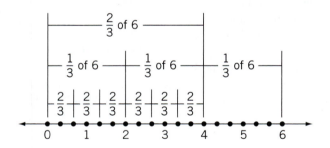

In this way, the commutative property of multiplication is clearly illustrated:

$$6 \times \frac{2}{3} = \frac{2}{3} \times 6$$

The number line can be used as a teaching aid, without difficulty, to illustrate multiplication examples in which one of the factors is a whole number. The number line is not the best model, however, to explain situations in which neither factor can be written as a whole number—for example, $\frac{2}{3} \times \frac{4}{5} = \square$ and $\frac{7}{21} \times \frac{2}{9} = \square$. To illustrate examples like these, we can make better use of a region model.

To explore the way in which regions are used to illustrate multiplication of fractional numbers, let's first look at the example $6 \times \frac{2}{3} = \square$ once again.

UNIT REGION

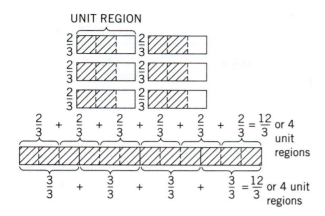

$$6 \times \frac{2}{3} = \frac{2}{3} + \frac{2}{3} + \frac{2}{3} + \frac{2}{3} + \frac{2}{3} + \frac{2}{3}$$

This illustration indicates the way in which multiplication can be modeled as repeated, or successive, addition. Thus:

$$6 \times \frac{2}{3} = \frac{2}{3} + \frac{2}{3} + \frac{2}{3} + \frac{2}{3} + \frac{2}{3} + \frac{2}{3}$$
$$= \frac{12}{3}$$
$$= 4$$

We can count the number of shaded parts (one-thirds) and see that there are 12 one-thirds, $\frac{12}{3}$. Another name for $\frac{12}{3}$ is 4.

$$\frac{12}{3} = \frac{3}{3} + \frac{3}{3} + \frac{3}{3} + \frac{3}{3} = 1 + 1 + 1 + 1 = 4$$

But, as stated earlier, the repeated addition model is not an efficient or appropriate model to use for exercises such as $\frac{1}{2} \times \frac{1}{3}$. A different approach to the use of regions is called for when the product of two fractions is involved.

A valuable device to teach multiplication of fractions is a unit square, a square with each side one unit long. The unit square may be subdivided into smaller squares. Let's examine the following models:

UNIT SQUARES

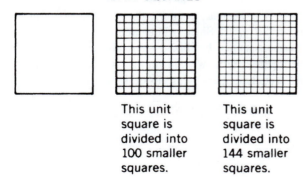

This unit square is divided into 100 smaller squares.

This unit square is divided into 144 smaller squares.

By strategically placing a colored rubber band across a unit card, we can illustrate $\frac{1}{2}$ of the card, $\frac{1}{4}$ of the card, or several other fractions. Using rubber bands and the unit card, let's consider this example:

$$\frac{1}{2} \times \frac{1}{3} = \square$$

First we construct a unit square.

UNIT SQUARE

Next we divide the unit square horizontally into halves.

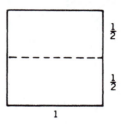

Then we divide the unit square vertically into thirds.

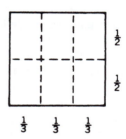

Examining the unit square, we see that it has been partitioned into 6 congruent (equal) regions. To show the result of $\frac{1}{2} \times \frac{1}{3}$ on the following region, we shade any $\frac{1}{3}$ of the unit square (shading one direction); then we shade either the lower or the upper $\frac{1}{2}$ of the unit square (shading a different direction). By observation, we can see that one part of the unit square has been shaded twice.

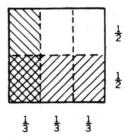

Comparing the double-shaded region with the total square, we see that one of the six parts (smaller regions) has been shaded twice. This leads us to the conclusion that $\frac{1}{2} \times \frac{1}{3} = \frac{1}{6}$. The same diagram, or one similar to the following, can be used to illustrate $\frac{1}{3} \times \frac{1}{2} = \frac{1}{6}$. This is another example of the commutative property of multiplication.

To explore multiplication of fractions using a unit square, use the *Rectangle Multiplication of Fractions 12.3b* virtual manipulative to model $\frac{1}{2} \times \frac{1}{3}$. Change the virtual manipulative to illustrate $\frac{1}{4} \times \frac{2}{3}$. Now try $\frac{3}{5} \times \frac{2}{3}$. These three examples are present on the accompanying CD.

　　Click on the "New Problem" button to model and explore other multiplication of fractions exercises.

VM 12.3b

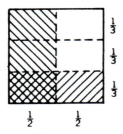

Now let's see how we can use the same sort of reasoning to find the product of two fractions whose values are both greater than 1.

$$\frac{3}{2} \times \frac{4}{3} = \square$$

First we construct a unit square, dividing the square horizontally into halves and vertically into thirds. We divide the square into halves and thirds because they are the fractional parts being considered (indicated by the denominators) in this particular example.

Notice that the square is now divided into six congruent parts. Since we have established our unit square, we can extend it horizontally and vertically to form a region that is $\frac{3}{2}$ by $\frac{4}{3}$ in size. We do this because $\frac{3}{2}$ and $\frac{4}{3}$ are the two factors being considered.

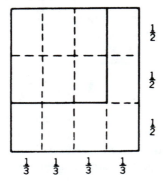

Again, notice that each small region is actually $\frac{1}{6}$ of a unit square. In this case, we have more small

regions than are necessary to make up one unit square. In fact, there are 12 small regions, or $\frac{12}{6}$ of a unit square. Since $\frac{12}{6}$ is another name for 2, we can see that there are actually enough small regions to complete two unit squares. Consequently, $\frac{3}{2} \times \frac{4}{3} = \frac{12}{6} = 2$. (NOTE: It might be advantageous to use centimeter graph paper for this model. A unit square can be marked off on part of the graph paper. Then, when it comes time to add on to the unit square, you will be able to do so by enlarging the boundary of the unit square on the graph paper.)

After children have solved many examples of this kind and have developed an understanding of multiplication of fractions, the more familiar algorithm for multiplying fractions can be introduced. Children should be led to generalize for themselves that when multiplying two fractions, they can multiply the numerators of the two factors to obtain the numerator of the product, and multiply the denominators of the two factors to obtain the denominator of the product. The last two examples can be solved using this algorithm as follows:

$$\frac{1}{2} \times \frac{1}{3} = \frac{1 \times 1}{2 \times 3} = \frac{1}{6}$$

$$\frac{3}{2} \times \frac{4}{3} = \frac{3 \times 4}{2 \times 3} = \frac{12}{6} \text{ or } 2$$

In each case, we get the same answer that we obtained by using regions. Notice that after we have determined the numerator and denominator of the product, we may wish to rewrite the product in another form (as an equivalent fraction or as a whole number, for instance).

In the second example, the product $\frac{12}{6}$ can be rewritten as 2. Since whole numbers and fractional numbers named by mixed numerals can be expressed in fraction form, we can find the product of any two fractional numbers by means of the algorithm.

$$6 \times \frac{2}{3} = \frac{6}{1} \times \frac{2}{3} \qquad 3 \times \frac{1}{4} = \frac{3}{1} \times \frac{1}{4}$$
$$= \frac{6 \times 2}{1 \times 3} \qquad\qquad = \frac{3 \times 1}{1 \times 4}$$
$$= \frac{12}{3} \text{ or } 4 \qquad\qquad = \frac{3}{4}$$

$$2\frac{1}{2} \times \frac{1}{3} = \frac{5}{2} \times \frac{1}{3} \qquad 2 \times 5 = \frac{2}{1} \times \frac{5}{1}$$
$$= \frac{5 \times 1}{2 \times 3} \qquad\qquad = \frac{2 \times 5}{1 \times 1}$$
$$= \frac{5}{6} \qquad\qquad = \frac{10}{1} \text{ or } 10$$

We can now generalize that to multiply any two fractions (whole numbers are understood here to be fractions having the denominator 1), the following steps should be performed:

1. Multiply the numerators of the factors to obtain the numerator of the product.

2. Multiply the denominators of the factors to obtain the denominator of the product.

3. If desired, rename the product (as an equivalent fraction or whole number numeral, for example).

If $\frac{a}{b}$ and $\frac{c}{d}$ are any two fractions such that $b \neq 0$ and $d \neq 0$, then
$$\frac{a}{b} \times \frac{c}{d} = \frac{a \times c}{b \times d}$$

After completing a multiplication example, it may be necessary to simplify the product. For instance:

$$\frac{2}{3} \times \frac{3}{4} = \frac{2 \times 3}{3 \times 4} = \frac{6}{12} = \frac{1 \times 6}{2 \times 6} = \frac{1}{2}$$

It may be much easier if the example is simplified before multiplying. Consider the example $\frac{2}{3} \times \frac{3}{4}$ again.

$$\frac{2}{3} \times \frac{3}{4} = \frac{2 \times 3}{3 \times 2 \times 2} \qquad \text{Factor}$$
$$= \frac{3 \times 2 \times 1}{3 \times 2 \times 2} \qquad \text{Rewrite}$$
$$= \frac{3}{3} \times \frac{2}{2} \times \frac{1}{2} \qquad \text{Rewrite}$$
$$= 1 \times 1 \times \frac{1}{2} \qquad \text{Rename}$$
$$= \frac{1}{2}$$

Factor the numerator and denominator completely. Look for values of 1. Thus you have simplified the example prior to multiplication.

$$\frac{5}{6} \times \frac{3}{10} = \frac{1 \times 5 \times 3}{2 \times 3 \times 5 \times 2}$$
$$= \frac{1 \times 3 \times 5 \times 1}{2 \times 3 \times 5 \times 2}$$
$$= \frac{1}{2} \times 1 \times 1 \times \frac{1}{2}$$
$$= \frac{1}{4}$$

Before going on to division of fractions, let's look at the example $\frac{1}{2} \times \square = 1$. Clearly, $\square = 2$ (or $\frac{2}{1}$), since $\frac{1}{2} \times \frac{2}{1} = \frac{2}{2} = 1$. If we work through some additional examples like this one, we begin to see a pattern emerge:

$$\frac{1}{5} \times \square = 1 \rightarrow \square = \frac{5}{1} \qquad \therefore \frac{1}{5} \times \frac{5}{1} = 1$$
$$\frac{4}{7} \times \square = 1 \rightarrow \square = \frac{7}{4} \qquad \therefore \frac{4}{7} \times \frac{7}{4} = 1$$
$$\frac{5}{3} \times \square = 1 \rightarrow \square = \frac{3}{5} \qquad \therefore \frac{5}{3} \times \frac{3}{5} = 1$$
$$\square \times \frac{11}{4} = 1 \rightarrow \square = \frac{4}{11} \qquad \therefore \frac{4}{11} \times \frac{11}{4} = 1$$

In each of these examples, we discover a pair of fractional numbers whose product is equal to 1. (Recall that the number 1 is called the identity element for

multiplication of whole numbers. We will see later in this chapter that 1 is also the identity element for multiplication of fractions.) Two numbers whose product is 1 are called **reciprocals** or **multiplicative inverses** of each other. For instance, the last three examples show that the reciprocal (or multiplicative inverse) of $\frac{4}{7}$ is $\frac{7}{4}$, that the reciprocal of $\frac{3}{5}$ is $\frac{5}{3}$, and that the reciprocal of $\frac{4}{11}$ is $\frac{11}{4}$. We also observe that for the fractions in each of these examples, the numerator of the first fraction equals the denominator of the second, and the denominator of the first equals the numerator of the second.

Is it possible to use this idea to find reciprocals? Let's see. If we interchange the numerator and denominator in the fraction $\frac{2}{3}$, we obtain $\frac{3}{2}$. Is $\frac{3}{2}$ the reciprocal of $\frac{2}{3}$? That is, does $\frac{3}{2} \times \frac{2}{3}$ equal 1? Yes, since $\frac{3}{2} \times \frac{2}{3} = \frac{6}{6} = 1$. Is it always true that if $\frac{a}{b}$ is a fraction, then its reciprocal is $\frac{b}{a}$? We might ask this question in a slightly different way: Is it true, for every fraction $\frac{a}{b}$, that $\frac{a}{b} \times \frac{b}{a} = 1$? The answer is yes, provided neither a nor b is equal to zero. (Why must we exclude these cases?)

Thus we have the following procedure for finding the reciprocal (or multiplicative inverse) of a nonzero fractional number:

1. Express the given number in fraction form.

2. Interchange the numerator and denominator of the fraction in step 1. The result is the reciprocal (or multiplicative inverse) of that fraction.

What is the reciprocal of $2\frac{3}{8}$? Use the procedure suggested.

First write the mixed numerals in fractional form:

$$2\frac{3}{8} = 2 + \frac{3}{8} = \frac{16}{8} + \frac{3}{8} = \frac{19}{8}$$

Then interchange the numerator and denominator of the fraction $\frac{19}{8}$. This gives the fraction $\frac{8}{19}$. Clearly, $\frac{8}{19}$ is the reciprocal of $2\frac{3}{8}$ since $2\frac{3}{8} \times \frac{8}{19} = \frac{19}{8} \times \frac{8}{19} = \frac{152}{152} = 1$.

Returning to our discussion of multiplying fractions, let's consider the multiplication example $3 \times 2\frac{1}{2} = \square$. We might choose to solve this example by expressing the factors in fraction form and multiplying as we would any two fractions.

$$3 \times 2\frac{1}{2} = \frac{3}{1} \times \frac{5}{2} \qquad \text{Renaming}$$
$$= \frac{3 \times 5}{1 \times 2} \qquad \text{Procedure for multiplying with fractions}$$
$$= \frac{15}{2} \qquad \text{Multiplication}$$
$$= \frac{14}{2} + \frac{1}{2} \qquad \text{Renaming}$$
$$= 7 + \frac{1}{2} \text{ or } 7\frac{1}{2} \qquad \text{Renaming}$$

However, there is another way of solving this example if we remember that a mixed numeral names the sum of a whole number and a fraction. That is, $2\frac{1}{2}$ can be written as $2 + \frac{1}{2}$.

$3 \times 2\frac{1}{2} = 3 \times (2 + \frac{1}{2})$	Renaming
$= (3 \times 2) + (3 \times \frac{1}{2})$	Distributive property of multiplicaton over addition
$= 6 + \frac{3}{2}$	Multiplication
$= 6 + (\frac{2}{2} + \frac{1}{2})$	Renaming
$= 6 + (1 + \frac{1}{2})$	Renaming
$= (6 + 1) + \frac{1}{2}$	Associative property
$= 7 + \frac{1}{2}$	Addition
$= 7\frac{1}{2}$	Renaming

Therefore, $3 \times 2\frac{1}{2} = 7\frac{1}{2}$.

As with other examples of this type, the intermediate steps need not be recorded with such detail by children—indeed, they shouldn't be. Instead, it is sufficient for them to comprehend the underlying process and note that "three times two and one-half is the same as three times two added to three times one-half, or six added to three-halves, or seven and one-half."

Now let's try another example: $3 \times 7\frac{1}{8} = \square$. We *could* choose to rewrite the first number as $\frac{3}{1}$ and the second as $\frac{57}{8}$ and then multiply these two fractions. Alternatively, let's examine the exercise as, perhaps, a more meaningful expression. We might then determine the answer to this, as described in the previous paragraph, by mentally renaming the second number as the sum of a whole number and a fraction. This approach allows us to interpret $3 \times 7\frac{1}{8}$ as the sum of three groups of 7 (or 21) and three groups of $\frac{1}{8}$ (or $\frac{3}{8}$), or $21 + \frac{3}{8}$, which can be written as $21\frac{3}{8}$.

Apply the same sort of reasoning described in the preceding examples, with a challenging twist, to solve $4\frac{1}{2} \times 6\frac{1}{4} = \square$. (Be careful: Here we would need to not only multiply 4×6 and $4 \times \frac{1}{4}$, we would also need to multiply $\frac{1}{2} \times 6$ and $\frac{1}{2} \times \frac{1}{4}$ for a total of $24 + 1 + 3 + \frac{1}{8}$ or $28\frac{1}{8}$.)

Teaching multiplication of numbers named by mixed numerals is really no more than an extension of what has been taught previously. Multiplication with mixed numerals should provide an opportunity for children to apply basic structure and discover how to solve seemingly new, but related examples.

Division of Fractional Numbers

Now let's examine the inverse of multiplication—division—with respect to fractions. This is often as challenging a topic for children to master as it is for teachers to develop in a meaningful manner. Actually, division of fractions is not very relevant to the everyday life of a child (or many adults, for that matter). Try, for example, to create a real-life story problem, meaningful to an elementary school child, which involves the division of two fractions. (Be careful with recipe examples: Most of these involve either the division of a fraction by a whole number or the multiplication of two fractions—not the division of a fraction by a fraction.) Certainly, examples can be found in construction, fashion design, and so on (have you thought of one yet?), but these examples are often contrived and commonly replaced by estimation and alternative algorithms when encountered in practice.

Recall that division on whole numbers was described in Chapter 8 as finding the missing factor, $\square$, in a sentence such as $A \times \square = B$. Let's apply this same description of division to the set of fractions. Consider the example $\frac{1}{4} \div \frac{1}{2} = \square$. The missing factor definition of division suggests that we can rewrite this example as the multiplication sentence $\frac{1}{2} \times \square = \frac{1}{4}$. Written in this form, the example asks us to find a number that will yield a product of $\frac{1}{4}$ when multiplied by $\frac{1}{2}$.

The example can also be expressed as follows:

$$\frac{1 \times \Diamond}{2 \times \triangle} = \frac{1}{4}$$

Because we know that $1 \times 1 = 1$, the numerator of the missing factor is clearly 1. Since we know that $2 \times 2 = 4$, the denominator is 2. Therefore, the answer is $\frac{1}{2}$.

$$\frac{1 \times 1}{2 \times 2} = \frac{1}{4} \qquad \frac{1}{2} \times \frac{1}{2} = \frac{1}{4} \quad \text{or} \quad \frac{1}{4} \div \frac{1}{2} = \frac{1}{2}$$

Consider the example $\frac{3}{4} \times \square = \frac{6}{16}$. It can be expressed in this form:

$$\frac{3 \times \Diamond}{4 \times \triangle} = \frac{6}{16}$$

The answer here is $\frac{2}{4}$, which can be renamed as $\frac{1}{2}$.

$$\frac{3}{4} \times \frac{2}{4} = \frac{6}{16} \qquad \text{or} \qquad \frac{3}{4} \times \frac{1}{2} = \frac{3}{8}$$

This procedure has been successful so far, but some examples might become difficult if no alternative procedure were available. Consider the example $\frac{3}{7} \times \square = \frac{5}{9}$, which can be rewritten as follows:

$$\frac{3 \times \Diamond}{7 \times \triangle} = \frac{5}{9}$$

Three times what number equals 5, and seven times what number equals 9? This method gives us a cumbersome, but nevertheless correct, answer.

$$\frac{1\frac{2}{3}}{1\frac{2}{7}}$$

How can children begin to comprehend the meaning of such a fraction? How can they possibly translate it into something with more meaning for them? We clearly need another method for division of fractions.

The meaning of division, as related to rational numbers expressed as fractions, may be thought of in another way. The children are familiar with the "division box" symbol, $\overline{)}$, which they have learned to interpret as division; they are also familiar with division of whole numbers. With these two ideas as prerequisites, children are ready for the division of rational numbers expressed as fractions using division boxes by paralleling the discussion of the division of whole numbers with the division of fractions. First, review a whole number example such as, "What does $2\overline{)6}$ mean?" This example can be interpreted to mean that we have 6 things and we want to know how many groups of 2 can be made using these six things.

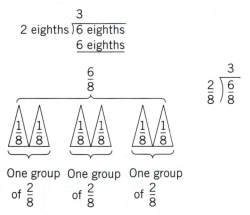

Thus, three groups of 2 can be made from 6 things.

If we have 6 eighths, how many groups of 2 eighths can we make?

$$2\text{ eighths}\overline{)6\text{ eighths}}$$
$$\underline{6\text{ eighths}}$$
with quotient 3

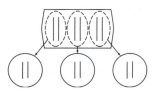

$$2\tfrac{6}{8}\,\overline{)\,\tfrac{6}{8}}$$ with quotient 3

One group   One group   One group
of $\frac{2}{8}$ of $\frac{2}{8}$ of $\frac{2}{8}$

On the concrete level, by using sectors of a circle, we can show that there are three groups of $\frac{2}{8}$ each made from a group of $\frac{6}{8}$. Thus, $\frac{6}{8} \div \frac{2}{8} = 3$.

Alternatively, consider the pattern block figures that follow to help interpret $\frac{1}{3} \div \frac{1}{6} = \square$. Use pattern blocks with the yellow hexagon representing one whole unit.

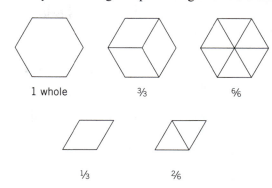

1 whole   ⅔   6/6

⅓   2/6

Then, a blue rhombus would have a value of $\frac{1}{3}$ and a green triangle would have a value of $\frac{1}{6}$. To determine the answer to $\frac{1}{3} \div \frac{1}{6}$, we need to determine how many groups of $\frac{1}{6}$ there are in $\frac{1}{3}$. Clearly, there are two groups of $\frac{1}{6}$ in $\frac{1}{3}$. Thus the answer to $\frac{1}{3} \div \frac{1}{6} = \square$ is 2.

Let's compare another division example using fractions with an example using whole numbers, specifically, $9 \div 3$ and $\frac{9}{10} \div \frac{3}{10}$.

$$3\overline{)9}$$ with quotient 3

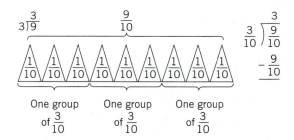

$$\tfrac{3}{10}\,\overline{)\,\tfrac{9}{10}}$$
$$\underline{-\tfrac{9}{10}}$$

One group   One group   One group
of $\frac{3}{10}$ of $\frac{3}{10}$ of $\frac{3}{10}$

Thus we can see that there are three groups of $\frac{3}{10}$ in $\frac{9}{10}$. Sometimes an example does not divide evenly. For instance:

$$2\overline{)9}$$
$$\underline{-8}$$
$$1$$
with quotient $4\tfrac{1}{2}$

Now relate this example to $\frac{2}{10}\,\overline{)\,\tfrac{9}{10}}$.

$$\frac{9}{10}$$

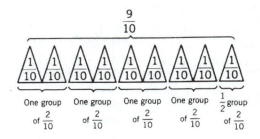

One group   One group   One group   One group $\frac{1}{2}$ group
of $\frac{2}{10}$ of $\frac{2}{10}$ of $\frac{2}{10}$ of $\frac{2}{10}$ of $\frac{2}{10}$

Thus:

$$
\begin{array}{r}
4\frac{1}{2} \\
\frac{2}{10}\overline{\smash{\big)}\,\frac{9}{10}} \\
\underline{\frac{8}{10}} \\
\frac{1}{10}
\end{array}
$$

The $\frac{1}{10}$ "remainder" is $\frac{1}{2}$ a group of $\frac{2}{10}$.

In developing an alternative method for division of fractions, we *must* understand the meaning of division by 1. Consider this example:

$$\tfrac{3}{5} \div 1 = \tfrac{3}{5}$$

From this example and others like it, we can generalize that any fraction divided by 1 is equal to the number itself. That is, division by 1 leaves the value of any fraction unchanged. Now we are prepared to develop another method for dividing fractions.

Let's reconsider the following example:

$$\tfrac{5}{9} \div \tfrac{3}{7} = \square$$

We know that $\frac{5}{9} \div \frac{3}{7}$ can be written in complex fraction form as

$$\dfrac{\frac{5}{9}}{\frac{3}{7}}$$

Since the identity element for multiplication, 1, is a valid concept in the set of fractions, just as it is in the set of whole numbers, we can multiply

$$\dfrac{\frac{5}{9}}{\frac{3}{7}}$$

by 1, written in a special form, and by doing so, translate the example into a new form:

$$\tfrac{5}{9} \div \tfrac{3}{7} = \dfrac{\frac{5}{9}}{\frac{3}{7}} = \dfrac{\frac{5}{9}}{\frac{3}{7}} \times 1$$

$$= \dfrac{\frac{5}{9}}{\frac{3}{7}} \times \dfrac{\frac{7}{3}}{\frac{7}{3}}$$

We know that the reciprocal of the denominator $\frac{3}{7}$ is $\frac{7}{3}$, and if we multiply any number by its reciprocal the result is 1. Thus we choose here to multiply the fractional number $\dfrac{\frac{5}{9}}{\frac{3}{7}}$ by $\dfrac{\frac{7}{3}}{\frac{7}{3}}$ (another name for 1).

$$= \dfrac{\frac{5}{9} \times \frac{7}{3}}{\frac{3}{7} \times \frac{7}{3}}$$

$$= \dfrac{\frac{5}{9} \times \frac{7}{3}}{1} \quad \text{(The product of reciprocals is 1.)}$$

$$= \tfrac{5}{9} \times \tfrac{7}{3} \quad \text{(Division by 1)}$$

In this manner the example $\frac{5}{9} \div \frac{3}{7} = \square$ has been rewritten as $\frac{5}{9} \times \frac{7}{3} = \square$. So, we have translated the division example into a multiplication example (which we already know how to solve) by changing the division sign into a multiplication sign and by replacing the fraction following the operation sign ($\frac{3}{7}$) with its reciprocal ($\frac{7}{3}$). Thus we can determine the quotient for $\frac{5}{9} \div \frac{3}{7} = \square$.

$$\tfrac{5}{9} \div \tfrac{3}{7} = \tfrac{5}{9} \times \tfrac{7}{3}$$

$$= \tfrac{5\times7}{9\times3}$$

$$= \tfrac{35}{27}$$

Intermediate steps could have been omitted in the determination of the answer. Whenever one fraction is to be divided by another, we can bypass these steps by inverting the second fraction and multiplying (instead of dividing).

> If $\frac{a}{b}$ and $\frac{c}{d}$ are any two fractions such that $b \neq 0$ and $c \neq 0$, then
> $$\frac{a}{b} \div \frac{c}{d} = \frac{a}{b} \times \frac{d}{c}$$

It is important to note that children should not be directed to such abstract rules during initial instruction. It is not necessarily easy for children to understand division of fractions; only after they have developed such an understanding should they use shortcuts—and, even then, they should know what they are doing and be able to verbalize, in their own words, what is taking place. It is counterproductive to expose them to shortcuts such as

VM 12.4a

To explore division of fractions using division as the inverse of multiplication, use the *Fraction Bars 12.4a* virtual manipulative to model $\frac{1}{4} \div \frac{1}{2}$ by converting this expression to $\frac{1}{2} \times \square = \frac{1}{4}$.

The virtual manipulative may also be used to determine the answer to $\frac{6}{8} \div \frac{2}{8} = \square$ by building a number line model showing that three groups of $\frac{2}{8}$ can be placed in $\frac{6}{8}$.

Still another variation of *Fraction Bars 12.4a* allows the user to model division of fractions using the common denominator method. The exercise $\frac{9}{10} \div \frac{3}{10}$ is explored as 9 (tenths) ÷ 3(tenths) = 3. Use this virtual manipulative to show the answer to $\frac{5}{6} \div \frac{1}{4} = \square$ by first modeling $\frac{10}{12} \div \frac{3}{12} = \square$ and then determining that the answer to 10 (twelfths) ÷3 (twelfths) is $3\frac{1}{3}$.

"invert and multiply" until they have demonstrated some understanding of division of fractions using models. In general, mathematical shortcuts should not be presented without first exploring an adequate explanation of their use, purpose, and why they work. Such shortcuts usually lead to more time spent repeating instruction and, in reality, less meaningful and long-lasting learning.

Closure

At this point of their mathematical development, children have used whole numbers in the study of the operations of addition and multiplication and in the study of the inverse operations, subtraction and division. Prior to the study of operations on fractions students should have the basic facts of addition and subtraction internalized and the basic facts of multiplication and division nearly memorized. The basic structure of number systems (properties) should be understood and operable. With the introduction of operations on fractions, we are applying what the students already know to another set of numbers—an extension of known concepts to an extension of the whole number system.

We have carefully examined some basic structures (properties) related to addition, subtraction, multiplication, and division with fractions. Regarding the properties of fractional numbers, we find the following:

1. Addition and multiplication of fractions are commutative, but subtraction and division are not commutative.

2. Addition and multiplication of fractions are associative, but subtraction and division are not associative.

3. The number 0 is the identity element for addition with fractions. The number 1 is the identity element for multiplication with fractions.

4. Multiplication is distributive over addition and subtraction for fractions.

5. Division is not distributive over addition or subtraction for fractions.

Finding an effective approach to addition and subtraction of fractions can be a challenge for some teachers. Rather than trying to develop an understanding of the underlying concepts, some too often resort to providing mechanical techniques or algorithms that do provide students with a route to a correct answer without touching on what is happening conceptually. Explaining how to do several examples and then providing children with practice to mimic what the teacher has shown are not acceptable techniques for teaching. The "follow me" approach does not provide students with a solid foundation for mathematics. Concrete models focusing on meaning are essential to help children see what is really happening when they multiply and divide fractions.

Most adults have a vague understanding of what division of fractions means in the real world, and it is true that our occasions to use division of fractions in the real world are rare. Nevertheless, this text suggests models that clearly illustrate what the division of fractions means. Although it becomes difficult to model examples other than the simplest ones, the concepts can become clearer after seeing even a few examples solved by manipulating sectors of circular-shaped regions.

Children need many examples of addition, subtraction, multiplication, and division of fractions before they can perform these operations abstractly. Such examples should be on concrete, semiconcrete, and semiabstract levels first, in that order. Real objects should be used to show parts of groups and regions. The number line is also an excellent model to help children understand addition and subtraction of fractions.

Children need many experiences with diagrams—shading fractional parts and determining the intersection of these parts. It is important to remember that as long as children need to refer to diagrams to understand a concept, they should be encouraged to do so. It is also important to allow children who already understand a concept to apply what they have learned; holding them back by not extending their thinking to abstractions when they are ready can be just as harmful as pushing them into abstractions before they're ready.

Children should not be presented with shortcuts to operations with fractions before they have an understanding of how the operations work; this lack of understanding can confuse them and rob them of the joy of discovering for themselves why the operations function as they do. If they understand the basic concepts involved, they can develop a true level of proficiency in working with operations on fractions.

Student facility with operations on fractional numbers is not as critical as it once was thought to be—albeit still useful, particularly in advanced mathematics. Students will find that fraction algorithms will serve them well as they explore algebra and other advanced topics in their mathematical development. Ratio and proportion, percents, probability, polynomial expressions, linear and quadratic equations, and the slope of lines and curves are but a few of the areas in which students will again encounter the material found in this chapter. Perhaps we shouldn't exaggerate the role of computations with fractional numbers, but we shouldn't underestimate it either. Certainly, the concepts underlying operations involving rational numbers are fundamental to success in mathematics.

PRACTICE EXERCISES FOR TEACHERS

These exercises are designed for the reader of this book, not for the children the reader may teach. Although some are suitable for use in an elementary or middle school classroom, they should not necessarily be given to children in the form presented here. Ideas appropriate for classroom activities on the concepts and ideas discussed in this chapter can be found in a later section of this chapter and on the CD that accompanies the text.

1. Write an addition sentence for each of the following models.

     a)

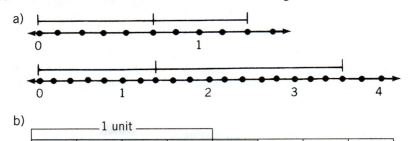

     b)

2. Complete the table; write all entries in simplest form.

							Addends							
A d d e n d s	+	$\frac{5}{12}$	$\frac{1}{12}$	$\frac{7}{12}$	$\frac{11}{12}$	$\frac{1}{4}$	$\frac{17}{12}$	$\frac{2}{3}$	$\frac{5}{6}$	$\frac{2}{5}$	$\frac{1}{2}$	$\frac{1}{3}$	$\frac{3}{4}$	$\frac{1}{7}$
	$\frac{3}{12}$													
	$\frac{3}{4}$													

VM 12.1a

3. Solve each of the following examples and model each example using both number lines and regions. Additional practice on these and similar items is available using the VM—*Fraction Bars—Addition*.

     a) $\frac{3}{16} + \frac{7}{16} = \square$ b) $\frac{6}{7} + \frac{5}{7} = \square$ c) $\frac{7}{8} + \frac{3}{8} = \square$ d) $\frac{2}{9} + \frac{7}{9} = \square$

VM 12.1b

4. Consider the following numbers as denominators. Find the least common multiple for each group of denominators. Additional practice on similar items is available using the VM—*Finding Common Denominator*.

     a) 4, 6   b) 15, 12   c) 8, 12   d) 3, 5, 9   e) 6, 15, 10

5. Write a subtraction sentence for each of the following models.

     a)

     b)

c)

6. Solve each of the following examples. Model each one on the number line and with regions. Additional practice on these and similar items is available using the VM—*Fraction Bars—Subtraction*.

VM 12.2a

a) $\frac{4}{5} - \frac{3}{10} = \square$ b) $\frac{7}{8} - \frac{3}{4} = \square$ c) $\frac{5}{6} - \frac{1}{3} = \square$ d) $\frac{2}{3} - \frac{1}{4} = \square$

7. Model each of the following multiplication examples on the number line. Additional practice on these and similar items is available using the VM—*Fraction Bars—Multiplication*.

VM 12.3a

a) $3 \times \frac{1}{4} = \square$ b) $4 \times \frac{2}{5} = \square$ c) $5 \times \frac{2}{3} = \square$

d) $6 \times \frac{1}{2} = \square$ e) $8 \times \frac{5}{6} = \square$ f) $5 \times \frac{3}{4} = \square$

8. Model each of the following multiplication examples by using regions. Additional practice on these and similar items is available using the VM—*Rectangle Multiplication of Fractions*.

VM 12.3b

a) $\frac{1}{2} \times \frac{3}{4} = \square$ b) $\frac{2}{3} \times \frac{1}{4} = \square$ c) $\frac{2}{5} \times \frac{1}{6} = \square$

d) $\frac{5}{6} \times \frac{1}{8} = \square$ e) $\frac{3}{8} \times \frac{4}{5} = \square$ f) $\frac{2}{3} \times \frac{4}{5} = \square$

9. Solve each of the following division examples by using a drawing.

a) $\frac{2}{9}\overline{)\frac{8}{9}}$ b) $\frac{1}{4}\overline{)\frac{3}{4}}$ c) $\frac{5}{11}\overline{)\frac{10}{11}}$ d) $\frac{1}{4}\overline{)\frac{3}{8}}$ e) $\frac{2}{3}\overline{)\frac{5}{6}}$ f) $\frac{4}{5}\overline{)\frac{4}{3}}$

10. Name the reciprocal of each of the following numbers.

a) $\frac{3}{5}$ b) $\frac{1}{4}$ c) $\frac{5}{6}$ d) $\frac{9}{5}$

e) 17 f) $2\frac{1}{4}$ g) $6\frac{7}{8}$ h) $3\frac{4}{9}$

11. Solve the following examples by rewriting each one in the form $(\frac{a}{b})/(\frac{c}{d})$. Then multiply the numerator and denominator by the reciprocal of $\frac{c}{d}$.

a) $\frac{2}{9} \div \frac{8}{9} = \square$ b) $\frac{3}{4} \div \frac{1}{4} = \square$ c) $\frac{10}{11} \div \frac{5}{11} = \square$

d) $\frac{3}{8} \div \frac{1}{4} = \square$ e) $\frac{5}{6} \div \frac{2}{3} = \square$ f) $\frac{4}{3} \div \frac{4}{5} = \square$

12. Suppose that $\frac{x}{z}$ and $\frac{y}{z}$ represent two fractional numbers. Complete each of the following statements by supplying the correct relation symbol ($=$, $<$, or $>$) in the blank.

a) If $x < y$, then $\frac{x}{z}$ _____ $\frac{y}{z}$

b) If $x = y$, then $\frac{x}{z}$ _____ $\frac{y}{z}$

c) If $x > y$, then $\frac{x}{z}$ _____ $\frac{y}{z}$

13. If a, b, c, and d are any counting numbers and $a \times d < b \times c$, then $\frac{a}{b} < \frac{c}{d}$. This fact enables us to compare two fractional numbers by comparing products of counting numbers. Use this test to decide which is the lesser of each of the following pairs of fractional numbers.

a) $\frac{13}{27}, \frac{27}{55}$ b) $\frac{71}{81}, \frac{18}{21}$ c) $\frac{6}{17}, \frac{23}{67}$

14. Solve each of the following examples.

a) $(\frac{3}{4} \times \frac{5}{6}) \div \frac{2}{3} = \square$ b) $(\frac{7}{8} \div \frac{4}{5}) \times \frac{1}{2} = \square$

c) $\frac{2}{5} \times (\frac{2}{3} \div \frac{3}{4}) = \square$ d) $\frac{5}{7} \div (\frac{4}{9} \times \frac{2}{5}) = \square$

15. Internally simplify each of the following examples before multiplying.

a) $\frac{7}{9} \times \frac{3}{8} = \square$ b) $\frac{4}{5} \times \frac{15}{28} = \square$ c) $\frac{6}{7} \div \frac{4}{5} = \square$ d) $\frac{8}{9} \div \frac{4}{18} = \square$

e) $\frac{5}{6} \div \frac{20}{21} = \square$ f) $\frac{3}{11} \times 2\frac{4}{9} = \square$ g) $2\frac{5}{6} \div 3\frac{1}{4} = \square$ h) $1\frac{3}{8} \times 4\frac{2}{3} = \square$

16. If a room measures $12\frac{1}{2}$ feet by $11\frac{3}{4}$ feet, how many square yards of carpeting will be needed to cover the entire floor?

TEACHING COMPETENCIES AND SELF-ASSESSMENT TASKS

The following questions and statements are designed to reflect the teaching competencies that appeared at the beginning of this chapter and, in some cases, to expose you to deeper aspects of the concepts presented. Take a moment to consider your response to each of these in light of what you've read and learned.

1. Identify teaching materials and aids that can be used to teach children both the meaning and the process of operations with fractions. What are the most effective means of developing children's understanding of operations on fractions?

2. Discuss important concepts that children must comprehend before the teacher introduces division with fractions.

3. Defend the relative importance of learning the operations with fractions as we increase the use of metric measure, calculators, and computers.

4. Describe the difficulties that children encounter when attempting to use certain calculators and computers for operations on fractions. Do all calculators or computers handle operations with fractions in the same manner?

5. Discuss the relationships between ratios and fractions. How are they alike? How are they different? Use real-life examples to compare and contrast the standard algorithm for adding fractions to an algorithm for adding ratios.

6. Discuss the relationship between regrouping with whole numbers and regrouping using fractions. How are they alike? How are they different?

7. Make a list of instances in which the identity element of multiplication is used with fractions. How important is the identity element of multiplication in operations with fractions?

8. What are the advantages and disadvantages of allowing children to develop and use their own fraction kits? Should such home-made kits be constructed with circular or rectangular regions (or both)?

SAMPLE INSTRUCTIONAL AND ASSESSMENT ACTIVITIES

These activities and more are available on the CD that accompanies this text.

VM 12.1a

1. In the primary grades, we use a variety of activities to prepare children to work with fractions; they should not, of course, be expected to perform operations with abstract fraction symbols. Instead, the children should manipulate concrete objects to show the relations involved in discovering that equivalent fractions exist, how they relate to one another, and how they compare. Provide physical models, such as Cuisenaire rods, pattern blocks, and circular fraction pieces to expose primary school children to meaningful examples of the process of adding and subtracting fractions. For some children, the pictorial qualities of virtual manipulatives may help develop conceptual understanding. See, for example, VM—*Fraction Bar Addition—1*.

2. Discuss how many of certain EQUAL pieces of something make up the whole—that is, that it takes 3 one-thirds (for instance) to make one whole item. Point out counterexamples in which three unequal pieces still form a whole but don't represent thirds.

VM 12.1a

3. Using the fraction kit described in Chapter 11 or VM—*Fraction Bar—Addition*, have the student concretely model:

a) $\frac{1}{3} + \frac{1}{3}$ b) $\frac{1}{3} + \frac{1}{3} + \frac{1}{3}$ c) $\frac{1}{2} + \frac{1}{4}$ d) $\frac{3}{6} + \frac{1}{2}$

4. Using the fraction kit described in Chapter 11 or VM—*Fraction Bar—Subtraction*, have the student model:

a) $\frac{5}{8} - \frac{2}{8}$ b) $\frac{1}{2} - \frac{1}{4}$ c) $\frac{5}{6} - \frac{1}{2}$

VM 12.1a
VM 12.2a

5. Have students make number line diagrams or use the VM—*Fraction Bars—Addition* or *Subtraction* to help solve the following examples:

a) $\frac{1}{4} + \frac{1}{4} = \square$ b) $\frac{1}{6} - \frac{1}{6} = \square$ c) $\frac{2}{4} + \frac{1}{4} = \square$ d) $\frac{2}{6} + \frac{1}{6} = \square$

e) $\frac{3}{4} - \frac{1}{4} = \square$ f) $\frac{3}{6} + \frac{1}{6} = \square$ g) $\frac{4}{6} + \frac{1}{6} = \square$ h) $\frac{5}{6} - \frac{1}{6} = \square$

VM 12.1a
VM 12.2b

6. Ask students to draw diagrams to help complete each equation. Alternatively, use *Fraction Bars—Addition* or *Fraction Bars Subtraction—Missing Addend* to complete these exercises.

a) $\frac{1}{4} + \frac{1}{2} = \square$ b) $\frac{3}{8} + \frac{2}{8} = \square$ c) $\frac{1}{2} + \square = \frac{4}{6}$

d) $\frac{5}{8} + \frac{1}{4} = \square$ e) $\frac{1}{2} + \frac{0}{4} = \square$ f) $\frac{2}{4} + \square = \frac{3}{4}$

g) $\frac{1}{2} + \frac{1}{3} = \square$ h) $\frac{5}{8} + \square = \frac{3}{4}$ i) $\frac{1}{6} + \square = \frac{1}{3}$

7. Children in the intermediate grades should be able to translate simple problem situations involving fractions into appropriate mathematical sentences. Have children write a mathematical sentence for each of the following and then solve the problems.

a) It took Lewis $2\frac{1}{2}$ hours to mow Mrs. Shih's lawn. It took him $1\frac{3}{4}$ hours to mow Mrs. Hall's lawn. How much more time did he spend on Mrs. Shih's lawn?

b) Linda's library books weighed $2\frac{1}{4}$ pounds. Diane's weighed $3\frac{1}{4}$ pounds. Henry carried both stacks of books for the girls. How many pounds of books did he carry?

c) Fred fed $2\frac{1}{4}$ bags of peanuts to the elephants and $3\frac{3}{4}$ bags to the monkeys. He kept 1 bag for himself. How many bags of peanuts did Fred buy?

d) Michelle picked 3 rows of corn on Monday and 8 rows on Tuesday. There were 18 rows of corn in the garden. What fractional part of the corn did she have left to pick?

VM 12.1a
VM 12.2a

8. Using the fraction kit described in the activities for Chapter 11 or VM—*Fraction Bars—Addition* or *Subtraction*, have the student model:

a) $\frac{5}{8} + \frac{2}{8}$ b) $\frac{5}{6} - \frac{2}{6}$ c) $\frac{7}{10} + \frac{1}{5}$ d) $\frac{1}{2} - \frac{1}{4}$

9. Have students determine the greatest common factor of the numerator and denominator of each fraction. You may also want students to explore GCF and LCD by using the VM—*Finding Common Denominators*.

a) $\frac{6}{9}$ b) $\frac{8}{12}$ c) $\frac{16}{12}$ d) $\frac{25}{15}$ e) $\frac{8}{8}$ f) $\frac{64}{80}$

10. The number line is an excellent device to use for developing an understanding of the division of fractions

How many one-thirds are there in 2? You can readily see that there are 6 one-thirds in 2. Thus, 2 divided by $\frac{1}{3}$ is 6. Have students draw a number line to show how many three-fourths are in 1.

chapter 13

Rational Numbers Expressed as Decimals

TEACHING COMPETENCIES

Upon completing this chapter, you will be able to:

- Use base ten blocks, regions, money, the number line, and other models to develop an understanding of decimals and operations on decimals.

- Write any rational number in fraction form, decimal form, or expanded notation and describe situations in which one form may be more useful or appropriate than another.

- Perform operations and inverse operations on rational numbers expressed in decimal form.

- Express numbers in scientific notation form.

- Use ratio and proportion to describe problem situations and to solve percentage problems.

- Rewrite any terminating or repeating decimal in fraction form.

- Design lessons for elementary and/or middle school students that incorporate meaningful models for rational numbers expressed as decimals.

VIRTUAL MANIPULATIVES

Upon completing this chapter, you will be able to use virtual manipulatives on the accompanying CD to:

- Develop an understanding of decimals by using *Representing Decimal Numbers*. **(VM 13.1)**

- Illustrate the concept of adding using *Addition with Decimals*. **(VM 13.2)**

- Model the concept of subtracting using *Subtracting with Decimals*. **(VM 13.3)**

- Explore different ways to express comparisons in *Relating Fractions, Ratios, Decimals, and Percents*. **(VM 13.4)**

Numbered CD icons throughout the chapter refer to the virtual manipulatives in this list.

Why are decimal numbers so widely used in science, industry, and commerce and in applications involving the metric system, calculators, and computers? Why is it that rational numbers expressed as fractions do not play a greater role in such situations? A major reason is that decimal numbers provide a convenient and efficient form of expressing rational numbers for both comparison and computational purposes. The use of rational numbers expressed as decimals permits the application of the place-value notation used for whole numbers to be extended to rational numbers.

Models That Give Decimals Meaning

A beginning step in teaching children about rational numbers expressed as decimals is to develop an understanding of what a given decimal number represents. Several models can be used with students. Let's begin to develop an understanding of decimals by using base ten blocks.

Review whole number place-value concepts before beginning the exploration of decimals. With whole numbers, children understand the value of the base ten blocks as illustrated:

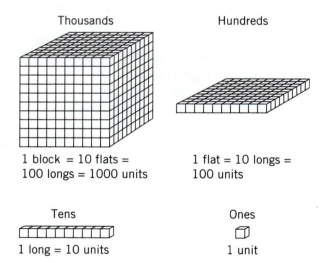

Thousands   Hundreds

1 block = 10 flats =   1 flat = 10 longs =
100 longs = 1000 units   100 units

Tens   Ones

1 long = 10 units   1 unit

At this stage of development, students should have had many experiences with base ten blocks in learning the concept of place value applied to whole numbers.

Now, let's redefine the values of the blocks. Base ten blocks should always be defined in terms of the block that is being used to represent the ones place. When a particular block is defined as being one unit, the other blocks of a base ten set are then defined accordingly. Begin by redefining the large block to be one unit.

Ones

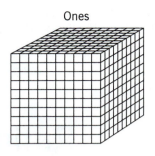

Then discuss with the children the relationships among the remaining blocks, as tenths, hundredths, and thousandths are defined. If a large block is defined to be equal to one, then a flat is one-tenth of a large block because one large block is equivalent to 10 flats. A long is one-tenth of a flat because there are 10 longs in a flat. And, a small cube is one-tenth of a long because there are 10 cubes in a long. VM 13.1

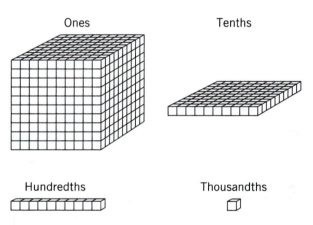

Ones   Tenths

Hundredths   Thousandths

More commonly (and more "naturally") teachers often choose to use the flat block to represent one unit when discussing decimal numbers. In such case, a long is then one-tenth of a flat and a cube is one-hundredth (one-tenth of one-tenth). This value assignment has the advantage of using the flat as 100 small cubes when discussing whole numbers and a small cube as one-hundredth of a flat when considering decimal numbers. Also, 10 longs are equivalent to a flat, so a long is one-tenth of a flat. VM 13.1

Students need to manipulate the blocks, see the new relationship, extend the place-value chart, and discuss the extension of the place-value system. This is not a new concept for the students: It only extends a concept developed in earlier grades. If decimals are introduced before fractions, then the use of base ten blocks and the concept of place value provide an excellent procedure for introducing rational numbers expressed as decimals.

Another tool that should be used with students is a graph paper model of decimal numbers. Graph paper models are more dependent on fractions than base ten blocks are. Let's examine the models and their usefulness for introducing students to decimals.

If students have worked with fractions, they should understand fractions representing tenths and hundredths. Graph paper is an effective way to illustrate $\frac{1}{10}$ and $\frac{1}{100}$ (and, consequently, .1 and .01).

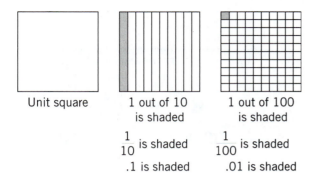

Unit square	1 out of 10 is shaded	1 out of 100 is shaded
	$\frac{1}{10}$ is shaded	$\frac{1}{100}$ is shaded
	.1 is shaded	.01 is shaded

Circular regions can be used in a similar manner.

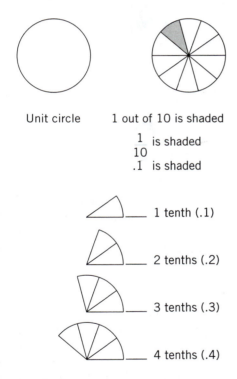

Unit circle   1 out of 10 is shaded

$\frac{1}{10}$ is shaded

.1 is shaded

1 tenth (.1)

2 tenths (.2)

3 tenths (.3)

4 tenths (.4)

Students may have modeled many fractions on the number line. After doing halves, thirds, fourths, fifths, sixths, and eighths, students will find it easy to model tenths on a number line.

Even though graph paper and regions can be useful when discussing decimals, let's return to the place-value approach and examine it further. The concept of place value is fundamental to an understanding of decimals.

So that students may be able to discover the meaning of decimals for themselves, it is necessary for them to examine and make use of place value.

Place Value—A Foundation for Decimals

Let's examine a procedure that might be used to teach understanding of decimals. Write a numeral for a three- or four-place whole number on the chalkboard. Label the place-value name above each digit of the numeral. Using a heuristic approach, review the relation between the value of each of the places. For example:

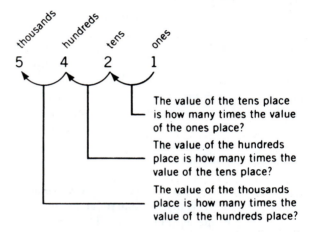

The value of the tens place is how many times the value of the ones place?

The value of the hundreds place is how many times the value of the tens place?

The value of the thousands place is how many times the value of the hundreds place?

The children's responses to each of these questions should be that each place value is 10 times the place value on its right.

Now, using the same procedure, compare the value of each place to the value of the place to its immediate right.

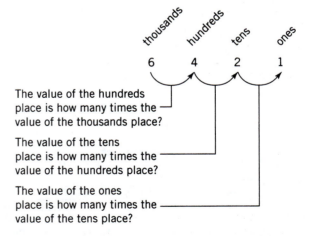

The value of the hundreds place is how many times the value of the thousands place?

The value of the tens place is how many times the value of the hundreds place?

The value of the ones place is how many times the value of the tens place?

The answers to each of these three questions should be that the place value on the right is $\frac{1}{10}$ of the place value on its immediate left.

These questions merely reflect the place-value understanding that children should have already developed in exploring whole numbers. Now ask the children to imagine that there is a place to the right of the ones place. What relationship might exist between the ones place and this new place? Permit the children to discuss their ideas about this new place.

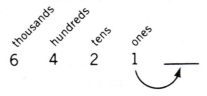

The students should respond, assuming that the same pattern continues, that the value of the new place should be $\frac{1}{10}$ that of the value of the ones place. From their understanding of fractions, the children know that $\frac{1}{10} \times 1 = \frac{1}{10}$. Therefore, we agree to call this new place the tenths place. What about the next place to the right of the tenths place? What relation exists between this new place and the tenths place? The value of this new place should be $\frac{1}{10}$ the value of the tenths place. Since $\frac{1}{10}$ of $\frac{1}{10}$ is $\frac{1}{100}$, we can name this place the hundredths place. Using the developing pattern, we can continue this procedure to find the values of as many decimal places as we wish to examine.

Since all the places to the right of the ones place represent fractional parts of 1, we need a way to indicate this fact. We do this with a **decimal point**, our reference point to indicate the separation of whole number values from fractional number values in a decimal (base ten) numeral. The decimal point is marked between the ones place and the tenths place.

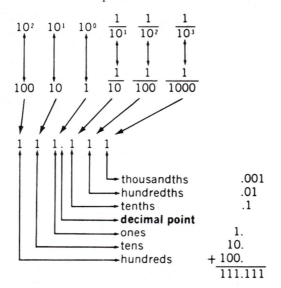

Take a moment to continue this place-value scheme to both the left and the right. Name, for example, the first six places to the right of the decimal point. Using the pattern developed, you should be able to name each of these places and, in so doing, see clearly the structure and meaning of the decimal system of notation.

Money should also be used to help develop an understanding of tenths and hundredths. Place a $1 bill in the ones place; a dime is $\frac{1}{10}$ of a dollar, and a penny is $\frac{1}{100}$ a dollar. A dime is written in decimal form as .10, and a penny is written as .01.

Ones

Dollar

Tenths

Dime

Hundredths

Penny

Discuss money with the children, and relate the writing of money values to the place-value system. Using money can be particularly useful in comparing the relative value of different one- and two-place decimals and in beginning discussions of addition and subtraction of decimals.

Numeral expanders can also be used to help children understand decimal notation (see the discussion of numeral expanders in Chapter 6). To use a numeral expander to explore place value, put a numeral expander that has the zeros printed on it in front of you. Make sure that the small section of the numeral expander is on the left and that the longer sections are on the right. (This is the opposite of the way that the numeral expander is placed for whole numbers.) Using the special marking pencil, mark a large dot, so that everyone in the classroom can see it, in the lower left-hand corner of the small section. This dot will be used as the decimal point.

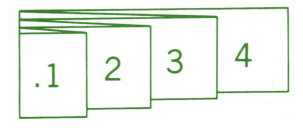

On each of the next three panels with zeros printed on them, mark a large dot in the lower left-hand corner. Also, write a large numeral on each of the four panels.

When the numeral expander is ready for use with decimals in expanded form, it will look like the above model. Note that four decimal points have been written on the numeral expander—one on the tenths panel, one on the hundredths panel, one on the thousandths panel, and one on the ten-thousandths panel.

Now, use the prepared numeral expander with the decimal points marked. Hold the numeral expander as illustrated, so that the tenths and hundredths places face the students.

Next fold back the thousandths and ten-thousandths places so that they do not show. Now the tenths and hundredths places can be expanded by unfolding these two places.

Have the students write the number in standard notation when the expanded notation is shown and in expanded notation when the standard notation is shown.

Children Are Shown	Children Write
.4 + .07	.4 + .07 = .47
.2 + .09	.2 + .09 = .29
.36	.36 = .3 + .06
.23	.23 = .2 + .03

When the children have a firm understanding of tenths and hundredths, they are then ready to consider additional places. Use similar procedures to develop standard notation for tenths, hundredths, thousandths, and ten-thousandths. The numeral expander will help children understand the standard and expanded notation for these four places.[1]

Exponential Notation

In our discussion of the structure of place-value numeration systems, we saw that every whole number can be renamed in several ways. For example, 427 can be written in expanded notation:

$$427 = 400 + 20 + 7$$

We can also write 427 using exponential notation:

$$427 = (4 \times 10^2) + (2 \times 10^1) + (7 \times 10^0)$$

Can all decimal numerals be written in similar alternative forms? Yes, this is possible. Consider, for example, the numeral 23.56; we can rewrite it in expanded notation as follows:

$$23.56 = 20 + 3 + .5 + .06$$

We can continue and write the numeral in several other forms:

$$
\begin{aligned}
23.56 &= 20 + 3 + .5 + .06 \\
&= 20 + 3 + \tfrac{5}{10} + \tfrac{6}{100} \\
&= (2 \times 10) + (3 \times 1) + (5 \times \tfrac{1}{10}) + (6 \times \tfrac{1}{100}) \\
&= (2 \times 10^1) + (3 \times 10^0) + (5 \times 10^{-1}) \\
&\quad + (6 \times 10^{-2})
\end{aligned}
$$

Students in the intermediate grades should be able to rewrite decimal numerals in these alternative forms to demonstrate an understanding of place value in decimal numerals. Some students in the middle grades may be ready to use negative exponents to write decimals in yet another form. If the students understand the meaning of negative integers, you might use the patterns in the following chart to help the children discover the meaning of 10^{-1}, 10^{-2}, and so on:

Decimal	Exponential Notation
1000	10^3
100	10^2
10	10^1
1	10^0
.1	$10^?$
.01	$10^?$
.001	$10^?$

[1](NOTE: Information on purchasing two plastic numeral expanders (one with zeros and the other with word names for place values), a 24-page teacher's booklet, and an erasable marking pencil can be obtained by contacting Dr. William Speer, Curriculum and Instruction, ms 3005, University of Nevada, Las Vegas, Nevada 89154-3005.)

Students should be familiar with the way exponential notation is used in the first four rows of the chart. Which exponents should we use to complete the pattern in the right-hand column of powers of ten? We observe that as we go down the right-hand column, the exponents decrease by 1 each time. If this pattern continues, which exponent should we use to replace the first question mark? Yes, $^-1$ (the integer that is 1 less than 0). Which integer should replace the second question mark? Clearly the answer is $^-2$ since $^-2$ is the integer that is 1 less than $^-1$. Which integer should replace the third question mark? Yes, $^-3$. In this way, the children can discover the following about negative exponents:

$$10^{-1} = \quad .1 = \tfrac{1}{10} \text{ or } \tfrac{1}{10^1}$$
$$10^{-2} = \quad .01 = \tfrac{1}{100} \text{ or } \tfrac{1}{10^2}$$
$$10^{-3} = .001 = \tfrac{1}{1000} \text{ or } \tfrac{1}{10^3}$$

From these and similar facts, the children should be able to make the generalization that for any whole number n:

$$10^{-n} = \frac{1}{10^n}$$

Expanded notation and powers of ten that involve negative exponents can be used to reinforce ideas about place value. For example:

$$
\begin{aligned}
34.1 &= 30 + 4 + .1 \\
&= (3 \times 10) + (4 \times 1) + (1 \times \tfrac{1}{10}) \\
&= (3 \times 10^1) + (4 \times 10^0) + (1 \times 10^{-1}) \\
234.12 &= 200 + 30 + 4 + .1 + .02 \\
&= (2 \times 100) + (3 \times 10) + (4 \times 1) \\
&\quad + (1 \times \tfrac{1}{10}) + (2 \times \tfrac{1}{100}) \\
&= (2 \times 10^2) + (3 \times 10^1) \\
&\quad + (4 \times 10^0)(1 \times 10^{-1}) + (2 \times 10^{-2}) \\
764.123 &= 700 + 60 + 4 + .1 + .02 + .003 \\
&= (7 \times 100) + (6 \times 10) + (4 \times 1) \\
&\quad + (1 \times \tfrac{1}{10}) + (2 \times \tfrac{1}{100}) + (3 \times \tfrac{1}{1000}) \\
&= (7 \times 10^2) + (6 \times 10^1) + (4 \times 10^0) \\
&\quad + (1 \times 10^{-1}) + (2 \times 10^{-2}) \\
&\quad + (3 \times 10^{-3})
\end{aligned}
$$

(NOTE: Do not ask children to write out each of these steps. These steps have been written here primarily to help you understand the concepts. Teachers should be able to understand and write these steps. This use of expanded notation should further clarify the meaning of decimals in our number system—a base ten or decimal system.)

Addition with Decimal Numbers

Students who have studied fractions, place value, and addition of whole numbers should find that adding decimal numbers is merely an extension of prior

knowledge. Let's look at an addition example involving decimals by comparing it to regions of a circle. Using tenths of a circle, let's explore the example. $2 + .3 = \square$. The students that understand basic addition know that

2 tenths + 3 tenths = 5 tenths

We can write the following:

$$.2 + .3 = .5 \quad \text{or} \quad
\begin{array}{r} 2 \text{ tenths} \\ + 3 \text{ tenths} \\ \hline 5 \text{ tenths} \end{array}
\quad \text{or} \quad
\begin{array}{r} .2 \\ + .3 \\ \hline .5 \end{array}$$

Now, let's look at the same example modeled on the number line, illustrated just like any other addition example.

Begin at 0, the point called the origin. Mark off an addend of 2 tenths, then mark off an addend of 3 tenths, and you arrive at the point we call the sum, which, in this case, is 5 tenths. Therefore,. $2 + .3 = .5$.

Another approach to the addition of decimals uses a logical extension of the process of adding wholenumbers and does not require prior experience with adding fractions. Base ten blocks can be a valuable manipulative device for illustrating the addition process as it applies to decimals. To do this, define the value of the blocks (as was done earlier in this chapter) so that the flat block represents one unit, or one whole. The long block would then be one-tenth of the flat block, and the small cube block would be one-hundredth of the flat block. Using this scheme, the addition example $1.45 + .7$ would appear as shown.

VM 13.2

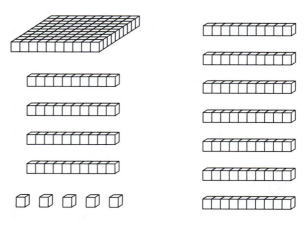

By putting the blocks together and adding similar blocks, we can easily see that the result would be 1 flat block, 11 longs, and 5 cubes. The 11 longs could be renamed as 1 flat block and 1 long. Therefore, the total can be renamed as 2 flat blocks, 1 long, and 5 cubes. A variety of exercises such as this should be used, both with and without the notion of renaming.

When adding whole numbers, similar place values are added. That is, ones are aligned in the ones column, tens in the tens column, and so on. The same idea applies to addition of decimals. Tenths are added to tenths and are aligned in the tenths column; hundredths are added to hundredths and are aligned in the hundredths column; and so on. If the children understand place value and similar terms, they should then understand that in the addition of decimals, the decimal points end up being aligned as a result of adding similar terms. The meaning of place value should be reviewed and stressed as often as necessary when introducing children to rational numbers in decimal form.

If the child has had prior experience with adding fractions, then you may wish to take advantage of this knowledge. Consider another addition example:

$$\frac{3}{10} + \frac{4}{10} = \frac{7}{10}$$

After the study of fractions, this example should not prove to be too challenging. We know from our examination of decimals that we can rewrite these fractions as follows:

$$\frac{3}{10} = .3$$
$$+\frac{4}{10} = +.4$$
$$\frac{7}{10} = .7$$

Thus another way to add $\frac{3}{10}$ and $\frac{4}{10}$ is to rewrite these fractions as decimals.

$$.3 \text{ (three − tenths)}$$
$$+.4 \text{ (four − tenths)}$$
$$.7 \text{ (seven − tenths)}$$

Take another example:

$$\frac{23}{100} + \frac{14}{100} = \frac{37}{100}$$

Another way of stating this example is:

$$.23 \text{ (twenty − three hundredths)}$$
$$+.14 \text{ (fourteen hundredths)}$$
$$.37 \text{ (thirty − seven hundredths)}$$

A longer example illustrates the procedure more clearly:

$$.234 = \frac{234}{1000} = \frac{2340}{10000} = .2340$$
$$.1742 = = \frac{1742}{1000} = .1742$$
$$+.11 = +\frac{11}{100} = \frac{1100}{10000} = +.1100$$
$$ \frac{5182}{1000} = .5182$$

(Again, do not ask children to write out these steps.)

By working through a number of similar examples, students should soon realize why decimal points end up being aligned in addition and subtraction. Alignment of decimal points is comparable to finding a common denominator, as we saw in the preceding example. A shorter analysis of the example is shown here. Notice the use of zeros in illustrating place value.

$$.234$$
$$.1742$$
$$+ .11$$
$$.5182$$

$2 \times \frac{1}{10,000}$ or .0002

$8 \times \frac{1}{1000}$ or .008

$1 \times \frac{1}{100}$ or .01

$5 \times \frac{1}{10}$ or .5

Notice that in the hundredths column, we obtain a sum of .11, or $\frac{11}{100}$. We record the .01 $\frac{1}{100}$ in the hundredths column and add the 0.1 $\frac{1}{10}$ to the tenths column; we add this .1 to the .4 and indicate the sum, .5, in the tenths column.

Consider this example:. $8 + .6 = \square$. We can solve this example as follows:

$$.8$$
$$+.6$$

We know that $\frac{8}{10} + \frac{6}{10} = \frac{14}{10} = 1\frac{4}{10}$ or $1 + \frac{4}{10}$. Therefore:

$$.8$$
$$+.6$$
$$1.4 \text{ or } 1 + .4$$

After working many such examples involving decimals, students should discover that the decimal points are always aligned in addition and, more important, that numerals must be expressed with their proper place value just as in addition of whole numbers. If children know the basic addition facts and can relate fractions and decimals, they should have little difficulty with addition of decimals. The basic structure of whole numbers and fractional numbers is merely applied in a new way.

Subtraction with Decimal Numbers

From a knowledge base of addition, students should be able to formulate some generalizations concerning subtraction of decimals. As might be expected, they should explore the subtraction of decimals using models of some sort.

Let's consider an example: $.5 - .3 = \square$. Once again, base ten blocks are an effective model for subtraction

VM 13.3

(with or without renaming). This manipulative approach to $.5 - .3 = \square$ can be accomplished using either the take-away or the missing addend interpretation of subtraction as shown. (For this particular exercise, we'll use flats as representing one-tenth of a large block. See illustration at the bottom of this page.)

Of course, circular regions can also be used. In this case, each pie-shaped piece represents one-tenth of a circular region.

When using the number line as a model, we always begin at 0. In the example $.5 - .3 = \square$, the .3 is an addend and .5 is the sum. From 0, we mark the addend .3 and then mark the sum .5. What is the missing addend?

Thus, we can see that $.5 - .3 = .2$.

Students should discover that the decimal points are always aligned in subtraction and, more important, that the numbers must be expressed with their proper place

value, just as in addition of decimals. This is illustrated in these examples:

$$\frac{7}{10} - \frac{3}{10} = \frac{4}{10} \qquad \begin{array}{r} .7 \\ -.3 \\ \hline .4 \end{array}$$

$$\frac{29}{100} - \frac{12}{100} = \frac{17}{100} \qquad \begin{array}{r} .29 \\ -.12 \\ \hline .17 \end{array}$$

Another example illustrates the conversion of fractions with unlike denominators:

$$\begin{array}{rcccl} .73 & = & \frac{73}{100} & = & \frac{73}{100} \quad \text{or} \quad .73 \\ -.4 & = & -\frac{4}{10} & = & -\frac{40}{100} \quad \text{or} \quad -.40 \\ & & & & \frac{33}{100} \quad \text{or} \quad .33 \end{array}$$

Again, alignment of decimal points is associated with finding a common denominator. By aligning tenths under tenths and hundredths under hundredths, we are subtracting numbers named with like denominators.

$$\begin{aligned} .73 - .4 &= (.7 + .03) - .4 \\ &= (.7 - .4) + .03 \\ &= .3 + .03 \\ &= .33 \end{aligned}$$
$$\begin{aligned} .73 - .4 &= \left(\frac{7}{10} + \frac{3}{100}\right) - \frac{4}{10} \\ &= \left(\frac{7}{10} - \frac{4}{10}\right) + \frac{3}{100} \\ &= \frac{3}{10} + \frac{3}{100} \\ &= \frac{30}{100} + \frac{3}{100} \\ &= \frac{33}{100} \\ &= .33 \end{aligned}$$

After exploring a number of similar examples and developing place-value generalizations, children should be provided with practice exercises until the process is clear. Students need practice in subtraction involving

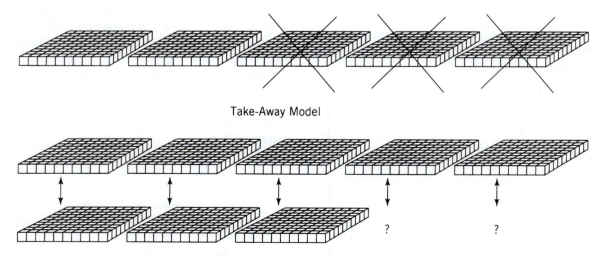

Take-Away Model

Missing-Addend Model

"ragged" decimals and decimals with more places, as in these examples:

$$
\begin{array}{cccc}
27.4 & 42.78 & 74.2 & 80 \\
-3.5 & -17.2 & -38.176 & -29.63 \\
\hline
\end{array}
$$

These exercises give the students the opportunity to compare and contrast the benefits of using fraction notation, expanded notation, regrouping, and models such as base ten blocks. These exercises also provide the teacher with an opportunity to evaluate the students' knowledge of basic subtraction facts and knowledge of place value.

Multiplication with Decimal Numbers

Now, let's consider multiplication of decimals. Begin with models on the concrete level. Consider the example $3 \times .2 = \square$. What does this mean? It means you have three groups with 2 tenths in each group. If represents 1 tenth of a circle, then you have 2 of these in each of three groups.

By observation, we can conclude that three groups of 2 tenths will equal 6 tenths. We write

$$
3 \times .2 = .6 \quad \text{or} \quad
\begin{array}{r}
2 \text{ tenths} \\
\times 3 \\
\hline
6 \text{ tenths}
\end{array}
\quad \text{or} \quad
\begin{array}{r}
.2 \\
\times .3 \\
\hline
.6
\end{array}
$$

The same example can also be modeled on a number line.

Thus, $3 \times .2 = .6$.

Another approach to teaching multiplication with decimals is to have children make use of what they have learned about multiplication with fractions. Suppose we are given a multiplication example in which both factors are written as decimals. It is possible to rewrite the decimals as fractions and multiply as usual, and the result will be the product expressed in fraction form. You can then rewrite this fraction as a decimal; this

gives the answer for the original example expressed in decimal form.

Let's look at an example that is solved using this procedure. Suppose we wish to solve the example $2.7 \times .3 = \square$.

1. Use place-value and basic properties to help rewrite the decimals as fractions.

$$
\overbrace{2.7 \times .3}^{\text{Decimals}} = 2\tfrac{7}{10} \times \tfrac{3}{10}
$$
$$
= (2 + \tfrac{7}{10}) \times \tfrac{3}{10}
$$
$$
= (\tfrac{20}{10} + \tfrac{7}{10}) \times \tfrac{3}{10}
$$
$$
= \underbrace{\tfrac{27}{10} \times \tfrac{3}{10}}_{\text{Fractions}}
$$

2. Using the fraction form, multiply as usual according to the short-form algorithm (i.e., numerator times numerator, denominator times denominator).

$$
\tfrac{27}{10} \times \tfrac{3}{10} = \tfrac{27 \times 3}{10 \times 10}
$$
$$
= \tfrac{81}{100}
$$

3. Rewrite the fraction obtained in step 2 as a decimal to get the final answer.

$$
\tfrac{81}{100} = .81
$$

Therefore, $2.7 \times .3 = .81$

Now, let's use the same procedure to solve $14.5 \times 2.17 = \square$.

1. Write the example in fraction form.

$$
14.5 \times 2.17 = 14\tfrac{5}{10} \times 2\tfrac{17}{100}
$$
$$
= (\tfrac{140}{10} + \tfrac{5}{10}) \times (\tfrac{200}{100} + \tfrac{17}{100})
$$
$$
= \tfrac{145}{10} \times \tfrac{217}{100}
$$

2. Multiply.

$$
\tfrac{145}{10} \times \tfrac{217}{100} = \tfrac{145 \times 217}{10 \times 100}
$$
$$
= \tfrac{31,465}{1000}
$$

3. Rewrite the example in decimal form:

$$
\frac{31465}{1000} = 31.465
$$

Therefore, $14.5 \times 2.17 = 31.465$

Students who understand and practice this procedure are not as likely as those who do not to encounter the difficulty of not knowing where to put the decimal point. Eventually the children can make the transition to the usual short-form algorithm for multiplying decimal numbers:

$$16.2 \quad \frac{162}{10} \quad \times \quad \frac{357}{1000} \quad = \quad \frac{57,834}{10,000}$$

$$\begin{array}{r} \times .357 \\ \hline 1134 \end{array}$$

8100 tenths × thousandths = ten-thousandths

$$\begin{array}{r} 48,600 \\ \hline 5,7834 \end{array}$$

Tenths times thousandths gives ten-thousandths, so the final digit in the answer should occupy the ten-thousandths place. After practice with several examples of this sort, the students can be led to verbalize that to determine the location of the decimal point, we count to see how many digits are to the right of the decimal points in the factors.

This method will provide students with insight as to why this rule of counting decimal places is used in multiplication of decimals. When pupils come to understand multiplication of decimals thoroughly and discover that they can determine the location of the decimal point by counting the number of places in the factors, then they can then make use of this particular shortcut rule.

Division with Decimal Numbers

Division of decimals can also begin with models. Let us examine $.2\overline{)}.6$. What does it mean? It might mean that 6 tenths are to be separated into two groups. Suppose that $\triangleright$ represents 1 tenth of a circular region. Then:

6 tenths

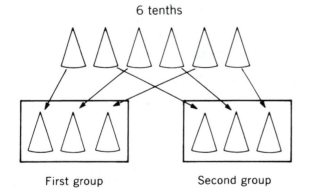

First group   Second group

Thus, when 6 tenths are separated into two groups, there are 3 tenths in each group.

$$.2\overline{)}.6 \rightarrow \begin{array}{c} .3 \\ 2\overline{)}.6 \end{array}$$

We can also use the number line to demonstrate. Mark off the product (.6), and then separate this line segment into 2 equivalent segments.

One group   One group
of 3   of 3
tenths   tenths

There are two groups of .3 in .6.

$$\begin{array}{c} .3 \\ 2\overline{)}.6 \end{array}$$

Now consider .6 divided by .2. That is, $.2\overline{)}.6$. This can be interpreted to mean that we have a product of .6 and want to make groups of .2. How many groups of .2 can we make from a group of .6?

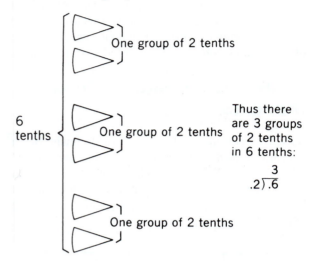

6 tenths

One group of 2 tenths

One group of 2 tenths

One group of 2 tenths

Thus there are 3 groups of 2 tenths in 6 tenths:

$$\begin{array}{c} 3 \\ .2\overline{)}.6 \end{array}$$

We can also use the number line. Mark off a product of 6 tenths, and then mark off groups of 2 tenths from 0 until you reach 6 tenths.

One   One   One
group   group   group
of 2   of 2   of 2
tenths   tenths   tenths   → Product

There are three groups of .2 in .6:

$$\begin{array}{c} 3 \\ .2\overline{)}.6 \end{array}$$

Now consider an example such as $\frac{.8}{.4} = \square$. We know that we can multiply the numerator and the denominator by the same number to get an equivalent fraction (i.e., we can multiply by 1 in the form of $\frac{a}{a}$, where $a \neq 0$). In this case, let's multiply by $\frac{10}{10}$

$$\frac{.8}{.4} \times \frac{10}{10} = \frac{8}{4} = 2$$

What about an example such as. $\frac{.84}{.21} = \square$? We can multiply by 1 in the form of $\frac{100}{100}$

$$\frac{.84}{.21} \times \frac{100}{100} = \frac{84}{21} = 4$$

Let's relate this to the long division format: $.21\overline{)}.84$. In this case, we should multiply both the product and the known factor by 100 to obtain a whole number divisor.

$$\begin{array}{c} 4 \\ 21\overline{)}84 \end{array}$$

In this way, we rationalize by using the traditional shortcut process of "moving" the decimal point in long division to obtain a whole number divisor. By multiplying both the dividend and the divisor by 100, we are actually multiplying the entire indicated division exercise by 1, in the form of $\frac{100}{100}$. Connect this procedure to the use of common denominators for division of rational numbers expressed in fraction form.

Relating Decimals and Fractions

Now we are ready to take a closer look at the relation between decimals and fractions written in the form $\frac{a}{b}$ (where $b \neq 0$). We have said that any fractional number, $\frac{a}{b}$, can be thought of as a quotient obtained from the division of a whole number a by a counting number b. This can also be stated another way: A **fractional number** is any number y that satisfies an equation of the form $b \times y = a$, where a is a whole number and b is a counting number. For such an equation, the solution can be expressed either as $y = a \div b$ or as $y = \frac{a}{b}$. Thus, the fraction $\frac{a}{b}$ means the same thing as $a \div b$. That is, $\frac{6}{2}$ is the same as $6 \div 2$, and $\frac{.6}{.2}$ is the same as. $6 \div .2$.

We have seen that any fraction whose numerator is a whole number and whose denominator is a power of ten (1, 10, 100, 1000, etc) can be easily expressed as a decimal. What about other fractions that aren't written with a denominator of a power of ten? Are all other fractions easily changed to be expressed with denominators of powers of ten? Consider the fraction $\frac{1}{4}$.

$$\begin{aligned} \frac{1}{4} &= \frac{1}{4} \times 1 \\ &= \frac{1}{4} \times \frac{25}{25} \\ &= \frac{25}{100} \\ &= .25 \end{aligned}$$

We could also find the decimal for $\frac{1}{4}$ by recalling that $\frac{1}{4}$ means 1 divided by 4 ($1 \div 4$).

$$\begin{array}{r} .25 \\ 4)\overline{1.00} \\ -80 \\ \hline 20 \\ -20 \\ \hline 0 \end{array}$$

In view of this, let's ask, "What is the decimal name for $\frac{5}{8}$?"

$$\begin{aligned} \frac{5}{8} &= \frac{5}{8} \times \frac{125}{125} \\ &= \frac{5 \times 125}{8 \times 125} \\ &= \frac{625}{1000} \\ &= .625 \end{aligned}$$ We chose $\frac{125}{125}$, another name for 1, because 125 is the least number that when multiplied by 8 will give a product in the denominator that is a power of ten: $8 \times 125 = 1000$.

But since $\frac{5}{8}$ can be interpreted as the indicated division, 5 divided by 8, let's examine the division form.

$$\begin{array}{r} .625 \\ 8)\overline{5.000} \\ -4800 \\ \hline 200 \\ -160 \\ \hline 40 \\ -40 \\ \hline 0 \end{array}$$

The decimal for $\frac{5}{8}$, then, is .625 (six hundred twenty-five thousandths).

What are the decimal names for the following common fractions?

$$\text{a)}\frac{3}{8} \qquad \text{b)}\frac{4}{5} \qquad \text{c)}\frac{3}{4}$$

$$\text{a)}\frac{3}{8} = \frac{3}{8} \times \frac{125}{125} = \frac{375}{1000} = .375$$

or

$$\begin{array}{r} .375 \\ 8)\overline{3.000} \\ -2\,4 \\ \hline 60 \\ -56 \\ \hline 40 \\ -40 \\ \hline 0 \end{array}$$

$$\text{b)}\frac{4}{5} = \frac{4}{5} \times \frac{2}{2} = \frac{8}{10} = .8$$

or

$$\begin{array}{r} .8 \\ 5)\overline{4.0} \\ -4\,0 \\ \hline 0 \end{array}$$

$$\text{c)}\frac{3}{4} = \frac{3}{4} \times \frac{25}{25} = \frac{75}{100} = .75$$

or

$$\begin{array}{r} .75 \\ 4)\overline{3.00} \\ -2\,8 \\ \hline 20 \\ -20 \\ \hline 0 \end{array}$$

Note that in many cases the division method is far simpler to use, as in this example: $\frac{21}{32}$

$$\begin{array}{r} .65625 \\ 32)\overline{21.00000} \\ -19\,2 \\ \hline 1\,80 \\ -1\,60 \\ \hline 200 \\ -192 \\ \hline 80 \\ -64 \\ \hline 160 \\ -160 \\ \hline 0 \end{array}$$

We can readily discover that certain fractions, when renamed as decimals, do not terminate, but yield a quotient that repeats endlessly. An example is $\frac{1}{3}$.

$$\frac{.333\ldots}{3)\overline{1.000}}$$

We put three dots (called an *ellipsis*) after the third digit in the quotient to show that the pattern continues in the same way—an endless succession of 3s. We can never get a remainder of zero, regardless of how many places we calculate in the quotient.

Observe the result in performing the indicated division in $\frac{3}{7}$ or $3 \div 7$. We obtain the quotient .42857142857 .... Again, we can never obtain a zero remainder, regardless of how many decimal places we calculate in the quotient (since that would mean the division terminated). Notice, however, that in this quotient a particular sequence of numerals occurs repeatedly: the sequence 428571 repeats over and over again. A fractional number whose quotient repeats a particular sequence of digits is called a **periodic decimal** or **repeating decimal**. A repeating decimal is often indicated by a bar over the digits that repeat—for example, $.\overline{428571}$. All fractions whose decimal forms do not terminate are periodic. (Although we do not prove this here, it may be an interesting challenge for you to pursue by considering examples and searching for counterexamples.) Thus we see that fractional numbers named in decimal form give either repeating decimals (in which one or more digits repeat endlessly) or **terminating decimals** (in which the quotient terminates—that is, eventually has a zero remainder).

We can easily determine whether the decimal for a fraction terminates or repeats by inspecting the prime factorization of its denominator.

Fraction	Prime Factorization of Denominator	Decimal
$\frac{1}{4}$	2×2	.250 or .25
$\frac{1}{2}$	2	.50 or .5
$\frac{1}{10}$	2×5	.10 or .1
$\frac{1}{20}$	$2 \times 2 \times 5$	.050 or .05
$\frac{1}{50}$	$2 \times 5 \times 5$	.020 or .02

Notice that each prime factorization on the preceding table contains only factors that are also factors of 10, the base of our number system. Fractions that have been simplified and whose denominators, when factored into primes, contain only 2s and 5s as factors form terminating decimals.

Let's examine some fractions whose denominators contain factors other than 2s and 5s.

Fraction	Prime Factorization of Denominator	Decimal
$\frac{1}{3}$	3	.333 ...
$\frac{1}{6}$	2×3	.1666 ...
$\frac{1}{12}$	$2 \times 2 \times 3$	.08333 ...

These fractions contain, in the prime factorization of their denominators, factors other than 2 or 5. Fractions of this kind form repeating decimals. Note that we usually round off repeating decimals such as .333.... We *sometimes* refer to this by approximation or rounding as simply .33, but it very important to recognize that .33 is only an approximation, not an exact value for the number $\frac{1}{3}$ or .333....

Decimal fractions can be indicated on the number line in the same manner as whole numbers or common fractions.

Note that points on the number line are now named in decimal form. We can see that

$$\frac{1}{5} = \frac{2}{10} = .2$$
$$\frac{2}{2} = \frac{5}{10} = .5$$
$$1 = \frac{2}{2} = \frac{5}{5} = \frac{10}{10} = 1.0$$

and so on.

Other number lines can be drawn that show other decimal names. For example:

The number line is an extremely useful device for demonstrating order relationships between different decimals—for example, to show that .5 > .375 and that .125 < .625. It is also useful for showing the decimal equivalents of common fractions, as was the case on the preceding number line. How would we locate the point named by a repeating decimal? This is not difficult if we have a method for converting a repeating decimal into a fraction.

You might approach the task of relating fractions to repeating decimals by asking children to explore patterns generated through performing the indicated division that certain fractions represent. For example, using a calculator (or paper and pencil, if you prefer), calculate the decimal equivalent for $\frac{1}{9}$. The indicated division yields .1111 .... (Note that depending on the calculator you use, you may get eight 1s preceded by a decimal point. It's important to recognize that this is only an approximation. The actual answer is a decimal number with repeating 1s. This can be verified by the paper-and-pencil division method if need be.) If you calculate the decimal equivalent for $\frac{2}{9}$, you'll get .222 ... for the answer. Can you predict the decimal equivalent for $\frac{3}{9}$ (or $\frac{1}{3}$)? What about $\frac{4}{9}$? What about $\frac{7}{9}$? Conduct a similar experiment for $\frac{1}{7}$, $\frac{2}{7}$, $\frac{3}{7}$, $\frac{4}{7}$, and so on.

An algebraic approach can also be used to convert a repeating decimal to an equivalent fraction. Let's examine how this is done by writing the periodic decimal .636363... as a fraction. If we let n equal the repeating decimal .636363..., we can find the value of $100 \times n$ by multiplying $.63\overline{)63}$ by 100.

$$n = .636\overline{363}\ldots$$
$$100 \times n = 63.636\overline{363}\ldots$$

Now, we subtract the first of these two equations from the second.

$$
\begin{array}{r}
100 \times n = 63.63\overline{63}\ldots \\
-\quad n = (\ \ .63\overline{63}\ldots) \\
\hline
99n = 63
\end{array}
$$

We find that if $99 \times n = 63$, then $n = \frac{63}{99}$. Translating this into simplest form, we find that $n = \frac{7}{11}$. We can now write the repeating decimal .636363 ... as the fraction $\frac{7}{11}$.

Now try converting .333 ... and .037037... into fraction form. First multiply .3333 ... by 10 and .037037 ... by 1000. (Notice that in the first example, the single digit 3 is repeated, so we multiply the decimal by 10^1, or 10. But in the second example, three digits, .037, are repeated, so we multiply the decimal by 10^3, or 1000.) After proceeding as before to solve these two examples (getting $\frac{1}{3}$ and $\frac{1}{27}$ for answers), we can draw some generalizations for changing periodic decimals into fraction form:

1. Assign an unknown (such as n) to represent the repeating decimal.

2. Multiply the equation in step 1 by some power of 10 so that the decimal point is shifted to the right as many places as there are digits that repeat.

3. Subtract the equation in step 1 from the equation in step 2.

4. Solve the new equation obtained in step 3; write the solution as a fraction.

Apply these generalizations to the periodic decimal .015015....

1. Let $n = .015\overline{015}$

2. Multiply the equation in step 1 by 1000 so that the decimal point is moved three places to the right (since there are three digits, 015, in the repeating period).

$$1000 \times n = 015.015\overline{015}$$

3. Subtract the equation in step 1 from the equation in step 2.

$$
\begin{array}{r}
1000 \times n = 015.015\overline{015} \\
-\quad (n = \quad\ .015\overline{015}) \\
\hline
999 \times n = 15
\end{array}
$$

4. Solve the equation obtained in step 3.

$$N = \frac{15}{999} = \frac{5}{333}$$

Scientific Notation

We have shown that in our number system, we can name numbers in many ways. One of the ways we found earlier to rename numbers is using expanded notation. For example, 123 can be written as $100 + 20 + 3$. We might also choose to express 123 in terms of powers of 10.

$$1 \times (10 \times 10) + 2 \times (10) + 3$$

Consider another way to name 123. If we are multiplying two 10s together, we can use exponential notation, as we did in discussing place value (see Chapter 6). Thus we can write 10^2 for 10×10 (the 2 as it is used here is called an *exponent*). Using exponential notation, we write 123 as follows:

$$123 = (1 \times 10^2) + (2 \times 10^1) + (3 \times 10^0)$$

There are many other ways of using exponents in naming 123. For example:

$$
\begin{array}{llll}
12.3 & \times & 10 & \text{or} \quad 12.3 \times 10^1 \\
1.23 & \times & 100 & \text{or} \quad 1.23 \times 10^2 \\
.123 & \times & 1000 & \text{or} \quad .123 \times 10^3
\end{array}
$$

If the number 123 is expressed as 1.23×10^2, it is said to be expressed in scientific notation. The following table shows some numbers expressed in scientific notation:

Number	Scientific Notation
24	2.4×10^1
324	3.24×10^2
1324	1.324×10^3
12,000	1.2×10^4
140,000	1.4×10^5
1,750,000	1.75×10^6

Examine these numbers expressed in scientific notation. What generalization can we make about writing numerals in this way? In **scientific notation**, a number is always expressed as some number equal to or greater than 1 and less than 10 that is multiplied by 10 raised to a certain power. For example, 24 is expressed in scientific notation as 2.4 (a number greater than 1 and less than 10) multiplied by 10^1, or 2.4×10^1. Similarly, the number 140,000 is expressed as 1.4 (again, a number greater than 1 and less than 10) multiplied by 10^5, or 1.4×10^5. Because 10^5 equals 100,000 we have:

$$\times 10^5 = 1.4 \times 100,000$$
$$= 140,000$$

Scientific notation, as the name suggests, is an efficient way for people in technical fields to express and work with very large quantities. The following table lists some astronomical distances expressed in scientific notation:

Planet	Distance from the Sun (in miles)
Mercury	3.6×10^7
Venus	6.71×10^7
Earth	9.29×10^7
Mars	1.42×10^8
Jupiter	4.83×10^8
Saturn	8.86×10^8
Uranus	1.78×10^9
Neptune	2.79×10^9
Pluto	3.67×10^9

Just as numbers representing great quantities can be expressed conveniently in scientific notation, so can numbers representing small quantities. We have examined fractional parts expressed in decimal form and, earlier, the use of negative exponents to name fractional parts. Now, let's examine the use of scientific notation to express very small numbers. First, we have seen that $\frac{1}{10}$ can be expressed as .1 or 10^{-1}. (Recall that 10^{-1} means $\frac{1}{10^1}$ or $\frac{1}{10}$, since any number raised to the first power is equal to the number itself.) Then $\frac{1}{100} = .01 = \frac{1}{10^2}$. Again, 10^{-2} means $\frac{1}{10^2}$ or $\frac{1}{100}$. If we continued in this way, we could make a chart such as the following:

Fraction	Decimal	Scientific Notation
$\frac{1}{10}$	.1	1×10^{-1}
$\frac{1}{100}$	.01	1×10^{-2}
$\frac{1}{1000}$	.001	1×10^{-3}
$\frac{1}{10,000}$	.0001	1×10^{-4}
$\frac{1}{100,000}$	.00001	1×10^{-5}
$\frac{1}{1,000,000}$	.000001	1×10^{-6}
$\frac{1}{10,000,000}$	.0000001	1×10^{-7}
$\vdots$	$\vdots$	$\vdots$

The pattern here is evident. Now, let's simply apply our knowledge of scientific notation to this sequence. In scientific notation, we express a number as the product expression of a number between 1 and 10, and 10 raised to some power. For example, 300,000 is expressed as 3×10^5. How could we express $\frac{3}{100000}$? This rather awkward fraction could be rewritten as follows:

$$3 \times 10^{-5}$$

The relation of this numeral to the fraction form is

Now suppose you wished to express the time required for a computer to perform one addition operation. Some older computers require 115 nanoseconds per processing step. This would be written as .000000115 or, in fraction form, as $\frac{115}{1000000000}$ (115 billionths). Scientific notation, 1.15×10^{-7} is a much simpler way of referring to and using this number.

Ratio, Proportion, and Percent

Many elementary and middle school mathematics programs introduce and teach the concept of ratio in conjunction with rational numbers expressed as fractions. We have chosen to introduce ratios at this point in the mathematics program as a means of reviewing fraction ideas and as a vehicle for teaching percents. The concept of ratio is another aspect of rational numbers that is useful in solving a variety of examples.

Look at a problem such as this:

Balloons are sold at the rate of 2 balloons for 5¢.

How many balloons can you buy for 10¢?

This problem can be interpreted this way: "Two balloons for five cents" suggests a fixed rate (a comparison between two numbers), which we can call a **ratio**. If this ratio is constant, we should be able to find out how many balloons we can buy for 10 cents or 20 cents, or how much it would cost to buy 4 balloons or 6 balloons.

One way we can express the ratio of balloons to cents is 2:5 (2 balloons for 5 cents). A somewhat more convenient notation is the familiar fraction form:

$\frac{2}{5}$ (two balloons)
(five cents)

Young students need to manipulate real objects so that they can easily see and then understand this relationship. For example:

Two balloons

Per nickel

2 for 5¢   6 for 15¢   10 for 25¢
          4 for 10¢   8 for 20¢

Now suppose we want to find the number of balloons we can buy for 10 cents. If "two balloons for 5 cents" can be expressed as a ratio, $\frac{2}{5}$ (often read "two to five" in this context), then there is some number of balloons that we can buy for 10 cents. Suppose we let n stand for the number of balloons we can buy for 10 cents. Then we can write:

$$\frac{n(n \text{ balloons})}{10(\text{ten cents})}$$

Thus we see that we can buy 2 balloons for 5 cents, 4 balloons for 10 cents, and so on. We can write $\frac{2}{5}, \frac{4}{10}, \frac{6}{15}, \frac{8}{20}, \frac{10}{25}, \ldots$. These are *equivalent ratios* because each ratio expresses the same relationship: The relationship 2 to 5 is the same as the relationship 4 to 10, and so on.

An equation of two equivalent ratios, such as $\frac{2}{5} = \frac{n}{10}$, is called a **proportion**. When the problem is stated in this way, we can see that if $\frac{n}{10}$ is equal to $\frac{2}{5}$, then the numerator and denominator of $\frac{2}{5}$ must be multiplied by 1 in the form of $\frac{a}{a}$, where $a \neq 0$, to obtain $\frac{n}{10}$. The form of $\frac{a}{a}$ in this case is $\frac{2}{2}$ because the denominator, 5, must be multiplied by 2 to get 10, and so must the numerator, 2, be multiplied by 2. The value of n, then, is clearly 2 × 2, or 4. We can buy 4 balloons for 10 cents.

$$\frac{2}{5} = \frac{4}{10}$$

Helping students look for patterns is an excellent technique for locating missing numbers in a proportion. Let's examine ratio patterns in several different ways:

Relationship Between Denominators and Between Numerators

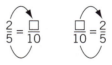

Since one denominator is twice the other, the corresponding numerator must be twice the other.

RESEARCH SNAPSHOT

What mathematical knowledge is needed to develop children's concepts of ratio and proportion?

In a study of a fifth grader, Lo and Watanabe (1997) found that the following mathematical knowledge was useful in the development of the concepts of ratio and proportion:

- number structures, such as multiples and divisors
- a conceptual basis of multiplication and division
- familiarity with a variety of multiplication and division situations
- meaningful multiplication and division algorithms
- the integration of this knowledge with rational number concepts

The authors also suggest that ratio and proportion instruction should start with situations that are meaningful for students.

Which kinds of mathematical experiences do you think would help children develop more sophisticated understandings of ratio and proportion?

Lo, J., & Watanabe, T. (1997). Developing ratio and proportion schemes: A story of a fifth grader. *Journal for Research in Mathematics Education, 28,* 216–236.

For additional research briefs, "ERIC Digests" lets you search more than 2000 short syntheses of research on a range of education topics. The syntheses were produced by the Educational Resources Information Center (ERIC). Check http://www.ericfacility.net/ericdigests/index/.

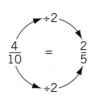

Relationship Between Numerator and Denominator

Since the numerator is one-half of the denominator in one ratio, it must be one-half in the other.

Since the denominator is twice as large as the numerator in one ratio, it must be twice as large in the other.

As we mentioned, when two equivalent ratios are expressed as an equality, they form a proportion. A proportion is a mathematical sentence.

$$\frac{2}{5} = \frac{4}{10}$$

This proportion is read, "Two is to five as four is to ten." Because a ratio always expresses a relation between two quantities, this proportion means, "Two balloons for five cents indicates the same price ratio as four balloons for ten cents."

If we use notation of the form $a{:}b$ to express the ratios, then the proportion $\frac{2}{5} = \frac{4}{10}$ would be written $2{:}5 = 4{:}10$. Some textbook authors prefer to use the symbol ($::$) in place of the equal sign ($=$) when ratios are expressed in the form $a{:}b$. Using this notation, the proportion would then be written $2{:}5{::}4{:}10$. However, such symbolism serves more to confuse elementary school children than to enlighten them. We want to exploit the connections between ratios and fractions—not hide them in abstractions that aren't needed until much later.

We can, by use of the ratio method, find the cost of any number of balloons or the quantity of balloons we can buy for any given amount of money.

$$\frac{2}{5} = \frac{4}{10} \quad \leftarrow \left[\begin{array}{l} \text{2 balloons for 5¢} \\ \text{4 balloons for 10¢} \end{array}\right.$$

Therefore, $\frac{2}{5} = \frac{40}{100}$ ← 40 balloons for 100¢

Establish a pattern with children by first setting up a table to find the cost of 2, 4, 6, 8, ... balloons.

Number of Balloons	Cost
2	5¢
4	10¢
6	15¢
8	20¢
10	25¢
12	30¢
14	35¢
⋮	⋮

Children can see that the ratio is always $\frac{2}{5}$ and that different proportions can be set up.

$$\frac{2}{5} = \frac{4}{10} \quad \frac{2}{5} = \frac{8}{20} \quad \frac{2}{5} = \frac{14}{35} \quad \text{and so on}$$

A ratio is an expressed relation between two numbers: 2 tickets for $3 (e.g., $\frac{2}{3}$). A proportion is a statement of equality for two ratios:

$$\frac{2}{5} = \frac{4}{10} \quad \frac{3}{7} = \frac{21}{49} \quad \frac{1}{3} = \frac{4}{12}$$

An interesting property is commonly used in solving proportions: If two equivalent ratios are written in fraction form, then the two products formed by multiplying the numerator of one fraction by the denominator of the other are equal. In symbols we can say:

$$\text{If } \frac{a}{b} = \frac{d}{c}, \text{ then } a \times d = c \times b$$

To see why this is always true, multiply both sides of $\frac{a}{b} = \frac{c}{d}$ by the product of the denominators ($b \times d$).

$$\frac{a}{b} \times (b \times d) = \frac{c}{d} \times (b \times d)$$

$$\frac{a \times (b \times d)}{b} = \frac{c \times (b \times d)}{d}$$

$$\frac{(a \times d) \times b}{b} = \frac{(c \times b) \times d}{d}$$

$$(a \times d) \times \frac{b}{b} = (c \times b) \times \frac{d}{d}$$

But $\frac{b}{b} = 1$ and $\frac{d}{d} = 1$, so the last equation simplifies to:

$$(a \times d) \times 1 = (c \times b) \times 1$$
$$\text{or}$$
$$\times d = c \times b$$

The products $a \times d$ and $c \times b$ are often called **cross products** because they are formed according to this scheme:

$$\frac{a}{b} \rightleftharpoons \frac{c}{d}$$

Use simpler proportions and patterns to assist students in the discovery of cross products. Provide students with many examples of simple proportions such as $\frac{1}{2} = \frac{2}{4}$, $\frac{1}{3} = \frac{2}{6}$, $\frac{2}{3} = \frac{6}{9}$, and so on. Encourage students to look for patterns in the relationships between the numerators and the denominators. Challenge the students to look for a relationship or pattern that yields $4 = 4$ (for the first pair) or $6 = 6$ (for the second) or $18 = 18$ (for the third).

Let's solve some proportions by using both patterns and the cross-product method. Consider this example: "Suppose 3 waitresses can serve a total of 17 tables. How many waitresses are needed to serve 51 tables?" This problem can be expressed by the following proportion:

$$\frac{3}{17} = \frac{w}{51}$$

Looking for patterns, we might recognize that $17 \times 3 = 51$.

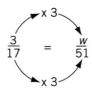

If the denominator of the second ratio is 3 times the denominator of the first ratio, then the numerator of the second ratio must be 3 times the numerator of the first ratio.

$$\frac{3}{17} \times 1 = \frac{w}{51}$$
$$\frac{3}{17} \times \frac{3}{3} = \frac{w}{51}$$
$$\frac{3}{17} \times \frac{3}{3} = \frac{9}{51}$$

Using the cross-product method, we find that:

$$3 \times 51 = w \times 17 \text{ or } w \times 17 = 153$$

Therefore,

$$w = 153 \div 17 \text{ or } w = 9$$

Thus, 9 waitresses are needed to serve 51 tables, if 3 waitresses are needed for 17 tables.

Comparing the two techniques for solving ratio examples, many find using patterns to be simpler if one term of a proportion is a multiple of another term of the proportion. The following example also points out the importance of clearly identifying the specific relationship that the ratio is intended to convey:

If a class has 4 boys and 6 girls, then how many boys would we expect in a class of 30 students?

The temptation might be strong to set up the following proportion and solve for n:

$$\frac{4}{6} = \frac{n}{30}$$

However, careful consideration of the problem should suggest that the ratio of boys to classmates should be expressed by $\frac{4}{10}$, not $\frac{4}{6}$. That is, there are 10 classmates and this question asks for a comparison of the number of boys to the number of classmates, not to the number of girls. Therefore, the problem should be solved by the following proportion:

$$\frac{4}{10} = \frac{n}{30}$$

therefore, $n = 12$. That is, if there are 4 boys for every 6 girls, then there would be 12 boys in a class of 30 children.

Consider a common example of ratio in action: "Marilyn Sue kept a record of the number of hits for the total official times at bat. She found that she had 8 hits for 40 official times at bat. At this rate, how many hits should she have for 45 official times at bat?" The example can be expressed by the following proportion:

$$\frac{8}{40} = \frac{h}{45}$$

Use of the cross-product method gives

$$8 \times 45 = h \times 40 \quad \text{or} \quad h \times 40 = 360$$

Therefore,

$$h = 360 \div 40 = 9$$

Thus, Marilyn Sue can expect 9 hits out of 45 official times at bat. This is a representation of Marilyn Sue's hitting ability. How might we compare her hitting with the hitting of another player?

In studying baseball facts, the following information was gathered:

Player	Hits	Times at Bat	Ratio
Mary Ann	6	24	$\frac{6}{24}$
Cecelia	4	10	$\frac{4}{10}$
Tom	3	30	$\frac{3}{30}$
Dan	5	25	$\frac{5}{25}$
Jim	2	8	$\frac{2}{8}$

Which player has the best batting average? A batting average is calculated by comparing the number of hits to the number of official times at bat. It is very difficult to simply compare the ratios for these players to determine the best batter because each ratio is based on a different number of official times at bat. To compare the batting averages, we may choose to rewrite the ratios so that they all have the same second term or denominator. For convenience, let's select 100 as a common denominator.

Player	Ratio	Rewritten Ratio
Mary Ann	$\frac{6}{24}$	$\frac{25}{100}$
Cecelia	$\frac{4}{10}$	$\frac{40}{100}$
Tom	$\frac{3}{30}$	$\frac{10}{100}$
Dan	$\frac{5}{25}$	$\frac{20}{100}$
Jim	$\frac{2}{8}$	$\frac{25}{100}$

Now that the ratios have been written with a common denominator, 100 in this case, we can compare them and can easily see that Cecelia has the best batting average and Tom has the poorest. Ratios that have a common denominator of 100 are often called *percentages*. The symbol for percent is %. The word *percent* comes from the Latin *per centum*, meaning "for a hundred." By **percent** we mean "per hundred," or "parts of a hundred." Thus, 1% means "one per hundred" or "one out of every hundred" ($\frac{1}{100}$ or .01); 25% means "twenty-five per hundred," or "twenty-five out of every hundred" ($\frac{25}{100}$ or .25); and 50% means "fifty per hundred," or "fifty out of every hundred" ($\frac{50}{100}$ or .50).

An effective way of modeling percent is to use base ten blocks, specifically, the flat block as 1 whole, or 100%. Long blocks can then be used to signify 10%, and small cubes to represent 1%. We can easily show that 50% equals $\frac{1}{2}$ by showing that 5 longs are the same as one-half of a flat.

Another related, but perhaps more readily available, method is to use graph paper with 100 squares to represent 100%. Yet another model for developing children's understanding of percentage is a hundreds board. Use a heavy cardboard square and divide it into 100 smaller squares.

Children may want to draw on graph paper by marking off $10 = by = 10$ squares. By definition, the entire card represents 100%—that is, all of the squares.

In the square on the left, 1 small square is shaded. We can see that $\frac{1}{100}$ of the square is shaded. Changing the fraction to a decimal, we see that .01 of the square is shaded. Each small square on the card is 1%. In the center square, 10 small squares are shaded; $\frac{10}{100}$ of the large square is shaded. The fraction $\frac{10}{100}$ is another name for $\frac{1}{10}$. Thus, we can say that .1, .10, or 10% of the center square is shaded. A rubber band or ribbon could be stretched around the large square to illustrate 10%. The square on the right has a rubber band up two rows from the bottom. This card shows 20% below the rubber band and 80% above the rubber band.

Students need to work with other shapes and objects to understand the concept that all of something is 100%. For example:

Which percentage of each of the following regions is shaded?

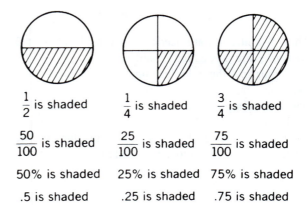

$\frac{1}{2}$ is shaded $\frac{1}{4}$ is shaded $\frac{3}{4}$ is shaded

$\frac{50}{100}$ is shaded $\frac{25}{100}$ is shaded $\frac{75}{100}$ is shaded

50% is shaded   25% is shaded   75% is shaded

.5 is shaded   .25 is shaded   .75 is shaded

We have seen that .01, $\frac{1}{100}$ and 1% are three names for the same number (one one-hundredth). Similarly, the number seventeen one-hundredths can be represented as a decimal, as a fraction, or as a percent: .17, $\frac{17}{100}$, or 17%. Each of these numerals can be thought of as expressing a ratio (17 per 100).

Several different ways may be used to express each comparison—a fraction, a ratio, a decimal, or a percent. For example, we say that $\frac{1}{2}$, $\frac{50}{100}$, .50, and 50% are equivalent. We often have the need to name the likelihood of an event in a probability situation, such as tossing a coin for heads or tails, by using fractions (say, $\frac{1}{2}$), percent (say, 50%), and decimals (say, .5). The following table shows some equivalent names for percents:

Fractions	Ratios	Decimals	Percents
$\frac{1}{2}$	$\frac{50}{100}$	.50	50%
$\frac{1}{4}$	$\frac{25}{100}$	.25	25%
$\frac{1}{3}$	$33\frac{1}{3}/100$	.333...	$33\frac{1}{3}\%$
$\frac{1}{8}$	$12\frac{1}{2}/100$	.125	$12\frac{1}{2}\%$
$\frac{3}{4}$	$\frac{75}{100}$	.75	75%

When one form or name for a percent is known, how do we find the other forms? One of the basic structures of mathematics that we might use is the identity element of multiplication. Consider a pack of gum that contains 5 sticks. If a child is chewing 2 sticks of gum, which part or percent of the pack is the child chewing? Since the child is chewing 2 sticks out of a pack of 5, we would say that the child is chewing $\frac{2}{5}$ of the pack. How can we find the ratio for $\frac{2}{5}$ that has a denominator of 100? We know that $\frac{2}{5} \times 1 = \frac{2}{5}$ and that 1 has many names, such as $\frac{2}{2}$, $\frac{3}{3}$, $\frac{4}{4}$, and so on. Which value for 1 should we select so that the denominator of the original ratio, $\frac{2}{5}$, becomes 100? Since $5 \times 20 = 100$, we should select $\frac{20}{20}$ as the form for 1 to use here. Now, since $\frac{2}{5} \times 1 = \frac{2}{5}$ and $1 = \frac{20}{20}$, we write $\frac{2}{5} \times \frac{20}{20} = \frac{40}{100}$. Therefore, the fraction $\frac{2}{5}$ can be written as an equivalent ratio of $\frac{40}{100}$. From our study of decimals, we know that $\frac{40}{100}$ can be written as .40 and that .40 can be written as 40%.

Some fractions have denominators that are not factors of 100. How are these fractions changed to ratios, decimals, and percents? Either of the two techniques learned earlier in this chapter may be applied in this situation. We know that the fraction bar can also be interpreted as an indicated division, so we can change a fraction to a decimal by dividing the numerator by the denominator. We also know that when an element is missing in a proportion, we can find it by using the cross-product method.

For example, consider the fraction $\frac{5}{6}$. We see that 6 is not a factor of 100. Using the first method, we divide the numerator by the denominator.

$$.83\frac{2}{6} = .83\frac{1}{3} = 83\frac{1}{3}\%$$
$$\frac{5}{6} = 6\overline{)5.00}$$

Thus we say that $\frac{5}{6}$ equals $83\frac{1}{3}$% Now let's consider the cross-product method.

$$\frac{5}{6} = \frac{n}{100}$$
$$5 \times 100 = n \times 6$$
$$500 = n \times 6$$
$$500 \times \frac{1}{6} = n \times 6 \times \frac{1}{6}$$
$$\frac{250}{500} \times \frac{1}{\cancel{6}_3} = n$$
$$250 \div 3 = n$$
$$83\frac{1}{3} = n$$

Thus:

$$\frac{5}{6} = \frac{83\frac{1}{3}}{100} = .83\frac{1}{3} = 83\frac{1}{3}\%$$

Ratio and proportion play a major role in the study of percentage. In more traditional mathematics programs, three rather mechanical approaches to percentage problems were commonly taught. Today a single, more meaningful approach is usually presented. By defining percent as parts of a hundred, we eliminate the tedious, mechanical formula requiring children to move decimal points back and forth and to drop and add percent signs. The following examples use the ratio approach to percent:

Example a: 20% of 10 = n
Example b: n% of 10 = 2
Example c: 20% of n = 2

Consider Example a, 20% of 10 = n. In some programs, 20% is expressed as $\frac{20}{100}$ or 20 per 100. Therefore, 20% of some number (in this case, 10) can be expressed by equivalent ratios: 20 per 100 is equivalent to some number n per 10.

$$\frac{20}{100} = \frac{n}{10} \text{ or } \frac{n}{10} = \frac{20}{100}$$

The numerator and denominator of $\frac{n}{10}$ must both be multiplied by the same number to get $\frac{20}{100}$. Since the denominator, 10, must be multiplied by 10 to get 100, the numerator, n, must also be multiplied by 10 to get 20.

$$n \times 10 = 20$$
$$n = 2$$

Thus, n is equal to 2:

$$\frac{2}{10} = \frac{20}{100}$$

and so 20% of 10 = 2.

VM13.4

Models play an important role in understanding the relationships among percent, fraction, and decimal notation. The VM titled *Relating Fractions, Ratios, Decimals and Percents* on the CD that accompanies this text allows the user to input part, whole, or percent and then shows the amount in both a rectangular and circular region. Which percent values create an image that is shaded more than one-half but less than three-fourths? Which fraction values represent between 40% and 50%? Which fraction values would yield percents between 70% and 71%? Use the VM to show that $\frac{1}{2}$% does not equal 50%. How would the VM have to be changed to show 200%?

Now, consider Example b, n% of 10 = 2. We can solve examples of this kind by recognizing that the percent is not known but can be expressed as some part, n, of 100. We see that 2 out of 10 is equivalent to some part, n, of 100.

$$\frac{n}{100} = \frac{2}{10} \quad \text{or} \quad \frac{2}{10} = \frac{n}{100}$$

The value of n is clearly 20, and $\frac{20}{100}$ can be expressed as 20%.

$$20\% \text{ of } 10 = 2$$

Finally, let's look at Example c, 20% of n = 2. This example should be written as follows:

$$\frac{20}{100} = \frac{2}{n} \quad \text{or} \quad \frac{2}{n} = \frac{20}{100}$$

We can determine the value of n by examining the proportion in terms of equivalent fractions. The value of n is thus shown to be 10.

Simple examples involving percent, such as those just given, are often more easily understood in the elementary or middle grades when interpreted by means of proportions (equivalent ratios). Moreover, since ratio can be a rather complex topic, it is not elaborated at this point in the curriculum but is nevertheless introduced to students in terms of a familiar topic—equivalent fractions.

Ratio is just one method taught to students to solve percentage problems. Let's examine another method that is closely tied to elementary algebraic thinking. After students have used models such as graph paper and have an understanding of the meaning of percentage, then a formula method may be introduced. In the formula method, students must learn to identify the rate, base, and percentage. Consider this example:

$$20\% \text{ of } 40 = 8$$

In such situations, the **rate** is 20%, the **base** is 40, and the **percentage** is 8. The algebraic formula the student must learn is $r \times b = p$, which stands for "rate

times base equals percentage." Consider the following problem:

Sam correctly solved 60% of the 30 mathematics examples on the last test. How many examples did Sam solve correctly?

In this problem, 60% is the rate, 30 is the base, and the percentage needs to be found. Substitute the values in the algebraic percentage formula, and solve the example. Remember that we may express 60% as .60 to help us keep track of the decimal point when calculating.

$$r \times b = p$$
$$.60 \times 30 = p$$
$$18.00 = p$$

Therefore, Sam solved 18 examples correctly.

Let's change the example to illustrate another case of percentage.

On a mathematics test, Sam solved 18 out of 30 examples correctly. What percentage of the mathematics examples did Sam solve correctly?

In this problem, 30 is the base, 18 is the percentage, and we are to find the rate. Now we can substitute the values in the algebraic percentage formula and solve for the rate.

$$r \times b = p$$
$$r \times 30 = 18$$

When given a product and a factor, the student should understand how to solve the example.

$$\square \times 30 = 18$$
$$\square = \frac{18}{30} = \frac{3 \times 6}{5 \times 6} = \frac{3}{5} \times \frac{6}{6}$$
$$\frac{3}{5} \times 1 = .60$$
$$.60 = 60\%$$

Thus, Sam solved 60% of the mathematics examples correctly.

If Sam solved 60% of the examples correctly and he solved 18 correctly, how many examples are on the entire mathematics test? The rate is 60%, which can be written as .60. The percentage is 18. Substituting these values in the percentage formula $r \times b = p$, we get

$$r \times b = p$$
$$.60 \times b = 18$$

The product is 18, and .60 is a factor.

$$b = \frac{18}{.60}$$
$$\text{so, } b = 30$$

There are a total of 30 examples on Sam's mathematics test.

Closure

As the United States continues to adapt to and use the metric system, we must reconsider the practical need and value of rational numbers expressed as fractions and those expressed as decimals in our society. Since the metric system is based on powers of ten—the same as our decimal number system—undoubtedly more emphasis needs to be placed on decimals and, perhaps, less emphasis on fractions. However, it will always be necessary to relate fractions and decimals—parents will continue to cut candy bars in "half," the business world will continue to use percent and relate percents to fractions and decimals, and the study of more advanced mathematics will be predicated on knowledge of the rational number system. We can't afford to do anything less than prepare students for a world that makes frequent use of both fraction and decimal notation and concepts.

Too often teachers begin teaching about decimals on the abstract level and children become lost very quickly. More emphasis needs to be placed on the concrete level as students develop an understanding of rational numbers expressed as decimals. When teachers build a better foundation, they find that they need to devote less time to the operations that involve decimals. Since the basic facts of addition, subtraction, multiplication, and division are the same for decimals as for whole numbers, it's important for all to recognize that the study of decimals presents an extended application of whole number concepts the children already understand. Children soon realize that the basic facts they have memorized also apply to decimals, and thus there are no new basic facts to memorize. The place-value generalization is simply extended to the right of the decimal point.

Students should realize, with the aid of a teacher's focused questions, that the fraction-decimal-percent relation is merely a matter of renaming a number in different ways. This approach eliminates a great deal of the confusion and misunderstanding that was common in many "disconnected" elementary school mathematics programs.

Children already have an understanding of fractions, and the number line provides an excellent visual presentation of the relation between fraction and decimal forms. The place-value grid, or chart, and squared graph paper are other aids used to present this relationship.

Another way of preparing students to understand decimals is to use real money—dollars and cents are expressed in decimals. You can "buy" some item, such as shoes or books or cell phones, from the children at the beginning of the class period with real money; then they can buy it back at the end of the period.

With continuing emphasis on place value and understanding of our number system, there is no reason children should approach decimals with the idea that decimals are something completely isolated from concepts that they have already discovered and used. What children should discover is the relationships of decimal numbers to the structure of our number system. When they begin to recognize that operations with decimals can be more convenient than operations with fractions in many situations, they will realize the importance of decimal notation and facility with decimal operations.

We leave this chapter with an interesting and curious example of ratios, fractions, decimals, and percent that conveys the importance of their relationships to each other.

Jeff and Ryan are two baseball players. In one month, Jeff gets 20 hits in 25 at bats (20 for 25, or 80%), and Ryan gets 19 hits in 25 at bats (19 for 25 or 76%). Clearly, Jeff is the better hitter for that month, even if only by one hit. In the next month, neither player gets much playing time because of injuries. Still, Jeff continues to do a little better than Ryan, getting 3 hits in 10 at bats (3 for 10 or 30%) while Ryan gets 1 hit in 5 at bats (1 for 5 or 20%). How is it, then, since Jeff had better averages both months, that Ryan has the better average overall (20 for 30 or $66\frac{2}{3}$% for Ryan versus 23 for 35 or 65.71% for Jeff)?

Problems such as this one can bring about new discussion on what a ratio represents and how ratio may be different from a fraction.

PRACTICE EXERCISES FOR TEACHERS

These exercises are designed for the reader of this book, not for the children the reader may teach. Although some of these examples are suitable for use in the elementary or middle school classroom, they should not necessarily be given to children in the form presented here. Ideas appropriate for classroom activities on the concepts and ideas discussed in this chapter can be found in a later section of this chapter and on the CD that accompanies this text.

1. Write 346.128 in expanded form.

2. Translate each of the following decimals into a fraction.

   a) 2.1896   b) .003201   c) .1212   d) .4646

   e) .88 . . .   f) .25   g) .358   h) .072072

3. Translate each of the following fractions into a decimal.

   a) $\frac{4}{7}$ b) $1\frac{12}{13}$ c) $\frac{8}{11}$

   d) $\frac{11}{12}$ e) $\frac{5}{15}$ f) $\frac{2}{3}$

4. Is it possible that there is a fraction with a whole number numerator and a counting number denominator that when changed to a decimal, is neither terminating nor repeating? How can you be sure of your answer?

5. Complete the indicated operation in each of the following examples.

   a) $2.34 + 17.1 + .0234 + .123$ b) $43.7 - 12.684$

   c) 7.43×2.1 d) $6.2\overline{)8.928}$

6. Solve each of the following problems by using ratios.

   a) Tomato juice is on sale at 3 cans for 97 cents. How much must you pay for a dozen cans?

   b) Mr. Shih's class is going to the art museum. If 5 children can ride in each car, how many cars are needed to carry all 35 children in the class?

   c) If 100 centimeters measures the same length as 1 meter, how many centimeters are needed to measure the same length as 3 meters?

   d) If 1 kilometer is approximately .6 mile, how many kilometers will measure the same length as 1 mile?

7. Solve each of the following problems by using ratios and proportions.

   a) A chair that normally sells for $150.00 has been marked down to sell for $100.00. What is the percent of discount?

   b) The price for unleaded gasoline has increased at a particular station from 342.9 cents per gallon to 433.9 cents per gallon. What percent increase has there been at that station?

   c) In a fourth-grade class, 10% of the children received perfect scores on an arithmetic test. If 33 children received perfect scores, how many children took the test?

   d) At Boulder Elementary School, 56% of the students walk to school every day. How many students walk to school if there are 500 pupils in the school?

   e) At Greenspin School, 391 children attended the school play. If this is 17% of the number of children in the school, what is the total number of children who attend Greenspin School?

8. Use the percentage formula to solve each of the problems in the previous exercise. Describe how the solutions differ.

9. Express each of the following with an ordinary base ten numeral:

    a) 9.38×10^5 b) 2.37×10^4 c) 4.66×10^9 d) 5.3×10^6

    e) 8.31×10^{-2} f) 3.641×10^{-6} g) 2.2×10^{-3} h) 4.681×10^{-5}

10. Express each of the following numbers in scientific notation.

    a) 7300   b) 24,000,000   c) 8,900,000,000

    d) 123   e) 16,432   f) 437.56

11. Change each of these fractions, $\frac{1}{3}$, $\frac{5}{7}$, and $\frac{6}{13}$, to decimals. How often does the sequence of digits repeat? Formulate a general rule that allows you to predict the maximum number of decimal places that can occur before a digit is repeated. (HINT: Consider the denominator of each example.)

12. How might you use a 10-by-10 square cut from graph paper to show that $\frac{1}{2}$ and $\frac{1}{2}\%$ are different concepts?

13. Translate each of the following fractions into a percent.

VM 13.4

    a) $\frac{7}{8}$ b) $\frac{9}{11}$ c) $\frac{3}{15}$

    d) $\frac{7}{13}$ e) $\frac{3}{4}$ f) $\frac{8}{9}$

TEACHING COMPETENCIES AND SELF-ASSESSMENT TASKS

The following questions and statements are designed to reflect the teaching competencies that appeared at the beginning of this chapter and, in some cases, to expose you to deeper aspects of the concepts presented. Take a moment to consider your response to each of these in light of what you're read and learned.

1. Examine a number of elementary school mathematics textbooks at different grade levels; compare and contrast the techniques for introducing decimals to children.

2. Which home-made or commercial teaching aids are effective in developing an understanding of decimals?

3. Discuss the use of decimals in society today. Which is more useful—decimals or fractions? Why?

4. List the advantages of using decimals instead of fractions with a calculator or a computer.

5. Compare the common characteristics of a specific operation on decimals with that same operation on whole numbers.

6. Discuss why, when dividing 1 by 6, some calculators might display .1666666 and others .16666667. What is the "real" value, and how do we write it?

7. Compare the pencil-and-paper algorithm for multiplying the following factors to one using the scientific notation representation of the factors.

    a) 24×57 b) $34,000 \times 2800$ c) $809,000 \times 45,600,000$

    d) 2.3×34.675 e) $0.0003 \times .00405$

8. Discuss the similarities and differences between ratios and fractions. Is it possible to add ratios meaningfully? If so, is adding ratios the same as adding fractions?

9. Debate whether .9999 . . . is equal to 1, or simply very close to 1. Structure your debate to use the decimal equivalents of $\frac{1}{3}$ and $\frac{2}{3}$ and the fact that $\frac{1}{3} + \frac{2}{3} = \frac{3}{3}$, or 1.

10. Discuss the prerequisite knowledge necessary for studying concepts and operations on decimals.

11. Discuss useful evaluation techniques for assessing the understanding of decimals on the concrete level.

12. Discuss the advantages of teaching decimals before fractions and teaching fractions before decimals.

SAMPLE INSTRUCTIONAL AND ASSESSMENT ACTIVITIES

These activities and more are available on the CD that accompanies this text

1. Construct a deck of cards with the numerals .10 through .99. Relate this to money notation by marking one side with the $ sign (e.g., $.30) and the other with the ¢ sign (e.g., 30¢). Shuffle the deck and pull out two cards, one for each player. The player with the greater number value on the cards gets to take the card from the other player. The player who has the most cards at the end is declared the winner.

2. When children play with a calculator, they will often press keys just to experiment. In this process, they will likely divide a smaller number by a larger number. Many calculators will display the results of 1 ÷ 6 as .16666666, and this result can be used to initiate questions about the need for decimals.

3. Have children write simple verbal problems involving ratios. This is an excellent way to find out whether they understand the basic ideas. For example, in a certain classroom, the ratio of boys to girls is 2 to 3. If there are a total of 12 boys in the classroom, how many girls are there? If there are 25 children in the classroom, how many are boys? Could there be 33 children in the classroom? Why or why not? Give them opportunities to discuss the problems and explain their thinking.

VM 13.4

4. A game using cardboard dominoes can be helpful in learning to recognize equivalent fractions and decimals. Make a set of 28 dominoes, each of which shows numerals for positive rational numbers as fractions, decimals, or both. For example:

Some of the cards should be doubles. For example:

Place dominoes facedown on the table and shuffle. Each player selects five dominoes; the remaining dominoes are left on the table in a pile. The player with the greatest double begins by placing it on the table. The player to the left may play a domino if he or she has one with a numeral equal to the sum of the two on the double, or if he or she has one with a numeral naming a fraction or decimal equivalent to the original domino. If the child cannot play, he or she must draw from the pile until a play results. The next player may play either on the other side of the double, if he or she has the sum, or on the last domino played, if he or she has a fraction or decimal equal to the open end or equal to the sum of the two fractions or decimals. The game is ended when one player runs out of dominoes. Each player gets one point per play.

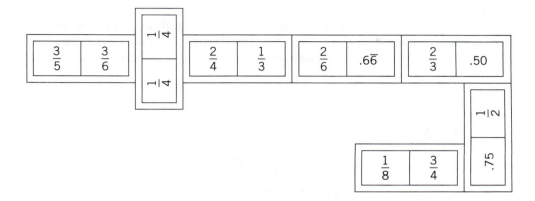

5. Mark 40 cards with numerals expressed as decimals. For example:

One person mixes the cards and deals one at a time, facedown, until each player has three cards. When the dealer says "Grab," each player then picks up his or her cards and arranges them in the correct order. The first person to declare "Between" and display the correct sequence wins a point. A person who says "Between" first but illustrates an incorrect sequence loses 2 points. The first person to get 12 points is the winner.

6. Teachers can easily construct a place-value pocket chart by using a piece of tagboard 24 inches by $5\frac{1}{2}$ inches, folded $1\frac{1}{2}$ inches and stapled or sewn as marked.

To use this place-value pocket chart, call a number, such as 258.025. The student then places the numerals 2, 5, 8, 0, 2, and 5 in the correct pockets.

7. A variety of problems can be presented that will reinforce basic concepts of measurement and help children understand some of the uses and advantages of decimal notation. For example, have the children draw polygons on pieces of paper. Ask them to measure the sides of the polygons to the nearest centimeter and nearest inch. Which measurements are easier to make? Have the children calculate the perimeters of the polygons they drew in centimeters and in inches (using the measurements they have obtained). Which measurements are easier to add?

8. When 9 is divided by 17, many calculator display screens will read .5294117. How can the example be entered into the calculator so that you will know the eighth decimal place?

VM 13.4

9. Stress the comparison between fraction and decimal notation frequently as children begin to extend their working knowledge in the operations of arithmetic. This is not to imply that every example must be translated from one form into the other, which would defeat the purpose of using the most efficient form. When a child understands the relation and can select the notation that is most efficient in a given situation, then the purpose has been accomplished.

This is particularly true in the operations of multiplication and division involving decimals. The memorized rules of counting the decimal places and moving the decimal point should be replaced by sound mathematical reasoning that can be justified. Study and complete the following examples:

a) $.1 \times 6 = \dfrac{\square}{10} \times 6$

b) $.25 \times .3 = \dfrac{25}{\square} \times \dfrac{3}{\square}$

c)

```
  .36   =                    3 tenths  6 hundredths
× 4                    ×                4 ones
                         12 tenths 24 hundredths
                         14 tenths___hundredths
                  ___ones___tenths___hundredths
```

d)

```
  .26   =                    2 tenths  6 hundredths
× .4                   ×               4 tenths
                         8 hundredths 24 thousandths
                         ___hundredths___thousandths
                  ___tenths___hundredths___thousandths
```

e)

```
   .25
 × .34
  .0020
  .0080
  .0150
  .0600
   □
```

$\dfrac{4}{100} \times \dfrac{5}{100} = \dfrac{20}{10000}$ $\dfrac{20}{10000}$

$\dfrac{4}{100} \times \dfrac{2}{10} = \dfrac{8}{1000}$ $\dfrac{8}{1000}$

$\dfrac{3}{10} \times \dfrac{5}{100} = \dfrac{15}{1000}$ $\dfrac{15}{1000}$

$\dfrac{3}{10} \times \dfrac{2}{10} = \dfrac{6}{100}$ $+ \dfrac{6}{100}$

$\square$

f)

```
   .34
 × .08
```

14

Data Analysis: Graphs, Statistics, and Probability

TEACHING COMPETENCIES

Upon completing this chapter, you will be able to:

- Define the statistical terms *range*, *mean*, *median*, and *mode* and calculate these measures for a given collection of data.

- Design and construct graphs (frequency polygons, histograms, bar graphs, line graphs, pictographs, or circle graphs) for a given set of data.

- Construct stem-and-leaf plots and/or box-and-whisker plots from data collections.

- Determine the possible outcomes in a simple probability experiment and the theoretical probability that certain events will occur.

- Describe ways in which statistics and probability are used in life situations and identify ways in which statistics and probability might be misused or misinterpreted.

- Use Pascal's Triangle and/or geometric arguments to calculate probability.

- Design instructional activities that incorporate data gathering, handling, and interpretation in a manner appropriate for elementary or middle school children.

VIRTUAL MANIPULATIVES

Upon completing this chapter, you will be able to use virtual manipulatives on the accompanying CD to:

- Compare and contrast different representations of data with histograms and box-and-whisker plots using *Classroom Size*. **(VM 14.1)**

- Examine measures of central tendency using *Histogram and Box Plot*. **(VM 14.2)**

- Represent data using *Circle Graph*. **(VM 14.3)**

- Examine the effects of data changes in circle graphs using *Pie Chart*. **(VM 14.4)**

- Explore probability, patterns, and permutations and combinations using *Combinations and Pascal's Triangle*. **(VM 14.5)**

- Model experimental probability and compare the results to theoretical probability using simulation games *Lots of Tosses and Spinner*. **(VM 14.6a; VM 14.6b)**

Numbered CD icons throughout the chapter refer to the virtual manipulatives in this list.

The amount and type of data available to us are rapidly expanding. To obtain maximum benefit from this information explosion, it is absolutely essential that we develop efficient and effective means of organizing, analyzing, and interpreting this information. Clearly, data handling and analysis have extensive applications in the physical and biological sciences, the social sciences, and business. Computer manufacturers, for example, use statistics to assess and project the buying habits of the population: How many computers should be produced this year to meet public demand? Which portion of the population will purchase laptop computers? Which portion of the businesses in the United States will use computers for inventory control? Which portion of the computer business can each manufacturer expect to capture this year? These and similar questions in other industries are being asked every day.

Statistics helps people find answers to questions by making available intelligent methods for organizing and handling limited amounts of data in order to make predictions. **Statistics** is the analysis of numerical and qualitative data to determine the relationships that exist among the data (such as central tendencies, dispersion, or scatter). The National Council of Teachers of Mathematics (NCTM) *Principles and Standards for School Mathematics* recognizes and emphasizes the roles played by data analysis in the mathematical literacy of children (and adults).

Instructional programs from pre-kindergarten through grade 12 should enable all students to—

- Formulate questions that can be addressed with data and collect, organize, and display relevant data to answer them.

- Select and use appropriate statistical methods to analyze data.

- Develop and evaluate inferences and predictions that are based on data.

- Understand and apply basic concepts of probability.

According to NCTM, "A thorough grounding in statistics and probability provides tools and ways of thinking that will be useful throughout students' lives. Because some things children learn in school seem to be predetermined and rule bound, it is critical that they also learn that some problems involve solutions that depend on assumptions and have some degree of uncertainty" (NCTM, 2000, p. 71). Students—in fact, *all of us*—stand to benefit from the ability to deal intelligently and rationally with assumption, variation, and uncertainty.

A Child's View of Statistics

Young children will benefit from an introduction to basic concepts of data handling and analysis. Teaching problem solving, beginning in kindergarten, helps create a foundation on which basic statistical concepts can be developed. An exposure to methods of gathering and organizing data should be a part of each child's mathematical experience. In most cases, work with statistics can be tied quite naturally to activities in science, social studies, sports, and so on, to give insight into the relevance of mathematics and real-world applications in many different areas.

Let's think about the number of children assigned to a typical classroom. This number, of course, will vary from one classroom to another and from one part of the country to another. Suppose, just for the sake of argument, that we were able to list every one of the classrooms across the nation as well as the numbers of students assigned to each of these classrooms. We would then have a complete collection of information. Data are collections of numerical facts. (Data is the plural form; datum is singular.)

The total population for the data we are considering in this example would be enormous. In view of the size of the entire population, we would do better to work with only a subset or sample of the population. In selecting a sample to work with, we must be careful to ensure that the sample will have characteristics similar to those of the total population. Careful selection of this sample is important in any situation in which statistics is being used to illustrate a point, support an argument, or make a prediction. The sampling technique will vary with the type of study being conducted and the questions to be answered, but in order to draw valid conclusions, it is essential that it yield a representative sample of the population from which it is drawn.

Let's return to our example of classroom size as described by the number of students in a classroom. Once we have collected the data we need about the numbers of students in the sample classrooms, we must have some way to put that data in a useful form. In other words, we must organize the data. One way to organize data is to arrange them in a tabular form. For example, suppose we have obtained data on the 21 classrooms in Cortland School. In this school there are 3 classrooms for each grade level, K through 6. The data collected are listed in the table by grade, teacher, and number of students.

K	Mrs. Forde	27
K	Ms. Usnicki	26
K	Mrs. Dixxon	29
1	Ms. Fenway	34

1	Mr. Shih	33
1	Mrs. Mose	32
2	Miss Friedlund	30
2	Mr. Brayer	29
2	Mrs. Toady	31
3	Ms. LoTadams	29
3	Ms. Maxbetter	32
3	Ms. Close	31
4	Ms. Nocigar	36
4	Mrs. Calvin	34
4	Mrs. Short	35
5	Ms. Thin	32
5	Mr. Wide	31
5	Mr. Gallie	33
6	Mrs. Wrigley	28
6	Mr. Hynes	29
6	Ms. Hobbes	27

Our interest is focused on the number of children in each classroom. Thus, the data in the table might be further organized as follows:

Children per Classroom	Tally	Number of Classrooms
36	I	1
35	I	1
34	II	2
33	II	2
32	III	3
31	III	3
30	I	1
29	IIII	4
28	I	1
27	II	2
26	I	1

This table gives the specific number of children in various classrooms and tells how many classrooms contain that number of children. The number of classrooms containing a given number of students might be referred to as a frequency. A **frequency** tells us how many times a particular datum occurs.

Measures of Central Tendency in Data

Depending on the purpose for collecting data, we may be interested in the scattering (or dispersion) of the data, or in its central tendencies. One measure of dispersion is the *range*. The range of the data from the table in the preceding section is from a low of 26 students per classroom to a high of 36 students per classroom. The **range** is usually thought of as simply the difference between the least and the greatest measure. In our example, the range would be 10. At times, the range can be a useful measure, particularly when the lowest and highest scores are revealed—not just the difference between them. However, no matter which interpretation of range is used, the range will tell us nothing about the positions of inner data points. Unusually high or low bits of datum, called *outliers*, may render this statistical descriptor practically useless.

The most common measure of central tendency is the *mean*. The mean for the classroom size situation we are considering would be the number of students per classroom if the school population were evenly distributed, with the same number of students in each classroom. The **mean** is also referred to as the arithmetic mean or, sometimes, simply as the *average*. (Although any measure of central tendency can legitimately be called an average, we will restrict the use of that term here to be equivalent to the mean.) What is the average number of students per classroom at Cortland School? We can calculate the mean by adding the measures and dividing by the number of measures.

$$\frac{\text{Sum of measures}}{\text{Number of measures}} = \text{Mean or average}$$

In our example, the mean is the sum: $27 + 26 + 29 + 34 + 33 + 32 + 30 + 29 + 31 + 29 + 32 + 31 + 36 + 34 + 35 + 32 + 31 + 33 + 28 + 29 + 27$, divided by 21 (the number of classrooms). When we add these measures, we get a sum of 648. Dividing this by the total number of classes, we get an average of nearly 31 students per class.

$$\text{Therefore, the average} = \frac{648}{21}$$
or about 31 children per classroom.

The mean can also be thought of as the numerical balancing point for a set of data. That is, if the students could be easily transferred from one class to another, without regard for grade level, then all classes would be balanced at about 31 students per classroom. Note that the actual computed average for this set of data is 30.857142 . . ., or 30 students with 18 students left over.

Certainly, in this particular case, an approximate average is quite usable. Note that for these data, the actual computed average is not the same as any of the individual class enrollments. Sometimes, the average of a collection of data will be found within that data (e.g., the average of 4, 5, 8, and 15 is exactly 8), but sometimes, as in the preceding classroom enrollment example, the average will not actually be one of the data points. One thing is certain, however: The average must always fall within the extremes of the data.

The mean is often, but not always, a good measure for describing the central tendency of a collection of data. It is most reliable when the range of the data is not too great. If the range is great, the mean may be misleading. For example, if one of the classrooms in Cortland School had contained 100 children, the mean would have been almost 34 children per classroom, when actually the figure of 31 is a better description than 34 of the actual situation in the school. To overcome the difficulties that arise from atypically or unusually large or small extreme measures, we often use a different measure of central

tendency known as the *median*. When the data are listed in order of size, the **median** is the middle measure. To find the median class size for Cortland School, we can again use the frequency table.

Since the number 11 is halfway between 1 and 21, we can count down from the top (or up from the bottom) to find the middle measure. We find that the eleventh measure, or median, for this set of data is 31. If we consider our earlier hypothetical situation in which one classroom had 100 children instead of 35, the median would still be equal to 31. Note that this one extreme measure may have a great effect on the mean or average, but little or no effect on the median. But knowing how to find the median is not valuable unless you also know when to use it.

This points out that the best measure of central tendency to use in a given situation depends on the distribution of the measures. If the measures are rather close together, with no notable extreme cases, then the mean is likely to be an appropriate measure of central tendency. If there are one or two scores that are extremely high or

RESEARCH SNAPSHOT

What does research say about children's development of notions of average?

Using more than 90 student interviews, Watson and Mortiz (2000) showed that students' conceptions of average followed a developmental path that begins with "stories," then proceeds to "mosts and middles," and finally ends with the mean as "representative" of a data set. They conducted follow-up interviews with these students three to four years later and found that the students had maintained their level of thinking about average.

Mokros and Russell (1995) interviewed 21 students from grades 4, 6, and 8 to examine their notions of average. Five predominant approaches to solving the open-ended problems were found. Two of the approaches taken by the students did not recognize the notion of values being representative (average as the mode, average as an algorithmic procedure), while the other three approaches embodied an idea of representativeness (average as what is reasonable, average as midpoint, average as a mathematical point of balance).

The youngest students in the study who viewed the average as the mode did not treat the data set as an entity, but as a list of values of numbers. Their idea of representativeness was limited to the mode, or the value with the most data.

To help develop children's knowledge of representativeness, the authors encourage giving students opportunities to describe and compare data sets, to compare different concepts of the "middle," and to introduce other measures of central tendency, such as the median, that connect with emerging concepts.

Which specific data sets from the students' real-life experiences might you suggest as being appropriate to the developmental and experiential level of children within the elementary grade levels of preK to 2, 3 to 5, and 6 to 8?

Mokros, J., & Russell, S.J. (1995). Children's concepts of average and representativeness. *Journal for Research in Mathematics Education, 26*, 20–39.   Watson, J. M. & Moritz, J. B. (2000). The longitudinal development of understanding of average. *Mathematical Thinking and Learning, 2*, 11–50.

For additional research briefs, "ERIC Digests" lets you search more than 2000 short syntheses of research on a range of education topics. The syntheses were produced by the Educational Resources Information Center (ERIC). Check http://www.ericfacility.net/ericdigests/index/.

extremely low, the more appropriate measure of central tendency to use is likely to be the median.

A third measure of central tendency is the **mode**, the measure that occurs most often in a set of data—that is, with the greatest frequency. The mode at Cortland School is 29 students per classroom because more classrooms have that number of students than any other number of students. If a sample has two measures that occur with the same frequency (and more than all the others), then the distribution is said to be *bimodal*. A set of data could have many modes.

Organizing and Interpreting Data

One approach to introducing children to the measures that we apply to data is to begin with concrete graphs. These are graphs made by using real objects to represent, say, preferences or choices that children might make. Children might be asked to choose their favorite fruit drink and to show each choice by stacking the cup that each child used behind labels for each flavor, thereby forming an actual graph. Alternatively, you might use photographs or children's drawings of their pets arranged into a graph by putting the pictures side by side next to a label indicating the pet type.

Teachers often take individual pictures of the students in their classrooms and then use these pictures throughout the year to form "snapshot bar graphs" of month of birth; height; or other identifiable and distinguishing characteristics such as favorite pets, number of siblings, or amount of television watched each week. Other materials that might be used to form a concrete graph include strings of paper clips made to specified lengths as well as buttons or inexpensive plastic disks glued to posterboard to match given criteria. Students can also use stacking cubes to form the bars of a bar graph or stretch a length of rope or yarn across the front of the room from which cards (or student pictures) representing data points may be hung.

A graph is one of the most convenient devices for organizing and presenting data. Well-constructed graphs make it possible to present a great deal of information, literally at a glance. Graphs give a view of the shape of the data that is difficult, if not impossible, to get in other ways. One great advantage in using a graph to analyze data is the visual impact that many graphs have. This quick conveyance of information is a prime reason newspapers and other popular media make heavy use of graphs—they present a lot of information in a small space.

VM 14.1

Let's look at a graph showing the enrollments for the 21 classrooms at Cortland School. The kind of graph shown in the following illustration is called a **bar graph**.

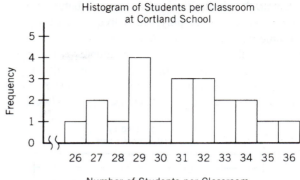

Histogram of Students per Classroom at Cortland School

Number of Students per Classroom

Graphs are essentially pictures designed to illustrate relationships among data so that the reader can easily interpret the data shown. A graph must have a title and be labeled in such a way as to indicate clearly to the reader what the graph is attempting to describe. The bar graph is only one of several different types of graphs. The type of graph one should select depends on the data collected and how that data can best be presented to the reader.

Another common method for representing data is to group data in intervals and plot the frequencies of the data in each interval. A bar graph representing a grouped frequency distribution is called a *histogram*. The bars showing the frequencies for each interval are centered over the midpoint of the interval. In a **histogram**, the individual data points "disappear" into the intervals. Since intervals are used, only approximate data can be retrieved.

A histogram is a special type of bar graph, usually with no space or gaps between the bars. A bar graph does not have to use data clumped into intervals as a histogram does. A bar graph can consist of parallel bars in which the *length of each bar* is proportional to certain quantities given in a set of data. In a histogram, the *area of each interval bar* is proportional to the number of observations that that interval contains.

Let's look at another type of graph, a **frequency polygon**. The following frequency polygon was made by connecting the midpoints of the tops of the bars in the bar graph of the students per classroom at Cortland School.

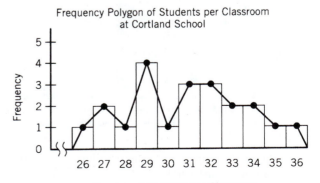

Frequency Polygon of Students per Classroom at Cortland School

Number of Students per Classroom

Note the similarities and differences between a bar graph and frequency polygon. A frequency polygon is commonly referred to as a *line graph*.

Let's take a closer look at bar graphs. A bar graph may be oriented either horizontally or vertically. Using the following bar graph, we can compare the amount of money collected by each grade in Cortland School.

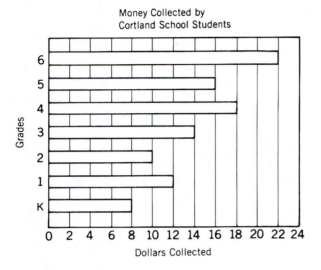

At a glance, you can tell which class collected the most money, which class collected the least, and which classes, if any, collected the same amount.

Sometimes several bar graphs are combined to make either a side-by-side multiple bar graph or a stacked bar graph. A side-by-side bar graph is commonly used to compare two different groups of data on the same characteristics. For example, the graph that follows illustrates residence hall versus off-campus housing preferences for college freshmen, sophomores, juniors, and seniors.

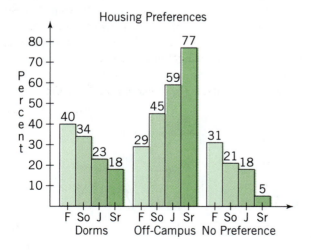

A stacked bar graph is often used to show how two or more parts make up a whole bar. As an example, consider a graph that shows gender preferences for different

colors. Note that the individual bars are composed of two distinct sections. To interpret these graphs, you must realize that one section is literally stacked on the other, as opposed to both portions of a stack beginning at zero.

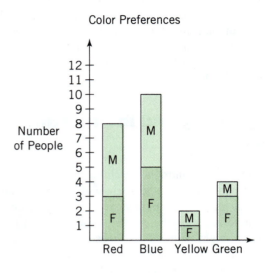

Bar graphs are suited to *discrete* data—that is, data that are noncontinuous, distinct, countable, and separate from other information, such as the number of pets in a household, the different colors of cars in a parking lot, or the number of people who like particular types of music.

We can make a line graph by taking the bars off a bar graph and connecting the center point of the top of each bar. This method might be used to change the money bar graph previously shown into a line graph. However, a line graph is more suited to continuous data such as temperature change or a person's height over a period of time—that is, data that do not change by jumps but by a constant, fluid process. A line graph can, for example, show fluctuation, such as the change in temperature illustrated in the following graph:

One of the major difficulties in constructing a line graph is the selection of a proper scale for one or both of the axes. The scale, of course, must be able to accommodate the collected data. To do this, the scale must provide for the variance between greatest and least values to be graphed, and it must reflect the degree of accuracy required. Let's examine the growth of a seedling. Each morning at 9:00 A.M., a person measures the height of a bean plant. The data are then placed on a graph as shown.

Growth of a Bean Plant

The horizontal and vertical axes serve as the reference points for the graph. The horizontal axis is the reference line for the days of the week. The vertical axis is the reference line for the height of the plant. Note that the scale is marked in centimeters and that the height is approximated for each day.

Consider the exact same information plotted on exactly the same graph, with one very notable exception—the vertical axis in the graph now has a scale of decimeters instead of centimeters (1 decimeter = 10 centimeters).

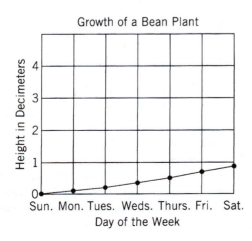

Growth of a Bean Plant

Notice that if you quickly glanced at this graph, you might come to a very different conclusion about the growth rate of the seedling than you might have from the first graph. Data, and the graphs resulting from the data, must be carefully handled and interpreted. Too often data can be manipulated in correct but misleading ways to show whatever point the designer of the graph wants to emphasize. This is an indication of a *biased representation of data*.

As mentioned earlier, young children often create graphs using real objects, such as drink cups stacked on a table or a chalkboard tray to show the children's preferences in juice flavor. In this activity, each cup represents one vote for a particular flavor. If we drew a picture of such a physical graph and let each cup represent several children's choices, then we'd have a natural extension to graphing as it develops in the upper elementary grades.

When an actual concrete graph using real objects is drawn representatively, it is commonly referred to as *a pictograph*. A **pictograph** is a graph in which pictures represent values or quantities; for instance, a picture of a car may represent a certain number of cars sold. Numbers are commonly rounded off for convenience. For example, in the pictograph, the symbol 🚗 represents 100 cars; thus, 🚗 car represents 50 cars.

This pictograph has a title, a scale, and pictures representing the number of cars sold.

Cars Sold by Shih Agency, 2005–2008

🚗 = 100 cars

Year

2008 🚗 🚗 🚗 🚗 🚗 🚗

2007 🚗 🚗 🚗 🚗 🚗 🚗 🚗

2006 🚗 🚗 🚗 🚗 🚗 🚗

2005 🚗 🚗 🚗 🚗 🚗 🚗 🚗 🚗

The first line of the pictograph represents the Shih Agency car sales for 2008. There are $5\frac{1}{4}$ units shown on the line, each unit representing 100 cars. Multiplying

$5\frac{1}{4}$ times the scale of 100 indicates that the Shih Agency sold approximately 525 cars during 2008. The second line of the graph indicates that $6\frac{1}{2}$ 100-car units were sold during 2007. Multiply $6\frac{1}{2}$ by 100; this indicates that the Shih Agency sold approximately 650 cars in 2007. Using the same procedure to interpret the number of cars sold during 2006 and 2005, we find that approximately 600 cars were sold in 2006 and approximately 800 in 2005.

 VM 14.3   A **circle graph** can be used similarly, with sectors of a circle representing percentages of the data being studied. To construct such a graph, students need to have some understanding of both angular measurement and percentage. The following circle graph shows the data in the table concerning John's earnings in a week:

Money Earned by John in a Week			
	Money Earned	Percent of Earnings	Measure of Sector
Lawn mowing	$12.00	40%	40% of 300° = 144°
Weeding garden	7.00	23%	23% of 300° = 83°
Selling vegetables	9.50	32%	32% of 300° = 115°
Collecting trash	1.50	5%	5% of 300° = 16°
Total earned	$30.00		

 VM 14.4   A circle graph is typically easy to read because one can see at a glance the relative value of each item shown. However, like some other types of graphs, circle graphs can be constructed in a manner that misleads the viewer. If the circle graph is "tilted" on its side, the perspective of the various sectors can distort the actual proportion. Consider the following two identical representations of a circle divided into four equal regions.

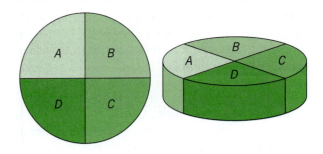

In the first view, this relationship is obvious. In the second view, it appears that sections B and D are larger than sections A and C.

Stem-and-leaf plots are an efficient and relatively easy way of displaying and comparing raw data. These are commonly used when the data can be represented by numbers over a range of tens and ones (or hundreds and tens, thousands and hundreds, etc.). Individual measures are preserved in the display of a stem-and-leaf plot, but the manner in which the data are recorded shows the shape of the entire set. Consider the following data representing the distances achieved (in meters) in a softball throwing contest:

73, 30, 57, 45, 33, 33, 38,
74, 62, 30, 35, 62, 56, 46

As listed, it is difficult to make any quick statements about the data and any measures of central tendency. If these raw data are organized into a stem-and-leaf plot, then certain aspects become more visible. In the following figure, the stem is the digit in the tens place of each number, and the leaves are the digits in the ones place. For example, the second row of the figure represents two scores, 45 and 46, while the fourth row represents two scores that are the same, 62. The first row represents six scores. What are they? What is the lowest score?

Softball Throwing Contest Results
(in meters)

Stem		Leaf				
3		0	0	3	3	5	8
4		5	6			
5		6	7			
6		2	2			
7		3	4			

It's relatively easy to see the individual data points in such an arrangement, but you also can quickly see the range (30 to 74) and any modes (30, 33, and 62). You can quickly count to get the median (45.5, halfway between 45 and 46), and you can get an approximate sense of the mean (a little less than 50).

Side-by-side stem-and-leaf plots are an excellent way of comparing two distinct sets of raw data. Such arrangements often appear as shown in the following double stem-and-leaf plot. What conclusions can you draw about the data?

Test Score Comparisons

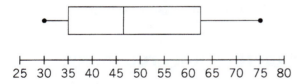

Fourth Grade					Third Grade			
	6 7 8	|5|	2 4				
	4 6	|6|	1 7 8				
	4	|7|	5 5 5 7 8			
	5 7	|8|	0 0 2 2 8			
2 3 3 5 8		|9|	3 4				

(NOTE: In a side-by-side stem-and-leaf plot, the center column is the leading digit. Consequently, the first row for fourth grade has scores of 56, 57, and 58, while the first row for third grade is 52 and 54.)

VM 14.1 **Box-and-whisker** plots are another visual means of displaying the range, quartiles, median, and distribution of a data set. Such graphs are usually reserved for upper grades due to their more complex construction as compared to stem-and-leaf plots. Nevertheless, we can benefit from examining data in this manner. The data from the preceding softball-throwing example have been arranged into a box-and-whisker plot here:

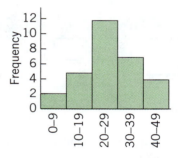

Close examination of the graph shows the data split into four distinct sections, called *quartiles*. When the data are arranged in numerical order, **quartile** is the name given to each successive one-fourth of the data. The "box" in the graph represents the two middle quartiles (the middle 50% of the scores), and the "whiskers" show the lower and upper quartiles (the lowest 25% of the scores and the highest 25% of the scores, respectively). The box and whiskers give you a quick picture of the shape of the data. For example, at a glance you can see that the scores of the entire data set lie between approximately 30 and 75. You can also see that 25% of the scores are between 30 and 35 and that the middle 50% of the group have scores falling between 35 and approximately 62. The vertical line in the box represents the median, about 46. Which other pieces of information can you glean from a box-and-whisker plot?

Box-and-whisker plots are a visual means of displaying the range, quartiles, median, and distribution *(dispersion)* of a data set. Such graphs can be used to

lead students into a discussion of percentiles, normal distributions (normal curves), and standard deviation. A **normal distribution (normal curve)** is a symmetrical distribution with the mean, median, and mode all being equal.

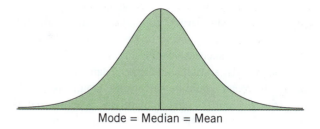

Mode = Median = Mean

The concept is often used when a sample set of data is compared with an entire population. For example, the scores on a mathematics quiz for students in a particular fourth grade might be collected and graphed on a frequency bar graph.

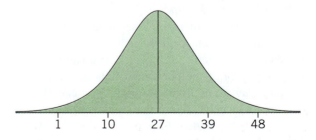

You'll note some interesting aspects of this small sample. The graph shows that a score between 20 and 29 was achieved by 12 students while a total of 7 students scored below 20. The overall distribution of scores indicates that some students did well, some did poorly, but most were somewhere in the middle. This sort of dispersion would be similar to one expected from data for the larger population. If our sample is representative and if we were to collect data on test performance from the general population of all fourth graders, then we would get a graph that looked something like the following normal curve:

Close examination of a normal curve shows that the data may be split into distinct sections. These sections are defined by the *standard deviation* for the data. **Standard deviation** measures the dispersion of data from the mean and can be used to discuss the performance of an individual with respect to the mean for the population. The boundaries of each section are defined as a number of standard deviations above or below the mean. Each section contains a certain percentage of the larger population that would fall within that particular section. **Percentile** is the name given to each successive one-hundredth of the data. In other words, a student scoring 1 standard deviation below the mean would be performing at approximately the 16th *percentile*—that student has a score that is better than approximately 16% of the population.

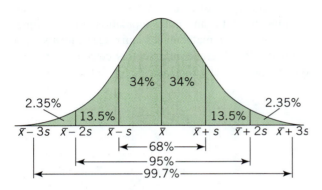

The sections that are 1 standard deviation above or below the mean (+/−1) each contain 34% or the normal population. The sections in the graph that are +/−1 standard deviation from the mean represent the middle 68% (34 + 34) of the scores.

The sections that are more than +/−1 standard deviation from the mean include the lower and upper scores representing a total of approximately 32% of the scores (the lowest 15.85% of the scores and the highest 15.85% of the scores, respectively).

The sections that are more than +/−2 standard deviations from the mean include the lower and upper scores representing a total of approximately 5% of the scores (the lowest 2.35% of the scores and the highest 2.35% of the scores, respectively).

The comparison of a sample set of data to the normal curve can give you a quick picture of the shape of the data. For example, at a glance, you can see that a total of 99.7% of the population falls between +/−3 standard deviations from the mean. You can also see that approximately 15% of the scores are at or below 19 and that the middle 68% of the group has scores falling between 20 and approximately 39. The vertical line in the graph represents the mean, about 27. What other pieces of information can you glean from a normal curve comparison to a sample?

Taking a "Chance"

The concept of probability is part of our everyday lives: "I will probably get a B on the test." "The odds are even for the UCLA–USC game this year." "The Cubs have a chance to win the pennant." "I'll bet two to one that it rains tomorrow."

As we've discussed so far, graphs are valuable in providing visual models of data. Graphs can also be used for making conjectures about likelihood. For example, a graph representing temperatures throughout the year for a given location can be used to predict temperatures for next year's vacation. In this sense, graphs may be used as an introduction to informal probability notions.

A contemporary mathematics program should provide an opportunity for children to learn more about probability and to use it in effective and meaningful ways to assist in the decision-making processes they so often face. Probability is a familiar part of the business world, and when presented properly, children will recognize it as an important part of their future lives.

The mathematics of probability can be complex—but need not be. The material in this chapter is intended as a foundational introduction for teachers, but elementary students should be led to discover intuitively many of the basic and fundamental aspects of probability. The topic is much too important to be considered as "just enrichment material" at any grade level.

Experimental Probability

Today, mathematics programs at all grade levels should include an examination of probability. To be successful, such an introduction should be accompanied by experimentation with physical objects. By examining the results of their experiments and comparing these results with theoretical data, children can develop a greater understanding of probability—and often be quite surprised by variations from expectations due to chance.

We suggest that you use an experimental approach to probability and interpret the results in light of our discussion of theoretical data. We will use checkers in our discussion, but you can use any objects (coins, for example) that can be easily flipped and have a different pattern on each side so that you can easily distinguish which side falls facing up.

Consider a checker that has a star on one side and circles on the other.

If we flip the checker in the air and let it fall on a table, will the star side or the circle side be facing up? Clearly, these are the only two reasonable possibilities. (We assume throughout that the checker or coin does not land on its edge and that the object used is balanced fairly or "is honest.") Because only one of two possible results can be obtained by flipping a checker once, a star or a circle, we can express this by the ratio $\frac{1}{2}$. This ratio states that there is one chance out of two possibilities that the star will come up (or, equally likely, one chance out of two possibilities that the circle will come up). The ratio $\frac{1}{2}$ is an expression of the probability that a star (or a circle) will be obtained by flipping the checker once. (You might find it interesting to note that while the probability of getting a star is $\frac{1}{2}$, the odds of getting a star are $\frac{1}{1}$. This difference occurs because *odds* are typically defined as the ratio of the number of possible ways something will occur to the number of possible ways that it won't occur, while *probability* is defined as the ratio of the number of ways something can occur compared to all of the possible occurrences.)

In speaking of probabilities, obtaining a star is one "event," and obtaining a circle is another event. In one toss of the checker, only one of these two events can occur, and the two possible events are equally probable. On one toss, the probability of obtaining a star is $\frac{1}{2}$ (one chance out of two possibilities), and the probability of obtaining a circle is $\frac{1}{2}$ (one chance out of two possibilities).

Probability, then, is a numerical measure of the chance that a particular event will occur, compared with the total number of events that could possibly occur. The probability of a particular event occurring is the ratio of the number of ways that particular event can occur to the total number of possible events. We can express the ratio mathematically as follows:

$$\text{Probability of a particular event occurring} = \frac{\text{Number of ways the event can occur}}{\text{Total number of possible events}}$$

When a checker is flipped once, the total number of possible events is two. Since the probability of obtaining a star is $\frac{1}{2}$ and the probability of obtaining a circle is $\frac{1}{2}$, what conclusion can we make about the nature of probability from our experiment? The sum of the probabilities of all the possible events is always 1—in this case, $\frac{1}{2} + \frac{1}{2}$ or $\frac{2}{2}$, or 1. This agrees with our common sense: If we flip a checker, it has to result in one of the possible events (since we have barred the possibility of the checker's landing on its edge).

To illustrate another aspect of this situation, imagine that you have a checker with a star on both sides. What is the probability of obtaining a circle by flipping the checker?

$$\text{Probability of a particular event occurring} = \frac{\text{Number of ways the event can occur}}{\text{Total number of possible events}} = \frac{0}{2} = 0$$

In short, this event cannot happen. If the checker had a circle on both sides, however, then the probability of obtaining a circle by flipping the checker would be $\frac{2}{2}$ or 1, meaning that this event would happen without fail.

By performing experiments, we can test whether our theoretical data seem to hold true. However, all experimental data on probability are based on a "long run"—that is, a large number of trials. The greater the number of trials we make (the "longer the run"), the more likely it is that our experimental data will approximate our expected theoretical data. For example, the familiar expression "fifty-fifty chance" simply means that out of 100 trials (e.g., flipping a checker 100 times), the number of stars (or circles) we are likely to see will be close to 50. However, this is one of the most misunderstood points about experimental versus theoretical probability. It could happen (though it is highly unlikely) that we would get 99 stars consecutively.

If we were lucky enough to have gotten 99 stars in a row, what would be the probability of obtaining a star on the next toss? It would still be one-half. The probability of obtaining a star is one-half on each flip. If, instead, you asked what the probability would be of getting 99 stars in a row (before having made your first toss), then the answer is quite small indeed: 1 divided by 2 raised to the ninety-ninth power! But even if we did obtain 99 stars and 1 circle out of 100 tosses, it is likely that in a run of 1000 trials, we would still come close to 500 stars and 500 circles. Students are often fascinated with the comparison of experimental results to "expected" theoretical results.

Theoretical Probability

There are some other aspects about probability that we must be familiar with before we can properly interpret our data. We can obtain theoretical probability by computation. For example, we have said that the probability of obtaining a star by flipping a checker once is $\frac{1}{2}$ (or one out of two possibilities). Suppose we flip the checker twice in succession. What are the possible outcomes for this two-flip experiment? Four results are possible, as seen in the table.

FIRST TOSS	SECOND TOSS	POSSIBLE RESULTS
S	S	Star on first toss Star on second toss
C	S	Circle on first toss Star on second toss
S	C	Star on first toss Circle on second toss
C	C	Circle on first toss Circle on second toss

The table shows that for two flips, the probability of getting one star and one circle is greater than that of getting two stars or two circles. What are the chances that flipping one checker two times will turn up a star both times? One out of four chances, or $\frac{1}{4}$. What are the chances that the two tosses will turn up a circle both times? One out of four chances, or $\frac{1}{4}$. What are the chances that the two tosses will turn up one star and one circle? Two out of four chances, or $\frac{4}{2}$. However, suppose we designated order as a part of the event. Suppose we had one red checker and one black checker and then asked, "What is the probability of obtaining a star on the red checker and a circle on the black checker?"

Red Checker	Black Checker
Star	Star
Star	Circle
Circle	Star
Circle	Circle

Clearly, there is a probability of $\frac{1}{4}$, or one out of four chances, of obtaining this combination. Notice that when we use one red checker and one black checker, the event of one red star and one black circle is different from the event of one red circle and one black star.

Permutations and Combinations

You may have heard the terms *permutation* and *combination* in other discussions about probability. The preceding discussion represents an application of a permutation because the order in which events occur is important. If we remove order from consideration, then it can be said that there are only three different combinations, or outcomes, that are possible, namely,

two stars, two circles, or a star and a circle; but if order is important, then there are four different outcomes that are possible, namely, two stars, two circles, a star and a circle, or a circle and a star.

Consider this distinction in terms of dice. A single die has six sides, representing values from 1 through 6. What is the probability of obtaining a 3 if you roll a die once? One chance out of six, or $\frac{1}{6}$.

If you roll two dice, one red die and one blue die, what is the probability that you will roll a 5 on the red die and a 6 on the blue die?

We see from the diagram, often referred to as a *tree diagram*, that there are six possible outcomes for one roll of a single die. But when rolling two dice, we see that there are 36 possible outcomes.

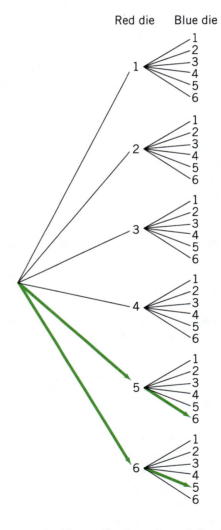

For example, if we roll a 1 on the red die, there are still six possibilities for the blue die. If we roll a 2 on the red die, there are still six possibilities for the blue die. In other words, for each possible outcome of the red die, there are six possibilities for the blue die. Because there are six possibilities for the red die, there are 6×6, or 36, possibilities for the two dice together. The dice are independent of each other, so the number that comes up on one die does not affect the number that will come up on the other die. Therefore, the probability of a 5 appearing on the red die is $\frac{1}{6}$, and the probability that a 6 will come up on the blue die is also $\frac{1}{6}$. The combined probability that the red die will have a 5 and the blue die a 6 is the product of the two probabilities, or $\frac{1}{6} \times \frac{1}{6} = \frac{1}{36}$. If order does not matter, the probability that on a roll of two dice one die will be 5 and the other die a 6 is $\frac{2}{36}$.

We can also examine the possibilities resulting from tossing a single checker twice. Note that tossing one checker two times in a row is the same as tossing two checkers at one time. In both situations the same combinations occur (as long as order does not matter).

1. One checker tossed twice gives the possible outcomes we have already examined.

FIRST TOSS	SECOND TOSS
★	★
○	★
★	○
○	○

2. Two checkers tossed at once can land in only the same four possible ways (when order matters).

First	★	★
Second	○	★
Third	★	○
Fourth	○	○

3. Now flip three checkers at once. What are the possible ways the checkers might land (when order matters)?

	First Checker	Second Checker	Third Checker
A	Circle	Circle	Circle
B	Circle	Circle	Star
C	Circle	Star	Circle
D	Circle	Star	Star
E	Star	Circle	Circle
F	Star	Circle	Star
G	Star	Star	Circle
H	Star	Star	Star

How many possible ways can the three checkers land? Eight. What are the chances that all three checkers will be circles (row A)? One out of eight chances, or $\frac{1}{8}$. What are the chances that two will be circles and one will be a star (rows B, C, and E)? Three out of eight chances, or $\frac{3}{8}$. What are the chances that two will be stars and one will be a circle (rows D, F, and G)? Three out of eight chances, or $\frac{3}{8}$. What are the chances that all three will be stars (row H)? One out of eight chances, or $\frac{1}{8}$. Taking 3 checkers at a time, there are four possible combinations, or ways they can be put together. Notice that again the sum of the probabilities is 1. (As we have noted, this will always be the case.)

$$\frac{1}{8} + \frac{3}{8} + \frac{3}{8} + \frac{1}{8} = \frac{8}{8}, \text{ or } 1$$

Now flip a single checker 10 times, and record the results. Then try 20 times, 50 times, 100 times. Record your results in a table. (One hundred trials can be considered a long run for this experiment.)

Number of Trials	Circle	Star
1		
2		
3		
⋮	⋮	⋮
100		

What are your experimental results? How many circles did you get? How many stars? Your long-run results should be very close to the theoretical probabilities we have already examined. It would be interesting if each student in the class would flip a checker 20 or 25 times. You could then combine the results obtained by all the students into one set of data. This would give a long run in the least amount of time.

VM 14.6a

Models for Exploring Probability

Probability has long fascinated mathematicians and others. Blaise Pascal, a seventeenth-century French mathematician, made use of a diagram of probability that was previously employed by others but is known today as *Pascal's Triangle*. To answer the questions of a friend who was a gambler, Pascal spent some time exploring the mathematics of gambling (which, of course, is based on probability). Pascal's Triangle is a means of representing the probability of the occurrence of a particular event.

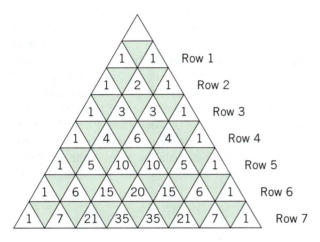

VM 14.5   In examining the patterns in the triangle, you will notice that a given number in any row can be determined by adding the numbers named in the two adjacent triangles in the row above the given number. For example, look at the numeral 6 in row 4. The two numbers named in the triangles adjacent to 6 in the preceding row are 3 and 3, and $3 + 3 = 6$. Since the triangle could be continued in the same manner, you should be able to use this pattern to name the numbers that would appear in the eighth row (1, 8, 28, 56, 70, 56, 28, 8, 1).

VM 14.5   Another interesting pattern can be found by shading certain elements in Pascal's Triangle. For example, shade those numbers in the triangle that are even to see an interesting visual pattern. Try shading the multiples of three. What happens when you expand the number of visible entries in the triangle and then shade the prime numbers? Let's review the information that we obtained from a long run of testing. When 2 checkers are flipped, the probability is that $\frac{1}{4}$ of the total events are circles, $\frac{2}{4}$ (or $\frac{1}{2}$) are a circle and a star, and $\frac{1}{4}$ are stars. These ratios are read, "one out of four," "two out of four," and so on. When 3 checkers are flipped, $\frac{1}{8}$ of the total events are circles, $\frac{3}{8}$ are two circles and one star, $\frac{3}{8}$ are one circle and two stars, and $\frac{1}{8}$ are stars.

In the following table, the center column names the numerator of the probability ratios, and the right-hand column names the denominator of the probability ratios. For example, when 4 checkers are tossed, the probability ratios of the five different ways the checker could fall are $\frac{1}{16}$, $\frac{4}{16}$, $\frac{6}{16}$, $\frac{4}{16}$, and $\frac{1}{16}$.

Number of Checkers Tossed	Combinations	Number of Combinations
1	1, 1	2
2	1, 2, 1	4
3	1, 3, 3, 1	8
4	1, 4, 6, 4, 1	16
5	1, 5, 10, 10, 5, 1	32
6	1, 6, 15, 20, 15, 6, 1	64
7	1, 7, 21, 35, 35, 21, 7, 1	128
8	1, 8, 28, 56, 70, 56, 28, 8, 1	256

Notice that our table is arranged in the form of Pascal's Triangle. Look at the table and consider the meaning of the rows. Assume that we are tossing a coin. Let's correlate the possible combinations (heads or tails) with the number patterns in the table.

■ Row 1: 1 coin, 1 toss
    2 possible combinations

    $(1 + 1 = 2)$

H	T

Heads: $\frac{1}{2}$ or 1 out of 2 chances
Tails: $\frac{1}{2}$ or 1 out of 2 chances

■ Row 2: 1 coin, 2 tosses
    4 possible combinations

    $(1 + 2 + 1 = 4)$

H H	T H
H T	T T

2 heads: $\frac{1}{4}$ or 1 out of 4 chances
1 head and 1 tail: $\frac{2}{4}$ or 2 out of 4 chances
2 tails: $\frac{1}{4}$ or 1 out of 4 chances

■ Row 3: 1 coin, 3 tosses
    8 possible combinations

    $(1 + 3 + 3 + 1 = 8)$

H H H	T T T
H H T	T T H
H T H	T H H
H T T	T H T

Each row can be examined in much the same way to determine all the possible combinations, and new rows could be added to the table indefinitely.

This data can also be explored using *geometric probability*. That is, geometric probability arguments organize the data set in such a way that visual geometric interpretations help us make sense of the likelihood of an event. For example, consider a random drive from south to north in a valley that has three villages you might wish to visit: Kurlee, Moe, and La-ree.

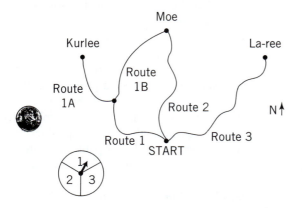

There are roads leading into the valley, and you decide to choose which one to take by flipping a coin (when you have two choices) and spinning a fair spinner (when you have three choices). What is the probability that you'll end up at the village of Moe?

At the start of your trip, you have three possible directions in which you could go, two of which could lead you to the village of Moe; therefore, you have a $\frac{2}{3}$ probability of heading in that direction on your random drive. (The chance of picking the direct route is $\frac{1}{3}$ and the chance of picking the other possible route to Moe is also $\frac{1}{3}$.) If we let the entire shape shown here represent the probability of reaching any village, then the probability of reaching Moe directly at this point can be shown by shading a total of one-third of the shape.

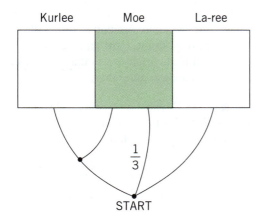

If the spin of the spinner does not result in the direct route, but instead sends you to the fork in the road, then you have only two options available, one of which leads you to Moe. So, at this point, you have a probability of $\frac{1}{2}$ that you'll choose the road that takes you to Moe. This can be shown by shading one-half of the one-third representing that route.

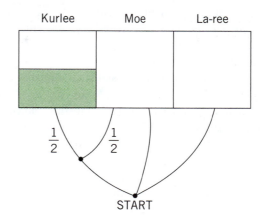

What is the overall probability before you begin your drive of choosing roads that allow you to reach Moe? The answer to this question can be found by combining the two shaded pieces that represent reaching Moe and interpreting the geometric representation of these probabilities as $\frac{1}{3} + (\frac{1}{2}$ of $\frac{1}{3})$. That is, $\frac{1}{3} + \frac{1}{6}$ or $\frac{3}{6}$.

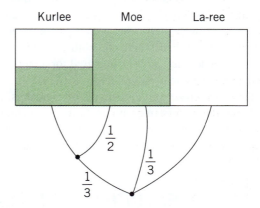

The diagram shows that the probability of reaching Moe on a random drive from south to north is $\frac{1}{2}$, since one-half of the entire region has been shaded. Use a similar argument to determine the probability of ending up at the village of Kurlee.

Closure

Many college students preparing to teach elementary or middle school children may recall little or no introduction to either statistics or probability in their own elementary mathematics development—possibly because the topics of statistics and probability are sometimes placed as the last chapter in a child's mathematics textbook, and many classes never get to them. Because of the lack of content knowledge coupled with little opportunity to develop competency with statistics and probability, you may have found this short introduction chapter to, perhaps, be a bit of a challenge. However, you should have also found the introduction of these concepts to be intriguing and motivating—particularly with many experiences explored on the concrete level and systematically moving through the semiconcrete, semiabstract, and abstract levels of development.

The underlying concepts of statistics are likely more familiar than those of probability. Many of us are ill prepared to function successfully with statistics, and yet the basic concepts are not difficult to comprehend or calculate. Approaching statistics with real data, studying the data, and then arriving at generalizations seem to offer less frustration than using a rule-based approach. Often we can go well into the study of statistics by just asking interesting questions and seeking answers. Probability, although commonly used, is less well recognized as a topic of study in the elementary school and may be approached in a less biased manner than statistics.

An experimental approach to both statistics and probability is perhaps the most beneficial for elementary or middle school children. Situations that can be reenacted in the classroom provide motivation and enjoyment. Children should be encouraged to design and perform their own experiments and keep careful records of data. Many statistics and probability activities can be placed on activity cards or prepared for a laboratory approach to mathematics.

Many elementary/middle school mathematics programs begin the study of graphing by teaching children how to read graphs. We suggest that children will develop a better understanding of graphs and graphing if they are actively involved in constructing the graphs they are asked to read and interpret. These early experiences, as well as later ones, should involve concrete graphing before the formal graphs in this chapter are discussed. That is, children should have many opportunities to use real objects set out in rows or columns. For example, the children in one class might be asked to stand behind birth-month signs while the children of another class use this human graph to make statements about the data.

This chapter may be readily coordinated with science or social studies topics, as well as topics from other school disciplines. The uses for statistics and probability are becoming more familiar to children through television and newspapers. Space travel has posed new problems in probability. What are the chances that a shuttle will achieve a given orbit? What are the chances that the weather will be suitable for liftoff? Industry has used statistics and probability to determine the chances that certain products are defective; the Department of Labor publishes statistics on employment. Many other sources of data are available for interesting class activities.

Both statistics and probability are intertwined with the data analysis that we must undertake if we are to rationally interpret events that occur in our daily lives. In fact, "daily" may be too weak of a descriptor for the frequency with which we encounter these topics. A glance at nearly any section of the newspaper will readily reveal our need to understand data and weigh the evidence. The exploration of topics described in this chapter are not diversions from the mathematics curriculum; they are, in fact, essential to the development of a mathematically literate society that creates thoughtful arguments and makes reasoned decisions.

PRACTICE EXERCISES FOR TEACHERS

These exercises are designed for the reader of this book, not for the children the reader may teach. Although some of these examples are suitable for use in an elementary or middle school classroom, they should not necessarily be given to children in the form presented here. Ideas appropriate for classroom activities on the concepts and ideas discussed in this chapter can be found in a later section of this chapter and on the CD that accompanies this text.

1. If you flip 4 pennies at one time, what is the probability that all 4 coins will show heads? If you flip 5 pennies, what is the probability that all 5 pennies will show heads? If you flip 6 pennies, what is the probability that all 6 pennies will show heads?

VM 14.5

2. Which different combinations are possible for 10 pennies flipped at one time? Indicate the ratio for each combination. (HINT: Use Pascal's Triangle.) Additional practice on similar items is available using the VM—*Combinations and Pascal's Triangle.*

3. Take three slips of paper. On one, write the numeral 1; on the second, the numeral 2; and on the third, the numeral 3. Place all three slips of paper in a hat or box.

   a) What is the probability that you will draw the 1 on the first draw?

   b) On the second draw, what is the probability that you will draw the 2 if you drew the 3 on the first draw and did not replace it?

   c) What is the probability that you will draw the 3 on the first draw, the 2 on the second draw, and the 1 on the third draw?

   d) What is the probability that you will draw an odd number on the first draw?

   e) What is the probability that you will draw an even number on the first draw?

4. If you toss a single die,

   a) what is the probability that you will roll a 6? a 4? a 3?

   b) What is the probability that either a 1 or a 6 will be rolled?

   c) What is the probability that a 2, 4, or 6 will be rolled?

   d) What is the probability that a 1, 2, 3, or 4 will be rolled?

   e) What is the probability that a 1, 2, 3, 4, or 5 will be rolled?

5. If you place 5 red marbles, 2 blue marbles, and 1 white marble in a bag, what is the probability that on the first draw, you will draw a red marble? a blue marble? a white marble?

VM 14.2

6. Suppose you toss 4 pennies 32 times. Each time you record the number of heads and obtain the following frequency table (or you could also use the virtual manipulative on the CD to solve this problem).

Number of Heads	Tally	Frequency
0	||	2
1	ЖТ ||	7
2	ЖТ ЖТ |||	13
3	ЖТ |	6
4	||||	4

   a) What is the mean for this collection of data?

   b) What is the median? The mode? The range?

   c) Make a frequency polygon for this collection of data.

   Additional practice on similar items is available using the VM—*Histogram and Box Plot.*

7. Your piggy bank contains 7 quarters, 10 dimes, and 5 nickels. You turn the piggy bank upside down to shake out a coin. (Assume that the size and weight of the coins do not affect this experiment.)

   a) What is the probability of getting a quarter?

   b) What is the probability of getting a dime?

   c) What is the probability of getting a nickel?

8. A regular dodecahedron (a three dimensional figure with 12 faces) has a calendar printed on it such that one month is printed on each face. If you roll the dodecahedron, what are the chances of rolling each of the following?

   a) the month of January

   b) a winter month

   c) a month between January and August

9. Use a deck of 52 regular playing cards without the jokers. What are the chances that if you draw one card, it will be one of the following?

   a) the ace of spades   b) a jack   c) a diamond

   d) a face card   e) between 3 and 9

10. A drawer contains 12 navy blue socks and 12 black socks. You wish to get either a pair of navy blue socks or a pair of black socks. If you are reaching into the drawer without looking, how many socks must you remove to be sure you have one matched pair?

VM 14.3

11. Draw a circle graph or use the *Circle Graph* virtual manipulative based on the following results of rolling a die 100 times; show proportionately how many times each number was rolled.

Number Rolled	Number of Times Number Was Rolled
1	14
2	5
3	15
4	32
5	24
6	10

12. Construct a pictogram using the following data concerning the number of years 5 retired players of the Kansas City Chiefs played in the National Football League.

Player	Years
Jim Lynch, linebacker	8
Mo Moorman, guard	7
Ed Podolak, running back	6
Willie Lanier, linebacker	8
Elmo Wright, wide receiver	4

TEACHING COMPETENCIES AND SELF-ASSESSMENT TASKS

The following questions and statements are designed to reflect the teaching competencies that appeared at the beginning of this chapter and, in some cases, to expose you to deeper aspects of the concepts presented. Take a moment to consider your response to each of these in light of what you've read and learned.

1. Create a data set in which the mean, median, mode, and range are all identical. Adjust the data set so that the mean, median, mode, and range are all different. Create a new data set in which the range is 20, the mean is 15, the median is 18, and the modes are 21 and 16.

2. Discuss the nature of data most appropriate for display in each type of graph discussed in this chapter.

3. Design a single data set representing a real-life situation that can be convincingly displayed on either a bar graph, line graph, or circle graph. Which issues and questions are raised as you create this data set?

4. Identify a real-life data set that is suitable for a stem-and-leaf plot and create such a display. Indicate the mode and range. Identify a real-life data set that is suitable for a box-and-whisker plot and create such a display. Indicate the median, range, and the upper and lower quartiles.

5. Conduct an experiment to determine how frequently a paper cup dropped from a height of 5 feet will land upside down. Express your result as a probability and test it over a larger sample. Make any appropriate revisions in your conclusion. Adjust the height of the drop and examine changes in the result.

6. Identify at least 10 situations in which we might encounter statistics and/or probability in our daily lives. In what ways are these situations alike? Different?

7. Objects are frequently used to represent amounts in pictographs. In this chapter, for example, pictures of cars were used to represent sales of 100 cars. Suppose a pictograph were drawn using pictures of cereal boxes to represent sales of 1000 boxes. If sales were to double, should the number of pictures of boxes be doubled? Should the size of the boxes (volume) be doubled? Should only the height or width be doubled? Do all of these variations accurately represent the real situation?

8. Research the literature to find uses of Pascal's Triangle, other than probability, in elementary mathematics. Discuss your findings with the class.

9. Discuss appropriate graphing experiences in the kindergarten and/or first-grade classroom.

10. Which aspects of probability should be included in the primary mathematics program? Why do you believe others should be excluded?

SAMPLE INSTRUCTIONAL AND ASSESSMENT ACTIVITIES

These activities and more are available on the CD that accompanies this text

1. Provide children with plastic or wooden cubes to represent each of their pets. (NOTE: We are asking the children to function on the semiabstract level, since cubes will be used to *represent* pets.) Place a chart in front of the children with columns labeled for each type of pet. The chart might look like this:

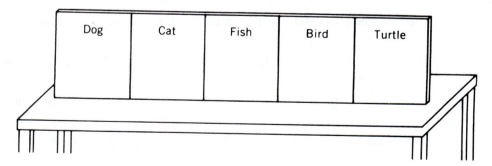

| Dog | Cat | Fish | Bird | Turtle |

Have each child place his/her block on a stack in front of the appropriate pet category. The heights of the stacks can be compared to analyze the class data.

2. This is a game for two players or teams. You'll need a track similar to that shown here and a coin. Both teams start at the beginning and alternate turns flipping the coin. If heads comes up, then the team moves ahead one space. If tails comes up, then the team moves ahead two spaces. Each team tries to reach the end first. Mark the paths with Hs and Ts as heads and tails are flipped. Does the same team win this game if it's played several times? What can be said about the tosses of the winning team?

Start

Finish

3. The computer may prove to be more useful than the calculator in the context of manipulation of data, because the data that it is capable of handling include words as well as numbers. Database software is readily available for all grade levels. This software allows the user to search data for common characteristics or traits. These common elements can then often be tallied, and sometimes graphed, within the software itself. When this is not the case, the information can usually be translated into graph form by the user. Children can gather and enter their own data, or the teacher can locate precollected data packages. Readers are encouraged to examine database software locally available for the computer system they are using.

4. Have the children collect and bring into the classroom graphs from newspapers and magazines to put on a bulletin board. Discuss similarities. Use examples and counterexamples of effective graphs.

5. Encourage the children to collect information about school lunches for a period of time. They should identify different beverages available, different main entrees, different vegetables, different fruits, different breads, and different desserts. The children can then enter the data into a database program and analyze the data by using the various aspects of the database. For example, children can use the database to determine the fruit most commonly offered. Follow-up "studies" can be done regarding the favorite dessert of the class and the frequency with which it is served. The children could also explore the probability of certain items appearing together or on certain days of the week.

6. Suppose you have five red poker chips, four blue chips, and three white chips in a bag.

a) What is the probability of getting a blue chip on the first draw?

b) What is the probability of getting a white chip on the first draw?

c) What is the probability of not getting a white chip on the first draw?

d) Suppose you got a red chip on the first draw. What is the probability of getting another red chip on the next draw?

e) If you know that the probability of getting a yellow chip is 0, what does this tell you about the colors of the chips in the bag?

f) Write fractions (probability ratios) to represent the probabilities for parts a through d.

7. Make a set of cards with the letters A, B, C, D, and E, one on each card. Make a total of 14 A cards, 8 B cards, 6 C cards, 6 D cards, and 2 E cards. If you shuffle the cards and draw one card, what are the chances of getting an A card? What are the chances of getting an E card? Which cards would have equal chances? Make a simple chart to record this experiment. Guess which type of card you will get. Write it down. Draw a card and write down the letter of the card you actually got. See how many times you win.

VM 14.6b

8. You have probably played games that have a spinner like the one pictured. If you do not have one, make one similar to it with cardboard, a paper clip, and a thumbtack. Use stiff, flat cardboard and make sure the spinner turns freely. Alternatively, use the *Spinner* VM to complete these exercises.

Numeral	1	2	3	4	5	6
Occurs						

If you spin the spinner just one time, what are the chances of landing on 6? What are the chances of landing on 3? Spin the spinner 20 times and keep a record of the results.

a) Which numeral occurred the greatest number of times?

b) Which numeral occurred the least number of times?

c) Which numerals occurred about the same number of times?

d) According to your experiment, which numeral seems most likely to occur?

e) Which numeral seems least likely to occur?

f) Try this experiment two more times; compare the three records. Has your opinion changed?

9. Last month the temperatures recorded in Gallic City at 5:00 P.M. were 75, 62, 54, 68, 72, 52, 62, 63, 71, 72, 65, 80, 74, 69, 64, 72, 82, 80, 69, 70, 59, 64, 69, 72, 67, 75, 62, 71, 74, and 54.

a) Make a chart with this information, giving the temperature and the tally (the number of times each temperature was recorded). What is the range?

b) Find the mean, the median, and the mode.

c) What is the best indicator of the measure of central tendency for this information?

d) Check your newspaper each day and graph the maximum and minimum temperatures for a week or a month. Discuss which type of graph best represents the data (and why).

10. Use the "find" or "search" capability of a word-processing package to identify how many times certain words appear in a previously typed passage. Can you find the mode? If your word processor has a word count capacity, can you find the average number of words per paragraph? How might the phrase "average paragraph" be interpreted?

11. Ask students to construct a bar graph, line graph, circle graph, pictograph, stem-and-leaf plot, and box-and-whisker plot from the same set of data. What characteristics must be present in the data to make all of these different graphs? Are some types of graphs more appropriate than others for certain data?

15

Measurement

TEACHING COMPETENCIES

Upon completing this chapter, you will be able to:

- Describe various characteristics and applications of nonstandard and standard units of measure.
- Relate some of the historical development of measures and measurement.
- Describe various aspects of the metric and U.S. customary systems of measurement.
- Describe the relationship among and between different measuring units and different measurement instruments.
- Add, subtract, multiply, and divide using denominate numbers.
- Enumerate steps in student's acquisition of money concepts.
- Describe an effective and efficient approach for teaching time concepts to children.
- Prepare lessons integrating measurement with other topics within mathematics and with other subject areas in the elementary and middle school school curriculum.

VIRTUAL MANIPULATIVES

Upon completing this chapter, you will be able to use virtual manipulatives on the accompanying CD to:

- Develop an understanding of the relative sizes of measures and conversion of measurements in *Converting Units*. **(VM 15.1)**
- Explore various combinations of coins that are equivalent in value in *Make Twenty-five Cents, Make Fifty Cents*, and *Make a Dollar*. **(VM 15.2a; VM15.2b; VM 15.2c)**
- Illustrate the concept of making change using *Count Change*. **(VM 15.3)**
- Match the time of a digital clock with an analog (circular) clock in *Match Clocks*. **(VM 15.4)**
- Explore the notion of elapsed time in *What Time Will It Be/Was It?* **(VM 15.5)**

Numbered CD icons throughout the chapter refer to the virtual manipulatives in this list.

Some people think that measurement is just something you do with a ruler, a scale, or a container.

Maybe there's more to it. Consider the following situation as described by a seventh grader:

It was 10 minutes to two on Friday, May 23rd. My 4 friends and I were on the way to the third floor to our social studies class to take a test. I got a score of 85 on my last test so I needed to get at least a score of 95 on this one to keep my A average. I wasn't as worried as I was the last time because I knew I could do better.

Last week I tried to talk my parents into giving me a $5.00 raise in my allowance if I earned an A in this class. They said they would consider it if I would agree to save half of it each week.

When I got within 10 feet of the classroom door, I could feel the tension begin to build. I reminded myself that I knew the material, but it was almost 80 degrees in the classroom that day—how could I concentrate? At least I drank a 12-ounce can of soda before class to keep from dehydrating! (It wasn't sugar free—I needed all the energy I could get.)

The sentences of this story have a common thread. Did you notice that each and every sentence included some sort of reference to a measure or to a measurement? Some references are more obvious than others. For example, the reference to "sugar free" is a measure showing the lack of sugar content in a soft drink, while the reference to "within 10 feet of the classroom door" is clearly an example of measuring approximate distance. The statement about needing "at least a score of 95" on the test is a measure, of sorts, of the student's knowledge (or test-taking ability). What about the statements "10 minutes to two," "May 23rd," "last week," and "$5.00 raise"? These are measures of time and money. The comment about saving "half of it" is a comparative form of measuring an amount of money. The reference to the "third floor" is a measure of location, and the comment about "4 friends" is a measure of numberness. Finally, even the sentence in the first paragraph "I wasn't as worried ... because I knew I could do better" is a measure, albeit subjective, of the student's confidence. The point? Measurement is pervasive in our lives. Take a moment to consider, and perhaps list, all the forms of measurement you engage in during a single day.

Because measurement is so important due to its practicality and application in so many aspects of everyday life, the National Council of Teachers of Mathematics (NCTM) has included the study of measurement as one of the five content standards put forth in the *Principles and Standards for School Mathematics* (2000). The preK–12 measurement standards reads:

Instructional programs from pre-kindergarten through grade 12 should enable all students to—

● Understand measurable attributes of objects and the units, systems, and processes of measurement.

● Apply appropriate techniques, tools, and formulas to determine measurements.

The study of measurement, when effectively structured, serves as a connector to other areas of the mathematics curriculum. For example, the study of measurement provides a context for visiting and/or reviewing topics such as number operations, geometric concepts, statistical concepts, algebraic concepts, and general problem-solving situations: "Measurement is an important vehicle for highlighting mathematical connections—not only within mathematics itself, but to areas too often viewed as 'outside of mathematics' such as social studies, science, art, physical education, and the student's own interests and experiences" (NCTM, 2000, p. 70).

The Historical Development of Measurement Systems

One of the first mathematical needs of any society is a system of standard measurement. Even primitive people developed some rudimentary way to mark the passage of time or describe the distance from one place to another—for example, the distance from the tribe's camp to a herd of animals that could provide food and clothing.

Ancient Egyptian and Babylonian civilizations developed the first recorded systems of measurement in the Western world. The Egyptians were concerned with agriculture, particularly along the fertile Nile River. Consequently, they developed an elaborate system of land measurement for laying out crops and marking the annual loss and subsequent restoration of land resulting from the great floods of the Nile. They also developed a system for measuring volume—for them, the amount of grain in a container—but this system of volume measurement was extremely complex and awkward to use.

The Babylonians advanced the science of measurement. They calculated the length of the sidereal year to be 365 days, 6 hours, and 11 minutes—a figure that is within 3 minutes of the modern calculation.

(The sidereal year is computed from the apparent movement of the stars, which gives a more accurate measurement of time than the earth's movement around the sun. Even today, such astronomical observations and scientific measurements help standardize the measure of time to a high degree of precision.)

The development of systems of measure by peoples of the ancient world was closely tied to the creation of the science of geometry. The English word *geometry* is derived from the Greek *geo*, meaning "earth," and *metron*, meaning "measure," and thus *geometry* means "earth measure." This suggests that the practical activity of measurement was critical to the origin of the abstract discipline of geometry.

The Egyptians and the Babylonians, as well as the ancient Greeks and Romans, used units of measure that, for the most part, were derived from dimensions of the human body. For example, the length of the forearm, called a *cubit*, was used as a measure by the Babylonians and other early peoples. Some of the units that early civilizations used for measuring length were the length of a foot, the width of a finger, the width of the palm of a hand, and the length of a soldier's stride.

For centuries, units of measure continued to be derived from the human body. In the early Middle Ages, the following units of length were commonly used:

fathom: the distance between a person's hands with arms outstretched

cubit: the distance from the elbow to the tip of the middle finger

hand: the width of the hand

digit: the width of the index finger

foot: the distance from the heel of the foot to the tip of the great toe

yard: the length of the arm from shoulder to the tip of the middle finger

The limitations of these units of measure become evident with a little thought. The distance from the elbow to the tip of the middle finger varies from person to person. The width of the hand is greater for a large person than for a small person. Not all people have feet of the same length. In short, these units of measure were inconsistent in that they varied from person to person, and these differences were responsible for errors in communicating measures. Measurement would not be invariant until people devised a system of **standard measure**—units of measure that would be the same reference for everyone.

During the late medieval period, attempts were made to establish some standard units of measure. The length of a standard yard was originally determined in the following way: The length of 3 barleycorns was to be an inch; 12 inches were to be a foot; 3 feet were to be a yard. Later, Henry I of England (1068–1135) decreed that the distance from his nose to the thumb of his outstretched arm would be one yard. Edward I of England (1239–1307) established the first fixed standard—one that didn't change based on whoever happened to be king at the time—an iron rod whose length was defined as one yard.

During the last three centuries, with the evolution of machine tools and more accurate instruments, measurement has become an extremely, but not completely, precise science. So much so, in fact, that in the nineteenth century, England, France, and the United States established bureaus of standards to maintain fixed units of standard measure. Not only units of linear measurement, but also those for weight, time, and other aspects of measure have been standardized by defining standard units.

Contemporary Measurement Systems

There are two commonly used systems of measurement today: the U.S. customary system and the metric system. The U.S. customary system, with which many of us are *somewhat* familiar, is the system most used by laypersons in the United States but in few other places in the world. The United Kingdom began conversion to the metric system in 1965; Australia followed in 1970; and Canada, in 1971. The metric system is used throughout other countries of the world and in the scientific work of all nations.

The U.S. customary system of measurement is, in many cases, difficult to work with because of the odd relations between the various units. This confusion is primarily due to the long historical development of the system, which has its roots in units of measure that were in use before the development of standard measure.

Even standardized measurement presents difficulties; for instance, a dry quart is larger than a liquid quart, and a British quart is smaller than either the dry quart or the liquid quart. An ounce that measures liquid is not the same as an ounce that is used to measure dry material; also, the avoirdupois ounce (which we normally use) is lighter than the troy ounce or the apothecaries' ounce.

The table shows some of the principal units of the U.S. customary system that you might recognize.

Length
12 inches = 1 foot
3 feet = 1 yard
$5\frac{1}{2}$ yards = 1 rod
40 rods = 1 furlong
8 furlongs = 1 mile

Area
144 square inches = 1 square foot
9 square feet = 1 square yard
4840 square yards = 1 acre
640 acres = 1 square mile

Volume
3 teaspoons = 1 tablespoon
16 tablespoons = 1 cup
2 cups = 1 pint
2 pints = 1 quart
4 quarts = 1 gallon
2 gallons = 1 peck
4 pecks = 1 bushel

Weight
$437\frac{1}{2}$ grains = 1 ounce
16 ounces = 1 pound
100 pounds = 1 hundred weight
20 hundred weights = 1 ton

As we examine the table, we are unable to identify a clear and logical pattern of relations among the various units. This accounts for the awkwardness of the U.S. customary system. The growth of science and industry in the eighteenth century, however, required an efficient and convenient way to measure length, weight, and volume. The metric system of measurement was created to satisfy this need.

The metric system did not evolve out of the capricious customs of the ancient and medieval worlds but was first suggested by various French scientists in the late eighteenth century (shortly after Thomas Jefferson proposed a similar system of measure for the young United States). A number of countries, including France, came to adopt the metric system. In 1866, the U.S. Congress officially recognized the legal status of the metric system in the United States. In 1875, the International Bureau of Weights and Measures was established through the Treaty of the Meter in an attempt to create a uniform and efficient system of measurement. The system that was adopted by the bureau is the metric system. In 1893, Congress adopted the metric standards as the standards for all measurement in the United States. For example, a *foot* is presently defined to be 0.3048 meter and a *pound* is defined as 453.59237 grams.

Almost all countries of the world have adopted the metric system and made it the official system of measurement. Moreover, scientists throughout the world do their work with metric units. Consequently, as American society becomes more scientifically and technologically oriented, it becomes necessary, even critical, for us to understand and make use of the metric system. For this reason, the metric system continues to be an important part of mathematics and science programs in elementary and middle schools.

It's interesting to note that the United States officially adopted the metric system in 1875, but it was little used by the citizenry. In 1975, Gerald Ford, then president, signed the Metric Conversion Act, which called for a voluntary conversion to the metric system and established the U.S. Metric Board to handle the coordination of the conversion. Immediately after the passage of the act, there was enthusiasm for change, but the momentum waned, primarily because conversion was not made mandatory.

Many today believe that the "metric movement" in the United States is dead, but a great many changes have already occurred, and will continue to occur, in how we measure our world. For example, the U.S. military uses metric measures, as does the medical profession. Many sporting events use metric units to measure distance and mass. A large number of major businesses, such as those in the automobile and high-tech industries, are heavily metricized. Products in our stores are labeled metrically; the film we buy is measured in millimeters; and our weather reports and our road signs often reflect both metric and U.S. customary measures.

So, although we have not had what might be termed an "overnight explosion of metric measurements" thrust on us, we have adapted well and continue to expand our use of the metric system to include those areas that have traditionally been measured using the U.S. customary system. The simple fact is that if a company (or a society) is to be competitive in a global economy, then it must adapt to the metric system of measurement.

The metric system has evolved over the decades and has been modified into what it is today. The metric system, called *le système international d'unités*, is known as SI. SI provides eight basic units, listed in the following table.

Measurement	Standard Unit	Symbol
Length	meter	m
Capacity	liter	l
Mass	gram	g
Temperature	Kelvin	K
Time	second	s
Electric current	ampere	A
Amount of substance	mole	mol
Luminous intensity	candela	cd

In elementary and middle school measurement, we commonly teach only length, capacity, mass, temperature, and time. The temperature we teach, however, is usually Celsius or Fahrenheit, not the Kelvin scale. Kelvin measure is more commonly used in certain science applications.

The basic unit of linear measurement (length) in the metric system is the *meter*. Originally, the standard meter was based on a calculation of one ten-millionth of the distance between the North Pole and the equator, through Paris. Today, having more precise instruments of measurement, we know that this measurement is slightly inaccurate.

The meter has been redefined as the distance between two microscopic lines engraved on a particular platinum-iridium bar maintained under specified conditions at the International Bureau of Weights and Measures at Sèvres, France. A meter was alternatively defined as the length of 1,553,164.13 wavelengths of red cadmium light waves under specified conditions. In 1969, members of the General Conference on Weights and Measures defined the meter as 1,650,763.73 wavelengths of the orange-red line of krypton 86. A more recent definition of a meter is the distance traveled by light in .000000003335640952 seconds.

These modern definitions serve to determine the length of the meter to a phenomenally high degree of precision. (Of course, this information is provided only for the teacher's understanding of continued attempts to increase the level of precision—it is not intended that children be exposed to such formal definitions.) Teachers are reminded of the variability and uncertainty of "the distance from a king's nose to his outstretched thumb" as compared to the scientific definitions given here.

The other units of length in the metric system are related to the meter by powers of ten. The names of the units of length based on the meter are composed of two parts, the base meter and a prefix that indicates the relation of the unit to the meter. For example, *kilo* is a prefix meaning "one thousand," so the term *kilometer* designates a unit of length equal to one thousand meters. Most foreign automobile speedometers measure speed in kilometers per hour, just as ours measure speed in miles per hour. (In fact, almost all speedometers are calibrated in both systems.) Similarly, *centi* is a prefix meaning "one-hundredth," so the term *centimeter* designates a unit of length equal to one-hundredth of a meter. Notice the clear and logical pattern of relations among the various units; this makes for ease and efficiency in scientific work.

We do not teach children all the prefixes—there is no need to do so at this stage of development. In elementary school, we usually teach only *kilo, deci, centi,* and *milli.* Other prefixes are sometimes introduced at the middle school level. The full listing of prefixes in the table are to familiarize you with the complete system of naming measures. You should not find it necessary to memorize the entire table. We too often forget that we do not memorize all the measures in our familiar U.S. customary system of measurement, either.

EM 1 exameter	=	1 000 000 000 000 000 000.	meters
Pm 1 petameter	=	1 000 000 000 000 000.	meters
Tm 1 terameter	=	1 000 000 000 000.	meters
Gm 1 gigameter	=	1 000 000 000.	meters
Mm 1 megameter	=	1 000 000.	meters
km 1 kilometer	=	1 000.	meters
hm 1 hectometer	=	100.	meters
dam 1 dekameter	=	10.	meters
m1 meter	**=**	**1.**	**meter**
dm 1 decimeter	=	.1	meter
cm 1 centimeter	=	.01	meter
mm 1 millimeter	=	.001	meter
um 1 micrometer	=	.000 001	meter
nm 1 nanometer	=	.000 000 001	meter
pm 1 picometer	=	.000 000 000 001	meter
fm 1 femtometer	=	.000 000 000 000 001	meter
am 1 attometer	=	.000 000 000 000 000 001	meter

From the eight basic units of the SI, all other measurements are developed. The accompanying table shows the most commonly used measurements:

Quantity	Common Units	Symbol
Length	kilometer	km
	meter	m
	centimeter	cm
	millimeter	mm
Area	square kilometer	km^2
	square meter	m^2
	square centimeter	cm^2
	square millimeter	mm^2
Volume	cubic meter cubic	m^3
	decimeter cubic	dm^3
	centimeter	cm^3
Mass	kilogram	kg
	gram	g
Temperature	degree Celsius	°C

Now let's examine some of these different metric measures. Units of area in the metric system are based on the convenient relation of powers of ten. Area measure involves the use of squares. For example, one square meter is the amount of area covered by a square one meter on a side.

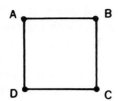

$$m\overline{AB} = m\overline{BC} = m\overline{CD} = m\overline{DA} = 1 \text{ meter}$$
Area of square ABCD = 1 square meter

Thus we can arrange a table to show square metric units.

sq km	1 square kilometer	= (1000.)²	square meters
sq m	**1 square meter**	**= 1.**	**square meter**
sq dm	1 square decimeter	= (.1)²	square meter
sq cm	1 square centimeter	= (.01)²	square meter
sq mm	1 square millimeter	= (.001)²	square meter

It is advisable to suggest (or have students identify) some real-world approximations for the various units of measure that are being discussed. These referents are intended only as approximations that will help the students relate an otherwise abstract expression, such as "three square meters," with something real to them. For this reason, it is important that such referents be clearly understood. For instance, an example that might prove helpful when discussing a square meter would be an area similar to that covered by half of a typical classroom door or, perhaps, a card table.

The metric system uses the kilogram and gram instead of the U.S. customary units of pounds, ounces, and so forth. Originally, the *gram* was defined as the weight of one cubic centimeter of pure water under specified conditions (a cubic centimeter being the volume contained by a cube one centimeter on a side). Today, using more precise instruments, scientists have redefined the gram as one-thousandth of the weight of a particular platinum-iridium cylinder maintained under specified conditions. The gram is the basic unit of weight in the metric system. The other units of weight are related to the gram by powers of ten as shown in the following table. (From this point on, we will show only the most commonly used units. You may expand the tables as necessary.)

kg	kilogram	=	1000	grams
g	**1 gram**	**=**	**1.**	**gram**

The names of the units of weight other than the gram are composed of two parts: the base *gram* and a prefix that indicates the relation of the unit to the gram. For example, *mega* is a prefix meaning "one million," so the

term *megagram* names a unit equal to one million grams. Similarly, the prefix *micro* means "one-millionth," so the term *microgram* designates a unit of weight equal to one-millionth of a gram. Again, a clear and logical pattern exists in the relations among the various units.

A representation that is often used as a referent for a gram is a single M&M's candy or a nickel. A referent model to use for a kilogram might be a classroom dictionary or some other appropriate classroom object, such as a box of manipulatives. Whatever is selected, weigh it ahead of time to be certain that it is reasonably close to a kilogram in weight.

The basic unit of volume in the metric system is the *liter*, which is defined as the volume of one kilogram of pure water under specified conditions. The standard liter was originally intended to equal one-thousandth of a cubic meter, or one cubic decimeter, but because of the inaccuracy in fixing the units of weight, this equality is only approximate. As shown in the accompanying table, the other units of volume in the metric system are related to the liter by powers of ten. (Again, we will not complete the entire table; you can complete additional parts of the table as necessary.)

l	**1 liter**	**=**	**1.**	**liter**
cl	1 centiliter	=	.01	liter
ml	1 milliliter	=	.001	liter

The names of the other units of volume have two parts, the base *liter* and a prefix indicating the relation of the unit to the liter. For example, *deka* is a prefix meaning "ten," so the term *dekaliter* names a unit of volume equal to ten liters. Similarly, the prefix *deci* means "tenth," so the term *deciliter* names a unit of volume equal to one-tenth of a liter. Notice, once again, the clear and logical pattern of relations among the various units.

Many children are familiar with two-liter bottles of soda. You can also use a quart container to represent and demonstrate that a quart is a little less than a liter.

The relations among the metric units of length, weight, and volume are summarized in the following table.

Because the units of the metric system are related in a simple and logical way by powers of ten, it is easy to change from one unit to another. We need only multiply or divide by the appropriate power of ten. Consider, for example, 2 farmhouses that are 1300 meters apart. Suppose we want to express this distance in kilometers. We know that 1000 meters is equal to 1 kilometer and that each meter is equal to $\frac{1}{1000}$ of a kilometer. Therefore we can multiply 1300 by $\frac{1}{1000}$ (or .001) and obtain 1.3, which is the distance between the 2 farmhouses in kilometers.

VM 15.1

$$1300 \text{ meters} = 1.3 \text{ kilometers}$$

Prefix	Linear Measure	Weight	Volume or Capacity
10^3 × base	kilometer	kilogram	kiloliter
10^2 × base	hectometer	hectogram	hectoliter
10^1 × base	dekameter	dekagram	dekaliter
100 × base	**meter**	**gram**	**liter**
10^{-1} × base	decimeter	decigram	deciliter
10^{-2} × base	centimeter	centigram	centiliter
10^{-3} × base	millimeter	milligram	milliliter

(Of course, we could have solved this by dividing 1300 by 1000—a process equivalent to multiplying 1300 by $\frac{1}{1000}$). Clearly, by using appropriate powers of ten, it is quite easy to change units in the metric system.

VM 15.1

In the U.S. customary system, however, it is much more cumbersome to change units. Suppose, for example, that the 2 farmhouses are 1.3 miles apart and that we wish to express this distance in feet. There are 5280 feet in one mile. So, we must multiply 1.3 by 5280 to find the distance in feet between the 2 farmhouses.

$$1 \text{ mile} = 5280 \text{ feet}$$
$$1.3 \text{ miles} = 1.3 \times 5280 = 6864 \text{ feet}$$

$$
\begin{array}{r}
5280 \\
\times \quad 1.3 \\
\hline
1584.0 \quad (.3 \times 5280) \\
5280 \quad (1 \times 5280) \\
\hline
6864.0
\end{array}
$$

Therefore, 1.3 miles is equal to 6864 feet, so the 2 farmhouses are 6864 feet apart.

At this point we can begin to appreciate the efficiency of the metric system. To convert 1.3 miles into 6864 feet, we had to perform a three-step mathematical operation. Even if we had memorized the fact that there are 5280 feet in 1 mile, we would still have had to multiply 1.3 by 5280. But to convert 1300 meters into 1.3 kilometers, we had only to multiply 1300 by $\frac{1}{1000}$ (or divide 1300 by 1000). Converting one metric measure to another metric measure is a process that often requires only a minimal amount of mental mathematics.

If a measurement is expressed in metric units, a computation can be performed to express the same measurement in U.S. customary units. Similarly, if a measurement is expressed in U.S. customary units, a computation can be performed to convert the measurement into metric units. The most common relations between metric and U.S. customary units are listed in the accompanying

table. Although these relations are only approximate, they are adequate for most practical purposes. The symbol ($\approx$) is read as "approximately equal to."

Linear Measure			
1 meter	$\approx$ 39.37 inches	1 centimeter	$\approx$ .3937 inch
1 meter	$\approx$ 3.28 feet	1 centimeter	$\approx$ .0328 foot
1 meter	$\approx$ 1.09 yards	1 centimeter	$\approx$ .0109 yard
1 kilometer	$\approx$ .62 mile		
	1 inch $\approx$ 2.54 centimeters $\approx$ .0254 meter		
	1 foot $\approx$ 30.48 centimeters $\approx$ .3048 meter		
	1 yard $\approx$ 91.44 centimeters $\approx$ .9144 meter		
	1 mile $\approx$ 1609 meters $\approx$ 1.609 kilometers		
Weight			
1 gram	$\approx$ .035 ounce $\approx$ .0022 pound		
1 kilogram	$\approx$ 2.2 pounds		
1 pound	$\approx$ 453.6 grams $\approx$ .4536 kilogram		
1 ounce	$\approx$ 28.35 grams $\approx$ .02835 kilogram		
Volume			
1 liter	$\approx$ 61.025 cubic inches		
1 liter	$\approx$ .264 gallon		
1 liter	$\approx$ 1.057 quarts		
1 gallon	$\approx$ 231 cubic inches $\approx$ 3.785 liters		
1 quart	$\approx$ 57.75 cubic inches $\approx$ .946 liter		

Even though the conversion of measurements within a given system of measure is essential, conversion of measurements from one system to a different system is not normally taught as part of the elementary school mathematics program. Students need only an understanding of the relative sizes of the measures. Usually, if a measure is given in metric units, the calculating will also be done in metric measure. Although comparison is certainly appropriate, do not ask children to convert from one system of measurement to another.

The Process of Measurement

So far in this chapter, we have discussed measurement in ways that we all recognize, but we have avoided an explanation of what we mean by the term. What is measurement? **Measurement** is the determination of the size of an object, or a comparison between some aspect of an object and a standard unit. When we determine the height of a building, we are using measurement. When we determine the time it takes to run a race, we are using measurement. When we count the number of students in a classroom, we are using measurement. In each of these situations, our measurement is expressed by a combination of two things:

1. The measure, which shows us "how many"

2. A standard unit, which shows us the unit of measurement with which the quantity to be measured is compared

For instance, consider these examples:

The building is 350 feet high.

The racetrack is 100 meters long.

The race took 17 seconds.

In the first example, the unit of measurement is feet and the measure is 350; in the second, the unit of measurement is meters and the measure is 100; in the third, the unit of measurement is seconds and the measure is 17.

Let's develop the idea of measurement with respect to linear measurement. **Linear measurement**, as the name suggests, is concerned with measurement of length. Children in the primary grades can begin to develop some concept of linear measurement by using any suitable object as a measuring device. A child could measure a desk using the length of a pencil, an eraser, a book, or a card, for example. One child might measure the desk as "7 pencils long," and another child might measure it as "14 erasers long." Through a discussion and comparison of such measurements, children will soon realize the need for standard units of measurement to communicate results—a measure of "10" doesn't mean much unless you also know the unit being used.

Each class might develop its own standard unit of measurement; one class might use a Popsicle stick, for example. These children will soon discover that if 2 of them use the same measuring instrument carefully, they will arrive at the same (or very nearly the same) measurement of a given object. Each pupil might find that his or her desk is 6 Popsicle sticks long.

After spending a considerable amount of time manipulating familiar objects, children are ready for the more abstract level of comparing line segments, choosing one line segment as a standard unit. Students should be asked to compare the lengths of the following two line segments.

They can do this by tracing segment AB on another sheet of paper and then placing this tracing on top of segment YZ. Clearly, segment AB is shorter than segment YZ, or $m(AB) < m(YZ)$. The letter m in front of (AB) is read "the measure of." We can therefore read the sentence $m(AB) < m(YZ)$ as "The measure of line segment AB is less than the measure of line segment YZ." In the same manner, the following two line segments can be compared in length:

This time the two line segments are of equal length: $m(MN) = m(PQ)$. Children should be encouraged to make a number of such comparisons so that they can gain an understanding of relative (or comparative) lengths.

Now let's introduce a standard unit of length. Let the distance between points S and T, the length of segment ST, be called a *unit length*.

Students can compare the length of the following line segment GH with this standard unit:

They should trace segment ST on another sheet of paper and label the tracing S′T′. Then they should place S′T′ on the top of segment GH so that points G and S′ coincide. The point on GH that coincides with point T′ can be labeled A.

Children should then place segment S′T′ on top of segment GH so that points A and S′ coincide and so that point T′ coincides with a point to the right of point A (i.e., between points A and H). The point that coincides with T′ can be labeled E.

Then, by placing segment S′T′ on top of segment GH so that points E and S′ coincide, children will discover that points H and T′ also coincide. Children can thus see that the length of segment GH is three times the length of segment S′T′. Since we have defined the length of ST to be a unit length, we can say that the length of segment GH is 3 unit lengths.

The process just described for measuring the length of segment GH is, admittedly, a bit awkward. It would be much easier if we had a line segment such as the following:

The distance in unit lengths between the point labeled 0 and any other labeled point on the line segment is equal to the number naming the other point. For example, the distance between the points labeled 0 and 2 is 2 unit lengths, the distance between the points labeled 0 and 4 is 4 unit lengths, and so on. If we place the relabeled segment on top of segment GH so that point G and the point labeled 0 coincide, point H coincides with the point labeled 3. The distance between the points labeled 0 and 3 is 3 unit lengths. Therefore, the length of segment GH is also 3 unit lengths.

We have now developed a standard unit for measuring distance—the unit length. We can measure the distance between any two points and the dimensions of any object by comparing the appropriate distances to this standard unit of measure. Such measurements have meaning because the unit length is a fixed unit of measure—it has the same length today as it did yesterday and will have the same length tomorrow—and because a quantitative relation exists between any distance and the unit length. For example, the height of a particular building is equal to 2300 unit lengths.

We use a number of different units for measuring length or distance. We have already discussed the most important of these—the inch, the foot, the meter, and so on. An understanding of these units can be developed in much the same way that understanding of the unit length was developed. For example, children can construct a line segment AB such that the distance between the end points is 1 inch:

Then they can construct a line segment such as the following, which is composed of three smaller segments, each 1 inch long:

Each of these smaller segments is congruent to segment AB. If segment TW is matched with the whole numbers 0 through 3, as in the following illustration, then we can use it to measure distance in inches, just as we used a similar line segment 3 unit lengths long to measure distances in unit lengths.

Let's create a segment, XY, that is 1 centimeter long, another standard unit of measurement. If we use segment XY four consecutive times, we say that the segment is 4 centimeters long.

By developing the idea of measure in this way, we can enable children to understand much more clearly what they are doing when they use a ruler marked off in inches or centimeters to measure an object. Other units of length

can now be developed in terms of this understanding. For example, having gained an understanding of what inches are, children will be better prepared to comprehend the meaning of feet, yards, miles, and so on. Their understanding of the metric units of linear measurement (centimeter, meter, millimeter, and kilometer) can be developed in much the same manner. (It is interesting to note that this process of converting within a given measurement system provides an effective example of the concept of function discussed in algebra. That is, every yard Y of measure is equal to 3 feet F. The algebraic equation $Y = 3 \times F$ describes this function relationship.)

Children in grade 1 should be introduced to inches, feet, centimeters, and meters as standard units of linear measure. Rulers in this grade should have only the points marking inches or centimeters. Units smaller than an inch (e.g., half inches and quarter inches) will probably only confuse young children at this level. If the number line has been used to develop basic number concepts, children should easily be able to apply these concepts to linear measurement. In fact, a ruler really is simply a concrete number line. Both yardsticks and metersticks can be considered extended number lines.

When measuring a distance with a ruler, we are making a **direct measurement**, which is any measurement that is obtained by placing a measuring instrument directly on the object whose dimensions are to be measured. When we move a yardstick or a meterstick along the floor to find the length and width of a room, we are making a direct measurement. When we compare the dimensions of two windows by applying a tape measure to each of them, we are again making a direct measurement. An **indirect measurement**, on the other hand, is any measurement that is not a direct measurement. For example, if we wish to determine the distance across a wide river, we may have to employ scientific instruments or a mathematical technique; we cannot simply place a yardstick, meterstick, or tape measure on the surface of the water.

The teacher should provide many opportunities for children to measure objects in the classroom. First, the children should be asked to estimate the measure of the object. Not only does estimating provide them with the experience of "guessing and checking," it also provides a real reason for measuring—to verify the estimate.

In measuring a line segment, we place the edge of the ruler along the line segment as illustrated in the following drawing:

A common mistake made by children is to place the ruler on the segment to be measured in such a way that the left end of the segment lines up with the 1 on the ruler as opposed to the left end of the ruler itself. Some rulers are even made in such a way that the zero point is indented and written on the ruler. For example:

The measurement we have just made is only an approximation. In fact, it is impossible to measure any distance exactly. Any ruler or tape measure cannot be other than an imperfect instrument. The marks on a ruler or tape measure are physical marks (i.e., they have length and width), and a geometric point cannot be exactly represented by a mark that has dimensions. Moreover, the human eye is incapable of perceiving the precise points at which an object to be measured begins and ends. Even if we used the most precise and perfect tool to measure, it would still be our human frailty that would cause the measurement to be approximate rather than exact.

In addition to these barriers to exact measurement, there is another difficulty. Examine the following drawing:

The length of segment MN is greater than 1 inch, but it is less than 2 inches. There is no whole number of inches that represents exactly the length of segment MN. The best estimate we can make is that the length of segment MN is approximately 2 inches—that is, it is closer to 2 inches than to any other whole number of inches. This is hardly an exact measurement, but most of the measurements that children make are obviously approximate in this same manner.

As students progress through elementary school and are introduced to fractional numbers on the number line, they should also be introduced to partial units of linear measure. The half-inch can be introduced in grade 2, the quarter-inch in grade 3, and the eighth-inch and sixteenth-inch whenever the children have developed a sufficient understanding of the number line and rational numbers.

In the metric system, measures of centimeter and meter can be presented in grade 1. Millimeters can be introduced in grade 2. The units should be used independently: Other metric units should not be presented until children have had some experience with decimals.

Now let's return to the measurement of segment MN. When we measured this line segment before, we found that its length was approximately 2 inches. Once children have become familiar with half inches, however, they can measure segment MN again, this time with a ruler that is marked to indicate half inches. For example:

On this ruler, the long lines labeled with numerals indicate inches, while the unlabeled short lines indicate half inches. For example, the distance between the zero mark and the line labeled 2 is 2 inches, and the distance between the zero mark and the unlabeled short line just to the left of the line labeled 2 is $1\frac{1}{2}$ inches. Clearly, the length of MN cannot be expressed exactly in terms of whole inches and half inches. However, it is closer to $1\frac{1}{2}$ inches than to 2 inches. Therefore, we can say that the length of segment MN is approximately $1\frac{1}{2}$ inches.

But this poses a problem. Our first measurement indicates that the length of MN is approximately 2 inches, whereas our second measurement indicates that this same length is approximately $1\frac{1}{2}$ inches. How can we reconcile these two measurements? The key to answering this question is the difference in the precision of the measurements. The first measurement was made in terms of whole inches, the second in terms of half inches. The second measurement is more precise than the first, although both are approximately correct. To the nearest inch, the length of segment MN is 2 inches. To the nearest half-inch, the length of MN is $1\frac{1}{2}$ inches. Now, let's measure the length of segment MN to the nearest quarter-inch. This time we must use a ruler, such as the following one, with each 1-inch interval divided into four equivalent parts.

Each small interval is therefore one-quarter of an inch long. Examining this drawing, we see that the length of segment MN is less than $1\frac{3}{4}$ inches but greater than

$1\frac{1}{2}$ (or $1\frac{2}{4}$) inches and that it is closer to $1\frac{3}{4}$ than it is to $1\frac{1}{2}$. Thus, the length of MN is approximately $1\frac{3}{4}$ inches. This is more precise than either of the previous two measurements.

Let's now measure the length of MN to the nearest eighth-inch.

Clearly, of all the lengths indicated in the preceding drawings, $1\frac{3}{4}$ (or $1\frac{6}{8}$) inches best approximates the length of segment MN. To the nearest eighth-inch, segment MN is $1\frac{6}{8}$ inches long. The smaller the unit of measure used, the more precise the measurement.

At this point, we should note that the first step in the measurement process is to select the units to be used. A measurement is always made in terms of units. It is therefore impossible for children to measure something until they have decided whether they are going to use inches or meters or days or dollars or something else. It is also important that the units be appropriate for the situation. It would be ridiculous to use inches for finding the distance between New York and Los Angeles. It would be equally ridiculous to weigh a small bag of candy on the scales at a truck-weighing station. The first step therefore is to select a unit of measurement appropriate for the situation at hand.

Another step in the measurement process is to analyze the reasonableness of the measure. We may, for example, determine that the appropriate unit to use to measure the distance from Los Angeles to New York as being miles (or kilometers), but it is certainly unreasonable to suggest that the distance is 200 miles (or, say, 320 kilometers).

Many children have a tendency to be careless in naming units of measure. In solving a word problem, they may want to give the answer as a measure (a number) without naming the units. For example, consider the following problem:

> If John weighs 89 pounds and Peter weighs 82 pounds, how much do John and Peter weigh together?

When asked the answer to this problem, children may reply, "171." But this incomplete response is not appropriate. Do they mean "171 yards," "171 days," "171 apples," or what? The reply "171" is insufficient because a measurement is always made in terms of some unit. A measurement therefore must always be expressed as a measure and a unit of measure.

The numerical answer to this word problem is thus "171 pounds" ("171" shows the measure; "pounds" shows the unit of measurement). This point must be emphasized. Remember, as discussed in Chapter 5, that a word problem should be answered with a complete sentence. Therefore the complete answer to this particular story problem would be, "Together, John and Peter weigh 171 pounds."

Computing with Denominate Numbers

The phrase **denominate numbers** applies to quantities expressed using both a numeral and a unit of measure. Some people criticize work with denominate numbers on the grounds that we cannot perform operations on measurements—we can only operate on numbers. In one sense, this argument is correct. Yet, if we look at the real world, we see many practical situations in which we must deal with measurements assigned to real things and hence with denominate numbers. Denominate numbers are not numbers in the mathematical sense: They are measurements of attributes of objects, and we use operations on numbers to help us compare and operate with these measurements.

Children should be given the opportunity to work many problems involving units of measure. These may or may not be in the form of word problems, such as the preceding example. Consider this addition example:

$$\begin{array}{r} 1 \text{ foot } 5 \text{ inches} \\ + \ 1 \text{ foot } 2 \text{ inches} \end{array}$$

This example is not expressed in terms of a single unit. Rather, the measurements have been made in two units—feet and inches. This is, of course, quite acceptable. We can solve this example by adding the numbers expressed in the feet column and then adding the numbers expressed in the inches column separately.

$$\begin{array}{r} 1 \text{ foot } 5 \text{ inches} \\ + \ 1 \text{ foot } 2 \text{ inches} \\ \hline 2 \text{ feet } 7 \text{ inches} \end{array}$$

The sum, in this case, is clearly 2 feet 7 inches.

Here is another example, this time using metric measures:

$$\begin{array}{r} 3 \text{ meters } 34 \text{ centimeters} \\ + \ 3 \text{ meters } 27 \text{ centimeters} \\ \hline 5 \text{ meters } 61 \text{ centimeters} \end{array}$$

Using metric measures, consider how easy it would be to rewrite the example all in one unit and then add the numbers. We can change 3 meters 34 centimeters to

334 centimeters, and we can change 2 meters 27 centimeters to 227 centimeters. Now the example becomes

$$\begin{array}{r} 334 \text{ centimeters} \\ + \ 227 \text{ centimeters} \\ \hline 561 \text{ centimeters} \end{array}$$

Note that the addition of metric measure can conveniently be changed to an addition example that is quite familiar to most children. Adding denominate numbers is usually much easier using metric measure than U.S. customary measure.

Now let's consider another example using U.S. customary units for weight:

$$\begin{array}{r} 4 \text{ pounds } 10 \text{ ounces} \\ + \ 3 \text{ pounds } \ \ 9 \text{ ounces} \\ \hline \end{array}$$

The answer here is 7 pounds 19 ounces. But 19 ounces is equal to 1 pound 3 ounces. The answer can therefore be expressed as 8 pounds 3 ounces.

$$\left.\begin{array}{l} 7 \text{ pounds} \\ 19 \text{ ounces} \end{array}\right\} = 7 \text{ pounds} + 19 \text{ ounces}$$
$$= 7 \text{ pounds} + (1 \text{ pound} + 3 \text{ ounces})$$
$$= (7 \text{ pounds} + 1 \text{ pound}) + 3 \text{ ounces}$$
$$= 8 \text{ pounds} + 3 \text{ ounces}$$
$$= 8 \text{ pounds } 3 \text{ ounces}$$

Note that the concept of regrouping as used with place value can be applied to regrouping here: Since 16 ounces equals 1 pound, then 19 ounces becomes 1 pound 3 ounces. The answer to the preceding example can be written in a number of different ways. For example:

8 pounds 3 ounces
7 pounds 19 ounces
6 pounds 35 ounces, and so on.

It is more convenient, however, to write the answer as 8 pounds 3 ounces. If we write the answer with a lesser number of pounds, the expression for ounces would necessarily be more cumbersome. In general, as a matter of convenience, when a measurement is expressed in two or more units, the larger unit is written with as great a number as possible.

Children often have a difficult time regrouping measurements, even if they normally can regroup in base ten effectively. One technique that seems to help is to provide them with concrete opportunities. For example, students can use gallon and quart containers, along with some rice or sand, to actually carry out the process of regrouping in an exercise such as the

following:

$$\begin{array}{r} 2 \text{ gallons } 3 \text{ quarts} \\ + \ 1 \text{ gallon } 2 \text{ quarts} \\ \hline \end{array}$$

Three more examples follow in which the answers have been expressed in the most convenient form:

(a)
$$\begin{array}{r} 4 \text{ yards } 2 \text{ feet } \ \ 5 \text{ inches} \\ \times \ 5 \\ \hline 20 \text{ yards } 10 \text{ feet } 25 \text{ inches} \end{array}$$
$$= 20 \text{ yards} + 10 \text{ feet } + 25 \text{ inches}$$
$$= 20 \text{ yards} + 10 \text{ feet } + (2 \text{ feet } + 1 \text{ inch})$$
$$= 20 \text{ yards} + (10 \text{ feet } + 2 \text{ feet}) + 1 \text{ inch}$$
$$= 20 \text{ yards} + 12 \text{ feet } + 1 \text{ inch}$$
$$= (20 \text{ yards} + 4 \text{ yards}) + 1 \text{ inch}$$
$$= 24 \text{ yards} + 1 \text{ inch}$$
$$= 24 \text{ yards } 1 \text{ inch}$$

(NOTE: It is not intended that children write the chain of equations seen here. These are presented to illustrate to the teacher the equivalence between the initial and final answers.)

(b)
$$8 \times 77¢ = \square$$
$$8 \times 77¢ = \$6.16$$
$$\begin{array}{r} \$.77 \\ \times \ 8 \\ \hline \$6.16 \end{array}$$

(c)
$$\begin{array}{r} 7 \text{ grams } \ 4 \text{ decigrams} \\ \times 6 \\ \hline 42 \text{ grams } 24 \text{ decigrams} \end{array}$$
$$= 44 \text{ grams } 4 \text{ decigrams}$$

OR, more conveniently, use 7.4 (since 7 grams 4 decigrams = 7.4 grams)

$$\begin{array}{r} 7.4 \\ \times \ 6 \\ \hline 44.4 \text{ grams } (\text{ or } 444 \text{ decigrams}) \end{array}$$

Notice that in example c, 7 grams 4 decigrams is rewritten as 7.4 grams before the indicated multiplication is performed. This is not necessary, but computation is generally easier in that form. Such simplification is possible because the metric system is based on powers of ten. The expression "4 decigrams" can be rewritten as ".4 grams"; the sum of 7 grams and .4 grams can be expressed as 7.4 grams.

Money and Time as Measures

Money represents a countable system of measurement of value or worth. Children should be introduced to the concept of measuring money early—beginning in kindergarten. First have the children sort picture files or attribute blocks to focus on their different characteristics; then have them separate a collection of coins into piles that are alike. Successfully separating the coins into different piles indicates that the child can identify those that are alike and those that are different. Have the children examine each of the different coins and discuss the similarities and the differences with other coins.

The next stage requires the children to recognize the relative value of the coins. How many pennies does it take to have the same value as a nickel? (NOTE: Do not say to young children, "How many pennies are there in a nickel?" We are interested in the relative value of the coins—there are no pennies *in* a nickel, strictly speaking. Instead, a nickel has the same value as 5 pennies.) The children can construct a table such as the following:

Nickel	Dime	Quarter	
5 pennies	10 pennies	25 pennies	3 nickels
			1 dime
	2 nickels	5 nickels	
			3 nickels
	5 pennies	2 dimes	10 pennies
	1 nickel	1 nickel	
			2 nickels
		1 dime	15 pennies
		15 pennies	
			1 dime
			2 nickels
		1 dime	5 pennies
		1 nickel	
		10 pennies	
		(and so on)	

VM 15.2a

Next, children need to recognize the various combinations of coins that are equivalent in value. Ask the children, "What different combinations of coins have the same value as 25 cents?" A variety of numberness skills will come into play as children do this. For example, they will need to practice grouping, counting, addition, subtraction, trading, and renaming.

VM 15.3

The concept of making change should be presented next. Use real objects with price tags on them and have the children pretend to buy and sell them. The prices should be realistic so that the children also begin to develop a concept of value. Money notation with the use of ¢ and $ can then be introduced.

Additional concepts involving money are addressed in Chapters 5, 6, 13, and 14, in which you will find discussions of how money notation provides an excellent forum for examining whole number and decimal place value. Money also serves as a motivating denominate context for exploring operations in word problems. Consequently developmentally appropriate problem-solving experiences that involve money should be present throughout the elementary school curriculum.

Another aspect of measurement that children should be familiar with is time. Children generally have some knowledge of time when they enter school. Time has regulated their lives since birth, so they have developed an intuitive understanding of it; for example, they may seldom miss their favorite television shows.

Readiness activities necessary for an understanding of how time is measured and how to read a clock should begin in kindergarten. By the end of the primary grades, all children should be able to read an analog (circular) clock to the nearest minute.

VM 15.4

Informal development of time concepts usually begins in pre-kindergarten and continues more formally each year thereafter through the elementary grades. Begin to develop an understanding of day and week through conversation with the children. In grades 1 and 2, month and year can be developed, and "A.M.," "P.M.," and the calendar can be introduced.

After children have some understanding of numbers, the teacher can begin to use a clock to show times to do certain activities. At this point, it is better to use even hours, such as two o'clock or three o'clock, rather than two-thirty or four-fifteen.

Do not rush children into reading clocks—it can be a very abstract and difficult task for some. Do not use the terminology *quarter after*, *half past*, or *quarter to* until the later grades. A young child knows a "quarter" as twenty-five cents; suddenly the teacher wants the child to know a quarter as 15 minutes. So as not to confuse children, reserve the word *quarter* for money at this point. Also, since young children have not been formally introduced to rational numbers, they cannot easily comprehend "one-half" as "half past an hour."

Children should be exposed to both the traditional circular clock with hands as well as the digital clock. Teaching children how to read a digital clock is relatively straightforward: They read the numerals left to right as either a one- or a two-digit number with the (:) as a break followed by the next number. That is, "10:34" is read, of course, as "ten thirty-four." The only real difficulty occurs with a time such as "2:03" when the zero must be read as "oh."

A Valuable Tool for Helping Children Learn to Read a Standard Analog Clock

A child is not ready to learn to read a standard analog clock until he or she can

1. Understand a number line segment from 0 to 60
2. Visualize number lines
3. Count by fives from 0 to 60

With these prerequisites, the following paragraphs describe an outstanding method for helping children learn to read a standard clock.

Cut twelve 2-inch-by-5-inch rectangles from colored cardboard or acetate. From the same color of cardboard, cut an arrow-shaped hand for the clock. With a paper

RESEARCH SNAPSHOT

How can the concept of elapsed time be incorporated into problem-solving situations?

Carpenter, Fennema, Franke, Levi, and Empson (1999) classified rate problems that involve elapsed time as special types of multiplication and division problems.

For example: A baby elephant gains 5 pounds each day. How many pounds will the baby elephant gain in 7 days?

In this problem, the 7 days are not really groups, and the student solving the problem would use 5 counters to represent the 5 pounds gained after one day has passed. It is important to provide your students opportunities to solve problems that involve different kinds of quantities.

What other contexts with measurement could be used to write similar problems?

Carpenter, T. P., Fennema, E., Franke, M. L., Levi, L., & Empson, S. B. (1999). *Children's mathematics: Cognitively guided instruction*. Portsmouth, NH: Heinemann.

For additional research briefs, "ERIC Digests" lets you search more than 2000 short syntheses of research on a range of education topics. The syntheses were produced by the Educational Resources Information Center (ERIC). Check http://www.ericfacility.net/ericdigests/index/.

---

punch, punch holes uniformly in the lower left-hand and right-hand corners of each rectangle. Use brass fasteners to hook the twelve cards together. Write one numeral on the upper left-hand corner of each card. Thus you have a flexible number line segment from 1 to 12.

Introduce the children to the number line segment in a horizontal position by laying it on the floor, placing it in the chalk or marker trough, or on a flannel board. Place the arrow so that it points directly at a numeral, and have the children read the numeral.

Now place the arrow so that it is pointing somewhere between two numerals.

The children need to be led to agree that when the arrow is pointing in between two numerals, then the number is read as the least value until the hand reaches the next number.

After the children are successful in reading the arrow pointing to the horizontal number line segment, connect the two ends with a brass fastener to make a circular shape and place it on the floor or on a flannel board. Place the arrow, perhaps now referred to as a "hand," in the center, and have the children practice reading the numeral the hand is pointing toward. You may need to make another set of cards with the numerals 4 to 8 oriented correctly (as opposed to being upside down as in the figure).

For the next step in teaching how to read an analog clock, introduce counting by fives beginning with 5 and counting to 55. Cut 12 more 2-inch-by-5-inch cards from a different color of cardboard. Punch holes in their lower left-hand corners, and fasten them with brass fasteners. Print the numerals 5, 10, 15, ... , 55 on the upper left-hand corner of the cards, and place five equally spaced marks on each card. Cut a longer arrow (hand) out of the same color of cardboard as this number line segment.

Give the children practice in reading the number the arrow is pointing toward.

Read this point as 27.

Continue having the children practice reading the arrow as it points toward marks between the numerals written on the number line segment. After the children are successful in reading the number line segment horizontally, change the arrangement to a circular one.

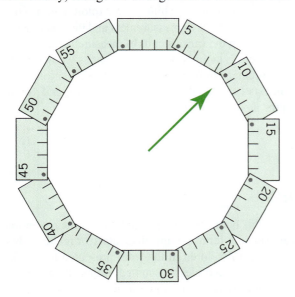

Place the long arrow, now referred to as a hand, in the middle of the clock and have the children practice reading the number the hand is pointing toward.

Now place the number line segment with numerals from 1 to 12 on top of the segment that has numerals from 5 to 55. Place the two arrows or hands together, and discuss how they are different. The hands are not "big" and "little"; one is called the "short hand" and the other the "long hand". Read the short hand first with the top number line segment; then read the long hand using the number line segment that is underneath. For example, this clock is read as 5:10:

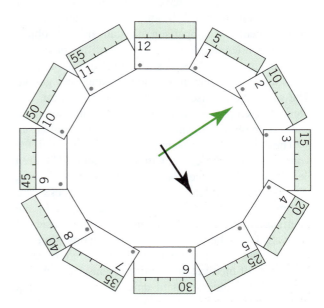

Now the children have developed all the necessary skills they need to read a clock. Continually provide opportunities for them to tell time.

After they have become efficient in reading the clock, the idea of "to the hour" may be introduced. It is much more difficult for children to understand this, so wait until they are proficient in reading "after the hour" before introducing to the hour.

One other aspect of time that should be explored is the notion of elapsed time. For example, if the students **VM 15.5** go to school from 9:00 A.M. to 3:15 P.M., how many hours and minutes are they in school? There are a number of mental strategies that they can incorporate here. For example, they can determine how long until noon, determine how long after noon, and then add the two results together.

Closure

Engineers and scientists have considerable need for measuring instruments. Should these instruments be calibrated in U.S. customary units or in metric units? The average American adult needs measurement to consider "which one is longer?" "which one is the best buy?" "which one is heavier?" and so on. Should the average American use U.S. customary or metric measurements as he or she makes these decisions?

Most people are able to use a ruler to measure length and a scale to measure weight, but does the average American have a solid understanding of what measurement is? If an individual understands measurement as a comparison of a standard to an object of unknown length, does it make any difference if the units are metric or U.S. customary? Through use, we develop an understanding of foot, pound, and gallon. The same should also be true for a meter, gram, and liter. More emphasis should be placed on measurement and less emphasis on which set of units we should use.

The concepts of measurement should begin with the young child's experiences with real measures. Children need many experiences experimenting with measuring devices such as rulers, scales, containers, clocks, and thermometers. As measurement is developed in the intermediate grades, children should develop tables of equivalencies. They should decide on the precision and the accuracy of measure needed for different tasks. New units of measure are continually inserted into the program, including standard units for measuring area and standard units for measuring volume.

The exploration of measurement is well suited to a laboratory approach. Children learn measurement best by measuring. Provide many materials for children to use in experimenting and discovering relationships. Children can begin to measure with crude instruments and then continually refine the instruments as more precise measurements are required. Children enjoy making their own measuring instruments. A teacher might construct a ruler and set up a place in the room called the "Bureau of Standards" to house that ruler. From the standard ruler at the Bureau of Standards, each child may construct his or her own measuring device. Standard units for surface measure and volume can also be developed and placed in the Bureau of Standards.

To young children, the concept of measurement is most meaningful when it is expressed in terms of concepts such as *longer, shorter, taller, later*, and *farther*. In the spring, they realize that the days are longer and they are allowed to play outside later. In winter, the days are shorter, and it seems that children must go to bed earlier. They know that some children are taller than others, that some stores are farther away than others, and that some people are older than others. All of these familiar situations create a perfect setting for developing the concepts of measurement.

When faced with a simple situation that demands measurement of length, a child should understand the need for measuring and be able to decide on the proper units to use and perform the measurement with a degree of accuracy appropriate to the child's age and maturity.

In this chapter, we have concentrated on linear measurement. However, all the most common types of measurement—length, area, volume, weight, time, and money—should be developed in the elementary and middle grades. For the most effective teaching, these concepts should be developed with real materials. Ideas can then be discovered and understood rather than superficially learned and mechanically applied. Time must be provided for children to explore and discover the basic concepts of measurement and the relations that exist among the various units of measurement. The time spent here is an important investment as we will revisit measurement through many applications and in many contexts (such as through perimeter, area, and volume in the next chapters).

PRACTICE EXERCISES FOR TEACHERS

These exercises are designed for the reader of this book, not for the children that the reader may teach. Although some of these examples are suitable for use in the elementary or middle school classroom, they should not necessarily be given to children in the form presented here. Ideas appropriate for classroom activities on the concepts and ideas discussed in this chapter can be found in a later section of this chapter and on the CD accompanying this text.

1. Measure each of the following line segments to the nearest half-inch, then to the nearest centimeter.

a) A————————————————————B

b) M————————————————————————————————————N

c) X————————————Y

d) C————————————————————D

2. Place the $(<)$, $(=)$, or $(>)$ symbol in between the two statements to make each complete statement true.

a) 5 centimeters _____ 52 millimeters

b) 1 meter _____ 99 centimeters

c) 1 yard _____ 36 feet

d) 4 liters _____ 401 milliliters

e) 1 mile _____ 5280 feet

f) 4 kilograms _____ 453.6 grams

g) 23 centimeters _____ 2.3 millimeters

h) 7 decimeters _____ 1 meter

i) 1 bushel _____ 2 pecks

j) 8 pints _____ 1 gallon

k) 9 pounds _____ 140 ounces

l) 2 feet _____ .5 yard

m) 3 meters _____ 300 centimeters

3. Write each of the following measures in meters. Use the reference chart in this chapter to help you.

a) 72 decimeters

b) 41 dekameters

c) 5000 centimeters

d) .0672 hectometer

e) .8 decimeter

f) .04 hectometer

g) 92 centimeters

h) 1241 millimeters

i) 824 hectometers

4. Write the equivalent of 720 milliliters in each unit as indicated. Use the reference chart in this chapter to help you.

a) liters

b) centiliters

c) deciliters

d) dekaliters

e) hectoliters

f) kiloliters

5. Solve each of the following examples using denominate numbers. Rewrite the metric examples to make them easier to solve. For example, in part h, 3 cm 8 mm = 38 mm; thus the example should be written as 3×38 mm. (What happens when you try to do the same for those written in U.S. customary units?)

a)   3 ft 4 in.
      7 ft 9 in.
   $+$ 6 ft 5 in.

b)   8 hr 43 min
   $+$ 1 hr 39 min

c) $4\overline{)\,6\text{ m }8\text{ cm}}$

d)   2 rd 9 ft
   $\times$ 6

e)   17 ft 7 in.
   $-$ 6 ft 9 in.

f)   5 m 23 cm
   $-$ 1 m 67 cm

g)   7 yd 3 in.
   $-$ 2 yd 8 in.

h)   3 cm 8 mm
   $\times$ 3

i) $5\overline{)\,12\text{ gal }3\text{ pt}}$

j)   4 m 54 cm
      6 m 63 cm
      9 m 37 cm
   $+$ 1 m 52 cm

6. Express each of the following measurements in the units indicated.

a) 17 feet = ____ yards

b) $1\frac{3}{4}$ yards = ____ inches

c) 20 pints = ____ gallons

d) $1\frac{3}{8}$ pounds = ____ ounces

e) 3 cups = ____ tablespoons

f) 7 miles = ____ feet

g) 1815 square yards = ____ acre

h) 43 cups = ____ pints

i) 49 square yards = ____ square feet

j) 3 gallons = ____ cups

7. Express each of the following measurements in the units indicated. Use the reference chart in this chapter to help you.

a) 5.4 meters = ____ centimeters

b) 81 kilometers = ____ meters

c) 1 megaliter = ____ microliters

d) 5497 grams = ____ kilograms

e) 72 liters = ____ microliters

f) 524 milliliters = ____ deciliters

g) 2473 micrograms = ____ grams

h) 7 meters = ____ decimeters

8. Answer each of the following statements true or false.
a) Most countries of the world use the U.S. customary system of measurement.
b) The metric system is a base ten system.
c) The metric system is compatible with our place-value system.
d) The metric system is much older than the U.S. customary system.
e) All linear measurement is approximate.
f) The smaller the unit of measure, the more precise the measure.

VM 15.2b

9. List all the possible combinations of coins that will make 50 cents if only dimes, nickels, and quarters are used.

VM 15.2c

10. List all possible combinations of coins that will make one dollar if only dimes, nickels, and quarters are used.

11. Use a metric ruler calibrated in millimeters to calculate the thickness of a penny. (HINT: You might want to develop a strategy that uses more than one penny.)

12. Use a metric ruler calibrated in millimeters to calculate the thickness of a dime.

13. What is the greatest amount of money you could have in U.S. coins and still not have change for a dollar?

TEACHING COMPETENCIES
AND SELF-ASSESSMENT TASKS

The following questions and statements are designed to reflect the teaching competencies that appeared at the beginning of this chapter and, in some cases, to expose you to deeper aspects of the concepts presented. Take a moment to consider your response to each of these in light of what you've read and learned.

1. Discuss measurement situations in which standard units of measure are typically NOT used.

2. Develop your own linear measurement system and discuss the difficulties you might encounter as you use this system.

3. Discuss the advantages and disadvantages of the United States adopting the metric system.

4. Discuss measurement situations in which fractions are most useful and situations when decimals are most useful.

5. Discuss appropriate measuring instruments for each grade level range—preK to 2, 3 to 5, 6 to 8.

6. Discuss the similarities and differences between addition of whole numbers and addition of denominate numbers.

7. Compare and contrast addition of measures in U.S. customary units and addition of measures in metric units.

8. Discuss and compare operations using U.S. customary measurement with those using the metric system.

9. Describe two models you might create to help convince a child of the relative values of coins and groups of coins.

10. Examine how several elementary school mathematics textbooks teach children how to tell time. Discuss the similarities and differences between methods used by other elementary textbooks and the method used in this text to introduce the concepts of time.

11. In what ways would you integrate measurement topics with other subjects explored at the preK to 2, 3 to 5, and 6 to 8 grade levels?

12. Identify and discuss the uses of a metric interest center (mathematics metric lab) within the classroom.

SAMPLE INSTRUCTIONAL AND ASSESSMENT ACTIVITIES

These activities and more are available on the CD that accompanies this text

1. Have sticks of various lengths available. Ask children to measure the width of the room in stick-length units. Repeat the activity using sticks of greater length and sticks of shorter length. Have children compare and discuss the results; then decide which stick length is the most practical to use for this project. Give children ample time to follow through on this activity. Have groups of three or four children work together measuring various objects or distances in the classroom. Ask them to compare their results and present their findings to the class for discussion.

2. Select groups to work together measuring objects that you have already measured. Have each group record its results and then check to see if its measurements are reasonably correct. Take into account that many children may lack the dexterity and coordination needed to obtain fairly accurate results.

VM 15.1

3. Allow the children to discover the relationships among standard units of liquid measure (gallon, quart, pint). Provide the children with standard-sized containers, and let them pour sand from the smaller containers into the larger containers. Be sure to have the children keep records of their findings.

4. Present a variety of activities related to the number line from 0 to 12. You can present many addition and subtraction activities that will develop readiness for telling time.

After these activities, review counting by fives, and present many experiences that involve counting by fives from 0 to 60. Supplement these activities with work on the number line from 0 to 60. Label only those points that correspond to multiples of five.

Relate the two number line diagrams. Be sure that children do not become confused by the use of different unit lengths in the two number line diagrams.

5. In teaching children about money, use real money. If play money is used, the children must jump to one more level of abstraction to associate each unit of play money with the corresponding unit of real money. To avoid loss of money, try "buying" something from the child (such as a shoe) for a fixed amount (say, 75 cents). Place a large box in the room, and have each child put one shoe in it; then give each child 75 cents. At the end of the period when each child returns the 75 cents, he or she gets the shoe back.

6. Multiple-use overhead transparencies are valuable in working with children. Make two transparencies, one with clock faces and one with the hands of the clock. The centers of the clocks and the hands should be positioned at the vertices of a square, as in the following example:

    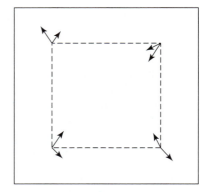

The dotted lines should not be on the transparency; these are only shown to help you make the transparency. Note that the transparency with the hands can be rotated so that it can be placed on the clock faces four different ways. If you rotate the transparency with the clock hands 90 degrees, you will have 4 more clock faces for children to read. This will provide 4 clocks to read in each position, and with four positions you have 16 clocks to read.

Now you can flip over the transparency and place it on the clocks again. Rotate the transparency; you will have another 16 clocks for the children to read. This will provide a total of 32 clock faces for the children.

7. Allow the children to compare the weights of various objects in the classroom to a 1-pound weight or a 1-ounce weight. Use this activity only to compare weights, not to determine the actual weight of an object. You may also want to have the children use metric weights, such as a kilogram, but, as with U.S. customary measures, the emphasis should be exclusively on heavier or lighter, not on actual measure.

8. The grocery store has three brands of soup. Brand A weighs 539 grams and costs $.69. Brand B weighs 305 grams and costs $.32. Brand C weighs 553 grams and costs $1.29. Which brand is the best buy? Use the unit price to make a valid comparison.

Brand A .69/539 = .0012801

Brand B .32/305 = .0010491

Brand C 1 .29/553 = .0023327

Brand B seems to be the best buy, since you pay. 0010491 cent (less than a penny) per ounce for the soup. Which other factors would you consider in order to determine what you think would be the best buy?

9. Use the constant key and set up the calculator to solve many examples of changing feet to yards. Enter the following into the calculator:

$$\boxed{1}\ \boxed{2}\ \boxed{\div}\ \boxed{3}\ \boxed{=}$$

$$(12 \div 3 =)$$

Now you can enter any number of feet and press the equals key; the display screen will show the number of yards. Try using

$$\boxed{2}\ \boxed{4}\ \boxed{=}$$

$$(24 =)$$

An 8 should appear on the display screen. This is the number of yards that equals 24 feet. Try several more examples.

16

Geometry: Basic Concepts and Structures

TEACHING COMPETENCIES

Upon completing this chapter, you will be able to:

- Justify the importance of geometry in the elementary and middle school curriculum.
- Use correct terminology and mathematical notation for figures such as lines, line segments, rays, and angles.
- Classify angles according to their measures and according to their relationship to one another.
- Identify and describe various models and materials that can be used with children to explore geometric concepts.
- Use a straightedge and compass to produce basic geometric constructions.
- Describe fundamental concepts and properties of symmetry.
- Describe fundamental concepts and properties of transformational geometry.
- Prepare lessons on the development of foundational geometric concepts, structures, and terminology for children in grades preK to 2, 3 to 5, and 6 to 8.

VIRTUAL MANIPULATIVES

Upon completing this chapter, you will be able to use virtual manipulatives on the accompanying CD to:

- Develop spatial perception using *Space Blocks*. **(VM 16.1)**
- Examine transformational geometry concepts such as symmetry, slides, flips, and turns using *Translations, Reflections, Rotations*. **(VM 16.2a; VM16.2b; VM 16.2c)**
- Explore a variety of basic geometric concepts using *Geoboard*. **(VM 16.3)**
- Investigate spatial perception and basic geometric concepts using *Tangrams*. **(VM 16.4)**

Numbered CD icons throughout the chapter refer to the virtual manipulatives in this list.

Consider the following excerpt, adapted from the IDEAS section of an issue of National Council of Teachers of Mathematics (NCTM) journal *Teaching Children Mathematics*:

A child lives at the corner of First Avenue and Elm Street. The school is at Fourth and Oak. In order to walk to school the child needs to follow the streets shown on the map below. Because of houses, fences, and other obstacles it isn't possible to take any shortcuts through the blocks. There are lots of different ways to go, but a direct route from home to school always goes east or south, never west or north.

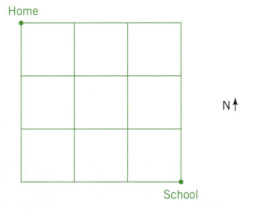

Find a direct route and determine how many blocks long it is. How many different direct routes are there?

Is there one direct route that is shorter than any other?

The next day the child decides to take the school bus. The figure below shows the locations of the bus stops between the child's home and the school. Luckily, the last stop the bus makes before heading back to school is right in front of the child's house! Trace any route that goes from the school through all of the bus stops and back to school. (The bus can travel north, south, east, or west.)

Is the route you traced the shortest route? Describe the shortest route that goes through each stop. What is the minimum length of a school bus route that goes through each stop, but goes through stop A first?

What does this activity have to do with basic geometric concepts? You may recognize the street maps as grids made up of line segments. The locations of the

RESEARCH SNAPSHOT

How might knowledge of the van Hiele model influence a teacher's classroom decision-making?

In Chapter 1, the van Hiele model, a theory that identifies five levels of thinking in geometry, was introduced. Van Hiele characterized his model as hierarchical. That is, thinking at level 2 is not possible without mastery of level 1. As you read about the geometric concepts in Chapters 16 and 17, think about how you might use the van Hiele model in your classroom.

In a study of 309 students, ages 11 to 18, Gutierrez and Jaime (1998) identified different processes of reasoning as characteristics of several van Hiele levels: use of definitions, formulation of definitions, classification, and proof.

Results showed that students were not at specific van Hiele levels but could show progress in some ability at higher levels without complete acquisition of lower levels. So, instead of the classical belief that a student was at either level 1 or level 2, students were assessed in the study using some of the processes that underlie the van Hiele levels. What sort of activities might you structure to assist you in identifying the van Hiele levels of children in the classroom?

Gutierrez, A., & Jaime, A. (1998). On the assessment of the van Hiele levels of reasoning. *Focus on Learning Problems in Mathematics, 20*, 27–46.

For additional research briefs, "ERIC Digests" lets you search more than 2000 short syntheses of research on a range of education topics. The syntheses were produced by the Educational Resources Information Center (ERIC). Check http://www.ericfacility.net/ericdigests/index/.

house, school, and bus stops can all be represented by points on these segments. The routes can be thought of as paths or networks that traverse these grids and form either simple or nonsimple, closed or open curves. In fact, the subject of network theory is one branch of the important field of discrete mathematics that deals with practical concerns such as optimizing schedules and routes for airlines, trucking companies, and the like. Most young children are familiar with the underlying concepts of network theory through informal activities such as finding different ways to walk or ride to a friend's house or the mall.

It has been found that children develop a sense of their world by observing geometric concepts and shapes around them; they learn by observation and intuitive processes rather than by complex or formal analysis. According to the NCTM *Principles and Standards for School Mathematics*, the development of geometric and spatial knowledge begins before schooling and is stimulated by exploration of shapes and structures in the child's environment. Foundational geometric ideas discussed in this chapter help children represent, describe, and communicate an understanding of the mathematics of their world.

Early Experiences in Geometry

Children have had many experiences with geometry before they enter school. The blocks that children play with are often cubes, prisms, and cylinders. Children develop informal, intuitive understandings about geometry from their own play and observation, but they usually do not have ample opportunities and, sometimes, are not developmentally ready to verbalize their discoveries. For instance, when building a tower, children often select an appropriate block for their immediate building needs and yet may not be able to use even unsophisticated geometric vocabulary to explain the reasons for their choice.

Consider the following:

In the drawing on the left, the top block is unstable; on the right, it is stable. Children usually perceive this and choose the configuration of blocks on the right as a base on which they continue to build. Intuitively, with experience manipulating various objects, children learn

to compare blocks and develop the ability to visualize the geometric shapes.

In addition to helping children develop the vocabulary needed to describe their observations and actions, teachers also need to help children develop spatial perception. The development of spatial perception seems a logical component of elementary mathematics curricula since, according to Piagetian theory, many elementary-age children are still in the sensorimotor or concrete operational stages: They learn by interacting with their environment. Several skills or abilities have been identified as components of spatial perception. Those that seem to have a particular relevance to the study of geometry are eye-motor coordination, figure-ground perception, perceptual constancy, position-in-space perception, visual discrimination, visual memory, and perception of spatial relationships. A description and example of each follows.

Eye-motor coordination involves the ability to match visual inputs with appropriate motor responses. In the activity previously described in which children place a block across the top of two other blocks, children with poor eye-motor coordination would find balancing the crossbar laborious, even if the upright blocks are the same height. These students may have difficulty focusing on geometric concepts since they use working memory to concentrate on motor skills and movements rather than the geometric concepts that may be embedded within the activity.

Figure-ground perception is the ability to locate figures hidden in a complex background. An example of an activity that uses this skill is the hidden figures puzzles that appear in children's magazines or the puzzles that ask children to determine, for example, how many triangles are shown in this figure (five).

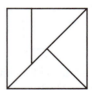

Perceptual constancy refers to the ability to recognize a shape regardless of size, shadings, or orientation in space. Until about age 8, many children recognize a square when one edge is in a horizontal position but claim it is no longer a square when it has been rotated so that it "stands on a point" as in the following figure:

square   square?

Position-in-space perception is the ability to relate an object's position to one's own position. Terms such as *before/behind*, *left/right*, and *above/below* involve position-in-space perception. Primary-age children who demonstrate reversals in reading or writing words or numerals typically have poor position-in-space perception. Perception of spatial relationships is a more advanced ability. It involves not only the ability to relate objects to one's own position, but also the ability to relate the positions of two or more objects to each other. Both of these spatial abilities come into play when children work with manipulative materials and may even affect their learning of nongeometric topics, such as place value or computational algorithms.

Visual discrimination is the ability to perceive similarities and differences, while visual memory is the ability to accurately recall objects no longer in view. Children's activity books often have games and puzzles that develop these skills. For example, visual discrimination is involved when children are shown several pictures, two of which are identical, and are asked to find the matching pair. In a game involving visual memory, children are shown a tray filled with common objects and given one or two minutes to memorize the objects on the tray. While the children are not looking, an object is then removed from the tray, and they must determine which object was removed.

To help children develop **spatial perception**, let them make use of three blocks, such as a cube, a prism, and a pyramid, and provide them with directions to follow in arranging the blocks—for example:

Place the pyramid in front of the cube.   Place the cube on top of the prism.   Place the prism behind the cube.

Using blocks or pictures of common items, illustrate words of position and spatial arrangement for the children. A suggested list of contrasting descriptors might include the following:

under/over	above/below	first/last
in front of/behind	high/low	far/near
right/left	inside/outside	

Also include positional situations that have more than two descriptors, such as beside/by/next to and bottom/middle/top.

Although generally defined and discussed in isolation, activities designed to develop one particular spatial skill often serve to enhance others. Development of these skills also provides teachers with many opportunities to integrate mathematics with other content areas, such as art or physical education. Even though several of the spatial skills discussed here are considered most appropriate for the early childhood curriculum, upper elementary and middle-grade teachers should include them in their curricula since spatial thinking is related to success in higher-level mathematics, such as high school geometry and calculus.

Spatial perception skills can be a challenge and a source of anxiety for some students. As a means of building a foundation for future success with visualization, it is wise to provide children with many formal and informal experiences in sorting, classifying, and 'playing' with materials such as attribute pieces, pattern blocks, and geoblocks. Check teachers' manuals and articles in the bibliography for this chapter on the accompanying CD for instructions on using these materials. Also, the use of the virtual manipulative *Space Blocks* (provided with this text on the accompanying CD) will offer children experiences that will assist with the development of spatial perception.

The "Building Blocks" of Geometry

Certain basic concepts of geometry—such as *point, space, curve, line, line segment, ray, angle,* and numerous *polygons* and *polyhedra*—must be explored before students are ready for the formal study of geometry that typically occurs in high school. There are at least two sequences that might be followed to introduce students to these concepts.

One sequence, which relies heavily on child development levels, begins with three-dimensional shapes, since they can be represented by concrete materials; builds understanding of two-dimensional shapes through studying the faces and edges of the three-dimensional figures; and concludes with the abstract concepts of one-dimensional and zero-dimensional figures—that is, line, line segment, ray, and point.

Another sequence, based more on mathematical structure and logic and less on child development, begins with the abstract concept of *point*. Under this organization, one-dimensional figures are studied as a collection of points. Two-dimensional and three-dimensional figures logically follow.

It is the opinion of the authors of this text that a developmentally appropriate organization is best used with children. However, since this text is designed for preservice and inservice teachers, rather than children directly, the more mathematical sequence (beginning with point and progressing to three-dimensional figures) is the one followed here. We highly recommend that teachers in the primary grades consider initiating the exploration of geometric concepts with young children by beginning with examples of everyday models of three-dimensional figures and, eventually, working backward to the notion of point.

Some fundamental geometric concepts, such as point, are undefined terms. Such terms provide a foundation for the development of the language of geometry and the base from which conjectures can grow. We can attach meaning to these undefined terms only by assuming particular properties about them. Basic statements, assumed to be true, that express these fundamental assumptions in geometry are called **axioms** or **postulates**.

As mentioned earlier, the term *point* is an example of an undefined term in geometry. Although this is not a definition, a geometric **point** can be thought of as an immovable or fixed location in geometric space. Similarly, geometric **space**, which is also undefined, can be thought of as the set of all points. Geometric space and geometric points, like numbers, are abstractions—they don't *physically* exist in the real world.

We cannot see a geometric point because, unlike a pencil point or chalk mark, a geometric point has no physical length, width, or thickness—only a position. When we pinpoint the location of an object, we are specifying its position as precisely as we know how. We can think of a geometric point as providing the most precise way possible of specifying a particular position.

Geometric points and geometric space are ideas with no actual physical existence. In constructing figures, however, we often illustrate geometric ideas by using physical representations—dots and lines drawn on paper or the chalkboard. Just as a number is an idea, physically represented by a numeral, so is a geometric point an idea, physically represented by a dot. The dot we draw is a convenient representation. No matter how small we make our physical dot, it still represents infinitely many geometric points; nevertheless, a dot is the most satisfactory way we have of representing the concept of a geometric point. Points represented by dots are usually labeled with capital letters, as in the following example:

- A   (read, "point A")

What is a plane? To understand the concept of a geometric **plane**, think of a flat tabletop. Imagine the surface of the tabletop extending horizontally in all directions limitlessly.

The flat surface of this table extended horizontally in all directions without end suggests a model of a geometric plane. Like all other geometric figures, a plane is a set of points. A plane is a subset of space. An elementary school child is best introduced to the concept of plane through physical representations of parts of planes. The simplest representations for a child to understand are the surfaces of a desk, a wall, a chalkboard, a sheet of paper, a book cover, the floor of a basketball court, and so on. If your classroom has a large window, you might use it as a starting model of a plane region and have children note that if it were removed, the place (points) where it was still remains. Now imagine this set of points extended in all directions (left, right, up, and down) indefinitely. This exercise should help you develop an understanding of a geometric plane.

A small sheet of cardboard, even an index card, may also be used to represent a part of a plane. Have two students each hold a sharpened pencil with the point up. Attempts to balance the cardboard (representing a plane) on the two pencil points (representing two points) will not be successful. But if another student holds a third pencil relatively near the other two (but not in line with them), the cardboard will rest steadily on the three pencils.

Teachers can reinforce this fact by asking why a three-legged stool never wobbles, even if each of the three legs has a different length. If you have access to a photographic tripod, you might also demonstrate this property. Each of these situations emphasizes an important geometric fact: Any three points not in a straight line determine a unique plane (or flat surface). That is, if three points are not in a straight line, how many planes can be passed through them? Only one. It is not possible to place a different cardboard on the three pencil points—it would lie in the same plane as the first sheet of cardboard.

The shortest or most direct path between two given points in space is called a *line segment*. A **line segment** is a set of points in a plane that represents the shortest distance between two given points. A line segment has a first (or initial) point and a last (or terminal) point. These are called the end points. A line segment has a definite length—the distance between the two end points. The symbol for the line segment from point A to point B (with the end points included) is $\overline{AB}$ and is read "line segment AB." A tightly stretched string is a good physical representation of a line segment. Many students will recognize the line segments drawn on roadways that separate traffic lanes. Other models include the edges of a chalkboard, the edges of a page, and so on. What others can you think of?

The concept of line is also undefined in geometry. A **line** is a set of points and therefore a subset of space. If we draw a representation of a line segment on paper with pencil and straightedge and imagine that this representation is extended endlessly in opposite directions, the result can be thought of as a geometric line. To help children understand the concept of a line, ask them to imagine line segments extending from their pencil points to

1. The doorknob (have the end points named in each case)
2. The top of the school flagpole
3. The top of the Washington Monument, the Empire State Building, or some other prominent (and pointed) landmark with which they are familiar
4. A distant star

Having stretched their imaginations to envision the two end points of an imaginary line segment, the children should now be ready for the broader concept of line.

A line has no end points but continues endlessly in each of two opposite directions. To represent a line, we draw a line segment and place arrowheads at each end to show that the line has no end points but extends endlessly in both directions.

We often name a line by using a single lowercase letter or by labeling two points on the line. We can refer to the figure in the drawing below as "line RS" or "line Sr."

Line RS is also indicated by the symbol $\overleftrightarrow{RS}$. When we name two points on a line, we have also named a line segment—in this case, line segment RS, or $\overline{RS}$. Every line segment is a subset of a line. It would be helpful to explain to children that *segment* means "part." Line segment RS is a subset, or part, of line RS.

Extending the Basics—Curves, Regions, and Rays

We have established that a line segment consists of a set of points in a plane and is therefore a subset of space. As mentioned, line segment AB is also described as the *shortest path* between the two points, A and B, in a plane.

A •————————————• B

There are other paths, however, between points A and B. Some of these are illustrated in the following diagram:

All of the paths connecting any two given points are examples of curves. In the previous diagram, the curves that are represented are called *simple curves* because the curve doesn't pass through the same point twice. A **simple curve** is defined as a curve that passes through no point more than once. A line segment is a special kind of simple curve. The mathematical term *curve* is defined differently than the everyday use of the word. A mathematical curve *might* be a straight line or line segment, while, for example, a highway curve brings a different image to mind.

A **closed curve** is a curve that returns to its starting point. A closed curve has no end points. A **simple closed curve**, then, is a curve that returns to its starting point without crossing itself at any point. Is a triangle a simple closed curve? Yes. Some other examples of simple closed curves are represented in the following diagram:

Students should practice drawing simple closed curves, including simple closed curves that pass through one, two, three, or more given points.

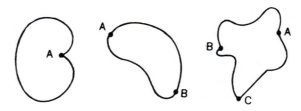

The possibilities are limitless.

Careful notice should be taken of the fact that a curve that crosses itself does not form a simple closed curve. None of the following is a simple closed curve:

Any curve that forms a simple closed curve separates the plane in which it lies into three sets of points:

1. The set of points comprising the simple closed curve itself

2. The set of points comprising the interior of the simple closed curve

3. The set of points comprising the exterior of the simple closed curve

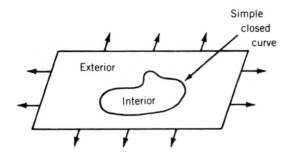

The set of points formed by the union of a simple closed curve and its interior is referred to as a *simple closed region*.

A **ray** is another subset of a line. It consists of a point on the line and all points on the line extending in one direction from that point.

The point from which the ray extends is part of the ray and is called the end point, or the initial point, of the ray. For example, on the following line, we have marked point A:

This point is the end point (or initial point) of two rays, one beginning at point A and extending endlessly to the right, the other beginning at point A and extending endlessly to the left. Obviously, an infinite number of rays are contained in a line, since any point on the line can be selected as an end point and there are an infinite number of points on the line.

By naming a point on either side of point A, we can now name the two rays (sometimes referred to as opposite rays) that extend from this point.

We can name a ray with two letters, representing two points, as $\overrightarrow{AB}$. This name represents the ray that starts at point A and extends endlessly to the right (through point B). The bar with one arrowhead on it indicates that a ray

is being named, and the fact that there is no arrowhead above the A indicates that point A is the end point of the ray. Similarly, $\overleftarrow{AC}$. represents the ray that starts at point A and extends endlessly to the left (through point C). It is interesting to note that the two rays, ray AB and ray AC, have only one point in common, that being point A.

A commonly used physical representation of a ray is a flashlight or searchlight beam. A child can readily imagine a beam of light beginning at the flashlight and continuing endlessly in space in one direction.

With these concepts in mind, children's intuitive perception can be developed. With pencil and straightedge, they can practice drawing lines on paper and, as symbols are introduced, add these to their drawings. Note that the lines do not always have to be drawn horizontally—in fact, doing so may give a false impression—any direction is, of course, satisfactory.

Remember that when a student uses a straightedge to draw a line segment (or any other geometric figure), he or she is picturing only a representation of the abstract geometric figure. It is no more correct to say that what has been drawn is a line segment than it is to say that a sketch of a person is a human being. Again, the distinction between words in mathematical language and words in everyday language must be made. A question to deliberate is, "At what developmental level should we try to make this distinction clear to children?"

Next, children should practice drawing lines through a given point. They may discover that there is (theoretically) no limit to the number of lines that they can draw through any one point. An interesting discussion may ensue by having children draw several lines through a point, first using a blunt crayon, then a dull pencil, and finally an ultrafine-point pen. This activity should help them realize that their ability to draw many lines through a point is influenced by the thickness of the instrument used. Infinitely many abstract lines can be drawn through a given point since abstract lines have no thickness.

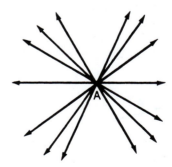

At this stage, children are ready to examine a line through two distinct points. Have them mark two points on a sheet of paper and label them. Then have them draw lines through the two points. They soon realize that only one straight line can be drawn through two points. Because they are marking dots with a pencil to represent points, children may try to draw two or more lines through two points. Remind them that their pencil-drawn dots should be as small as possible (they will still cover many geometric points) so that only one line will pass through two points.

In these exercises, the lines children draw through two points should extend beyond the points. The children can then reinforce the concept of a line segment by drawing a figure that does not extend beyond two points. When drawn this way, it is evident that the segment has a definite length (between the end points). The children can emphasize this fact by drawing more line segments between any two marked points. Practice in drawing geometric figures should be given through exercises such as the following:

1. Draw a line, mark and name four points on the line, and use these points to name the line in several different ways.

(↔AB, ↔AR, ↔AS, ↔BR, ↔BS, and ↔RS)

2. Given point A, draw lines through point A.

3. Given two points, A and B, draw a line through them.

4. Draw a line segment, name seven points on the line segment, and then use these points to name different line segments.

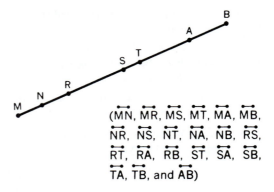

(↔MN, ↔MR, ↔MS, ↔MT, ↔MA, ↔MB, ↔NR, ↔NS, ↔NT, ↔NA, ↔NB, ↔RS, ↔RT, ↔RA, ↔RB, ↔ST, ↔SA, ↔SB, ↔TA, ↔TB, and ↔AB)

5. Given point R, draw a ray with point R as the end point, and name the ray by naming any other point on the ray.

This is ray RT. The first letter always indicates the end point of a ray.

If children understand what these drawings represent, they will have no difficulty with later drawings and concepts. All figures are built with the basic building blocks that we have studied so far in this chapter. They are illustrated in the following diagram:

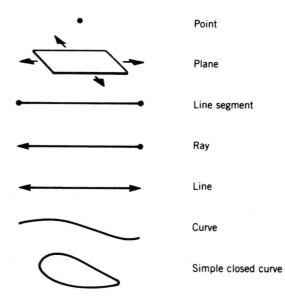

By way of review, although books differ, this text leaves the concepts of space and point as undefined. Space is understood to be the set of all points. Conversely points are understood to be locations in space. A line segment is defined as a set of points that forms the shortest path between two points. A geometric line is undefined. It extends endlessly in opposite directions. A ray is defined as part of a line consisting of a point on the line and all the points on the line extending endlessly in one direction from the initial point.

Angles and Angle Measure

An **angle** is defined in most mathematics programs as the union of two rays that have a common end point. The common end point of the two rays is called the **vertex** of the angle, and each of the two rays is called a **side** of the angle. To name an angle, we usually name three points on the angle—the vertex and a point on each of the two sides. In the following diagram, the angle is named by the three points C, A, and B:

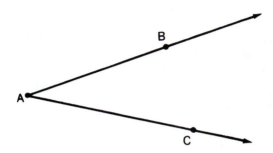

In symbols, we can name the angle as ∠BAC. Notice that the vertex, labeled A, is the second point named in the expression ∠BAC. When we name any angle this way, the vertex is always listed between two other points. This angle could also be named ∠CAB.

Any angle divides the plane in which it lies into three sets of points:

1. The set of points comprising the angle itself
2. The set of points comprising the interior of the angle
3. The set of points comprising the exterior of the angle

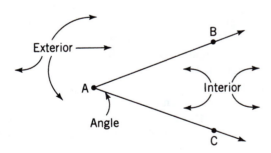

One standard unit of angle measure is called a **degree**. The number of degrees measures the amount of rotation between the sides of an angle. In more advanced mathematics, this rotation may be clockwise or counterclockwise and may range from 0 to 360 degrees (and even more). In the elementary grades, we *most commonly* measure angles as counterclockwise rotations from an initial ray to a terminal ray with angle measure ranging from greater than 0 degrees to less than or equal to 180 degrees. For example:

A young child will not typically be concerned with the measurement of angles. By grades 3, 4, or 5, however, the student should be able to use a simple **protractor** to draw angles of a given measure or to determine angle measure. It is probably best to use a single-scale protractor with counterclockwise measures. When using a single-scale protractor, position it so that the initial ray of the angle to be measured is set on the zero mark. To determine the measure of an angle, place the protractor with its horizontal center point on the vertex of the angle (B in the figure) and its base parallel to one of the sides (ray BC in the figure). In the following diagram, the measure of ∠ABC (50°) is read directly on the inside semicircular scale:

The symbol *m*∠ABC represents the measure of ∠ABC. Thus, *m*∠ABC = 50°. [NOTE: The use of a protractor with a "double scale" (as in the figure) may be inappropriate at this point due to confusion over which scale to use—the counterclockwise or the clockwise.]

Since many primary-school children have an intuitive understanding of the concept of angle, they should practice drawing angles of all sizes. To learn that an angle is the union of two rays with a common end point, they should practice by naming a point and then drawing any two rays from that point. For example:

Again, encourage the children to draw angles that open in different directions. Teachers tend to draw angles on chalkboards with a horizontal ray or base. They should give themselves the same freedom to draw angles in many positions on the chalkboard.

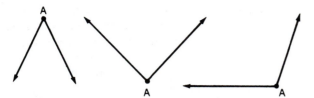

Note that drawings such as the following are incorrect (by our definition of angle) and should be discouraged. These are not two rays sharing a common end point.

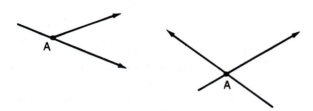

Suppose we have two angles such as the following and we wish to compare them to see whether they have the same size (or measure):

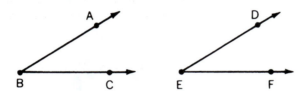

On another sheet of paper, trace ∠ABC and call it ∠A'B'C' (read "angle A prime, B prime, C prime"). We can compare ∠ABC with ∠DEF by putting the tracing ∠A'B'C' on top of ∠DEF. If we place the tracing ∠A'B'C' on ∠DEF so that $\vec{B'C'}$ falls on $\vec{EF}$, we can decide whether ∠ABC has the same measure as ∠DEF. If, after we have placed point B' over point E and $\vec{B'C'}$ over $\vec{EF}$, we find that $\vec{B'A'}$ coincides with $\vec{ED}$, then we know that the two angles have the same measure. If ∠ABC and ∠DEF have the same measure, we say that they are **congruent** or that ∠ABC "is congruent to" ∠DEF. The symbol (≅) is used to indicate congruence, so we can write ∠ABC ≅ ∠DEF. This is read, "angle ABC is congruent to angle DEF." That is, *m* ∠ABC = *m* ∠DEF.

Angles are sometimes classified according to their properties, some of which we will now examine. Consider $\overleftrightarrow{AB}$. Point C on $\overleftrightarrow{AB}$ and point D not on $\overleftrightarrow{AB}$. Point C is marked directly under point D.

Now draw ray CD.

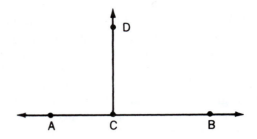

Ray CD determines two angles, ∠ACD and ∠BCD. If these two angles are congruent, then they are called right angles, and $\overleftrightarrow{CD}$ is said to be **perpendicular** to $\overleftrightarrow{AB}$ (in mathematical symbols, $\overleftrightarrow{CD} \perp \overleftrightarrow{AB}$). A right angle has a measure of 90°.

Consider $\overleftrightarrow{XY}$, point O not on $\overleftrightarrow{XY}$, and point Z on $\overleftrightarrow{XY}$. Ray ZO is drawn.

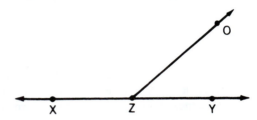

Trace ∠YZO on another sheet of paper, and label the tracing ∠Y'Z'O'. Then compare the tracing ∠Y'Z'O' with ∠BCD (the right angle in the previous example). Place the tracing so that point Z' falls on point C and $\vec{Z'Y'}$ falls on $\overleftrightarrow{CB}$. Clearly, ∠Y'Z'O' is not congruent to ∠BCD; therefore ∠YZO is not congruent to ∠BCD. Since ∠YZO is less than a right angle, we call ∠YZO an **acute angle**, which can be defined as an angle that is less than a right angle, or an angle whose measure is less than 90°. Using symbols, we can compare the measures of angle BCD and angle YZO in the following way: *m*∠YZO < *m*∠DCB. This is read "the measure in degrees of angle YZO is less than the measure in degrees of angle DCB" or simply "angle YZO is less than angle DCB."

Now let's examine another situation in which we have line MN and point E on $\overleftrightarrow{MN}$. Another point, G, not on $\overleftrightarrow{MN}$ is marked, and $\overleftrightarrow{EG}$ is drawn.

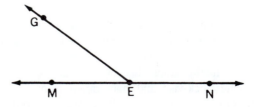

Trace ∠NEG on another sheet of paper, and label the tracing ∠N'E'G'. Compare ∠N'E'G' with ∠BCD (the right angle in the earlier example) by placing point E' on point C and $\vec{E'N'}$ on $\overleftrightarrow{CB}$. Clearly, ∠N'E'G' is not congruent to ∠BCD, and therefore ∠NEG is not congruent to ∠BCD. Since angle NEG has a measure greater than a right angle but less than 180°, we call angle NEG an *obtuse angle*. Using symbols, we can compare the measures of angle NEG and angle BCD as follows: *m*∠NEG > *m*∠BCD. This is read, "the measure in degrees of angle NEG is greater than the measure in degrees of angle BCD" or simply "angle NEG is greater than angle BCD." An **obtuse angle** can be defined as an angle whose measure is greater than 90° but less than 180°. (An angle with a measure of exactly 180° is usually called a **straight angle**. Consequently, a line is a representation of a straight angle.)

We can point out physical representations of right angles in the classroom. The corner of the room, for example, suggests several right angles.

The corners of a window or a chalkboard are also convenient representations of right angles. Another representation of a right angle is the corner of a sheet of paper such as a page of this book. Children will probably see the notion of right angle best as the "square corner" of some object. They should be able to draw approximate representations of right angles using any object with a rigid square corner.

Let's consider names for angle relationships that are based on their relative positions and measures. What statements can we make about the following angles: ∠DOC and ∠COB?

We see that angle DOC and angle COB have a common vertex, point O. The two angles also have a common ray, $\overrightarrow{OC}$, between them. Two angles with a common vertex and a common ray (or side) between them are called **adjacent angles**. In the preceding diagram, angle DOC is adjacent to angle COB.

Whenever two lines intersect, four angles are formed. The angles that are opposite each other are called **vertical angles**. ∠XOY and ∠WOZ are vertical angles and ∠YOW and ∠XOZ are vertical angles.

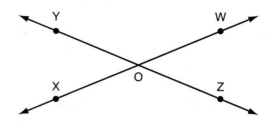

∠XOY and ∠WOZ are vertical angles and ∠YOW and ∠XOZ are vertical angles

If the sum of the measures of two angles is equal to the measure of a right angle (90°), the two angles are said to be **complementary angles**. In the following diagram, if $\overleftrightarrow{OU}$ is perpendicular to $\overleftrightarrow{ST}$, that is, if ∠SOU and ∠UOT are right angles, then ∠UOV and ∠VOT are complementary angles, since the sum of the measures of ∠UOV and ∠VOT is equal to the measure of the right angle UOT.

$$m(\angle UOV) + m(\angle VOT) = m(\angle UOT)$$

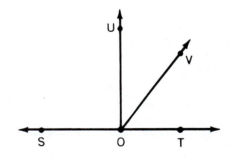

Two angles do not have to be adjacent (as angle UOV and angle VOT are) to be complementary angles. In the following diagram, angle JEK and angle LEM are complementary, because the sum of their measures is 90°:

If the sum of the measures of two angles is equal to 180°, then the two angles are said to be **supplementary angles**. In the following diagram, angle BEC and angle CED are supplementary because the sum of their measures is equal to 180°.

$$m(\angle BEC) + m(\angle CED) = 180°$$

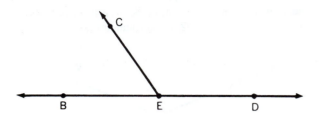

In this case, angle BEC and angle CED are also adjacent angles, but two angles that are not adjacent can still be supplementary. In the following diagram, angle NUP and angle QUR are supplementary because the sum of their measures is 180°, even though they're not adjacent.

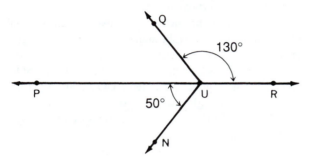

In some instances, adjacent angles may be congruent. For example, consider the following diagram:

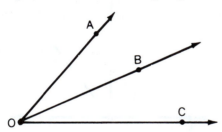

Clearly, angle AOB and angle BOC are adjacent angles. Trace ∠AOB and label the tracing ∠A′O′B′. Place the tracing so that O′ falls on point O and ray O′B′ falls on ray OC. We see that angle AOB is congruent to angle BOC. Since ∠AOB is congruent to ∠BOC, ray OB is said to bisect ∠AOC. To **bisect** is to divide in half. Since ∠AOB is congruent to ∠BOC, the measures of these two angles are equal. Therefore ray OB bisects angle AOC.

Exploring Geometric Constructions

As well as knowing the vocabulary related to lines and angles, older elementary-school and middle-school children should examine basic procedures for constructing lines and angles. This examination should occur in two distinct ways—one way is to make use of the technology at hand to perform these procedures and the other should

include the exploration of the use of more classical tools. Several excellent, relatively inexpensive computer software packages are available that incorporate elements of computer-assisted design to perform these constructions (see Chapter 4). For example, Geometer's Sketchpad, Electronic Geoboard, and Elastic Lines include, among other things, the capabilities of constructing parallels, perpendiculars, and angles of various sizes and types. These programs are tools that alleviate the potential drudgery of some constructions and allow the user to concentrate on the underlying problem or concept.

Consider the following question:

What is the definition of a median of a triangle?

A student might locate a mathematics text and discover that, in that particular book, a median is defined as a segment joining a vertex of a triangle to the midpoint of the opposite side. Examination of other books may lead to alternative definitions. Not all books define geometric terms in the same way.

As an alternative to looking up the answer to the question in one or many books, the student might use a software package to explore the meaning of the term by directing the computer to draw a median in triangle DEF from angle E.

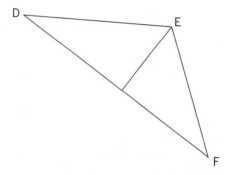

The student could then use the features of the software to measure the side cut by the median and note that it is divided into two equivalent segments. Furthermore, the student might then discover that the two new triangles formed by the construction of the median have equal areas. Will this *always* be the case?

A major advantage to such software packages is that they create an environment that encourages formulating hypotheses and making conjectures. Each of the software packages can generate a given construction many times over. Through the use of this repetitive feature, the student can easily recreate this process and measurement on various triangles to discover that, indeed, it appears that a median cuts a triangle into two triangles of equal area. The student has discovered an alternative definition of median that would not have been found if only the textbook had been consulted. This is an example of an informal approach to geometry in the elementary grades that provides a base for a more structured look at proof in later grades.

Although it is possible to model geometric constructions with dynamic drawing software packages, the classical tools for geometric constructions include the straightedge, the compass, and a sharp pencil. (A straightedge is simply a ruler without numerals or other marks on it. A **compass** is a scribing device with an adjustable radius used for drawing arcs.) A challenge in constructing geometric models in this manner lies in trying to draw accurate models without the use of a ruler (to measure lengths) or protractor (to measure angles).

Given the benefits derived from the use of technology in modeling the construction indicated in the example on medians, you may wonder why a student would ever resort to the use of traditional tools. The reason lies in the purpose. The technology performs the process for the user and allows the user the freedom to explore consequences. The use of a straightedge and compass focuses attention on the process itself and allows the student the opportunity to encounter basic structures as emerging concepts.

Let's begin with a simple exercise. Use a straightedge to construct a line segment, $\overleftrightarrow{AB}$.

Using the straightedge, construct another line segment, $\overleftrightarrow{XY}$, longer than $\overleftrightarrow{AB}$. Label any point C on the line segment.

Now, adjust your compass so that the fixed point is at point A on $\overleftrightarrow{AB}$ and the pencil of the compass falls on point B. The arc made by the compass should pass exactly through point B. Move the fixed compass point to point C, and draw an arc so that it intersects the line segment containing point C. Label this point of intersection point D.

We can say now that $\overleftrightarrow{CD}$ is congruent to $\overleftrightarrow{AB}$.

Now let's construct an angle, ∠JEF, congruent to a given angle, ∠ABC.

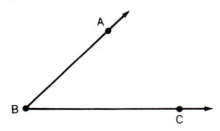

First, draw a ray and label it $\overrightarrow{EF}$.

With the fixed point on point B, set the compass at any convenient radius and draw an arc through the sides of angle ABC. Label the points of intersection of this arc and the sides of the angle as points G and H.

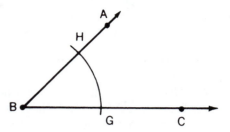

Using this same radius, set the fixed compass point on E, and draw an arc that intersects ray EF.

Label the point of intersection of the arc with $\overleftrightarrow{EF}$ as point I. With the compass, measure the distance from point G to point H. Using this measurement, draw an arc from point I that intersects the first arc we drew on this diagram. Label this intersection point J, and draw ray EJ with a straightedge and pencil.

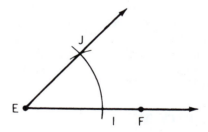

We can now say that ∠JEF is congruent to ∠ABC. (Note that arc GH in the earlier figure defines how wide the angle is open in much the same way as arc IJ does for the preceding figure.) For practice in construction, use this procedure to draw several other angles congruent to given angles.

Now let's consider the following angle, ∠RST, and construct the bisector of ∠RST:

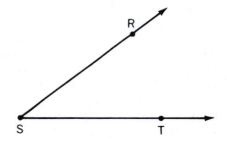

Placing the fixed point of the compass at point S, draw an arc so that it intersects ray SR and ray ST. Label the two points of intersection as point U and point V.

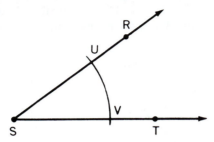

Placing the fixed point of the compass at point U, draw an arc between $\overleftrightarrow{ST}$ and $\overleftrightarrow{SR}$. Then, using the same setting on the compass, draw an arc from point V that intersects the arc made from point U. Label the intersection point M. Connect points S and M by means of a straightedge and pencil. The ray SM is the bisector of angle RST.

$$\angle RSM \cong \angle TSM$$

Exploring basic geometric constructions can provide students with a view of geometry that will serve them well in later studies. The structural nature of classic constructions can help them recognize the logic and connections applied in building paths from the simple to the complex—a foundational component of any axiomatic system.

Symmetry and Transformational Geometry

In high school, the student of geometry has the opportunity to study a deductive mathematical system in which results can be obtained through careful step-by-step logical reasoning, starting from basic assumptions called *axioms* or *postulates*. In the elementary grades, geometry is usually presented in an intuitive manner—a more informal approach. As such, elementary and middle-school children rely heavily on a visual approach to geometry. We want the students to become acquainted with some of the terminology of geometry, and we want them to perceive various kinds of relationships and properties between and among geometric figures.

An effective way to help students develop in these areas is to introduce some of the basic ideas of symmetry and geometric transformations. These ideas are helpful in exploring the properties of geometric figures.

According to the NCTM *Principles and Standards for School Mathematics*, "instructional programs should include attention to geometry and spatial sense so that all students recognize the usefulness of transformations and symmetry in analyzing mathematical situations" (NCTM, 2000, p. 61).

Most of us are familiar with figures that are symmetric about a line. In each of the following figures, the given figure is symmetric about the dotted line. The dotted line is called a **line of symmetry** for the figure.

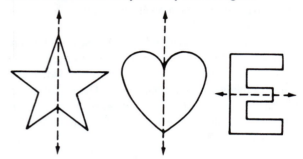

Have the children place a mirror on the line of symmetry of a figure and compare the figure and its reflection.

The Mira Math device is another excellent aid to use when introducing both geometric constructions and symmetry. "Mira" is the commercial name for a red plastic device that has a reflective as well as a transparent quality. It can be held in such a way as to display a reflection of a figure drawn on paper.

A Mira is especially helpful in studying **transformational geometry**—the geometry of flips (reflections), slides (translations), turns (rotations), and scaling (dilation). A Mira can also be used for the study of congruence; line segments; angles geometric shapes; and other geometric concepts, such as parallel and perpendicular lines. Consult the Mira Math teachers' manual for detailed instructions for teaching geometry with this unique device.

A Mira can also be used as an alternative to a straightedge and compass for numerous traditional construction activities. In that context, this device is used to verify constructions by reflections, rotations, and translations. For example, place a Mira vertical to the paper in many different places. How do you know when you have placed the Mira on a line of symmetry? If you were to trace any one of these figures, cut the figure out, and fold it along the dotted line, you would find that the parts on either side of the dotted line match perfectly. The part of the figure on one side of the dotted line is the "mirror image" of the part on the other side.

Symmetry with respect to a line can be described in mathematical terms. A figure is symmetric with respect to a line if each point P of the figure (where P is not on the line) has a matching point P′ on the other side of the line such that the line bisects $\overleftrightarrow{PP'}$ and is perpendicular to $\overleftrightarrow{PP'}$.

For example, consider the following heart-shaped figure:

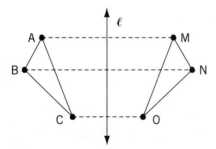

The point P′ is called the *image* of P in the line (or the image of P under **reflection** in the line). Similarly, the image of Q is Q′, the image of R is R′, and so on. We could also think of P as the image of P′, of Q as the image of Q′, and so on. The point V at the tip of the figure can be thought of as its own image; so can the point W labeled at the top of the figure. The word **flip** is often used in discussing the image or reflection of a figure about a line.

Now, look at the following diagram:

If we flip triangle ABC over the line, point A will fall on point M, point B will fall on point N, and point C will fall on point O. Thus we can speak of triangle MNO as the flip image of triangle ABC. The operation of flipping triangle ABC over the line to obtain triangle MNO is an example of a geometric transformation. For each point of the original figure, there is a matching point in the flip image.

Another kind of geometric transformation is known as a **translation**. Consider the following rectangle ABCD. Suppose we transform ABCD by matching each vertex with a point 2 units of measure farther down on the page.

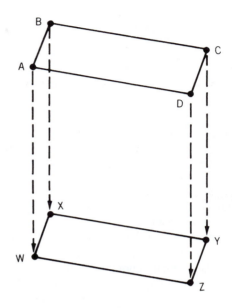

In a similar fashion, we can match every point on ABCD with a point 2 units lower. The resulting figure, WXYZ, is called the image of ABCD under a translation. When we use a translation of a figure, we are finding the figure that we would obtain if it were possible to give the rectangle a straight shove in a given direction and through a given distance. Some authors recommend that translations simply be called **slides**—a word suggesting an intuitive meaning of the concept of translation.

We can use an arrow to indicate both the direction and the distance of a translation. For example, we can indicate a translation of $1\frac{1}{2}$ inches to the right by an arrow $1\frac{1}{2}$ inches in length and pointing to the right. If we use such a translation on the following polygon ABCDEF, we get polygon RSTUVW as the image under the translation:

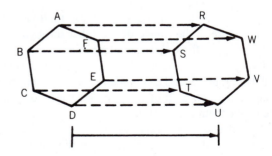

Each point of the image polygon is $1\frac{1}{2}$ inches to the right of its corresponding point in the given polygon. The arrow below the diagrams of the two polygons indicates how far and in which direction ABCDEF moves under the translation.

VM 16.2c

Another transformation we can use on a geometric figure is a **rotation**, sometimes simply called a **turn**. If we apply a counterclockwise one-quarter turn to the triangle ABC, as shown in the following diagram, we get AB'C' as the image figure:

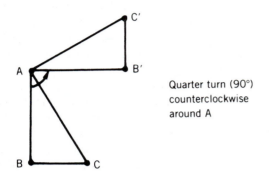

Quarter turn (90°)
counterclockwise
around A

The point about which the given figure is turned is called the *center* of the turn. The curved arrow indicates the direction of the rotation.

Here are some more diagrams that show a given figure and its image under a turn transformation. Because all points of the original figure remain at the same distance from the center of rotation after rotation, the image figure has the same size and shape as the original.

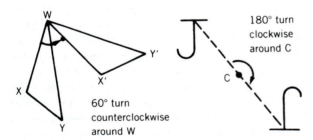

60° turn
counterclockwise
around W

180° turn
clockwise
around C

Flips, slides, and turns are connected with the important geometric concept of congruence—in fact, these actions can be used to generate an alternative definition of the term. Namely, if one figure is the image of another with respect to one of these motions or a combination of these motions, then the figures are congruent. Also, if two figures are congruent, then you can get from one figure to the other by a flip, a slide, a turn, or a combination of these motions. That is, one figure is the image of the other through some combination of flips, slides, and/or turns.

To see this, you might ask students to model shapes on dot or graph paper. Have students form two congruent triangles, one on each of two separate sheets of paper. Then have them rotate, slide, and even flip the triangles to show that the two triangles are actually congruent. You may need a mirror to show the flip, or you can physically cut out one shape and actually flip it to match the other.

Flips, slides, and turns move figures from one position to another, but they do not change them in any other way.

Figures stay the same size and the same shape, which is exactly what congruence means. For this reason, flips, slides, and turns are called *rigid motions*. Another type of transformation, **scaling** (or **dilation**) uses a scaling factor other than 1 and is a nonrigid motion. This scaling transformation changes the relative size of the figure being transformed by stretching or shrinking it. The resulting figure will be *similar* to the initial figure. That is, the resulting figure will be the same shape but a different size than the original.

Basic ideas of geometric transformations can be presented to children to help them understand a variety of ideas in geometry. This approach provides many opportunities for children to manipulate cutouts and tracings of geometric figures or other familiar shapes. A formal development of the ideas of geometric transformations, however, should not be the goal at the elementary level—informal, intuitive experiences with these concepts are more beneficial.

Other Devices for Exploring Geometric Concepts

An excellent device for presenting basic geometric concepts to children is the geoboard. A *geoboard* is usually a piece of material in which an array of nails or pegs has been placed. Very often a geoboard is made from a square piece of plywood in which an array of nails has been driven partway into the wood. The nails should protrude about 1 centimeter.

10 centimeters

10 centimeters

First row
one centimeter
from edge of
geoboard

Two centimeters
between nails

To make the nails a uniform height, use pliers to hold the nails from the side and drive the nails in until they hit the top of the pliers. Since the first row of nails is positioned 1 centimeter from the edge and the nails are 2 centimeters apart, several geoboards can be placed side by side to make a large board or to be used as a model for the *xy* coordinate plane.

Geoboards, for the primary grades, should probably have a total of 25 or 36 pegs (5 by 5 or 6 by 6). Upper-grade students can use boards with up to 10-by-10 pegs to model more complex figures and designs.

By placing rubber bands around the nails driven into the geoboard, the students can represent line segments, squares, rectangles, triangles, and angles. Ask students to perform various tasks and answer questions using the geoboard. Examples of more open-ended questions and activities follow:

1. Have the children show a line segment on their geoboards. Using the nails, see who can make the longest line segment and who can make the shortest line segment. In a class discussion, have children show why they think their line segment is the longest or shortest.

2. After the children have had time to experiment with making angles on the geoboard, ask them to make an angle with the fewest number of degrees. Have different children show why their angle contains the fewest degrees. Will you accept an angle of $0°$?

3. Have the children make an angle with the greatest number of degrees. Will you accept an angle that a child says contains $390°$? $190°$?

4. Have the children make an acute angle that contains the greatest number of degrees.

5. Have the children make an obtuse angle that contains the greatest number of degrees. Does a $360°$ angle fit the request?

6. After making open and closed curves, have the children make a closed curve that has the greatest interior and a closed curve that has the smallest interior.

Tangrams are an effective manipulative for children when developing concepts of spatial relations. A *tangram* set has 7 pieces that fit together as shown:

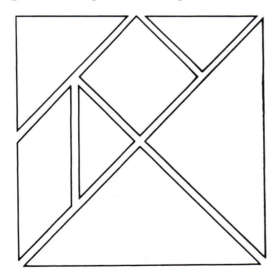

The 7 pieces can be put together in hundreds of different ways. Often it is useful to give the students an outline of a figure and ask them to put the 7 pieces inside the outline. Tangrams can help teach children about whole-part relationships, spatial relationships, congruence, similarity, perimeter, and area.

Closure

This chapter presents geometric terms and concepts that are fundamental building blocks for the study of geometry. To function successfully in geometry, a firm foundation and a basic vocabulary must be developed. Students need to learn the symbolism that corresponds with the terminology and how to put these symbols together to construct geometric ideas and relevant hypotheses.

Many geometric terms are misused in daily conversation. For instance, the term *line* is often incorrectly used as a synonym for line segment or ray. Some students find geometry to be more difficult than other areas of mathematics because of such confusion in the use of terms. Also, geometry is too often associated with the process of memorizing a series of steps in a procedure or proof that must be repeated word for word.

Many of today's teachers were introduced to geometry at the secondary level in a traditional geometry course that utilized formal proof. Because of this narrow view of geometry, some teachers find it difficult to acknowledge that many basic ideas of geometry have an important place in the elementary-school curriculum.

Many of the concepts found in this chapter are presented to the reader as abstractions, but observation suggests that young children can't easily work with abstract notions such as point, line, and line segment. Any consideration of these concepts at elementary or middle-grade levels should be based more on the child's intuitive understanding of the concepts and less on textbook descriptions or formal characterizations by means of axioms or postulates. An intuitive approach to geometry permits you to use a wealth of activities that can be exciting as well as mathematically sound. Rather than memorizing a set of formulas with little or no meaning, a student needs to understand what a formula represents and how it was developed.

Familiarity with basic geometric concepts is an essential component of how a child comes to know and relate to his or her physical environment. The basic terminology encountered and developed through the exploration of geometry provides a foundation for the communication of ideas, hypotheses, and connections. To analyze and generalize and to convey relationships, characteristics, and properties among and between observations, it is critical that students be engaged in activities outlined in this chapter and on the CD accompanying this text.

These basic concepts and structures of geometry— the "building blocks" of geometry—are expanded and extended in the next chapter as we explore polygons (two-dimensional figures) and polyhedra (three-dimensional figures).

PRACTICE EXERCISES FOR TEACHERS

These exercises are designed for the reader of this book, not for the children the reader may teach. Although some are suitable for use in an elementary or middle-school classroom, they should not necessarily be given to children in the form presented here. Ideas appropriate for classroom activities on the concepts and ideas discussed in this chapter can be found in a later section of this chapter and on the CD that accompanies this text.

VM 16.3

1. Use a traditional geoboard or the virtual manipulative *Geoboard* to model some line segments of different lengths on a geoboard, or use dot paper.

VM 16.3

2. Model some open curves and some curves that are not open lengths on a geoboard, or use dot paper or the virtual manipulative *Geoboard*.

VM 16.3

3. Model the following types of angle lengths on a geoboard, or use dot paper or the *Geoboard* virtual manipulative.

    a) acute angle   b) right angle   c) obtuse angle

    d) pair of adjacent angles   e) supplementary angles

VM 16.3

4. Model two perpendicular line segments lengths on a geoboard, or use dot paper or the *Geoboard* virtual manipulative. Must these lines be vertical and horizontal?

5. a) Draw a representation of a point. Name it A. How many lines can be drawn through point A?

    b) Draw a representation for another point about 3 centimeters from point A. Name the second point B.

6. a) Make a tracing of angle PEN. Name your angle P′E′N′. Using a compass and straightedge, bisect angle P′E′N′. Since both angles have the same measure, we say that the two angles are (congruent) or (equivalent).

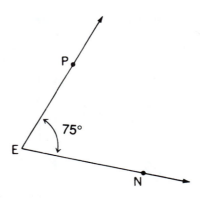

    b) Since angle PEN has a measure of less than 90°, we say that PEN is an (acute) or a (right) or (obtuse) angle.

7. Write the number of degrees for the complementary angle of each of the following angles.

    a) $m \angle MAC = 25°$ b) $m \angle DEC = 45°$ c) $m \angle CAT = 80°$

    d) $m \angle LOT = 73°$ e) $m \angle HAT = 3°$ f) $m \angle CAP = 86°$

8. Write the number of degrees for the supplementary angle of each of the following angles.

    a) $m \angle NOT = 40°$ b) $m \angle TOP = 90°$ c) $m \angle BUT = 150°$

    d) $m \angle LOW = 170°$ e) $m \angle INA = 45°$ f) $m \angle INA = 109°$

9. Make a drawing that represents an acute angle, labeling it ∠XYZ. Construct an angle congruent to ∠XYZ, and label it ∠X′Y′Z′.

10. Identify the geometric concept suggested by each of the following drawings. If the figure can be represented by a symbol, write the symbol.

a)
A

b)
F   G

c)
H   K

d)
Y
X
Z

e)
N
O   M

f)
S   T

g)
P
Q   R

h)
L
M
R
N

i)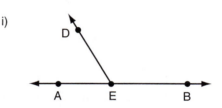
D
A   E   B

11. Determine whether each of the following statements is true or false.
a) Line segments, rays, and angles are sets of points.
b) A line is an infinite set of points.
c) A line segment is a finite set of points.
d) Two perpendicular lines form four right angles.
e) If you make diagrams to represent two lines, line AB and line CD, and the pencil lines you draw do not cross in the diagram, then the two lines cannot intersect.
f) If two angles are supplementary angles, then they are also adjacent angles.

12. Name all the line segments marked in this figure.

A   B   C   D   E   F

VM 16.3

13. Draw a square. Use dotted lines to show all lines of symmetry of the square. This activity might also be done using the *Geoboard* virtual manipulative.

VM 16.2a

14. Suppose that polygon A′B′C′D′E′ is the image of polygon ABCDE under a translation (slide). What can you say about the following?
a) the relationship between lines AA′, BB′, CC′, DD′, and EE′
b) the lengths of line segments AA′, BB′, CC′, DD′, and EE′
c) the sizes and shapes of ABCDE and A′B′C′D′E′

VM 16.2c

15. Trace the following figure on a sheet of paper. Then sketch the image of ABCDE under a quarter turn (i.e., a turn of 90°) in a counterclockwise direction with respect to point O. Use the virtual manipulative *Rotation* to explore this and similar activities.

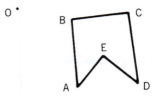

16. Draw each of the following figures after a rotation around point P as suggested under each drawing.

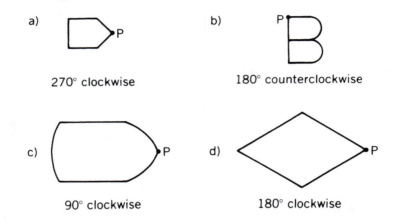

a) 270° clockwise

b) 180° counterclockwise

c) 90° clockwise

d) 180° clockwise

17. Draw all the lines of symmetry for each of the following figures.

a)

b)

c)

d)

18. Trace each of the following figures on a sheet of paper. Then flip the figure over a line. Use the virtual manipulative *Reflection* to explore this and similar activities.

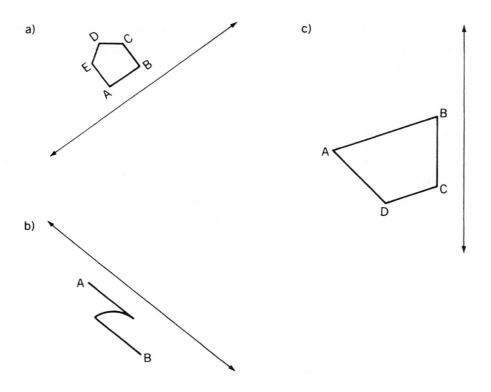

TEACHING COMPETENCIES
AND SELF-ASSESSMENT TASKS

The following questions and statements are designed to reflect the teaching competencies that appeared at the beginning of this chapter and, in some cases, to expose you to deeper aspects of the concepts presented. Take a moment to consider your response to each of these in light of what you've read and learned.

1. Why is the study of geometry essential for elementary and middle-school children? What are the benefits of the study of geometry to other topics in mathematics and to other subject areas?

2. Examine elementary and/or middle-school mathematics textbooks to determine the percentage of each program that is devoted to geometry. Is the geometric content of these mathematics programs adequate, or should it be increased or decreased? Is the geometry integrated with other mathematical subject matter?

3. Conduct a geometric scavenger hunt around the school by searching for physical representations of basic geometric concepts discussed in this chapter. Find at least three distinct examples of each concept and draw a sketch or take a digital picture that correctly names and labels the concept represented.

4. Locate a copy of the Geometer's Sketchpad computer software. Explore the capabilities of this program and the ways in which it represents and labels basic geometric concepts.

5. Make a list of at least 10 examples of angles in our environment, such as those suggested by intersecting roads, and classify your examples by angle types and angle relationships.

6. Research and then discuss the merits of using geoboards to teach the basic concepts of geometry such as those outlined in this chapter.

7. Locate information about the Mira Math aid discussed in this chapter and compare and contrast this device with traditional techniques for teaching geometry.

8. Use a compass and straightedge to construct a square. Describe the process to a friend and defend (justify) each stage of the construction. Use a compass and straightedge to create an abstract design that has several lines of symmetry. Color the design to emphasize the symmetry.

9. Compare and contrast Euclidean geometry and transformational geometry.

10. Discuss how the technical vocabulary of geometry should be handled in an elementary program.

11. Since the child's world is three-dimensional (blocks, balls, and so on), should a geometry program begin with solid geometry (three-dimensional) and then move to plane geometry (two-dimensional)? Argue both sides of this issue.

SAMPLE INSTRUCTIONAL AND ASSESSMENT ACTIVITIES

These activities and more are available on the CD that accompanies this text

VM 16.3

1. Some first graders have sufficient motor development to be able to work with a geoboard. Provide time for children to explore how different shapes and lines can be modeled on the geoboard. Alternatively, use the virtual manipulative *Geoboard* to give children the experience of modeling line segments.

VM 16.3

2. Make a simple design on a geoboard or on the *Geoboard* virtual manipulative included with the CD accompanying this text. Have students copy it to another geoboard. Then have students copy it to dot paper.

3. Have two children sit in such a way that they cannot observe each other. Provide both children with identical sets of pattern blocks. As one child builds with the blocks, he or she describes what he or she is building and gives instructions to the other child to imitate. For example, "Place a square in front of you, place a triangle on top of the square, place the trapezoid to the left of the square . . ." After using all the blocks, students compare the two displays of blocks to see if they are alike or how they differ.

VM 16.3

4. Use the geoboard or the virtual manipulative that is on the CD accompanying this text to show open and closed curves. Examine each model made by the children and discuss why it is an open or closed curve.

VM 16.3

5. Play a version of "Twenty Questions" by making a shape on a hidden geoboard or use the virtual manipulative *Geoboard* and have the children ask "yes or no" questions to determine the shape.

VM 16.3

6. Use a geoboard to make an angle with the greatest number of degrees possible. Compare different models and discuss which fits the criterion. Using the geoboard, make an angle with the fewest possible degrees. Alternatively, use the virtual manipulative *Geoboard*.

VM 16.2b

7. Trace each figure and the line shown with it. After you have done this, draw the flip image of the figure with respect to the line. Alternatively, use the virtual manipulative *Reflections* on the CD that accompanies this text.

VM 16.2c

8. Students can study rotations conveniently by using tracings of figures on overhead transparencies. Have students do a number of experiments to sketch the images of various figures under rotations of one-quarter turn, one-third turn, one-half turn, and so on. Alternatively, have the students use the virtual manipulative *Rotations* on the CD that accompanies this text. Have the students consider questions such as the following:

a) Does a clockwise rotation through one-half turn give the same image as a counterclockwise rotation through one-half turn? (Assume that the center of rotation stays the same.)

b) Around which point can a circle be rotated through a one-half turn clockwise so that the image of the circle is the circle itself?

c) Draw a square. Draw dotted line segments to join both pairs of opposite vertices. Label the point where the segments intersect with the letter C. What is the image of the square under a one-quarter turn clockwise around point C? Under a one-half turn clockwise around C? Under a three-quarter turn clockwise around C?

d) Draw other geometric figures that are their own images under one-quarter turns, one-half turns, and three-quarter turns.

VM 16.2b

9. In the first quadrant of a four-quadrant grid, draw a simple design with intersecting lines or shapes. Flip this design into the second and fourth quadrant, and then flip either of these into the third quadrant. Color the resulting design and indicate the symmetries. Alternatively, use the virtual manipulative *Reflections* on the CD that accompanies this text.

VM 16.2a

10. In which cases is the figure labeled "2" a slide image (i.e., an image under a translation) of the figure labeled "1"? Alternatively, use the virtual manipulative *Translations* on the CD that accompanies this text.

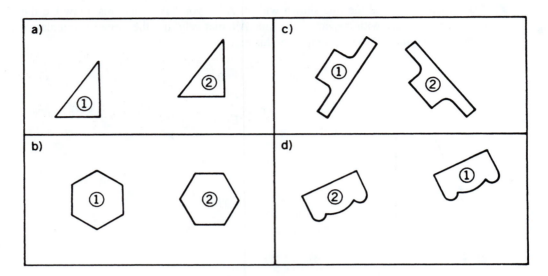

chapter **17**

Geometry: Polygons and Polyhedra

TEACHING COMPETENCIES

Upon completing this chapter, you will be able to:

- Classify polygons according to the number of sides they contain.
- Classify triangles according to the measures of their angles and/or according to the measures of their sides.
- Calculate perimeters and areas of squares, rectangles, parallelograms, and triangles and calculate the circumference and area of a circle, given its radius or diameter.
- Apply the Pythagorean theorem to find the length of any side of a right triangle, given the measures of the other two sides.
- Recognize and classify three-dimensional shapes such as prisms, pyramids, cylinders, cones, and spheres.
- Calculate the volume and surface area of three-dimensional shapes, given the necessary information about the dimensions of the shape.
- Prepare lessons that combine basic geometric concepts with the exploration of polygons and polyhedra and that integrate geometry with other topics of the mathematics curriculum and the broader elementary or middle school curriculum.

VIRTUAL MANIPULATIVES

Upon completing this chapter, you will be able to use virtual manipulatives on the accompanying CD to:

- Illustrate the Pythagorean theorem with a geoboard using *Pythagorean theorem*. **(VM 17.1)**
- Explore the interrelationships of quadrilaterals using *How Many Quadrilaterals?* **(VM 17.2)**
- Estimate the area of regions using *Approximating the Area of a Circle with the Geoboard*. **(VM 17.3)**
- Manipulate the volume and surface area of polyhedra using *Volume and Surface Area of Polyhedra*. **(VM 17.4)**

Numbered CD icons throughout the chapter refer to the virtual manipulatives in this list.

Children live in a geometric world—the buildings they see on the way to school, the food containers in the kitchen at home, and the toys they play with (especially blocks, balls, and even the boxes the toys came in) have geometric characteristics. In fact, almost every interaction children have with their world is in some way connected to geometry. Because of the geometric environment that surrounds us, it is logical that geometry should be emphasized at every grade level. Sadly some teachers either skip or downplay geometry in their implemented curriculum. There are two likely reasons for this: (1) elementary and middle school teachers may not have sound backgrounds in geometry as part of their own mathematical preparation and (2) some teachers may believe that basic operations and computational skill are more important than geometry in developing mathematical proficiency.

In today's world, however, we must reevaluate the significance of geometry in the elementary and middle school mathematics program. Geometry must not be viewed as a "course" that is usually relegated to grades 9 or 10. Primary, upper-elementary, and middle school children should be provided opportunities to explore geometric concepts through processes such as locating, orienting, measuring, drawing, modeling, classifying, and sorting. Readers are reminded of an important discussion in Chapter 2 that illustrates ways in which geometry might serve as a lens for studying other mathematical content in the elementary and/or middle school. Your attention is also drawn to the discussion of valuable information on the scope and sequence of geometry concepts across the grades found on the CD that accompanies this book.

According to the National Council of Teachers of Mathematics (NCTM) *Principles and Standards for School Mathematics:*

Instructional programs from pre-kindergarten through grade 12 should enable all students to—

- Analyze characteristics and properties of two- and three-dimensional geometric shapes and develop mathematical arguments about geometric relationships.
- Specify locations and describe spatial relationships using coordinate geometry and other representational systems.
- Apply transformations and use symmetry to analyze mathematical situations.
- Use visualization, spatial reasoning, and geometric modeling to solve problems.

In Chapter 15 we discussed measurement and in Chapter 16 we considered some of the basic concepts of geometry, including symmetry and transformations. In this chapter, we expand on these concepts and relate measurement to geometry. We are now ready to use the fundamental concepts and structure of geometry developed in these chapters to examine a variety of geometric shapes and relations.

Defining Polygons

Simple closed curves composed of three or more line segments (referred to as sides) are called **polygons**.

RESEARCH SNAPSHOT

What does research say about children's early conceptions of geometric shapes?

Clements, Swaminathan, Hannibal, and Sarama (1999) interviewed 97 children, ages 3 to 6, to investigate the criteria they used to identify and describe shapes. The preschool children exhibited working knowledge of simple geometric forms such as circles, squares, and, to a lesser degree, triangles and rectangles. The children tended to focus on the visual features of the shapes, rather than on the properties of the shapes.

The authors recommend that to help develop more explicit knowledge of the components and properties of shapes, teachers should encourage their students to describe why a figure belongs or does not belong to a shape category.

How else could you help your students discover the properties of shapes?

Clements D. H., Swaminathan S., Hannibal M. A. Z., & Sarama J. (1999). Young children's concepts of shape. *Journal for Research in Mathematics Education, 30,* 192–212.

For additional research briefs, "ERIC Digests" lets you search more than 2000 short syntheses of research on a range of education topics. The syntheses were produced by the Educational Resources Information Center (ERIC). Check http://ericfacility.net/ericdigests/index/.

"Poly" comes from the Greek word *polys*, meaning "many"; and "gon" comes from the Greek word *gonia*, meaning "angle." Therefore, a polygon is, literally, a shape with many angles. The following shapes are examples of polygons:

Polygons are simple closed curves formed by the union of three or more line segments that lie in the same plane and touch only at their end points. Remember that the interior of a polygon is not a part of the polygon itself. A polygon along with its interior is referred to as a **polygonal region**.

Polygons have special names according to the number of sides or angles they have. A three-sided (or three-angled) polygon, for example, is called a *triangle*, while a four-sided (or four-angled) polygon is called a *quadrilateral*. If all the sides of a polygon are congruent (i.e., have the same length) and all its angles are congruent (of equal measure), then it is called a **regular polygon**. If the sides of a polygon are not all congruent or if the angles are not all equal in measure, the polygon is referred to as an **irregular polygon**. Polygons can also be classified as either *convex* or *concave*. A polygon is called **convex** if all of its interior angles are less than $180°$. If at least one interior angle of a polygon is greater than $180°$, then the polygon is **concave**.

The following table names the more familiar polygons. We present this table to illustrate techniques used for naming polygons.

Number of Sides	Prefix	Name of Polygon	Name of Region
3	tri-	triangle	triangular region
4	quad-	quadrilateral	quadrilateral region
5	penta-	pentagon	pentagonal region
6	hexa-	hexagon	hexagonal region
7	hepta-	heptagon	heptagonal region
8	octa-	octagon	octagonal region
9	nona-	nonagon	nonagonal region
10	deca-	decagon	decagonal region
11	undeca-	undecagon	undecagonal region
12	dodeca-	dodecagon	dodecagonal region
...	...	...	...
many	poly-	polygon	polygonal region

It is not necessary that your students memorize all these names; require them to know only those names you determine are developmentally appropriate for them. (Keep in mind that very young children *do* use and understand some rather sophisticated words. Consider how many young children recognize and use "tyrannosaurus" when discussing dinosaurs.)

The geoboard is a useful tool for exploring basic geometric shapes (see Chapter 16). Each student should have his or her own geoboard with a supply of rubber bands. As each of the different geometric shapes is discussed, the student should be given ample opportunity to experiment and make the shape on the geoboard. Few children (or college students, for that matter) have enough experience actually creating polygons—more time is spent labeling existing shapes that were created by the teacher or textbook company. After students have each constructed a given polygon, have them compare with others and see how many different ways a given polygon can be made on a geoboard.

Let's discuss several of the specific polygons mentioned in the table. A **quadrilateral** is a polygon with four sides. It is a simple closed curve composed of four line segments, none of which lies on the same line.

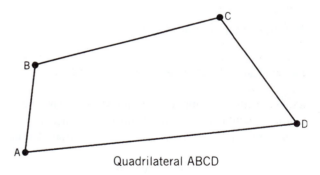

Quadrilateral ABCD

A **pentagon** is a polygon with five sides. It has five line segments lying in a plane and forming a simple closed curve.

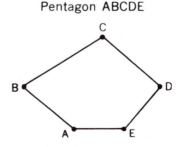

Pentagon ABCDE

Children may be familiar with the Pentagon building across the Potomac River from Washington, D.C.

A **hexagon** is a polygon with six line segments lying in a plane and forming a simple closed curve.

Hexagon ABCDEF

The heads of bolts are often, but not always, hexagonal.

An **octagon** is a polygon with eight sides. It has eight line segments lying in a plane and forming a simple closed curve.

Octagon ABCDEFGH

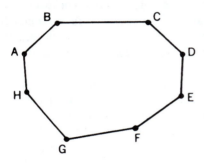

A stop sign, for example, is a regular octagon.

A Closer Look at Triangles

Mark any three points that are not on the same line, and connect the three points with line segments. The shape formed is a triangle. Let's look at triangles in detail.

We have said that an angle is two rays that have a common end point but do not lie on the same line. For example, in the following diagram, the two rays, ray AB and ray AC, determine the angle CAB (or angle BAC). Since there is only one angle represented in the figure with a vertex at A, you can also name this as angle A.

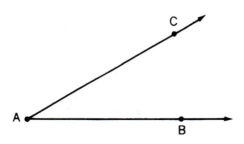

Now suppose that B is selected as the endpoint of another ray that passes through (or contains) point C. Then extend ray BA with B as an end point.

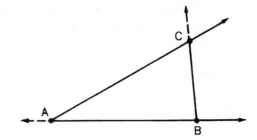

Clearly we have formed another angle. What can we name this angle whose vertex is point B? We can name it angle CBA or angle ABC.

A *closed plane region* is a set of points in one plane that is bounded by a closed curve (but not necessarily a *simple* closed curve). The boundary of the closed plane region formed in the preceding diagram is a triangle. The triangles discussed in this chapter are all planar triangles—that is, each triangle is considered to lie entirely within a plane. (It is interesting that there are other defined geometries in which this is not the case. You might find it worthwhile, for example, to explore the geometry of the sphere. How does the definition of a triangle change when it is drawn on a spherical object?)

Color the following triangle, ABC (read "triangle ABC"):

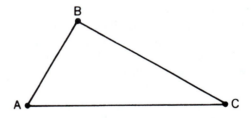

When you colored ABC, you should have colored *only* the line segments—AB, BC, and CA—because △ABC is the union of line segments that forms a triangle. When we use the term *triangle*, we mean only the set of points that comprise the closed curve. When we use the phrase *triangular region*, we mean the union of the closed curve and the interior. If you were to color the triangular region bounded by segments AB, BC, and CA, you would color both the line segments (the sides) and the interior of △ABC.

A triangle, then, can be seen as the boundary of a particular kind of closed plane region. A triangle partitions, or separates, a plane into three sets of points:

1. The set of points that makes up the line segments forming the sides of the triangle

2. The set of points that makes up the interior of the triangle

3. The set of points that makes up the exterior of the triangle

Since every triangle is made up of three line segments (called *sides*), we can name certain kinds of triangles according to the relations among the sides.

- **Equilateral triangle:** A triangle in which the sides are equal in length is called an equilateral triangle. Since line segments that are equal in length are said to be congruent, we can also say that an equilateral triangle is a triangle with three congruent sides. For example, the following is an equilateral triangle:

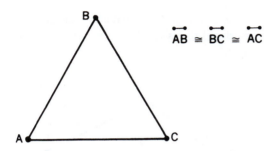

The statement is read, "Line segment AB is congruent to line segment BC, and line segment BC is congruent to line segment AC."

- **Isosceles triangle:** A triangle in which at least two sides are congruent is called an isosceles triangle.

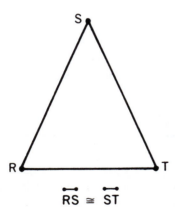

Are all equilateral triangles also isosceles triangles? Yes, because an isosceles triangle has at least two congruent sides and, so, could have all three congruent. (Be warned that some programs define isosceles triangles as having *exactly* two equal sides. In such cases, obviously, equilateral triangles are not considered to be isosceles triangles.)

- **Scalene triangle:** If no two sides of a triangle are congruent, we call the triangle a scalene triangle.

When we describe a triangle as being equilateral, isosceles, or scalene, we are describing it according to the relations that exist among its sides. We can also name triangles according to the relations that exist among the angles suggested by the line segments bounding the triangles. Consider the following definitions:

- **Right triangle:** A right triangle is a triangle that has a "square corner," referred to as a 90° angle or a right angle. Examples of this triangle are common in our environment.

$m(\angle BAC) = 90°$

Unfortunately, right triangles are too frequently drawn showing a horizontal base with the right angle on the left (as in the illustration shown). However, teachers should take care to show right triangles in many orientations. For example, use an overhead projector with a right triangle drawn on a transparency. After the triangle has been identified, move it to many different positions by rotating or flipping it; have the students explain why it is still a right triangle.

- **Equiangular triangle:** A triangle whose three angles are congruent is called an equiangular triangle.

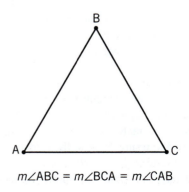

$m\angle ABC = m\angle BCA = m\angle CAB$

If we examine any equiangular triangle, we find that not only are all its angles equal in measure but that all its sides are also congruent. Consequently, any equiangular triangle is also an equilateral triangle.

● **Acute triangle:** We have already learned that an angle with a measure of less than 90° is called an acute angle. If all three of the angles of a triangle are acute, the triangle is called an acute triangle.

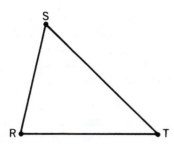

$$m\angle RST < 90°,\ m\angle STR < 90°,\ m\angle TRS < 90°$$

● **Obtuse triangle:** We have also learned that if an angle has a measure of more than 90° but less than 180°, it is called an obtuse angle. A triangle that has one obtuse angle is called an obtuse triangle.

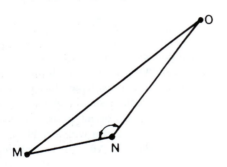

Can any triangle have more than one obtuse angle? Remember that an obtuse angle has a measure of more than 90° but less than 180°. In a triangle, the sum of the measures of the three angles is 180°. If the measure of one angle is more than 90° then the sum of the measures of the other two angles must be less than 90°. Consequently, the answer to the question is, "No, a triangle cannot have more than one obtuse angle."

To verify that the sum of the angles of a triangle is 180°, have upper-elementary or middle school children draw several large triangles on a sheet of paper and then use a protractor to determine the measures of the angles of the triangles. Ask them to take each triangle separately and add its angle measures. The results will depend on the accuracy with which the children use

their protractors, but they will find that the sum of the measures of the angles of a triangle is around 180°. Because of inaccuracy in their measurements, they may be off a few degrees, but they will be close enough to make an appropriate generalization. We should be able to generalize through inductive reasoning that in any plane triangle ABC, the sum of the measures of the angles is 180°. In mathematical symbols, we can write, in △ABC:

$$m\angle A + m\angle B + m\angle C = 180°$$

Another way to show that a triangle contains angles measuring 180° is to place a pencil on one side of a triangle.

Rotate the pencil through the angle CAB.

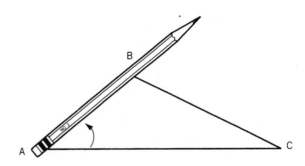

Then, holding the pencil fixed at B, rotate it through angle ABC.

Finally, holding the pencil fixed at C, rotate it through angle BCA.

Note that the pencil, having rotated through all three angles of ABC, has reversed direction—that is, it has made a 180 degree turn or turned through 180°.

Younger children can also discover through their own efforts at a cut-and-paste activity that the sum of the measures of the angles represented by any triangle is 180°. Have children draw triangles of many different sizes and types on paper. If they color the angles of a given triangle ABC and then tear off the corners, they will discover that the three angles of any one triangle, when placed together as shown here, form a straight line (sometimes thought of as a straight angle or an angle of 180°).

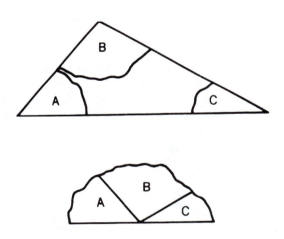

After several trials, children will discover that this is true for any triangle, no matter what its sides or angles measure.

The ancient Egyptian culture developed an extensive practical use for triangles. The Egyptians made use of geometry in surveying the land after the annual spring floods of the Nile River. The floods washed away landmarks, and some method of reestablishing boundaries was necessary. Historians have noted that one surveying tool used by the Egyptians was a rope with 13 equally spaced knots. If the first and thirteenth knots are joined and a stake is placed at the fourth, the eighth, and the thirteenth knot, a right triangle is constructed.

We also know that triangles of this kind were studied by a Greek geometer, Pythagoras, in the sixth century B.C. His statement on the relation between the lengths of the sides of right triangles is known as the *Pythagorean theorem*. Consider the following triangle, $\triangle ABC$, in which angle ACB is a right angle. In the diagram of this right triangle, we can mark the right angle by making a small square, as shown.

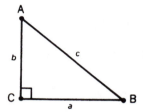

Because we label the vertices of a triangle with capital letters, we sometimes use lowercase letters to name the sides. By custom, the side opposite a given angle is named with the same letter as the angle, but using a lowercase letter. For example, in the preceding diagram, the side opposite angle A is labeled *a*. The longest side of a right triangle (the side opposite the right angle) is called the *hypotenuse*. The other two sides are called *legs*.

The **Pythagorean theorem** states that the square of the measure of one leg of a right triangle added to the square of the measure of the other leg is equal to the square of the measure of the hypotenuse. (Or, alternatively, the square of the measure of the hypotenuse of a right triangle is equal to the sum of the squares of the measures of the other two sides.) By the time they complete elementary school, students need to understand the meaning of this theorem and be able to state it in words and use it in simple applications. Committing a written formula to memory makes little sense without knowing what it represents. Nevertheless, using this drawing, we can state the theorem of Pythagoras mathematically as follows:

or
$$a^2 + b^2 = c^2$$
$$m(BC)^2 + m(AC)^2 = m(AB)^2$$

Suppose we assign the following unit lengths to the sides of right triangle ACB:

$$a = 4 \text{ units}$$
$$b = 3 \text{ units}$$
$$c = 5 \text{ units}$$

Substituting these values in the mathematical statement of the theorem and performing the indicated computation, we can illustrate the Pythagorean theorem.

$$a^2 + b^2 = c^2$$
$$(4 \times 4) + (3 \times 3) = (5 \times 5)$$
$$16 + 9 = 25$$
$$25 = 25$$

There are literally hundreds of proofs of the Pythagorean theorem. We will not attempt to give a general proof of this theorem here, but we will verify and discuss in detail an example that illustrates the theorem.

Consider right triangle ABC.

Using segment AC as one leg, construct the square ACMN.

Using segment CB as one leg, construct the square CBOP.

Using segment AB as the hypotenuse, construct the square ABRS.

a = 4 UNITS
b = 3 UNITS
c = 5 UNITS

VM 17.1

Each of the three square regions we have just constructed is subdivided into unit squares, as shown in the diagram. The number of small square regions along a particular side of the triangle indicates the length of that side. So, the number of small square regions in a particular square region on a side represents the square (a^2 or b^2) of the length of the side next to that particular square region. For example, the hypotenuse AB (named c in the diagram) has a length of 5 units, so the square (c^2) of the hypotenuse is 25; and the square region ABRS is divided into 25 smaller square regions. It can be observed visually that the number of small squares in square CBOP (16) added to the number of small squares in square ACMN (9) is equal to the number of small

squares in square ABRS (25).

$$a^2 + b^2 = c^2$$
$$4^2 + 3^2 = 5^2$$
$$16 + 9 = 25$$
$$25 = 25$$

The regions can be cut out and pasted together (or built using blocks) to demonstrate, even to very young children, the physical property of equivalent areas underlying the Pythagorean theorem.

Let's examine the following right triangles in light of the Pythagorean theorem.

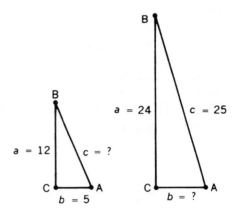

If you know the lengths of the legs of a right triangle, is it possible to find the length of the hypotenuse? Yes, by applying the Pythagorean theorem. If you know the lengths of the hypotenuse and one of the legs of a right triangle, can you find the length of the other leg? Yes, in much the same way. The necessary computations are illustrated in these diagrams.

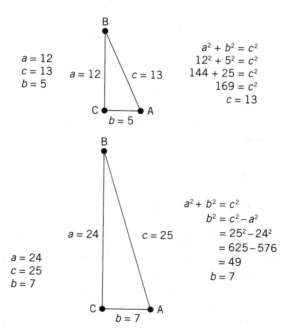

a = 12
c = 13
b = 5

$$a^2 + b^2 = c^2$$
$$12^2 + 5^2 = c^2$$
$$144 + 25 = c^2$$
$$169 = c^2$$
$$c = 13$$

a = 24
c = 25
b = 7

$$a^2 + b^2 = c^2$$
$$b^2 = c^2 - a^2$$
$$= 25^2 - 24^2$$
$$= 625 - 576$$
$$= 49$$
$$b = 7$$

You might discuss how the situation in the second figure shown could be interpreted as a wall 24 feet high with a ladder 25 feet long placed 7 feet from the base of the wall. Alternatively, you might think of a person at point B throwing a ball to a person at point C (a distance of 24 feet). How far would that person have to throw the ball to get it to the person at point A? What other applications or interpretations of the Pythagorean theorem can you devise that would prove to be useful with elementary or middle school children?

The term *congruent* was defined earlier with respect to angles. Let's see how we can apply the concept of congruence to triangles. **Congruent triangles** are defined as triangles that have the same size and shape. That is, their corresponding sides are congruent, and their corresponding angles are congruent. We define **similar triangles** as triangles that have the same shape but not necessarily the same size. Only the corresponding angles must be congruent; the corresponding sides may have equal or different, but proportional lengths.

Compare these three triangles:

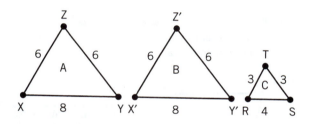

In the triangles pictured, the corresponding sides are as follows:

$$\overleftrightarrow{XZ} \text{ corresponds to } \overleftrightarrow{X'Z'} \text{ corresponds to } \overleftrightarrow{RT}.$$
$$\overleftrightarrow{YZ} \text{ corresponds to } \overleftrightarrow{Y'Z'} \text{ corresponds to } \overleftrightarrow{ST}.$$
$$\overleftrightarrow{XY} \text{ corresponds to } \overleftrightarrow{X'Y'} \text{ corresponds to } \overleftrightarrow{RS}.$$

Triangle A is congruent to triangle B because the corresponding sides of triangles A and B are congruent and the corresponding angles are congruent. Triangle C is similar to triangles A and B because it has the same shape but not the same size. The angles of triangle C are congruent to the corresponding angles of triangle B (and triangle A), but the corresponding sides are not congruent (i.e., they do not have the same length).

We can express these relations in the following manner. Because Triangle A is congruent to triangle B, we can, therefore, state that

$$m(\overleftrightarrow{XZ}) = m(\overleftrightarrow{X'Z'}) \quad m\angle X = \angle mX'$$
$$m(\overleftrightarrow{XY}) = m(\overleftrightarrow{X'Y'}) \quad m\angle Y = \angle mY'$$
$$m(\overleftrightarrow{YZ}) = m(\overleftrightarrow{Y'Z'}) \quad m\angle Z = \angle mZ'$$

Triangle C is similar to triangle B (and to triangle A). C ~ B. [The symbol (~) means "is similar to."]

Therefore,

$$m\angle X' = m\angle R$$
$$m\angle Y' = m\angle S$$
$$m\angle Z' = m\angle T$$

Let's compare the similar triangles ABC and DEF, pictured in the following diagram:

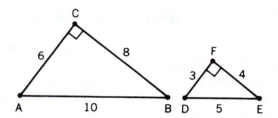

The line segment DF corresponds to line segment AC. The lengths of these two sides can be compared by a ratio, $\frac{3}{6} = \frac{1}{2}$. That is, the length of side DF is to the length of side AC as 3 is to 6 (or as 1 is to 2). The ratio of the lengths is 3:6, or 1:2. Compare the length of side EF with that of side BC. This ratio is 4:8 or 1:2. Similarly, comparing the lengths of sides DE and AB, we find that $\frac{5}{10} = \frac{1}{2}$. If two triangles are similar to each other, the lengths of their corresponding sides will have the same ratio. Applying this idea to $\triangle DEF$ and $\triangle ABC$, we see that the ratios of the lengths of corresponding sides is, in each case, $\frac{1}{2}$.

$$\frac{m(\overline{DF})}{m(\overline{AC})} = \frac{m(\overline{EF})}{m(\overline{BC})} = \frac{m(\overline{DE})}{m(\overline{AB})} = \frac{1}{2}$$

If we are given two similar triangles and are told the lengths of three sides of one of the triangles and the length of one side of the other triangle, we can easily determine the lengths of the other two sides of the second triangle. This is an application of the concepts of ratio and proportion, which were discussed in Chapter 13. For example, suppose we are given the following two similar triangles:

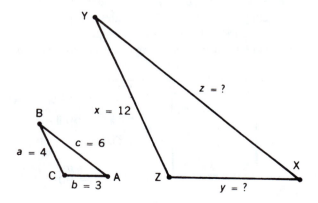

If we know that a and x are corresponding sides, then we know that the ratio of corresponding sides must be

$\frac{1}{3}$ (since $\frac{a}{x} = \frac{4}{12} = \frac{1}{3}$, and since the corresponding sides of similar triangles all have the same ratio). Therefore $y = 9$ and $z = 18$.

$$\frac{1}{3} = \frac{3}{y} \qquad y = 9 \left(\text{since } \frac{1 \times 3}{3 \times 3} = \frac{3}{9}\right)$$
$$\frac{1}{3} = \frac{6}{z} \qquad z = 18 \left(\text{since } \frac{1 \times 6}{3 \times 6} = \frac{6}{18}\right)$$

A Closer Look at Quadrilaterals

Before we discuss quadrilaterals, let's take a look at parallel lines. **Parallel lines** may be defined as two or more lines in the same plane that never intersect. Similarly, we can call two or more line segments parallel if they are subsets of parallel lines.

In the following diagram, line AB is parallel to line CD. Consequently, the two lines never intersect. This is written as AB ∥ CD, which is read, "Line AB is parallel to line CD."

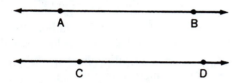

With this in mind, we can now discuss an important class of geometric shapes called quadrilaterals. A *quadrilateral* was defined earlier as a simple closed curve composed of four line segments, none of which lies on the same line. A quadrilateral should not be confused with a **quadrilateral region**, which is defined as a quadrilateral and its interior.

We earlier classified triangles according to angle measure and relative length of sides. Quadrilaterals are also classified according to the relations among their sides and angles. We can name several different kinds of quadrilaterals according to these relations.

- **Square:** A square is a quadrilateral having four congruent sides and four angles of equal measure. All four angles of a square are right angles—that is, each angle has a measure of 90°.

A line segment joining any two opposite vertices of square ABCD divides the square into two

right triangles. In fact, a line segment that joins any two nonadjacent vertices of a polygon is called a *diagonal* of the polygon. In square ABCD, we have marked diagonal AC, forming right triangles ABC and ADC.

- **Rectangle:** A rectangle is a quadrilateral in which sides opposite each other are both congruent (equal in length) and parallel, and each angle has a measure of 90°.

Notice that since all squares have opposite sides that are congruent and parallel, and since each angle has a measure of 90°, then all squares are also rectangles. However, not all rectangles are squares.

- **Parallelogram:** A parallelogram is a quadrilateral in which the opposite sides are congruent and parallel.

Notice that the parallelogram differs from the rectangle in that the angles of a parallelogram are not necessarily 90°. A parallelogram whose angles are all 90° is also a rectangle. Thus, all rectangles are parallelograms, but not all parallelograms are rectangles.

- **Rhombus:** A rhombus is a quadrilateral in which all four sides are congruent and the opposite sides are parallel.

Notice that the rhombus differs from the square in that the angles of a rhombus are not necessarily

90°. A rhombus whose angles are all 90° is a square. Thus, all squares are rhombuses, but not all rhombuses are squares. A rhombus is a special kind of parallelogram—a parallelogram in which all four sides are congruent.

- **Trapezoid:** A trapezoid is a quadrilateral in which one and only one pair of sides is parallel.

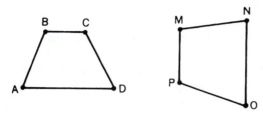

In trapezoid ABCD, $\overleftrightarrow{AD} \parallel \overleftrightarrow{BC}$.
In trapezoid MNOP, $\overleftrightarrow{PM} \parallel \overleftrightarrow{ON}$.

Some mathematics programs change this definition of a trapezoid to read, "at least one pair of parallel sides." How does this revised definition differ from the initial one given? What does this new definition do to the relationship between parallelograms and trapezoids? The relations among the various kinds of quadrilaterals can be shown clearly and quickly by means of a diagram. Suppose we consider all quadrilaterals and then name the subsets of this collection of all quadrilaterals.

Suppose that U represents the set of all quadrilaterals; and

that A represents the set of all parallelograms;

that B represents the set of all rectangles;

that C represents the set of all rhombuses;

that D represents the set of all squares;

that E represents the set of all trapezoids;

and that F represents the set of all other quadrilaterals.

Then we can draw the following diagram:

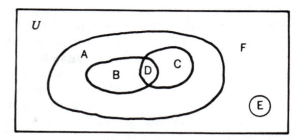

From this diagram we can make a number of observations:

1. All rectangles, rhombuses, and squares are also parallelograms.
2. All squares are both rhombuses (or rhombi) of a special type and rectangles of a special type.
3. There are no squares that cannot also be called both rhombi and rectangles; however, there are rectangles and rhombi that are not squares.
4. There are rhombi that are not rectangles.
5. There are rectangles that are not rhombi.
6. There are no trapezoids that can be called parallelograms, rectangles, rhombi, or squares.
7. The set of all other quadrilaterals includes all plane figures formed by four line segments of various lengths.

Understanding the interrelationships of polygons (e.g., that squares are "special" rectangles as well as being "special" rhombi) involves class inclusion—a characteristic of someone operating at van Hiele's third stage (see Chapter 1). This ability should emerge by the upper-elementary grades, but many high school students still lack this ability—possibly resulting from a lack of emphasis of geometry in early grades.

A Closer Look at Circles

Another important simple closed curve is the circle. A circle is not usually thought of as a polygon, although some programs refer to it as a polygon with infinitely many sides. A more common definition of a **circle** is that it is the set of all points in one plane that are an equal distance from a given point, called the *center*.

Use the "How Many Quadrilaterals?" virtual manipulative found on the CD that accompanies this text to explore the various types of quadrilaterals that can be drawn in a fixed space. How many other parallelograms can be drawn on the 9-peg geoboard? How many squares? How many trapezoids? Can you draw a rhombus on the 9-peg geoboard? How many other quadrilaterals can be drawn?

VM 17.2

A line segment from the center to any point on the circle is called a **radius** (the plural of radius is radii). A line segment extending from any point on the circle to another point on the circle and passing through the center of the circle is called a **diameter**. A diameter can therefore be thought of as two radii lying on the same line. Remember that a circle, like any other geometric shape, is an abstract concept, and the model drawn on paper is merely a representation of a circle.

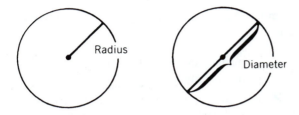

The distance around a circle is called the **circumference** of the circle. Any two points of a circle divide the circle into two parts. Either of these two parts is called an **arc**.

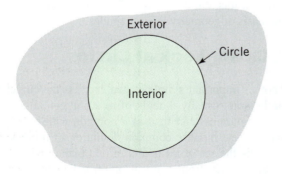

There are three distinct sets of points formed by a circle—the points forming the interior, the points forming the exterior, and the simple closed curve that forms the circle itself.

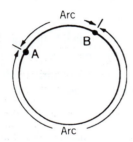

A **circular region** is the simple closed region formed by a circle and its interior—that is, by the points forming a circle and the points forming its interior.

There is an important relation between the diameter of a circle and its circumference—the ratio of circumference to diameter is always the same, no matter what size the circle. Children exploring concepts of area need to develop an understanding of this ratio, referred

to as **pi**, or π. Often π is introduced to children as a numerical value that they then mechanically use in a formula to determine the circumference and area of a circle without understanding its derivation or meaning. Programs today, however, often introduce the concept of π through experiences that provide children with the opportunity to discover what π actually represents. We will now describe a simple approach to this topic.

Provide a large circular object, such as a cardboard disk or pizza tray or pie pan, and a ruler. Use the ruler to measure the diameter of the circular object. We can then measure the approximate circumference (the distance around the rim or edge) of the circular object by rolling the circular object through one complete revolution and measuring the linear distance traveled. To do this, mark a dot at some point on the circumference, and place this dot on the table at point A. Then roll the circular object until the dot is again on the table, this time at point B. The distance between A and B (just over three full diameters of the object) approximates the circumference of the object.

Another method of determining pi would be to use a piece of string to measure around the circular object. A cloth tape measure would be helpful in getting accurate measurements. We can compare the diameter with the measured circumference by means of the following ratio:

$$\frac{\text{circumference}}{\text{diameter}}$$

This ratio, expressed as a decimal, is approximately 3.1. By comparing the circumferences of many circular objects with their diameters, children should draw the conclusion that π, the ratio of the circumference to the diameter of any circle, is a little more than 3, regardless of the size of the circular object. Children should be encouraged to use a calculator for dividing the circumference by the diameter to avoid clouding the important concept of the value of this ratio with needlessly tedious paper-and-pencil computations. When students have reached this conclusion, they can then be advised that mathematicians have a special symbol for this relationship and number, the Greek letter π.

Students sometimes wonder what the exact value of π is. Mathematicians have proved that π is an irrational number, a nonterminating, nonrepeating decimal. Thus, any fraction or decimal that we may write for π

is only an approximation for the actual value of π. Commonly used approximations for π are 3.14, 3.1416, and $\frac{22}{7}$. Supercomputers have been able to calculate approximations of π to many millions of decimal places. In fact, a computer's ability to quickly and accurately compute an approximation of pi to many places is one way for scientists and mathematicians to measure a computer's speed and efficiency.

Area, Perimeter, and Circumference Measurement

Another marriage of geometry and measurement that should be investigated by both elementary and middle school students is the concept of *area*. **Area** gives us a two-dimensional measure of a plane region. Area, like any other measurement, is always expressed by a number value coupled with an appropriate unit of measure. The object to be measured is compared with a standard unit measure. An area might be expressed, for example, as 6 square inches (or 6 sq in.). The standard unit of measure in this example is square inches, and the number value is 6, which indicates how many square inches.

The standard units for measuring area are square inches, square feet, square yards, square miles, square meters, square centimeters, and so forth. A square inch, by definition, is that area represented by a square region 1 inch on each side. Similarly, a square centimeter is that area represented by a square region 1 centimeter on each side.

In finding the area of a region, we ask, "How many square units are there in the given region?" Children could be asked to place square, color tiles, on a shape and count how many tiles it takes to fill the shape. As an example, consider a rectangular region that is 4 units wide and 6 units long. How can we find the area of this region?

Geoboards can also be useful in exploring area. Since most geoboard pegs split the board into square regions, the children can count the number of squares within a shape. The children can compare their calculated area with the counted area. The two answers should, of course, be the same.

A simple method for determining the area of a rectangular region is to use a ratio. There are 6 square units in one row. This fact can be stated by means of a ratio: 6/1, or "six square units per row." So, if there are 6 units per row, how many square units are there in 4 rows? This can be expressed as a proportion, using two equivalent ratios.

$$\frac{6}{1} = \frac{\square}{4}$$

The missing numerator is clearly 24.

$$\frac{6 \times 4}{1 \times 4} = \frac{\square}{4}$$
$$\square = 24$$

The denominator of the first ratio is multiplied by 4. So, to maintain the equivalence, the numerator must also be multiplied by 4. We see that there are 24 square units in the rectangular region. We can verify this fact by counting the number of square units in the region. If the unit is centimeters, then the area is 24 square centimeters; if the unit is inches, then the area is 24 square inches.

Consider another region.

If there are 18 square units in one row, how many square units are there in 8 rows?

$$\frac{18}{1} = \frac{\square}{8}$$
$$\frac{18 \times 8}{1 \times 8} = \frac{\square}{8}$$
$$\square = 144$$

There are 144 square units in 8 rows. Again, we can verify the answer by counting the number of square units in the region.

After children have found the areas of several rectangular regions, they should be able to generalize their findings. The number of units in the length times the number of units in the width gives the number of square units in the area. This fact can be expressed by the following formula:

$$A = L \times W$$

In this formula, A stands for area, L stands for length, and W stands for width.

Now, let's use the concepts of area and ratio to determine the area bounded by a parallelogram.

$$\triangle FDA \cong \triangle ECB$$
$$\therefore \text{ Area } \triangle FDA = \text{Area } \triangle ECB$$

Cut off the triangular region BEC, and move it to the other end of the parallelogram to form a rectangle. The area within the original parallelogram ABCD is exactly the same as the area within the new rectangle ABEF that is formed. Thus we can determine the area within parallelogram ABCD by determining the area of the rectangular region ABEF.

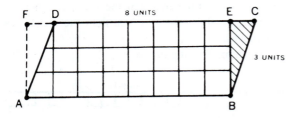

In the rectangular region ABEF, if there are 8 square units in one row, how many units are there in 3 rows?

$$\frac{8}{1} = \frac{\square}{3} \qquad A = l \times w$$
$$\frac{8 \times 3}{1 \times 3} = \frac{\square}{3} \qquad A = 8 \times 3$$
$$\square = 24 \qquad A = 24 \text{ square units}$$

The area within the parallelogram is therefore 24 square units.

We can generalize from this last example. If segment AB is called the *base* of the parallelogram (*b*), and if segment BE is called the *height* of the parallelogram (*h*), then the number of square units in the area (*A*) within the parallelogram is indicated by the product of the number of units in the base and the number of units in the height. We can express this fact by means of the following formula:

$$A = b \times h$$

Let's apply these concepts to finding the area of a triangular region.

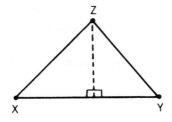

Make a tracing of $\triangle XYZ$, and label it $\triangle X'Y'Z'$. Place $\triangle X'Y'Z'$ next to $\triangle XYZ$, as in the following diagram:

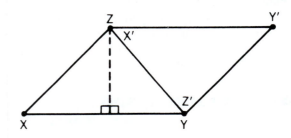

The area of one of the triangular regions is clearly one-half the area of the parallelogram. The formula for the area of the parallelogram is $A = b \times h$. Therefore the formula for determining the area of a triangle (one-half of a parallelogram) is

$$A = \tfrac{1}{2}(bh)$$

[Notice that this formula has been written without the multiplication symbol, ($\times$), between the *b* and the *h*. This is acceptable, and quite common, notation. The multiplication sign between two factors in a formula can always be omitted, provided the meaning of the expression or sentence remains clear.]

Consider the following triangular region RST, and determine its area:

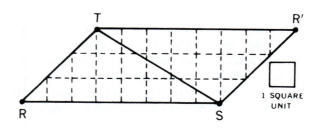

$$\begin{aligned}
A &= \tfrac{1}{2}bh \\
&= \tfrac{1}{2} \times 8 \times 3 \\
&= \left(\tfrac{1}{2} \times 8\right) \times 3 \\
&= 4 \times 3 \\
&= 12 \text{ square units}
\end{aligned}$$

The area of the triangular region is 12 square units. These basic principles can also be applied to finding the areas of other triangular regions.

The process of determining the area of a circular region is more challenging than determining the area of a polygonal region. One method, which will give an estimate of the area, is to place the circular region on a square grid and count the number of square units covered by the circular region.

RADIUS

ARC

r = length of radius

a = length of arc

If we count all the squares that fall completely within the boundary of the circle and compare that number to the number of squares that fall completely within and/or cross the boundary, we will have an approximation of the circle's area as between those two numbers. The smaller the square unit used, the more precisely the area of the circular region can be estimated.

A second method is to think of the circular region as being made up of many small congruent triangles, approximated by drawing a large number of radii to form many small regions that are triangular in shape. Notice that the radii must be drawn so that the resulting arcs of the circle are all equal in length if the small triangular regions are to be congruent.

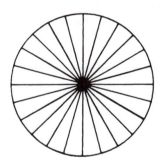

Let's consider this second method of determining the area of a circular region. Examine one of the small regions that has been formed.

We can use the formula $A = \frac{1}{2}(ra)$ to find the approximate area of this region. The shape of the region is very nearly triangular, with the arc as a base and the radius as a height. The area within a triangle, remember, is equal to one-half the product of the base and the height. Then, multiplying the area of this region by the total number of regions, we obtain an approximation of the area of the entire circular region. If we consider each small region to be a triangle (which is approximately the case), we can state that the area of the circular region (A) is equal to the area within the first triangle $\frac{1}{2}(ra_1)$ added to the area within the second triangle $\frac{1}{2}(ra_2)$ added to the area within the third triangle $\frac{1}{2}(ra_3)$ added to the area within the fourth triangle $\frac{1}{2}(ra_4)$, and so on.

$$A = \tfrac{1}{2}(ra_1) + \tfrac{1}{2}(ra_2) + \tfrac{1}{2}(ra_3) + \cdots + \tfrac{1}{2}(ra_n)$$

The term $\frac{1}{2}(ra_n)$ represents the area within the last triangle.

The sum of the lengths of the bases of the triangles is approximately equal to $a_1 + a_2 + a_3 + a_4 + \cdots + a_n$, which is the same length as the circumference of the circle. So the area within the circle can be expressed by the following equation:

$$A = \tfrac{1}{2}[r(a_1 + a_2 + a_3 + a_4 + \cdots + a_n)]$$
$$= \tfrac{1}{2}[r(\text{circumference})]$$

But we know that the circumference of a circle is used to calculate the value of π (pi). The value of π has been defined as the ratio of the circumference to the diameter.

$$\pi = \frac{\text{circumference}}{\text{diameter}}$$

Another estimate is obtained by drawing a polygonal region that entirely contains the circle. As in the example, the smaller the square unit, the more precisely the area of the circular region can be estimated.

Estimate the area of the circle on the geoboard by drawing two polygonal regions, one that is inside the circle and another that contains the circle. Measure the areas of the two polygonal regions and compute the estimates.

VM 17.3

Hence the circumference of a circle is equal to π times its diameter, or 2π times its radius (r).

$$\text{circumference} = \pi \times \text{diameter}$$
$$= \pi \times (2 \times \text{radius})$$
$$= 2\pi \times \text{radius}$$
$$= 2\pi r$$

Thus we can calculate the area within a circle to be equal to π times the square of its radius.

$$A = \tfrac{1}{2}[r(\text{circumference})]$$
$$= \tfrac{1}{2}[r(2\pi r)]$$
$$= \tfrac{1}{2} \times 2 \times (\pi \times r \times r)$$
$$= \pi r^2$$

Now, let's use this formula to determine the approximate area of a circular region with a radius of 10 units.

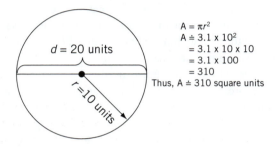

$A = \pi r^2$
$A \doteq 3.1 \times 10^2$
$\quad = 3.1 \times 10 \times 10$
$\quad = 3.1 \times 100$
$\quad = 310$
Thus, $A \doteq 310$ square units

The area of a circular region with a radius of 10 units is approximately 310 square units. Now determine the approximate circumference of the same circular region.

$$C = \pi \times d$$
$$= 3.1 \times 20$$
$$= 62 \text{ linear units}$$

The circumference is approximately 62 linear units.

The sum of the measures of the line segments that form a polygon is called the **perimeter** (P) of the polygon. We can determine the perimeter of a polygon, such as the following scalene triangle, by adding the lengths of the sides.

Perimeter $= m(\overrightarrow{AB}) + m(\overrightarrow{BC}) + m(\overrightarrow{CA})$

The perimeter of an equilateral triangle is equal to three times the measure of one side, since the three sides are all congruent (equal in measure).

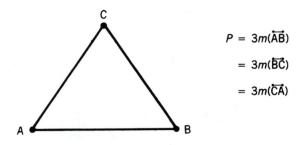

$P = 3m(\overrightarrow{AB})$
$\quad = 3m(\overrightarrow{BC})$
$\quad = 3m(\overrightarrow{CA})$

We can express this fact in symbols by writing $P = 3s$, where s stands for any of the three sides.

The perimeter of a square is equal to four times the measure of one side, since all four sides are congruent.

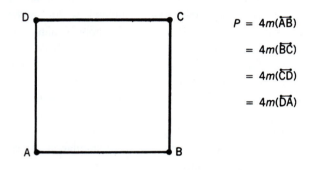

$P = 4m(\overrightarrow{AB})$
$\quad = 4m(\overrightarrow{BC})$
$\quad = 4m(\overrightarrow{CD})$
$\quad = 4m(\overrightarrow{DA})$

This fact can also be expressed in symbols as $P = 4s$, where s stands for the length of any of the four sides.

The perimeter of a rectangle is equal to twice the measure of one of the sides representing the length added to twice the measure of one of the sides representing the width.

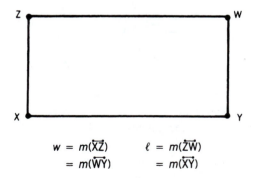

$w = m(\overrightarrow{XZ})$ $\ell = m(\overrightarrow{ZW})$
$\quad = m(\overrightarrow{WY})$ $\quad = m(\overrightarrow{XY})$

Let L equal the measure of the length and W equal the measure of the width. The perimeter, then, can be determined according to the following formula:

$$P = 2L + 2W$$

Note, however, that the formula is not as important as the concept it represents. Children who wish to simply add the lengths of the sides to determine the perimeter should not be criticized for this less efficient but conceptually correct approach.

Defining Polyhedra

So far in our discussion of geometry, we have considered only shapes lying entirely in one plane (two dimensions). Now we will examine shapes in three dimensions. **Three-dimensional shapes**, sometimes called *spatial shapes*, are geometric shapes that do not lie entirely in one plane.

Since the environment in which we live is three dimensional, children are more likely to be familiar with representations of three-dimensional shapes than they are with representations of plane shapes. Just as sheets of paper and chalkboards can be used to represent planes, so can shoe boxes, rooms, skyscrapers, soup cans, ice cream cones, and basketballs be used to represent various kinds of three-dimensional shapes.

An effective introductory approach to the topic of three-dimensional shapes is to lead children to become even more aware of familiar physical shapes around them and to associate these physical shapes with the geometric shapes that they suggest. For example, it is quite likely that the children are in a classroom with a floor, a ceiling, and four walls and that one pair of opposite walls is longer than the other pair. A room like this represents a particular kind of geometric three-dimensional shape.

Early in our study of two-dimensional shapes, we defined what is meant by a simple closed curve. Let's begin our study of three-dimensional shapes by defining a simple closed surface. A simple closed curve, we remember, consists of the points in a plane that divide the plane into three sets of points—the points forming the simple closed curve itself, the points forming the interior of the curve, and the points forming the exterior of the curve.

Analogously a **simple closed surface** consists of the points in space that divide space into three sets of points—the points forming the simple closed surface itself, the points forming the interior of the three-dimensional shape, and the points forming the exterior of the three-dimensional shape. For example:

When discussing plane regions, we defined the union of a simple closed curve and its interior as a plane region. In spatial geometry, we define the union of a simple closed surface and its interior as a three-dimensional region or space region.

If we examine the walls of a room, we see that the intersection of two walls can be thought of as representing a line segment. If we think of the two walls as representing or determining planes (remember that planes extend endlessly, without bounds), the intersection of these two planes is a line. We can generalize by noting that the intersection of any two planes is always a line, as shown in the following diagram:

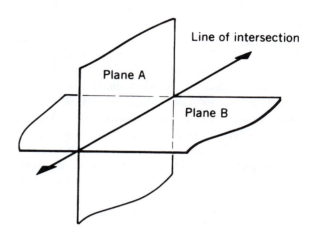

But planes do not always intersect. If we examine the opposite walls of most rooms, we see that they do not meet and would not meet if the walls were extended indefinitely. If we consider the planes that the two walls can be thought of as representing, we see that these planes do not intersect. Two planes that have no intersection (that never intersect) are called **parallel planes**.

We are now prepared to consider an important kind of simple closed surface, the prism. A **prism** can be defined as a simple closed surface formed by two congruent polygonal regions in parallel planes and three or more quadrilateral regions joining the two congruent polygonal regions so as to enclose the space between them completely. The following diagram illustrates one kind of prism:

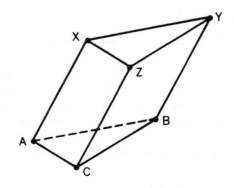

The triangular regions ABC and XYZ are the two congruent polygonal regions in parallel planes; AXZC,

CZYB, and BYXA are the quadrilateral regions joining triangular regions ABC and XYZ and enclosing completely the space between them.

The two congruent parallel polygonal regions are called the *bases* of the prism. In the prism pictured here, the triangular regions ABC and XYZ are the bases. The quadrilateral regions of a prism that join the two bases are called *lateral faces* or *sides*. In this prism, the quadrilateral regions AXZC, CZYB, and BYXA are the faces. All of the polygonal regions that form the prism (the lateral faces and the two bases) are called the *faces*. The line segment formed by the intersection of two sides (faces) is called an *edge*. Each point where three edges (or three faces) intersect is called a *vertex* (the plural of vertex is vertices). The prism shown has five faces (regions defined by ABC, AXZC, CZYB, BYXA, and XYZ), nine edges (segments defined by BC, AB, CA, XZ, YZ, XY, BY, AX, and CZ), and six vertices (points A, B, C, X, Y, and Z).

Many different kinds of three-dimensional shapes can be classified as prisms, and each is named according to the polygonal regions forming the bases. The table shows some of the principal types of prisms.

NAME OF PRISM	POLYGONAL REGIONS FORMING THE BASES	NUMBER OF FACES	NUMBER OF EDGES	NUMBER OF VERTICES
 TRIANGULAR PRISM	TRIANGULAR REGIONS	5	9	6
 QUADRILATERAL PRISM	QUADRILATERAL REGIONS	6	12	8
 HEXAGONAL PRISM	HEXAGONAL REGIONS	8	18	12

You may be interested in examining the columns displaying the number of faces (*f*), edges (*e*), and vertices (*v*) to see if you can find a relationship among these values. Leonhard Euler, a Swiss mathematician of the eighteenth century, derived a now-famous formula expressing this relationship:

$$f + v = e + 2$$

That is, the number of faces plus the number of vertices is equal to the number of edges plus 2.

Many prisms are shaped so that if we could imagine setting them horizontally on one of their bases, their sides and the edges joining the two bases would be perpendicular to the bases. (Because all the lateral edges of a prism are parallel, we need to know only that one of the lateral edges is perpendicular to the bases.) Such prisms are called **right prisms**. The prisms pictured in the preceding table and in the following shape are right prisms.

Other prisms are shaped so that if they are placed horizontally on one of their bases, their sides and the edges joining the bases are not all perpendicular to the bases.

Such prisms are not right prisms. The prisms that we explore in this chapter are dominantly right prisms.

A quadrilateral prism with rectangular bases is called a **rectangular prism**. The following diagram pictures a rectangular prism:

Like any other quadrilateral prism, it has six sides, twelve edges, and eight vertices. A rectangular prism that is also a right prism is referred to as a **right rectangular prism**. Children often refer to this shape simply as a box. The use of informal language should not be discouraged, but students in the upper-elementary and middle grades should begin to encounter and use more sophisticated terminology and vocabulary when discussing geometry.

Let's look at a specific kind of right rectangular prism. The sides of this particular prism are all congruent square regions, and all the edges of the prism are congruent. This three-dimensional shape is called a

cube—a quadrilateral prism in which the six faces are all congruent square regions. The following diagram shows a cube:

Just as area is an important measurement concept in two-dimensional geometry, an important measurement concept in spatial geometry is volume. **Volume** is a measure of the space occupied by a space region. The volume of an object is named by a numeral and an appropriate measure unit name—for example, 3 cubic feet or 4 cubic centimeters. Notice that the unit name is prefaced by "cubic." We always use cubic units in measuring volume—cubic inches, cubic feet, cubic centimeters, and so on.

What does "cubic feet" mean? Consider a cube whose edges are each 1 foot long. (Remember that the edges of a cube are all congruent, or equal in length.) The measure of the space enclosed by such a cube is defined as 1 cubic foot. We can define cubic inches or any other unit of volume in a similar way. What does "cubic centimeters" mean? A cube whose edges are each 1 centimeter in length is called a cubic centimeter. The unit cube from a set of base ten blocks or Cuisenaire rods is a cubic centimeter.

Now let's examine the following right rectangular prism:

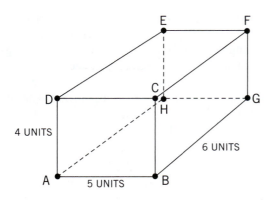

Let's see how we can determine the volume of this rectangular prism. To do this, we must determine how many cubic units can be fitted into the prism. How many cubic units can be placed end-to-end along the edge AB?

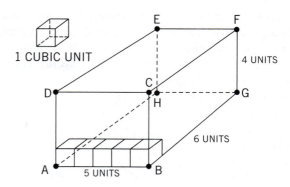

Five cubic units can be placed end-to-end along edge AB. How many cubic units can we place end-to-end along edge BG?

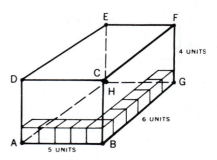

The answer is 6. How many cubic units can be placed on the lower base, that is, rectangle ABGH? If there are 5 cubic units in one row, how many cubic units are there in 6 rows?

$$\frac{5}{1} = \frac{\square}{6}$$

$$\frac{5 \times 6}{1 \times 6} = \frac{\square}{6}$$

$$\square = 30$$

Thus, 30 cubic units can be placed on the lower base.

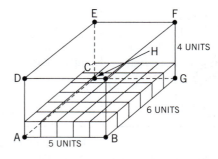

Since the prism is 4 units high, it can hold 4 layers of these cubic units. If there are 30 cubic units in 1 layer, then 4 layers contain 120 (or 4 × 30) cubic units.

After solving a number of similar exercises involving right rectangular prisms, both concretely with cubes and boxes and pictorially as shown here, students should be able to make a generalization about determining the volume of such spatial shapes. This generalization might be written as a formula. The volume, V, within a right rectangular prism is equal to the number of cubic units that can be placed along the length of the prism, L, times the number of cubic units that can be placed along the width, W, times the number of cubic units that can be placed along the height, H.

$$V = L \times W \times H$$
or
$$V = LWH$$

Using this formula, find the volume of a right rectangular prism 6 units wide, 15 units long, and 7 units high.

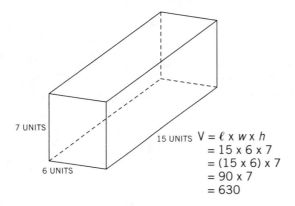

7 UNITS
15 UNITS
6 UNITS

$$V = \ell \times w \times h$$
$$= 15 \times 6 \times 7$$
$$= (15 \times 6) \times 7$$
$$= 90 \times 7$$
$$= 630$$

The volume of this prism is 630 cubic units.

The following formula is another way of expressing the volume within a right rectangular prism:

$$V = b \times h$$
or
$$V = bh$$

Using this formula, the volume, V, of a right rectangular prism is equal to the number of cubic units that can be placed on one of the bases, b, times the number of cubic units that can be placed along the height, h.

This formula is equivalent to the first formula, $V = LWH$, since the number of cubic units that can be placed on one of the bases of the prism (b) is determined by the product of the number of cubic units that can be placed along the length of the prism (L) and the number of cubic units that can be placed along the width (W). In the formula $V = L \times W \times H$, we simply replace $L \times W$ with its equivalent, b, to obtain:

$$V = L \times W \times H$$
or
$$V = b \times h$$

An advantage of the formula $V = bh$ is that it is valid for any right prism. It is not restricted to right rectangular prisms as is the other formula. For example, consider the following right triangular prism:

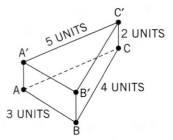

We know that the area of one of the bases (triangular region ABC or triangular region A′B′C′) is 6 square units ($\triangle$ABC and $\triangle$A′B′C′ are right triangles, so the area of the triangular region ABC or triangular region A′B′C′ is one-half the product of its legs: $\frac{1}{2} \times 3 \times 4$, or 6). Therefore we can fit 6 cubic units on one of the bases of the prism. But there are 2 layers of these cubic units because the height of the prism is 2 units. Consequently, 6×2, or 12, cubic units can be placed in the prism, so the volume of the right triangular prism is 12 cubic units. The same result can be obtained by using our second formula.

$$V = bh$$
$$= (\tfrac{1}{2} \times 3 \times 4) \times 2$$
$$= 6 \times 2$$
$$= 12 \text{ cubic units}$$

In a similar manner, we can determine the volume within any right prism.

A **pyramid** is a simple closed surface formed by a simple closed region, a point not in the plane of the region, and triangular regions joining the simple closed region and the point outside the region, completely enclosing the space between them. In the pyramid shown here, ABCD is the simple closed region, E is the point not in the plane of ABCD, and the triangular regions joining ABCD and point E are ABE, BCE, CDE, and DAE.

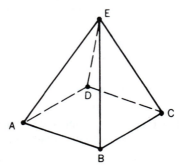

The simple closed region ABCD is called the *base* of the pyramid, and the triangular regions ABE, BCE, CDE, and DAE are called *lateral faces*. The naming of the parts of a pyramid is consistent with that of prisms. In the diagram of the pyramid, the plane regions ABCD, ABE, BCE, CDE, and DAE are the *faces;* the *segments* BC, DA, BE, DE are the *edges;* and the points A, B, C, D, and E are the *vertices*.

Pyramids are classified and named according to the polygonal region forming the base. For example, a quadrilateral pyramid whose base is formed by a rectangular region is called a **rectangular pyramid**. In the following diagram, the quadrilateral region WXYZ (the base) is rectangular; thus, the three-dimensional shape represented is a rectangular pyramid. A rectangular pyramid, like any other quadrilateral pyramid, has five faces, eight edges, and five vertices.

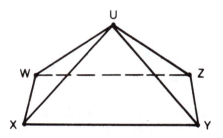

The following table shows some of the principal kinds of pyramids. (Note that Euler's formula, faces + vertices = edges + 2, mentioned earlier in this chapter, also applies to pyramids.)

NAME OF PYRAMID	POLYGONAL REGION FORMING BASE	NUMBER OF FACES	NUMBER OF EDGES	NUMBER OF VERTICES
TRIANGULAR PYRAMID	TRIANGULAR REGION	4	6	4
QUADRILATERAL PYRAMID	QUADRILATERAL REGION	5	8	5
HEXAGONAL PYRAMID	HEXAGONAL REGION	7	12	7

The formula for the volume of a sphere is more challenging to develop and understand than the formula for the volume of a prism. For illustration purposes, let's

use a special prism, a cube, as a model. The diagram attempts to show three congruent pyramids that you may notice will "fit" into this cube.

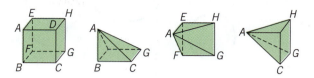

Since three congruent pyramids with a height equal to s, the side of the cube, and with bases equal in area, s^2, to a face of the cube will fit precisely into the cube with a volume of s^3, then the volume of one of the pyramids must be $\frac{1}{3}$ of the volume of the cube. That is,

$$V = \tfrac{1}{3}(Bh)$$

where B is the area of the base and h is the height of the pyramid.

Another simple closed surface that students have often seen is the cylinder. A **cylinder** is a simple closed surface formed by two congruent simple closed regions (not polygonal regions) in parallel planes and one or more surfaces (at least one of which is curved) formed by the union of the line segments that join corresponding points of the curves that bound the two congruent regions. The following drawings illustrate various kinds of cylinders:

The simple closed regions at the ends of a cylinder are called the *bases* of the cylinder. The surface or surfaces that join the two bases are called the *lateral faces*. The bases and lateral faces of a cylinder are illustrated in the following drawing:

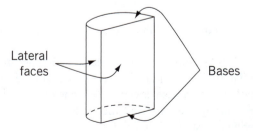

Note that a cylinder doesn't have to have a circular base—the base only needs to be a simple closed curve that is not a polygon. A few of the shapes that the bases of a cylinder might have are indicated in the following diagram:

If the bases are polygonal regions, the simple closed surface is a prism rather than a cylinder. (Remember that a polygon is a simple closed curve formed by the union of line segments and that a polygonal region is formed by the union of a polygon and its interior.) If a simple closed surface is a prism, the edges of its two bases are all line segments; but if a simple closed surface is a cylinder, the sides of its bases are not all line segments. This is the essential difference between a prism and a cylinder.

If the line segment joining the centers of the bases of a cylinder is perpendicular to the bases, then the cylinder is a **right cylinder**. A cylinder whose bases are circular regions is called a **circular cylinder**. School-age children, as well as some adults, often refer to this shape informally as a can.

In a right circular cylinder, the line segment joining the centers of the bases is perpendicular to both bases and parallel to the sides of the cylinder.

The volume of a cylinder can be found by determining the area of the base and multiplying this by the height of the cylinder. That is,

$$V = Bh$$

where B is the area of the base and h is the height of the cylinder.

A cone is another three-dimensional shape that is familiar to most children. A **cone** is a simple closed surface having a base, a vertex, and one or more lateral faces joining the base and the vertex. The following drawings illustrate various kinds of cones:

The *base* of a cone is a simple closed nonpolygonal plane region. The *vertex* is a point not in the plane of the base. The *lateral face* or *faces* consist of the surface(s) joining the vertex and the simple closed curve bounding the base. The base, vertex, and lateral faces of a cone are illustrated in the following drawing:

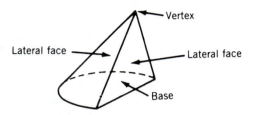

The base of a cone does not need to be circular. Some of the shapes that the base of a cone might have are indicated in the following drawings:

If a polygonal region forms the base, the simple closed surface is a pyramid rather than a cone. If a simple closed surface is a pyramid, the edges of the base are all line segments; if a simple closed surface is a cone, the edges of the base are not all line segments. This is the essential difference between a pyramid and a cone.

A cone whose base is a circular region is referred to as a **circular cone**. If the line segment joining the center of the base with the vertex of the cone is perpendicular to the base, then the circular cone is called a **right circular cone**.

 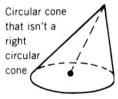

The volume of a cone can be found by relating our knowledge of cones to our knowledge of a pyramid. A cone can be thought of as a pyramid with a base that has infinitely many sides. Since the volume of any pyramid is $\frac{1}{3}$ of the volume of the prism in which it is embedded, the volume of a cylinder is $\frac{1}{3}$ the volume of the cylinder in which it is embedded. That is,

$$V = \tfrac{1}{3}(Bh)$$

where B is the area of the base of the cone and h is the height of the cone.

Another simple closed surface that is familiar to all children is the sphere. Young children have all played with balls or other toys that have suggested spheres, and they are therefore familiar with physical representations, or models, of spheres. A **sphere** is a simple closed surface that is the set of all points in space that are the same distance from a given point, called the *center*. A sphere divides space into three sets of points—the points forming the sphere itself, the points forming the interior of the sphere, and the points forming the exterior of the sphere.

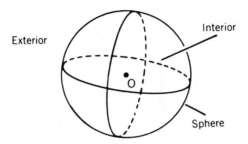

Any line that passes through the interior of a sphere intersects the sphere at two points. In the following diagram, A and B represent the points of intersection of a sphere with a line passing through the center, O, of the sphere:

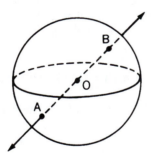

A line segment that passes through the center of a sphere and whose end points are points on the sphere is a *diameter* of the sphere. Hence, segment AB is a diameter of the sphere shown. A line segment whose end points are a point on a sphere and the center of the sphere is a *radius* of the sphere. In the sphere shown, segments OA and OB are *radii*.

The method of deriving the formula for the volume of a sphere is more complex than for many other space figures. Suffice it to say that we can imagine a sphere with diameter *2r* embedded within a right circular cylinder that has a height of *2r* and a base diameter of *2r*. The difference in volume of the two objects, the sphere and the cylinder, was discovered through experimentation by Archimedes to be $\frac{1}{3}$ the volume of the cylinder. That is, since the volume of this cylinder

is $2\pi r^2$ the volume of the embedded sphere must be

$$V = \tfrac{2}{3}(2\pi r^2)$$

or

$$V = \tfrac{4}{3}(\pi r^2)$$

Another important aspect of the measure of three-dimensional shapes is the concept of surface area. The **surface area** of a simple closed surface is the total area of the surfaces that form the shape. Consider the following right rectangular prism:

Imagine a physical model of this prism. If we cut the model along edges AA′, A′B′, B′C′, C′D′, AB, BC, and CD and flatten it out, it would look something like this:

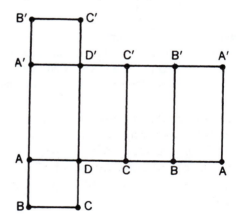

(Perhaps you might wish to model this with an empty cracker box that can be flattened.) We can see now that the surface area of a prism is the sum of the areas of all of the sides—in this case, the sum of the areas of the two congruent bases added to the areas of the four lateral faces.

Students need to have many experiences that help them see the meaning of surface area. This is more important than simply memorizing a formula. Nevertheless, how can we derive a formula that could be used to calculate the total surface area of a prism? Every prism has two congruent bases, so the surface area must contain the area of one base multiplied by 2 (*2b*, where *b* stands for the area of the base). It must also contain the area of the lateral faces. In the preceding right rectangular prism, the area of the lateral faces is calculated as follows:

Area of lateral faces
$$= (mAB \times mAA') + (mBC \times mBB')$$
$$+ (mCD \times mCC') + (mDA \times mDD')$$

In this formula, we use mAB, mAA', mBC, and so on, as abbreviations for the measure of segments AB, AA', BC, and so on. Since the prism is a right prism, we know that $AA' = BB' = CC' = DD' = h$, so area $= (AB \times h) + (BC \times h) + (CD \times h) + (DA \times h)$. By applying the distributive property, we can state:

$$area = (mAB + mBC + mCD + mDA) \times h$$

Then, since $(mAB + mBC + mCD + mDA)$ is equal to the perimeter of a base of the prism:

$$area = perimeter\ of\ a\ base \times height\ of\ the\ prism$$
$$= Ph$$

Since we are looking for the total surface area of the prism, we must include the area of the two bases as well as the area of the four vertical sides. Thus,

$$surface\ area = area\ of\ two\ bases$$
$$+ area\ of\ four\ sides$$
$$= 2 \times (AB \times BC) + Ph$$
$$= 2b + Ph$$

Now let's calculate the surface area of the following right rectangular prism, in which rectangular regions ABCD and A'B'C'D' are the bases. (Can you see why we don't need to label the lengths of all of the sides?)

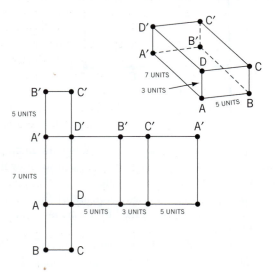

$$surface\ area = (2 \times area\ of\ a\ base) + (perimeter$$
$$of\ a\ base \times height)$$
$$= 2b + Ph$$
$$= [2 \times (3 \times 5)]$$
$$+ [(3 + 5 + 3 + 5) \times 7]$$

$$= [2 \times 15] + [16 \times 7]$$
$$= 30 + 112$$
$$= 142$$

The surface area is 142 square units.

We can use this same method to determine a formula for finding the surface area of a right triangular prism. Imagine cutting and flattening a physical model of the following right triangular prism:

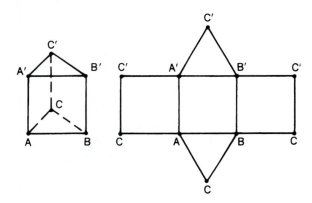

The surface area of this three-dimensional shape must contain the areas of the two bases—the area of the triangular region ABC plus the area of the triangular region A'B'C' ($\triangle ABC$ is congruent to $\triangle A'B'C'$)—which can be represented by $2b$, where b stands for the area of either of the two bases. It must also contain the area of the lateral faces, which are rectangular regions.

$$area = (AB \times AA') + (BC \times BB') + (CA \times CC')$$

Since $AA' = BB' = CC' = h$, we can write

$$area = (AB \times h) + (BC \times h) + (CA \times h)$$
$$= (AB + BC + CA) \times h$$

Since the perimeter (P) of the base is equal to $AB + BC + CA$, we can write

$$area = Ph$$

Therefore,

$$surface\ area = (2 \times area\ of\ a\ base) + (perimeter$$
$$of\ a\ base \times height)$$
$$= 2b + Ph$$

We can generalize from this by noting that the surface area *(SA)* of any right triangular prism is equal to the sum of the areas of its two bases ($2b$) and the product of the perimeter of one of the bases and the height of the prism *(Ph)*.

$$SA = 2b + Ph$$

Let's use this formula to determine the surface area of the following right triangular prism:

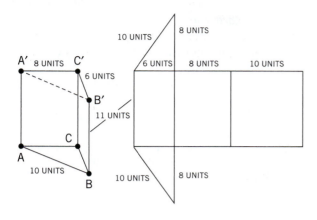

$$SA = 2b + Ph$$
$$= [2 \times (\tfrac{1}{2} \times 6 \times 8)] + [(6 + 8 + 10) \times 11]$$
$$= [2 \times 24] + [24 \times 11]$$
$$= 48 + 264$$
$$= 312$$

The surface area is 312 square units.

Closure

Renewed emphasis on geometry has become a part of most elementary and middle school mathematics programs. However, teachers sometimes believe that with some limited attention given to identifying squares, rectangles, triangles, and circles, they can skip geometry in favor of emphasis on the fundamental computation with whole numbers, fractions, and decimals. Of course, this approach does not provide children with either a well-balanced or effective mathematics program. It also does not give them background experiences needed for aspects of geometry that will be explored at the secondary level.

Young children's mathematics comes from the real world, and geometry certainly is a part of everyday life. Geometry is all around us and needs to be integrated with the mathematics of whole numbers and rational numbers. Exploring area and perimeter provides an excellent opportunity to bring together addition, multiplication, and measurement. Measuring for carpet or paint or some other common need offers a real situation involving the children and their parents.

Three-dimensional figures are more familiar to young children than are two-dimensional figures. Blocks, boxes, and many toys and objects from the child's environment are three-dimensional figures. From the faces of three-dimensional figures, children can identify the shape of a square, the shape of a rectangle, or the shape of a triangle. From this real-world approach children then draw pictures of the shapes. As children mature, their drawings begin to take on more of the characteristics of three-dimensional drawings.

When children play with blocks, they operate in a three-dimensional world. The teaching of geometric concepts must begin with having children manipulate concrete objects. Children need help in "seeing" the objects and their properties. Attribute blocks, Cuisenaire rods, base ten blocks, and other materials all are used to begin a mathematics program with manipulatory 3-D figures. The geoboard is a device for use on the semiconcrete level for modeling two-dimensional geometric shapes. The Mira can be used on the semiabstract level, when children can begin drawing models. String art, straw shapes, and other manipulatives can be used on the more abstract levels, when curves, perimeter, and volume are presented to the class. Many other mathematics concepts are also explored as the children learn the characteristics of the shapes merely because the materials are used as manipulatives. The concepts of thick and thin, big and little, and large and small can be learned, as can color, shape, and size.

As you study the mathematics programs available for elementary and middle school children, you will notice that there is a wide variation in grade placement of geometric concepts. Decisions as to which geometric concepts should be taught at specific grade levels must be made with attention to developmental readiness. The van Hieles' work with geometry and the young child, as well as that of others listed in the bibliography of this and the previous chapter on the CD, provide evidence that children can explore many geometric ideas at an early age.

Young children need ample opportunity to play with blocks that are cubes, rectangular prisms, pyramids, cones, and spheres. Older children need experiences cutting paper models and pasting them together to make solid three-dimensional shapes. Use clear plastic for the faces of three-dimensional shapes and use a strong glue

Use the "Volume and Surface Area of Polyhedra" virtual manipulative found on the CD accompanying this text to explore these concepts. Use eight blocks to build a polyhedron with maximum surface area. Use eight blocks to build a polyhedron with minimum surface area. What is its shape?

VM 17.4

to fasten Velcro (which can be purchased at a fabric store) along the edges. The pieces then may easily be put together and taken apart. For example, make six equivalent square regions out of clear plastic, and glue Velcro around each edge as follows:

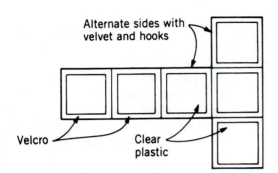

Alternate sides with velvet and hooks

Velcro

Clear plastic

Now fold the square regions into a cube. An interesting variation would be to arrange the six pieces on a tabletop in a number of different ways that would each yield a cube if folded into a three-dimensional shape. (By making faces of different shapes, you should be able to collect enough pieces to model a wide variety of prisms and pyramids.)

Geometry provides an opportunity to explore a different view of mathematics that aids in the development of a spatial sense. Through knowledge of geometry, we can solve problems from other topics in mathematics and from other fields, even within disciplines such as art and physical education. To gain full advantage and transfer of knowledge, be certain to integrate geometry into other curricular areas.

PRACTICE EXERCISES FOR TEACHERS

These exercises are designed for the reader of this book, not for the children the reader may teach. Although some examples are suitable for use in the elementary or middle school classroom, they should not necessarily be given to children in the form presented here. Ideas appropriate for classroom activities on the concepts and ideas discussed in this chapter can be found in a later section of this chapter and on the CD that accompanies this text.

VM 17.1

1. Classify each of the following triangular regions according to its sides. Classify each according to its angles. Then determine its area and perimeter.

a)

b)

c)

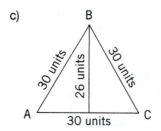

2. Use your knowledge of the area of a parallelogram to develop a formula for the area of a trapezoid. Use b_1 for the length of the lower base, b_2 for the length of the upper base (the bases are parallel sides), and h for the height of the trapezoid.

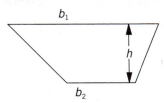

3. Classify each of the following quadrilaterals; then determine its area and perimeter.

a)

b)

c)

4. Construct a polygon congruent to each of the following shapes.

a)

b)
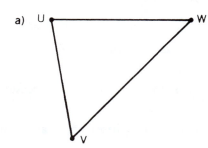

5. Determine the area and circumference of each of the following circles.

a)

b)

VM 17.1

6. Use the Pythagorean theorem to determine the measure of the indicated side in each of the following shapes.

a) Find the value of *a* by determining the length of segment BC.

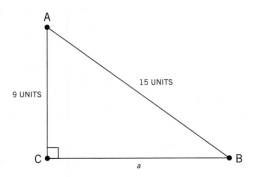

b) Find the value of *b* by determining the length of segment AC.

c) Find the value of *c* by determining the length of segment AB.

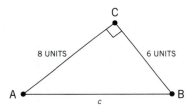

7. The measures of two angles of a triangle are 63° and 46°. What is the measure of the third angle?

8. Identify each of the following space regions, and list the bases, edges, and vertices for each region.

a)

c)

b)

d)

9. Find the volume of each of the following space regions.

VM 17.4

a)

b)

c)

10. Calculate the surface area (SA) of each of the following space regions.

VM 17.4

(The bases are right triangles.)

11. For each of the following descriptions, match the geometric three-dimensional shape or shapes.

a) A three-dimensional shape with $V = bh$ as the formula for volume   Sphere

b) A three-dimensional shape with all points equally distant from a single point   Pyramid

c) A three-dimensional shape whose lateral faces are rectangles   Prism

d) A three-dimensional shape with four faces   Cone

e) A three-dimensional shape whose lateral faces are triangles   Cylinder

12. If each of these regions were cut along the outer boundary and folded together, which three-dimensional shape could it make?

a)

b)

c)

d)

VM 17.4

13. Complete the following table.

Space Figure	Area of Base	Height	Volume
Cylinder	42 sq in.	10 in.	
Cube			125 cu cm
Triangular prism	37 sq in.		518 cu in.
Cylinder	24 sq m	50 dm	
Rectangular prism	27 sq mm		243 cu mm
Square prism	6 sq ft	18 in.	

TEACHING COMPETENCIES AND SELF-ASSESSMENT TASKS

The following questions and statements are designed to reflect the teaching competencies that appeared at the beginning of this chapter and, in some cases, to expose you to deeper aspects of the concepts presented. Take a moment to consider your response to each of these in light of what you've read and learned.

1. Go on a shape scavenger hunt around your neighborhood! Find different examples of distinctly different polygons and polyhedrons, make sketches, and sort the shapes in more than one way. Use a digital camera to record the images and make a collage display.

2. Keep a tally of triangular shapes that you see in your surroundings during a given day. Which types of triangles are more prevalent than others? Why?

3. Explain what we mean when we say that all linear measurements are approximate.

4. Describe a number of real-life applications of the Pythagorean theorem that children can explore. Include examples involving both indirect and direct measurement, as discussed in Chapter 15.

5. Raid your kitchen! Locate a number of products that are packaged in prisms, cylinders, and other spatial shapes. Check your local grocery store for other polyhedra.

6. Discuss the role of formulas in a geometry program. Should formulas be memorized? Should formulas be developed or should they be presented as fact to children?

7. Locate and discuss the recommendations for teaching geometry in elementary and middle school as reported in the *Principles and Standards for School Mathematics* published by the NCTMO. Include a discussion of the degree of emphasis that should be placed on geometry in an elementary and middle school mathematics program.

SAMPLE INSTRUCTIONAL AND ASSESSMENT ACTIVITIES

These activities and more are available on the CD that accompanies this text.

1. Attribute blocks and pattern blocks that are used in the primary grades for patterning and sequencing provide an excellent introduction to basic geometric shapes. Children need many experiences sorting the blocks according to shape, number of corners, and number of sides.

2. Students should be encouraged to verbalize their intuitive understandings of three-dimensional figures.

a) Who is inside the playhouse? (interior, exterior)

b) What is the shape of the front of your book? (shape)

c) How many sides does a cube have? (spatial perception)

3. On the chalkboard, draw a large square, a large rectangle, and a large triangle. Draw them so that their areas appear to be equal. Ask, "Which figure is smallest? Which is largest?" Solicit suggestions as to how we could actually determine if one of the figures covers more area than the others. Give students an opportunity to explain. Then draw horizontal and vertical lines over the figures to form equal squares, or use an overhead projector to project a grid onto the figure. Ask if this would give us a method that we could use to determine the largest figure. Let the children discuss how they would count only parts of some squares in determining the area of the triangle.

4. Mark off large figures on the playground blacktop with chalk. Students need many experiences actually seeing measurements such as 10 meters or 20 feet on the playground. Thus students will begin to develop a foundation for visualizing measurements in the real world. Seeing the actual 5 meters should mean much more than a short line segment drawn on a chalkboard to represent 5 meters.

VM 17.5

5. Use geoboards to calculate perimeters of figures. At this stage of development, remember to use only figures with right angles on the geoboard. Young students cannot calculate the length of diagonals. They can, however, compare this length to other lengths on the geoboard by using a card marked with those distances.

VM 17.5

6. Use a geoboard to model

a) geometric shape

b) an angle with the least number of degrees

c) an angle with the greatest number of degrees

d) a geometric shape with the greatest area

e) a geometric shape with the least amount of area

7. Study the diagram and answer the questions.

1 UNIT REGION

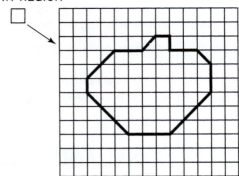

a) How many unit regions fit entirely within the polygonal region?

b) How many unit regions are necessary to cover the region?

c) The area of the polygonal region is exactly _____ units.

8. Have cutout models of a circle, a rectangle, a square, and a triangle available. Then introduce models of a cube, a sphere, a cone, a cylinder, and a pyramid. Compare the two-dimensional and the three-dimensional models. Ask students to explain the ways in which the figures are alike and the ways in which they are different. (Students should be able to identify the three-dimensional shapes by name.) Ask one student to think of one of the three-dimensional shapes. Have another student try to identify the shape about which the first student is thinking by asking a series of questions that can be answered only with yes or no. Continue the questions until the object is identified.

9. For each of the following exercises, draw rectangles on squared paper; record the measures of the rectangular regions and the measures of their sides. Use paper marked off in either square inches or square centimeters.

a) Draw three rectangles such that the measure of each rectangular region is 16 square inches.

b) Draw three rectangles such that the measure of each rectangular region is 18 square inches.

c) Draw four rectangles such that the measure of each rectangular region is 24 square inches.

10. Use models of a prism and a pyramid that have equal heights and congruent bases. Ask students to predict which will hold more. If possible, encourage them to guess how much more. Have them experiment by filling the pyramid with sand and then pouring it into the prism. Have students repeat the experiment enough times to indicate the validity of the test. This same experiment can be done with a cone and a cylinder having equal bases and equal heights.

Index